D1472743

Social Theory Revisited

Social Theory Revisited

Clinton Joyce Jesser
Northern Illinois University

THE DRYDEN PRESS
Hinsdale, Illinois

Library of Congress Cataloging in Publication Data

Jesser, Clinton J.   comp.
  Social theory revisited.

  Bibliography: p. 407
  Includes index.
  1. Sociology—Addresses, essays, lectures.
I. Title.
HM51.J47   301'.01   74-22007
ISBN 0-03-078005-5

Acknowledgments

Selection 1.1: Robert A. Nisbet. "Conservatism and Sociology." *American Journal of Sociology*, 58 (September 1952), 167–175. Copyright © 1952 by the University of Chicago Press and reproduced by permission.

Selection 2.1: David Cohen. "Comte's Changing Sociology." *American Journal of Sociology*, 71 (September 1965), 168–177. Copyright © 1965 by the University of Chicago Press and reproduced by permission.

Selection 2.2: E. E. Evans-Pritchard. *The Sociology of Comte: An Appreciation.* Manchester, England: Manchester University Press, 1970. 24 pp. Copyright © 1970 by Manchester University Press and reproduced by permission.

Selection 3.1: Werner Stark. "Herbert Spencer's Three Sociologies." *American Sociological Review*, 26 (August 1961), 515–521. Copyright © 1961 by the American Sociological Association and reprinted by permission.

Selection 4.1: Paul E. Mott. "Marx's Macroscopic Theory of Social Change" [Editor's title]. In Paul E. Mott, *Organization in Society*, © 1965. By permission of the author and Prentice-Hall, Inc., Englewood Cliffs, N.J.

Selection 4.2: Lewis A. Coser. "Karl Marx and Contemporary Sociology." In Lewis A. Coser, *Continuities in the Study of Social Conflict.* New York: Free Press, 1967. Pp. 137–151. Copyright © 1967 by Lewis A. Coser and reprinted by permission.

Selection 5.1: Stanislav Andreski. "Method and Substantive Theory in Max Weber." *British Journal of Sociology*, 15 (March 1964), 1–18. Copyright © 1964 by Routledge and Kegan Paul and reprinted by permission.

Selection 5.2: Reinhard Bendix. "Max Weber's Sociology Today." Reprinted from *International Social Science Journal*, XVII:1 by permission of Unesco, © Unesco 1965.

Selection 6.1: Theodore Abel. "The Contribution of Georg Simmel: A Reappraisal." *American Sociological Review*, 24 (August 1959), 473–479, with "Comment" by Robert A. Nisbet, 479–481. Copyright © 1959 by the American Sociological Association and reprinted by permission.

Selection 6.2: Murray S. Davis. "Georg Simmel and the Aesthetics of Social Reality." *Social Forces*, 51 (March 1973), 320–329. Copyright © 1973 by University of North Carolina Press and reprinted by permission.

Selection 7.1: J. A. Barnes. "Durkheim's Division of Labour in Society." *Man*, (N.S.) 1 (June 1966), 158–175. Copyright © 1966 by Macmillan Publishing Company and the Royal Anthropological Institute of Great Britain and Ireland.

Selection 7.2: Barclay D. Johnson. "Durkheim's One Cause of Suicide." *American Sociological Review*, 30 (December 1965), 875–886. Copyright © 1965 by the American Sociological Association and reprinted by permission.

Selection 7.3: Gregory P. Stone and Harvey A. Farberman. "On the Edge of Rapprochement: Was Durkheim Moving toward the Perspective of Symbolic Interaction?" *The Sociological Quarterly*, 8 (Spring 1967), 149–164. Copyright © 1967 by the Midwest Sociological Society and reproduced by permission.

Selection 8.1: Herbert Blumer. "Society as Symbolic Interaction." In Arnold M. Rose, *Human Behavior and Social Processes*. New York: Houghton Mifflin, 1962. Pp. 179–192. Copyright © 1962 by Houghton Mifflin and Routledge and Kegan Paul and reprinted by permission.

Selection 8.2: Herbert Blumer. "Sociological Implications of the Thought of George Herbert Mead." *American Journal of Sociology*, 71 (March 1966), 535–544. Copyright © 1966 by the University of Chicago Press and reproduced by permission.

Selection 8.3: William H. Desmonde. "G. H. Mead and Freud: American Social Psychology and Psychoanalysis." In *Psychoanalysis and the Future*. New York: National Psychological Association for Psychoanalysis, 1957. Pp. 31–50. Reprinted from *The Psychoanalytic Review*—(Psychoanalysis and the Future, 1957), through the courtesy of the Editors and Publishers, National Psychological Association for Psychoanalysis, New York, N.Y.

Selection 9.2: Gunter W. Remmling. "Karl Mannheim: Revision of an Intellectual Portrait." *Social Forces*, 40 (October 1961), 23–30. Copyright © 1961 by the University of North Carolina Press and reprinted by permission.

This book is dedicated to my mother and father, who toiled on a small farm in the hills of North Dakota.

PREFACE

How shall we communicate the works of social theorists? This is the main question that prompted the development of this book. The traditionally approved answer is to have the student read them in the original. The advantages claimed for this approach are that the freshness of the originals is retained and that no biases other than the student's own are introduced. Thus, it is thought that in this way the student makes up his own mind about the theorist's work. There are, however, a number of difficulties that are not often admitted. In the usual case, a student does not read all of the man's work—there isn't time for it—and, therefore, he comes away with a partial view. And, while it is true that he introduces only his own biases, these can be considerable, given his inexperience in reading theoretical materials, his lack of knowledge of the times during which they were written, his difficulty in reading the sometimes archaic style and vocabulary, and his exposure to the great store of stereotypes[1] about all these theorists.

Or one can use a text authored by a single writer that covers all the significant theorists. There are three serious difficulties with this approach, however: (1) a given writer is not likely to be equally knowledgeable about every subject and thus produces an unevenly written book; (2) the writer's biases, whatever they may be, permeate his entire text; and (3) any classifications of "schools" of theory, should he attempt them, may be highly misleading and superficial.[2]

The approach offered in this volume evolved in the classroom as students indicated a need for it. The book is a celebration of social theorists of the nineteenth century and part of the twentieth, besides being an evaluation and a reappraisal of their works. It is intended to *supplement* rather than replace reading of the works in the original. The theorists of this

---

[1] By a stereotype we mean some label that is widely used to identify some event, person, work, place, and so on, but that is used in such a way as to discourage acquiring any more than the minimal knowledge conveyed by the stereotype itself.

[2] See Stephen Fenton, "The Myth of Subjectivism as a Special Method in Sociology," *The Sociological Review*, 16 (November 1968), 333–349; and the review by Robin M. Williams, Jr., of *Community, Character, and Civilization* by Don Martindale in *American Journal of Sociology*, 70 (November 1964), 380, 381.

period are treated in secondary sources by writers who have studied their particular subject long and carefully and who are themselves working sociologists. Through their interpretations we gain more quickly, though not more superficially, a view of the theorist's work and, often, of his times, in a style and vocabulary more readable than the original. We also have the benefit of clarifications that have been made since the theorist wrote and pertinent evaluations in relation to present-day research and concerns in sociological theory. A greater diversity of interpretations and points of view is therefore possible. At the same time we have tried to give an adequate background for each chapter so that the readings can be more fully understood.

I would like to acknowledge my indebtedness to a number of people: to my students, who provided me with feedback on the articles herein presented;[3] to Charles P. Loomis, William F. Form, William Faunce, and Jay Artis, from whom I learned in the classroom; to Richard N. Adams in anthropology and Richard S. Rudner in philosophy, who also influenced me. I wish to give special thanks to Lewis Coser, who supplied considerable criticism on an earlier draft of this book. Many other colleagues to whom I am grateful I cannot name here; some I have come to know since my graduate studies, and some I know only through their works. Nathan, my ten-year-old, apparently believes this book to be an interdisciplinary work since he calls me a "socie-biologist!" Finally, I appreciate the considerable help given me by the late Caleb Smith of Holt, Rinehart and Winston and some much needed encouragement from Richard Owen, also of Holt, and my grateful thanks to Elyce Misher for all of her work on the manuscript.

DeKalb, Illinois   Clinton Joyce Jesser
October 1974

---

[3] Each chapter title page of this book contains a comment from a student about the particular theorist to be considered. I include these comments not because I wanted to create the first "hip reader" in sociological theory, but because I felt they might personalize the book and give a more human dimension to a topic that is often treated in a very pedantic manner.

CONTENTS

Social Theory Revisited

Introduction

Why Study Past Social Theorists?

Why should we study the classical theorists in sociology? For many reasons. Every science, if it is to be worthy of the name, must make its founders obsolete; but it must also incorporate their valid insights and ideas. That is, its accumulated strategies and probings should benefit from the founders' efforts, while new techniques and information should enable us to go beyond the old masters, to do better what they attempted, and should permit us to avoid their errors.[1] At the same time, an appreciation of the past is necessary if we are to see how each theorist's work opened new doors and served as a model (although an imperfect one in some cases) for future research.

When properly understood and criticized, these theorists' works can give us a starting point for pursuing many of the questions that still concern sociology. What are the effects of increasing development of science and industry in a society? What is the nature of society and its sources of social order? What are the major social divisions, the extent of inequality between them, and the causes and consequences of this? Where shall we look for the sources of great long-term change in a society, and how do they operate? Of what consequence to a social system are the antithetical principles of organization embodied in it? To what extent do normative patterns control the behavior of people when they have had little to do with their creation? Although there is certainly no need to venerate these scholars unduly, one cannot ignore the fact that they phrased important questions and accomplished analyses that are still worth knowing about today.

There can be no certainty as to what a particular author meant in one passage or another, nor that the emphasis we give a phrase was the one he intended. We interpret writings selectively, using and emphasizing

---

[1] Robert K. Merton, *On Theoretical Sociology* (New York: Free Press, 1967), 26–29.

what meets our or some group's intellectual and ideological[2] needs. Spencer may be "in" for a while, then Marx or Durkheim. There is, however, room for middle ground. An appreciation of the *various* questions a theorist pursued, of the shift in direction he may have taken, and of the place he occupied within the social structure of his society can help check the wild swings in fashion that discredit one man while extolling another.

How Study Social Theory?

How shall we study the works of past theorists? We have already indicated that a proper mixture of respect and criticism is necessary. The main objective in this book is to find out how their ideas stand today. We have also suggested that when a man's work is viewed in relation to his times and his social biography—his roles, audiences, friends, and adversaries—a fuller appreciation of it is gained. This is only an ancillary objective, but such an analysis requires some elaboration.

The sociology of knowledge takes as its basic working hypothesis the assertion that ideas, even those that become the legacy of sociology, are to a degree products of social life, just as material traits and inventions are. Therefore, a sociologist properly studies ideas by attempting to discover the extent to which they resulted from or were shaped by needs, conditions, debates, changes, and other factors, within the society to which the thinker belonged.

However, we must also appreciate the complexities and limitations of the sociology of knowledge. Our theorists may have assumed diverse roles: an apologist for conservative powers, a member of an alienated group, an official of a government, to cite a few possibilities. Their social life and times will not have *fully* determined the content of their ideas, the style in which they presented them, nor the techniques they used to analyze them; scholarly styles and ideas—especially explanatory ideas that employ the imagination—are too complex to be neatly fashioned in this way. By being critically introspective and exercising some detachment from their surroundings, writers *can*, to a degree, free themselves from the prevailing thoughtways and opinions of the day. And the ideas themselves, especially those that assert a relation between empirical events (hypotheses), can of course be determined to be true or false without consideration of the biases of their author or the times in which he lived. If, for example, a theorist asserts that formality increases as the size of

---

[2] One definition of ideology is the following: ". . . a system of beliefs that presents value-judgments as empirical truths in order to justify, with or without conscious intent, a particular socio-economic group's claim to material and prestigial rewards" (Walter P. Metzger, "Ideology and the Intellectual: A Study of Thorstein Veblen," *Philosophy of Science*, 16 [April, 1949], 125).

organizations increases, the validity of this hypothesis must depend solely on the evidence that shows this to be or not to be the case—not on the milieu that shows us how or why the theorist got interested in organizations or looked at them as he did. It is only when we ask why these types of ideas were expounded at a given time, or why this particular person formulated them, do we need to employ a sociology-of-knowledge study.

We can also study the works of the classical sociologists as history. Robert K. Merton recently issued the long-overdue complaint that sociologists are not very systematic in their analysis of the history of sociological theory—not as careful as they are in their analysis of sociological problems in the empirical world. "The historian of ideas runs the risk either of claiming to find a continuity where it did not in fact exist or of failing to identify continuity where it did exist."[3] For the analysis of theoretical, as well as other ideas, we need some more formal and precise criteria—some tools to work with—so that we will be better able to compare ideas of one theorist with those of another.

For example, in disputes over who "borrowed" whose idea, we will have to determine not only which writer enunciated it first and whether one or the other or both could have known of their common idea, but also whether the two ideas are really the same. Were the ramifications—the insights and deductions gleaned from the idea—the same? And did the theorists make the same use of the idea in their overall work? This is a question that the sociology of knowledge can help answer by showing some of the trends or problems from which the idea arose or to which it was addressed. Similarly, in the case of a theorist who was known to have been exposed to an earlier writer's work, the criteria of ramification and use will apply in judging how similar his ideas were to his predecessor's.

Not all the difficulty, it is admitted, resides in the historian of sociology and his inadequate tools. Often, as in the works being examined in this book, careful definitions of key terms are not developed and the total logical structure of the argument in which the terms appear is far from clear. The task of systematically comparing ideas is difficult, and we shall not pursue it to any large extent in this book, but Merton has words of wisdom and caution for those who would.[4] He feels that too often "adumbrationism," careless claims for similarity, characterizes the analysis of the history of social theory, where "the faintest shadow of resemblance between earlier and later ideas [is taken] as virtual identity."[5]

---

[3] Merton, *On Theoretical Sociology*, p. 8.

[4] Merton's tools would be needed if one were, for example, to judge the assertion by Andreski that Spencer can be regarded as the forerunner if not the true founder of cybernetics. (See Stanislav Andreski (Ed.), *Herbert Spencer* [London: Michael Joseph, 1971], p. 27.)

[5] Merton, *On Theoretical Sociology*, p. 21.

What Is Social Theory?

We believe that the men selected in this book qualify as social theorists because they all offered explanations or interpretations of problems or questions in the context of observable social phenomena. They turned their attention, as social analysts never before had, to the *actual* social world and appreciated the necessity of careful observation and data collection. They defined a field for and an approach to sociology and fashioned concepts for the analysis of societal phenomena. They tried to give coherence to the field of sociology and distinguish it from other disciplines. Their explanations are quite scientific and theoretical because, in contrast to the folkwisdom of earlier social thought, they are abstract and therefore organize observations of social phenomena. Furthermore, these explanations are (1) not intended to be immediately practical (i.e., to solve social problems whose dynamic patterns are not yet understood); (2) nor primarily prescriptive (i.e., to persuade toward ethical standards of how social phenomena and actors *ought* to behave); (3) nor indifferently parochial (i.e., to rest experience or observation on a narrow base in time and place.) And they attempt to answer the question, Why? Why do social phenomena come about, differentiate as they do, and change?

The explanations in the works presented here may not provide very satisfactory answers, but they are worthy of consideration. For example, although evolutionary theory is fraught with pitfalls when applied to social phenomena, it does at least give a plausible account of why and how societies grow and differentiate from one another. Marx did have some explanations for the formation and conflict of classes, even if these are imprecise, defective to a degree, and almost tautological.[6] And Weber did have a theory for the rapidity of Western capitalistic development, not withstanding the facts that the theory is strewn over two or three hundred pages of writing, is not subjected to a "crucial experiment," and somewhat neglects factors such as transportation and military and political technology in the West. Finally, Durkheim did attempt an explanation of differential suicide rates and conceived of the types of observations that would constitute a crucial test. Although the Jews possessed many characteristics which should have predisposed them to high suicide rates (such as being highly urbanized, attaining high educational levels, and being

---

[6] For example, in his hypothesis that major or radical changes in the organization and control of production will be followed by major changes in the class structure, he fails to define the two phenomena (changes in production and changes in class structure) independently of one another, to specify measurements for each change, and to hazard predictions on the basis of the hypothesis. It is too commonly assumed that when class structure changes, the mode of production has also changed; and where mode of production has changed *without* a change in class structure, the former is *alleged* not to have been radical enough. Here the closeness to tautology is evident.

engaged in commercial occupations to a large extent), Durkheim's theory still predicted low suicide rates because of their group cohesiveness.[7] This factor was crucial to the theory and was borne out in research.

Whatever else theory requires—and today, owing to the influence of considerations in sampling, measurement, testing, and formal models, the requirements are diverse and disputed—it requires imagination, at least in the early stages of development. By this we mean not the metaphysical / conjectural imagination unbridled by and indifferent to real social facts of order and change, but the *art* of probing questions about social life and process, discovering ideas that visualize novel connections and dynamics sometimes by assuming the existence of hidden or heretofore unnoticed factors (e.g., Weber's conception of the "Protestant ethic" or Durkheim's conception of "anomie") until their status can be inferred empirically. This type of imagination has the highest respect for the incontrovertibility of empirical fact—the final arbiter that makes or breaks a theory—but acknowledges that it is the power of the human intellect that makes sense of empirical facts. No one can tell another person exactly how he can develop the perception to see the puzzles in the social world around him. No one can teach another exactly how to find important questions to research—those that will lead to other important questions or unlock answers that will integrate a whole range of data, such as Durkheim's conception of group cohesiveness. And no one can stipulate an exact set of rules by which to seize upon new insights. But that theory requires vision and the art of understanding the hodge-podge social world few will deny.

The theories examined here differ in (1) their scale, (2) their degree of clarity and focus, and (3) their causal form.

1. By *scale* we mean the range of social phenomena to which the theorist confines his observations. For example, some men, known as macroscopic theorists, seek the key dynamics by which different changes in *whole* societies come about, a scope that everyone in this book, except Simmel and Mead, embraced.[8] Their approach might be either historical or evolutionary. The historical sociologist largely examines diverse and detailed historiographies with the aim of gleaning generalizations about social dynamics by comparing cases in which a given social development did occur with those in which it did not. The evolutionary sociologist constructs schemes of general stages of social development for societies as a whole, attempting to show how one stage is both a prerequisite and a

---

[7] Arthur L. Stinchcombe, *Constructing Social Theories* (New York: Harcourt Brace Jovanovich, 1968), pp. 17–25.

[8] See Helmut R. Wagner, "Displacement of Scope: A Problem of the Relationship between Small-Scale and Large-Scale Sociological Theories," *American Journal of Sociology*, 69 (May 1964), 571–584.

limitation of the next. Historical sociology should be possible without accepting evolutionary theory, whereas the construction of evolutionary theory requires historical sociology inasmuch as the theory must illuminate and be "tested" by historical fact. We see Max Weber as primarily a historical theorist and Herbert Spencer as an evolutionist, while Marx represents both modes of thought.

2.   The *clarity and focus* of a theory refers to the extent to which it has become crystalized into clear propositions and interrelations among these propositions.[9] The theories of the men considered in this book tend to be relatively non-extant. They were written at the informal, cursive level; so one must ferret out the theory's essentials from the many pages over which they tend to be scattered and then attempt to link up the propositions. Weber's work on religion and capitalism is of this nature. Durkheim's theory of suicide, on the other hand, is crystalized more easily. Theories are no less important for being non-extant, however. As mentioned above, most of the theorists in this period set themselves to explore social phenomena and to develop conceptual frameworks for examining their dynamics; explicit theory development was not usually a dominant orientation.

3.   Finally, we come to *causal form*, that is, the particular level or type of underlying causation that a theory emphasizes. This aspect is quite important, as it involves the theorist's conception of what is fundamental about social life and what social science should do to illuminate the social world. Although other terms might be more descriptive, we will call one type of theory *grounded theory*[10] and the other type *external theory*. We cannot go into all the philosophical antecedents of these two types here (some sections of the last chapter of this book are relevant to this discussion). Suffice it to say, however, that they quite clearly distinguish the way some sociologists conceive of theory and do their work today (and debate the issues in sociology).

The two types of theory are already seen in the way the men covered in this book conducted the sociological enterprise. But it is only in the last approximately thirty years, in the case of the development of external theory, and in the last ten years, in the case of the development of grounded theory, that the methodology of each (the logic by which theorizing proceeds) has been refined and new tools for constructing and using the theories in research have been added.

Grounded theorists, such as Weber, Simmel, and Mead, seek to depict

---

[9] See Richard G. Dumont and William J. Wilson, "Aspects of Concept Formation, Explication, and Theory Construction in Sociology," *American Sociological Review*, 32 (December 1967), 985–995.

[10] Barney Glaser and Anselm Strauss, *The Discovery of Grounded Theory: Strategies of Qualitative Methodology* (Chicago: Aldine, 1969).

and understand social life *at the level of the thinking, feeling, striving actor* and the way perceptions and meanings of events, emerging in some unique time order in the life of the actor, affect the course of his actions. When other actors are involved, their perceptions and meanings must be taken into account also, and we must find out how one actor influences the other. Unless very good life history documents exist, the sociologist must involve himself as a researcher / participant–observer in the life of the actors being studied, taking more the role of the researcher / *participant* as the situation permits, as the level of meaning to be grasped deepens, or as the group's ways are more foreign to the researcher. New techniques of observation, analysis, and theory construction (some borrowed from field work in anthropology) have been added to the contributions of Weber, Simmel, and Mead to make their approach a more complete and sophisticated methodology.[11]

Grounded theory is ultimately the construction of the researcher who, as much as possible, experiences the subject of investigation first-hand. Its goals are (1) to summarize cogently and sensitize us to the complexities that influence how the actors define their situations; (2) to understand the way they predicate their everyday lives on tacitly shared understanding that makes complex interaction possible; and (3) to describe the regularities manifested in such interaction. Theory in this sense is never finished; moreover, it avoids the pitfall of explaining social life mechanistically, by ignoring the symbol-mediated world of the actor. The world of social action is seen as complex and dynamic, man's existence being more sentient than that of other animals; hence, such theories are produced largely for heuristic purposes. They are constructions of the researcher summarizing the "mix" of the social world as seen and managed by the actor. An example of grounded theory in the work of Weber might be his depiction of how the religious definitions and strivings of Protestants worked their way into the actor's economic activities by infusing a rational view toward resources, industrious labor, and acquisitiveness. A modern instance would be the work of Manning[12] on the processes by which pregnant, unmarried women gradually decide that an abortion is necessary.

---

[11] See George McCall and J. L. Simmons (Eds.), *Issues in Participant Observation* (Reading, Mass.: Addison-Wesley, 1969); William J. Filstead (Ed.), *Qualitative Methodology* (Chicago: Markham, 1970); Jack D. Douglas (Ed.), *Understanding Everyday Life* (Chicago: Aldine, 1970).

[12] Peter K. Manning, "Fixing What You Feared: Notes on the Campus Abortion Search," in James M. Henslin (Ed.), *Studies in the Sociology of Sex* (New York: Appleton, 1971), pp. 137–166. An approximation of complete participation in the life of the actors being studied may be thwarted by a number of factors, such as distance, sex of the researcher, and so forth. But an attempt is made to get acquainted with the situation of the subjects.

Grounded theory is not necessarily adverse to statistical generalization. For example, the action being observed by the researcher can be described as having *x* meaning for *n* number of actors and occurring with a certain frequency. Nor is grounded theory carried out unsystematically; perceiving or inferring meaning and sequences of meaning requires carefully observing and querying the actor in different contexts. Neither is the theory always hidden or implicit. However, the more conscious effort to refine participant–observer techniques and to grasp meaning constellations and sequences has tended to make grounded theory microscopic rather than macroscopic. What grounded theorists shun is the attempt of external theorists (to whom we turn next) to apply a view of causation that sees the actor as circumscribed by or passive in face of larger material and social conditions, to give priority to concepts that omit the strivings and constructions of the actor, and to utilize a hypothesis-"testing" approach in which the strength of relationships between "variables" seems to be paramount.

External theory, one of the most prominent approaches to the construction of theory in sociology, largely leaves the actor out or *does not include him as the "significating" person in the way grounded theory does.* Here the explanatory goal is different, based on a different image of social life and the operation of causes. External theory draws more heavily on the physical science model in that it attempts to show how social processes and conditions, often viewed as operating outside the actor, limit his world or produce given consequences in his situation or overt behavior. The effects that such forces have on the actor are assumed to be predictable, and models are often employed to depict alternative guesses concerning the "paths" they follow. Hypothesis formulation seeks the connections between "variables" abstracted from social life or between units of activity irrespective of how these are experienced by the actor. A large body of data is usually sampled in order to determine which variables are statistically related.[13] An example of external theory in the work of Durkheim would be his idea that the variation in suicide rates depends on the presence or absence of anomie in society. An example today is the conception that various kinds of behavior (e.g., voting) are linked to status inconsistency.[14]

Since the main purpose of this book is to revisit and evaluate the ideas of major figures in the recent history of sociology, the above discussion serves to remind us that, where theories are advanced by the

---

[13] Many methods texts could be cited. See Hubert M. Blalock, Jr., (Ed.), *Methodology in Social Research* (New York: McGraw-Hill, 1968) or Blalock (Comp.), *Causal Models in the Social Sciences* (Chicago: Aldine, 1971).

[14] For example, see Gerhard E. Lenski, "Status Inconsistency and the Vote," *American Sociology Review*, 32 (April 1967), 298–301.

writers, the criteria by which they are evaluated should be reasonably *appropriate* to the type of theory developed.

Selection of Theorists and Articles

The objective of this book has already been stated in the preface: to acquaint the student with the works of social theorists in a summary form and to assess their present-day standing.

Obviously, the theorists presented here were selected for certain reasons. All except George Herbert Mead and Karl Mannheim wrote mainly during the nineteenth century, a period sometimes called the "classical" age[15] of sociology. During this time the discipline was cast in the mold of science, was institutionalized as a subject within colleges and universities, and was practiced according to synthesizing rather than compartmentalizing, fact-gathering methods that came to dominate the field later. And the theorists in this book usually identified themselves as sociologists or wrote major pieces considered to be sociological treatises, such as that of Karl Marx on technology and inequality. These works and the ideas they embody are discussed in the subsequent chapters.

There are other reasons for selecting these theorists. Auguste Comte, Herbert Spencer, and Emile Durkheim struggled with the organization of the discipline, trying to distinguish it from others in its approach and content and searching not only for a general set of concepts by which to organize the facts of society but also for the laws of its development. This problem is acute even today. Karl Marx provided much of the foundation, later built upon by Mannheim, for the sociology of knowledge, an analysis that is very popular today. Marx also provided one of the first macroscopic theories of social change that utilized some key analytical variables in bringing the "super- and the sub-structure" of society together.[16] Max Weber searched history for sociological generalizations and constructed abstract conceptual schemes for contrasting different social organizations. In a debate that persists to the present day, Weber was an early and sophisticated advocate of the view that explanation in social science poses problems not encountered in physical science. Emile Durkheim exhibited a highly disciplined analysis of societies, taking great care to give empirical base to his theories. He, like Weber, also stirred a controversy over explanation, this one on the question of reduction: are social facts irreducible to psychological facts, and are psychological variables, therefore, totally

---

[15] See Alvin Gouldner, *The Coming Crisis of Western Sociology* (New York: Basic Books, 1971), pp. 116–138.

[16] See Gert H. Muller's review of Gerhard Lenski's "Human Society." *Contemporary Sociology*, Vol. 1 (July 1972), 306–307.

irrelevant in the explanation of social facts? Finally George Simmel and Herbert Mead gave impetus in social science, as did Weber, to the development of concepts reflecting a view of the world as seen by the actor, a world in flux and change as a result of the actor's creativity.

We have already mentioned several criteria governing the choice of the articles. Preference was given to those secondary sources that not only presented a description of the theorist's basic ideas but also attempted an evaluation of them. It was desirable that the articles contain some reference to the times, to the sociocultural conditions and problems current when the theorist lived, although the major emphasis in this book is on *re-evaluation* of these scholars' works from our vantage point and not on a thorough understanding of them in relation to their own milieu. Where such descriptions of the times were lacking, we supplied them, particularly for Auguste Comte, Herbert Spencer, Karl Marx, and Max Weber. We seek to know the theorist whole—the full flavor of his life, times, and works, which has been ignored in previous theory texts. When we read a literary work, we want to know something about the author; why not when we read the works in sociology, too?

It was also important that some articles be included here in which the works of the theorist's entire career were treated so that any shifts in his thought could be detected and described. Such change is conspicuous in the lives of almost all of these men, especially Comte, Spencer, and Durkheim. Unless these new directions are noted, the old stereotypes, based on only one segment of the man's work, are nurtured. In Comte's case, the debate between the liberals and conservatives of his day played a part in his transformation; for Spencer, the alternating conceptions of society were significant; and in the case of Durkheim, the interplay of authority and autonomy became important.

Finally, criteria of readability and cogency guided the selection of the articles.

In summary, we have attempted in this introduction to explain the reasons for selecting persons called theorists in sociology, the meaning of theory, and the virtues of selecting secondary sources for this book. Much more could be written, but it is hoped that this brief sketch will suffice as a background for the examination of the works of the theorists and their times which follows in the next chapters.

It may be in order to explain briefly why the theorists are not taken up in strict chronological sequence. We feel that Spencer, rather than Marx, should follow the presentation on Comte because we wish to show the contrast between France and England and how it affected their sociologies. It is, we thought, proper for Simmel to follow Weber since, although their sociologies differ in methodology and conceptual focus, they share a concern for the survival of man's individuality in the modern world. Finally, we present Durkheim rather late in the book because he represents the theory / research approach that came to predominate in later (especially American) sociology and because it is convenient—especially in view of our choice of the Stone and Farberman article, Selection 7.3—to move from Durkheim directly into Mead.

**Theorists Covered in This Book and Dates
of One Major Sociological Work of Each**
Auguste Comte (*Positive Philosophy*, 1830–1842)
Herbert Spencer (*Principles of Sociology*, 1876–1896)
Karl Marx (*Capital*, 1867–1879)
Max Weber (*The Theory of Economic and Social Organization*, circa 1911–1920)
Georg Simmel (*Sociology*, 1908)
Emile Durkheim (*The Division of Labor in Society*, 1892)
George Herbert Mead (*Mind, Self, and Society*, posthumous, 1934).
Karl Mannheim (*Ideology and Utopia*, 1929).

ONE

Prelude to Comte: The Sociocultural Context of Nineteenth-Century Sociology in France

General Introduction

Social thought in every age is oriented to certain controlling ideas. Especially important are those that arise in periods of significant societal change and upheaval—periods termed *critical* by Auguste Comte and *axial* by Don Martindale[1]—and that become subjects of deep concern in the debates and analyses of social thinkers. Such ideas, Robert A. Nisbet[2] believes, are the concepts of community, authority, status, the sacred, and alienation. They preoccupied social thinkers interested in order and stability in such different arenas of wide-scale change as the Greek city-state, ancient Rome, and the early Christian church of St. Augustine and became most prominent again in nineteenth-century Europe as Comte appeared.

The fourteenth through the eighteenth centuries had brought the Age of Reason. Gradually, critical reason united with empirical science to produce the philosophy of the Enlightenment, diverse in its sources but exemplified in the works of such men as Montesquieu and Rousseau.[3] Montesquieu broke with the past by advancing a philosophy of history and

---

[1] See Don Martindale, *Social Life and Cultural Change* (Princeton, N.J.: Van Nostrand, 1962), pp. 66–71.

[2] Robert A. Nisbet, *The Sociological Tradition* (New York: Basic Books, 1966), pp. 6, 7.

[3] Irving M. Zeitlin, *Ideology and the Development of Sociological Theory* (Englewood Cliffs, N.J.: Prentice-Hall, 1968), pp. 11–32.

society that would discern social facts as they are, outline the interdependence of institutions, classify and compare societies, and identify the laws to which the real conditions of society are conformable. Error and ignorance operate at the human social level, however, and consequently men deviate from what the laws require; thus the full potential of what society ought to be is not realized. Rousseau gave more of a radical twist to his conception of society by invoking a hypothetical and pristine "state of nature" in which man might serve his minimal needs adequately by himself. He attempted to show that the only moral force capable of holding society together occurs when men are allowed to develop interdependencies on the basis of their real differences in talent and ability; moreover, they must be permitted to submit themselves *freely* to these relationships in accord with their reasonable conception of the "General Will," or the greater good of the group. Any other arrangement results in a corrupted and artificial society that can be held together only by force. Return to the original state of nature is not feasible, and perhaps, thought Rousseau, society itself need consist of nothing more than the condition that allows a man to expand his individual goodness through freely-entered-into contracts.

Such was the thrust of the philosophical analysis of society in the works of two representatives of Enlightenment thinking. Their immediate objectives were not to bring about any specific social change nor to deny the need for interdependencies between groups. But for several reasons they were pressed into the service of those who out of their own political or economic motives sought quick destruction of the old order. Montesquieu, in particular, warned that society might be astray from its real possibilities, the nature of which scientific research might disclose. Rousseau placed great faith in the potential for individual men to avert the tyranny of powerful institutions if given liberty. Both attacked tradition with the critical scalpel of reason and disliked corporate (medieval) society, which fettered the individual in his thought and commerce. Headily optimistic, they held that the faculties for an individual's direction and discoveries dwell within the individual himself rather than in religious authority and other time-honored institutions. Opposed to aristocracy and the monolithic control of the Church, they inclined instead toward political sovereignty, individual (natural) rights, and equality.

In the nineteenth century, although the current of thinking was still generally with the Enlightenment movement, a more sympathetic reconsideration of the virtues of medieval social order arose in the works of such men as Bonald and Maistre.[4] This reassessment was made more urgent by the severe social changes being wrought by the political and industrial revolutions in France. The political revolution, Nisbet reminds

---

[4] Ibid., pp. 43–55.

us, totally changed the broad goals of political power, secular rationalism, and moralistic ideology—it aspired to "save" man.[5] The industrial revolution was likewise severely disruptive; it altered the relations between man and his work, his community, and his family, brought new technology, the factory system, and changes in property relations, and swelled the population of cities.

In the midst of these far-reaching changes, different groups made very different diagnoses of what was happening and, especially, of what was to come. Liberals generally applauded the greater freedom of movement and commerce afforded individuals (especially those in the growing middle classes) and the rise of secularism, which permitted more freedom of thought. And radicals believed in the possibility that power, if purified and entrusted to the people, could be used in the service of building a new and more equitable social order based on the abolition of most forms of private property, even one that retained some benefits of the factory system.[6] It is the posture of the conservatives, however, that is described in the following article by Nisbet.

Introduction to Selection 1.1

In this essay Nisbet again reminds us that theoretical problems of the social sciences always have a significant relation to the moral aspirations of an age. He argues that the social philosophy of conservatism, which gained very little attention in the nineteenth century, importantly shapes the concerns of sociological thought even today. Conservatism in the nineteenth century was the product of a negative reaction to capitalism, political centralization, religious dissent, scientific rationalism, individualism, secularism, and equalitarianism. But conservatives remained largely unrecognized because of the then unfailing faith in the self-stabilizing, free individual and the presumed beneficence of historical change. These were taken as foregone conclusions, inherent "goods," and the conservatives could not sway opinion toward openly inspecting them. Today this faith has largely disappeared, and we are again concerned in sociology with institutional dislocations, psychological insecurities, and uncertainties of the social order.

Faced with the broad perspective of masses, alienation, and power—forces that alarmed many—the conservatives enunciated general assumptions about the nature of society and man that were designed to sober up the liberals. These Nisbet describes below: They upheld the idea that society is a product of long, slow, natural growth with an intricate relationship of parts. The individual is nothing apart from society, which

---

[5] Nisbet, *The Sociological Tradition*, pp. 33, 34.

[6] Ibid., pp. 9–31.

shapes even his conceptions of individual rights. Social institutions, even those of the Middle Ages, serve basic, timeless human needs. The functions of practices and beliefs in society are interrelated; the rational functions of certain of these are not readily apparent but nevertheless they foster group sentiments or cohesion at a deeper level. Historical change does not guarantee organizational harmony; in France, for instance, it succeeded in further severing the moral ties that bind an individual to his family and kin and in loosening the force of authority. Finally, interdependence in a society requires hierarchy.

Scientific social thinkers of the time were not completely unaffected by the import of these assumptions, however, and Nisbet closes by showing one of these lines of influence—that on the emergence of systematic sociology in France in the works of Comte, LePlay, and Durkheim.

Notice that Nisbet is not saying that sociology has become the *advocate* of conservative causes in any particular age, whatever they happen to be. He does believe, though, that in the problems it selects and in the concepts it fashions (such as status and cohesion) sociological research exhibits a concern for the questions raised by the conservatives of the nineteenth century as they reacted to social processes very much in motion today.

I.I

Conservatism and Sociology

ROBERT A. NISBET

To the contemporary social scientist, to be labeled a conservative is more often to be damned than to be praised. After all, does not the *New International Dictionary* define "conservatism" as the "disposition and tendency to preserve what is established" and, in effect, accuse the conservative of "tending to maintain existing institutions or views" and of being "opposed to change or innovation"? Put in this light the social scientist is likely to conclude that those qualities most essential to the humanist or scientist—originality, independence, audacity, and disdain for tradition—are the very opposite of conservatism.

But conservatism, in any full view, cannot be restricted to the psychological terms of attitude and evaluative response. In the contextual terms of history there are also conservative *ideas*. Such ideas as *status, cohesion, adjustment, function, norm, ritual, symbol*, are conservative ideas not merely in the superficial sense that each has as its referent an aspect of society that is plainly concerned with the maintenance or the *conserving* of order but in the important sense that all these words are integral parts of the intellectual history of European conservatism.

They are also integral concepts in the contemporary study of human behavior. More than one observer has been recently struck by the profound change that has taken place during the last generation in the general orientation of American sociology. Until a generation ago the principal interests of American sociologists lay in the study of *change*. Those aspects of society which Spencer and Ward had categorized as dynamic were foremost objects of study, and in almost all such studies the essentially organizational character of historical change was taken for granted. Allied with this faith in the beneficence of change was the conviction that the real unit of sociological investigation was the individual, regarded typically as self-sufficing in nature and as the most solid element of social reality. With very few exceptions, problems and hypotheses reflected a widespread moral conviction of the organizational direction of history and of the self-sufficing nature of the individual.

Today, we plainly find a radically different orientation. The major orientation is not change but *order*. Gone is the rationalist faith in the power of history to solve all organizational problems, and gone also is the rationalist myth of the autonomous, self-stabilizing individual. In the place

16

of these older certainties there now lies a widespread preoccupation with phenomena of institutional dislocation and psychological insecurity. More than any other, it is the concept of the social group that has become central in contemporary sociology. As a concept it covers the whole set of problems connected with integration and disintegration, security and insecurity, adjustment and maladjustment. It contrasts sharply with the primacy of the individual in earlier American sociology.

Doubtless, present theoretical interests in the social group and its psychological properties may be seen as manifestations of the moral imperatives of community which dominate so many areas of belief and longing at the present time. Theoretical problems in the social sciences always have a significant relation to the moral aspirations of an age. When, in the eighteenth and nineteenth centuries, there was widespread faith in moral and social progress and in the emancipation of individuals from old ways of action and belief, the prime theoretical problems of the social sciences were those of change, process, evolution, and the varied concepts of the self-driven, autonomous individual. In our own day, when a preoccupation with community and a fear of insecurity pervade almost every area of civilized life, it is not strange that the social sciences should deal so preponderantly with theoretical problems of group integration and disintegration.

But current ideas are related not only to current moral contexts; they have also a genetic relationship to earlier sequences of ideas. An idea system which possesses no decisive importance in one generation or century frequently provides the materials of the dominant intellectual perspective of the generation or century following. Such is the historical significance of the idea system of conservatism. As a historical structure of ideas, conservatism has received much less attention in the history of ideas than have individualism and rationalism, systems which so notably held the intellectual field in the nineteenth and early twentieth centuries. Yet, from an essentially minor position in the nineteenth century, conservatism has come to exert a profound influence upon the contemporary mind.

Three major perspectives stem from the writings of the early nineteenth-century conservatives in Europe. The first is the perspective of the *masses:* of populations relentlessly atomized socially and morally by the very economic and political forces which the liberals and radicals of the nineteenth century hailed as progressive. The second perspective is that of individual *alienation*: of widening aggregates of individuals rendered steadily more insecure and frustrated as the consequence of those moral and intellectual changes which the rationalists saw as leading to creative liberation from the net of custom. The third is the perspective of *power*: of monolithic power that arises from, and is nurtured by, the existence of masses of rootless individuals, turning with mounting desperation to centralized authority as a refuge from dislocation and moral emptiness.

These are the major intellectual legacies of conservatism. But within them lies a number of smaller, more specific, interests which can be seen in sharp contrast to the central ideas of nineteenth-century individualist

rationalism and which can be seen also as contributing to the very core
of a great deal of contemporary sociological thought. It is the argument
of this paper that present-day problems and hypotheses of social order,
group integration and disintegration, and the nature of personality are
rooted much more deeply in the conservative tradition in modern European
thought than in the liberal-radical systems of the nineteenth century
which are more commonly made the background of modern sociology.

Conservatism, as a distinguishable social philosophy, arose in direct
response to the French Revolution, which had something of the same
impact upon men's minds that the Communist and Nazi revolutions have
had in the twentieth century. In each instance the seizure of power, the
expropriation of old rulers, and the impact of new patterns of authority
upon old certainties led to a reexamination of ideas of freedom and order.
But it was not alone against the Revolution in France that the conservatives revolted. It was more fundamentally against the loss of status that
could be seen everywhere in western Europe as the consequence of economic change, moral secularism, and political centralization. For such men
as Burke and Bonald, the French Revolution was but the culmination of
historical process of social atomization that reached back to the beginning
of such doctrines as nominalism, religious dissent, scientific rationalism,
and to the destruction of those groups, institutions, and intellectual certainties which had been basic in the Middle Ages. In a significant sense,
modern conservatism goes back to medieval society for its inspiration and
for models against which to assess the modern world. Conservative criticisms of capitalism and political centralization were of a piece with de-
nunciations of individualism, secularism, and equalitarianism. In all these
historical forces the conservatives could see, not individual emancipation
and creative release, but mounting alienation and insecurity, the inevitable
products of dislocation in man's traditional associative ties.

From this critical view of history the conservatives were led to formulate certain general propositions concerning the nature of society and man
which diverged sharply from those views which the rationalists and
individualists had emphasized.

The first and most inclusive proposition has to do with the nature of
society. Society—what Burke called "legitimate" and Bonald "constituted"
society—is not a mechanical aggregate of individual particles subject to
whatever rearrangements may occur to the mind of the industrialist or the
governmental official. It is an organic entity, with internal laws of development and with infinitely subtle personal and institutional relationships.
Society cannot be created by individual reason, but it can be weakened by
those unmindful of its true nature, for it has deep roots in the past—roots
from which the present cannot escape through rational manipulation.
Society is, to paraphrase the celebrated words of Burke, a partnership of
the dead, the living, and the unborn. For the conservatives, especially in
France, the metaphysical reality of society, apart from all individual
human beings, was unquestioned; and this was perhaps the major proposition directed against the social nominalism of the Enlightenment.

Second, the conservatives insisted upon the primacy of society to the individual—historically, logically, and ethically. Bonald was led to work out a complex theory of symbolism and language development in order to prove that man and his ideas could never have preceded the institutions of society, institutions which had been created directly by God. "Man," wrote Bonald, "exists only in and for society. Society forms him only for himself. . . . Not only is it not true that the individual constitutes society, but it is society which constitutes the individual by *l'éducation sociale*." Hegel wrote critically of rationalist efforts to deal with "the isolated individual" and rejected strenuously what he called "the atomistic and abstract point of view." Apart from the constraints and representations embodied in society and its associative disciplines, there is no morality, and man is intellectually in a void. There are no instincts or prepotent reflexes in man by which thought and morality can be deduced. Only through society and its associative and symbolic manifestations does man become man at all.

From this it follows, in the third place, that society cannot be broken down, even for conceptual purposes, into individuals. The irreducible unit of society is and must be itself a manifestation of society, a relationship, something that is social. The individual, Lamennais declared, is but a fantasy, the shadow of a dream. We can never perceive what the rationalist calls "individuals." We see, rather, members of society—not "individuals" but fathers, sons, priests, church members, workers, masters, and so forth. Not even for purposes of politics, Hegel argued, should the reality of social membership be obscured. "The circles of association in civil society are already communities. To picture these communities as breaking up into a mere conglomerate of individuals as soon as they enter the field of politics is . . . to hang the latter in the air. . . ."

Fourth is the principle of interdependence of social phenomena. Since society is organismic in nature, there is always a delicate interrelation of belief, habit, membership, and institution in the life of any society. Each individual and each social trait are parts of a larger system of coherence. Efforts, however well-intended, to reform or remake one part of society inevitably violate the complex lines of relationship which exist and must exist in any stable society.

Fifth is the principle of needs. Not fictitious natural rights but unalterable *needs* of man, his "wants," as Burke termed them, are primary. Allowance for these, Burke wrote, "requires a deep knowledge of human nature and human necessities, and of the things which facilitate or obstruct the various ends which are to be pursued by the mechanisms of civil institutions." Every society and each of its parts is the response to certain timeless needs of human beings. Disrupt the mechanisms of satisfaction, and disorder and misery are the result.

Sixth is the principle of function. Every person, every custom, every institution, serves some basic need in human life or contributes some indispensable service to the existence of other institutions and customs. Even prejudice, Burke insisted in a striking passage, has, despite the contempt that it arouses in the mind of the rationalist, the indispensable function of holding together the structure of society, of providing a kind of emotional cement for beliefs and habits. There is, in prejudice, an indwelling wisdom that is the product of the centuries and of man's deep needs for security.

Seventh, the conservatives, in reaction to the individualistic Enlightenment, stressed the small social groups of society. The social group, not the individual, is the irreducible unit of society; it is the microcosm, *societas in parvo*. Internal social groups constitute the smaller allegiances of society, within which the whole society becomes meaningful. They are, Burke wrote, "our inns and resting places." The Revolution had exerted its most drastic powers against the traditional social loyalties, against the whole of that area of interpersonal relationships which had descended from the despised Middle Ages. But these are the true sources of society and morality. "No man was ever attached by a sense of pride, partiality, or real affection to a description of square measurements," Burke wrote in a hostile critique of French efforts to create new areas of administration and loyalty. "We begin our public affections in our families. . . . We pass on to our neighborhoods, and our habitual provincial connections."

The religious groups, family, neighborhood, occupational association— these, declared Bonald, are the necessary supports of men's lives. The reformers are in error when they strive to make men forget the values of this sphere of society and to live in terms of the rational dictates of will, based on scientific information. Abstract, impersonal relationships will never support a society; and where these principles tend to prevail in the population, there we find the strongest tendencies toward social and moral disorganization.

Weaken the traditional social relationships of men, whether by commerce or by governmental reform, argued the conservatives, and inevitably legitimate society will be replaced by an incoherent and distracted mass of individual atoms. Once individuals have become separated from traditional ties "and have got themselves loose, not from the restraint, but from the protection of all the principles of natural authority and legitimate subordination, they become the natural prey of imposters," wrote Burke. The conservatives in France made this the essence of a principle: man's reason, his goals, even his individuality, are dependent upon close affiliation with others and upon the structure of external values in society.

Lamennais, in a short essay on suicide,[1] wrote: "As man moves away from order, anguish presses around him. He is the king of his own misery, a degraded sovereign in revolt against himself, without duties, without bonds, without society. Alone, in the midst of the universe, he runs, or rather he seeks to run, into nothingness." To regard community as a check upon individuality is a monstrous error, for it is only within community that individuality can develop and be reinforced.

Eighth, the conservatives were led to recognize the reality of social

---

[1] This remarkable essay was published in 1819. See *Oeuvres complètes* (Brussels, 1839), Vol. II, p. 150–51. The same insight is to be found two decades later in Tocqueville's great study of democracy and at the end of the century in Durkheim's writings. I am indebted to Cesar Grana for directing my attention to this passage from Lamennais which he has translated for me.

disorganization. Liberals and radicals were not unmindful of the miseries and dislocations occasioned by the historical process, but they persisted in seeing the nature of history as inherently organizational in basic design. From the point of view of a Condorcet or a Bentham (and this remained true in the rationalist tradition through both the classical and the Marxian economists) there may have been intermittent *disorders*, but never disorganization in the large sense.

But the effects of revolutionary legislation upon traditional institutions created in the minds of the conservatives a deep preoccupation with disorganization. This was, for them, essentially a moral phenomenon, but it was inextricably related to historical dislocations of the legitimate interdependence of the functions and authorities of society. The consequence of revolutionary changes would not be higher forms of organization but rather an intensification of old processes of disorganization, culminating eventually in the atomization of all morality and society.

It was in these terms that the conservatives, especially in France, wrote bitterly of religious individualism. For them religious individualism was to be seen as the opposite side of social disorganization. Protestant depreciation of the corporate, ritualistic, and symbolic elements of religion could lead, like its historic attack upon the supremacy of Rome, only to the eventual sterilization of the religious impulse. The root meaning of the word "religion," Bonald declared, is social. What, indeed, does the parent-word, *religare*, mean but to bind together? To argue the supremacy of individual faith or belief is to argue the collapse of religion as a spiritual society.

The conservative view of urbanism and commerce was not different. All the conservatives were struck by the contrasting effects of town and country upon institutions and groups. Burke could see in urbanism and commerce certain leveling implications which weakened the basic resources of individuality. Hegel observed with alarm the disorganizing effects of English industrialism upon the personalities of men, through its destructive inroads upon family and local community. In a systematic study of the contrasting effects upon the family of urban and rural conditions, Bonald pointed to the dislocative impact upon the kinship ties of urban impersonality and industrialism. The city, he wrote, has the effect of congregating human beings but not of uniting them. The urban family is inherently a less stable form of organization than the rural, and so is the urban community. There is more genuine social solidarity in backward rural areas, despite the greater dispersion of the population than in the city.[2]

Ninth, the conservatives were led to insist upon the indispensable value of the sacred, nonrational, nonutilitarian elements of human existence. To argue that man may ever live by reason alone or by relationships founded solely upon reason is preposterous, the conservatives argued. To attempt to found society upon the purely secular and upon purely individualistic motivations of pure achievement is ruinous. Man lives and must

---

[2] *"De la famille agricole et de la famille industrielle,"* in *Oeuvres complètes*, ed. by Abbé Migne (Paris, 1859–64), II, 238 f.

always live through observances of ritual, ceremony, and worship. The onslaught of the Revolution against the *ancien régime* and the celebration of pure reason, both in legislative action and in popular decree, had dangerously weakened the sacred supports of society. Burke's famous words on the rationalist view of the political contract which is the state, his insistence upon the sacred, prerational foundations of all political association, were echoed in the writings of other conservatives. Apart from the *sacredness* of an institution or relationship it will not long hang together. Mere rationality is not sufficient.

Tenth was the principle of hierarchy and status. The revolutionary and rationalist emphasis upon equality must lead quickly, it was argued, to a leveling of social differences which will obliterate the natural channels of transmission of human values. Without hierarchy in society, there can be no stability. Classes of men in the larger society perform the same functions that are performed by ranks in an association, by the unequal status of father and child in the family. The very principle of interdependence of institutions in society carries with it, when one recognizes the different ages and capacities of individuals, the necessity of a similar interdependence of individuals. And this interdependence is necessarily hierarchical. In all associations the principle of hierarchy will assert itself; and, when men become aware of diminishing relationships between themselves and their accustomed status in this large social hierarchy, nothing but unhappiness and despair will be the result.

Finally, the conservatives emphasized the principle of legitimacy of authority. Authority is legitimate when it proceeds from the customs and traditions of a people, when it is formed by innumerable links in a chain that begins with the family, rises through community and class, and culminates in the large society. By its invasions of traditional areas of authority and its exaltation of the rational state, the Revolution had deprived human beings of the secure roots which come from legitimate authority and left them exposed to unstable compromises between chaos and extreme power. The legitimacy of authority proceeds, not from axioms of right and reason, but from beliefs and habits which are imbedded in the needs which are served by authority. Far from being an artificial thing, a necessary evil at best, as the liberals had argued, authority is the substance of every form of relationship. Authority does not degrade; it reinforces. It is force that degrades, the kind of force that must ensue when the normal authorities are dissolved. A generation later, Tocqueville gave perfect expression to the conservative theory of authority when he wrote: "Men are not corrupted by the exercise of power or debased by the habit of obedience, but by the exercise of power which they believe to be illegitimate, and by obedience to a rule which they consider usurped and oppressive."

It can scarcely be argued that conservatism exerted any widespread influence on thought in the nineteenth century. For this was the century of great hope, of faith in what seemed to be the ineluctable processes of history, of faith in the natural individual and in mass government. All the major tendencies of European history—the factor system included—were widely regarded as essentially liberating forces. By them, men would be emancipated from the ancient system of status and from communities within which initiative and freedom were stifled. For most minds in the nineteenth century, conservatism, with its essentially tragic conception of history, its fear of the free individual and the masses, and its emphasis upon community, hierarchy, and sacred patterns of belief, seemed but one final manifestation of that past from which Europe was everywhere being liberated.

Yet conservatism had its influence, and it is only today that we are becoming aware of the real extent of conservative ideas upon nineteenth-century thinkers and policy-makers. Here we can consider but one of these lines of influence, that which is a part of the rise of systematic sociology in France. Sociology may be regarded as the first of the social sciences to deal directly with the problems of dislocation involved in the appearance of a mass society. Economics, political science, psychology, and anthropology long remained in the nineteenth century faithful to the precepts and perspectives of eighteenth-century rationalism. Sociology, however, from the very beginning, borrowed heavily from the insights into the society that such men as Burke, Bonald, and Hegel had supplied. Thus, even in Comte's philosophical celebration of progress, there is a profound note of veneration for the past and of preoccupation with processes of status and security that is lacking in the writings of those for whom the rationalists of the eighteenth century formed the proper point of departure in the study of man.

The traditionalist quality of Comte's new science is not to be missed. His admiration for the structure of the Middle Ages is almost unbounded, and he tells us that the Catholic traditionalists deserve the eternal gratitude of positivists for having awakened men's minds to the greatness of medieval culture. Moreover, he praises the followers of Bonald for having actually used positivist principles in their own analysis of institutions. By their recognition of the inherent instability of individualism and the disorganizing social consequences of such dogmas as equality, popular sovereignty, and individual rights, and by their insistence upon the priority of society to the individual and the social dependence of man upon society's values and institutions, the traditionalists have earned the gratitude of all positivists.

Comte's aim was the creation of a science of society. He regarded his long study, *The Positive Polity*, as a treatise in sociology, as the compendium of the new science of society. The principles of positivism, he declared, when absorbed by everyone, would make forever unnecessary any reliance upon the tenets of historic religion. The science of human relations was to be the great organizing principle in society that would replace traditional Christianity. Comte himself was no scientist; but, through his romantic worship of science, the social structures of family, community, language, religion, and cultural association were removed from the frankly theological and reactionary context in which they lay in

Bonald's thought and were given the context and terminology, if not the substance, of science. However absurd many of Comte's ideas may have appeared even to some of his followers in France and England and however difficult it is to distinguish clearly between the positive approach and the conservative approach to human relations, the important fact here is that, by his veneration of science, Comte's work was the means of translating the conservative principles into a perspective more acceptable to later generations of social scientists.

If Comte gave most of the nomenclature and emotional appeal of science to the study of human relations, it was Pierre Frédéric LePlay, who some years later gave it a methodology and set of techniques for empirical investigation. LePlay was a devout Catholic, a reactionary by all standards of his time. Like the earlier conservatives, he found most of the ills in western Europe to be the product of the Revolution. He, too, was concerned with restoring the prestige of the family, church, and local community and correspondingly depreciated the role of the state and direct political action. Ideas of progress, equality, individual rights, popular sovereignty—all these were as detestable to LePlay as they had been to Bonald and Comte.

Yet, despite his outspoken traditionalism on all economic, social, and spiritual matters, the conclusion cannot be avoided that LePlay contributed more to the scientific study of human relationships than the science-worshipping Comte did. It is irrelevant to point out that most of the conclusions which LePlay drew from his massive study of the European working classes were conclusions hardly different from the basic prejudgments which he had inherited from his early environment, hardly different from the frankly reactionary ideas of Bonald and De Maistre. What is important from the point of view of historical analysis is that LePlay transformed the moral insights of the conservatives into a set of concrete problems calling for rigorous field investigation.

Les Ouviers européens is perhaps the supreme example in the nineteenth century of actual field research into the structural and functional aspects of human institutions. The heralded thinkers of the nineteenth century—Comte, Spencer, and Ward—were content, on the whole, to leave their readers in the terminological suburbs of science; the nomenclature of science was set in contexts alien to techniques of verification. But in LePlay's work we have something decidedly different. Making all allowance for the influence upon his field work of moral presuppositions and objectives which have nothing to do with science strictly regarded, the fact remains that it was LePlay, above all others, who took the study of the family, local community, occupation, and cultural association out of the theological, the romantic, or the evolutionary contexts in which others had set them, robbing them of reality, and put them in the tougher, richer perspectives of comparative research into the actual lives of peoples. With this comparative methodology went a complex of precise techniques for the detailed study of human beings in their institutional environments.

What is important in the present connection is simply to note that in

LePlay's work the basic insights and assumptions of philosophical conservatism become translated into an empirical study of human relationships. The essential content of conservatism remains; the methodological approach is changed significantly.

It is in the writings of Durkheim, however, at the very end of the nineteenth century that we find the most important link between conservatism and the contemporary study of human behavior. Durkheim shares with Freud a large part of the responsibility for turning social thought from the classic rationalist categories of volition, will, and individual consciousness to those aspects of behavior which are in a strict sense nonvolitional and nonrational. Until a few years ago Freud's was the more widely recognized influence in this respect. But it is impossible to miss the fact that Durkheim's reaction to individualistic rationalism is more radical than Freud's. Freud was virtually one with the rationalists in his acceptance of the primacy of the individual and of intra-individual forces. Nonrational influences upon behavior proceed, in Freud's system, from elements deeply imbedded in the individual, elements deriving essentially from man's racial past. The individual remains the *terminus a quo* in Freudian explanations. For Durkheim, however, the principal sources of human motivation, thought, and conduct lie in social conditions external to the individual; they lie in society and in the history of society. What we are given, in the study of human nature, as Durkheim tirelessly proclaimed, is a set of social facts, facts which stem from the primacy of society to the individual. It is this supreme emphasis upon society and all its mechanisms of constraint that makes Durkheim's reaction against individualistic rationalism more basic than Freud's, and it is this emphasis in all its ramifications that places Durkheim securely in the conservative tradition.

If Durkheim could not accept the basic premise of the French conservatives—the primacy of an omnipotent personal God to all society and culture—he was at least willing, in his final phases of thought, to ascribe to religion a determinative influence in human life that no theologian could improve upon. And it is hard to resist the conclusion that society, for Durkheim as for Bonald, takes on characteristics of exteriority and power that make it almost indistinguishable from a divine entity.

Like Bonald, Durkheim can declare that "society is a reality *sui generis*; it has its own peculiar characteristics, which are not found elsewhere and which are not met with again in the same form in all the rest of the universe." Almost in the words of Burke, Durkheim writes of collective representations that they "are the result of an immense cooperation, which stretches out not only into space but into time as well; to make them a multitude of minds have associated, united, and combined their ideas and sentiments; for them long generations have accumulated their experiences and knowledge. A special intellectual activity is therefore concentrated in them which is infinitely richer and complexer than that of the individual." And when he writes of crime that it is *necessary*, that "it is bound up with the fundamental conditions of all social life, and by that fact useful, because these conditions of which it is a part are themselves indispensable to the normal evolution of morality and law," he might be paraphrasing Burke's celebrated remarks on the necessity of prejudice in society.

We see the elements of conservatism in Durkheim's whole rationale of social constraint; in his demonstration of the noncontractual elements in contract; in his insistence upon the irreducibility of the moral "ought" to utilitarian considerations; in the moral basis that he gives to all social organization; in his dissection of morality into the two cardinal categories of discipline and group attachment; in his momentous division of all social phenomena into the sacred and the secular. We see the philosophical assumptions of conservatism in his profound stress upon the functional interdependence of all parts of society; in his derivation of the categories of human reason from sources in society. Durkheim's view of history is essentially the conservative view, with its stress upon the disorganizational and alienative aspects of modern European development and upon the creation of the masses, lying inert before an increasingly omnipotent state. And, finally, we cannot miss the conservative cast of his most articulate program of reform, the creation of new intermediary occupational organizations to fill the social vacuum caused by revolutionary liquidation of the guilds.

None of this derogates in any way from the scientific achievement of Durkheim. One may agree with many a reader of Durkheim's works that seldom has the scientific union between theory and empirical data been as rigorous and fruitful as it is in *Suicide*. What Durkheim did was to take the conservative view of society out of what was essentially a speculative frame of inquiry and translate it into certain hypotheses, which he sought to verify— at least in the case of rates of suicide—crucially. We assuredly cannot miss the scientific intent and perspective of much of Durkheim's work or the careful relation between theory and existent bodies of data. But neither can we miss the clear historical source of Durkheim's hypotheses regarding suicide that is to be found in earlier writings on the subject by Lamennais and Tocqueville and, for that matter, in the whole structure of the conservative view of society.

SUMMARY AND EVALUATION
OF CHAPTER ONE

While others concerned themselves with the effects of economic liberalism on the economy, industrialization on work, religious dissent on the Church, and individual rights and representation on politics, it was the conservatives who sensed the *social* implications of all of these developments. They perceived societal breakdown and pondered whether man from the fourteenth to the nineteenth centuries in his search for freedom, individualism, equality, modernity, and release from the traditional, close-knit groups of family, kin, guild, neighborhood, community, and church had escaped one set of tyrannies only to find himself caught in another. Mass society breeds evils of its own: rootlessness, alienation, atomization, constant change, a frustrating inability to provide something to believe in, the failure to live up to its own high standards of perfection and progress, yes, even the manipulation of the disoriented individual in its swings in fashion, large-scale, standardized mass media, and centraliza- tion of governmental power.

Sociologists of the period benefitted from this "creative paradox"[1] by turning the moral issues of the conservatives into research questions *while remaining themselves humanely and deeply concerned for the survival of modern man.* Comte was a liberal because he advocated the methods of science and even a near-radical because he believed in the large-scale reordering of society along "positivist" principles, although he shunned the idea of entrusting power to the common man. But he was more of a conservative in that he lamented moral decay and the breakdown of organic interdependence, decried the decline of such intermediary groups as the family and community, which tie the individual to the larger society and control his impulses, and feared rapid social change.

SELECTED BIBLIOGRAPHY

Anderson, Eugene N., and Pauline R. Anderson. *Political Institutions and Social Change in Continental Europe in the Nineteenth Century.* Berkeley: University of California Press, 1967.

Barber, Bernard. *Science and the Social Order.* New York: Crowell-Collier and Macmillan, 1962.

Barber, Bernard, and Walter Hirsch (Eds.). *The Sociology of Science.* New York: Free Press, 1962.

Barnes, Harry Elmer, (Ed.). *An Introduction to the History of Sociology.* Chicago: University of Chicago Press, 1948. Chap. I and II (also in abridged paperback version published in 1966 by same press).

Becker, Howard, and Harry Elmer Barnes. *Social Thought from Lore to Science.* 3d ed. New York: Dover, 1961. Vol. I, Chap. IV; Vol. II, Chap. XV.

Bendix, Rinehart. "Tradition and Modernity Reconsidered." *Comparative Studies in Society and History,* IX (April 1967), 292–346.

Berger, Peter L., and Thomas Luckmann. *The Social Construction of Reality: A Treatise in the Sociology of Knowledge.* Garden City, N. Y.: Doubleday, 1967. Anchor paperback.

Butterfield, Herbert. *The Origins of Modern Science: 1300–1800.* New York: Crowell-Collier-Macmillan, 1951.

Cahnman, Werner J., and Alvin Boskoff (Eds.). *Sociology and History.* New York: Free Press, 1964.

---

[1] Robert A. Nisbet, *The Sociological Tradition* (New York: Basic Books, 1966), p. 17. On a more popular level some conservatives seem to believe that man is basically evil and can be "tamed" or controlled only within society; some liberals, on the other hand, believe that man can make a more perfect environment of society and thereby perfect man himself or restore the freedom he supposedly lost on first entering into society.

Guerlac, Henry. "Science during the French Revolution." In Philip G. Frank (Ed.), *The Validation of Scientific Theories*. New York: Crowell-Collier-Macmillan, 1961. Pp. 159–176.

Holzner, Burkart. *Reality Construction in Society*. Cambridge, Mass.: Schenkman, 1968.

Kaplan, Norman, (Ed.). *Science and Society*. Skokie, Ill.: Rand McNally, 1965.

Lefebvre, Georges. *The Coming of the French Revolution*. New York: Vintage Books, 1947.

Marsak, Leonard M., (Ed.). *The Rise of Science in Relation to Society*. New York: Crowell-Collier-Macmillan, 1964. Paperback.

Martindale, Don. *Social Life and Cultural Change*. Princeton: Van Nostrand, 1962. See especially Pt. I.

Merton, Robert K. *Social Theory and Social Structure*. Rev. and enl. ed. New York: Free Press, 1957. Pt. IV. "Studies in the Sociology of Science."

Nisbet, Robert A. "The French Revolution and the Rise of Sociology in France." *American Journal of Sociology*, 49 (September 1943), 156–164.

Nisbet, Robert A. *The Sociological Tradition*. New York: Basic Books, 1966.

Torrey, Norman L., (Ed.). *Les Philosophes*. New York: Capricorn Books, 1960.

Von Martin, Alfred. *Sociology of the Renaissance*. New York: Harper Torchbooks, 1963.

Zeitlin, Irving. *Ideology and the Development of Sociological Theory*. Englewood Cliffs, N. J.: Prentice-Hall, 1968.

TWO

Auguste Comte

"I found particular relevance, or, I should say,
identification, with the situation of his [Comte's] generation.
The same bleak future in terms of job situations faces
my generation. Comte's subsequent spiritual malaise and
the vacuum of values parallels my own search for a set
of values and ideals that are not only valid to my 'ivory
tower' campus life, but which can fit and work in the much
more real world of my future."

—STUDENT COMMENT

General Introduction

As indicated in the previous chapter, Auguste Comte lived in a time
of great change and, to some, great promise. Feudalism had collapsed.
Political revolutions, spurred by Enlightenment and liberal economic philosophies, had shaken the class structure, traditional notions of government, and conceptions of men's rights. The industrial revolution was
changing man's relation to his work, family, and community and seemed
to promise a period of plenty for everyone. The grounds for the development of knowledge were being challenged, and a reconstruction was under
way. Practitioners of the physical sciences were disputing the authoritative
preachments of the clergy about the nature of the world and, by revealing
natural laws, offering the possibility of control over the physical domain.
Moreover, nationalism and the Reformation had weakened the Church.
Socialist thinkers, heady with the idea of man-directed change and convinced
of the existence of progress, were pressing for reform with hopes of usher-
ing Europe into an improved social order. Finally, revolutionaries were
demanding that intellectuals dissolve their guild-like boundaries and make

29

knowledge available to all and that they focus their studies on matters of national interest.[1]

Politically the scene in early nineteenth-century France was chaotic, with bourgeois republicans, Royalists, Bonapartists, socialists, Catholics, and anticlerical groups all clamoring to administer their particular nostrums to cure the ills of society. Governmental stability was threatened. The revolution of 1798 was followed by counterrevolution and then a Directorate rule. The first decade of the 1800s, Comte's early years, was dominated by the rise and fall of Napoleon, who was followed by the kings of the Bourbon Restoration. During their rule, the misery of the factory workers became especially acute and sparked further revolution from 1830 to 1848. In all of this Comte remained disenchanted. He condemned individualism, equalitarianism, and political sovereignty, those philosophies he considered responsible for fueling revolution; in addition, he chafed under the lack of opportunity for his own career during the Restoration period.

Comte (1798–1857) was born in Montpellier, France, of Catholic parents, who were said to be Royalists (supporters of the restoration of French royalty). When he was nine, he began his study at the Lycée of Montpellier, where he progressed very rapidly. He subsequently enrolled in the *Ecole Polytechnique* in Paris, which emphasized studies in mathematics and physics, and became something of a rebel in these disciplines. A friendship developed between Comte and one of the new progressive socialist thinkers of his day, Henri Comte de Saint-Simon, whom he served as secretary from 1817 to 1823 and from whom he broke in about 1824 with some bitterness. Shortly thereafter began a long period of tribulation: from 1826, when he fell ill, to about 1838, he suffered financial hardship, rejection from colleagues, and marital discord. Between 1845 and 1846 he established a friendship with Clotilde de Vaux, a woman whom he admired greatly. In 1848, after receiving insufficient acclaim for his scholarship and losing his job at the *Ecole Polytechnique*, he established the Positivist Society.[2]

---

[1] See Charles Coulston Gillispie, "Science in the French Revolution," in Werner J. Cahnman and Alvin Boskoff (Eds.), *Sociology and History* (New York: Free Press, 1964), pp. 89–97.

[2] Comte's main works are the following: First came "A System of Positive Polity," a pamphlet published in 1820). Next was *Plan of the Scientific Operations Necessary for the Reorganization of Society*, on which Saint-Simon collaborated. It was called by Comte "the great discovery of the year 1822," the date of publication. *Positive Philosophy* in six volumes, the first three of which deal with natural science, was produced from 1830 to 1842 and was alternatively titled *Course of Positive Philosophy*. Written while Comte was lonely and bitter but still aspiring to gain a scientific audience, it was an outgrowth of his lectures and his study with Saint-Simon. It is condensed into a single volume, entitled *The Positive Philosophy of Auguste Comte*, trans-

Comte's contributions include his ideas of (1) positivism;[3] (2) the law of three stages of intellectual evolution; (3) the filiation of the sciences—that is, the ordering of disciplines, which entails the recognition of what the higher disciplines owe to the lower—sociology being at the top because of its relevance to moral as well as physical phenomena (see Selection 2.2); and (4) the division of sociology into the study of statics, the laws governing the coherence of social phenomena (see Selection 2.1), and dynamics, the laws governing the movement and succession of such phenomena.

Positivism was Comte's term for his method of studying society, modeled largely on the technique of natural science. He advocated observation, comparison, experimentation, and, most importantly for social science, the study of history, which instills in man a proper appreciation for his debt to the past. Though controlled experiments in the social realm are not usually feasible, a type of quasi-experiment is sometimes possible when a "pathological" case occurs naturally (probably, in Comte's judgment, early nineteenth-century French society as a whole!). In such circumstances, we can improve our knowledge of society by comparing the "abnormal" state with the "normal."

Human progress, Comte believed, derives largely from intellectual evolution, and he thought he had detected the principle of this process in the *law of three stages*: the Theological, the Metaphysical, and the Positive, stages also noted by Turgot and Burdin. Comte claimed that when man first attempts to understand a realm of phenomena, he tends to ascribe its changes to the "immediate action of supernatural [fictitious] beings" (the Theological stage); next, man locates its causes in "abstract forces, veritable entities [that is], personified abstractions" of a less capricious sort (the Metaphysical stage); finally, the mind limits its explanations to the discoverable laws of "invariable relations of succession and resemblance," which the phenomena themselves disclose (the Positive stage). Thinking about the social realm still remained, according to Comte, in both the Theological (religious–speculative) and Metaphysical (philosophical–utopian) stages. He saw this as the result of man's tendency to analyze objectively first those phenomena from which he can most easily detach himself. Thus, astronomy enters the positive stage first and soci-

---

lated by Harriet Martineau. Finally Comte's *Positive Polity* appeared, also titled *System of Positive Polity*. It was published in four volumes between 1851 and 1854 and was dedicated to his beloved Clotilde. Three more of Comte's works are footnoted by David Cohen in Selection 2: *Religion of Humanity: Subjective Synthesis* (1856), *Opuscules de Philosophie Sociale* (1883), and *L'Industrie III* (with Saint-Simon, from 1817).

[3] For Comte's treatment of this idea as well as others described below, see mainly Harriet Martineau (Trans. and Ed.), *The Positive Philosophy of Auguste Comte* (New York: Calvin Blanchard, 1855), Bk. VI, Chaps. III–XI.

ology last because man's customs and values, being highly cherished and bound up with his very actions, are not easily scrutinized. The aim of positivism was "to help men develop a society in which positivistic consciousness determines social being."[4]

Comte's reference to the "filiation of the sciences" constitutes a claim that knowledge has entered the Positive stage in some areas before others, e.g., astronomy and physics. The higher disciplines, though entering the Positive stage later, are more complex and dependent upon the lower ones. The lower sciences can only "filiate" with the higher ones in an abstract sense; that is, they lay the groundwork for those above them. A new type of filiation must be observed at the level of sociology. Only at this level of analysis can one meaningfully use the historical method, which shows the continuous growth of society and the continuous influence of generations upon each other. Thus, the conservatism that required Comte to establish the whole before interpreting the parts, as in biology, now requires him to acknowledge the past within the present.

Comte's conception of sociology as *statics* and *dynamics,* stability and change, encouraged others to subject the discipline to serious investigation along these lines. This is his most important contribution. It is true that he tended to equate statics and dynamics with his moral concerns for order and progress and gave special emphasis to the idea that order must always precede progress. While this may diminish Comte's claims for his own objectivity, it does not, however, detract from his principal contribution of making sociology a self-conscious discipline.

But it is not enough simply to define what Comte meant by positivism, intellectual evolution, and sociology, for each must be viewed from the perspective of Comte's background, his times, and his goals. These will be discussed following the two selections for this chapter: an article by David Cohen (Selection 2.1) and one by E. E. Evans-Pritchard (Selection 2.2).

Introduction to Selections 2.1 and 2.2

The following two selections treat quite different aspects of Comte's works. Cohen considers heretofore unexamined questions: how Comte analyzed industrial activity and organization and how his encounter with conservative and traditionalist philosophies stimulated him to determine the social relations conducive to solidarity. The article is thus a logical extension of Nisbet's discussion in Chapter One. Evans-Pritchard takes another approach. Instead of discussing the influence of intellectual cur-

---

[4] George Simpson, *Auguste Comte: Sire of Sociology* (New York: Crowell, 1969), p. 8.

rents of the day on Comte's study of society, he clarifies Comte's major ideas themselves and assesses their standing today.

There is no substance to certain common notions about Comte. He did not remain a "science-worshipper" throughout his career or persist in the conviction that progress would insure internal order for society. Nor did he stay aloof from the actual examination of social relations. Cohen corrects these misconceptions. He is especially interested in Comte's later thought, which most sociologists have avoided, particularly some of his ideas on industry.

Comte's early concerns, according to Cohen, were mainly to define and defend the idea of a science of society and simply to assert the inevitability of social progress as science and industry increased. His "social physics" would ". . . allow a rational calculation of the action best suited to effect the transition" to a harmonious workshop of industrial organization in Europe, to be characterized, presumably, by rational mastery, moral autonomy for the individual, and social harmony. Then in the mid-1820s Comte encountered the works of the traditionalists and conservatives and was persuaded to their view that a genuine crisis existed; the "moral glue" holding French society together had indeed been dissolved. Comte adjusted by making a series of changes in his sociology that were to transform him from a naive believer in self-sustained dynamic progress to a proponent of the more sober view that society must be examined as it is here and now. He began to recognize that there are real limitations to what sociology alone can do in societal reconstruction.

Comte's first response to the crisis was simply to ask an extra duty of science: in addition to disclosing fact and connection, it must also reveal the appropriate morality that these require. Sociology, besides studying the progressing society, must also provide the consensus needed for social order. Comte would prescribe institutions to help remind the diverging interest groups of their common goals and make them aware of the new positivistic ideas. Just a little persuasion was needed to make people cooperate. Later, he came back to this thinking in his conception of a Church of Humanity, to be headed by wise, altruistic priest–sociologists.

It was to Comte's credit, however, that he saw the inadequacy of these views. He realized that sociology was more than faith in science, and that accedence to the exhortations of secular priests would not automatically bring about social solidarity. Therefore, around 1838 Comte turned to the task of discovering the elementary processes of social life that contain the seeds of cohesive relations. This study, called statics, explores how real societies function through the alignments of their different parts and how consensus is established so that these everyday operations can occur. Comte's analysis led him initially to examine industrialism and to produce, according to Cohen, the first "serious sociological account" of it. Comte recognized a paradox in the phenomenon of work, as did Durkheim later. On the one hand, work stems from man's egoistic need to stay alive and therefore fosters selfishness. But as industry becomes more specialized, individual skills consist more and more in performing only small segments of a large task. Thus, on the other hand, work also requires a cooperative effort that produces distinctly social tendencies. In recognizing the social aspects of work, Comte rejected both the liberal view that it was only an economic activity and the conservative view that industrial differentiation was singularly alien to solidarity and personality development.

But the possibility of divisive effects did concern Comte, so he pushed his study of social statics further, into another "involuntary" source of solidarity: the family. Here he found that as we labor with others in the intimate context of conjugal, paternal, filial, and fraternal relations, we develop "the sentiments to which there corresponds a similar affection outside . . . with similar effect."

Finally, Comte analyzed the state as an involuntary source of authority that enlarged on the coordinative and control processes already present in internally differentiated groups.

Comte's faith that the abstract forces of history would bring progress to society had crumbled. At the heart of his sociology now was the conviction that a concrete social order was *already* defined by the forces productive of social sentiments, namely work, the family, and the state. Consequently, progress from here on out for Comte would have to confine itself to the practical, but small, variations in the pace and direction of change that are possible in different social settings.

Finally, since Comte had analyzed only the sociological considerations of solidarity—that is, the social sentiments, and their manifestations in the larger society—he later attempted to outline a new, largely psychological discipline, *La Morale*. This science would complement sociology in that it would analyze two additional sources of solidarity: man's original nature and his individual variations. This, because of his death, he did not complete.

Evans-Pritchard, in Selection 2.2, undertakes the formidable task of examining the two major works of Comte's career: *Course of Positive Philosophy* (Comte as Aristotle) and *System of Positive Polity* (Comte as St. Paul). The "appreciation" takes the form of both praise and criticism. In his article, addressed to both sociologists and anthropologists today, Evans-Pritchard attempts to give the ideas in these treatises a fair hearing and thereby to clear up some misunderstandings about them.

In his consideration of *Course of Positive Philosophy*, Evans-Pritchard thinks, first, that Comte formulated the positive method to call attention to the fact that the essential method of all the sciences is the same. "Moral" (sometimes merely interpreted as "social") phenomena can and should be studied as "natural" phenomena, though Evans-Pritchard believes Comte could have clarified his position further by defining the status of natural phenomena. And Comte did not embrace *scientism*, the proposition that the instruments or techniques of science are more important than the questions it raises or the theories that guide an inquiry in the first place.

Next, Evans-Pritchard believes that Comte's scheme of the hierarchy of sciences was an original and illuminating piece of systematization, when viewed in terms of the *logical* connections between the different disciplines (the knowledge of the motions of phenomena in the lower, less complex disciplines, e.g. physics, does not depend on knowledge of the truths of the higher disciplines, e.g., biology) rather than an assertion of the unilinearity of their actual development. Psychology is omitted in Comte's scheme, probably, Evans-Pritchard contends, because there could in Comte's view be no bona fide place for a science of the individual since he cannot exist apart from society or humanity.

Then there is the matter of the law of three stages. In a general way, Evans-Pritchard believes, Comte was accurately describing how man's explanation of phenomena evolves from ascription to animistic forces (Theological and Metaphysical stages) to describing or explaining observable facts or conditions (Positive stage) both in the growth of humanity and in the life cycle of the individual. If the *Philosophes* deserved to be associated with the Metaphysical stage, it was because in Comte's view they did not properly understand that the problem of the time was a *moral* one, requiring not more critical and autonomous powers for the individual but, rather, a knowledge of society's requirements for solidarity. Comte tempered his condemnation of the early stages, however. He credited them with, essentially, acting as stepping stones for the next by providing examples of mistakes that must be corrected and attributed to the fetishism of the early theological stage the creation of the family. Similarly, he believed that critical periods, such as the one he lived through in France, are followed by organic periods in which knowledge complements the harmony of parts within a society.

Finally, Evans-Pritchard discusses Comte's conception of the laws of society. We must seek in history, Comte averred, not just any laws, but rather the laws of the general *direction* of society. Universal history of Humanity must give us a vision of where we are going, not merely dates and places. A description of the facts is not completed until it has imparted an understanding of both what they are and what they are becoming. Knowledge of laws in the social realm will be difficult to attain, Comte admitted. But they would allow man to change the pace of development a bit, to smooth out the "oscillations" that society experiences as it progresses, or to avert some of the minor crises that might occur.

In *System of Positive Polity,* Evans-Pritchard tells us, Comte (as

Saint Paul) considered the practical matter of a plan for reconstructing society; he attempted to coordinate sentiments (from which action springs) with reason (the knowledge about attaining goals that science can contribute). If sentiments alone cannot organize a society, and science itself cannot prescribe the right course of action, except to some extent by supplying knowledge of laws, exterior regulation and guidance must ensure that man performs his responsibilities to Humanity either out of love or duty. Evans-Pritchard concludes with the thought that the later works were not in contradiction with the earlier ones since there is always some place in sociology for philosophy.

2.1

Comte's Changing Sociology

DAVID COHEN

I

The historical significance of Comte's sociology has never been a matter of particular controversy. His work has usually been regarded as an early step toward an empirical science of society, where we find the application of scientific method to social phenomena united with a theory of scientific and social progress. The unifying element—common enough in late eighteenth- and early nineteenth-century thought—was his assumption that man's intellectual history was a steadily progressive development which would finally culminate in the extension of scientific method from nature to human society and culture. However imperfect his execution of the idea may be judged to have been, the significance of his work has generally been seen to lie in the effort to define the social fact and the laws of social movement scientifically.[1]

It is also commonly held, and correctly so, that this is true largely of Comte's earlier thought, that his later ideas moved in rather a different direction. With few exceptions, the social theory associated with his Religion of Humanity has seemed to sociologists less a significant aspect of their discipline's history than a denial of its scientific spirit. Most of all in British and American studies, the tendency has been studiously to avoid serious examination of his later thought.[2]

Yet this approach has yielded an inadequate view of both Comte's sociology and the social situation in which it developed. In reality, his

---

[1] A few of the studies that adopt this view are H. Gouhier, *La Jeunesse d'Auguste Comte et la formation du positivisme* (3 vols.; Paris, 1933–41), II, 5–62; L. Levy-Bruhl, *The Philosophy of Comte*, trans. Beaumont-Klein (London, 1903), p. 260; and A. Saloman, *The Tyranny of Progress* (New York, 1955), pp. 58–62. Sociologists, though often more sensitive to Comte's "organismic" ideas, still tend to the same attitude. See, e.g., D. Martindale, *The Nature and Types of Sociological Theory* (Boston, 1960), pp. 63–65.

[2] There is no worthwhile study in English of Comte's later work. The best study is P. Arbousse-Bastide, *La Doctrine de l'éducation universelle dans la philosophie d'Auguste Comte* (2 vols.; Paris, 1957).

entire conception of sociology changed radically as a result of his confrontation with two important facts of early nineteenth-century life. One
was the Industrial Revolution and the debate over its social effects; the
other was the challenge to ideas of scientific and social progress embodied in the conservative thought after the French Revolution.[3]

Comte began with a naïve, mechanical, and utopian conception of
sociology and its object in inevitable scientific and social progress. As a
result of his confrontation with the implications of industrialism and conservative ideas, he gradually evolved a more complex, non-mechanical, and
markedly less utopian conception of sociology and its object in social
solidarity. One very striking result of that movement was his virtual
abandonment of the evolutionary and methodological ideas associated with
his early thought. Another result, even less recognized, was that he developed a novel and substantial approach to industrialism and its social
consequences. In effect, his changing sociology represents the first effort
to take serious sociological account of the phenomenon known as industrialism. The development of his sociology is thus of particular interest in
the history of that science. It is of more general interest as an important
step in the evolution of the metaphors and concepts still employed to
understand and criticize industrial society.

II

From its inception, Comte's sociology embodied a basic tension, characteristic both of his work and of the general intellectual situation in
post-Revolutionary France. From the Enlightenment and the French school
of liberal economic thought he had absorbed the conviction that a golden
age of science and industry lay in the immediate future of European
society. There all knowledge would be humanized and positivized, purged
of the misleading transcendental fantasies of religion and metaphysics.
The confusion which marked all prescientific thought would be supplanted
with the careful procedures of mature empirical science. At the same time,
society would be totally industrialized. Industrial production, inherently a
peaceful and cooperative form of social organization, would transform
Europe into a vast and entirely harmonious workshop, centrally directed
by humane financiers. Oppression would be replaced by co-operation, war
by peace, conflict by harmony. As a result, the clash of opinion and power
would cease. In an age of intellectual certainty and social harmony,
political conflict and domination would have little or no place. Both the

---

[3] The impact of conservative ideas on early nineteenth-century social thought
has been treated well by R. Nisbet, in "The French Revolution and the Rise
of Sociology," *American Journal of Sociology* (1943), pp. 156–64; and in
"Conservatism and Sociology," *ibid.* (1952), pp. 167–75. There is no coherent
treatment of the early debate over industrialism in France; there are scattered
materials in the standard histories of socialism and the working-class movement. It is the non-socialist sources that are more interesting and less studied.
See P. Moon, *The Labor Problem and the Social Catholic Movement in France*
(New York, 1921), pp. 6–37; E. Martin St.-Léon, *Histoire de corporations des
métiers* (Paris, 1897), pp. 510–663; M. Elbow, *French Corporative Theory,
1789–1948* (New York, 1953), pp. 16–32.

state as an instrument of domination and otherworldly aspirations would evaporate. In science and industry men would concretely manifest their mastery of self and nature.[4]

All that remained in the 1820's was for some member of the European scientific community scientifically to describe and reveal the means of attaining this new age. Again in the tradition of the Enlightenment, Comte called for the creation of a predictive science of human progress. "The proper object of political science . . . is a general determination of society's future."[5] He proposed a new "social physics, to reveal the steps lying between Europe and the new order, which would allow a rational calculation of the action best suited to effect the transition. Taking societies as social wholes, he sought to examine their historical development in order to construct a proof of inevitable progress and a prediction of its future course. Society-in-motion was the chief social fact, and sociology was a weapon in the service of progress. It was a scientifically demonstrable program, a theory of social practice.[6]

At the same time, however, Comte also accepted the most significant and widely diffused element in the conservative reaction against science, social reform, and revolution. It was from Saint-Simon that he first absorbed the notion of society as a community of communities, constituted and sustained not by the rational assessment of self-interest, but rather by a body of communal values and beliefs. In the conservative view, here was the key to both social theory and practice. To grasp the common beliefs of a society was to penetrate to its very essence. Alter or dissolve that and you have changed or destroyed society itself.[7]

In his earliest writings (1817–22) the tension between these two elements was latent and only slowly rose to the surface. Since he equated the advance of science and industry with social progress, it seemed natural at first to represent their solvent effects upon earlier stages of European society as necessary and even happy consequences of man's evolution. In 1820 he regarded the dissolution of the *ancien régime* as a prerequisite of progress and a bright promise of the future.[8]

Two years later he took a somewhat more serious view of the question. Europe was deep in a fundamental crisis, resulting from the dissolution of an entire historic system of religious and social values. While

---

[4] Comte, *Opuscules de philosophie sociale* (hereinafter cited as *"Opuscules"*) (Paris, 1883), No. 2, pp. 5–62. Comte's early ideas on industry can be found in a series of essays entitled *L'Industrie III*, on which he collaborated with Saint-Simon; they date from 1817, and have been published in *Évolution originale d'Auguste Comte* (hereinafter cited as *"EO"*), ed. T. Mendes (Rio de Janeiro, 1913), pp. 93–162. (All translations mine.)

[5] *Opuscules*, No. 3, p. 186.

[6] Comte's first efforts toward a science of history lie in two fragmentary essays of 1819: "Ce que c'est la politique positive"; "De la division qui a existé jusqu'à présent entre la morale et la politique" (*EO*, pp. 447–54).

[7] See works by Nisbet cited in n. 3.

[8] *Opuscules*, No. 2, pp. 5–59.

science and industry had dissolved the old order, neither was yet sufficiently organized to supplant what had been destroyed.[9]

In 1824 Comte read the Traditionalists for the first time, with the consequence that his view was marked with a more acute sense of crisis. Society had been stripped of its constitutive element, and thus in political life "there remains no other expedient [for governments] than force or corruption."[10] A centralized, mechanical, and despotic state expanded into the void left by the breakdown of common values and intermediate associations. In individual life the absence of any social norms promoted the emergence of an autarchic individualism. Society, he argued, was in a state of continuing inner warfare; "social sentiment, searching vainly [for] some fixed and exact notion of what constitutes the common good . . . finishes by degenerating into a vague philanthropic intention, incapable of having any real influence."[11]

The critique was penetrating—it is still classical—and was drawn in substance from the literature of Traditionalism. Yet it was entirely typical of Comte's early thought that he should see the solution purely in science. The point he labored to make in the essays of the 1820's was that an entire new system of scientific ideas had developed, and lacked only a science of society to be complete. Once sociology was established, European civilization would once again rest on the solid ground of a common intellectual culture.[12]

Comte was thus in the curious position of arguing that science would cure the very disease it caused. The source of this paradox is not obscure. His sociology had initially been conceived as a proof of the inevitable advance and future triumph of science. Yet his attention had partly shifted from demonstrating progress to reconstructing consensus. Since there had been no corresponding shift in the structure of sociology, the new science was pressed into the service of both causes at once.

This tension was sharpened by his development, in this same period, of a new view of industrialism. While he did not suddenly abandon his earlier position, he did articulate some serious reservations. In particular, he came to regard the industrial division of labor as a mixed blessing. By the mid-1820's he was familiar with critics of the new economic order, and agreed with many that increasing specialization of function forced individuals to "a more and more limited point of view . . . animated by increasingly special interests."[13] By itself this view was not unusual, for it only echoed concerns over the psychic impact of the division of labor in industry dating back at least to Adam Smith.[14] However, Comte came to the problem precisely at the time he was first digesting the conservative

---

[9] *Ibid.*, No. 3, p. 88.

[10] *Ibid.*, No. 5, pp. 251–52. On the Traditionalists see Gouhier, *op. cit.*, III, 333–34.

[11] *Opuscules*, No. 5, pp. 247–48.

[12] *Ibid.*, No. 3, pp. 120–24.

[13] *Ibid.*, No. 5, p. 266. Gouhier, III, 110–57.

[14] *Wealth of Nations* (2 vols.; London, 1892), II, 301–8. Comte was familiar with Smith; see *EO*, pp. 573–74.

analysis of social disorganization and plea for the reconstruction of organic social cohesion. Thus, in 1824–25 he approached industrialism, having clearly in mind the idea of solidarity so prominent in Traditionalist thought. The result was that he moved from a consideration of the impact of specialized labor on the worker's psyche to reflections on its general social effects. He concluded that the industrial division of labor would result in men's inability to grasp "the relation of [their] special activity to the totality of social activity.[15] Social fragmentation would therefore proceed apace with the industrialization of European society; "what sociability gained in extent it lost in energy."[16] By 1825 Comte had concluded that social disorganization was an inevitable consequence of industrialism. The bright promise of a spontaneously integrated and harmonious social workshop had suddenly faded.

His immediate response had nothing to do with sociology. Comte called for new institutions, "having as their special purpose to recall to a general point of view minds disposed always to diverge, and . . . activities which tend always to deviate." A new spiritual power would be required to promulgate the new system of scientific ideas in forms accessible to the European masses. It would provide a comprehensive moral government, guiding thought and action always to the common good.[17]

The lack of any apparent connection between this proposal and Comte's sociology of progress is the clearest evidence of his dilemma. While the new spiritual power occupied a substantial portion of the essays of 1824–25, it plainly had no foundation whatever in his sociology. The form and content of the sociology of progress were not congruent either with the new problems which had drawn Comte's attention, or with the solution he began to elaborate. This was to be expected, for the very assumptions underlying his early sociology had been called into serious question. Having begun with the idea that Europe stood on the threshold of a scientific and industrial utopia, he had come to see in science and industry fundamental threats to the basis of society itself. It was not simply the sociology of progress, but his unexamined assumption of the compatability of science and industry with the reconstruction of organic solidarity which had been directly undermined. His interest had shifted without his sociology following suit.

III

Although Comte was reluctant to admit the subsequent changes that his thought underwent, he was not unaware of them.[18] Gradually the structure of his social theory moved into focus with his new concerns.

Regarding science, he finally arrived at the view that a new system of

---

[15] *Opuscules*, No. 5, p. 266.

[16] *Ibid.*

[17] *Ibid.*, pp. 267–68.

[18] See, e.g., Comte's letter to a Dr. Audiffrent, from 1857, published in *Auguste Comte Méconnu* (Paris, 1898), pp. 293–94. There Comte wishes he had never published the *Cours de philosophie positive,* which is usually regarded as his most important work. He clearly expressed the view that it seemed inconsistent with his later work.

communal ideas could not be based on science as he had earlier understood the term. Though initially he had conceived science as an ordered body of knowledge which represented nature only insofar as it could be known empirically, Comte changed the concept until it came to mean a constructed body of poetic fictions, teleological myths, "laws," all intended not to offer an empirical and objective representation of nature but rather to foster a generalized sense of universal community. Once he had adopted the conservative idea that the common experience of belief and communal emotion was the elementary social bond, he could hardly long persist in the search for a purely scientific system of communal beliefs. His original positivism had been sacrificed to the requirements of organic solidarity.[19]

The notion of a new spiritual power and this transformation of science required some justification. Here the three-stage law was worse than useless, for it expressed his earlier conviction that not only religion and metaphysics but myth and poetry as well would be supplanted by pure positive science. The law of man's increasing objectivity could hardly be employed as the rationale for a sudden increase in his subjectivity; particularly at the very moment when Europe was supposed to be moving into an age of wholly positive thought. The sociology of progress, which was nothing but an elaboration of the three-stage law of increasing objectivity, would be an inadequate theoretical foundation for these new ideas.

The problem was sharpened by Comte's growing conviction that even a new system of spiritual government would be inadequate to account fully for social solidarity. Reconstruction would require more than a new doctrine and a new spiritual power. It would be necessary to go deeper and to reveal the elementary forms and processes of social life in which solidary relations arose.[20]

The combination of these difficulties led Comte to sketch the outline of a wholly new sociology in 1838. "Social statics" would analyze the "conditions of social existence," seeking a "positive conception of social harmony," a determination of the basis of social cohesion.[21] This new science would delineate the sources of the "fundamental solidarity among all the parts of the social organism."[22] By defining the various involuntary sources of solidarity, social statics would reveal the matrix within which *voluntary* sources of solidarity might be established, thus providing a

---

[19] Comte's views changed slowly over a period of nearly twenty years. His later views are best summed up in *Synthèse subjective* (Paris, 1857), pp. 3–25. The changes can best be seen by contrast with some of his earlier pronouncements, where science is specifically characterized as a perfectly objective view of reality, in which the facts and generalizations cannot be altered or arranged to suit man's emotional or practical needs; see *Cours*, III, 187–88. For an excellent general treatment of these changes see J. Delvolvé, *Réflexions sur la pensée Comtienne* (Paris, 1932).

[20] *Système de politique positive* (4 vols.; Paris, 1895), II, 3.

[21] *Cours*, IV, 231, 251.

[22] *Ibid.*, p. 237.

theoretical basis for the new spiritual power.[23] Statics would therefore provide exactly what was missing in Comte's work thus far—an account of the nature and sources of social solidarity.

His discussion began on the conviction that the roots of most major social problems sprang from the egoistic drives generated by the pure necessities of sustaining physical existence. All activities aimed at satisfying these necessities must be self-regarding. Consequently, as long as practical concerns dominate man's life, as long as the mastery and transformation of the environment is a primary need, egoism will present a serious problem. This, Comte argued, becomes clear if social life is envisioned with the burdens of productive activity omitted. If nourishment, shelter, etc., were abundant and free, "then the great problem of human life would be resolved spontaneously." Such was the case because the dominance of egoism was due only to the "constant stimulus of physical needs. Deprived of such a stimulus [we would] particularly develop the only instincts which allow a perfect limitless, almost universal expansion . . . the sympathetic feelings."[24] In this ideal model of labor-free existence neither science nor industry would exist, for both arise to satisfy material needs. In their stead men would follow their inclination toward artistic play. "Actions would be transformed into games, which in place of preparations for practical life would constitute simple modes of expression and exercise." Men would devote themselves to "festivals, to express and develop the common affections."[25]

This juxtaposition of play and production has led some to argue that Comte regarded human labor as objectionable, or, what amounts to the same thing, merely an aspect of the world of necessity soon to be overcome by history's inexorable advance.[26] Yet he saw no end to productive activity and, what is more important, saw in it certain distinctly social tendencies. It is the need to produce which gives rise to the division of labor, that is, to production of a specifically social character. The division of labor, he insisted, was eminently suited to develop . . . the social instinct, by spontaneously inspiring in each a just sense of close dependence toward all others."[27] He saw an intimate reciprocal relation, where specialization intensified solidarity, which in turn allowed further differen-

[23] *Ibid.*, pp. 251–52.

[24] *Système de politique positive*, II, 142.

[25] *Ibid.*, pp. 144–45.

[26] This point of view has been most clearly expressed by Frank Manuel in *The Prophets of Paris* (Cambridge, Mass., 1962), esp. pp. 294, 313. See also J. Lacroix, *La Sociologie d'Auguste Comte* (Paris, 1956), pp. 82–100. For comments, see n. 30, below.

[27] *Cours*, IV, 421. There is no hint in any of Comte's work regarding the source of this, one of his most novel ideas. However, in 1821 Saint-Simon published (with Comte's aid) *Du Système industriel*, in the Preface to which he noted that in an industrial society men depend on others less as individuals, and more upon the mass of society. It may be that that was the germ of Comte's view.

tiation and growth. Indeed, the proliferation of work and more specialized skills meant that "social organization tends increasingly to rest upon an exact appreciation of individual diversity."[28] From this point of view, then, the division of labor stimulated a fuller development of individual personality at the same time as it deepened and extended solidarity.

Comte's treatment of productive activity was thus paradoxical. Although production arises to meet the demands of physical necessity, and always has a specifically egoistic character originally, it is precisely the productive process through which egoism is sublimated into social sentiments, and in which the burdens of physical necessity are lightened. Concerning the ideal model of a labor-free society, Comte had commented: "The irresistible needs which our activity must serve being personal, our practical life at first cannot display any other character . . . exciting the selfish while it represses the sympathetic development."[29] His point was simply that such a model was only ideal—emancipation from natural necessity and the sublimation of egoism could never occur spontaneously. They could only take place as a result of the productive process; they were the consequence of labor, not its denial. The notion of a labor-free society was a utopia only in a purely formal sense. It served as an ideal type designed to illuminate reality.[30]

The paradoxical quality of Comte's discussion was highlighted by his continuing contention that along with the solidarity-producing effects of the division of labor there would inevitably be some contrary consequences. It was probably as a direct result of the idea that socialized labor in itself would never generate sufficient solidarity to sustain society that

---

[28] *Cours*, IV, 426. (Italics mine.) The similarity to Émile Durkheim's defense of the industrial division of labor against critics of specialization is striking. Durkheim himself has been alone in seeing this *(Division of Labor in Society,* trans. G. Simpson [Glencoe, Ill.: Free Press, n.d.]), pp. 402–9.

[29] *Système de politique positive*, II, 149.

[30] Manuel takes a peculiar tack on this question. He argues that for Comte labor was merely "part of the transitional world of necessity from whose fetters the man of the future would be freed." Comte was "skeptical of the meaningfulness of this outer-directed activity [labor] in changing man's inner being" *(op. cit.,* p. 313). Yet the whole point of Comte's argument as summarized above is precisely the opposite. What appears to lie at the root of Manuel's view is his desire to represent Comte as an almost fantastic utopian. Manuel writes that Comte was a "dry, obsessively precise mathematics teacher" who threw "his textbooks out the celestial windows, and abandoned himself to the Italian operas" in his social theory *(ibid.,* p. 294). The result of this interpretation is, among other things, a mistranslation of Comte. When Comte wrote, regarding the model of a labor-free society, that we must "apprécier ce que deviendrait alors notre existence intellectuelle" *(Système de politique positive,* II, 142), Manuel translates "evaluate what our intellectual existence *will be*" *(op. cit.,* 194). Thus, Comte's conditional becomes the future tense, which of course makes it seem that Comte was proposing, rather than supposing. To my mind this throws serious doubt on Manuel's view.

he pushed the study of social statics further. His two main objects of inquiry were family and political relationships.

In the family, he argued, "man really begins to leave behind his pure personality, and first learns to live for others . . . it constitutes an indispensable preparation for social life."[31] The family presented the fundamental process common to all levels of human association. There, purely egoistic individual drives are transformed into the stuff of sociability by virtue of the active co-operation which family life demands. "It is only in these . . . intimate relations that labor first makes us appreciate sufficiently the obligation and satisfaction of living for others. [In] larger associations . . . the same necessity . . . tends to the same general results."[32] Thus, analysis of the family is crucial because it is the elementary social unit, and "the natural laws of all human association should be explained first regarding the most basic form."[33] The family presents a prototype of the various social processes—present in all varieties of association—in which sociability is imprinted on the primary egotistic human materials.

Comte's analysis of those processes centered on four types of relation and sentiment which developed in the family and ramified throughout society: paternal, filial, conjugal, and fraternal. The last of these he regarded as a "simple attachment" which constituted the most elementary and universal form of social affection. This relation, and the sentiment it generates, are most easily expanded beyond the family and are elementary to the development of social solidarity: they furnish a direct link between family and society. The filial relation, on the other hand, reaches across generations, producing "veneration," which extends solidarity beyond the merely contemporary forms of social relationship. It is the source and prototype of tradition. The paternal relation, which originates in affection for offspring, provides another "natural transition between the ties of the family . . . and the connections of society."[34] Through such extra-familial relations as apprenticeship it is transformed into a generalized social sentiment. Finally, in the conjugal relation Comte saw embodied the highest type of social sentiment, which finds clearest expression in the woman's cultivation of altruistic love. In its pure form such feeling is unattainable for anyone engaged in productive labor. In woman's love Comte saw the clearest approximation of pure altruism, and thus it represented the least adulterated form of social sentiment.

The family, then, was a training ground for the various sentiments which form part of the ground of social solidarity. To each of the relations and sentiments developed therein, there "corresponds a similar affection outside . . . with a similar effect."[35] As in the case of productive activity,

---

[31] *Cours*, IV, 399.

[32] *Système de politique positive*, II, 150, 170.

[33] *Ibid.*, p. 182.

[34] *Ibid.*, p. 201.

[35] *Ibid.*, p. 202. For Comte's entire discussion of this subject, see pp. 170–202.

Comte's interest lay in the processes through which elementary egoistic drives are transformed into the sentiments and relations productive of social solidarity. The family was a prototype; Comte had elaborated "in the most elementary case . . . the positive ideas . . . which will suffice for the whole of society."[36]

Finally, he sought to consider the social grounds of involuntary authority. The discussion was a far cry from his earlier utopianism, for now political domination and the state were accepted as natural aspects of all association, rather than being regarded as ephemeral forms of social life destined to decay with the advent of industrialism. [Force, he now argued, was a fact of social life and a constitutive element in all association.] Relationships involving some forms of domination were essential to group function, arising from various inequalities which will always persist. Such relationships—which Comte referred to generally as government— arise spontaneously "following the development [of] the separation of social functions."[37] They emerge first in the various groupings of social functions; such groupings naturally "give rise, in each group, to its particular government, which on a small scale controls and directs." More extensive government arises from the combinations of these elementary forms, culminating in what came to be known as the state.[38] Thus, secular government, Comte's "temporal power," arises from all forms of social activity, and lends direction and coherence at every level of human association. As society expands and grows more complex, such functions become increasingly large and necessary. The state is merely an organic extension of political relationships inherent in any social group. At the same time, Comte argued that the existing European state system, characterized by large territorial units, standing armies, immense bureaucracy, and mechanical administration, should not serve as a model for political organization. He found the ideal pattern in the smaller city-state, whose size, coherent population, and social compactness made it appear a more viable and cohesive political unit. The oppressive mechanisms of modern bureaucracy were less likely to flourish in smaller, more highly integrated social groupings.[39]

This concluded Comte's account of various involuntary sources of social solidarity. It remains only to say that it was still axiomatic with him that all practical activity required moral control and regulation. The highest aspect of social specialization would be the distinction between secular and spiritual government, which was, of course, the foundation of the new spiritual power. It would offer moral guidance designed to reinforce all the existing sources of solidarity, by promulgating a social

---

[36] *Ibid.*, pp. 194–95.

[37] *Ibid.*, pp. 294–95.

[38] *Ibid.*, pp. 297–98.

[39] *Ibid.*, pp. 304–6. Manuel argues (*op. cit.*, pp. 305–6), however, that Comte was fanatical for centralized organization, and had no appreciation of the significance of intermediate association. Since the assertion is made with no evidence, and in view of Comte's vehemence in precisely the other direction, Manuel's view is dubious.

morality designed to inculcate altruistic sentiments.[40] Comte held out hope that at some time solidarity might become so intense as partially to replace power in the constitution of society, and thus he looked forward to a possible diminishment in state activity. Yet he did not forget that productive activity in an industrial age entailed competition as well as co-operation, division as well as solidarity. Man's distinguishing characteristic was the creative transformation and mastery of nature, and therefore domination of some sort would be an inevitable aspect of human existence.

IV

The changes in Comte's thought amounted to a new view of sociology and its objects. The science was no longer grounded in a deterministic theory of inevitable historical advance, but rather in a quest for the grounds of social solidarity. His early view of society as merely the locus of "a general and combined action"[41] was supplanted by a much more subtle and complicated view. The object of sociology was no longer a mechanical series of inexorable periodic advances in science and society, but rather it was the processes typically constitutive of society itself. As a result, Comte's early social dynamics—the sociology of progress—was relegated to a minor role in his final conception. Since the fundamental processes underlying social structure and change had been identified, and the normal course of their development analyzed in social statics, all that remained for the sociology of progress was to determine the small variations of pace and direction which would arise in different social settings. Comte still held to the idea of social progress and still conceived dynamics as a predictive science, but it was no longer the theoretical basis of sociology. Social dynamics progress could be viewed only "as the development of an order already defined." It was of purely practical interest, and had no theoretical importance.[42] Indeed, in his later work Comte's interest in history centered much more in the area of tradition as a source of transgenerational solidarity than in any theoretical aspect.[43]

In Comte's new view, then, it was the determinants of solidarity, not determined historical progress, that were the focus of attention. It was for that very reason, however, that his speculation moved even beyond the formal limits of sociology itself. That science, he argued, grasped solidarity and the processes in which it arose as collective manifestations. The facts proper to sociology, therefore, lay in the various *social transformations* of human sentiment and activity. He came increasingly to feel, however, that this omitted two significant aspects of the analysis of social cohesion: the original materials which in society are transformed into the stuff of sociability, and individual variations in the effects of social process. Both of these would by definition be beyond the reach of a science

---

[40] *Système de politique positive*, II, 351–52.

[41] *Opuscules*, No. 3, p. 81.

[42] *Système de politique positive*, II, 1–4, 471; III, 3–5. However, Comte had earlier written that "social organization should not be considered, either in the past or the present, isolated from the state of civilization" (*Opuscules*, No. 3, p. 114).

[43] *Système de politique positive*, III, 2.

of the social and collective. Therefore he proposed the creation of a new science—*La Morale*—and sketched in its outlines. It would, in the first place, determine and analyze the specific elements in human nature which undergo transformation in social existence. *La Morale* would reveal the superior force of selfish over altruistic drives, and document the dominance of irrational over rational impulses. Second, it would seek to understand the impact upon individuals of variations in social and organic conditions.[44] While sociology dealt with the social transformations of man, this new science would consider his original constitution. While sociology dealt with collective manifestations, *La Morale* would consider individual variations. In its outline, then, the new science was at once a classical study of human nature and a groping toward psychology.

Comte's conception appears confused, and because of his death he never had the opportunity for any clarification. What is important is that in contrast to all his earlier pronouncements, where facts of an individual or non-social character are by definition impossible, Comte came to see such things as essential to the analysis of solidarity.[45] If nothing else, this is evidence both of the seriousness of his interest in solidarity and of the extent to which it changed the basic forms of his social theory.

Finally, it is necessary to assess Comte's position on the question of industrialism itself. In general, his work represented an effort to reconcile the idea of an industrial society with his vision of organic community and social solidarity. His ideas unfolded against a background in which these two views were sharply polarized. The liberal economists' argument that society was a field for free productive and commercial activity had been self-consciously and distinctly opposed to the conservative conception of society as a grouping of semiautonomous, solidary communities. For the liberal, these communities—the intermediate associations—could only impede production, trade, and expansion of industry, and the free play of man's competitive aggression. The conservative critics of industrialism and liberal economic thought agreed that this had been the case, and added only that it should be so in the future as well. These associations, solidary and quasi-independent, they saw as the veritable fabric of society; their function, among others, was to restrain and perhaps stifle industrial production and conflict. To the liberal ideal of specialized labor, competition, and a high degree of economic freedom, the conservatives had juxtaposed the ideals of social cohesion, order, and cooperation, embodied in organic communities. The liberals exalted individual economic freedom and man's conquest of nature; the conservatives exalted social solidarity, finding in it the ground and determinants of human growth.[46]

---

[44] *Ibid.*, II, 435–37; IV, 230–35.

[45] Earlier he had written that "the scientific spirit forbids regarding human society as being actually composed of individuals" (*Cours*, IV, 398).

[46] For the views of the conservatives see n. 3, above. Perhaps the best summary of the liberals' ideas can be found in one of E. Allix's many articles on the period: "J.-B. Say et les origines de l'industrialisme," *Revue d'économie politique* (1910), pp. 303–13, 341–63.

Comte self-consciously sought to avoid approaching the problem of industrialism from an economic point of view, for he regarded that as a narrow and unfruitful perspective. Rather, as Durkheim recognized, Comte aimed to deal with the problem from a specifically sociological point of view, to approach it in terms of that science's most fundamental concept—social solidarity.[47] As a consequence he was forced to synthesize elements from both traditions and thus to transform some of the basic concepts in question. He rejected the conservative attack on the division of labor, arguing that it was a fundamental source of co-operation and solidarity. Similarly, he moved beyond the liberals' purely economic conception of society and the division of labor and argued that, far from being a simply economic phenomenon, the specialization of work gave rise to a fuller differentiation and development of personality. Perhaps most significantly, he rejected the view held on both sides that the essence of a commercial and industrial society was a free-ranging competitive egoism. Socialized labor, by its very nature co-operative and solidary, and intermediate associations seemed to him the mechanisms in which egoistic drives were transformed into the stuff of social life; the ground of social and economic diversification was not egoism, but rather the social institutions and processes in which solidarity arose. In the Comtean sociology, industrialism and the division of labor no longer stand opposed to organic community and the realization of individual personality but, instead, close to their very source. Therein lies the uniqueness both of his sociology and of his approach to the problem of industrialism.

---

[47] Durkheim is, to my knowledge, alone in seeing this as the very essence of Comte's sociology (see his *Division of Labor*, pp. 62–63).

2.2

The Sociology of Comte: An Appreciation

E. E. EVANS-PRITCHARD

This is not an attempt to present a biography of Auguste Comte, however brief. That has been very well done by others and would in any case have to take into more detailed account all sorts of things without a knowledge of which much of what he wrote cannot be fully understood, for they coloured his work to the point of dominating its themes: his royalist and Catholic family (he was always a paradox: a republican royalist, aristocratic proletarian, Catholic freethinker); also his acute paranoia, reaching heights of suicidal madness, and the megalomania that so often accompanies it, which rendered him intolerable to anyone who might have thought of helping him attain academic status and a painful experience to those of his family and friends who sought to ease his condition only to have vented on them malice of an almost Corvoesque intensity. And then of course his women: the mistress passion of his youth, Pauline (the mother of his child), the ex-prostitute Caroline Massin, with whom in 1825 he made a disastrous marriage (in a ceremony well described as *lugubre*), a long-suffering lady who took much and could take more no longer and left him in 1842; and lastly in 1844 the beautiful (if we may judge by her picture) lady Clotilde de Vaux (her husband appears to have been in prison) whose rôle would scarcely be accepted as a character of make-believe, the Beatrice—his *'sainte patronne'*—who inspired the near lunacy of his last writings. (The poor lady endured listening to his lectures, from which even her death in the following year did not release her, for Comte continued to deliver discourses at her graveside; yet who can read the *Dédicace* to the *Système* or its *Invocation finale* without being deeply moved?)

Then, Comte's opinions and even his character were very much shaped by the events of his time. France, bled almost to death in the Napoleonic wars, had to endure many vicissitudes and uncertainties also in the years which followed, troublous years (1814, 1815, 1830, 1848, 1851) which drove Comte to near despair and convinced him more and more that the basic issues were not political but moral and could be decided only by a combination of the scientific study of the social problems involved with a radical regeneration of the French people—a sincere acceptance of altruistic standards, values and sentiments. France was defeated and defeatist and could, and must, rise again but this could be achieved only if knowledge and duty joined hands. So also Durkheim saw the challenge to the France of after 1870.

Then again, Comte's contribution to social studies must be seen in the perspective of the general history of ideas if the originality of his thought is to be appreciated, and his claim to be the founder of sociology upheld. Clearly, he was deeply influenced by Montesquieu, Turgot, Diderot and the Encyclopaedists in general, and above all by Condorcet; also by de Maistre, and by Hume, Adam Ferguson, and Adam Smith—to mention a few names—and by contemporary socialist propaganda. He was, of course, profoundly influenced also by Saint-Simon, whose secretary and collaborator he was for seven years, from 1817 to 1824 (and heaven forbid that we should enter into the tangled relationship between the two men). Equally clearly, much of what he regarded as his most inspired discovery— the positivist approach to the study of social institutions—was almost a commonplace among eighteenth century philosophers, and his insistence on the need to reconcile such studies with an acceptance of order and authority was a familiar topic, especially in Catholic France of the Restoration—indeed, a claim might be put forward on behalf of the triumvirate Bonald (1754–1840)–de Maistre (1754–1821)–Chateaubriand (1768–1848) for some of the credit that has gone to Comte.

But whatever claims might be advocated on behalf of others and however much he was both the intellectual child of his time and heir to the past—and no one in this broad sense can be regarded as an entirely original thinker—there can be no doubt about his enormous influence on nineteenth century ways of looking at social affairs, an influence easy to discern in the writings of men like Herbert Spencer, J. S. Mill, Lecky and Morley in this country* and Lévy-Bruhl and Durkheim in his own— none of whom were little fish. We can see his influence also on such historians as Mommsen and Grote and, so it is said, Taine and Renan—also not little fish. And in other countries, Spain, Portugal, and South America in particular.[1]

But all this, however essential it would be to take it into consideration in a biographical sketch, can be set aside in giving an answer to the question here asked: what in Comte's writings have significance for social anthropologists and sociologists, and not only for their historical interest but also for their relevance to our problems today, for many of the issues he raised are still unsettled, many of the questions he asked still unanswered, or at any rate still disputed.

Born in 1798 and dead in 1857, Comte did not have a very long life, and considering also how it was beset by poverty, sickness and *dissentiments conjugaux* and acrimonious quarrels of one sort or another it is

---

* England.—Ed.

[1] No modern European philosopher has had so great an influence in Latin America as Comte (Leopoldo Zea in *Bull. de la Soc. française de Phil.*, 1958, p. 27).

surprising what he accomplished: six volumes of the *Cours de philosophie positive* (1830–1842), four volumes of the *Système de politique positive* (1851–1854), the *Catéchisme positiviste* (1852) and many *opuscules*.[2] Much also has been written about him.

For our purposes we may give our attention mainly, though not exclusively, to the *Cours*, a monstrosity of 2,582 pages and probably near a million words, and stylistically repellent, which makes its prolixity and didacticism an added aggravation to a test of endurance. The first three volumes of this vast encyclopaedia of the sum of human knowledge (he and Spencer were the last two men who aspired to universal knowledge) deal with what today would be termed the natural sciences—inorganic and organic—and only the last three with social institutions and morals. The natural science volumes cannot, however, be ignored by the social scientist, because they form a prologue to the social science volumes and are a necessary introduction to them in two respects. Firstly, in Comte's view, some acquaintance with the natural sciences is required because the essential methodology of all the sciences is the same and the correct use of procedures of observation and analysis in the social sciences could therefore best be studied in those sciences which had preceded them and were more developed. Secondly, the sciences have a logical structure which must also be a chronological order and can therefore be best presented in a hierarchy of increasing complexity of content, with mathematics at one end and sociology[3] at the other. The logical structure and chronological sequence of the series is inevitable because each depends on the truths of those which precede it.

J. S. Mill states Comte's argument succinctly: 'Thus, the truths of number are true of all things, and depend only on their own laws; the science, therefore, of Number, consisting of Arithmetic and Algebra, may be studied without reference to any other science. The truths of Geometry presuppose the laws of Number, and a more special class of laws peculiar to extended bodies, but require no others: Geometry, therefore, can be studied independently of all sciences except that of Number'. And so on: 'The phaenomena of human society obey laws of their own, but do not depend solely upon these: they depend upon all the laws of organic and animal life, together with those of inorganic nature, these last influencing society not only through their influence on life, but by determining the physical conditions under which society has to be carried on.[4]

The phenomena of each science are thus more complex than those of the preceding one, and if this is true—for it has been questioned[5]—it is in consequence increasingly difficult as we ascend the scale to formulate

---

[2] He did not live to write various other works he had planned to write, on logic, mathematics, morals, education, and others (*Système*, IV, p. 542).

[3] It was Comte who first used the term 'sociology.' He had earlier, following Condorcet, spoken of '*physique sociale*.' The analogy he mostly used was, however, that of an organism.

[4] John Stuart Mill, *Auguste Comte and Positivism*, 1961 edn., pp. 37–38.

[5] For example, by Leslie A. White, *The Science of Culture*, 1949, pp. 55 *sq.*

any laws governing the phenomena being investigated and even if, therefore, sociology finally succeeds in making general statements about its subject matter they are likely to have a smaller degree of generality than those in the inorganic and organic sciences and will anyhow, and inevitably, be reached last of the sciences and only when the organic sciences, its immediate foundations as it were, have attained a high point of development. This does not mean, however, that the subject matter of any science in the ascending scale of the sciences can be organized and explained in terms found to be conceptually appropriate in the science preceding it. Each science is a new phenomenal level demanding its own explanations in its own specific terms, for each has its own specific, autonomous, character. The struggle to mark out an exclusive domain of inquiry in the social sciences—to determine what constitutes a social fact which is not any other kind of fact, what are sociological phenomena which are not any other kind of phenomena—was still a battle being fought by Durkheim more than half a century later in his manifesto *Les règles de la méthode sociologique.*

Here we may pause and ask some questions, but before asking them it has to be noticed, and of course often has been, that Comte does not include psychology in his series (to the annoyance, among others, of Mill and Spencer) and indeed expresses his utmost contempt for it—which made it easier to endow social phenomena with specificity. His contempt for the introspective observations which passed as psychology in his day may well have been deserved, but my impression is that he held that on logical grounds there could be no such science. Man is born into the world an animal. His moral and intellectual functions are what are implanted on the organism by society, the products of culture. Consequently one must not define 'humanity' by 'man' but 'man' by 'humanity'. Furthermore it is quite irrational to try to explain society, even in its simplest fetishistic stage, in terms of individual needs, it being the most vicious of metaphysical (Comte's dirtiest word) theories which derives faculties from needs of the individual.[6] Men only respond to needs by creating new institutions when social conditions determine the response.

So all in all what place could there be for an autonomous science of psychology in between physiology and sociology? What people might call psychology was to Comte a branch of physiology, what he called cerebral physiology, and he later, much to the embarrassment of some of his erstwhile admirers, advocated phrenology as the most appropriate means of studying mental phenomena. Leaving out the phrenology, it seems to me that Durkheim took up much the same position, that there is no place for an intermediate science between the organic and the social sciences, though, so far as I know, he never actually said this in so many words.

What, now, about the hierarchy of the sciences based on the increasing complexity of their subject matter? Comte's classification of the sciences

---

[6] Comte, indeed, more or less ignores the individual, to him an abstraction: *'La société humaine se compose de familles, et non d'individus.'* (*Système,* II, p. 181.) The family is the true unit (*élément*) of society.

was for the time he made it, it seems to me (though Karl Pearson did not think much of it), an original and illuminating piece of systematization, and as a logical paradigm it is convincing; though, as oversimplified by Comte, it is scarcely acceptable as a historical record of a unilinear order of development of the sciences, as Spencer was to point out.

The whole scheme makes certain basic assumptions which, though they seem to be still taken for granted by some anthropologists, are nevertheless questionable. The fundamental dogma is one shared by most eighteenth century moral philosophers (Rousseau was an exception), that social institutions are just as much part of 'nature' (one of their favourite metaphysical terms) as the phenomena studied by physicists and chemists. Comte states this without any equivocation, if not without evident contradictions. Earlier ideas about social institutions were either theological fictions, happily in decay, or, what was far worse, metaphysical entities, still alas only too much in evidence and just theology (for which one could have some respect) gone bad. The Reformation and the Revolution had destroyed the Catholico–feudal structure of Europe, and the metaphysical notions which served to undermine its intellectual and moral basis were such rubbish that they could only be transitory, critical, negative and illusory (I wish I could do full justice to Comte's vituperative epithets). What was wanted, and had to come, was a rational and scientific study of social life. Once theological dogmas and metaphysical jargon had given way to sober scientific research into the physical universe and the structure and functions of living organisms, man had acquired real knowledge, a knowledge of the laws of their existence, which he could apply to ammeliorate, at any rate to some extent, his circumstances. The old division of the Greeks between natural philosophy and moral philosophy must therefore go for ever. The pioneers of positive philosophy had long ago pointed to the path which must be pursued—Bacon, Galileo, Descartes; Bacon above all. We had now reached the point in the development of thought at which social phenomena could, and should, be studied by the same methods as had yielded such remarkable results in the natural sciences, and comparable results might be expected. The techniques employed, as distinct from the methods, would of course have to vary according to the nature of the phenomena under investigation. The methods are observation (including experiment), comparison, and generalization (which, when one comes to think of it, are processes common and essential to all thought, scientific or any other). The inductive method to be pursued in the social sciences is that of concomitant variation. The techniques employed will vary according to the situation in which observations are to be recorded. This is really mainly what Comte meant by 'positive philosophy'—that we should in inquiring into the nature of social life be rigorously scientific, basing our procedures on the model of the well established natural sciences.[7] And I may add here that Comte has often

---

[7] In an interesting footnote in his 1825 opuscule (*Système, Appendice Général*, p. 146) Comte wrote: '*Le langage, qui, examiné historiquement, présente un tableau fidèle des révolutions de l'esprit humain, nous offre de celle-ci un témoignage très-sensible. Le mot "sciences," qui d'abord*

been so misrepresented that he might have said that he was not a Comtist (positivist), as Marx had to say that he was not a Marxist;[8] though, as Dr. Charlton remarks, to inquire how far Comte was a consistent positivist may seem not unlike asking whether the Pope is a Catholic.[9]

But what about the little word with the big—and, it seems to me, ambiguous—sense, 'nature'? In one way of looking at the matter, everything which exists is 'natural' and is also part of a system and has a structure, and can therefore be studied as such. But in this sense the concept is so amorphous, so all-embracing, that it is of doubtful utility. When a word means everything it can also mean nothing. It is true that in this sense the planetary system and an Act of Parliament are equally parts of nature but they are phenomena of such different orders that one may indeed question whether much is gained by making the statement. To give any precision to the term 'natural' it seems to me what is required is to define what is 'non-natural' and to furnish some examples to illustrate the use of that term. After all, Comte's scientific (positivist) philosophy is no less 'natural', in the sense of being determined—as positivist philosophy must hold—by social conditions, than the theological and metaphysical philosophies he rejected—as indeed he might have admitted—so we are back to the old dilemma of the science of knowledge, a mirror facing a mirror with nothing in between. Who is the potter, pray, and who the pot?

But there is more to Comte than an insistence on scientific rigour in our study of social institutions if we are to discover the laws of their development. He claimed to have discovered the most fundamental of these laws, that of the famous three stages (or states)—actually first enunciated by Turgot.[10] According to Comte, man first conceives of the

---

n'avait été appliqué qu'aux spéculations théologiques et métaphysiques, et plus tard aux recherches de pure érudition qu'elles ont engendrées, ne désigne plus aujourd'hui, quand il est isolé, même dans l'acception vulgaire, que les connaissances positives. Lorsqu'on veut tenter de lui donner une autre signification. on est obligé, pour se faire entendre, de recourir à des périphrases dont l'emploi montre bien que, aux yeux du public actuel, c'est en cela seul que consiste le véritable "savoir." '

[8] P. A. Sorokin, *Sociological Theories of Today*, 1966, p. 156: 'Soon after Comte introduced the term 'positivism,' it acquired a 'singularistic–atomistic' meaning entirely different from the 'systematic' meaning given to it by Comte.' Positivism is not at all the same as scientism. Comte has well enough defined what he meant by positivism: *'Dans l'état positif, l'esprit humain, reconnaissant l'impossibilité d'obtenir des notions absolues, renonce à chercher l'origine et la destination de l'univers et à connaître les causes intimes des phénomènes, pour s'attacher uniquement à découvrir, par l'usage bien combiné du raisonnement et de l'observation, leurs lois effectives, c'est-à-dire leurs relations invariables de succession et de similitude'* (*Cours*, I, p. 3). For some of the different senses of the word 'positivism' see André Lalande, *Vocabulaire de la Philosophie*, 1932, pp. 598–600.

[9] D. G. Charlton, *Positivist Thought in France during the Second Empire*, 1959, p. 24.

[10] It is very clearly stated by Comte in the opuscule of 1825, reprinted in the *Système, Appendice Général*, pp. 137–138.

world theologically, that is, anthropomorphically, first in the form of Comte's idea of what fetishism was;[11] then polytheistically; then mono-theistically. Monotheism in modern Europe faded after nationalism had ruined the Catholic Church and under the impact of the anarchy of prot-estantism and rationalist criticism, deism, and finally a hotch-potch of absurd metaphysical notions advanced as explanations: ends, principles, causes, Nature, substance, essence, virtues, form and, on the political side, such sterile rubbish as liberty, equality, fraternity, the state of nature and what have you! His particular dislike of lawyers was, among other things, on account of their constant talk about natural rights, a meaningless con-ception they got from Roman law.

Even the greatest philosophers of the seventeenth and eighteenth cen-turies belonged to this negative and sterile category; Hobbes, Locke, Voltaire, Helvetius and Rousseau. They could not understand that the crisis of their time was a moral and spiritual one, so they thought their diffi-culties could be overcome by legislation. Their mistake was to suppose that intelligence and learning could by themselves do the trick: the worst of all illusions, the Greek utopian illusion. A *pédantocratie* (a word coined —in its English form—by J. S. Mill) just will not work. 'Legitimate social supremacy does not belong, properly speaking, either to force or to reason, but to morality, dominating equally the acts of the one and the counsels of the other' (*Cours*, VI, p. 312).

Full justice has not been done to Comte in this matter of the three stages.[12] He was saying little more than what was the thesis of his best biographer, Lucien Lévy-Bruhl, in his many books, that on the whole we may say that primitive and barbarous peoples tend to attribute events to what are commonly called supernatural forces of one kind or another (magic and religion) and that such interpretations slowly give way to rational-positive or scientific ones in the course of cultural progress; and he tried to show, which Lévy-Bruhl did not, how this development might have come about. Who can, in a broad view, deny that he was right?

---

[11] I suppose that Comte got his ideas about fetishism mainly from De Brosses. He certainly provides little evidence of having read much of first-hand travel accounts of primitive peoples. Although he placed fetishism at the dawn of human thought, he had more respect for it than for later theological (polytheistic and monotheistic) and philosophical (metaphysical) systems, and he came to think that there would have to be some kind of fusion between fetishism and positivism (*Système*, IV, pp. 42–44). There was a spontaneity about fetishism which permitted the development of reason and the impact of sentiment, and in a way that made it more akin to positivism than the arid, artificial and obstructive systems that the theologians and philosophers had erected, systems which by their pompous conceit impeded any progress of the mind, (*Système*, III, Chap. 2). However, both fetishism and theology had their rôles to play in the evolution of society: fetishism constituted the family, theocracy organized the society (*Système*, III, p. 500).

[12] The triadic concept goes a long way back, e.g. Vico. One finds it in various forms in Hegel, Marx, Frazer and Freud as well as in Comte.

Whether he was justified also in equating the ontogenetic and the phylo-genetic, as Freud did in his theory of the libido, is another question: 'Then, each of us, in contemplating his own history, does he not remember that he has been successively, with regard to his most important ideas, *theologian* in his infancy, *metaphysician* in his youth, and *natural philosopher* in his manhood' (*Cours*, I, p. 4).

It further follows from the logic of his argument that the theological or imaginative (*fictif*) type of explanation and the metaphysical or abstract type of explanation—in that order—of phenomena are ousted in favour of rational and experimental or positive ones in the sciences in their historical sequence: first in the inorganic sciences, then in the organic sciences, leaving only the social sciences cluttered up with a lot of idiotic verbiage which still passed, and passes, fraudulently as rational interpretation. Things are a bit more complicated than Comte made them out to be, but with certain reservations[13] we may here again accept his thesis in broad outline. Nor did Comte hold, as some have given the impression that he did, that the three stages, or states, in cultural development—the theological, the metaphysical, and the positivist—were closed and exclusive systems of thought. This would have been nonsense to him, for his whole point was that while one of them is the dominant philosophy of each phase and tends to exclude explanations of phenomena which run directly counter to it the other ways of thinking are found together with it, and indeed must be, since the sciences advance from the theological phase to the positivist phase in chronological order. Moreover there could otherwise have been no progress, because progress comes about by the maturing in one phase of the seed which will come to flower in succeeding phases; so what appears as decadence may equally be viewed as commencement of new birth and what appears as the height of development in any stage may equally be viewed as an advanced symptom of its decline. Unless the seed die (*Cor.* 15. 36). . . . Also Comte was under no illusions about current theological and metaphysical ideas co-existing with positivist ones; and indeed when we cast a brief look at the *Système* we shall abundantly appreciate that he, in his rather peculiar way of looking at things, understood that this must always be so.

Comte has, I think, also sometimes been misunderstood with regard to his attitude to the theological and the metaphysical. Naturally, he regarded the positivist philosophy as the best, both because it came last in the evolutionary series (evolution and progress were all the same for him) and because it had a more rational understanding of nature; but he also

---

[13] J. Fiske, *Outlines of Cosmic Philosophy*, vol. I, 1894 edn., p. 204, quotes Herbert Spencer: Comte's fundamental error was in not recognizing 'the constant effect of progress in each class upon *all* other classes; but only on the class succeeding it in his hierarchial scale. He leaves the impression that, with trifling exceptions, the sciences aid each other only in the order of their alleged succession. But in fact there has been a continuous helping of each division by all others, and of all by each.' Also it is surely not the case that the progress of generalization has always been from the simple to the complex, e.g. Aristotle's *Politics*.

regarded the earlier stages in which different outlooks on the world were prevalent as inevitable and indispensable stages in the development of thought, and therefore, in an historical sense, as beneficial. Moreover, if there had not been a good deal of purely rational thought and empirical knowledge in the theological stage modern science could never have come into being. And was not religion the mother of culture and social order? So even protestantism and metaphysical conceptions had to be, in that they played their part in the undermining of the Catholico–feudal society of Europe and, negative, anarchical, abhorrent and puerile though they were to Comte, they performed this essential service, as a *lacune néces-saire*, as *provisoires*, and thereby brought about the emergence of the new positivist order, which was to be seen as a terminus, just as the dictator-ship of the proletariat and the withering away of the State is envisaged as the final situation by Marxists. The inexorable, ineluctable laws of prog-ress—against which it is useless to fight, our only freedom being to recognize them—seem to stop operating at this point. Man is master of the universe and master of man. But, as we shall see, Comte became increasingly convinced that it was an over-simplification—indeed, wishful thinking—to suppose that knowledge could by itself bring about an ordered social life demanded if science were to be applied to the amelioration of the appalling moral decadence and intellectual confusion he saw all around him in the France of his time. Only religion could do that—but not *La religion révélée*; only *La religion démontrée*,[14] a sort of humanistic morality.

It will have been observed that Comte's whole thesis is a philosophy of history (as well as being a history of philosophy)—not just a philosophy of science but a philosophy of the development of thought in the history of mankind. We must be clear in our minds on this point what Comte and his contemporaries and immediate forerunners, and indeed also the anthro-pologists of the nineteenth century in general, understood by the sort of history they thought worth pursuing, for their perspective has been largely lost, possibly to the detriment of our subject (social anthropology), which may have to some extent abandoned thereby what gave it its bearings and its consistency.

According to Comte, social studies consist ideally of two branches: social statics dealing with the laws of co-existence and social dynamics dealing with the laws of succession.[15] He regarded this as a fundamental distinction found throughout the sciences, for example, in biology between anatomy and physiology; and it is necessary to distinguish radically, with

---

[14] *D'abord spontanée, puis inspirée, et ensuite révélée, la religion devient enfin démontrée'* (*Système*, II, p. 7). Comte had, as is well known, un-bounded respect for the Catholic Church as an institution, but he did not subscribe to its dogmas. He was not a Christian—he might be called a Catholic atheist; he did not have the solace of the precious doubt of which Unamuno speaks so eloquently.

[15] In his blueprint for the future, social statics and social dynamics cor-respond to the notions of order and progress, which have somehow to be reconciled.

regard to each political subject, 'between the fundamental study of the conditions of existence of the society and that of the laws of its continuous movement' (*Cours*, IV, p. 167). But he thought that in practice in social studies it would be premature and inopportune at the time he wrote to try to keep them apart (and nobody has been able to do so successfully since). He tells us about social statics little more than that all social activities form a harmonious whole, a consensus: that economic, legal religious, aesthetic, etc., facts cannot be understood in isolation but only in their relation to one another, but beyond this somewhat bland assertion, this enunciation of what Mauss was to call a *fait total*, of which he gives by way of illustrative examples in support little more than some very broad observations about such phenomena as militarism and industrialism. But he has plenty to say about the evolution of civilization, holding that it is on account of the nature of human society and culture that the method of analysis must be historical, for unlike biology (genetics?), for instance, sociology is concerned with the influence of different generations on those which follow them, a process of gradual but continuous accumulation; and this is true of both social dynamics and social statics, for the laws of co-existence manifest themselves above all in movement.

Earlier writers had the idea of law but they did not possess the essential concept of progress without which the idea of law is sterile, since the laws regulating social phenomena are essentially those of development or evolution or progress; or one can at least say that until the diachronic laws are discovered the synchronic ones cannot be discovered either. The 'incomparable' Aristotle, for instance, or Montesquieu, had not grasped the idea of progress, which alone could have given them a true understanding of the nature of social institutions, the meaning of which is to be seen in their movement in a certain direction. Without the notion of progress they were bogged down in vague and chimerical conceptions of oscillatory or circular movements. The idea of a definite and continuous movement in one direction was first brought about, according to Comte, by Christianity, but it did not go very far because social conditions were adverse and the natural sciences still nascent. The credit for the first consistent attempt to formulate laws of social progress must go to Condorcet. It was he who was, if not the first, the clearest exponent of what a sociological law should be: a formula derived from a study of cultural development. It was certainly one of Comte's contributions to social studies that he saw that to understand social phenomena it must be recognized that they are always in movement and can only be studied as such. The past is in the present and the present is in the future. Therefore no history, no sociology. As Lévy-Bruhl, in discussing Comte, puts it, 'Man has knowledge of himself when he puts himself back in the evolution of humanity.[16]

History, we must emphasize, did not convey the sense to Comte that it conveys to the modern reader of a book on the political history of a

---

[16] Lucien Lévy-Bruhl, *La Philosophie d'Auguste Comte*, fourth edn., 1921, p. 243.

people. For the historical writings of his day he had nothing but scorn—literary, narrative, almost anecdotal exercises—but he would also have shown little appreciation of the historical writings of today either, or most of them. They would have been for him mere chronicles of events, and of persons of no great significance. In the social histories of Comte and his eighteenth century precursors there are no particular events or persons. You look in vain for dates and names and even for mention of peoples in Adam Ferguson (except in his history of the Roman Republic), Condorcet or Comte. What does it matter who invented printing or precisely when it was invented? These details are accidents not worth recording. There is no history worth recording other than universal history. There cannot be a history of mathematics for one side of the Alps and another for the other side.

And in all this Comte was very far from holding a materialist view of history.[17] The vast social movements he was interested in are indeed brought about largely by economic—in the earliest stages, bionomic—changes, but these cannot be isolated from spiritual developments: 'The grave error of historical philosophy . . . results evidently, in fact, from an exaggerated and almost exclusive preoccupation with the temporal point of view of human events . . .' (*Cours*, V, p. 47). Then again he tells us 'It is ideas which govern and disturb the world . . . All the social mechanism rests finally on opinions . . . The great political and moral crisis of present-day societies, derives, in the last analysis, from the intellectual anarchy' (*Cours*, I, p. 26). No one is agreed on the fundamental ideas and values, without which agreement stable social life is impossible. Once Comte starts chasing that hare there is no stopping him—we shall have a further look at the hare later.

In one respect Comte's view of history might shock many modern social scientists. In spite of all he says about the need for use of the comparative method (what he calls *la méthode historique*) in reaching general conclusions, he pretty well confines himself to the conjecture, common to social philosophers of the time, that all peoples, being all alike, fundamentally progress in the same manner; though some, for reasons of climate or race or other 'inevitable secondary differences' (*Cours*, IV, p. 232), as he calls them, or because conditions may for a while be affected by (his darling phrase) 'exceptional perturbations', progress slower or faster than others. Consequently he reaches the conclusion that to study the development of social institutions in general it is sufficient to trace their evolution to its highest point—the civilization of Western Europe (*la civilisation occidentale*), and in particular France—'*centre normal de l'Occident*' (*Système*, I, p. 62). This may be a fiction but it is methodologically required. To bother about the history of India and China would merely create confusion and be a vain concession to concreteness and a display of sterile erudition. It is indispensible to have the

---

[17] J. A. Froude, *Short Studies on Great Subjects*, Second series, 1903, vol. II, p. 594, gives a false assessment when he speaks of 'the positive or materialistic' philosophy of history of M. Comte.

hypothesis of a single people to whom can be ideally related all the consecutive social modifications actually observed among distinct populations. Without this abstraction, this rational fiction, this theoretical framework, sociology would be no more than a barren, pointless, merely empirical collection of endless facts—a vain accumulation of incoherent monographs—which is what he would have said it very largely is, and what social anthropology could become.

Science is essentially composed of laws and not of facts.[18] Mere accumulation of facts leads nowhere. Individual histories have no meaning except when viewed in the light of universal history and the laws of its determination. Bossuet understood this, although he was a theologian; so did Turgot and Condorcet. The particularities of history do not give us its laws; it is the laws which will ultimately account for the particularities, make them significant, even give them meaning for him who contemplates them: *'la notion philosophique de "loi" naturelle consiste toujours à saisir la constance dans la variété'* (*Système*, II, p. 41). Particular histories are only useful to provide sociology with data for the testing of hypotheses and with illustrations for its theoretical conclusions; and they do not even do that if their authors are unaware of the hypotheses in the first place. All this is indeed sound reasoning, if, as Comte supposed, social phenomena are of the same order as those of the physical world: an apple falling or the trajectile of a bullet are to be understood in the light of well established laws of physics of one sort or another. Certainly Comte is right when he says that no observation is really possible at all except in so far as it is directed and interpreted by some theory; people who think that theory arises from bare observations themselves are quite wrong. Even in the simplest researches, scientific observations have to be preceded by some conception of the corresponding phenomena.

Even so, if all this be accepted—and in general much of it has to be— we must not expect results from the application of scientific methods of research to social facts commensurate with what has been achieved in the natural sciences. Social facts are much more complex, and in any case we are, says Comte, speaking of his time (and he might have said the same today), only at the threshold of positivist sociology, the situation being exactly like it was before astronomy replaced astrology, chemistry alchemy, and a system of medical studies the search for a universal panacea. We must not therefore expect to reach, perhaps ever, laws of a high level of generality; and even to reach generalizations on any level some modifications in general methodological conceptions are required in dealing with social phenomena.

The first and fundamental adjustment is necessitated by the very nature of these phenomena. In the inorganic sciences, even in the biological sciences, one seeks to study the simplest phenomena first and

---

[18] *'La science se compose de lois, et non de faits'* (quoted by Lévy-Bruhl, op. cit., p. 78). Comte has sometimes been wrongly presented as a bleak empiricist interested only in "facts" in the narrowest sense of that word. He was quite the opposite.

then the more complex, to break complex reality into simpler and simpler elements, so isolated for study. An analysis of this kind is inappropriate in the case of social phenomena, which are completely meaningless when broken into elements and can only be studied as wholes. What we know is the whole, so one should follow the sound rule of science, that one should proceed from the known to the unknown, and hence in the social sciences one should reverse the procedure of the inorganic sciences and proceed from the complex to the simple. Consequently every social fact 'is explained, in the true scientific sense of the term, when it has been suitably connected with either the totality of the corresponding situation or the totality of the preceding situation' (*Cours*, IV p. 214). It follows from this idea of a total situation that social relations, ideas and customs form a system in which every part is functionally dependent on every other part for both its operation and, for the observer, its meaning: 'This preliminary aspect of the science of politics supposes then evidently, of complete necessity, that contrary to present-day philosophical habits, each of the numerous social elements, ceasing to be envisaged in an absolute and independent manner, must always be exclusively conceived of as relative to all the others, with which it is intimately and always bound up in a fundamental solidarity' (*Cours*, IV, p. 171). 'Then, the scientific principle of the general relation consists essentially in the evident spontaneous harmony which must always tend to rule between the whole and the parts of the social system, of which the elements cannot avoid being finally combined among themselves in a manner fully conforming to their own nature' (*Cours*, IV, p. 176).

In other words, and as earlier said, at any stage political, moral, economic, domestic, religious, intellectual and aesthetic phenomena all hang together and form a complex unity the solidarity of which is derived from some dominant principle. There is an *'intime solidarité nécessaire entre les divers aspects quelconques du mouvement humain'* (*Cours*, VI, p. 61). This was Montesquieu's thesis[19] and it is still, or was till recently, a dogma, or at any rate a methodological axiom, among many social anthropologists. Comte saw that this is a very difficult proposition and that—I must say it again—to combine static with dynamic studies—in a very general sense, sociological with historical studies—is easier said than done, for the data are not only those at any one time existing but also those from which they have evolved, and they have furthermore to be viewed in relation to their evolutionary potentialities, what they are becoming or are to become.

I do not pursue Comte's discussion into the social phase of positivism, for he was speculating on the future—even more hazardous than speculating on the past—and he more or less regarded himself, with his usual superb self-confidence, as the only person who had knowledge of it: of the new world of science and technology, of rationalism, humanism,

---

[19] Though without the notion of 'stage'; the dominant principle being for Montesquieu a political one (types of government), for Comte a philosophical one (modes of thought).

agnosticism, industrialism, pacifism, altruism, etc. We will rather ask what was supposed to be the outcome and purpose of this lengthy inquiry.

The outcome was to be the establishment of the laws of social life, it being understood that such laws are never absolute but relative to our knowledge at any given stage—absolute knowledge of reality is unachievable. There are two kinds of natural sciences: the one abstract, general (nomothetic), which has for object the discovery of the laws which govern the different classes of phenomena (Comte's use of the concept of 'law' seems to me to come perilously near to what he denigrated as 'metaphysical'); the other, concrete, particular (ideographic) and descriptive, consists in the application of these laws to the effective history of the different existing beings. I regard this distinction as being in practice hard to maintain[20] and serving little useful purpose; but for Comte the first, the speculative sciences, are fundamental (one of his four-starred words) and the second, the applied, are secondary. Now Comte, the philosopher, was concerned only with the speculative and general. It can be said that he gave us excellent directions how to find these laws but it cannot be said that he discovered any—the so-called law of the three stages, even if true, is scarcely a law in the sense the word can be used in the natural sciences, and as defined by him. In the absence of a developed body of theory he held, as is understandable, that while the natural and advanced sciences may be taught dogmatically, the social sciences, being in a nascent stage, should be taught historically.

But in spite of his personal interest in the speculative, he considered it a complete waste of time to acquire knowledge of the laws of social life unless there could be based upon them an applied science of sociology. Not that he believed that research for useful ends at the expense of speculative research was anything but a mistake, even from the point of view of utility itself. But knowledge, to be worth pursuing, must be applicable. His oft-quoted formula was *'Science, d'où prévoyance; prévoyance d'où action!'* He would have agreed with what is written on Karl Marx's headstone in Highgate Cemetery, his famous 'The philosophers have only interpreted the world in various ways: the point, however, is to change it.'

But, says Comte, one can only modify social conditions to a very slight extent by a scientific study of them, and what can be done can only affect the pace of development and not its direction or outcome, which are determined by inexorable natural laws. There is plasticity only in so far as, since social progress does not follow a straight line but advances by a series of oscillations, an exact knowledge of these movements enables us to diminish the oscillations and the gropings (*tatonnements*), procedures by trial and error, which correspond to them; and also to exercise some control over lesser crises by rational prevision. Not, he hastens to add, that any hope can be expected from statesmen and other men of

---

[20] Also he did not, it seems to me, adequately define 'method,' 'law,' 'theory,' 'hypothesis,' 'explanation' and so on. Who can blame him? Philosophers still give different meanings to these terms.

affairs, who are under the illusion that social phenomena can be indefinitely and arbitrarily modified. All that results from their fumbling is disorderly experimentation. Comte's attitude in this matter resembles in general that of the Marxists, or what used to be their attitude: we must on the whole admit and accept our impotence when confronted with great social and cultural movements.

We may say about all this that while it is evident that one cannot have developed applied science until one has a developed theoretical science to apply—a developed medicine, for example, without a developed physiology—empirical knowledge is capable of application up to a point, and always has been; and it can be further held that learning may be useful in other than a strictly (and perhaps narrowly) positivist sense. Comte scarcely enters into these questions but it is evident from the *Système* that the moral regeneration he proposes to impose can in no conceivable way be said to arise from sociological inquiries into social phenomena nor from the hoped-for laws that are supposed to govern them.

So far we have considered a few points made by Comte in his vast *Cours*, such points as it would seem still as worth emphasizing today as when he made them. We cannot accept all of them without reservations; and we must pass judgment on him for his almost total disregard of facts (it comes almost as a surprise when he begins in the third volume of the *Système* to record some of the events in European history or perhaps we should say his estimation of them). But we must not judge him too severely on this score, for he was delivering lectures on the philosophy of science and on the history of science—he may be said to have been the first historian of science—and not on science. He has also been often rebuked for his mania for systematization, his *'esprit de système'* as Renan called it. The most damaging criticism is, I think, his *post factum* interpretation of history—and of a limited history in a particular region and restricted in time—as a sequence of events which was 'inevitable,' 'inexorable,' 'necessary' (metaphysical terms if ever there were any!), allowing nothing to choice and intention, making man the spectator and not the shaper of his destiny. It has fairly been asked whether Comte could, with all his talk of methodology and laws, have predicted any event in history, even events of fundamental significance in the history of mankind, those great movements of which he spoke so much. Certainly his predictions were very wide of the mark. 'The owl of Minerva spreads its wings only with the falling of the dusk.'

But in spite of all its defects it is true what John Morley said of the *Cours*, that 'This analysis of social evolution will continue to be regarded as one of the great achievements of human intellect.'[21] As social anthropologists we may reflect on the vast influence he has had on our subject, both directly and indirectly. It is customary, and right, for us to pay tribute to Durkheim but there is little of general methodological or theoretical significance in his writings that we do not find in Comte if we are earnest

---

[21] John Morley, Art, Comte, *Encyclopaedia Britannica*, vol. VI, p. 194.

and persevering enough to look for it; and I would go so far as to say, though he was not a person of Durkheim's stature, that there is nothing in Radcliffe-Brown's theoretical formulations of a century later that is not as clearly and cogently enunciated by Comte.[22] We may leave him now at the end of the first part of his journey with: 'Now that the human mind has founded celestial physics, terrestrial physics, both mechanical and chemical, organic physics, both vegetable and animal, it remains for it to complete the system of the sciences of observation in founding *social physics*' (*Cours*, I, p. 12).

What about the second part of his journey, the *Système*? He himself contrasts what he calls his two *carrières*, the Aristotle–Comte of the *Cours* and the St Paul–Comte of the *Système*, the scientist and the prophet.[23] But there was no blinding light on the road to Damascus. All the essential ideas of the *Système* (another 2,613 pages!) are to be found in embryo in his earliest writings, as they are in those of St Simon also; so that the surprised indignation of some of his friends, such as Littré and Mill, at what appeared to them to be a sudden conversion and recantation is scarcely warranted. Much of it is indeed a polemical and rather turgid repetition of what was said in the *Cours*, with the addition of a rather tedious prescription for the future of society. All the same, one can understand the dismay with which some of his admirers greeted it; and it must be admitted that Comte was a bit mad—madder even than Saint-Simon and Fourier had been—or at any rate that most people would have regarded his later actions and writings as symptoms of instability, what Littré called a '*crise de folie.*' Look at his portrait: 'His eyes have all the seeming of a demon's that is dreaming.' One need not go into details; one or two examples of his obsessional state will suffice. There was nothing unreasonable in his conviction that science and Catholicism were natural allies, but it was going a bit far in his efforts to combine positivism with moral regeneration to dispatch an emissary to arrange an understanding with the General of the Jesuits (whom he regarded as the real head of the Church, the Pope being little more than the bishop of Rome).[24] Comte, like Renan, never ceased to be a Catholic of a kind. His whole proposed organization for his Religion of Humanity, with its liturgical calendar and its sacraments (for Comte cult came before dogma), was

---

[22] There is a good deal of truth in the statement by the editors (Robert A. Manners and David Kaplan) of *Theory in Anthropology* (1968, p. II) that 'Theory-building in cultural anthropology comes to resemble slash-and-burn agriculture . . . (quoting Wallace) "After cultivating a field for a while, the natives move on to a new one and let the bush take over; they then return, slash and burn and raise crops in the old field again." '

[23] For Comte the founder of Christianity was not Jesus but Paul: '*Le vrai fondateur de ce qu'on nomme improprement le christianisme.*' (*Système*, I, pp. 102–103).

[24] Unfortunately the Father instructed to discuss Comte's proposals was deaf and also confused him with an economist of the same name.

modelled on the structure of the Church of Rome.[25] One need not be surprised that towards the end of his life the *Imitation* was his daily reading. Then, his new society ruled by industrialists in the place of warriors, and scientists in the place of priests, representing the temporal and the spiritual powers (another of Comte's notions taken from mediaeval times), was to be regulated on a scale communists might envy. Every person was required before the age of 21 to have a knowledge of all the abstract sciences, also Greek and Latin and the five principal modern languages. Mill also complained in sorrow that Comte had selected 150 volumes of science, philosophy, poetry, history and general knowledge (not at all a bad selection) and proposed a systematic holocaust of all books except these. He had also made a rule for himself to abstain from all reading whatsoever, except a few favourite poets, for the sake of mental health (*hygiène cérébrale*)—which Mill regarded as evidence of decline, but might on the contrary be regarded as a very salutary regimen to adopt. But though some of these aberrations could be regarded as no more than eccentricities, more serious symptoms of derangement could be thought to be his increasing passion for systematization to the point of mania, systematization both intellectual—I have earlier alluded to that—and moral.

It might be thought that a treatise containing so many what may seem to be odd ideas, and those mostly lacking in scientific interest, is not worth further consideration; though what he has to say on some topics, e.g., the family and language, is of value. However, I speak of the *Système*, if only briefly, for two main reasons. Firstly, Comte understood that science is by itself neutral. It can discover for us facts and the laws which determine them but it cannot decide for us how we are to act on our knowledge (there is here an obvious contradiction, for if there are inexorable laws we have no choice). It can, so Comte thought, even inform us of the inevitable course of social evolution but it cannot ensure that there will be any society to evolve (again a contradiction). For science to be of benefit to man there must be social harmony, which derives not from positivist philosophy alone, or even at all, but from a morality which arises from a sense of duty (the emphasis is on duties, not on rights, which are an obnoxious metaphysical concept), and charity and love.[26] We must live for others (*vivre pour autrui*). It is true, as Aron says,[27] that for Comte

---

[25] *Système*, IV, p. 159 and opp. p. 402. His attitude was not unlike that of G. K. Chesterton's eccentric Fleet Street friend who remarked to him 'The only little difficulty that I have about joining the Catholic Church is that I do not think I believe in God. All the rest of the Catholic system is so obviously right and so obviously superior to anything else that I cannot imagine anyone having any doubt about it' (G. K. Chesterton, *Autobiography*, 1937, p. 187).

[26] The motto of positivism was to be '*L'amour pour principe, l'ordre pour base, et le progrès pour but . . .*' (*Système*, I, p. 321). Also: '*On se lasse de penser, et même d'agir; jamais on se lasse d'aimer*' (*Système*, I, p. 690).

[27] R. Aron, *Les étapes de la pensée sociologique*, 1967, p. 89 *sq.*

history must be the development of human intelligence, but it is also the development of sentiment and morality, for what determines action is sentiment; intelligence serves only to attain the ends: '*Agir par affection, et penser pour agir*' (*Système*, I, p. 688). There must be a synthesis of heart and mind, but the heart must lead, the intellect follow. There is a *logique de l'esprit* and a *logique du coeur*; and '*Le sentiment . . . doit toujours dominer l'intelligence*' (*Système*, I, p. 435). Other—many—philosophers have said much the same, e.g. Hume, Bergson, Pareto, Weber, Unamuno.[28]

But morality ultimately rests not just on love, necessary, ultimate and final though love is, but also on direction, discipline, regimentation, force. I suppose that in modern terminology Comte might be labelled by some a 'fascist' for, for him, institutions stem from beliefs and have vigour and stability only if everybody accepts—is made to accept in the absence of any others—the same imposed and obligatory beliefs.[29] The fanatical harshness and arbitrariness of such rule was in some way to be softened by the influence of women in their rôles of mother, sister, spouse and daughter; a wife being the '*Centre moral de la famille*' (*Système*, II, p. 204). In the positivist society sentiment, reason and action will correspond exactly to the three '*Eléments nécessaires, fémenin, philosophique, et populaire, de l'alliance régénératice*' (*Système*, I, p. 215). Comte was not being sentimental about women, and it should be understood that for him marriage must be both monogamous and indissoluble; and the wife must be subordinate to the husband, for there can be harmony only if one commands and the other obeys (needless to say, he and Mill did not see eye to eye in this matter). It must also be said that in Comte's wild and magnificent imaginings his proposed reforms and Madame de Vaux were mixed up together.[30] At the end of the *Système* he wrote: '*Des 1845 j'avais pleinement apprécié, sous sa sainte influence, l'ensemble de ma carrière, dont la seconde moitié devait transformer la philosophie en religion, comme la première avait changé la science en philosophie* (*Système*, IV, pp. 529–30). So if there was no blinding light there was an angelic vision.

The second reason why I speak briefly of the *Système* is that Comte had the idea of history as the evolution of humanity, the Great Being (*Grand-Être*), of which the dead and the living both form part: in his memorable words '*L'Humanité se compose de plus de morts que de vivants*'

---

[28] In Comte's case the opposite terms are somewhat obscured by the further terms 'objective' and 'subjective' to denote two ways of viewing society and history. By 'subjective' he meant '*L'univers doit être étudié non pour lui-même, mais pour l'homme, ou plutôt pour l'humanité. Tout autre dessein serait, au fond, aussi peu rationnel que peu moral*' (*Système*, I, p. 36).

[29] To do Comte justice, he does say that '*Cet assentiment volontaire*' which is given to the conclusions of the natural sciences will be extended without doubt to moral rules when they will be recognized as susceptible of unchallengable proofs (*Système*, I, p. 100).

[30] '*Cette sainte harmonie entre la vie privée et la vie publique . . .*' (*Système*, Préface, I, p. 10).

and '*Les morts gouvernent de plus en plus les vivants.*' As individuals we do not exist, but where the mystic might say that we exist in God in whom we are all members one of another, for Comte we exist only in the Great Being humanity, in whom our little separate beings are merged and in which, if we have given what we have to give to humanity and not just taken what we could take, we are immortal, that is, our name is immortal, not our person (a not very satisfactory solution to the problem of survival for those who give and are forgotten). This was Comte's positivist conception of the Church Militant, the Church Suffering and the Church Triumphant. As I have said earlier, the individual for Comte is an abstraction. Society, in the widest sense of humanity, is the reality. Art, philosophy, science may get labelled with the names of individuals but properly conceived of they are the creation of humanity,[31] even though their collective nature has to be expressed through individuals (cf. Marxist writers, e.g., Plekhanov). Famous men in history are heirs, not authors; they do not make history, history makes them. Surely it is from Comte that Durkheim derived his theory of religion, that it is society men venerate when it is gods they think they worship, an illusion Comte wanted to make a reality; and that he took from the same source his whole conception of culture and society as collectively created and for the individual obligatory. Some may regard the *Grand-Être* as sentimentality. I would prefer to say sentiment, and to regard it as a great conception of history— ethical, if you like, rather than scientific—which far from conflicting with the positivist programme of the *Cours* seems to me to be a restatement of it in terms of morality, charity and poetry, but if we so regard it, it is only in a very vague and peculiar sense that, for all his talk of inevitability, Comte can be said to be a determinist.

You may ask yourselves as I conclude this lecture what is the point of digging up the past. Comte has himself answered that question as far as social studies are concerned: one can only understand ideas about social life when one knows something of the history of their development. For anthropologists it teaches also I hope a lesson in humility. 'After me cometh a builder. Tell him, I too have known!'

SUMMARY AND EVALUATION
OF CHAPTER TWO

Comte is often referred to as the "sire of sociology." Although this claim is generally accepted, we must weigh it, for its validity depends on what we perceive to be the essential qualifications of sociology as a discipline. Actually, there are three different versions of where and when

---

[31] Then language itself and all thought is collectively created. Nothing could be more stupid than the metaphysicians on this point when they represent '*Comme essentiellement individuelle une institution aussi pleinment sociale que celle du langage*' (*Système*, II, p. 237). Also: *Le public humain est donc le véritable auteur du langage comme son vrai conservateur*' (*Système*, II, p. 259).

sociology emerged.[1] Some say that sociology was known to the Greeks of classical times since they seriously opened and formulated fundamental questions about social man. A second view contends that sociology did not emerge until the doctrine of naturalism was prevalent and a logico-empirical method was at hand. Into this category, of course, falls the sociology embraced by Auguste Comte. Others hold that sociology did not arise until scholars such as Durkheim actually began to build the discipline by formulating more testable theory and seriously gathering empirical data in a careful and systematic way. These views are not necessarily contradictory. They only emphasize different aspects of the discipline. A wide range of opinion favors the view that sociology in the West was conceived clearly and fully around the time of Comte.

The conservative cast of Comte's works is undeniable and has been noted elsewhere.[2] Although his positivism soundly emphasized the elements of the scientific approach and properly shifted attention away from the absolutist metaphysical analysis to which thinking in the realm of social phenomena had been so long tied, it was, nevertheless, a tool of his conservative goals. Whereas the *Philosophes* used the method of science as a vehicle for the *critical* examinaton of medieval society, conservatives used it for "demonstrating" the needs of orderly progress. Science would disclose and legitimate, Comte believed, the truth of the conservative principles that society is an organismiclike unity requiring first of all interdependence among parts rather than the fulfillment of individualistic needs or rights. Historically, science would show that society has a character of its own, anterior to the individual, deeply rooted in the past from which it has slowly evolved and from which it derives its strengths.

Just as biology properly proceeds in its mode of analysis from the whole to the part, so, too, sociology, being most closely related to biology in the filiated order of the sciences, would show what each of the parts (and classes) owes to the others and to the whole. For ages it was accepted that society is of God or that man is social in a God-given society. But now the historical religion that provided the moral obligations had crumbled, and Comte railed only against those conservatives who still attempted to adduce the metaphysical reasons given by historical religion for the requirements of order instead of the positivistic reasons.

His faith in progress with science at the fore derived, as did Mon-

---

[1] See the following: Harry Elmer Barnes, "Social Thought in Early Modern Times," in Barnes (Ed.), *An Introduction to the History of Sociology* (Chicago: University of Chicago Press, 1948), pp. 71–76; Alvin Boskoff, "From Social Thought to Sociological Theory," in Howard Becker and Alvin Boskoff (Eds.), *Modern Sociological Theory* (New York: Holt, Rinehart and Winston, 1957), pp. 3–7; and Howard Becker and Harry Elmer Barnes, *Social Thought from Lore to Science* (New York: Dover, 1961), pp. 565–567.

[2] See Irving M. Zeitlin, *Ideology and the Development of Sociological Theory* (Englewood Cliffs, N.J.: Prentice-Hall, 1968), pp. 70–79; and Bernhard J. Stern, *Historical Sociology* (New York: Citadel, 1959), pp. 191–199.

tesquieu's, from the belief that social laws once disclosed would show what the "real nature" of society required to insure order and progress in a particular situation. As soon as man had knowledge of such laws, he would use them to his advantage by charting his social arrangements more along their course. Progress without order was not possible in Comte's view, and order would have to gain its bases from the more demonstrable truth of science (positivism) rather than the discredited fictions of religious and other utopian philosophers of the past.

Comte's positivism would be used against the short-sighted critics of medieval social structure (the *Philosophes*), the utilitarians, and all those who would hastily remake society without certified knowledge of its conditions. For positivism would demonstrate certain truths about society: that harmony among its parts is necessary, that it is more than a collection of utilitarian contracts, and that it is complex and must be modified only in accord with its real conditions and necessary course of development. Comte anticipated the fear that positivism, being a relative doctrine that could only gradually uncover the real laws of societal order through methods of continual correction, might not fill the gap that was left after the absolute spirit of traditional religious thoughtways had been abandoned. But Comte quieted such apprehensions with the assurance that, though the method was relative, it was nevertheless not *arbitrary*; chaos or turmoil would not result from its institutionalization. So complex are social phenomena, however, that only the few elite who are capable of theory should be entrusted with the job of studying society and making recommendations for its change.

Two sides to Comte's personality have been noticed in this chapter. One was the flamboyant and overly confident Comte, he who in attempting to establish the scientific method in societal analysis had to overstate his case and drive various enemies of positivism from the scene. He berated those who in their eager and unbridled utopianism would presume to change society at will, without regard for its social facts or laws, and claimed that the positive method, *if given the chance*, would avert their disasters. However, his own impatience prompted him finally to fashion plans for a society built on love, which failed to come to grips with important questions about the breakdown of social control, dissension, and the shortcomings of developing collective sentiments by mere ritual and observances.

The other side of Comte was analytic and introspective and perhaps needs greatest emphasis because his truculent, true-believer nature has received most of the attention up to this time. Comte began to examine real society, especially, as Cohen shows, those relations from which social sentiments emerge, the consequences of a highly differentiated division of labor, and the real problems of social control.

One school of thought today advocates that sociology should consist of a method and an analysis and have an ennobling influence on man. This kind of thinking is a product of Comte's influence. In this chapter we have noted Comte's attempts to inculcate positivistic consciousness into social analysis, in reaction to the abrupt social change of his time. Evans-

Pritchard finds Comte's *Course of Positive Philosophy* and his *System of Positive Polity* to be more compatible than generally supposed; in the former he inspires reliance on the factual method and naturalistic laws of science and in the latter he envisions the ennoblement of man in his rededication to Humanity. Between the composition of these works, according to Cohen, Comte undertook an often overlooked analysis of actual societal processes. In so doing, though his concern for social order understandably remained dominant throughout his life, Comte reached beyond both the Enlightenment faith in progress and conservative disdain for postrevolutionary French society. He analyzed the sources of social sentiment in industry and the family and the practical considerations for social change that these entailed. He may even have begun the outlines of a psychology, which remained unfinished at his death.

Criticisms of Comte's works are not lacking.[3] Most find fault with the emphasis he gave to certain matters. For example, he stressed certified knowledge of society as a replacement for the religious morality of the past and paid less attention to the social conflicts that occur even when the contending parties have accurate knowledge; he also pushed for early acceptance of the positivistic principles in the circles of government, while neglecting the necessarily slow development of science as it clarifies these principles.

Some writers have said that little in Comte is original.[4] He appeared on the scene when some important new ideas were coalescing. The idea of continuity and progress in history had been espoused by Montesquieu, Condorcet, and Turgot. The belief in science as the basic instrument for accomplishing progressive change was forcefully espoused by many, including Saint-Simon, from whom Comte acquired other convictions and orientations as well. Nevertheless, the urgency of his desire to initiate societal reform on the basis of more reliable knowledge, his flair for synthesis, and his thirst for comprehensive explanation give him a distinction not fully appreciated even today.[5]

Some common set of beliefs is necessary if a society is to survive, a requirement of which Comte was acutely aware. No purpose in life can be maintained if these beliefs are lacking. Beliefs concerning a particular area of life rest on accuracy of knowledge about it; but they also rest on faith and commitment. In a sense, when faith and meaning in life dissolve, God is killed. Comte took upon himself the hazardous and extrascientific task of using science to guide a society to something it can believe in. That task is still urgent today.[6]

---

[3] See Mary Farmer, "The Positivist Movement and the Development of English Sociology," *The Sociological Review*, 15 (March 1967), 5–20.

[4] See Becker and Barnes, *Social Thought from Lore to Science*, p. 565.

[5] See George Simpson, *Auguste Comte: Sire of Sociology* (New York: Crowell, 1969), pp. v–viii.

[6] See Edmund R. Leach's very provocative statement along these lines: "We Scientists Have the Right To Play God," *The Saturday Evening Post*, November 16, 1968, pp. 16, 20.

In the next chapter we shift to late eighteenth-century England. There the social conditions were quite different from those in France, and their effects on Spencer's sociology were as noticeable as the effects of the French milieu were on Comte's.

SELECTED BIBLIOGRAPHY

Aron, Raymond. *Main Currents in Sociological Thought I.* Garden City, N.Y.: Doubleday, 1968.

Barnes, Harry Elmer, (Ed.). *An Introduction to the History of Sociology.* Chicago: University of Chicago Press, 1948. Chap. III, "The Social and Political Philosophy of Auguste Comte: Positivist Utopia and the Religion of Humanity," pp. 81–109 (this article is omitted from the abridged, paperback edition).

Becker, Howard, and Harry Elmer Barnes. *Social Thought from Lore to Science.* Vol. II. New York: Dover, 1961. See especially Chap. XV.

Comte, Auguste. *Introduction to Positive Philosophy.* Translated and edited by Frederick Ferré. Indianapolis: Bobbs-Merrill, 1970.

Comte, Auguste. *Positive Philosophy.* Translated and condensed by Harriet Martineau. New York: Calvin Blanchard, 1855.

Iggers, Georg G., (Trans.). *The Doctrine of Saint-Simon.* New York: Schocken Books, 1972.

Lichtenberger, James P. *Development of Social Thought.* New York: The Century Company, 1925. See especially Chap. X.

Manuel, Frank E. *The New World of Henri Saint-Simon.* Cambridge, Mass.: Harvard University Press, 1956.

Mill, John Stuart. *Auguste Comte and Positivism.* Ann Arbor: Ann Arbor Paperbacks, The University of Michigan Press, 1965.

Simon, W. M. *European Positivism in the Nineteenth Century.* Ithaca, N.Y.: Cornell University Press, 1963.

Simpson, George. *Auguste Comte: Sire of Sociology.* New York: Crowell, 1969.

Zeitlin, Irving M. *Ideology and the Development of Sociological Theory.* Englewood Cliffs, N.J.: Prentice-Hall, 1968.

THREE

Herbert Spencer

"How can Spencer hold very contradictory concepts,
i.e., the state should devote its energies to the rights of
individuals and the survival-of-the-fittest concept? This is like
saying that blacks should have equal opportunity in society
and then blocking off any chance of their ever attaining it."

—STUDENT COMMENT

General Introduction

Herbert Spencer (1820–1903) was born in Derby, England.[1] Though his father, William, was a private teacher, Spencer received little formal education. At the age of thirteen he went to study informally with his uncle, a clergyman, who whetted his interest in mathematics and science. His interests in social affairs began to surface around 1842, when he wrote a series of articles on the proper sphere of government. Thereafter he served as a civil engineer until 1848, then turned again, this time more seriously, to writing on political, economic, and social topics as subeditor of an influential weekly London newspaper, the *Economist*. His position allowed him considerable time and exposed him to contacts with outstanding intellectual figures. In 1853 his uncle left him a stipend, which, along with free-lance writing for journals and the sale of his books, enabled him to support himself. During the remainder of his life, which proved to be a long one, Spencer wrote a great deal.[2]

---

[1] See J. D. Y. Peel's *Herbert Spencer: The Evolution of a Sociologist* (New York: Basic Books, 1971) for a discussion of the relationship between Spencer and the times in which he lived.

[2] The general character of his whole life's work was already intimated in the articles Spencer wrote from 1852 to 1855, such as "The Development Hypothesis" and "The Universal Postulate." Spencer's major writings began to appear

Spencer was brought up in the tradition of the Dissenters to which his parents and forebears adhered. In this sect one finds an interesting accommodation of science to religion and the encouragement of individualistic character. Specifically, Dissenters, drawing their membership from people aspiring to the new middle classes, objected to doctrinal restraints, advocated the development of the scientific, disciplined, naturalistic, and comprehensive frame of mind, and sought freedom in human, especially economic, activity. On the personal level the virtues of emotional restraint (rather than the greater indulgence in experience condoned by earlier Methodism), objectivity, self-sufficiency, singularity of purpose and perseverance, and sober industriousness were extolled.

In Spencer's immediate environment there was plenty of intellectual freedom and stimulation. His father was secretary of the Derby Philosophical Society, which had been founded in 1783 by Dr. Erasmus Darwin, Charles Darwin's grandfather.[3] The Society was modeled upon one in which Darwin had earlier participated, The Lunar Society of Birmingham, and promoted what was termed "practical and playful science." As a result of such influences, Spencer developed a wide-ranging curiosity about all matters of the natural world. He was less interested in practical affairs, though he attempted some inventions, than in the pursuit of abstract comprehension.

A largely self-educated man, Spencer regarded his ideas highly, felt protective of them, and stuck doggedly by the schemes he devised to synthesize them. He made some efforts at radical politics but ". . . his passionate and utopian belief in progress meant that he could not be wholly serious about political agitation."[4]

His bachelorhood and sexual abstention might possibly have had something to do with his nervous breakdown in 1855, but more probably

---

in 1854 with the publication of *Principles of Psychology* and *Social Statics* (actually written a few years earlier). The former became part of the overall work called *The Synthetic Philosophy*, the outlines of which were sketched in 1858. Later, the publication of Darwin's *The Origin of Species*—which relied on some of Spencer's ideas—gave Spencer the motivation to fill out the detail of *The Synthetic Philosophy*. This he did when he added *First Principles* (1862), *Principles of Biology* (1864–1867), *Principles of Sociology* (1876–1896), and *Principles of Ethics* (1879–1896). *Descriptive Sociology* was a series published from 1873, which classified large numbers of ethnographic facts from various societies according to structure and function. Among his other works are *The Study of Sociology* (1873), *The Man versus the State* (1884), and an article titled "Progress: Its Law and Cause" (1857). For a complete listing see Jay Rumney, *Herbert Spencer's Sociology* (New York: Atherton Press, 1966), 311–351.

[3] Peel, *Herbert Spencer*, p. 43.

[4] Ibid., p. 11.

it was the strain of hard work, financial insecurity, and his irritation with the criticism of his writings—criticism he took very personally.

While Spencer had many friends and intellectual colleagues (even though he had no university appointment), he became, especially after the breakdown, a very self-pitying, cantankerous, and rigid man. His popular fame was quite great, particularly in the United States between 1860 and 1890. J. D. Y. Peel tells that once a letter arrived at Spencer's home addressed to " 'Herbt. Spencer, England, and if the postman doesn't know where he lives, why, he ought to.' "[5] Yet, because of the relative decline of England's dominance in the world market and the emergence of the welfare state, described below, Spencer toward the end of his life became quite uncertain about the worth of his work.

Indeed, in 1937 Talcott Parsons asked, "Who now reads Spencer?"[6] His point was that Spencer's great evolutionism, incorporating his faith in Progress, was dead. Later, however, Parsons acknowledged some of Spencer's important contributions to sociological theory and analysis.[7] We agree that Spencer cannot be overlooked; even his evolutionary theory, when properly qualified, deserves attention. Below we shall present the social history of nineteenth-century England, discuss Spencer's approach to sociology, give his contrasting analyses of societies in Selection 3.1, and, in the Summary, evaluate evolutionism.

England in the Nineteenth Century:
Historical Background

England in the nineteenth century was, like France, undergoing rapid and far-reaching changes, but it did not fall prey to the violent revolution and the subsequent lengthy period of governmental floundering that occurred across the Channel. The conditions in the two countries are often compared in order not only to understand this difference but also to comprehend better why Auguste Comte and Herbert Spencer produced different sociologies. The transformations brought about by industrialization and the growing middle classes appear to have been quite similar in both France and England. The two countries differed, however, in their responses to these conditions and thus demonstrated very distinct results.

By the time England entered the nineteenth century, the Enclosure Acts had forced the small landholders to either drift into the swelling cities or become the laborers and tenants of the landed gentry who had gained

---

[5] Ibid., p. 2.

[6] Talcott Parsons, *The Structure of Social Action* (New York: Free Press, 1949), p. 3.

[7] Herbert Spencer, *The Study of Sociology* (Ann Arbor: The University of Michigan Press, 1966), pp. v–x.

ownership of their holdings. Cottagers, too, had lost much of their means of livelihood. The criminal code defined no less than 220 offenses as worthy of capital punishment. The government was still substantially the one that had developed out of the feudal order, but agitation for reform was growing because the landed gentry and aristocracy dominated political parties. Two forces feuling this movement were rapidly emerging: on the one hand, industrial and commercial growth accompanied by scientific agriculture and breeding, and, on the other, the philosophy known as Benthamism,[8] which was to play a great role later in arguments for free trade and social–political reform. David Thomson notes that England in 1815

> was on the brink of an era of prosperity and greatness unrivaled in her whole history. . . . At the same time, she was entering upon a period of remarkable social distress and unrest, of economic crises and political change. Her new wealth and her world supremacy rested on foundations of harsh sweated labour, appalling slum conditions in her new towns, and immense human misery. . . . much of her subsequent history has been the story of successive but not always successful efforts to reconcile her ideals of political democracy and universal happiness with the realities of economic distress and oppression. To bridge this enormous gulf she gradually devised the complex apparatus of the modern social-service State [to which Spencer objected—Ed.].[9]

This state of affairs, with its admixture of prosperity and distress and the consequent development of conflicting interest groups, noted below, became known as the "condition of England question." The response to this question and the means used to resolve it resulted in a more peaceful set of changes in England than in France.

Shortly after the turn of the century, some of the sources of change that lay ahead were clear. One, as might be expected, was the growing antipathy between employers and employees in the factories. Although the conditions of the workers, among whom were many children, were objectively no worse, and perhaps even better, than those of their ancestors, they were, nevertheless, deplorable and conspicuous. The first reactions to worker uprisings were repressive ones, sanctioned by the Combination Laws and the Six Acts; the former prohibited the formation of large assemblies of workers, while the latter sought to control or kill the radical press. However, these reactions soon gave way to the passage of a series of Factory Acts, which considerably improved the lot of the workers. Whether these were passed as a gesture of direct concern for the workers,

---

[8] Roughly, the doctrine that holds that the common good consists in the greatest happiness for the greatest number of people.

[9] David Thomson, *England in the Nineteenth Century* (Baltimore, Md.: Penguin, 1950), p. 32.

or whether, as also is suggested, they were promoted by wealthy land-holders in their attempt to curb the growing wealth of manufacturing and commercial interests by forcing them to pay more for labor, is not important. Robert Owen's model labor–management shops had demonstrated to some employers that they could both treat laborers better *and* retain high profits, and even that they might increase productivity and profits by improving working conditions. Furthermore, manufacturers were not unequivocally against the formation of worker unions, which were to grow in a later period, because they also believed that a society of plenty and harmony lay ahead.

The price of corn became a second source of change. On this issue both the factory workers and owners stood in opposition to the growers. The growers, who had produced corn in the national interest during the Napoleonic Wars, which had just concluded in 1815, now demanded and obtained tariffs on corn imported from other countries in order that they might continue to receive a high price for their own crop in England. However, it was obviously in the interest of workers to have the price of corn low so that their wages spent for food would go further. Factory owners disliked high corn prices not only because wages would have to keep pace but, more importantly perhaps, because tariffs were abnega-tions of free-trade and competition ideologies. And if other countries could not export corn to England, they in turn would have no means with which to purchase England's growing exports of industrial goods. It was not until 1845, however, after a period of famine, that the corn and (re-strictive) navigation laws were repealed—a cause Spencer helped to promote.

Next, a period of constitutional and political reforms took place. The conditions that prompted these were in large part those described above: the emergence of the new industrial and commercial groups together with the shift of population to new areas of the country. The state of government at the beginning of the nineteenth century is described by Thomson:

> The landed gentry had votes as 40s. [shillings] freeholders in the counties and often held great power as the local magistrates: a goodly proportion of their number sat in the House of Commons, and their sons had access to trade, politics, or the professions as they chose. The big landowners enjoyed great wealth from their extensive estates, the agricultural pros-perity of the enclosures, and the general stability of the national economy. They dominated the House of Lords and the councils of the king, con-trolled foreign policy, served as lords-lieutenant of the counties in charge of the local militia, and nominated large retinues of relations and dependents to place in the Commons, the Church, the Army, and indeed all public services.[10]

---

[10] Ibid., p. 56.

The most drastic change was demanded by the radicals, who wanted nothing less than a complete overhaul of the parliamentary system and representation based on people rather than property. This did not materialize completely until 1928. What did emerge was the Reform Bill of 1832, which successfully modified the system by granting a more favorable distribution of seats in the House of Commons to the new manufacturing and merchant classes. This bill heralded the passage of more such reform legislation between 1841 and 1872.

Other reforms in the 1830s further curtailed the power of the gentry, the big landowners, and the parish vestries and Justice of the Peace Offices through which such power was frequently exercised. At the heart of the law-and-order and poverty questions of the day was the ineffective, unrepresentative nature of local town government. Amendments to the criminal code resulted in a sharp reduction in the number of crimes punishable by death, and the police reorganization of 1829 instituted a more central control of operations, thereby making law enforcement more efficient. Riots were prevented and a police rate tax was levied. In 1834 the Poor Law Amendment provided for a new system to administer the help and care of the poor and made the aid programs more uniform by nationalizing them. It discriminated among the different needs of the poor and gradually put an end to their state of perpetual pauperism and dependency, as well as to the practice of pushing them back and forth between the city and the country in order to escape responsibility for them. Control over such programs became tighter and more centralized, and even more important for reducing the power of the aristocracy, local bodies were elected to work with Poor Law Commissioners. In 1835, the Municipal Reform Act further reduced the aristocracy's participation in government by requiring the election of borough councils by rate payers. Position on the borough councils could no longer be automatically usurped by the landed gentry but now had to be filled through election by rate payers.

Meanwhile a series of acts from 1820 to 1871 separated church and state by granting, with a few exceptions, equality of opportunity to Dissenters and Nonconformists of the Anglican Church of England in areas ranging from politics to education. This equality was later extended to Catholics. Such legislation received impetus from advocates of Benthamism, who managed to prevail over supporters of laissez-faire. The latter held that a government best serves its people when it abstains from interference in their economic and social affairs and could well have impeded reform.

Enfranchisement still required the holding of property, however. Stirred by this injustice, in 1838 the London Working Men's Association, a trade union established in 1836, started becoming more politicized. From it emerged the *People's Charter*, which called for ". . . universal male suffrage; equal electoral districts; removal of the property qualification for members of Parliament; payment of members of Parliament; secret ballot; and annual general elections."[11] Though the Chartist movement lost force by 1848, partly as the result of new prosperity after famine and internal disagreements over tactics, it inspired a seriousness over the conditions it assailed, and the first five of its points were incorporated into the Constitution of England by 1918.

By 1848 the drain on resources caused by a growing population was slowed by emigration, and a period of optimism, lasting until about 1880 and spanning most of Spencer's writings, was ushered in. This optimism developed despite the economic threat to England that such powers as the United States, Germany, and Portugal were now beginning to pose. As it turned out, this threat later proved a reality and resulted in the decreased popularity of Spencer's writings toward the end of his life.

While the confidence lasted, however, economic liberalism, with its emphasis on free trade and competition, was needed not so much to oppose welfare programs as to strengthen the new industrial and business class interests with which Spencer was in sympathy. He was not unequivocally against government correction and protection programs in economic or social life, but was rather skeptical of their development and implementation because he was convinced that so little was known about how to handle them and what their effects would be. Undoubtedly the conditions of the poor touched him, but he believed that intervention might actually *worsen* the situation in the long run.[12] Indeed, he felt, the operation of natural laws, which were assumed to work quite automatically, was leading to progressive improvement anyway.

If, as Spencer thought, self-regulated, disciplined men like him could take care of their own affairs without abridging others' rights, why could not this same principle operate in society generally? And since the middle classes in England had proven their responsibility by their peaceful, growing industriousness, large governmental involvement was clearly unneces-

---

[11] Ibid., p. 84.

[12] One of Spencer's famous quotes on the matter is this one:
> You see that this wrought-iron plate is not quite flat: it sticks up a little here towards the left—"Cockles," as we say. How shall we flatten it? Obviously, you reply, by hitting down on the part that is prominent. Well, here is a hammer and I give the plate a blow as you advise. Harder, you say. Still no effect. Another stroke? Well, there is one, and another, and another. The prominence remains, you see: the evil is as great as ever—greater, indeed. But this is not all. Look at the warp which the plate has got near the opposite edge. Where it was flat before it is now curved. A pretty bungle we have made of it. Instead of curing the original defect, we have produced a second. . . . What, then, shall we say about a society? . . . . Is humanity more readily straightened than an iron plate? [See Spencer, *The Study of Sociology*, pp. 245–246.]

sary, and violent political activity was unlikely from their sector. The middle classes feared revolution, in fact, and were consequently motivated to ally themselves with the aristocracy against the lower classes. Therefore, just as religion and the state should be separated, so, too, should the industriousness of the righteous, which was creating the great industrial output, be free of governmental fetters. These new middle classes would even provide for the lower classes without governmental programs. Overall, Spencer assumed that capitalist enterprise, based on a system that rewards competition, would enlarge the common good.

Because of the relative prosperity and stability in England and because of his Dissenter upbringing, which taught control in one's personal life, Spencer did not become as much of a diagnostician of social problems in his sociological theory as Comte did; he became, rather, the advocate of radical individual freedom. Moreover, whereas Catholicism became the bulwark of conservatism in France, sanctifying the good of the larger organic collectivity and the reciprocal moral obligations on which feudalism had been based, it wielded less influence in England, where the dominant force of Calvinism actually favored capitalistic–industrial activities. In this climate Spencer developed a more *secular-individualistic* analysis of social phenomena. Although both theorists believed in progress,[13] Comte had faith in the capacity of man to control his social environment to some extent by the use of his intellect. Spencer was much more skeptical of this and, instead, believed in the purposiveness of material evolution itself. The detail in which Spencer worked out his evolutionary framework is, of course, absent from Comte's work.

Spencer's Societal Analysis within the Evolutionary Framework

Spencer reflected the tendency of the time either to find a broad intellectual order in the accumulating facts about the world or to impose one on them. In 1853, Sir Charles Lyell, the geologist, had expounded the view that the earth's surface had evolved naturalistically over a long period of time. It was from such thought that Spencer drew the inspiration to rest his larger evolutionary scheme on the basic insight that motion (energy) pervades the universe. While energy is transferred through inorganic matter, it is *captured* by organic matter.

Beginning with certain assumptions such as the persistence of force, the indestructibility of matter, and the continuity of motion—all very abstract but, he thought indisputable laws—Spencer held that life and its

---

[13] For a comparison see Kenneth E. Bock, "Theories of Progress and Evolution," in Werner J. Cahnman and Alvin Boskoff (Eds.), *Sociology and History* (New York: Free Press, 1964), pp. 32–35.

off-shoot culture (the superorganic level) move from an incoherent *homogeneity* to a coherent, definite *heterogeneity* since every cause has several effects. From these assumptions Spencer deduced the development of societies. As differentiation of matter occurs, motion is absorbed (captured), and as *integration* of matter occurs, motion is dissipated (i.e., the area of its operation is widened). As this change occurs within an organism (or an aggregate or species),[14] the *equilibrium* among its parts or between it and the environment is disturbed, and a new equilibrium must be attained. (One indication that such is occurring would be the existence of conflict, although Spencer gave less emphasis to this process than the social Darwinists did later.) Spencer ultimately explained this movement as the result of an inherent instability in homogeneity. If these laws are true of nature, thought Spencer, they must be true of society also since it is simply a superorganic aspect of nature.

Spencer condemned those who attempted to solve social problems with moralistic preachments that prescribed what man *should be*. Yet, influenced as he was by such men as Adam Smith and Jeremy Bentham, Spencer did treat the phenomenon of happiness in his own analysis and philosophy. In his work, *Social Statics*, he equated unhappiness with *maladaptation*, which he believed was frequently nurtured and prolonged by man's shortsighted efforts at social correction. To him the evolutionary process was highly complex and intricate, and he tended to endow the adaptation process with a wisdom that, if allowed to follow its own course, would presumably result in a good state of affairs consonant with man's conception of happiness. Adaptation is always necessary since the conditions of a social state, although fixed at any one particular moment, change from time to time and place certain requirements on its members.

Spencer speculated that the social state evolved from some primitive (undifferentiated) horde, wherein one sacrificed the welfare of the other to one's own well-being. In contrast to this, the social state requires one's sympathy for the other, a code that finally should enable one to obtain full satisfaction for every desire without diminishing the power of the other to obtain the same. The individual's voluntary limitation of his own freedom was central to Spencer's laissez-faire. He believed that the more social man—disposed to work well with others—would outlive the less social man because he would better adapt to the requirements of society.

The social nature required of human beings changes as society changes, however. Personal freedom should increase as society differentiates, provided outside threats are minimal. In this same vein, Spencer suggested that different societies would engender different types of char-

---

[14] Although he recognized the possibility that development from the homogeneous to the heterogeneous occurs in species as well as in the individual organism, the latter remained the chief subject of his analysis.

acter; for example, whereas a military state would produce aggressiveness, bravery, and so on, an industrial one would encourage a more sympathetic nature. This insight foreshadowed the present studies of social structure and national character. Spencer thought that militaristic societies and thus war, with the centralized social control over the individual that it requires, were presumably on the wane.[15]

Societies were seen by Spencer as superorganic aggregates that obey the laws of differentiation and integration as they grow.[16] The quest for food is a main factor contributing to their growth. Once simple societies, "headless clusters" that lack government, exceed about one hundred in population, they undergo their first social differentiation: the formation of a ruling agency. Next, Spencer believed, a degree of operative differentiation (as between the sexes) takes place. As slaves are taken captive and work is allocated to them, a further differentiation within the society begins. The whole process is one in which first broad, simple contrasts (unlikenesses) of parts occur. Specialized structures develop especially in the areas of sustenance, distribution, and regulation. Later, a head is needed to hold these together, then a head of heads, as further unlikenesses occur, and so on. In such a way, Spencer believed, social organization is compounded and integrated.

The analysis of society as an interdependence of institutions was little developed before Spencer. His most important insight was that the structures in society gradually differentiate and specialize in function, thus necessitating an integration of these new functions within a new whole. In simple, largely undifferentiated societies those structures that do exist, for example, the family, perform multiple functions concerning economy, education, religion, tension management, politics, and other areas of life. Sometimes these functions are carried out within a large organization of a number of such structures, such as several families or lineages together.

---

[15] That militarism has remained a characteristic of some industrialized societies because of the existence of outside threats, indicates the extent to which a mix of Spencer's types is possible. See Rumney, *Herbert Spencer's Sociology*, p. 89. It is true that both optimism and a degree of pessimism can be noted in Spencer's works, and, to a large extent, which feeling is conveyed depends on which of the two schemes—the evolutionary or the military/industrial—is under consideration. Although he recognized retrogression and stagnation in particular societies, he thought that overall evolution was progressive. But because during the latter part of his lifetime he also saw the imposition of coercive regulation in England, a characteristic of military societies, in that respect he was less optimistic about the future.

[16] See Spencer's *Principles of Sociology I* (New York: Appleton, 1897), pp. 470–490, 549–575, 593–596. Whereas Malthus was gloomy about the prospect of population growth, which he thought would tend to outrun food supplies, Spencer believed that, as people multiply, more ingenuity would be required to stay alive, and thus man's intelligence would be raised.

However, in complex societies, which have undergone considerable differentiation, new structures have been created to perform specialized functions. Thus, the school has been developed to impart education; welfare bureaus, to administer the needs of the indigent; councils (constituted independently of kinship groups), to adjudicate; and so forth.

To summarize, then, Spencer developed two different classifications of society: one, a dichotomy consisting of the militaristic and the industrial, and the other, his main one, a system of several categories—simple, compound, double and trebly compound societies—based on his insights of expanding differentiation.

Introduction to Selection 3.1

If we do not fully appreciate Herbert Spencer, it may be because we misread or unfairly stereotyped him or, as Werner Stark indicates, because he vacillated from one perspective to another. Spencer's involvement in the social criticism of his day[17] may have contributed to some of the confusion, since he attempted to add force and dignity to his criticism by trying to justify it scientifically.

In his article, "Herbert Spencer's Three Sociologies," Stark discusses some of Spencer's perspectives of society. He shows, first, that when Spencer regarded society as a unity (according to the doctrine of realism), he believed the functions of the parts for the benefit of the whole to be of primary importance. Spencer drew an analogy between the working of society's parts and the working of the organs within an organism or the working of the units within a physical system. We might note that Spencer had for some time been an engineer and must have noticed the effects of new communication technologies. He could even explain competition as a form of cooperation.

When Spencer took the opposite view, conceiving of society as a multiplicity (from the standpoint of nominalism), he found the basic reality to be individuals in their transactions with each other.[18] In this frame of mind he now pointed to the deficiencies of the society-as-an-organism analogy. He also handled the problem of social order differently: whereas in his society-as-a-unity conception order is expected to occur because the activities of the specialized parts must fulfill the requirements of the whole, in his society-as-a-multiplicity conception order is expected to occur as a result of voluntary individual efforts; hence all remain free to do together those things that one cannot do for oneself.

---

[17] See his *Essays: Scientific, Political, and Speculative I, II, III* (New York: Appleton, 1899).

[18] Durkheim later attacked this "individuals-in-their-transactions" view of society.

In Stark's judgment, Spencer's third view was more tenable than the others, for it explored the idea that, through socialization, one desires to accommodate the wishes of others, the result being some unity among individuals. Spencer's references to "ego-altruism" and to behavior acquisition through pleasure and pain is part of this idea. It remained for later scholars such as George Herbert Mead to render a more sophisticated analysis of the relationship between self and society.

Despite the critical tone of his comments, Stark would undoubtedly agree that much of Spencer's work is quite worthwhile. If, as the poet Ralph Waldo Emerson once stated, consistency is a product of a small mind, then Spencer must be judged to have had a large mind since, according to Stark, he adopted conflicting points of view. And perhaps it was because of the tension between his different ideas that he pushed further into sociology than he might have with a consistent, one-sided attitude.

Stark's article is a comparison of passages that show the conflicting observations Spencer made as a result of viewing society both as a unity and as a multiplicity. Stark does not go into why Spencer formulated both sociologies or what in society may have influenced him. Actually, two doctrines, organicism and Utilitarianism, were of major importance in shaping his ideas. Both views were strong in England at the time. As organicist, Spencer saw the part in relation to the whole. The parts must function to satisfy the requirements of the whole, and those that do not presumably disappear, for they are badly adjusted and cannot be nourished by the other parts, which work together for the survival of the whole system. Out of such ideas came the society-as-a-unity perspective. As Utilitarian, however, Spencer saw the matter differently. In Utilitarianism, which derives from Benthamism, rationality is used to assess the efficiency of actions or their usefulness to the ends of individual actors. What is good and useful depends upon the individual's goals, not upon the requirements of some collectivity or system. To a Utilitarian the greatest good is still the greatest good for the greatest number of *individuals*. Here was the source of the society-as-a-multiplicity idea. Chiefly through these two competing doctrines the times left their mark on Spencer's work.

3.1

Herbert Spencer's Three Sociologies*
WERNER STARK

All of us are agreed that consistency is a very great virtue in a sociologist—a virtue as indispensable to him as it is to any other scholar or scientist. Yet it can happen once in a hundred years that a sociologist deserves to be called great, not because he is consistent, not because he embraces a certain principle of interpretation and analysis and drives it forward to its ultimate conclusions, but, on the contrary, because he tries a number of possible approaches and moves with an open mind along several different avenues. This precisely is the case of Herbert Spencer. Unlike LePlay, unlike Durkheim, unlike so many others that could be named, he has left behind no integrated school, no sons, as it were, to perpetuate his name. But in a sense we all belong to his family.

It is, I think, obvious that in the last analysis there are, and there can be, only three basic types of sociological theory. A society is, by definition, at the same time both a unity and a multiplicity, and for this reason the theoretician can either take the view that it is a unity rather than a multiplicity, that it is one rather than many; or he can take the view that it is a multiplicity rather than a unity, that it is many rather than one; or, finally, he can regard it as initially a multiplicity, but a multiplicity which tends to develop into a unity, which, through the operation of an inner life-principle, achieves increasing integration. It is the characteristic weakness and the characteristic strength of Spencer that he entertained all three opinions at the same time.

"Principles of Sociology"

The first alternative, the alternative which puts the emphasis on the essential unity of the social whole, has classically been formulated by saying that society is an organism, and Spencer, in his "Principles of Sociology," makes himself the conscious exponent of this organismic, quasi-biological conception. If there is any difference between him and

---

* This paper was originally read to the American Sociological Association's Spencer "Centenary Meeting" within the framework of the fifty-fifth annual meeting in New York City on the evening of August 26, 1960.

85

his predecessors it is this: he gives to the basic equation between society and organism a narrower, that is to say, less metaphorical, more literal meaning. A society *is* an organism, he maintains, because it obeys all the laws of structure, function and development which are characteristic, and which are constitutive, of organic life.

The core of Spencer's exposition is the second part of the first volume, entitled "The Introductions of Sociology," and here he immediately raises the question: what is a society? Two answers, he replies, are possible. "It may be said," he writes, "that a society is but a collective name for a number of individuals. Carrying the controversy between nominalism and realism into another sphere, a nominalist might affirm that just as there exist only the members of a species, while the species considered apart from them has no existence; so the units of a society alone exist, while the existence of the society is but verbal."[1] This nominalism, this definition of society as a multiplicity, this insistence that society is in the last analysis merely a word, a linguistic fiction, appears to him entirely erroneous. No, we must plump for the other alternative. We must say that society is an entity, a tangible reality, and only if we take this view are we in accord with the facts. It is interesting to note that Spencer is not satisfied at this point where the theoretical issue is considered, with saying that society is a unity in the sense in which the human body is a unit. To drive home his point, he uses an even stronger simile. He compares society to a house. It is true that a house is built of individual bricks, but what is left of the individuality of these bricks once the house has been built? Surely the dominant reality is now the reality of the whole. In his anxiety that nobody should misunderstand him, that nobody should suspect him of nominalism, overt or covert, Spencer goes so far as to define society as a thing. "The constant relations among its parts," he writes, "make it an entity," and "it is this trait which yields," and ought to yield, "our idea of a society."[2]

Of course, after having risen to these metaphysical heights, Spencer has to come down to a somewhat more sober level, and in the next paragraph he introduces his definition with which he then works throughout "The Inductions of Sociology"—the definition of society as an organism. Every single paragraph that now follows, with only one lone exception, presents a proof, or rather fancied proof, for the assertion that the cooperation of men in society is of the same nature (the word nature taken in a strict, scientific sense) as the cooperation of organs in the body physical. Turning Spencer's pages, one is constantly struck by two things: his ingenuity and his irrationality. Only a supremely ingenious man could have discovered so many parallels between social structure and social function on the one hand, physical structure and physical function on the other. And only a supremely irrational man could have taken the matter to such lengths. Sometimes, it must be confessed, Spencer's comparisons

---

[1] *Synthetic Philosophy of Herbert Spencer, The Principles of Sociology,* vol. I/2. Westminster Edition. New York: Appleton, n.d., p. 477.

[2] *Loc. cit.,* p. 448.

are more than strained. To give only one example: when a society goes over from road transport to rail transport, it achieves, he says, a decisive step forward in the career of evolution. It ceases to be "a cold-blooded creature with feeble circulation" and turns into "a warm-blooded creature with efficient vascular system."[3] The same happens when the electric telegraph is introduced. "Rudimentary nerves" become "a developed nervous apparatus." This last piece of fancy is particularly revealing. It shows that a good deal of Spencer's argument is merely verbal—merely a bad kind of poetry, I should almost say. What have the nerves within us in common with the telegraph wires outside us? They are both "internuncial agencies," Spencer says.[4] Alas! "Internuncial agency" is merely a word which shams identity where in reality there is contrast—at any rate more contrast than identity. Philosophers have in recent years opened our eyes wide to the pitfalls of language. We could never blame them if they made an example of Herbert Spencer—an example and a warning!

However, there are a few contexts in which the real issue is not complicated and covered up by a problematic form of verbal presentation, and they show us better than any other how deeply Spencer appears to have committed himself to the definition of society as a unity rather than a multiplicity. Most people would say that there is at least one process in social life which goes to show that a society is a multiplicity rather than a unity, namely the process of competition. In competition, man stands against man, interest against interest, and will against will. Cooperation, when it comes, will be the result of compromises, of contracts; it will be secondary, emergent, not primary and pre-existent. Those who have made the study of competition their special concern, the economists, have for this reason, practically without exception, been individualists, atomists, contractualists, and mechanists in social theory. Not so Herbert Spencer. He sticks to his organicism even when he comes to tackle the great phenomenon of competition, of competitive strife. Briefly, his submission is that competition is only an aspect of co-operation, of organic co-operation, to be exact. In the body physical each organ takes out of the blood-stream what it needs, for repair and growth; what *it* takes out, others cannot take out, and to that extent there is competition between them. But the final result is, in the healthy organism at any rate, the optimal apportionment of resources to needs, optimal from the point of view of the welfare of the whole. So also in society. What organs are and do in the body physical, that, Spencer asserts, industries are and do in the body social." In both cases," he writes, "these structures, competing with one another for their shares of the circulating stock of consumable matters, are enabled to appropriate, to repair themselves, and to grow in proportion to their performances of functions."[5] One need not absolutely deny that there is a parallel here between body physical and body social, in so far as both show a division and integration of labor. But, surely, the great difference is,

---

[3] *Loc. cit.*, pp. 507 *et seq.*

[4] *Loc. cit.*, p. 537.

[5] *Loc. cit.*, p. 518.

that in the body physical integration precedes, and is stronger than, division, whereas in the body social it is the other way round. This fact could not for ever remain unknown to so keen a mind as Herbert Spencer, and it comes to the fore in other parts of his work. It is even more prominent in a later work of his, "The Man *versus* the State," of 1884. The curious thing is that he never abandoned his organicism. He simply developed a second social theory, diametrically opposed to the first, and set it beside the other, as if two so hostile brethren could peacefully coexist under the same roof!

"The Man versus the State"

This second theory, just like the first, is essentially a modernized version of an older mode of thought. It is akin to that contractual explanation of the social bond which we find, not only in Jean-Jacques Rousseau, but in many writers of the eighteenth century. It is true that Spencer, in one or two passages, seems to reject the whole idea of a *contrat social*, but if one looks more closely, one sees soon enough that he objects only to two secondary features of the theory, not to the essential submission of the theory itself. He does not believe—and who could blame him?—that the *contrat social* was a historical fact, that there ever was a day and a place where it was concluded; and he protests against the use or abuse of this contractual conception for the justification of government and governmental tyranny, as if people had ever bound themselves to obey those who happen to control the state.[6] But all this does not mean that he finds the main thesis of contractualism inacceptable. On the contrary, he accepts it and he develops it. This main thesis is the definition of the social order as a network of contracts or quasi-contracts between individuals, and if one collects together all the passages in which this definition is used and elaborated, one sees that it plays at least as great a part in his thinking as the opposite theory, organicism.

Indeed, it can be shown that Spencer had to throw himself into the arms of this conractualism, because he was at heart an extreme individualist. In a crucial paragraph which does not blend with, but does jar against, the organological argument of "The Inductions of Sociology," Spencer admits that there can be no comparison between body physical and body social after all, because the body physical has only one seat of consciousness, thought and feeling, namely the brain, whereas in the body social every cell, that is to say, every individual, has consciousness and thinks and feels for himself.[7] In another passage, he himself pronounces the doom of that organismic theory, of that definition of society as a unity rather than a multiplicity, which he himself has so carefully elaborated. "Though, in foregoing chapters, comparison of social structures and functions to structures and functions in the human body, have in many cases

---

[6] *The Man versus the State*, edited with an introduction by Albert Jay Nock, Caldwell, Idaho: Caxton, 1945, pp. 176 *et seq.*

[7] *Loc. cit.*, pp. 460 *et seq.*

been made," he says with great candor, but, I am afraid, with little logic, "the social organism, discrete instead of concrete, asymmetrical instead of symmetrical, sensitive in all its units instead of having a single sensitive centre, is not comparable to any particular type of individual organism."[8] This clearly amounts to saying that a society is after all a multiplicity rather than a unity, and if this view is taken, then it is very difficult to account for the existence and for the coherence of social life without using, in some way and to some extent, the concepts of contractualism.

In "The Man *versus* the State," and especially in the fourth chapter of that book, Spencer then develops this contractual theory without remembering the contents of his "Principles of Sociology," indeed, without apparently being aware that he is contradicting himself. Once again he asks the question, what is a society? But this time he has a new answer: it is no more, he says, than "the mutual limitation of [individual] activities."[9] In other words, society is nothing in itself. It is not a scheme which exists before the individuals and into which they must fit themselves; it is not a kind of organism endowed with ontological reality; it is not a thing. It is merely the mutual relationships which obtain between the individuals —the individuals who alone are real in the ontological sense of the word, it is the system of mutual restraints which the individuals force on each other in their attempt to coexist; it is—to use more technical language— an equilibrium system between individual forces. Spencer has finally crossed his Rubicon: he has abandoned organicism and embraced mechanism. And he shows himself as radical a mechanist, as he had been an organicist. Society would not even exist, he tells us, if it were not useful to the men who join it. Far from being a form of life, it is an artifact—a tool which the individuals fashion in order to use it for their purposes, and which is justified in its existence only because, and insofar as, it is subservient to individual welfare. This is what Spencer writes: "Though mere love of companionship prompts primitive men to live in groups, yet the chief prompter is experience of the advantages to be derived from co-operation. On what condition only can co-operation arise? Evidently on condition that those who join their efforts severally gain by doing so." The word "severally" is particularly significant in this context. And, four pages later, he writes again: "The life of a society . . . depends on maintenance of individual rights. If it is nothing more than the sum of the lives of citizens, the implication is obvious. If it consists of those many unlike activities which citizens carry on in mutual dependence, still this aggregate impersonal life rises or falls according as the rights of individuals are enforced and denied."[10]

It is manifest from all this that a split goes right across Spencer's sociological thinking. We can note in passing that it would have been easy for him to save the coherence and consistency of his thought by bringing in here the distinction he draws elsewhere between militant and industrial

---

[8] *Loc. cit.*, p. 592.

[9] *Loc. cit.*, p. 198.

[10] *Loc. cit.*, pp. 199 and 203.

society, and saying that a militant society, fighting, as a whole, against other societies, is more like a unity than like a multiplicity, whereas an industrial society, which subserves individual welfare, is more like a multiplicity than like a unity. If he had taken this line, he would have anticipated, in its essentials, the deep insights which Ferdinand Tönnies was soon to present to the world. But it is a fact that he does not take this line; on the contrary, he bars the avenue of escape which would have been open to him. In "The Principles of Sociology" he says expressly that both militant and industrial society are organisms, only that in militant society the limbs, the outer limbs, the arms, are better developed than the digestive tract, and in industrial society it is the other way round, the digestive tract is better developed than are the limbs. And in "The Man *versus* the State" he insists that *every* society without distinction is a network of contracts. Militancy, he observes, obscures the contractual nature of social life but does not abolish it. Even the slave gets food, clothing and protection in exchange, in quasi-contractual exchange, for the work he does in his master's service. No society without contract; no society, therefore, that would not essentially be a multiplicity.[11]

"Social Statics"

Spencer was so little aware of his inconsistency that he even managed to present both contradictory points of view within the framework of one and the same book. That book was called "Social Statics" and first came out in 1850. He speaks there in terms of evolutionary tendencies rather than in terms of philosophical conceptualization, but that makes very little difference so far as logic is concerned. On page 497 he asserts that society becomes increasingly unified, more and more like an organism, like a thing. "We find," he says literally, "not only that the analogy between a society and a living creature is borne out to a degree quite unsuspected by those who commonly draw it, but also, that the same definition of life applies to both. This union of many men into one community—this increasing mutual dependence of units which were originally independent—this growth of an organism . . . may all be generalized under the law of individuation. The development of society . . . may be described as a tendency to individuate—to become a thing." But on p. 476 he had described multiplicity, lasting and irreducible multiplicity, as the end point of social development "Mankind are progressing," he had written, towards "that condition in which the individuality of each may be unfolded without limit, save the like individualities of others," a "condition of things dictated by the law of equal freedom." However carefully and charitably one may interpret these two passages, the hard fact remains that they are irreconcilable. Society may conceivably travel towards the maximum, or it may travel towards the minimum, of integration. It cannot do both things at the same time.

---

[11] *The Principles of Sociology*, esp. vol. I/2, pp. 519 *et seq.*; *The Man versus the State, loc. cit.*, pp. 199 *et seq.*

Clearly, then, Spencer was in the same predicament as the hero in Goethe's "Faust": "Two souls, alas, are dwelling in my breast!" It is instructive to ask, *why* he was so divided against himself. The answer to this question reveals the two greatest dangers which lie in wait for the naive, unwary sociologist. Spencer insisted that a society is many rather than one, that everything depends on the maintenance of individual rights, because he was an extreme liberal, even a near-anarchist. Man must not be cramped; he must not be coerced by others into doing what he does not want to do; therefore society must be regarded as essentially a coexistence, a coordination, of individual liberties. The contractual theory is simply inspired by a political creed. The psychological roots of the organismic argument are perhaps a little more difficult to discover, but even they do not lie very far under the surface. In Spencer's day biology was the queen of the sciences. You gained prestige by being a biologist of a kind. And the easiest way of making sociology into a kind of biology was to take the traditional body-metaphor, so beloved of the ancient and medieval philosophers, and give it a modern scientific twist and meaning. If this implied accepting the proposition that society was one rather than many, this could not be helped; the price was not too high to be paid— or so Spencer felt. The biologist's clothes do not really fit the social scientist, in fact, he is apt to look a little ridiculous in them; but Spencer would not have changed them for any other garb.

"Principles of Psychology"

I have compared Spencer to Goethe's Faust, torn hither and thither by conflicting loyalties. In fact, his plight was even more serious than that of the unhappy man, for he had yet a third tendency in him—the tendency towards a sociology neither organismic nor contractual, but cultural; a sociology very different from the two others, because it makes the sociality of man the product of human forces, forces operative in history, not of natural forces, be they vital or mechanical, which operate outside history and are independent of it. To find this third theory—and it is well worth looking for—we must go beyond his professedly sociological writings and turn to his "Principles of Psychology." It is none the less interesting for us for being presented in that particular framework; and I am convinced that it has had more influence on the main stream of sociological thought than either of its rivals.

It was one of Spencer's firmest convictions that man as he comes from the hands of nature is not really a social being—not yet at any rate. He may be potentially social; he is not at first actually so. There is in this respect no difference between the savage and the child. Both are entirely self-centered; both have not yet learned how to discipline themselves, how to behave and conduct themselves in the circle of their fellows. This comparison between the savage and the child is typical nineteenth century. It strikes us today as rather child-like, not to say childish. But it is worth analyzing because it teaches us a good deal about Spencer and his individualism, atomism, mechanism, and contractualism.

Society is not there from the beginning; in the beginning there is the individual, and sociality is merely a later addition—a secondary phenomenon. But it is, strange to say, also characteristic of his biologism. In his opinion, the social development—the socialization—of the child repeats the social development—the socialization—of the race. Clearly, we have before us here an attempt on Spencer's part to take one of the laws of contemporary biology and transfer it bodily, so to speak, to sociology. Baer and Haeckel had taught the biologists just before Spencer appeared on the scene to understand ontogeny—the evolution of the individual, his physical, and in particular his pre-natal physical evolution—as a recapitulation of phylogeny, the evolution of man as a species from some pre-historical subhuman ancestor to his present state. Spencer assumed that this law of biology must be a law of sociology also. What is true of the body physical, must needs be equally true of the body social—a very characteristic conviction on his part. But what is most significant—perhaps what is most exciting—about this whole complex of ideas is that it shows us Spencer entering a new field and following a new track. If the infant and if the primitive are not genetically social, then their sociality must be learned; then it must be due to education, that is to say, a cultural process. Then sociology cannot be modelled either on biology or on mechanics; then it must be a deeply human study. Then nature becomes merely a background to the social system, and in the foreground stands man himself, man as he raises himself by his own effort from a merely physical existence to the level of social, and that is to say, civilized and cultured life.

The technical label which Spencer stuck on to this, his third sociology, was "the theory of the ego-altruistic sentiments."[12] Man may have in him a certain purely altruistic strain, a certain, at first largely dormant strain of sympathy, but, by and large, as he emerges from the assembly lines of evolution, he is characterized and dominated by purely egoistic leanings. Every baby, Spencer thought, can prove that this is so. But then the baby is born into a social situation, and in this situation, because it is social, he has to add to his natural a definite social behavior, a social behavior which will not only modify his habitual mode of action, but ultimately his very self. Experience will teach him that there are some lines of conduct which will call out the hostility and the active ill-will of his fellowmen, while there are others which will arouse, not hostility, but approval, not ill-will, but good will. Hostility and ill-will mean pain, or at least the threat of it. Approval and good will mean pleasure, or at least the promise of it. Therefore the very selfishness of the agent will lead him to pursue socially acceptable lines of action and to shun such as are socially not acceptable. The very selfishness of the agent will induce him to embrace a life-policy which pursues personal aims by socially approved means, in other words, so to shape his behavior that it becomes compatible with the corresponding behavior of those around him—that it becomes social-

---

[12] *Synthetic Philosophy of Herbert Spencer. The Principles of Psychology,* vol. II/2. Westminster Edition. New York: Appleton, n.d., pp. 592 *et seq.*

ized, that it becomes social.[13] An ego-altruistic self comes into being and overlays the basic egoistic self; and, as it does so, multiplicity gives way to unity: the many become one. Now, insofar as the ego-altruistic sentiments are the fruits of experience, they are not products of natural facts or forces, but man-made phenomena, part and parcel of history and culture. Spencer's third social theory is philosophically worlds apart from the two others. It shows us a mode of sociological thinking which is no longer in thrall to the natural sciences but has gained its independence and found its true mission and its true stature and dignity.

The implications of Spencer's third attitude are tremendous, and he himself did not bring them fully out. But there is one important conclusion which he did draw. If social conduct is learned conduct, if it arises in and through education and experience, then there is nothing pre-determined about social life, then the measureless variety of social forms ceases to be a matter for surprise,[14] as it must be if it is regarded as a fixed pattern like an organism or an equally fixed pattern like an equilibrium system. Spencer moves to the very brink of the realization that a society is an order underlaid by comparative freedom, not an order dominated by comparative necessity. Not all the seeds he has sown blossom under his hands; but they are there all the same.

In the history of sociological thought, Spencer's third theory has played a far more significant part than either of the other two. To prove this, it is necessary to mention only one name—William Graham Sumner. Sumner's folkway concept is directly inspired by, and based on, Spencer's concept of egoaltruistic sentiments. It was through Sumner that what is most vital in Spencer's sociology entered into American sociology, and through American sociology into world sociology. In this case, the son was probably greater than the father; but we who are the son's sons, do well to remember our father's father. His inspiration is still with us, and so it will remain, a treasured possession, even in days to come.

SUMMARY AND EVALUATION
OF CHAPTER THREE

Any evaluation of Spencer's work must include an examination of his theory of evolutionism, different types of which were embraced by other writers of his day, such as Lewis H. Morgan. An additional reason for giving this theory special consideration here is that it is reemerging in anthropology and sociology today in the form of neoevolutionism.

J. D. Y. Peel suggests that evolutionism served "to reconcile men to a process of change [the specialization of function in England's expanding industrial complex] which was already well in motion and largely complete"[1] in Spencer's time. Evolutionism also permitted the English to

---

[13] *Loc. cit.*, pp. 598 *et seq.*

[14] *Loc. cit.*, pp. 602 *et seq.*

[1] J. D. Y. Peel, *Herbert Spencer: The Evolution of a Sociologist* (New York: Basic Books), 1971, p. 257.

reassert their judgment of England's superiority over other countries since specialization, which was progressing most rapidly in their midst, was presumably linked to progress.[2] But legitimation and nationalistic chauvinism were only the ideological uses of evolutionism. There were scientific, intellectual uses as well.

The laudatory aim of evolutionism was to synthesize the welter of facts about different, sometimes bizarre, societies all over the world. This burgeoning information crowded in on the minds of thinkers such as Spencer,[3] who felt the need to make sense of it. Science had to find some way of comparing and generalizing if it was to avoid getting bogged down in the discrete, innumerable detail of each case. Evolutionism served this purpose by plausibly explaining how the growth, differentiation, and individuation of different societies came about.[4] Its orientation was naturalistic in that it identified material conditions, not some esoteric forces of history or vitalistic forces of life, as causes of social growth and adaptation. Spencer helped us see that one cannot obtain an understanding of an individual structure of a society without understanding its material function.

Adherents of this theory of development interpreted evolution both as a specific and as a general phenomenon. *Specific* evolution explains the change that occurs within a particular system mainly through adaptation. That is, given variation and selection—concepts not well developed by Spencer but more fully explained later by Darwin—and pressures such as competition or environmental demands, only the variety of system that has an adaptive advantage over other varieties will survive. An example from biology illustrates how this process works: if variation exists in the potential speed of horses inhabiting a given locale, and adaptive pressure is exerted on them by predators, then, other things being equal, it is likely that the faster running horses will have a better chance for survival.[5] *General* evolution is the cumulative change in all like systems

[2] Today such optimism is rapidly fading, as the large industrial giants of the Communist and Western Countries stand ready, on the one hand, to blow each other up with their overkill weapons, and on the other hand, to strangle themselves in their own pollution.

[3] For his day, Spencer's data on preliterate societies were especially broad. Spencer's *Descriptive Sociology*, compiled in the late 1860s, was a vast array of facts about different societies arranged by structure and function. Even if Spencer did not always heed these facts, his compilation gave a seriousness to sociology not hitherto recognized. See Jay Rumney, *Herbert Spencer's Sociology* (New York: Atherton Press, 1966).

[4] Michael Scriven claims that evolutionary theory is really a *post*dictive (giving a plausible account by looking *back* on the development of systems) rather than a *predictive* theory. See his "Explanation and Prediction in Evolutionary Theory," *Science*, 130, No. 3374 (August 1959), 447–482.

[5] It is also possible, as Darwin recognized, that competition for sexual access to females might do harm to the species, as, for example, when the monopoly behavior of dominant stags deters from adequate caring for the young.

in general, that is, in all animal species or all societies *taken as a whole.* The theories of specific and general evolution both have their virtues when applied to a sociocultural system (as in the case of specific evolution) or sociocultural systems (the comparison that is made, as in the case of general evolution), but both also have their shortcomings.

It is difficult, for instance, to explain a surviving social characteristic as the result of adaptive superiority. But the specific evolution approach properly encourages the theorist to examine the real pressures that affect the development of a society and forces him to ask specific questions: Are there problems of adaptation in a culture or a society? What are they? What happens if they are not solved? The great variation possible in both adaptive pressures and social responses is bewildering, however. Look at marriage patterns, for example. Could the existence of cross-cousin marriage in a society be explained as the product of adaptive pressures? If so, what would these have been, and what alternatives to cross-cousin marriage might have resulted instead? If only a very loose connection between pressures and responses can be demonstrated to exist on the sociocultural level, as seems to be true in many cases, is not the explanatory value of this evolution theory then considerably weakened? But even if sociocultural traits do in some way represent adaptive responses, it must be recognized that they in turn may act as boundaries for further selections both social and biological.

The theory of general evolution explains social development differently. According to this view, society as a whole goes through general stages of growth, one stage being a prerequisite for the next and acting to limit it. Spencer believed that the evolution of societies taken individually appears multi-lineal since each grows in directions determined by its own adaptive pressures and responses;[6] however, the evolution of societies taken as a whole is unilineal in that a series of general stages can be detected. "First," he said, "let us mark that the course of civilization could not have been other than it has been";[7] thus, ". . . taking the entire assemblage of societies, evolution may be held inevitable."[8]

Excepting the faith in inevitable progress, then, the general evolution approach appears to have merit also. It is quite evident, according to Percy S. Cohen, that "some stages of development must be achieved for human society as a whole, before others are achieved"; for example, agriculture must precede industrialization.[9] Unfortunately, such formulations are not very precise because they do not tell us exactly how or when these changes occur. Moreover, the general evolution approach is not likely to establish the sequences of events that determined human institutions such as the family and can sometimes arrive at false con-

---

[6] Forward as well as backward development was acknowledged.

[7] Herbert Spencer, *Social Statics* (New York: Appleton, 1903), p. 234.

[8] Herbert Spencer, *The Principles of Sociology* I (New York: Appleton, 1896), p. 96.

[9] Percy S. Cohen, *Modern Social Theory* (New York: Basic Books, 1968), pp. 214, 215.

clusions; for instance, the first family form was probably not the matri-archy, as some evolutionary thinkers in Spencer's time argued. But on the whole it is difficult to deny that society passes through certain stages in a definite sequence and that each stage limits the options for the next. The demise of evolutionism, its discreditation in the early nineteenth century by critics such as Franz Boas in anthropology, resulted from its excesses, its lack of caution, and its tie to racism in some quarters.

Evolutionists gave insufficient attention to the basic criterion of the evolutionary *development* of a society (was it simply differentiation and integration?) and to the question of *how* different social stages came about. Furthermore, they sometimes made careless analogies between an organism and society, as when Spencer saw telegraph wires as the "nerves" of society. A principle that applied to the development of bio-logical phenomena does not necessarily apply to the development of social phenomena as well, even if the principle, for example, differenti-ation and integration, *seems* to govern both realms.[10]

The theory of evolution took shape too quickly, without regard for potential challenges to it. Built on the presumption that development meant *betterment*, it became a doctrine accepted on faith. Eventually, the theoretical groundwork of the evolutionists was shaken, as anthropologists began to take field work seriously and improve their methods of obser-vation in remote societies.

Today, however, evolution is enjoying a resurgence in both sociology and anthropology. Sociologists presently studying the growth of modernity, the creation of certain kinds of political and economic institutions in underdeveloped areas, suspect that certain social developments, such as a degree of literacy, must precede others, such as participatory democracy or industrial expansion, although the actual routes to these goals may vary in different societies.[11] In anthropology, neoevolutionism has been most prominent in the works of Leslie White and his students, who take culture to be a relatively autonomous, evolving system. They believe that evolutionary development occurs in a society as the amount and transfor-mation efficiency of energy increases. In their judgment, this thesis is universally applicable since energy is a resource that all cultures require and one that can be measured.[12]

---

[10] See V. Gordon Childe's *Social Evolution* (Cleveland: Meridian Books, 1963) for some tenable, heuristic analogies between biological and social evolution (esp. Chap. 12). See also G. Ledyard Stebbins's excellent article: "Pitfalls and Guideposts in Comparing Organic and Social Evolution," *The Pacific Sociological Review*, 8 (Spring 1965), 3–10.

[11] See, e.g., Neil J. Smelser, *The Sociology of Economic Life* (Englewood Cliffs, N.J.: Prentice-Hall, 1963), esp. Chap. 5; and Wilbert E. Moore, *The Impact of Industry* (same publisher, 1965).

[12] But see Marshall D. Sahlins and Elman R. Service (Eds.), *Evolution and Culture* (Ann Arbor: University of Michigan Press, 1960). Their point is that an increase in energy is not always put to the use of greater structural differentiation in society.

Though the sociology of Herbert Spencer suffered the fate of other philosophies of optimistic progress, some important contributions endure. Because of his individualistic leanings, nurtured by Utilitarianism, and his orientation to society as a superorganic system, Spencer formulated several different views of society, each identifying a different source of social order. His interest in both the development and the integration of societies, led to some insights on social structure and function that are still useful today: the rise and growth of new structures can be explained in part by their functions; further, as new structures form, functions are redistributed, and a new interrelation among the structures occurs.[13] Finally, since his aspirations ultimately lay with deductive reasoning established on the broad laws assumed to be operating in all of nature, he advanced the study of evolutionary change, a topic of continuing interest today.

Although Spencer compiled much data to support his view of society as an organism progressively multiplying in structure while specializing and integrating in function, his general evolutionary approach largely failed to take all of these data into account. As we mentioned in the introduction to this chapter, he modeled his evolutionary thinking, rather, on certain broad, indisputable truths of physical science: the persistence of force, the subdivision of a force as it falls on a mass, and the integration of matter and dissipation of motion. Accordingly, when he compared societies in concrete detail, it was largely for the purpose of substantiating the application of these truths to social phenomena; of illustrating the "fact" that different stages of evolution are evident the world over. To him the whole evolutionary record was to be found in existing societies variations of which bear witness to these indisputable truths. This approach marks Spencer's sociology as predominantly evolutionary and distinguishes it from the historical sociology of, for example, Marx or Weber, whose main objective was first to analyze the historical social record and then to develop from it generalizations about process and change.

The works of Spencer (or, shall we say, caricatures of them) were held in high regard by the American public in the postbellum period. His popularity peaked in 1882 when he made a memorable visit to the United States and was hailed as a hero. Spencer's science justified the "success ethic" as environmental exploitation gained momentum. If the bigger companies swallowed up the smaller ones, this trend could be interpreted as a necessity in terms of the law of survival of the fittest.[14]

The last half of the nineteenth century and the first decade of the twentieth was a period of considerable social and economic change in the United States. The Civil War was followed by a period of industrial

---

[13] Since "laws of nature" were thought to be responsible for this process of unification, Spencer has been called a positivistic organicist. See Don Martindale, *The Nature and Types of Sociological Theory* (Boston: Houghton Mifflin, 1960), pp. 79–81.

[14] See Richard Hofstadter, *Social Darwinism in American Thought* (Boston: Beacon, 1955), p. 45.

stagnation in the North during the 1870s. Urban areas increased rapidly from 10.8 percent of the total population in 1840 to 45.7 percent in 1910. This was due partly to heavy immigration and partly to the shortage of manpower, especially during the Civil War, which encouraged the mechanization of agriculture. While some people were crowding into the cities, then, others continued spreading out, rapidly expanding the country westward. Poverty existed amid plenty, and it is said that this period manifested "the greatest corruption and inefficiency in American state and national government during the entire nineteenth century."[15] As a result of such conditions, moral and religious reform movements were common. Above all, this was a time when Americans believed in the possibility of technological mastery over nature and in the benefits of education, ideas that predisposed them to Spencer.

William Graham Sumner taught one of the first sociology courses in America, and his approach was very much Spencerian. In his famous work *Folkways* (1907), Sumner based his sociology on the observations that human life encounters formidable obstacles and threats to survival, words that have a new ring of truth in this age of the "energy crisis"! There is a fundamental struggle to "win" (to use one of Sumner's favorite words) a livelihood within the conditions imposed by nature. In this process man always competes, indirectly at least, with others: "Every man who stands on the earth's surface excludes every one else from so much of it as he covers; every one who eats a loaf of bread appropriates to himself for the time-being the exclusive use and enjoyment of so many square feet of the earth's surface as were required to raise the wheat."[16]

The struggle *against* nature and competition for life *between* individuals were somewhat separate concepts for Sumner. Competition between individuals in the state of nature is raised to the level of antagonistic cooperation in society, which requires the subjugation of individual interest in the pursuit of a great common interest. When a person has the opportunity and abilities to win over nature he should be free to take advantage of them; Sumner deplored governmental intervention in this process. Men put a buffer between themselves and nature's monopoly on resources only when they create capital, for in capital surplus energy is gained by man's ingenuity. "If . . . we build houses several stories high so that several men can, in effect, stand on the same square feet of the earth's surface, or if we make the same number of square feet bear two loaves of bread instead of one, we break the monopoly of nature."[17] However, Sumner did not condone privilege for anyone who takes from one person the opportunity to master nature (or the fruits of his mastery) and gives it to another on bases unrelated to their abilities.

Sumner believed that social problems stem largely from wrong de-

---

[15] Howard Becker and Harry Elmer Barnes, *Social Thought from Lore to Science*, Vol. III, New York: Dover, 1961, p. 972.

[16] Albert Galloway Keller (Ed.), *Essays of William Graham Sumner I* (New Haven: Yale University Press, 1934, p. 386.

[17] Ibid., p. 387.

cisions. Nature herself rewards those who are enterprising by yielding to their efforts. In a limited land space, under conditions of high population, the small differences between people in practical adaptability will count for the most: "[Under these conditions] the rewards of prudence, energy, enterprise, foresight, sagacity, and all other industrial virtues is [sic] greatest; on the other hand, the penalties of folly, weakness, error, and vice are most terrible. Pauperism, prostitution, and crime are the attendants of a state of society in which science, art, and literature reach their highest developments."[18] Sumner also believed that much of our cherished philosophy of democracy, equality, and so on—even progress—was largely a reflection of the ease of livelihood at a given time depending on the land / population ratio at a given stage of technology.

Spencer's sociology was largely modeled on the processes of differentiation, integration, and equilibrium, while Sumner's was based on the concepts of variation, adaptation, and selection. Both believed that social adaptation, like biological adaptation, is essentially characterized by slow progress over a long time period, the complexity of subtle and intricate processes, and self-, or "natural," direction. Though the concept of competition was certainly present in Spencer's work, it was Sumner who linked competition to the emergence of virtues presumed to be answers to the struggle against nature—virtues such as thriftiness and hard work. Sumner praised capital formation and efficient management and believed that social systems reward the practices that win in man's struggle against nature.

Other American social theorists rejected Social Darwinism completely. The most articulate of them in Sumner's time was Lester F. Ward. Ward mounted his attack on the basis of the simple but important distinction between physical, or animal, evolution without purposiveness, and mental, or human, evolution decisively modified by purposive action, which he termed social "telesis." According to Richard Hofstadter, Ward sensed a new trend in the country: "It was natural enough to oppose governmental interference when government was in the hands of autocrats, but it is folly to cling to this opposition in an age of representative government when the popular will can be exerted through legislative action. . . . The laws of trade result in enormous inequalities in the distribution of wealth, which are founded in accidents of birth or strokes of low cunning rather than superior intelligence or industry."[19]

Ward further argued that free competition could be secured *only* by regulation. He believed that a planned society was not only possible—it was necessary. He assaulted the laissez-fairists by showing that nature was really a highly *in*efficient system: if a species could only *learn* to protect its ova or accomplish reproduction in a different way, it would not have to produce a billion or more ova in order to insure the survival of a handful of the offspring! Moreover, as Ward pointed out, competition

---

[18] William Graham Sumner, *War and Other Essays* (New Haven: Yale University Press, 1911), p. 185.

[19] Hofstadter, *Social Darwinism*, pp. 72, 73.

sometimes resulted in the fittest *not* surviving at all. The term natural was in fact only a label the laissez-fairists affixed to a value judgment for the purpose of justifying those arrangements they approved of. To Ward, the argument that the unfit fail, and failure is an unmistakable sign of unfitness was circular and without meaning. Such criticism reflected the growing interest in human purpose and a guided, regulated society for the benefit of the whole, which advocates deemed just as "natural" as a "nature-regulated" one.

SELECTED BIBLIOGRAPHY

Alland, Jr., Alexander. *Evolution and Human Behavior.* Garden City, N.Y.: The Natural History Press, 1967.

Barnes, Harry Elmer, (Ed.). *An Introduction to the History of Sociology.* Chicago: University of Chicago Press, 1948. Chap. IV.

Barringer, Herbert R., George I. Blanksten, and Raymond W. Mack (Eds.). *Social Change in Developing Areas.* Cambridge, Mass. Schenkman, 1965.

Becker, Howard, and Harry Elmer Barnes. *Social Thought from Lore to Science.* 3d ed. Vol. II. New York: Dover, 1961. See especially Chap. XVIII, "Positivism Merges with Evolutionary Philosophy: Spencer and the Organismic School," pp. 664–692.

Boulding, Kenneth E. "Towards a General Theory of Growth." *Canadian Journal of Economics and Political Science,* 19, No. 3 (August, 1953), 326–340 (reprinted as S-350, Bobbs-Merrill Reprint Series in the Social Sciences).

Buckley, Walter. *Sociology and Modern Systems Theory.* Englewood Cliffs, N.J.: Prentice-Hall, 1967. 11–17.

Burrow, J. W. *Evolution and Society.* New York: Cambridge University Press, 1966.

Carneiro, Robert L., (Ed.). *The Evolution of Society: Selections from Herbert Spencer's Principles of Sociology.* Chicago: University of Chicago Press, 1967.

Dole, Gertrude E., and Robert L. Carneiro (Eds.). *Essays in the Science of Culture.* New York: Crowell, 1960.

Goldschmidt, Walter. *Man's Way.* New York: Holt, Rinehart and Winston, 1959. See especially pp. 33–38.

Harris, Marvin. *The Rise of Anthropological Theory.* New York: Crowell, 1968.

Kardiner, Abram. *They Studied Man.* Cleveland: World Publishing, 1961.

Lichtenberger, James P. *Development of Social Thought.* New York: Century Company, 1925. Chap. XII.

Mead, Margaret. *Continuities in Cultural Evolution.* New Haven: Yale University Press, 1964.

Peel, J. D. Y., (Ed.). *Herbert Spencer: The Evolution of a Sociologist.* New York: Basic Books, 1971.

Peel, J. D. Y., (Ed.). *Herbert Spencer on Social Evolution.* Chicago: University of Chicago Press, 1972.

Rumney, Jay. *Herbert Spencer's Sociology.* New York: Atherton Press, 1966 (paperback).

Sahlins, Marshall D., and Elman R. Service (Eds.). *Evolution and Culture.* Ann Arbor, Mich.: The University of Michigan Press, 1960.

Scriven, Michael. "Explanation and Predication in Evolutionary Theory." *Science,* 130, No. 3374 (August 1959), 477–482.

Spencer, Herbert. *The Man Versus the State.* Donald MacRae (Ed.). Baltimore: Penguin, 1969.

Spencer, Herbert. *Principles of Sociology.* Stanislav Andreski (Ed.). Hamden, Conn.: Anchor Books, 1969.

Spencer, Herbert. *Structure, Function, and Evolution.* Stanislav Andreski (Ed.). London: Michael Joseph, 1971.

Spencer, Herbert. *The Study of Sociology.* Introd. by Talcott Parsons. Ann Arbor, Mich.: Ann Arbor Paperbacks, The University of Michigan Press, 1966.

Stebbins, G. Ledyard. "Pitfalls and Guideposts in Comparing Organic and Social Evolution." *The Pacific Sociological Review,* 8 (Spring 1965), 3–10.

Steward, Julian H. *Theory of Culture Change.* Urbana: University of Illinois Press, 1955.

Teggart, F. J. *The Idea of Progress.* Berkeley and Los Angeles: University of California Press, 1949.

Williams, George C. *Adaptation and Natural Selection: A Critique of Some Current Evolutionary Thought.* Princeton, N.J.: Princeton University Press, 1966.

FOUR

Karl Marx

"I don't agree that capitalists are so competitive they can't unite to protect themselves."

—STUDENT COMMENT

General Introduction

Karl Marx (1818–1883) was born in Trier, a town in the Rhineland of Germany. He studied first at the Universities of Bonn and Berlin. He shifted from law to philosophy at Berlin, where he was highly respected among his Bohemian friends and among the critics of Hegel. (Marx himself retained a high regard for Hegel's thought in spite of his own departures from it, however.) He received his doctorate from Jena in 1841 after writing a dissertation on the Greek philosophers, Democritus and Epicurus. Not able to secure a university position, in 1842 he became editor of the *Rheinische Zeitung*, which was suppressed soon thereafter. In 1843 he married and moved to Paris, the citadel of intellectual activity. Here he met Friedrich Engels, who became a lifelong friend, and other socialist thinkers. Engels later wrote with Marx, popularized and defended some of his ideas, and at times supported him financially. Within a few years Marx was exiled to Brussels. It was there that, in 1846, he joined the Communist League, which began to bring together radical thinkers from different countries for the purpose of promoting revolutions on an international scale.

A few revolutions in different countries did break out in 1848, but the League's role in them is not known. Marx did, however, write the League's platform during its second Congress in London, just before these revolutions broke out.[1] This document became known as the *Communist*

---

[1] Actually both Marx and Engels were tapped to write the platform; and it was Engels who wrote the first draft. But Marx was so dissatisfied with this draft that he completely rewrote it himself.

Manifesto or *Manifesto of the Communist Party.* It contained his ideas on class struggle between the proletariat and bourgeoisie.

After being arrested, tried, and freed in Germany,[2] Marx, not able to return to France, found asylum in London, where he lived the rest of his life and wrote *Capital (Das Kapital)* between 1867 and 1879. It contained two chapters of his earlier *Critique of Political Economy* (1859). Two more volumes of *Capital* were published after Marx's death. Between 1843 and 1849 Marx had rubbed shoulders with many working people, including refugees, and had become more and more disenchanted with traditional critical philosophical analysis. After this time, until about 1867, he had set himself to long hours of study of the condition of workers, resisting temptations by others to promote insurrections ("I am not a Marxist," he once exclaimed to those who wanted to make a doctrine out of his views and start a band of true-believers). In 1863 he had organized the First International Workingmen's Association, which helped him get considerable acclaim on the Continent for *Capital*.[3]

Marx, never a permanent resident of any country for very long, was touched by the evident human misery about him, which he perceived to be the result of private ownership, the narrow concern of the employer for the employee, and the rapid social and technological changes of the nineteenth century. Perhaps the social setting to which he reacted was mainly that of nineteenth-century England (which was described in the preceding chapter on Spencer). There, he thought, industrial forces were operating in a less restricted way than on the Continent, and England therefore offered the "purer" case for study. Marx was against promoting the dissolution of the family by the absorption of women and children into the labor force. He was deeply concerned about man's welfare. Though he was not religious, he saw little use in simply criticizing religion as the leftist-Hegelians did. It gave a false sense of victory. Marx saw the individual's problems in the context of the social system to which he belonged. He understood the connection between individual problems and the organization of economic activities. Without an understanding of the social system, there can be no understanding of the social problems since they are products of that system. His position seemed to be that the

---

[2] It was perhaps not so much that Marx was troublesome as that Germany, especially, was so repressive. According to Lewis A. Coser, fear of unsettling revolutions of the type that had occurred in France led to immense censorship and the denial of civil rights (*Masters of Sociological Thought* [New York: Harcourt Brace Jovanovich, 1971], pp. 76, 77).

[3] Some other works by Marx alone, or with Engels, are the following: *Economic and Philosophic Manuscripts of 1844, The Poverty of Philosophy, The German Ideology,* and *Selected Correspondence, 1846–1895.* Some very useful collections of Marx and Engels's writings are noted in the bibliography at the end of this chapter.

decadence of capitalistic industrialism could be endured—its high productivity of goods might even be emulated—since he thought it constituted a stepping-stone to a better economic order.[4] On March 14, 1883, while sitting in his easychair, Marx died gently, having been worn down by bronchitis and, finally, a tumor in the lung. His wife, much beloved by him, had died earlier.[5]

The central tasks of Marx were to reorient historical analysis toward a new conception of social change, to document the economic arrangements and forces in society, to promote the interests of workers by providing them with a scientific account of the conditions of labor and forces of production, and to forecast the future.

Marx noted that as man acts, he externalizes his experience, that is, he creates concepts and material objects that represent his existence. Marx differed critically with Hegel over how best to explain the condition of man's real existence. Hegel's interpretation was a metaphysical one: the *real* is continually striving to embody the Divine *Ideal*. Thus, Hegelians ascribed what they saw as man's alienation to his having separated himself from his true spiritual essence.

Not so for Marx. His view was that the cause of man's alienation lies in his own labors—in the separation from his labor and the products of it—not in the separation from some fictitious absolute proposed by an interpreting philosopher such as Hegel. Marx sought to direct historical analysis of the condition of man away from the prescribed Ideal, to which Hegelians assumed man's strivings were moving, toward the laboring condition of real man himself.

For Marx, analysis properly begins with man's actions to master nature in the pursuit of a livelihood. This is man's first requirement. Production is the appropriation of nature by the individual within and through a certain form of society. It is the process of satisfying needs and eventually creating new needs. Moreover, in laboring, man not only engages in his main form of self-realization, but he also enters into relations with others. Therefore, work in a society requires the reorganization of people as well as materials and tools. Both the material means of production and the social relations of production constitute the *materialist* outlook for which Marx's writings have become so popular. The way people are used in production and the benefits they derive from it were his central concerns. He further believed that just as the important reality in the establishment of a social system is the *organization* of production, so, too, we shall soon explain, the transformation of a social system,

---

[4] Machines might produce plenty for everyone—if it was properly distributed —and free man for other activities.

[5] The most intimate account of Marx's life is Isaiah Berlin's *Karl Marx: His Life and Environment* (New York: Oxford University Press, 1948).

especially the final one, occurs in the *organization* of the social class and interclass struggle.

According to Marx, a given social order consists of the productive forces and social arrangements within it at a particular time. Each stage in history embodies new forces and brings about its own classes, which are formed by the constraints of the new social order. The instruments employed in production, the form of cooperation required, and the relations(especially property relations) that result between the worker and the means and products of production distinguish one economic system from another. Class antagonism arises in each order as a result of the conflict between the property relations and the new social relations of production. A given social order reaches its terminus and will change when all the productive forces for which there is room have developed, when the social forces of production conflict seriously enough with existing property relations, and when the material conditions necessary for the change are already in embryo. The exploited people in each stage will not necessarily be victorious over their exploiters; for this to happen, they must represent a mode of production that will dominate in the future.

Scarcity is omnipresent in nature. Man creates things and ideas of value by his labor, and these are scarce, too. For this reason conflict occurs; but, more importantly, it occurs because within the division of socialized labor itself different classes arise, groups of people whose economic interests clash. Antagonism is present between man and nature, on the one hand, *and* between man and man, on the other. Thus, Marx manifested a pessimistic view of man's social nature—along with his belief in the ultimate victory of the proletariat—that sharply contrasted with the Utilitarian economic view that man's function in the division of labor works for the good of all. Marx saw men and classes competing and seeking to stake out as much of the share of rewards, or life chances, for themselves as possible.

This dynamic of class conflict, generated by the organization of production in given historical settings, constitutes the core of Marx's theory of social change. The theory involves the idea that underlying and shaping the social organization of production are productive forces, which Marx broadly defined initially as land, resources, skills, and any material techniques used in appropriating nature; later, he expanded his definition to include the social relations of production themselves. Always existing within the social organization of production is some antipathy between groups, particularly with respect to property relations, an antipathy that becomes all the more stark as the productive forces in society change. Conflict increases when the bourgeoisie and the proletariat emerge from the capitalistic factory system, the productive forces of which arose in the latter phases of feudalism. Marx termed the mechanism of social change at work in such processes a *dialectic negativity*, meaning that *every* social system creates the productive forces for its own destruction.[6] Conflict between the bourgeoisie and the proletariat reaches an intense level toward the end of the capitalistic factory phase and brings about its downfall.

Marx borrowed this idea of dialectic negativity from Fichte but modified it for the purpose of opposing Hegelian analysis. Whereas Hegelians recognized the dialectic forces of philosophical reason—that is, criticism and countercriticism, the actual spirit at war with itself—in the spiritual strivings to lift society to a higher level, Marx found the dialectic forces in society itself: the *thesis* of a system (its existing productive forces), its *antithesis* (the evolution of new forces as an outgrowth of the previous system), and the *synthesis* (the overthrow of the old system and establishment of the new). The idea of class conflict, which Marx saw as the medium of societal change had already been developed by French historians. Marx's contribution was that each system contains within *itself* the seeds of its own destruction, its own contradiction, though not all of the forces changing a system need come from within it. Marx explained this anomaly nowhere better than in his analysis of the development and final demise of the capitalistic factory system, the destruction of which its creators, the bourgeoisie themselves, engineer.

How does this take place? The broad outlines of the dialectic process are found in the *Communist Manifesto*. In it Marx defined the *bourgeoisie* as the class of modern capitalists who own the means of social production and employ wage labor. The *proletariat* is the class of modern wage laborers who, having no means of production of their own, must sell their labor power in order to live. The bourgeoisie arose in the latter phase of feudalism largely by breaking from traditional occupations and traditional economic restraints and pursuing free trade. They devised a gigantic division of labor for production geared to the extensive use of machinery in centralized, factory, locations.

Whereas in the cottage-industry system of feudalism a producer usually appropriated his own raw materials, conducted his work under his own roof, owned his own tools, finished a product, and controlled his own work pace, in the factory system the laborer is only a wage earner without control or ownership of the means of production. He is estranged from his own labor, both physical and mental, because it is performed strictly for the use of the capitalists, but his class consciousness is awakened as a result of the forces the bourgeoisie have set in motion: First, since workers must now form or augment capital (in this function they are indispensable to the bourgeoisie) and have no other means of livelihood, they are all forced into the same condition—dependence on

---

[6] Preliterate societies may be excepted because of a lack of capital, and in some societies, such as China, stagnation may occur for long periods.

wages. This gives workers some common basis for class consciousness. Second, because the bourgeoisie concentrate large numbers of them in factories—the transport to which is accomplished by rail introduced by the bourgeoisie—so as to make them compete against one another, workers interact more frequently with one another. This also promotes their realization that they constitute a working class. Third, in becoming a wage earner, the laborer has become an object in whom the bourgeoisie must take only a minimum maintenance-cost interest. In other words, the bourgeoisie searches for ways to pay only enough to keep the laborer alive and enable him to reproduce his race. This tendency, along with other forces in the factory, eventually pauperizes large sections of workers, who become further confirmed in their feelings of solidarity as a result.

Fourth, since the bourgeoisie in their ascendence to power must win some battles over other groups such as the aristocracy, they may temporarily need the support of the proletariat. But in using the proletariat for this purpose, they allow them insight into the political process the bourgeoisie are beginning to control and provide them with some access to the educational resources of society. This may enhance the workers' awareness of their plight, suggest new communication procedures, and arouse their moral outrage. Fifth, because no other responsibility for the worker beyond the payment of his wages *when he works* is exercised, and because the capitalists overproduce and markets fluctuate, the workers are at times left with no means of support; the crisis in the society that the bourgeoisie have created deepens until they themselves cannot seem to change their course of insatiable capital gains and workers see them as unfit to rule.

Finally, in becoming larger by investing in larger amounts of constant capital (raw material and machines), which gradually reduces the variable of labor (the number of laborers tending to or operating the machine), the bourgeoisie drive some articulate people into the ranks of the proletariat where they raise the consciousness of the worker further and plan a course of action against the bourgeoisie.

In his succeeding works, especially *Capital*, Marx went on to describe in more detail the development of the factory system and the antagonism between the proletariat and the bourgeoisie that it ultimately fosters.[7] He was especially interested in the way the organization of capitalistic production uses workers, the role played by machinery, and the concepts of alienation and exploitation.

Capitalism, Marx reminded us, emerged only when there appeared in the later stage of feudalism a class of individuals with adequate means of production and money and a class of free laborers. It is the peculiar

---

[7] The next four paragraphs draw heavily on Irving M. Zeitlin's *Marxism: A Reexamination* (Princeton, N.J.: Van Nostrand, 1967).

relation between these two groups that sharply sets capitalism off from its forebear, feudalism. Capitalists are moneyed people who sell for profit commodities that have been produced by the labor power purchased from workers who toil within the means of production owned by the capitalist. What is distinctive about this relationship is that, for the duration of the employment, the capitalist owns the place on which many workers are dependent for locations that allow cooperative labor. The laborer is free in that he is readily available and has no means of production of his own.

The capitalist has a fetish for commodities because these have ex-change value. He seeks to increase *surplus value,* the products he has left to sell *after* he has sold enough to pay the subsistence cost of the worker, the depreciation of machines, and cost of the raw material. He can achieve surplus because he *owns* the labor power of the worker, can calculate his costs, and can require hours of work from the employee in excess of what he needs to break even.

The social relations of capitalist production are embodied in the factory system, each part of which is a human being. The division of functions into smaller and more numerous specialties required a capitalist to hire large numbers of workers even before the Industrial Revolution. Initially it is to the capitalist's advantage to multiply the output of this system by hiring greater numbers of detail laborers. Gradually, however, the social relations of production change until the worker performs one particular task over and over. This means that he never has to change tools, a process that slows down production. At this point, the second stage of industrialization has been reached, and it is to the capitalist's advantage to substitute specialized machines for specialized tools. The knowledge, judgment, and will of the worker are now usurped by the central control of the organization. For the sake of greater productivity, the organization, not the individual, exercises its "mind."

Alienation sets in. For Marx it was the condition of separation that a worker perceives to exist between himself—his authentic being—and the products of his physical or mental laboring; it is impossible for him to identify with what he has created, so that, for example, he fails to under-stand or feel any connection between his economic function and the overall economy. The use of money as an impersonal medium of exchange and the force of money in setting priorities and exploiting the worker in other aspects of his life—rent, clothing, and so on—add to the condition of alienation. The machine uses the worker (not the other way around), and the expansion of machinery, though initially creating a few more jobs, eventually displaces more and more workers while the capitalist extracts greater amounts of surplus value. These displaced groups constitute the reserve labor force that can be admitted to or rejected from production, as the fluctuations of the capitalistic system require.

Marx's theory of social change is twofold. First, it contains the concept that property relations, backed by the laws of the state, are rigid; that is, they are unable to change once the productive forces that the owners embody have run their course. Therefore, the class that embodies the new productive force must destroy the outmoded relations. Second, the theory advances the idea that economic conditions generally, in addition to property relations, in the long run determine the other aspects of the social structure (other institutions such as politics, education, religion, etc.), so that as the former change, the latter change also.

Marx's sociology of knowledge should also be mentioned, for he pioneered in this area and laid the groundwork upon which Karl Mannheim (Chapter Nine) built. His position on the role of ideas in social life is consistent with the whole historical analysis that sets him apart from Hegel. Marx was interested largely in the *use* that ideas serve in relation to man's economic activities and perquisites. Even though idea complexes and the economic substructure may interact, it is largely from the latter that the main direction of change is seen. The source of consciousness is in the social relations to the material means of production: "From the socially established way in which man makes bread or cobbles shoes, his conscious activity, however complex, could be explained."[8] Man is therefore not a disinterested user of ideas; ideas are a reflection of the reality of labor, and they may be a tool for the defense of special privileges within the economic order.

Marx's insight on knowledge is that the outlook on the world (*Weltanschauung*) of a category of people, is formed by their class position and that the dominant ideas of an age are the ideas of the ruling class. It is possible for a person to develop a false consciousness, that is, to espouse ideas out of line with his material condition. Illusions that encourage misperceptions of material circumstances or opiates such as religion, which direct attention away from these realities may be present. Ideas relate ultimately to staying alive and involve power.

At last Marx "took the bull by the horns." If systems can be created which master and victimize man, systems can be changed so as to serve man. Marx's optimism and humanism asserted themselves; he had faith in technological progress and in the ultimate victory of the large class of workers responsible for the technological advances of society. A more perfect social order is promised when power has been purified (i.e., diffused). Human welfare must accompany technological improvement. He saw in his day a trend in the development of capital that, if unchecked, could only result in the collision of the swelling ranks of increasingly pauperized workers with the giant bourgeoisie. New forces in a society can be fully freed only when the restraints of the old system are destroyed.

---

[8] Jacques Barzun, *Darwin, Marx, Wagner* (Garden City, N.Y.: Doubleday, Anchor Books, 1958), p. 133.

Such conflict leads to progress, Marx believed, and in the end the workers, at last unified, would wrest all capital from the bourgeoisie and temporarily create the dictatorship of the proletariat by centralizing production in the state as a prelude to a more idealistic communism. Classes, which are products of the division of labor itself, would be abolished; with the end of class conflict, the medium of social change, would come the end of social evolution. Man would then be at last free to make his own history.[9] Capitalistic private property, which had succeeded individual property, would give way to socialized property of the many on whose labors it rests. A socialism planned and regulated for the development of man's highest potential, especially as man is freed from want, would come to pass.

Introduction to Selections 4.1 and 4.2

In Selection 4.1, Paul Mott presents a succinct account of Marx's theory of large-scale social change, which, according to Marx, began taking place in Europe within the feudal social structure. The class structure changed as new developments in the material means of production and markets occurred. Throughout his commentary Mott explains the dialectic pattern of thesis, antithesis, and synthesis. Even though Marx's writings overemphasized certain points, Mott concludes that some germs of truth remain; we will build upon his summary of these enduring virtues at the end of this chapter. Mott also shows that some of Marx's predictions have not come true for modern society because he did not envisage some alternative arrangements between employers and employees, as well as the broader role that the state is capable of assuming in economic affairs.

In Selection 4.2, "Karl Marx and Contemporary Sociology," Lewis Coser concludes that sociological analysis of certain problems of modern society can be illuminated when informed with some of Marx's insights. Coser places Marx's contributions against the background of two diverging points of view in sociology today: Some believe that society is the product of *"consensus,"* that social order derives principally from the existence of a set of integrated moral norms shared by the majority of society's members. These norms, when internalized in the personalities of various actors, make cooperation between individuals a matter of duty and legitimate the institutionalized arrangements of society. Others hold that society is in fact an arena of *conflict* among very diverse groupings. Consensus as to whose rules are valid for the legitimation of social arrangements (including reward distribution) is lacking, and therefore force and power are primary sources of social order.

---

[9] One may then, Marx says, fish or hunt without *becoming* a fisherman or a hunter. Rousseau's view of *voluntary* cooperation can be noted here.

Coser starts by describing Marx's fundamental insight that scarcity exists in all societies and is a potential source of conflict between groups. Such an interpretation, Coser feels, is required to balance the weight of those analysts, such as Talcott Parsons, who tend to give primacy to shared values through which roles are integrated and from which consensus derives.

Coser notes that Marx conceived of class as a collective thing: it arises only when individuals similarly related to the organization of the mode of production become aware, through communication, of their similar life chances and develop a consciousness of themselves as a unit. Such conditions enable individuals to act in concert and sometimes to sacrifice self-interest for the good of the class.

4.1

Marx's Macroscopic Theory of Social Change*

PAUL E. MOTT

Marx's major contribution to sociology and economics was his theory of social change. At the core of this theory were several assumptions besides that of the societal sources of human morality. First, he assumed that history moved in a dialectic pattern from *thesis* to *antithesis* to *synthesis*. Any given society is labeled a *thesis*. But every society (thesis) contains defects—the seeds of its own destruction (the antithesis). The interaction of these social forces would yield a new or modified society, called the synthesis. Second, the major forces of change in a society originate in its economy. Marx's theory has been given the label dialectic materialism because of this fundamental emphasis on the economy and the dialectic processes of history. Third, the *sine qua non* or essential characteristic of a society is its system of social classes. Fourth, the basis on which people can be assigned to social class positions is their relationship to the means of production: in other words, their occupations. Marx also defines the concept of *state* in a way that is uncommon to us. The state according to Marx is the instruments of violence and coercion found in a society.

Using these assumptions, we can trace Marx's theory of social change. Marx's thesis is classic feudal society found in Europe before 1350 A.D. Since the essential characteristic of society is its system of social classes and one's position in that system is determined by one's relationship to the means of production, then the class system in feudal society had the following status levels:

Thesis: Feudal Society
Feudal lords
Vassals
Guild-masters
Journeymen
Apprentices
Serfs

---

* Title supplied by editor.

But every system contains the seeds of its own destruction, and these seeds are located in the economy. The economic force that was to alter feudal society drastically was the revival of commerce with the East and the consequent growth of the new merchant class. Even the old guild system would be undermined by the newer factory system, because the guild system was too inadequate a productive mechanism to keep up with the demand for goods. The rapidly growing economic influence of the new merchant-industrial class—the bourgeoisie—was accompanied by increasing political influence. The eventual ascendance of the bourgeoisie resulted in a new synthesis: the capitalist nation-state. Since the essential characteristic of any society is its social classes, and positions in that system are a function of the person's occupation, the capitalist nation-state can be represented as follows:

Synthesis: The Capitalist Nation-State
Bourgeoisie
Professionals
Small businessmen (petit bourgeoisie)
Proletariat

The proletariat includes all of the industrial laborers. But every system contains the seeds of its own destruction, says Marx, and the capitalist nation-state is no exception. The economic forces that lead to the destruction of the capitalist nation-state are overproduction and the profit motive. The techniques of modern industry permit the production of goods on a scale more vast than ever before in human history. But the workers cannot consume as much as they produce because of the profit system that pays the worker less for making the commodity than he can buy it for himself. Marx's thinking on this point was based on the best economic theory available during his time, but from the point of view of modern economics it was not sufficiently sophisticated or accurate.

The problem of overproduction causes the bourgeoisie to search for new markets: a search that is facilitated by achievements in the fields of transportation and commerce. The efforts of the bourgeoisie result in exploitation of colonial areas for raw materials and as a place for selling manufactured goods. In this worldwide distribution and consumption system only the very large industrial organizations can continue to exist. Therefore, worldwide monopolies or cartels develop, whose leaders control the societies in which they do business. Small businessmen are driven into bankruptcy, and craftsmen and professionals are forced to work for the great monopolies rather than for themselves. As a result, the middle class is forced into the proletariat. The result is the social structure known as finance-imperialism.[1] The social class system of this new synthesis can be represented as follows:

---

[1] The term "finance-imperialism" was not used by Marx himself; it was applied by subsequent generations of economists and revolutionary thinkers.

Synthesis: Finance-Imperialist Society
Bourgeoisie
Proletariat

The bourgeoisie decrease in number as the less successful competitors are driven out of business and their organizations are absorbed into the larger ones. But the influence and wealth of this class increases at the expense of the proletariat. For its part, the proletariat gets poorer and less influential. The social distance between the two classes increases steadily. The members of the proletariat cannot improve their situation by peaceful means because the bourgeoisie control the state.

Every system contains the seeds of its own destruction, however. The defect in the finance-imperialist system is the economic oppression of the proletariat and forcing the middle classes into the proletariat. The more intellectual members of the old middle class provide the sense of direction, the inspiration, and the leadership to galvanize the less imaginative factory workers into a revolutionary force. Violent overthrow of the bourgeoisie is the only course open to the proletariat, says Marx, because the bourgeoisie control the state. Such a revolution could never occur in an agrarian society, according to Marx, because the means of communication are too primitive for the organization of a revolution. The violent overthrow of the bourgeoisie by sheer weight of numbers can occur only in an urban-industrial society that is a world rather than a national organization. After the revolution, a new synthesis—the dictatorship of the proletariat—is set up. In this system there are only two classes: the dictators and the proletariat. The dictators are the leaders of the revolution who must create the moral social organization—which you will note will be a worldwide society—and prepare the proletariat to live in it. The cornerstone of the new system is the negation of private property and profits. They are replaced by public ownership of the means of production. The proletariat is educated for the new society, and deviants are removed from the population. As society and man become increasingly moral, the state or the instruments of violence become less necessary. Gradually and irrevocably the state withers away and the dictatorship of the proletariat gives way to a new synthesis: the world communist society. In this society man is moral because he has a social consciousness—an internal gyroscope that keeps him on a moral path—and because the society is moral. The instruments of violence are unnecessary.

The Value of Marxian Theory

Marx actually had very little to say about the ultimate communist society: that task remained for Lenin and the neo-Marxists. But the outcome of the dialectic is not so important to us here as some of the earlier and more fundamental aspects of his reasoning. Marx's interpretation of the shift from feudal to industrial society agrees with modern interpretation on many major points. It agrees with newer versions because there are many useful elements in his assumptions about the process of social change. His assumption that conflict among social classes is inevitable still wins modified adherence in sociology.[2] Support for this assumption is modified because sociologists disagree about a definition of the concept of social class itself.

The importance of the economy in shaping the other parts of the society is also recognized. This assumption is the cornerstone of a type of sociological theory called human ecology [. . .].[3] Studies of community and national elites generally support this assumption. However, Marx's doctrinaire assumption that the economy affects the rest of the social structure but that nothing of importance arises independently of the economy and that the noneconomic aspects of society have no effect on the economic structures is no longer considered tenable by most sociologists. Noneconomic institutions can have effects on the society, although not so fundamental as those of the economy. Churches can obtain the passage of legislation to prohibit some kinds of economic activity completely or to limit it to certain days of the week. One social scientist has shown that Japan industrialized before China for reasons lodged in the value systems of the two countries and not primarily in the economy.[4] Modern sociology accepts the notion that the economy has a fundamental role in shaping the rest of the society. But it also holds that the other parts of the society have effects on the structure and functioning of the economy.

Marx's notion that the occupational system (one's relationship to the means of production) is the core of the system of social classes in a society receives modified concurrence today. Occupation is still considered by most social scientists to be the best single *indicator* of social class position. The problem arises in defining social class. Most social scientists do agree, however, that regardless of what it is, social class is a more complex concept than Marx made it.

This point of view is overdone sometimes. Some social scientists contend that certain occupational roles, such as physician, for example, have greater influence than one would expect from Marxian theory because the population *values* that occupation. In this dissent, a partially noneconomic factor—the prestige of the occupation—affects amount of influence. The choice of the physician as an example by the advocates of a less Marxian orientation is unfortunate. In medieval societies, the role of physician was neither influential nor prestigious. The physician's prestige and influence have grown as his success at treating human ailments has increased. It is undeniable that the successful treatment of illness is an important activity in a society. Also, the ability of the physicians to organize into associations and use their collective influence has been overlooked. By using their influence to obtain the passage of legislation

---

[2] D. H. Wrong, "The Functional Theory of Stratification: Some Neglected Considerations," *American Sociological Review*, 24 (1959), 772–82.

[3] A. H. Hawley, *Human Ecology* (New York: Ronald, 1950).

[4] Marion J. Levy, Jr., "Contrasting Factors in the Modernization of China and Japan," *Economic Development and Cultural Change*, 2 (1953), 161–197.

restricting certain activities to themselves, they have been able to increase their influence. Finally, the central value system of physicians is similar in many respects to those of the persons in the major centers of influence in our society—the economic elite. The natural alliance of these two groups on some issues has sustained the influence of the physicians.

The real usefulness of occupational prestige rank systems is that they are a relatively easy way to approximate the amount of influence possessed by a role. But they are at best only an approximation. An ex-President or ex-President's wife has far more prestige in the society than influence. The concept is also a social-psychological one that is concerned with people's attitudes about other people, not about how they behave.

The Limitations of Marxian Theory

In spite of its usefulness, the fact is that Marx's predictions were not correct. Instead of a mass society with a decreasing middle class, industrial societies have developed large and growing middle classes. The conditions of the workers improved rather than worsened, and no violent overthrow of a world-sprawling capitalism has occurred.

Marx had expected the workers to develop a class consciousness, but they did not. In England the Conservative Party gets a large proportion of its vote from the working class. In the United States the worker has disregarded the pleas of union leaders to be militant, exhibit solidarity, and attend union meetings.

Marx erred because, like so many social class theorists, he failed to appreciate the ability of aggregates of low influence status to increase their influence by peaceful means. Violent encounters between workers and owners have occurred, but they have been sporadic battles and skirmishes rather than outright wars. Labor conflict was prevalent during the nineteenth century in all western societies, but these encounters resulted in significant concessions from the owners of industries and from the government. The most fundamental of these concessions was the right to vote. The possession of this right is a very powerful source of influence: *one that can invert the influence ranking system at election time.*[5] The workers have many more votes than the economic elite; if they mobilize them, they can use the agencies of government as a means of winning further concessions from the economic elite. Many members of the economic elite recognized this fact and sought to use their resources to win the labor vote. During the latter half of the nineteenth century they were successful with this tactic. But in the twentieth century the government has emerged as a *third force* in relationships between labor and management. Among the concessions that were won by the workers (who were allied with the farm organizations at the turn of the century) was

---

[5] B. Walter, "Political Decision Making in Arcadia," in F. S. Chapin and S. F. Weiss (Eds.), *Urban Growth Dynamics in a Regional Cluster of Cities* (New York: Wiley, 1962).

antitrust legislation that eventually blunted the growth of the industrial organizations in American society.

The Emergence of Welfare-Bureaucratic Society

To account for the development of modern industrial society, we must move beyond Marxian theory and examine three major trends in some detail. The first is the shift from small to large subgroups, particularly in the economy. Marx predicted this trend, but he did not anticipate that growth would stop short of or retreat from the formation of monopolies or cartels. The second trend is the shift from a mass to an integrated form of social organization,* which Marx did not predict at all. Finally, there has been a trend away from an individualist value system to a welfare-collectivist one: an equally un-Marxian occurrence.

---

* Mass social organization is characterized by rootlessness among people and chaos in society. It existed in Europe during the transition from estate to class society and during the Industrial Revolution, which changed the relationship of people to family, community, and work. From mass social organization developed a more integrated form, in which there exists between the individual and the state a host of secondary associations that anchor him to norms and draw him into the mainstream of social life (this is a reference to Emile Durkheim's thought).—Ed.

4.2

Karl Marx and Contemporary Sociology
LEWIS A. COSER

Karl Marx is the classical theorist of social conflict. His whole contribution is based on the premise that collective interests and concomitant confrontations of power are central determinants of social process. The chapter that follows attempts to highlight this key component of Marx's work. It is not an assessment of his whole contribution, but rather a more modest attempt to emphasize one major aspect of his work that seems important for sociological inquiry today.

In the complex thought of Karl Marx there are many different strains that have been stressed at different times. With ideas of the past it is as with general history; "Every generation," wrote Carl L. Becker, "writes the same history in a new way, and it puts upon it a new construction. . . . We build our conceptions of history partly out of our present needs and purposes. The past is a kind of screen upon which we project our vision of the future."[1] Every generation reinterprets its intellectual inheritance and appropriates those ideas of past thinkers that are most peculiarly in turn with present needs. This is why mere inventories of our inheritance of ideas are never enough; we need to select and to sift if we are truly to incorporate inherited ideas into our present thought structures and thus make them our permanent possessions.

As a complicated and multi-faceted thinker, Karl Marx has been especially subject to the propensity of different periods and different groupings to refashion his image in record with their own needs. Thus the generation of Lenin would hardly recognize *their* Marx in the psychologized version of Marx's message that is projected by certain contemporary thinkers. Indeed, this process recently has been pushed to absurdity when, for example, Erich Fromm sees Marx as being mainly concerned with the psychological alienation of modern man and relates him to Zen Buddhism in his alleged concern for the curing of souls. For Marx, the alienation of modern man was not a psychological condition to be cured, but a consequence of social contradictions that could be abolished only through class conflict.

---

[1] Carl L. Becker, "What are Historical Facts," in Hans Meyerhoff, Ed., *The Philosophy of History in Our Time.* Garden City, N.Y.: Doubleday, Anchor Books, 1959, pp. 132–133.

Marx's stress on the function of social interests in the historical process can serve as a counterargument to those who claim that a functional orientation precludes concern with power and social change. These strictures may indeed be warranted when normative functionalism is under consideration, but I see no reason why other types of functional analysis might not be able to deal with these factors. Indeed, an eminent modern anthropologist of the functional school, the late S. F. Nadel, felt that "command over one another's actions" and "command over existing benefits or resources" were the main criteria to be used in the analysis of social roles and social structures.[2] The fact remains, however, that current sociological theorizing, whether functional in orientation or not, has too often neglected the dimensions of power and interests. The incorporation of certain of Marx's key ideas into the body of current theory will, I feel, be an important corrective in this respect. It will help right a balance that has been inclined excessively in the direction of normative integration and homeostatic balance.

Every sociological theory typically rests on some key variables that are thought to account in major part for the functioning of social systems. More particularly, norms and values, power, and interests may be said to be central factors on which various sociological theorists have focused their attention. The relative weight given to these factors, however, and their specific combinations, varies considerably. Thus, whereas normative functionalism, from Durkheim to Parsons, emphasizes common norms and values, it slights the importance of the allocation of scarce power and scarce resources as major explanatory variables. Conversely, Paretian sociology, although not unaware of the importance of the normative order as well as of economic determinants, focuses its major attention on the contest for power. Marx's sociology, in turn, though by no means oblivious of the functions of norms and values, is mainly concerned with the systematic consequences of the unequal allocation of scarce resources within a social system, one of these consequences being the unequal allocation of scarce power. Marx's major independent variable in the study of social systems turns out to be the character of interests that are systematically generated by the structure of productive relations, that is by a given system of allocation of scarce resources. Marxian sociology focuses on class interests just as Paretian sociology focuses on the striving for power, and normative functionalism on common-value integration.

Concentration on one set of variables, although it may be exceedingly valuable and productive of insights, always carries with it the inherent danger of wittingly or unwittingly slighting the importance of others. The fallacy of believing that explanations for a certain set of data are adequate for all scientific purposes lurked especially large in the case of major creative social theorists who felt justifiably that "their" variables did indeed have a great deal of explanatory power. They were prone to be-

---

[2] S. F. Nadel, *The Theory of Social Structure.* New York: Free Press, 1957, p. 115.

lieve that, as Talcott Parsons has argued in his first book, their logically closed system of theory referred to an empirically closed system.[3] This is why it behooves later generations of sociologists continuously to reassess their heritage and to attempt to determine the degree to which preponderant emphasis on one or the other set of variables may not hinder the understanding of the full operation of social systems even as it may brilliantly illuminate certain of their aspects.

Even though, and perhaps just because, theorizing in the dominant mode of normative functionalism has permitted American sociology to reach a level of sophistication hitherto unattained in any other sociological enterprise, it is time to help redress the balance by emphasizing the explanatory value of neglected conceptualizations of the factors of interests and power. This is, I take it, why Marx's sociology should again be accorded serious attention both as a corrective for certain prevailing emphases and as a major theoretical scheme in its own right.

Marx's analytical focus on the ways in which the relationships between men are shaped by their relative positions in regard to the means of production, that is, by their differential access to scarce resources and scarce power, carries with it, it stands to reason, an emphasis on clash, conflict, and contention as constitutive elements of any differentiated society. Marx was aware of the fact that unequal access must not at all times and under all conditions lead to active struggles, as his description of the century-long stasis of societies operating under Asiatic modes of production testifies. He nevertheless assumed that the potential for social conflicts is inherent in every differentiated society since it systematically generates conflicts of interests between persons and groups differentially located within the social structure.

To Marx, societal equilibrium was a special case of disequilibrium, whereas to current normative functionalism, disequilibrium is a special case of equilibrium. This is why it turns out that social change has typically presented special difficulties to normative functionalism whereas, in contrast, in the Marxian mode of analysis it is difficult to account for continued societal functioning under relatively stable conditions. The notion of intrinsic contradictions within the social order has been a mainstay of Marxist types of explanations, whereas current normative functionalism has clung to the idea of the integration of all component actors within a common system of norms and values. It is in this respect also that a reexamination of the Marxian scheme has some urgency. Even if there are certain relatively stable social systems for the analysis of which the integrative model would seem appropriate, sociologists would deprive themselves of a most valuable tool for the understanding of social systems such as those, say, of present-day South Africa,[4] Latin America, or the American South, were they to forego the opportunity of utilizing certain

---

[3] Talcott Parsons, *The Structure of Social Action*. New York: Free Press, 1949, p. 476.

[4] Cf., Pierre L. van den Berghe, *South Africa, a Study in Conflict*, Middletown, Conn.: Wesleyan University Press, 1965.

approaches that Marxian sociology provides for them. Not that opposed sociological theories variously premised on the ubiquity of social order or of social conflict are likely to be most productive in the long run, but a mature theoretical scheme will have to take both factors into account if it is to elaborate a full theoretical armatorium. This is another reason why I suspect that a reexamination of Marxian sociological categories can only benefit the further development of modern sociological theory.

A prerequisite for the understanding of the Marxian concept of class interests is the realization that Marx was not concerned with the maximization of individual self-interest upon which utilitarian interest theories commonly rest. He was not concerned with the private drives and propensities of individuals but rather with the collective interests of particular categories of men playing their peculiar roles on the social scene. "Individuals are dealt with only in so far as they are the personifications of economic categories," he says in the Preface to *Kapital*, "embodiments of particular class relations and class interests." Or, to put it into modern language, Marx was concerned with the way in which specific positions in the social structure tended to shape the social experiences of their incumbents and to predispose them to actions oriented to maximize their collective life chances.

Class interests in Marxian sociology are not given *ab initio*. They develop through the exposure of the incumbents of particular social positions to particular social circumstances. Thus competition divides the personal interests of "a crowd of people who are unknown to each other" in early industrial enterprises. "But the maintenance of their wages, this common interest which they have against their employer, brings them together again in the same idea of resistance-*combination*. Thus combination has always a double aim, that of putting an end to competition among themselves, to enable them to compete as a whole with the capitalist."[5] This is why Marx made fun of those utilitarian economists who were wont to wonder why workers might sacrifice a substantial part of their wages during strikes or in the effort to build a union. This behavior, Marx contended, could be easily understood if it was realized that these workers, far from maximizing their short-run private interests, were engaged in building organizations that could defend their long-term collective interests.

The collective or class interests which were in the center of Marx's concern were not simply *given*, they did not as such call forth action directly. Interests provided meaningful motivation for action only if translated into a collective assessment of the communality of life chances. This could arise only under specified conditions of which the most important one is communication between individuals similarly placed in the social structure. "The small peasants," he writes with regard to the French peasantry of the middle of the nineteenth century, "form a vast mass, the

---

[5] Quoted in Karl Marx, *Selected Writings in Sociology and Social Philosophy*, ed. by T. B. Bottomore and Maximilien Rubel. New York. McGraw-Hill, 1964, pp. 186–187.

members of which live in similar conditions, but without entering into manifold relations with one another. Their mode of production isolates them from one another, instead of bringing them into mutual intercourse. . . . Insofar as millions of families live under economic conditions of existence that divide their mode of life, their interests, and their culture from those of the other classes and put them into hostile contrast to the latter, they form a class. Insofar as there is only a local interconnection among these peasants, and the identity of their interests begets no unity, no national union, and no political organization, they do not form a class."[6]

To Marx, then, potential common interests of a particular stratum can be said to derive from the location of that stratum within a particular social structure. But potentiality is transformed into actuality, *Klasse an sich* into *Klass fuer sich* only when communication, common involvement in common struggle, and the formation of a consciousness of common fate ties individuals to a cohesive class that consciously articulates common interests. A cohesive class requires of its members the commonly assumed burden of letting the demands of class action take priority over the urges of private self-interest. Class action channels and restrains self-interest. It is a form of social control and hence helps class integration. It has disciplinary functions.

Moreover, Marx was well aware that "particular individuals are not 'always' influenced in their attitude by the class to which they belong."[7] That is, he admitted that particular individuals may not be interested in their class interests. Whether individuals would indeed transcend their individual self-interests and develop class interests was hence to Marx an empirical question—though he assumed, of course, that most of them would indeed do so. He showed hardly any concern with the processes of individual social mobility, since to him nontranscended individual interests, though they might hinder the formation of collective interests, were not a historically transforming social force.

In contrast to the utilitarians, who see self-interest as a regulator of harmonious society, Marx sees individual self-interest as destructive of class interest in general, and leading specifically to the self-destruction of capitalism. The very fact that each capitalist acts rationally in his own self-interest leads to the destruction of the interest common to all. Capitalists are doomed since their structural position does not permit them to arrive at a consistent assertion of common interests. As Raymond Aron has recently said, "For Marx, each man working in his own interest, contributes both to the necessary functioning and to the final destruction of the regime."[8] The very fact that the competitive mode of production of capitalism does not allow the emergence of a common class interest except as a defensive mechanism, the fact that capitalist entrepreneurs,

---

[6] Quoted in Lewis A. Coser and Bernard Rosenberg, *Sociological Theory*, 2d ed. New York: Crowell-Collier-Macmillan, 1964, p. 396.

[7] Quoted in Karl Marx, *Selected Writings, op. cit.*, p. 202.

[8] Raymond Aron, *Main Currents in Sociological Thought*. New York: Basic Books, 1965, pp. 134–135.

due to their structural position, are unable to transcend individual competition among themselves, leads them to their doom. Correlatively, the workers are seen as the agents of change and of destruction of the capitalist order precisely because their structural condition predisposes them to transcend their individual interests and to evolve a consciousness of common class interests.

Marx allowed that capitalists also found it possible to transcend their immediate self-interest, but he thought this possible only in the political and ideological rather than in the economic sphere. Capitalists, divided by their economic competition among themselves, evolved a justifying ideology and a political system of domination that served their collective interests. Political power and ideology thus seem to be serving the same functions for capitalists that class consciousness serves for the working class. But this symmetry is only apparent. To Marx the economic sphere is always the finally decisive realm. And within this realm, the bourgeoisie is always the victim of the competitiveness of its very mode of economic existence. It can evolve a consciousness, but it is always a "false consciousness," that is, a consciousness that does not transcend its rootedness in an economically competitive mode of production. The bourgeoisie engenders a repressive state machinery, but this machinery cannot come to grips with an economic process based on self-interest. Hence neither the bourgeois state nor bourgeois ideology can serve truly to transcend bourgeois self-interest in the same manner as working-class consciousness transcends the self-interests of the underprivileged.

Marx's analytical focus was on those points in the social structure at which a transformation of individual interests into collective interests could be predicted. He concluded that the structural position of the bourgeoisie did not let it attain a true collectivization of interests whereas the very position of the working class brought forth true collectivization.

Marx directs our attention on the differential distribution of resources and power and the chances that such differences will lead to the emergence of social conflicts over their retention, alleviation, or abolition. He argues that these conflicts will bring about the transcendence of self-interest among the deprived. Marx focuses attention upon those social processes in which alienative tendencies and counter-ideologies among the deprived are systematically generated by the distribution of statuses and powers upon which the social organization rests.

In the Marxian view, the nuclear cell of capitalist society, the factory, embodies within it that fatal contradiction of interests that will lead to the destruction of the capitalist enterprise. The capitalist mode of production is premised upon unequal access to resources on the part of different classes and it is equally premised on an unequal access to power. The institutional framework of capitalism is built upon systematic inequalities that, in turn, through their cumulative impact upon the life chances of the actors involved, lead to the activization of alienative tendencies among the deprived strata and ultimately to the breakdown on the capitalist system.

One need not share Marx's certainties, or at least hopes, concerning the breakdown of the capitalist system, in order to recognize the importance of the analytical tool he has provided for us. In fact, nothing seems lost for sociological purposes if Marx's deterministic scheme is couched in a probabilistic framework. One need not agree that unequal life chances must lead to a common consciousness and common political action in capitalist or any other society and yet accept the notion that one is most likely to find alienative and disruptive tendencies among those whose life chances have been impaired by the operation of a particular system. Similarly, it is profitable to investigate to what degree countercultures develop through communication and contact with men involved in similar social situations and located in similar structural positions that are depriving them of significant life chances. At the very least Marx has provided us with a program of research for investigating systematically those factors that might lead to the transformation of social system through the mobilization of the energy of those whom it exploits.

It is probably true, as Arnold Feldman has recently argued, that Marx "often correctly identified the contradictions within industrial societies, but that he uniformly overestimated the extent to which such contradictions could only be resolved through revolution of counterrevolutions."[9] But it is hardly difficult, though Marx would have disapproved, to separate Marx's eschatological hopes from his analytical scheme.

Marx remains the most powerful analyst of asymmetrical relationships. In contrast to the social theorists who cling to a harmony model of society and stress symmetry in the mutual orientation of actors, Marx is concerned with the facts of unilateral dependence and hence of exploitation, and the denial of reciprocity. Complementarity can be found in every type of society, even in a totalitarian one. Autocrats and dictators engage in complementary interactions with their subjects, even while they exploit them. In fact, institutionalized exploitation, the "right to something for nothing," to use Veblen's telling phrase, is usually hidden under a veil of claims to the complementarity of the roles of rulers and ruled. Marx helps to reject these conceits. He shows why, when economic resources or power positions are unequal, the resultant relationship is likely to be unbalanced, unilateral rather than multilateral.[10]

We have seen so far that Marx's social theory focuses attention on three interrelated conceptualizations. He stresses the importance of common interests and analyzes structural conditions that lead to the emergence of such common interests; he discusses the ways in which particular positions within the social structure predispose toward the development of alienative tendencies, and he analyzes unilateral relations of power as they emerge out of unequal access to scarce resources and scarce positions of power. These analytical concepts remain of high value even though Marx's concrete predictions as to, for example, an impending socialist revolution in highly developed industrial societies have been

---

[9] Arnold Feldman, "Violence and Volatility" in *Internal War*, ed. by Harry Eckstein. New York: Free Press, 1964, p. 126.

[10] Cf., Alvin Gouldner, "The Norm of Reciprocity," *American Sociological Review*, April 1960, Vol. 25, 2, especially pp. 165 and 169.

proven invalid. Unfortunately, those who opposed Marx for ideological reasons as well as his own followers and epigones have tended to focus their attention on concrete historical examples and predictions rather than on the concepts that informed Marx's analysis of social structure. This becomes evident if we confront Marx's conceptualization with certain present-day events. Let me give a few concrete illustrations:

Marx certainly had very little to say, concretely, on the turning point in American race relations that we experience today. Yet a Marxian type of analysis would be most helpful for its understanding. The fact that American sociology was so ruefully unprepared for the civil rights revolution of the last few years is connected with its systematic neglect of social conflict and of the mobilization of power and interests in racial contentions. Being wedded to the belief that only increased understanding between the races and successful mobilization of guilt about the American dilemma among the dominant racial majority would lead to the gradual erosion of prejudice and discrimination, American sociology was by and large unprepared for the emergence of a situation in which a major part of the initiative for change did not come from the white man but rather from the black. American sociology has systematically neglected analysis of the conditions that gradually led to the emergence of a new self-consciousness among younger Negroes and to the development not only of alienative tendencies in the Negro community but of a militant type of alienation as well. Much professional embarrassment might well have been avoided had attention been paid to certain Marxian leads; for example, to the process of communication through which individuals gradually came to submerge their initially separate and competitive self-interests in favor of overriding common interests and collective actions for revolutionary change in the status order. Similarly it would have been less easy to brush off Marxian leads as useless nineteenth-century utilitarianism had it been grasped that Marxian sociology, far from being predicated on the idea that human actors are always predisposed to act in terms of individual self-interest, is concerned with precisely those climactic situations in which men transcend self-interest and accept the sacrifices involved in the struggle for collective interests. It would hardly have come as a surprise to Marx that so many Negroes are disposed to sacrifice their own individual life chances, to postpone present satisfaction in the collective pursuit of common long-range goals. He knew that only men who articulate their common interests through common action have a chance to change their collective destiny.

The usefulness of the Marxian perspective does not stop with the understanding of the posture of the underprivileged within a specific social structure. It can be of equal help, as Marx himself showed, to understand the orientations of those who have vested interests in the maintenance of the social order. One need not neglect the importance of legal norms, of national values, and of appeals to conscience to grasp the impact on the Southern *status quo* of such mundane matters as the flow of federal funds, the prospective sales of bond issue, the direction of the flow of new capital into private enterprise. In the South one also finds principled racists who happen not to be interested in their economic interests, but the majority of Southern dominants *are* so interested. The threat faced by businessmen of losing customers or credit, or the threat faced by politicians of losing votes if dependent on a large Negro constituency, are efficient solvents of the cake of Southern custom. Even a cursory reading of the daily news about the South—and the North as well—revives the conviction that it is entirely too early to relegate Marxian thinking to the heap of historically obsolete dogmatic constructions. We still ought to listen to the man who wrote, "Morality, religion, metaphysics, and other ideologies, and their corresponding forms of consciousness, no longer retain . . . their appearance of autonomous existence. . . . It is men, who, in developing their material production and their material intercourse, change, along with their real existence, their thinking and the products of their thinking. Life is not determined by consciousness, but consciousness by life."[11]

Marx suffered from the misfortune of having been born in the nineteenth and not in the twentieth century, and much of his thinking is inevitably historically obsolete. In fact, I believe that a thinker who was so concerned with emphasizing the principle of historical specificity would have been the first to agree. Many of Marx's problems are no longer ours, few of his solutions can be ours, and even his methods of analysis are only partly usable today. More particularly, messianic and eschatological elements loom large in Marx's overall work and must be eliminated if his contribution to the science of society is to be recognized and utilized.

Moreover, it seems necessary to reject Marx's reductionist tendencies, his propensity, for example, to see in the political order only a reflection of the economic order.

Marx's economic reductionism, as Ralf Dahrendorf, among others, has shown,[12] led him to neglect the analysis of those power relations that are not derived from property relations. To Marx, power flowed from command over economic resources; he did not entertain the idea that command over economic resources might result from access to powerful positions. He understood, to cite Ignazio Silone's insightful quip, the role of plutocrats but was unable to foretell the advent of the "cratopluts" of the twentieth century.

Similarly, Marx's powerful analysis of unilateral relationships and his theory of exploitation remained too narrowly focused on the economic framework. Let me end with a quote from a young sociologist, himself clearly not a Marxian, Donald McKinley: ". . . perhaps Marx was, in part, right. His focus on exploitation was, however, too narrowly economic, and his predicated aggressive counterresponse, too narrowly political. Perhaps more importantly, the exploitation in a highly industrialized and differentiated society is of an emotional and moral nature and the alien-

---

[11] *Karl Marx, op. cit.*, p. 75.

[12] Ralf Dahrendorf, *Class and Class Conflict in Industrial Society*. Stanford, Calif.: Stanford University Press, 1959.

ated and aggressive response is of a like kind—family disorganization, crime, and political apathy."[13]

Here, as elsewhere, Marx did not go far enough, no doubt. But it behooves us to push farther in a direction in which he did some pioneering explorations. The cumulative enterprise of scientific inquiry is best served if we honor the contributions of our ancestors by selectively incorporating them into the body of our theories, while utilizing their leads to penetrate into realms that, to them, were yet virgin territory.

---

[13] Donald McKinley, *Social Class and Family Life*, New York. Free Press, 1964, p. 266.

SUMMARY AND EVALUATION
OF CHAPTER FOUR

A great deal has been written in criticism of Marx, and most of the points that have been raised are fairly well known by now. However, many of the criticisms are muted if one accepts, first, that Marx was making a *trend* analysis, not affirming "iron" laws, of economic changes in a particular period of history and, second, that the *spirit* rather than the letter of his writings should be followed in analyzing industrial processes in other times and places. Even the heat of controversy over Marx's predictions of the future is reduced when these caveats are heeded.

One of the most comprehensive and up-to-date evaluations of Marx's sociology has been done by Irving M. Zeitlin.[1] His discussion also has the merit of stating Marx's assumptions explicitly. These assumptions (presented in paraphrased form) and Zeitlin's and our evaluations of them are stated below.

Assumptions 1, 2, and 3: *The economic sphere of a society, the totality of the relations of production, give a society its character and its people its psychology. Social change is the product of tension between the developing forces of production and existing property relations; and class conflict (socially manifested) is an expression of objective conflict of interests (economically manifested) between classes.*[2] The crux of these assumptions is that a society is a system of interrelated institutional spheres and that change in the economic sphere has the potential of creating change in the others through the medium of class conflict. Zeitlin believes Marx was correct here, in that even though institutional spheres interpenetrate one another in real life, analytically it is acceptable to delineate each separately and consider its impact upon the others. Marx's choice of the term *substructure* may not have been the best, and he is not entirely clear on *how* the substructure of the economy ultimately

---

[1] Irving M. Zeitlin, *Marxism: A Reexamination* (Princeton, N.J.: Van Nostrand, 1967). See also Norman Birnbaum, "The Crisis in Marxist Sociology," in Hans Peter Dreitzel (Ed.), Recent Sociology (No. 1) (New York: Crowell-Collier-Macmillan, 1969), pp. 11–42.

[2] Ibid., pp. 79–87.

determines the superstructure of law, art, science, and so on. However, the determining influence of the economic sphere was in fact a tendency in countries of Western Europe, and even Max Weber's demonstration of a configuration of attitudes *compatible* with capitalistic development there supplemented rather than disproved Marx on this point.

Assumptions 4, 5, and 6: *The existence of private property determines the two fundamental classes in a society: workers and owners; and, in capitalist societies, conflict between them is inevitable, as is exploitation of the workers' labor.*[3] However, Marx himself recognized that class struggle might be manifested in ways other than revolution—through parliamentary action, for example. Moreover, while the ownership of property certainly cannot be ignored, it is not the only criterion determining the stratification of groups in the social order. Status is a criterion, too, and some groups are high in status without owning extensive property. It is true that the proportion of small owners *has* decreased drastically in the United States, making the distinction between owners and nonowners quite pronounced. However, the *authority* over production in large firms has come to reside in the hands of managers who may not have a large ownership interest; and the American union membership seems to have accommodated itself to working *within* the system for larger shares of benefits instead of striving for greater control over productivity (the recurrence of economic depression might well shake this complacency, of course).

Surplus value, as manifested in mounting surplus products, *is* a rather conspicuous characteristic of capitalist production. In order to judge whether it is the result of exploitation, however, one must ask how much control over production the worker has and to how much of the social product he is entitled after production, overhead, reserve costs, and other items have been covered.

Assumptions 7, 8, and 9: *With the advance of capitalism will come the increasing polarization of workers and the owners of the means of production, the increasing impoverishment of workers, and the inability to stabilize society and regulate its overproduction crisis.*[4] Polarization into two simple classes has not in fact occurred. Instead, the class structure has become much more complex, in large part because of the emergence of a large "salariat" (a group drawing salary rather than wages); their relation to the mode of production is somewhat different from that of wage earners since salaried jobs generally entail more authority and autonomy. At the other end of the social spectrum, as Norbert Wiley[5] has pointed out, one and the same person is not always a lender of money, a seller of commodities, and an owner of the means of production. On the contrary, different people often perform these functions, and they and

---

[3] Ibid., pp. 87–96.

[4] Ibid., pp. 96–103.

[5] Norbert Wiley, "America's Unique Class Politics: The Interplay of the Labor, Credit, and Commodity Markets," *American Sociological Review*, 32 (August 1967), 529–541.

their counterparts in society may be mixed. American class politics thus acquires its peculiar character: although the employee may indeed be in conflict with his employer over underlying economic inequalities or lack of work, he often chooses to express his dissatisfaction in the commodity market (e.g., through rent-strikes, lunch-counter sit-ins, and welfare rights demonstrations), a place where issues can be most easily crystalized.

Marx's prediction of the increasing impoverishment of workers must also be qualified in the sense that those who remain working may actually find their wages going up in the long run. However, Marx's essential thesis that the *proportion of workers actually thrown out of the production system entirely* determines the impoverishment of the whole class and leads to a crisis in the system has still not been tested. Whether the capitalist system can be regulated in such a way that lagging production in one area can be compensated by stimulating production in others and whether this action can be used indefinitely to forestall the crisis of overproduction accompanied by underemployment is an issue on which Marxists are themselves divided.[6]

Assumptions 10, 11, 12, and 13: *Exploitation of workers will eventually mold them into a class* for *itself (rather than a class* in *itself); their functional indispensability to production gives them political power that the state, which is an instrument of the bourgeoisie, will not let them exercise until they seize power—peacefully or by force—for themselves.*[7] Zeitlin thinks that Marx under-estimated the ability of workers to favor *other* interests over class interests, even as their objective situation seems to worsen. This is important, for, without consciousness of their misery, workers are not likely to collectivize their power and to organize for their struggles against the owners of production. As far as the state is concerned, it may in fact be capable of admitting some unprivileged classes of its own volition. Furthermore, Zeitlin feels that, with the advent of cybernated (self-regulating) machine automation, the worker may have lost the opportunity to seize power that he had when production still depended heavily on his labor. The critical period for capitalism may therefore lie *before* us. Whether new institutions and values will develop that will allow a larger proportion of the population to satisfy their economic wants more fully or whether property relations will hold sufficient sway to cause larger proportions of the population to go wanting is the critical question facing capitalism in the twentieth century, according to Zeitlin.

Kenneth Boulding, an influential interdisciplinary economist, has recently attacked Marxism along the lines of its feasibility for the socioeconomic development of nations.[8] Although many will disagree with both Boulding's own view of history and with his interpretation of the Marxist view of history, his main points are worth noting here. To begin with,

---

[6] Zeitlin, *Marxism: A Reexamination*, p. 102.

[7] Ibid., pp. 103–108.

[8] Kenneth E. Boulding, *A Primer on Social Dynamics: History as Dialectics and Development* (New York: Free Press, 1970).

Boulding charges that the dialectic view essentially employs the threat (rather than an exchange or integrative) system in organizing the activities of a society. It stirs up hatred and resentment between classes and nations (in the latter case, through nationalistic Marxism), often when there is no natural cleavage between them. The opponents seek, or are pushed, to destroy one another, while solutions to the nation's problems continue to be neglected. He claims, further, that the dialectic view, with its roots in the threat system, requires opponents to "ideologize" the rightness of their positions to such a degree that they can neither learn anything from one another nor solve their problems calmly and rationally. Moreover, Boulding believes that, in fact, virtually all revolutions and wars have cost society far more (in human lives, suffering, and postponed gross national product gain) than any ills they intended to cure could have, if left to follow a more normal course. He also asserts that as a result of the Marxist's tendency to locate surplus value in the labor of the worker, the efforts of organizers of production go unrewarded; consequently, countries with socialist philosophies experience socioeconomic stagnation. It is only during a brief period at the beginning of modernization, Boulding maintains, when a large amount of surplus value falls wholly into the hands of a small class of capitalists and landowners, that socialism is appealing—that, as he puts it, the "socialist bus" comes by. Afterward, if the country has, fortunately, missed the bus, it can continue to develop, and the differential between property and labor income narrows (why? we are not told). At any rate, continues Boulding, since the consumption of the idle rich in the United States amounts to only 5 percent of the national income, it is hardly worth a revolutionary upheaval to get rid of them. Finally, he admits that there is a place for the dialectic in history and in a philosophy for the future as a *minor motif* because some conflict or confrontation may be necessary in order to produce reform. But the larger and more important improvements, he avers, have already come and will continue to come as the result of a nondialectic, teleological (goal-directed), evolutionary (adaptive) approach, according to which men choose to solve their problems together rather than choose sides and fight.

Two additional problems and criticisms deserve brief mention. One concerns the labor theory of value—the idea that the value of a commodity for exchange in the market is a function of the units of labor put into it—and the other, the issue of objectivity in Marx's life. The soundness of the labor theory of value is largely a question for economists rather than sociologists to decide. However, his idea of exploitation—a concept deriving from the labor theory of value—is relevant to sociology. Neil J. Smelser has deemed it "too general and inclusive to explain the specifics of worker protests,"[9] despite his judgment that, overall, many of Marx's ideas on capital accumulation are valid.[10]

---

[9] Neil J. Smelser, *Sociological Theory: A Contemporary View* (New York: General Learning Press, 1971), p. 50.

[10] Ibid., p. 48.

The problem of Marx's objectivity, or lack of it, must be understood with reference to two of his tasks: specifically, he set out, in *Capital*, "to lay bare the economic law of motion of modern society";[11] more generally, he attempted to make himself, as a socialist theorist, a vehicle for the expression of what "in fact" was happening to the working class, to politicize their consciousness, and to help them understand their historic role in societal development. "Philosophers have only explained the world in different ways; what matters is that it should be changed," Marx once wrote. Was Marx objective? That is, did he, in accordance with the canons of scientific validity, allow a research question to be open to all the evidence relevant to its answer? On the one hand, it is generally agreed that he carried out his first task with extreme diligence and meticulous care as he searched for and brought to bear the various data on the operations and development of the capitalistic factory system of his time. What bothers some people, on the other hand, is that in his role as a socialist theorist, he was sympathetic to the working class and desirous that his studies contribute to their awakening and to the ultimate success of their struggle. We can conclude, however, that Marx's objectivity in his research was not seriously impaired by his commitments to the workers since he did not allow these commitments to distort his findings regarding the operations of the economic law of motion of modern society. The role of the scientist as an agent or blueprint designer of value-prescribed change will be discussed further in the next chapter on Weber.

What is more difficult to accept is Marx's claims to truth with reference to his own sociology (and suspicion) of ideas. How can *anyone*, even Marx, give a "true" account if ideas are the instruments by which one defends one's economic interests? If the ideas of the working class are correct (i.e., accurately reflective of their own material interests), then their interests must somehow be correct. But how is this determined? This is actually a problem beyond objectivity—a problem that involves discovering to what degree, and how, we can overcome certain types of ideology so we can develop a valid social science that is relatively universal. To this problem we will return in the chapter on Karl Mannheim.

The state has not withered away, as Marx predicted, especially not in socialist countries, as Marx might have predicted. The centralization of property seems necessarily to entail control by a small elite of people. Marx took the downfall of capitalist production to be imminent. But what can be meant by this if no pure capitalism exists anywhere or if both man and economic–political systems are in fact more malleable than Marx expected?

On the more positive and general side, it must be granted that Marx opened up some new and profitable areas of investigation: for example, (1) the interrelations among the forces of production, the social relations of production, and the character of a society's law, religion, philosophy,

---

[11] Karl Marx, *Capital*, Samuel Moore and Edward Aveling (Trans.) (London: G. Allen, 1949), p. xix.

and so on;[12] and (2) social stratification, involving the distribution of power and privilege,[13] revolutions,[14] and alienation.[15]

In summary we may say that Marx may have underestimated the ability of the capitalistic state to provide some degree of representation to unprivileged groups and failed to foresee the complication (rather than the simplification and inevitable polarization) of the class structure in advanced capitalistic industrial economics; however, Marx's mode of analysis—which focused attention on the impact of scarcity, the effect of the organization of the mode of production on the rest of the society, and the operation of dialectic forces in the economy—stands as a classic example of historical (longitudinal) scholarship in the dynamics of social change today. Furthermore, if we follow the spirit rather than the letter of his approach, it is likely to illuminate social change for some time to come.

SELECTED BIBLIOGRAPHY

Althusser, Louis, and Etienne Balibar. *Reading Capital.* Ben Brewster (Trans.). New York: Random House, 1970.

Anderson, Charles H. *Toward a New Sociology.* Homewood, Ill.: Dorsey Press, 1974.

Avineri, Shlomo. *The Social and Political Thought of Karl Marx.* New York: Cambridge University Press, 1968.

Barzun, Jacques. *Darwin, Marx, Wagner.* Garden City, N.Y.: Doubleday, Anchor Books, 1958.

Bendix, Reinhard, and Seymour Martin Lipset (Eds.). *Class, Status, and Power.* New York: Free Press, 1966.

Beqiraj, Mehmet. *Peasantry in Revolution.* Ithaca, N.Y.: Center for International Studies, Cornell University, 1966.

Berger, Peter, (Ed.). *Marxism and Sociology.* New York: Appleton, 1969.

Berlin, Isaiah. *Karl Marx: His Life and Environment.* New York: Oxford University Press, 1948.

---

[12] See, for example, George Dalton (Ed.), *Tribal and Peasant Economics* (Garden City, N.Y.: The Natural History Press, 1967).

[13] See Gerhard Lenski, *Power and Privilege* (New York: McGraw-Hill, 1966); and Reinhard Bendix and Seymour Martin Lipset, "Karl Marx's Theory of Social Classes," in Bendix and Lipset (Eds.), *Class, Status, and Power* (New York: Free Press, 1953), pp. 26–35.

[14] See James Chowning Davis (Ed.), *When Men Revolt and Why* (New York: Free Press, 1971). Revolution is a term not used with precision by Marx. Sometimes it means the changes brought about by the economically ascending class; at other times it means the violent overthrow of the entrenched dominant class.

[15] See Lewis S. Feuer, "What is Alienation? The Career of a Concept," *New Politics,* 1 (Spring, 1962), 116–134. See also Alfred McClung Lee, "An Obituary for 'Alienation,'" *Social Problems,* 20 (Summer 1972), 121–127. Another study, "Work in America," published by the United States Government in 1972 is currently unavailable but already controversial.

Brinton, Crane. "From Anatomy of Revolution." In H. Laurence Ross (Ed.), *Perspectives on the Social Order.* New York: McGraw-Hill, 1963. Pp. 431–436.

Christman, Henry M., (Ed.). *The American Journalism of Marx and Engels.* New York: New American Library, 1966.

Davies, James C. "Towards a Theory of Revolution." In H. Laurence Ross (Ed.), *Perspectives on the Social Order.* New York: McGraw-Hill, 1963. Pp. 437–450.

Feuer, Lewis S., (Ed.). *Marx and the Intellectuals.* Garden City, N.Y.: Doubleday, 1969.

Horowitz, Irving Louis, (Ed.). *The New Sociology.* New York: Oxford University Press, Galaxy paperback, 1965.

Israel, Joachim. *Alienation: From Marx to Modern Sociology.* Boston: Allyn and Bacon, 1971.

Kornhauser, William. "Revolutions." In Roger Little (Ed.), *Survey of Military Institutions.* Vol. 2. Chicago: University of Chicago Press, 1970. Pp. 404–441.

Laski, Harold J. *On The Communist Manifesto.* New York: Random House, Vintage Book, 1967.

Lefebvre, Henri. *The Sociology of Marx.* New York: Random House, 1968.

Lenski, Gerhard. *Power and Privilege.* New York: McGraw-Hill, 1966.

Marx, Karl. *Early Writings.* T. B. Bottomore (Trans. and Ed.). New York: McGraw-Hill, 1964.

Marx, Karl. *Selected Writings in Sociology and Social Philosophy.* T. B. Bottomore (Trans.) and Bottomore and Maximilian Rubel (Eds.). New York: McGraw-Hill, 1964.

Marx, Karl. *Das Kapital.* Friedrich Engels (Ed.) and condensed by Serge L. Levitsky. Chicago: Regnery, Gateway Edition, 1965.

Marx, Karl, and Friedrich Engels. *Marxist Social Thought.* Robert Freedman (Ed.). New York: Harcourt Brace Jovanovich, 1968.

Marx, Karl, and Friedrich Engels. *Writings on the Paris Commune.* Hal Draper (Ed.). New York: Monthly Review Press, 1971.

Mattick, Paul. *Marx and Keynes.* Boston: Porter Sargeant, 1969.

Parsons, Talcott. *The Structure of Social Action.* New York: Free Press, 1949.

Pirenne, Henri. *Economic and Social History of Medieval Europe.* New York: Harcourt Brace Jovanovich, Harvest Book, 1937.

Ruhle, Otto. *Karl Marx: His Life and Work.* Eden and Ceder Paul (Trans.). New York: New Home Library, 1943.

Sabine, George H. *A History of Political Theory.* New York: Holt, Rinehart and Winston, 1961. See especially Chaps. XXX and XXXIII.

Sahlins, Marshall. "Political Power and the Economy in Primitive Society." In Gertrude E. Dole and Robert L. Carneiro (Eds.), *Essays in the Science of Culture.* New York: Crowell, 1960. Pp. 390–415.

Schaff, Adam. *Marxism and the Human Individual.* New York: McGraw-Hill, 1970.

Stern, Bernard J. *Historical Sociology.* New York: Citadel, 1959.

Tucker, Robert C., (Ed.). *The Marx–Engels Reader.* New York: Norton, 1971.

Willer, David, and George K. Zollschan. "Prolegomenon to a Theory of Revolutions." In George K. Zollschan and Walter Hirsch (Eds.), *Explorations in Social Change.* Boston: Houghton Mifflin, 1964. Pp. 125–151.

Wilson, Edmund. *To the Finland Station.* Garden City, N.Y.: Doubleday, 1953.

Zeitlin, Irving M. *Marxism: A Reexamination.* Princeton, N.J.: Van Nostrand, 1967.

FIVE

Max Weber

"I found Weber's argument that the bureaucratization of the modern world led to its depersonalization relevant to today. People in our society are identified not by their facial features or individual characteristics but by their social security numbers and collective duties to society. 'The performance of each individual worker is mathematically measured, each man becomes a little cog in the machine and aware of this, his preoccupation is whether he can become a bigger cog.' "

—STUDENT COMMENT

General Introduction

Among American sociologists, Max Weber (1864–1920) is one of the most often-quoted scholars of the period from 1800 to about 1930. His father was a lawyer, a Protestant, and prominent in politics. Weber studied law at the University of Berlin; later, at Heidelberg, he wrote his doctoral dissertation on trading companies of the Middle Ages. He was a professor of economics at Freiburg in 1894 and at Heidelberg in 1896. In spite of the fact that Weber lived a relatively short life and that his work was interrupted for many years by a severe mental breakdown, his writing was prolific.[1]

---

[1] Works taken from Weber's large *Wirtschaft und Gesellschaft* include *The Theory of Social and Economic Organization*, A. M. Henderson and Talcott Parsons (Trans.) and Talcott Parsons (Ed.) (New York: The Free Press, 1964); *Max Weber on Law in Economy and Society*, Max Rheinstein (Ed. and Annot.) and Edward Shils and Max Rheinstein (Trans.) (New York: Simon and Schuster, 1967); *From Max Weber: Essays in Sociology*, H. H. Gerth and C. Wright Mills (Trans. and Eds.) (New York: Oxford University

135

Germany in Weber's Time

Weber, like Herbert Spencer and Auguste Comte, was concerned with the conditions in his own country and reflected this concern in the direction he took in his scholarly works. Interested in promoting the unity and ascendant cultural leadership of Germany,[2] Weber turned his attention to the condition of her ruling class, especially the Junkers, who held large land estates in Eastern Germany. He participated in the execution of a large survey-study of the condition of farm labor throughout the nation, conducted by the Association for Social Policy, and analyzed much of the data that came in from Eastern Germany. Through this analysis Weber gained a greater appreciation of the economic *and* social forces contributing to the agricultural problem and the interplay of these forces—subjects that occupied his attention in such later writings as *The Protestant Ethic and the Spirit of Capitalism.*

Germany's main agricultural problem at this time was falling domestic grain prices as a result of foreign grain imports. The Junkers' response to this situation was to obtain protective tariffs and to shift to some new

---

Press, 1958); *The City*, Don Martindale and Gertrude Neuwirth (Trans. and Eds.) (New York: The Free Press, 1958); and *The Sociology of Religion*, Ephraim Fischoff (Trans.) (Boston: Beacon Press, 1963). *Wirtschaft und Gesellschaft* is now available in English: *Economy and Society*, Guenther Roth and Claus Wittich (Trans. and Eds.) 3 vols. Totowa, N.J.: Bedminster Press, 1968). Weber died before finishing this work.

Weber's *Gesammelte Aufsätze zur Religionssoziologie* (*Collected Studies in the Sociology of Religion*, which he completed during the war years) is the source for all of the following works: *The Protestant Ethic and the Spirit of Capitalism*, Talcott Parsons (Trans.) (New York: Charles Scribner's Sons, 1958), completed and published in about 1904 and republished in Weber's larger work on *Religionssoziologie; The Religion of China: Confucianism and Taoism*, H. H. Gerth (Trans.) (New York: The Free Press, 1951); *Ancient Judaism*, H. H. Gerth and Don Martindale (Trans.) (New York: The Free Press, 1952); and *The Religion of India: The Sociology of Hinduism and Buddhism*, H. H. Gerth and Don Martindale (Trans.) (New York: The Free Press, 1958).

From Weber's *Gesammelte Aufsätze zur Wissenschaftslehre* (on the sociology of knowledge) comes *The Methodology of the Social Sciences*, Edward Shils and Henry A. Finch (Trans. and Eds.) (New York: The Free Press, 1949). Several of the essays in this book were written between 1903 and 1905, but most cover the whole period between 1903 and 1917.

Finally, there is S. N. Eisenstadt (Ed.), *Max Weber on Charisma and Institution Building* (Chicago: University of Chicago Press, 1968), which brings together essays from seven different areas of Weber's work. This is only a sample from the many works that exist.

[2] The following discussion on German labor and the Junkers is based largely on Reinhard Bendix, *Max Weber* (Garden City, N.Y.: Doubleday, 1962), pp. 1–48. See also Julien Freund, *The Sociology of Max Weber* (New York: Vintage Books, 1969).

methods of cultivation, more profitable crops, and new labor-use practices.

Weber noticed that the traditional arrangement of the annual contract, which gave farm laborers some security, was coming under pressure from a number of sources: decreasing profits; changing technology in agriculture; the growth of feelings of individualism among laborers, which sensitized them to the servitude of patronage; and the availability of Slavic laborers, who were willing to work for less. Morally and politically, Weber disapproved of the Junkers' proposal to solve the agricultural labor problem by the national financing of internal colonization (the importation and settlement of foreign laborers into the area). Weber believed this policy to be economically unsound because he thought that the ascendancy of the middle-class bourgeoisie, with whom he sympathized, would better serve the nation, and their need for labor and free trade ran counter to interests of the Junkers.

Weber also condemned the practice of holding land in trust (a scheme that further bolstered the Junkers' position) or preventing its sale to new capitalists who might manage and produce from it more efficiently. He disliked the way the Junkers cloaked their pursuit of their own interests in the rhetoric of patriotism; they should base any real claims to leadership, he thought, on economic rationality and growth, not on their military feat of the past. Nevertheless, Weber did credit the Junkers for the political and military leadership they asserted in the unification of Germany, which greatly facilitated her urban and industrial growth.[3] But he also saw that, in so doing, they had in fact undermined their own position (this was only one of the many anomalies Weber came to recognize in his studies of both history and social organization). It was the bourgeoisie who benefitted from Germany's new growth. Weber urged them to develop a capitalistic motive and ethic independent of politics and to refrain from groveling for admission to aristocratic circles, a practice that he thought corrupted their business. As a result of his observations, Weber felt that, indeed, any service to the national interests formerly gained from the solidarity between farm laborer and paternalistic employer seemed a thing of the past.

Weber made a number of studies that demonstrated to him the operation of *extra*economic considerations in ostensibly economic activities.

---

[3] According to S. M. Miller, in England, as reflected in the Glorious Revolution and, later, the anti-corn law, and in France, as reflected in the revolutions of 1789 and 1830, the industrial, commercial, and urban-elite sectors of the population gained political power commensurate with their economic power, thereby *diminishing* the political power of the agricultural elites. In Germany, during its compressed economic development, "the Junkers retained considerable political power despite the rise of capitalists, and the marriage of this military–agricultural group to the advanced technology encouraged the imperialistic activities of Germany and promoted a bellicose spirit" (S. M. Miller, *Max Weber* [New York: Crowell, 1963], p. 5.)

(This may be regarded as a rectification or expansion of the Marxian analysis.) He discovered, for instance, that the laborer struggled for status and independence; that the aristocratic Junkers also had status needs; and that factors such as tradition and the recruitment of traders from similar status groups (in which breaches of economic good faith reflected badly on one's respectability) regulated the workings of the stock market.

Weber admired Bismarck's nationalist ambitions for the greatness of Germany, specifically in culture and intellect, but he criticized the autocratic rule that inhibited leadership in underlings and forsook the development of representation for the common healthy man while developing social benefits for the sick and the weak. Weber also viewed with suspicion the growing bureaucratization in political affairs, which socialists encouraged. Even while admitting the technical superiority of bureaucratic administration in industry, he urged that its social effects on the liberty of men be continually scrutinized.

By 1909, according to T. S. Simey,[4] Weber was at odds with the Association for Social Policy because he had expressed his conviction that it was not dealing with issues objectively, as was its professed purpose. Rather, he contended that the Association was discussing and proposing matters in a manner useful to the existing establishment, an establishment from which he was becoming further estranged on account of its tyranny toward the common man. It was a curious and unfortunate way of expressing his disagreement with his opponents in the Association and led to further pronouncements on matters of fact and value. Instead of sticking to the honest view, which he seemed actually to hold, that his opponents' values were untenable, he proceeded to argue that they were entirely outside the bounds of science in arguing for any values at all.

Finally, his desire to give practical assistance to the causes of the common man was thwarted. He was gloomily convinced that the progression of *rationalization* (the conscious deliberation of social relations and the institutionalization of large bureaucratic organizations based on technical efficiency), which already pervaded all areas of life in Western civilization, would spread to other parts of the world also. Rationalization, Weber believed, was separating man from the immediate goals of his actions in all areas of social life (not just in the economic area analyzed by Marx). It prevented man from taking into his own hands the affairs he wished to control, and it stifled innovativeness.

The most comprehensive account of Weber's life has been written by Arthur Mitzman.[5] Though it relies rather heavily on some interpreta-

---

[4] T. S. Simey, "Max Weber: Man of Affairs or Theoretical Sociologist?" *Sociological Review*, 14 (November 1966), 303–327.

[5] Arthur Mitzman, *The Iron Cage: An Historical Interpretation of Max Weber* (New York: Knopf, 1970).

tions that are accepted on the basis of some questionable psychoanalytic suppositions, it nevertheless brings to light some tensions in Weber's life that might have contributed to his severe mental depression between 1900 and 1903 and gives some clues as to why he selected some of his major topics of scholarship. We are told, first, that Weber experienced some conflict in dealing with the hedonistic, authoritarian—especially in the home—life style of his father and the ascetic and principled standards of his mother. His scholarly interest in the social basis of authority through legitimacy may have come in part from his resentment of his father, as well as from his reaction to the Junkers themselves. In addition to this problem, Weber had apparent difficulty reconciling the sympathy that is required, for example, when accepting the affection of close friends with the discipline that is necessary to the role of the detached, impartial scientist (see the discussion below). Weber's early analysis of ascetic Protestantism gave way later to a more sympathetic interest in Old Testament mysticism and charisma as he began to relax the strictures of self-denial (an influence of his Calvinist mother) that he had imposed upon himself. Indeed, he seemed to begin to enjoy himself in the company of friends during his later scholarship. Finally, he was torn between attraction to heroic leadership in the political arena, of which he was capable, and the more reclusive life of disciplined, time-consuming scholarship. He later (especially between 1918 and 1920) did get involved in politics, but, more importantly, these two warring spirits within him undoubtedly had something to do with his scholarly views on the relation between facts and values, which is discussed further below.

Weber was a tormented and dynamic person. In 1897, shortly after the death of his father, Weber suffered a nervous collapse, which, except for intermittent periods of intense energy, deterred his teaching and scholarship for eighteen years. He was a highly critical man, making peace with virtually no person or trend of his day. He was disenchanted with the times. He would neither languish for the return of a romantic historical past, as the conservative did, nor reach out to embrace the promise of a golden future, as some radicals were doing. Ambivalence and defensive pessimism were his lot. Yet he was enormously impressive to the many who came to hear him speak. His constant groping for the *honest* intellectual response to events of the day often provoked strong opposition in return. Right-wingers sometimes tried to disrupt his classroom when they disagreed with him. The intense thunderstorm that occurred as Weber died was perhaps aptly symbolic of the intensity that had always characterized his own internal life.

Weber's task was quite different from Marx's even though they both focused on some common problems, such as the development of capitalism. Marx set himself to a reconstruction of history, the central features of which were the self-realization of man through his labor, the evolving productive forces or modes of production, and ultimately the emergence of a higher collective welfare for society. Even as an outsider, Marx was in the thick of political affairs. His moral judgments enlivened and directed his intellectual work. His method was to trace the causal forces of the mode of production and show where capitalist society was going. Although he gave meticulous attention to the corroboration of facts, he dwelt very little on how to explain the individual and society in such a way as to make more scientifically tenable the causal analysis of the historical process in which the *individual actor* operates. Nor did Marx deal self-consciously with the role of the social scientist in political affairs. Weber, however, gave a considerable amount of his attention to both of these areas. Further, in considering the relation of values to social science investigation, he also dealt with an epistemological matter (that is, one relating to the theory of the grounds for knowledge) in which Marx claimed little interest.

Weber was more the "establishment" sociologist with secure academic appointments. He only reluctantly identified himself as a sociologist, however (because he seemed to want to rescue sociology from its careless use of group-level abstractions, which had little bearing on individual action), and Marx never used the term sociology. Nevertheless, both made important contributions to the discipline. We turn first to Weber's philosophy of social science.[6]

We can simplify Weber's view of the mode of explanation of the social sciences by understanding it as both a product of and a reaction to a sort of positivistic psychology, on the one hand, and a historiography animated by the spiritual forces of human will, on the other hand. Positivistic psychologists approached man *nomothetically*; that is, they sought to develop lawlike, universal generalizations about him. However, they dealt with man only as manifested in his overt, repetitive behaviors, as though he were an object that always reacts in the same way when acted on by outside forces. In contrast, historiographers in the idealistic tradition viewed man *idiographically*; they attempted in other words, by confining their analysis to particular times and places, to show the uniqueness of actions or historical eras and to disclose in these the operation of human (cultural) volition or meaning. Since historiographers shunned generalization accomplished through comparison of cases, they relied instead on

---

[6] Weber's discussion of many of the points below is found in *The Methodology of the Social Sciences*. W. G. Runciman's *A Critique of Max Weber's Philosophy of Social Science* (New York: Cambridge University Press, 1972) was quite helpful here. See also H. Stuart Hughes, *Consciousness and Society* (New York: Vintage Books, 1961); Raymond Aron, *German Sociology* (New York: Free Press, 1964); Theodore Abel, *The Foundation of Sociological Theory* (New York: Random House, 1970); and Talcott Parsons, *The Structure of Social Action* (New York: Free Press, 1949), P. III.

private, unsound speculations in their zealousness to prove their thesis. Nor were they adequately aware that they were even employing such conceptual tools in locating and defining their so-called observed facts.

Weber attempted to establish a sort of middle ground by drawing from the virtues of each approach: he could accept the generalizing method and apply it to volitional actors. At the same time, he maintained that since the subject matter of social science was distinct from that of physical science, he had to construct more flexible and sensitive concepts and modify the generalizing method for human cultural studies. Weber's cautiousness in applying the method of science to man and his attempt to avoid many of the various methodologies or philosophies of his day makes his philosophy of social science very difficult to understand.

In the process of coming to a formulation of sociology, Weber first considered what distinguished social from physical phenomena and what effect this supposed difference should have on the approach to and investigation of social science. Weber acknowledged that both physical and social scientists *select* the phenomena they study; both see the world in terms of problems that they deem worthy of investigation. Weber believed, however, that humans have a special relationship to the social realm because they more fully create it according to their values and that it is one in which reactions and changes are constantly occurring—there are *more* different ways of taking interest in the social realm. Consequently, those kinds of things and events that social scientists study *inherently* invite evaluation from many different points of view; what investigators find important for analysis will therefore vary according to the values that define importance in the first place. Thus, while in the physical realm, gravity, for instance, has largely the same constancy and significance wherever it is detected, a kiss or an act of apparent conflict is subject to many interpretations.

The other reference to values in Weber's philosophy of social science is his reference to value-neutrality. As Robert A. Nisbet states in Chapter I of this book, Weber was deeply committed to the survival of man in the modern world. Weber's goal, however, was to explain what *is* rather than what *ought to be* and to build verified knowledge that was as free as possible of the wishful thinking of the investigator. He recognized, as we have said, that the scientist is *not* neutral in what he selects for investigation, but Weber urged that, having begun the inquiry, the scientist maintain an honest pursuit of truth, adhering scrupulously to the best principles of investigation.

Besides having to resist internal temptations to distort truth, the investigator must also fend off external pressures. Weber condemned efforts by the state to press the social scientist into its service in order to produce the "truths" it needed to remain credible or hold power. We mentioned above Weber's rather abrupt departure from the Association after accusing some of its members of being partial to state interests. Science, he contended, cannot rightfully claim the role of deciding the correctness of ultimate values, which are matters for the human spirit to weigh. Facts do not dictate their own evaluation. Facts and values are *logically* independent, although values certainly can be rationally scrutinized and judged with the aid of relevant facts. Science should be value-neutral in that it must not be swayed by this "party line" or that but should be singularly interested in demonstrable truth. The scientist might have to buffer himself from the state or even his close friends if these constitute impediments to his objectivity.

Weber contended that "sociology [in the sense in which this highly ambiguous word is used here] is a science which attempts the interpretive understanding of social action in order thereby to arrive at a causal explanation of its course and effects."[7] "Social action," he continued, "may be oriented to the past, present, or expected future behavior of others."[8] Weber distinguished among behavior, action, and social action: behavior is not action unless an actor, a set of actors, or a culture in general has assigned some meaning to it, and action is not social unless it is oriented toward others. Humans do not react mechanically; they respond to one another meaningfully, on the basis of shared expectations of mutual intentions. The events of social action then hang together by meanings (mental connections), and sequences or configurations of human events usually can be understood with reference to such meanings. In Weber's human action framework, actions are to be understood by reference to subjective categories of the actor, the imputation of motives, and the larger context of the action.

Before going further, we should consider Weber's rather confusing position on two questions: Do laws operate in the social realm? If they do, of what type are they? As generally understood today, laws in science are generalizations that assert a nonaccidental connection between two or more types of events and therefore provide a basis for prediction.[9]

As W. G. Runciman rightfully points out, although Weber originally held that the most general laws are the least useful in practice, he later admitted that sociology as a generalizing science is capable of contributing to an understanding of causality in history.[10] Weber may have had several reasons for shying away from references to laws. Previous sociologists and historiographers had indulged in enough idle speculation about "laws"

[7] Max Weber, *Social and Economic Organization*, p. 88.

[8] Ibid., p. 112.

[9] See Nelson Goodman, *Fact, Fiction, & Forecast* (Cambridge, Mass.: Harvard University Press, 1955).

[10] From Weber's *Economy and Society*, as cited in Runciman, *Max Weber's Philosophy of Social Science*, p. 18.

of the universe or "laws" of history that they assumed to be immanent, that is, automatically operating within the life process and directing it toward some terminus. This was teleology that science could do without. Also, Weber opposed narrow interpretations of social phenomena and consequently may have thought of laws as being exclusively mechanistic, implying a certitude that is not present in social dynamics or suggesting a view that abrogates the operation of mental events. He may have believed, too, that certain types of law function, but only on the individual level. Moreover, he seems to have held that a system of laws requires one to reduce social reality to a series of generalizations. In other words, he feared that one might mistake the generalizations for the events themselves or be confined by them to a *one*-sided view of the phenomena. Last, he may have felt that human events involve too much chance and too many antecedent factors to be conformable to lawlike generalizations, although he later recognized, as mentioned above, that maxims about behavior could help the investigator identify possible causes of a given action. In short, Weber claimed that it is simply not the main aim of social historical analysis to produce laws. Regardless of the reasons for his original opposition, however, once Weber had chosen to view social phenomena in a cause-and-effect manner, he was committed to accepting the existence of some kind of lawfulness since a law is simply an abstract formulation of the general or recurrent features of this cause-and-effect process. Furthermore, he believed that freedom of action involves the ability to bring about one's goals and realized that this can occur *only* in a predictable social universe.

According to Weber, the overall method in the social and physical sciences is the same; both seek the operations of causes and effect and employ the best canons of validation. Unlike the physical scientist, however, the social scientist can participate in the events of the world he investigates. An acting human being himself, he deals with the actions of other significating human beings singly or in groups, concretely or in the abstract terms of a constructed actor representing a given group, age, or historical period. And since social events are potentially more complex and changeable, it is not surprising that Weber suggested more than one way of comprehending human conduct.

Weber perceived a certain kind of conduct as rule-oriented behavior. For example, a priest performs rule-oriented behavior when he conducts mass by gesturing and speaking in a characteristic manner; we understand *what* he is doing because we know the rules for the situation. No laws are purportedly involved in this identification. The rules only direct the behavior, however; they cannot explain it. The priest is not conducting mass *because* he is gesturing and uttering words. We must still explain *why* the person who is said to be oriented to a rule performs the necessary behavior.

Weber viewed another type of conduct as motivated behavior. "A motive," he stated "is a complex of subjective meaning which seems to the actor himself or to the observer taking the actor's point of view an adequate ground for the conduct in question."[11] Again, to identify meaningful behavior as motivated is not to explain it; it must be used in explaining some other action on the basis of motive. In identifying the meaning of words or thoughts and in reconstructing the choices others may have confronted in taking courses of action *by analogy with our own experience*, we are using *verstehen*. That is, we interpret what is happening by assessing what meanings and motives might be present in the actions of other individuals in given situations and by comparing these with actions *with which we are familiar* or in which we ourselves may have participated.

Again, we understand that someone who swings an axe is chopping wood and that someone who adds numbers is balancing a ledger because we understand the rules for these actions. Our understanding of what a person is doing derives from the meaning we attach to his action. However, we must not only know what an individual is doing, but why he is doing it. The woodchopper may, Weber noted, be working off a rage (under the influence of an emotional motive) or he may simply wish to earn some money (under the influence of a rational motive).

One can adequately understand the operation of a motive directly at the level of meaning *if* the agent to whom it is imputed acts in a manner consistent with it. One can also attempt to explain the action causally by demonstrating that the motive as well as *other* factors *actually had an effect* on it. Weber's concern with this distinction between direct understanding and causal explanation represents virtually the hallmark of his work. He believed that the hypothetical constructions of action are developed in the *mind* of the investigator but that action occurs in the actual *world*, with all its complex features and many chains of causation. It is therefore important for the scientist both to examine his "mind pictures" carefully in their selections from the world and to use his mind for the understanding of the world itself. Sometimes he must visualize in his own mind some of the different chains of causation possible, since not all of them are represented in the empirical world, and must think them through in trying to understand why the action may have taken the course it did. These hypotheses must then be checked against *what took place*. One would do this in analyzing the causes of the Peloponnesian War, for example.

Weber's approach to concept formation was closely linked to his views on how understanding of human actions is attained and what the relationship between sociology and history is. Characteristic of the con-

---

[11] Weber, *Social and Economic Organization*, pp. 98–99.

cepts he fashioned for sociology were tentativeness, sensitivity, and many-sidedness. Tentativeness is well exhibited in his definition of a social relationship: a social relationship involves action oriented toward another and "consists entirely and exclusively in the existence of a *probability* [our emphasis] that there will be, in some meaningfully understandable sense, a course of social action."[12] And "[a] 'state' . . . ceases to exist in a sociologically relevant sense whenever there is no longer a probability that certain kinds of meaningfully oriented social action will take place."[13] In other words the existence of any social state of affairs is problematic; a meaning consistent with the expectations of the parties must be present for interaction to take place and for any activity that a state or any other body engages in to occur. Concepts must be sensitive, for social science proceeds by the "perpetual reconstruction of those concepts through which we seek to comprehend reality."[14] We have already mentioned Weber's view that if sociology is to deal with meaningful action, it must recognize change, the creation of new social realities through new meanings. This type of reality is difficult to grasp and entails much conceptual reformulation and the avoidance of conceptual closure. Finally, since concepts provide a way of looking and since the social world involves a multitude of meanings, Weber prescribed the use of opposing or complementing conceptual schemes, each of which presents a certain one-sided view of the social reality; by putting them together, one can then attain a many-sided perspective. Bendix discusses this technique in Selection 5.2.

Weber's formulation of what he called the *ideal* (constructed) *type*[15] is a little more difficult to understand.[16] He considered as ideal types all our concepts because in formulating them we make selections from the world and impose limitations on our way of seeing it; moreover, we can construct word pictures that *accentuate* certain elements to the point of deliberately making them unreal and can allow these elements to *interrelate logically* or form combinations that might never occur in the empirical world. Of course, we must always remember simply that noumena (concepts of the mind) are not phenomena; the type reminds us that the relationships it depicts are not the same as those that may be found in the empirical world. Weber was conscious of these caveats himself when he called his word pictures of "the Protestant Ethic," "the Western city," and "modern capitalism" ideal types; he felt that they constituted mental

---

[12] Ibid., p. 118.

[13] Ibid.

[14] Weber, *Methodology of the Social Sciences*, p. 105.

[15] Ibid., pp. 89–112.

[16] See Don Martindale, "Sociological Theory and the Ideal Type," in Llewellyn Gross (Ed.), *Symposium on Sociological Theory* (Evanston, Ill.: Harper & Row, 1959), pp. 57–91, for a comprehensive treatment.

selections of phenomena (from an explicit value position), assumed relations among their various presumed causes, and laid bare their distinctive (rather than, e.g., their common) features.

His *general* ideal types were the different empirical cases he constructed for the purpose of comparison with the type, in order to find out how closely they approximate it, and to develop generalizations about the patterns he found. These types can again open the interplay between sociology and history by allowing knowledge of the general case (the subject of sociological analysis) to illuminate the operations of the concrete case (the subject of historical analysis). Such knowledge can aid especially in imputing meaning more reliably to the concrete case. Ideal types are the general analytic tools social history had been lacking.

Special attention has been given to Weber's classifications of (1) types of social action, (2) types of authority, and (3) bureaucracy as an ideal type. These are, as Raymond Aron[17] suggests, auxiliary to Weber's basically historical analysis of social process with respect to its focus on the human actor.

1. Weber conceived of social action in terms of means and ends and defined four types: *zweckrational, wertrational, affektual,* and *traditional.*[18] *Zweckrational* action involves the deliberate assessment of ends (what one wants to do) and the choice of the most efficient means for accomplishing them. Such action is most rational because it is based on standards not determined by feelings or tradition. While *wertrational* action also entails a rational assessment of the most efficacious means, it simply accepts the end as given, without scrutiny. The end has sufficient worth in and of itself to compel action in pursuit of it. In *affektual* action, the internal state of the individual—his emotions and feelings—dictates the means of achieving the ends (e.g., a man chops wood in order to work off a rage). Finally, *traditional* action altogether lacks any conscious examination of means and ends according to rational standards.

2. Weber defined *power* as the "probability that one actor within a social relationship will be in a position to carry out his own will despite resistance regardless of the basis on which this probability rests."[19] Further on in the same text he terms it "the probability that a *command* [Weber's emphasis] will be obeyed."[20] *Legitimacy*, the quality that power has when individuals voluntarily submit themselves to a command, regardless of their motives, is what transforms power into *authority*. Weber distinguished three pure types of legitimate (imperative) authority: legal,

[17] *German Sociology*, p. 99.
[18] Weber, *Social and Economic Organization*, pp. 115–118.
[19] Ibid., p. 152.
[20] Ibid., p. 153.

traditional, and charismatic.[21] What is important in each is the nature of the belief that underlies the individual's submission to the command. *Legal authority* rests on rational grounds. The individual obeys because he believes that the command falls within the proper sphere of responsibility of the commander, who attained his position in accordance with agreed-upon rules. *Traditional authority* is based on the belief that he who commands does so in the name of traditions that are worthy of obedience. *Charismatic authority* relies on the subjects' perception of an exceptional quality within the personality of the commander, which in itself compels obedience. Weber also considered the use of force in bringing about compliance.

A community is a collectivity to which individuals conform out of a feeling of solidarity with the whole, whereas a society is a collectivity to which they conform out of considerations of rationality and self-interest. Estates are differentiated, rigidly separated groupings within society that are based on economic distinctions, but they become interdependent as the result of arrangements that their members do not question. The cooperation of classes is more antagonistic, however, because of their explicit recognition of scarcity, which induces competition, and the tenuousness of the contract that is necessary to hold classes together.[22]

3. Weber's characterization of bureaucracy parallels that of legal authority. Bureaucracy entails some distinctive characteristics of social organization not fully found anywhere except in Western civilization—and only *approximated* even there if bureaucracy is conceived of as an ideal type.[23] A bureaucracy is the embodiment of the rationality principle in social relations; that is, it employs rational rather than traditional criteria in fixing both the goals of the organization and the means to carry them out. Accordingly, offices are charged with specific responsibilities and linked by a chain of command, a regularized procedure is instituted for conducting the affairs of each office and recruiting individuals to it on the basis of merit, and surveillance systems are constantly used to ascertain whether or not the constructed organization produces the desired goals efficiently. Bureaucracies serve large numbers of people or produce large amounts of their specialized product, and, as they become larger, more centralization of authority and higher-order decision making tends to occur.

Finally, Weber asserted his abiding concern for the liberty of the individual in the face of institutions, which through increasing rationalization and hardening reduce the individual's spontaneity and the realm in which he expresses his own thoughts and will. "One of the most important

---

21 Ibid., pp. 328–363.

22 Gerth and Mills, *From Max Weber*, p. 183.

23 For a discussion of bureaucracy, *ibid.*, pp. 196–198.

aspects of the process of 'rationalization' of action," said Weber, "is the substitution for the unthinking acceptance of ancient custom, of deliberate adaptation to situations in terms of self-interest."[24] He could see the need for rationalization in a few areas where it was legitimate, but he observed that it was spreading everywhere in modern man's life. The interposition-ing of a host of rational rules of procedure between a man's action and the end it is intended to accomplish separates soldiers from the means of violence, scientists from the means of inquiry, civil servants from the means of administration—*as well as* laborers from the means of produc-tion, as Marx had indicated. Once rational procedures for doing some-thing have been set up, we follow them unthinkingly.

"Man is thus prepared for his absorption into the clattering process of bureaucratic machinery.[25] Weber's fear of rationalization stems largely from the separation he thought existed between knowledge and will, and, incidentally, from his disenchantment with the enlarging bureaucratic ma-chinery of the Bismarckian state and the men, like his father, who made peace with it. Rationality represented the march of knowledge; charisma represented the force of will and the human spirit. Only charismatic up-risings in history can put the individual back into direct contact with his institutions and change them. The charismatic leader might restore some awe, charm, and spirit to man's affairs after rationality had reduced them to a calculated set of techniques.[26] But Weber's hopes were not very high.

In summary we may say that Weber developed a historical, but scientifically analytical, approach to social process with reference to the human actor. (His brilliant social analysis of history is discussed in Selec-tion 5.1.) His focus on the self-conscious actor, whose response to the ac-tion of others is based on the meanings that he can ascribe to them sug-gested several ways of attaining an understanding of human action. Weber's social action typology, founded on an understanding of means and ends, is a notable contribution to sociology. While historical analysis focused on the complexes of meaning in action, sociological analysis examined these more fully by determining the various factors that shape and influ-ence the social actions in which meaning resides. Weber believed that the inevitable, even minimal, involvement of the social scientist in human affairs produced both opportunities and problems in explanation not en-countered by the physical scientist. In this connection, Weber was con-

---

24 Weber, *Social and Economic Organization*, p. 123.

25 Gerth and Mills, *From Max Weber*, p. 49.

26 As discussed by Ann Swidler, rationality has several distinct meanings in Weber's work and thought. See "The Concept of Rationality in the Work of Max Weber," *Sociological Inquiry*, 43 (Spring 1973), 35–42. Adversely, rationality was that process by which the "higher" values of the Enlighten-ment were being choked out by the emphasis being given to social and material technology in modern society.

stantly interested in the interplay between our mental conceptions of the happenings of the social world and the actual processes that occur there. He was deft at constructing conceptual interplays (dualities) that bring to light the anomalies of social change, as when the Junkers undermined their own status position, when the person driven by the Protestant ethic actually secularizes his life, or when both the elements of formality and informality adhere in a precarious balance in a set of social relations (see Selection 5.2).

Introduction to Selections 5.1 and 5.2

Weber mastered an enormous amount of historical data. He also had a deep appreciation for the requirements that the lawyer needed to meet in arguing cases in a court of law; the lawyer had to have well-defined terms and evidence to support the process of events that he claims took place. These two areas of expertise blend into the unique Weberian methodology that is illuminated in the following two articles. Stanislav Andreski summarizes the thesis that emerged from Weber's study of the link between the "worldly ascetic" ethic of Protestantism and the rapid growth of capitalism in the West and shows how Weber explored the thesis in his comparative historical studies of religion and economic life in non-Western countries. It stands as a truly great work of scholarship to this day in spite of some flaws. Reinhard Bendix, another well-versed analyst of Weber's works, discusses the way Weber's philosophy of concept formation and explanation worked its way into his general analysis of sociohistorical process. Weber created open-ended conceptual schemes that provide many different and fruitful starting points for the examination of the dynamic interplay of process in social reality.

Andreski opens his article with some observations on the tendency to stereotype Weber as the developer of a unique "interpretive" sociology based on empathy. This is not the case, as we have already noted in our discussion above. Andreski briefly discusses three other contributions to method: the anchoring of sociological concepts in the action of individuals, the paradigm of ethical neutrality, and the formulation of the ideal type. It is clear, however, from the space he gives it, that Andreski takes Weber's study of the relations between religion and economic activity in a society as one of Weber's outstanding achievements. Weber surpassed the erudition of other historians in that he not only compared social histories, but also compared the *functioning* of a particular institution such as religion over time in different societies. This is structural history framed in a way useful for sociology.

Worldly asceticism as embodied in Calvinism encouraged thrift, the accumulation of possessions as a sign of grace but the injunction against their use as luxuries, and the prescription of diligent, sober work as the only legitimate road to riches.[27] In support of Weber's thesis that these virtues of Calvinism augmented the growth of capitalism (though they did not constitute the only spur to its development) Andreski cites two arguments: one from harmony and one from co-variation. The argument from harmony is essentially that this ethic instilled in believers those characteristics favorable to capitalistic growth. The weakest part of this explanation, according to Andreski, is Weber's claim that the belief in predestination results in a motivation to expand economic enterprise for God's glory; one would expect, rather, the opposite—a *resignation* to things as they are. Andreski believes that Calvinists generally disregarded this element of Protestantism.

The co-variation argument, which is "proved" by comparative historical analysis, is that Protestants expanded economic enterprise to a farther extent *when they had the chance* than Catholics did when afforded similar opportunities. Weber was considering as enterprises small firms started by people who had little means to begin with. This thesis holds in countries where Protestants were in the minority, in the majority, or evenly balanced with Catholics and where Protestants emerged early or late as a group. Even Karl Kautsky's argument for reducing Calvinism to an irrelevant epiphenomenon cannot be fully accepted because, although the worldly ascetic ethic caught on best with people who as artisans and small businessmen were *shielded* in the city from feudal lords, when the ethic caught on where such threats were absent (e.g., among Scotsmen) the rapid accumulation and productive investment of capital still occurred.

Since Weber never stated his thesis in extreme form—that Calvinist religious virtues were *the* cause of rational capitalism—it is therefore not weakened by showing that the ethic may have been operating only *indirectly* in economic activity or that *other factors* also had an important effect. For example, a reasonable degree of political stability had to be present if there was to be any economic growth in a country at all; the Reformation helped put capital into circulation and make the use of interest respectable for the expansion of one's own economic enterprise; and the possession of the *civic* virtues of the Calvinists facilitated their economic productivity.

Andreski next considers Weber's examination of religious ethics in

---

[27] Weber showed that until the middle of the eighteenth century, although the economic firm was capitalistic in nature, the spirit animating the entrepreneur, the relationships between employer and employee and between seller and customer, and the pursuit of profit were defined and regulated by *traditional* (i.e., more nonrational) norms. Rational capitalism therefore represented a sharp break from the past in economic organization, as it confined economic activity within the strictures of rationalized enterprises that have an exact calculation of costs and profits, in the separation of the enterprise from the home, and so on. Above all Calvinism gave work and the making and saving of money a positive religious significance.

non-Western societies. Judaism could have had the same effect as the Calvinist ethic but—and this is what Weber neglected to note—it did not because Jews always remained in the minority and separated from specific outlets for their entrepreneurship in society. Only where Jews were not persecuted, and consequently did not feel compelled to show favoritism to one another and behave unethically toward gentiles, did they conduct expansionary business according to the same rational-universalistic principles that the Calvinists employed. Regarding Confucianism, Andreski believes Weber was somewhat mistaken. Nothing that the Confucian ethic said about economic affairs prohibited capitalist growth; it was practical and rational in outlook. That the real impediment was the fetters imposed on business by the bureaucratic state is shown by the business success of Chinese who emigrated to countries where conditions were more hospitable. Finally, in the case of Hinduism, Andreski accepts Weber's claim that capitalistic enterprise failed to develop because of a religiously prescribed abhorrence of worldly involvement and a disdain for the idea of the mastery of nature inherent in productivity.

Bendix's article is complicated because it undertakes to summarize the Weberian perspective that concerns the labyrinth of his conceptual distinctions, the elusive interplay between concepts and social process, and the many schools of thought that Weber drew strength from, challenged, or went beyond. The article harks back to Weber's belief that concrete social reality embodies a great richness of detail; that concept formation involves tentativeness, sensitivity, and many-sidedness; and that social forms represent at any one time only an incomplete, alternative embodiment of a meaning.

Bendix believes that Weber saw few, if any, straightforward developments in history. Even Weber's observation of the loss of awe, magic, and charm accompanying rationalization in the Occidental world was meant to aid in the analysis of problematical, shifting tendencies rather than to imply an inexorable, unilineal development. The course of development is never fixed. Process is many-faceted; it has a great number of different possible lines of development at different junctures.

The *consequences* of increased rationality can vary greatly, and they are often unintended. Fostered by the ancient Rabbinate, for example, the early growth of rationality was responsible for the creation of great values among the Jews, but these values later became encapsulated in perfunctory (irrational) rituals. Elsewhere, in Calvinism, rationality set the believer to the singular, systematic, and diligent pursuit of economic expansion. At the same time, however, it obfuscated comprehension of the Divine will ("don't contemplate the Divine plan; just get to work") and engendered an irrational fear of the loss of salvation. According to Bendix, Weber saw that as the Calvinist was driven by rationality in one area, he became a cripple in others; he was incapable of assessing his natural feelings, distrusted himself, and was insensitive. The theme of this part of Weber's work—the diversity of the forms, directions and consequences of rationality—contrasts sharply with the singlemindedness of the Marxian economic view.

The second strategy that Weber developed was the visualization of dual, *apparently* opposing tendencies within a single category. Bendix gives as an example Weber's formulation of patrimonial (traditional, nonrational) bureaucracy (antitraditional, rational); another is his *conceptual* separation of material and ideal forces in his view of the development of classes (unified by common types of goods) and estates (unified by common ideas and styles of living), society and the state. But Weber anticipated the *empirical* fusion of material and ideal interests in all of these cases. In actuality, these concepts may embody the different tensions and overlaps of material and ideal principles. Thus, Weber thought, while we may fashion our concepts ideally, that is, as images existing only within our own minds and simulating what we presume to be the indefiniteness and opposing and limiting forces of the social world, we must use them materially; we must, in other words, apply them to that world for heuristic purposes, to discover its changes, paradoxes, and particularities.

Finally, Bendix shows how Weber's versatility with concepts allows us to see the dynamic instability of social relations and groups. Weber formulated different types of legitimate authority, for instance, but these were not to be taken as depictions of social realities resting exclusively on a singular principle. Again, their precariousness is a product of the interplay between ideas and social machinery or forms. While the charismatic leader may be able to extract loyalty from his followers by means of the idea that he has a special endowment not found in ordinary men, the validity of that claim depends on his occasionally proving it through his deeds, for all his followers to see. Legal authority asserts legitimacy by reference to its ability to codify procedures in accordance with reason, but law-givers cannot ignore the larger corpus of customs, sentiments, and purposes of those whose compliance with the law they expect; against these sanctions even the law cannot move too rapidly, and within their boundaries it, too, must operate. Finally, the traditional leader may claim validity for his actions on the basis of tradition. However, tradition allows latitude and the tradition is also that the will of the ruler is unquestioned. How far the ruler may go with this latitude is the built-in limitation of traditional authority.

5.1

Method and Substantive Theory in Max Weber

STANISLAV ANDRESKI

Philosophical Foundations

The way in which most textbooks on the history of sociology classify Max Weber provides a good example of how people tend to affix labels by seizing on trifles: the pigeon hole assigned to him bears the label 'understanding sociology'—'verstehende soziologie.' If we take the word understanding at its usual connotation, we arrive at the conclusion that Max Weber had a monopoly on understanding society. This seems to be a slight exaggeration, although many sociological publications (including those which invoke Weber's name in vain) could very well be classified as 'non-understanding sociology.' Weber's distinction (not very clearly formulated) between 'understanding' and 'explaining' refers to something that has been known to philosophers for a very long time: namely, that we interpret actions of other human beings by attributing to them the feelings and thoughts which we should have if we carried out such actions. As Fichte showed, the validity of this procedure can never be proved; but neither can it be disproved, and nobody can utter its denial without contradicting himself, for the mere intent to communicate presupposes it. This analogy from subjective experience is not nowadays used in interpreting the behaviour of objects other than the higher animals. Its continuous application does distinguish the study of man and society from other branches of learning, but it in no way distinguishes the thought of Max Weber. In fact, dustmen, historians, detectives, pimps, philosophers all have to rely on their subjective experiences in order to be able to explain and predict the actions of others. Even the most astringent behaviourists, who avoid the humans and concentrate on rats, speak of organisms seeking and escaping.

Weber, naturally, never claimed that he invented the procedure of 'verstehen,' or that it was in any way peculiar to his way of thinking. It was the commentators who committed this folly. Moreover, when dealing with definite sociological problems as distinguished from the discussion of the method of sociology—Weber (as far as I can recall) never refers to the distinction in question. In *Wirtschaft and Gesellschaft* there are only a few phrases on this matter. Naturally, he devotes more space to it in his methodological writings, but I do not think that there is anything in that discussion which has not been said better and earlier by some philosopher. I must confess that in spite of my great admiration for Weber, I find his formulations of philosophical problems to be rather mediocre: he laboured under the baneful influence of the main current of German philosophy, with its habits of ponderous and elusive verbosity. (This was not so when it came to inductive theorizing, based on concrete data.) Notwithstanding this weakness, some of his thoughts on the methodology are of fundamental importance.

Three ideas constitute the essence of Weber's contribution to the methodology of the social sciences: firstly, the paradigm of reducibility of sociological concepts to actions of individuals; secondly, the paradigm of ethical neutrality; thirdly, the concept of the ideal type. The paradigm of reducibility amounts to a prophylactic rule. The practice of explaining the meaning of words denoting social conditions and positions in terms of the actions of individuals is as old as analytical thought. If we look up a dictionary for the meaning of 'unemployment,' we find it defined as 'a condition when large numbers of workers have no jobs.' 'Ruler' is given as 'one who rules,' and so on. Yet, abstract terms, which refer to phenomena which cannot be directly observed in their totality, tend to be bandied about without the least concern for their meaning. Millions of people (including many professional sociologists) talk about 'socialism,' 'democracy,' 'imperialism,' 'nationalization,' 'social integration' and what not, without ever stopping to consider what these words mean in terms of concrete actions of real persons. Formulating his paradigm, Weber simply erected into a methodological canon what always was the practice of all sound thinkers; but it was an important step forward because it makes a great difference whether a procedure is intuitive or reasoned out, and there is great merit in having said something that ought to have been obvious but was not, and still is not to most people. A further merit of Weber was that he stuck to methodology, and steered clear of the futile ontological problem, to which many of his contemporaries devoted their energies, which side-tracked even Durkheim, and which to this day haunts the precincts of some methodological seminars, namely the question of whether it is the society or the individuals that really exist. I cannot recall any statements of Weber on this point, but I feel sure by inference that he took it for granted that the parts existed just as 'really' as the wholes. Weber, however, was not unique in this respect, for Auguste Comte and Herbert Spencer had perfectly clear ideas on this matter, and the reification of social processes by the Durkheimians was a retrograde step.

The requirement of 'wertfreiheit'—which has been translated as value-freedom or ethical neutrality, but which I propose to call the paradigm of non-valuation—has often been misunderstood. Some people interpreted it as enjoining upon the sociologist an olympian indifference to the ills of mankind. Even apart from anything that Weber wrote, his passionate advocacy of various causes shows that this was not what he had in mind. His paradigm of non-hortation can best be regarded as a methodological and semantic rule for classifying propositions, in accordance with which we include in sociology only nonvaluative propositions. Naturally, in view of the emotional loading of all the words which describe human relations, the strict adherence to this ideal would silence us for ever. But this is no argument against trying to approach it, because the same is true of ideals such as logical consistency or clarity, which are universally upheld, though only intermittently attained. The validity of a methodological precept is not a matter of truth, but of heuristic utility, and by definition a precept cannot be 'wertfrei.' We must, then, examine the claim of this paradigm on the assumption that knowledge of social phenomena is valuable.

The first argument in its favour is that, when dealing with matters which arouse our emotions, we must discipline our reasoning, so as to avoid wishful or 'hate inspired' thinking. The adherence to the canon of non-valuation—i.e. careful separation of judgments of value from judgments of fact—is useful for this purpose. Secondly, the paradigm in question can be recommended on the grounds of semantic expediency. People differ considerably in their valuations, and it is often difficult to infer from the words of praise or denigration what features the objects exhibit, other than the capacity to please or displease the utterer. This difficulty might be obviated if all publications carried as preamble a full exposition of the author's values, but, plainly, the acceptance of the paradigm of non-valuation provides a far more economical solution. The third reason for recommending this paradigm is that by excluding numerous controversial issues, it enables people who disagree on many values, but share the wish to advance the knowledge of social phenomena, to collaborate in the furtherance of this end. In short, non-valuation in analysing social phenomena commends itself for the sake of objectivity. Objectivity, incidentally, can be defined as the freedom of reasoning from the influence of the desires, other than the desire to know the truth. Only in this sense can objectivity be approached, if not attained, for obviously, no reasoning can be independent of the concepts with which it operates, or of the knowledge on the basis of which it proceeds. Arguments for or against the admission of any given proposition into the body of accepted sociological knowledge cannot, of course, be free from judgments of value: they presuppose positive valuation of truth, consistency and of other ideals of scientific thought. They belong, however, not to sociology itself but to its meta-language,* to use the expression current among contemporary philosophers.

Ideal Types

The concept of ideal type is rather difficult. In the first place, it might be said that to talk about an ideal type is like talking about wet water, for any type, being an abstraction, is ideal and not real in the sense that a given material object is real: there exists this horse and that, but not a

---

* Broadly interpreted, metalanguage consists of statements about the inquiry or about the way the inquiry will proceed, not statements about the data or phenomena that are the subject of the inquiry.—Ed.

horse in general. The difference between an ideal type and a type pure and simple lies not in the abstractness of connotation but in the definiteness of denotation: whereas the types established by biological systematics have referents which fall under them, and nowhere else, this is not the case with ideal types. No horse in general ever lived, but there are many horses which satisfy perfectly the specifications of 'horsiness,' whilst nothing like a perfectly rational organization has ever been observed. The idea behind the concept of ideal type is that social phenomena, in virtue of their manifold and fluid nature, can be analysed solely in terms of the extreme forms of their characteristics, which can never be observed in their purity. This idea is perfectly sound but was presented in a manner somewhat lacking in clarity. It might be even argued that Pareto's treatment of the problem of conceptualization in sociology was less open to criticism. Pareto pointed out that all concepts of physical sciences are idealizations: that no movement without resistance of the medium has ever been observed (but only surmised in the case of celestial bodies), that nothing perfectly straight has ever been found, that vectorial analysis assumes movements which never take place, and that social sciences must proceed likewise. As far as social sciences are concerned, the most useful idealizations can be found in the most mature of them, which is not surprising: the concepts of economic theory, such as perfect competition or static equilibrium, provide the best examples of ideal types. On the other hand, there is nothing very 'ideal' about Weber's own typologies. When he talks about bureaucracy or feudalism or capitalism, he moves on the level of abstraction which is not very far removed from observable reality. Moreover, these concepts are taken at their current meaning. Altogether, there is nothing methodologically new in Weber's handling of typologies: he is doing exactly the same as did all the other good thinkers, beginning with Aristotle. The originality lay not in methodological novelty, but in substantive implications of the features, which on several occasions he singled out for consideration. For example his distinction between producing and consuming towns—'Produzentenstadt' and 'Konsumentenstadt'—is of fundamental importance to the problem of the conditions which permitted the rise of capitalism, but there is nothing logically distinctive about these concepts. The master's touch reveals itself in the way he uses them as the tools of analysis. On some occasions his typologies are less illuminating, or even useless: this is the case, I think, with his classification of the forms of rationality, as well as with that of the types of action. On these points common sense notions seem to be better.

Comparative Method

What I have said so far may have sounded almost as a denigration. This is far from being my intention. I regard Max Weber's contribution as the most monumental there has been to sociology, but I feel that the relatively less valuable parts of it have attracted the greater share of attention. To say that other parts of his works are more impressive is not to claim that the methodological writings are without importance. On the contrary, I am convinced that merely for formulating the methodological ideas discussed above Weber merits a place in the history of sociology. His supremacy, however, is due to his unsurpassed ability for making or suggesting inductive generalizations. This kind of work requires, in addition to a gift for theorizing, a profound knowledge of a wide range of factual data; and in this respect Weber was unrivalled. Nobody who glances through any of his major works can fail to be impressed by the astounding array of detailed information. True, the same can be said about writers like Frazer, Ratzel, Westermarck, Spengler and Toynbee, but there is a great difference between them and Weber. In the first place, they had nothing useful to say in the way of theoretical generalization. Frazer and Westermarck were interested in establishing a sequence of evolutionary stages, and Ratzel in showing the influence of geographical environment. Actually their works constitute useful encyclopaedias of customs, beliefs and institutions. Toynbee has a theory but it is vague, tautological and unverifiable; it could be propounded only by somebody unacquainted with the work of generations of thinkers who devoted their lives to the study of society. The *Study of History* has considerable value, but only as a source-book of recondite pieces of information. Whilst Frazer and Westermarck catalogued customs, and Spengler and Toynbee filled their books with spurious analogies between superficial features of mostly fictitious entities, Weber compared social structures and their functioning, noting differences as carefully as resemblances, and trying to relate isolated features to their structural contexts. When information on the structure of the society in which he was interested was lacking, he made truly herculean efforts to extract it from the sources. Each volume of his *Religionssoziologie* would merit praise even if it were the single product of life-long work. In spite of many serious errors, the parts devoted to China and India still stand unrivalled as 'holistic' (or, if you like, functionalist) analyses of these societies, revealing their inner springs, and showing the mutual dependence of culture and society. His original insights into the functioning of these societies are too numerous to be discussed here in detail, so one example must suffice: Weber was first to raise the problem of the distinctive features of the Chinese towns, and of how these were related to the structure of the state and of the economy. After fifty years there is still nothing better of this kind. Etienne Balazs—the sinologist who has done more than anybody else to fill this gap—recognizes Weber as the source of his inspiration. To appreciate the magnitude of Weber's achievement, it must be remembered that when he prepared his *Religionssoziologie* next to nothing was known about the social and economic history of China. He extracted his information on the structure of the Chinese society and its development from translated dynastic chronicles, reports of travellers, and the pages of the *Peking Gazette.* The amount of effort and perspicacity necessary for this task must have been prodigious. The same is true of his treatment of India. In the case of Ancient Israel his task was somewhat lighter because the subject has been better studied; and so the factual mistakes appear to be fewer. The history of the economic and political institutions of the ancient Mediterranean had been studied intensively even before Weber was born, and his contemporary Eduard Meyer attempted a synthesis in a remarkable essay on 'Economic Development in Antiquity.' During the sixty years since the appearance of *Agraverhaeltnisse in Altertum*, many excellent works appeared in this field, the most comprehensive being those of Roztovzeff and Heichelheim. Nevertheless Weber's sociological history, concealed under the modest title, remains unique. For it is neither an economic history, nor a social history (as it is commonly understood), nor a political nor a military, but a truly structural history, which shows how the economic changes influenced religion, how the innovations in tactics brought about the transformations of social stratification, how the distribution of political power impeded the growth of capitalism and so on. All the time he tries to trace dynamic relations between various aspects of social life. His treatment of historical data is just as much functionalist as were Malinowski's analyses of the Trobriand society; and in its light, the dispute between the functionalist and the historical schools of anthropology, which raged in the twenties and thirties, appears puerile.

Max Weber was a great historian, but, at least in his later years, he studied history mainly in order to make comparisons. His case studies are strewn with references to other situations, and with generalizations or hints at possible generalizations. When writing about the prophets of Ancient Israel, he presents a theory about relations between peasants and town traders and usurers, about the destruction of tribal solidarity by the monetary economy and the bureaucratic state, and about how social protest of the peasants tends to be connected with movements for religious reform. At the end of his analysis of the causes of the fall of the Roman empire he draws a comparison with the modern Occident, and throws in a prediction that 'as in the antiquity, the bureaucracy will become the master of capitalism in the modern world . . . for capitalism is now the chief agent of bureaucratization.' This was written before the end of the last century.

Weber was not the first to resort to comparisons in order to arrive at generalizations. Indeed, all the thinkers that have left their mark on the history of sociology did precisely that. Aristotle, Ibn-Khaldun, Bodin, Macchiavelli, Montesquieu, Buckle, Spencer, Roscher, Mosca and many others— they all used comparative method. The moral of this, incidentally, is that the aspirants to Weber's mantle should postpone their attempts to produce another *Economy and Society* until they acquire a comparable range of factual information. Weber's achievement shows, moreover, that the knowledge of other societies, and the consequent ability to compare, aids enormously the analysis of any given society, and particularly the discovery of causal relationships. His superiority over his most distinguished predecessors was largely due to the progress of historiography. Montesquieu could not have used similar data because they just were not available. Today it is possible to correct Weber on a number of points because during the forty years which have elapsed since his death relevant information has accumulated. His greatness can be measured by the profusion of extremely interesting hypotheses which can be found in his works. For instance: is it true, as he suggests in connection with his analysis of the Chinese intellectuals, that bureaucratic connections breed formalism in philosophy?

As is well known, all Weber's works are focussed, in one way or another, on the problem of the conditions which permitted the rise of capitalism. Almost needless to say, there was nothing original in this pre-occupation; it stems directly from Marx, and was shared by many scholars, particularly, in Germany. Marxists as well as the economists of the 'historical school' discussed it continuously, and the first edition of Werner Sombart's *Der Moderne Kapitalismus* appeared before Weber's articles in *Archiv fuer Sozialwissenschaft* (which were later incorporated into the volumes of *Religionssoziologie*). The originality of Weber's approach consisted, in the first place, in something very simple. In order to discover the causes of the rise of capitalism, other scholars studied in great detail the process of its growth, thus confining their attention to western Europe. He, on the other hand, conceived the brilliant idea of throwing light on this problem by concentrating on cases where capitalism failed to develop. This idea, it is true, would not amount to very much if he were not capable of carrying it out, but coupled with masterly execution, it gave to his works a stamp of uniqueness. The comparative point of view, moreover, saved him from pitfalls into which many others fell: unlike Sombart, for instance, he knew that neither the desire for pecuniary gain, nor vast accumulations of liquid wealth, were in any way peculiar to the countries where capitalism developed, and could not, therefore, be regarded as crucial factors.

The controversy over Weber's thesis has been centred around his assertions about the role which the Protestant ethics played in the development of capitalism in Europe, whilst the conjunction of his views on the impact of religions and economic life failed to attract a similar amount of attention. In what follows some comments on this wider issue are offered, but in the first place let us look at the economic impact of Protestantism within the setting of the European civilization.

Catholicism and Protestantism

Nothing contributed more to Weber's fame than his essay on the Protestant ethics and the rise of capitalism, although it contains no structural analysis, so characteristic of the bulk of his works. Whereas in his treatment of Hinduism, Judaism and of the Chinese religions he tries to relate religious beliefs to social institutions, viewing culture and society as an integrated whole, the *Protestant Ethics and the Rise of Capitalism* contains only rather disjointed references to the social circumstances. He nowhere claimed that the Calvinist ethic was the cause of the rise of capitalism, but treated in isolation from his other works the essay gives some justification to the reproach that he overstated his case.

There are two kinds of argument in favour of Weber's thesis: one of them can be described as the argument from harmony; the other as the argument from co-variation. Let us look at them in turn. The argument from harmony consists in showing that capitalism can be developed only by people endowed with certain traits of character, and that a given creed inculcates such traits.

It can be admitted as self-evident that capitalism cannot grow unless there are people who accumulate capital: that is to say, who do not spend everything they earn. The argument here is that Protestantism, and especially its Calvinist variety, taught thrift, whereas Catholicism did not. No religion, of course, has ever eradicated cupidity, but the disdain for material goods professed by the Catholic Church may have encouraged spending. Cupidity, after all, is something that comes naturally, whereas thrift is not. Thrift alone, however, is not enough.

An economic system whose propelling force is private accumulation of capital will not develop very fast if people are inclined to stop working as soon as they reach a certain level of affluence. Progress of such a system requires that those who have already enough for their needs should go on working and accumulating. The connection with Protestantism, particularly in its Calvinist variety, is that it taught people to regard work as a form of prayer, and the growth of possessions as the evidence of the state of grace. Another important influence of Protestantism was its insistence on work as the only legitimate road to riches. Other religions, of course, also prohibit robbery and theft, but Protestant puritanism is unique in condemning gambling. The religious ideals of work, thrift and enrichment without enjoyment and by means of work only, constitute what Weber calls 'worldly asceticism.' It is extremely plausible that a creed which preached such asceticism did in fact stimulate the growth of capitalism.

The argument that the Reformation first opened up possibilities of investment, by legitimizing interest on loans, carries less force because in reality interest-taking was very common during the late Middle Ages, and by no means limited to parasitic usury. Nevertheless, it might be claimed that by removing the need for subterfuges, the Reformation helped to direct investment into productive channels, for clandestine gains are more readily linked with parasitically exploitative than with productive employment of capital. We can debate how much weight should be assigned to this factor, but the direction of its influence is beyond dispute.

The weakest point in the argument from harmony is the assertion linking the doctrines of predestination with the acquisitive drive. It is difficult to see how an earnest belief that one's fate is determined by something absolutely beyond one's control could stimulate anybody to exert himself. Fatalism (that is to say, belief in predestination) is generally considered to be one of the greatest obstacles to economic development of the oriental lands—an attitude which saps entrepreneurial energies as well as the spirit of workmanship. What seems to have happened is that Protestants took as little to heart the doctrine of predestination as they did the old injunction to expose the other cheek to an assailant. It appears therefore that this tenet of Calvin's doctrine provided neither stimulus nor obstacle to the growth of capitalism.

The general conclusion which emerges from the foregoing analysis is that, although the doctrine of predestination constituted a neutral influence, the worldly asceticism ought to have stimulated the growth of capitalism. In order to obtain further light on this thesis, let us look at the argument from co-variation.

The data included in Weber's essay as well as those supplied by later investigators show clearly that in countries and regions where the Protestants and the Catholics live intermingled, the former occupy prominent positions in business in disproportionate numbers. In France, for instance, the influence of the Protestants in business is astonishing in view of the paucity of their numbers. In this case the explanation that their enthusiasm for business is due to being excluded from other fields of activity cannot be sustained because we would have to go right back to the 'ancient regime' to find bars against the entry of Protestants into official posts. There remains a possibility that the mere fact of being in a minority had a bracing effect upon them, but the predominance of the Protestants over the Catholics in the economic life of a country like Germany, with a more or less evenly balanced population, cannot be accounted for in this way. Only in the cases of Ireland and Prussian Poland can the economic inferiority of the Catholics be possibly explained by the fetters imposed upon them by their Protestant rulers. For this reason, these cases lend no support to Weber's thesis, but they do not contradict it either. It could be said that the predominance of the Protestants in American business is due to the fact that they descend mainly from the old-established population, whereas Catholics came more recently as poor immigrants, but for Canada and Holland this explanation plainly does not hold. The case of Holland is particularly significant because there the Catholics were a minority relegated to a political subordinate position but with ample opportunities for business activities. Their position resembled in some ways that of the Protestants in France after the end of legal discrimination. Nevertheless they furnished far fewer successful businessmen than either the Protestants or the Jews. Thus, even if we allow for the influence of other factors the data unambiguously suggest that Protestantism is more conducive to business activity than Catholicism.

We can adduce another argument from co-variation in support of Weber's thesis, using as our units of comparison states, instead of sections of populations located within the boundaries of one state, and pointing out that capitalism developed furthest and fastest in predominantly Protestant countries. In the world of today only the first part of this statement is true: the economies of the English-speaking countries, dominated by the Protestants, continue to represent the furthest stage in the evolution of capitalism, but their rates of growth are exceeded by those of France, Italy and Western Germany. The latter fact, however, does not invalidate the thesis of Weber, but only demands that we make explicit what is implicit: namely, that this thesis applies in full only to the situation where accumulation by private individuals constitutes the driving force of economic development. Once the giant concerns and trusts enter upon the scene, and the 'ploughing back' of their undistributed profits becomes (jointly with the financing by the state) the chief form of investment, worldly asceticism loses its importance because most of the saving becomes then in a sense 'forced.' It must be remembered, moreover, that Weber's analysis referred to an epoch when the margin of affluence was very much smaller than it is in the industrial countries of today, and as saving is more difficult for the less opulent, worldly asceticism sanctioned by religion was necessary for rapid accumulation and productive investment of the capital. The important point here is that capitalist enterprise of a non-predatory kind was developed by persons who did not have very much. There have always been large accumulations of liquid and real wealth in the hands of economically parasitic persons and corporations, but they contributed little to industrial growth, at least in its early stages. With the proviso, then, that it refers without qualifications only to economies consisting of small firms, the arguments from approximative covariation support Weber's thesis. Nevertheless, owing to the bewildering complexity of this problem, these comparative data lend themselves to other interpretations as well.

In his *Materialistische Geschichtsauffassung* (perhaps the greatest work of marxist historiography) Karl Kautsky attempted to invert Weber's argument in accordance with the marxist view that religion is a mere epiphenomenon without any causal efficacy—a view which is contradicted by Marx's statement that religion is the opium of the masses, for one cannot deny the power of opium. Narrating the spread of various heresies during the later Middle Ages, Kautsky shows how the class of artisans and petty businessmen provided a fertile ground for the conception and dissemination of ideas which found their final embodiment in Calvinism. For artisans and petty traders, fairly safe behind their walls from the depredations of feudal lords, hard work and saving were unique means of improving or even merely maintaining their positions. These conditions generated, according to Kautsky, the mentality which found its final sanction in Calvinism. This argument has considerable force: the evidence adduced by Kautsky and other writers does show that Calvinism struck roots above all in the cities where commerce and handicrafts prospered. The recent investigations show that the protagonists of Calvinism in German cities belonged to circles connected with business. Notwithstanding these new data, the thesis on the epiphenomenal character of Calvinism cannot be sustained because it fails to account for its spread among the Hungarian nobility, and above all, for the conversion of Scotland. At the time of John Knox, the Scotsmen, who later came to dominate the English finance, were semi-tribal rustics renowned for their dissolute ways. Knox and his followers made them into the most perfect examples of worldly asceticism. Here then the causation appears to have worked in the direction opposite to that suggested by Kautsky.

In Scotland Calvinism came to prevail without capitalism; in Italy capitalism failed to bring about religious schism of any kind. The case of Italy is particularly interesting because it contradicts not only Kautsky's thesis, but the extreme formulations of Weber's thesis as well: in Italy capitalism was born and prospered without any aid from the Protestant ethics and, in fact, the Papal See was one of the greatest centres of banking operations in the world. The Italians invented techniques so essential to capitalism as bill of exchange and double-entry book-keeping, and controlled banking in northern Europe until the seventeenth century: the main street of the district in London where headquarters of banks are located still bears the name of Lombard Street. At the times of Calvin and John Knox capitalism was vastly more developed in Florence and Venice than in Geneva or Edinburgh. Presumably one of the reasons why Protestantism had so little appeal to the Italian bourgeoisie was the close connection of the Italian bankers with the tributary machinery of the Church—the fact which might have had something to do with the external manifestations of piety for which Florence (the seat of high finance) was renowned. The second reason might have been the disinclination of the Italians to fight for their religious convictions: Macchiavelli maintained that the nearer a place was to Rome the less truly pious were its inhabitants. Be that as it may, the fact remains that the example of Italy shows that neither Protestantism in general nor Calvinism in particular can be regarded as mere epiphenomena of capitalism.

The thesis of Weber is affected only in the extreme formulations of some of its interpreters: for although the case of Italy proves that Calvinism could not have been a necessary condition of the emergence of capitalism, it does not rule out the possibility that Calvinism, had it been able to strike roots, could have given to the Italian capitalism greater impetus. Indeed the evidence from Italy supports the less extreme interpretation of this thesis because the Italian capitalism ceased to grow after the end of the sixteenth century, and began to decline thereafter. The causation of this withering of the economic impetus is very difficult to unravel: there were a number of factors involved such as the. loss of the importance of the Mediterranean as the trade route, foreign invasions and wars between the Italian states, and so on. The spirit of enterprise had waned but as at no time did it have a religious backing, there is little reason to attribute this to the changes in religious outlook—religion may have had something to do with it but in an indirect way.

When we look at the geographical distribution of the Catholic and Protestant populations, it seems so arbitrary that it is difficult to imagine that it could be the product of any such constant trend as the development of capitalism. A closer inspection of the process of the Reformation confirms this impression: a single battle often decided whether a country or a region were to remain Catholic or to become Protestant—and as is well known outcomes of battles often depend on accidents. The power of the princes to impose a creed of their choice upon their subjects—proclaimed in the sinister principle of 'cuius regio eius religio'—enlarged the scope of chance, because actions of single individuals exhibit less regularity than joint actions of large numbers.

Although in his writings on oriental religions Weber takes into account indirect effects of religious beliefs, the explicit stress throughout his *Religionssoziologie* is on what he calls 'economic ethics,' that is to say, on the influence upon the attitudes towards business of the code of behaviour prescribed by religion. But it might be argued that of greater consequence for the development of the economy was the influence of the ecclesiastical organization upon the distribution of power. Some writers have argued that the most far-reaching impact of the Reformation consisted in replacing an autocratic ecclesiastic organization by a looser one, thus weakening the conservative forces of society. Moreover, the Reformation has furthered the growth of capitalism by bringing about the confiscation of the gold in the possession of the churches and monasteries, and putting it into circulation, thus eliminating the greatest source of thesaurization, which must have acted as a brake upon productive investment.

There is another way in which Protestantism may have stimulated the growth of capitalism. A perfectly capitalist society is not viable: when the sole motive of individual actions is unbridled pursuit of gain the administration of the state becomes disorderly and corrupt, and the growth of capitalism is impeded thereby. This is not a purely deductive argument because we can see that the countries where capitalism developed furthest and fastest are blessed with more than average share of civic virtues. In the United States the great captains of capitalism may have been utterly ruthless and even dishonest, but on the whole the civic communal spirit is very strong there even today, and was much stronger at the time when capitalism began to develop. England, Holland and lately Sweden have for long been renowned as examples (relative, of course) of orderliness and civic virtues, and for the adherence to the principle that honesty is the best policy. The same can be said about the Germans, in spite of their authoritarian proclivities. Japan also exemplifies the usefulness of civic virtues to capitalism, but this case is irrelevant to the comparison of Catholicism with Protestantism. It must be noted, on the other hand, that all the so-called underdeveloped countries are conspicuous for the lack of public spirit.

Accepting as valid the assumption that capitalism requires a good measure of civic virtues if it is to prosper, we face the questions of whether this has anything to do with Protestantism, and of whether it is not entirely a matter of circular causation; for it might be argued that widespread poverty undermines civic virtues, and the lack of them makes poverty difficult to eliminate. It is a fact, however, that if we compare the Protestant with the Catholic lands, the difference in the prevalence of civic virtues is striking. Without going into the intricacies of possible causations, we must note the possibility that Protestantism might have stimulated the growth of capitalism indirectly, by fostering the civic virtues required for the smooth functioning of the state.

The contention that Protestantism stimulated the growth of capitalism in indirect ways which cannot be subsumed under Weber's concept of economic ethics, far from disproving Weber's thesis merely amplifies it.

Some weight must be assigned to the complete lack of arguments in favour of the contrary thesis that Catholicism is or was more propitious than Protestantism to the development of capitalism. At most it might be argued that under certain circumstances Calvinism fails to produce much spirit of capitalist enterprise. Among the examples which might be cited to this point the most conspicuous are those of the Calvinist Hungarian nobility and of the Boers of South Africa—although the Boers do show somewhat more inclination towards 'worldly asceticism' and business activity than the people who are in economically analogous positions in the Catholic lands. On the whole, then, if we bear in mind that Weber regarded Protestantism as a factor which fostered the development of capitalism, and not as *the* cause thereof, we can accept his thesis as valid.

Judaism

The volume of *Religionssoziologie* devoted to Judaism is unquestioningly a great work, full of illuminating insights and brilliant suggestions; nevertheless, its central theme sheds little light on the relation between religion and the rise of capitalism simply because as an economic force Judaism was negligible during its formative period and long afterwards. The Jews were a very small nation, leading a precarious interstitial existence, oppressed and pushed around by mighty nations and empires, and finding consolation in religious contemplation. As far as the evolution of ancient capitalism was concerned the nature of their religion was of no consequence: no matter how conducive to capitalist activity it might have been, the shaping of the economy (even of their own little country) was not in their hands.

During the earlier parts of the Middle Ages the primitive condition of society ruled out any development of capitalist enterprise regardless of whether the tenets of religion fostered 'the spirit of capitalism' or not. As soon as it became materially possible, the Jews began to play a prominent role in commerce and banking but, being restricted in residence and not allowed to own land, they were not in a position to take part in developing industry.

As soon as the restrictions imposed upon them ceased to be crippling, the Jews proved to be at least as successful in business as the Calvinists, and as the successful Jewish business men were as a rule just as pious as their Calvinist counterparts, there is no reason to think that the economic ethics of Judaism is in any way less propitious to capitalist activity than that of Calvinism. Indeed it would be strange if it were so, because the teachings of Protestantism (particularly of its puritanical varieties) consisted mainly of precepts of ancient Judaism.

The so-called 'double ethics' of the Jews (that is to say, the principle that it is sinful to cheat a co-religionist but not a Gentile), in which Weber saw a major obstacle to development of 'rational' business enterprise, does not belong to the core of Judaism and is perfectly explicable as a response to persecution and disdain. Where the Jews were not harrassed and achieved opulence, they usually conducted business just as respectably as anybody else.

In his famous book *The Jews and Modern Capitalism* Werber Sombart argued that the Jews were the true creators of capitalism. He based his contention on a number of instances in which an arrival of Jews in substantial numbers was followed by an efflorescence of business activity and a rapid growth of wealth. This was the case with Holland, Venice, the city of Frankfurt and many others. Contrariwise, expulsions of the Jews were in several instances followed by an economic decline of the city or even a whole country, as was the case with Spain. However, Sombart does not take into account the data which do not fit his thesis, such as the fact that in England the foundations of capitalism were laid during the period between the expulsion of the Jews and their return. It could even be argued that the presence of a very large number of Jews is fatal to development of capitalism on the ground that the Jews were much more numerous in the economically backward eastern Europe than in the countries of developed capitalism. The causation here is extremely involved.

Originally it was the economic backwardness which was the cause of the influx of the Jews into eastern Europe: objects of animosity from their Gentile competitors in more highly urbanized lands in western Europe, they were welcomed in the countries without a native trading class. However, their presence in large numbers acted subsequently as a brake upon commercial development because as soon as trade came to be monopolized by the Jews it became a depressed occupation. Being isolated from the surrounding population, the Jews were in a much weaker position than a bourgeoisie integrated with the rest of the society, and, therefore, they were unable to resist the encroachments of the nobility; which was the reason why the Polish and Hungarian nobles preferred them.

In spite of the startling achievements of its adherents in the field of business, Judaism could never become a decisive factor in development of capitalism because it was a religion of a minority of strangers which could never mould the character of any European nation. The Jews neither wished nor had the chance to convert to their faith the Christian majority; and it was out of the question that they should attain a truly dominating position in any country of the diaspora. In consequence, the Jews could use their aptitude for capitalist enterprise when the circumstances were propitious but were powerless to create them.

Weber was partly right: Judaism was not a crucial factor in the rise of capitalism; but he was wrong in imputing this to its economic ethics. This ethic was extremely favourable to capitalism but its influence was always severely limited by the non-proselitic character of Judaism.

Confucianism

Weber's volume on China constitutes an even greater contribution to sociology than his volume on Judaism, and nevertheless its general thesis seems to be wrong. True, everything influences everything in social life, and there can be little doubt that by contributing in some way to the maintenance of the structure of the traditional Chinese society, Confucianism somehow acted as an indirect brake upon the development of capitalism; but as far as the direct influence via the economic ethics is concerned, it does not appear that Confucianism in any way impeded capitalist activity. Analysing this problem along the lines similar to the foregoing treatment of Protestantism, let us first examine the argument from harmony—or rather disharmony.

In spite of what Weber says, I think that it is difficult to find among the tenets of Confucianism anything directly opposed to capitalist activity. Filial piety, patriarchalism and family solidarity do not hamper business very much, and were by no means absent from the European civilization at the time of the rise of capitalism. Ritualism (which is the factor which Weber stresses) was, it is true, very marked in traditional China, but it concerned personal relations—not economic activities. The general outlook of Confucianism was practical and rationalist. I think that Weber was wrong in maintaining that Christianity contributed to 'de-magicalization' (Entzauberung) of the view of the world.

The assignation of the low status to the merchants by the Confucianist literature cannot be regarded as an important factor for two reasons: firstly, because it was not uncommon in the ideological literature of the countries where capitalism was rising; and secondly, because it was an effect rather than a determinant of the existing distribution of power, as can be seen from the fact that the equally low status assigned to the soldiers in the Confucianist writings did not prevent them from attaining very high positions, and at times dominating the society.

Although many of its pre-conditions—such as well-developed transport and currency, wide area of peaceful commerce, and very high level of handicrafts—existed in China, capitalist industry could not develop there because of the fetters imposed upon business enterprise by the bureaucratic state. The officials always regarded the businessmen with resentment and employed many means to keep them down. Fiscal extortion prevented if not accumulation of profits, at least their regular investment in productive establishments, which was in any case difficult owing to official regulation of location and methods of production. That these factors, and not the economic ethics, were responsible for the arrest of capitalism in traditional China is demonstrated by the performance of the Chinese emigrants to the British and Dutch colonies, most of whom continued to adhere strictly to their traditional religion: within the institutional framework of these colonies, their religion constituted no impediment to capitalist enterprise, in which the Chinese immigrants were phenomenally successful.

Confucianism, then, did constitute a serious obstacle to the development of capitalism, but it did so not through the influence of its economic ethics upon the behaviour of those engaged in commerce and industry but in virtue of its fitness to serve as a political formula cementing the omnipotent bureaucratic state.

Hinduism

The central theme of Weber's volume on Hinduism—which like its companions could alone constitute a worthy achievement of life-long work—is less open to criticism. In reality, Hinduism did constitute a formidable obstacle to the rise of capitalism, owing to its numerous taboos prohibiting utilization of resources, and impeding collaboration in production by enjoining avoidance between persons of different castes. Although usury flourished in India since times immemorial, and large-scale financial operations were by no means unknown, the capitalist mode of production together with large-scale trade was first forcibly implanted by the British, and began to strike roots as a native growth only when the hold of Hinduism became less astringent, owing to the spread of laicism.

The esoteric mysticism of the Brahmins had, no doubt, something to do with the withering of the early buds of Hindu science, but as far as the shaping of the economy was concerned, more important was the support which Hinduism lent to social parasitism by making the toiling masses listless and utterly servile. As Weber rightly pointed out, with its promise of re-incarnation into a higher caste as the reward for keeping dutifully to one's station in life, Hinduism functioned as the most powerful 'opium of the people' ever invented. Other factors, too, fortified parasitism in India: frequent conquests, the instability of political order, ruthless fiscal extortion diverted energies and wealth from productive purposes.

Notwithstanding these qualifications, Weber's central thesis stands: not only indirectly via its influence on the structure of power, but also directly via its economic ethics, Hinduism was effective in preventing the rise of capitalism in India.

Weber's *Religionssoziologie* illustrates how a work can be truly great and nevertheless mistaken in some of its assertions; which only goes to show that science proceeds by successive approximations. Given the novelty, magnitude and complexity of the problems, insistence on more conclusive verification, and logically more rigorous formulation, would in all likelihood have prevented Weber from producing his works: the first outline had to be rough. It is not our merit but merely luck to be able to see certain points better by standing on his shoulders.

Even if, in some cases, Weber overestimated the efficacy of religious beliefs in directly determining behaviour in economic matters, the fact that he considers both directions of influence proves that it is completely unjust to accuse him of unilateralist interpretation. As mentioned above, he explains the stultification and decay of capitalism in the ancient world in terms of structures of power, without bringing in the 'economic ethics' as an independent factor. In order to obtain a balanced view of Weber's thought, we must realize that 'Agrarian Relations in Antiquity' is in no way less important than 'Sociology of Religions,' and constitutes its necessary complement.

In passing judgment on Max Weber as a thinker we must remember that he died before completing his main works. The final synthetic conclusions are mostly lacking. Even so, he is the towering figure of sociology. We shall never know what he would have achieved had he lived another twenty years.

5.2

Max Weber's Sociology Today[1]

REINHARD BENDIX

This centenary is a welcome occasion for an attempt to outline the general conception of Weber's work. Universal scholarly recognition of this work has made Max Weber a classic of modern sociology. He is, however, an extremely awkward authority, for his work excels neither in simplicity of ideas nor in clarity of exposition. It can so easily be spoken of at many different levels, and offers points of departure for the most varied interpretations. This is borne out by the fact that, in recent years, not only Weber's political ideas but also his concepts such as charisma, economic rationality, bureaucracy, etc., have been cited both in support of, and in opposition to, the tendencies of modern society towards democracy and towards dictatorship, as evidence for and against the progressive or the reactionary consequence of modern science and of so-called mass-society. Of relevance also are the strikingly dissimilar reactions in post-war Germany and America, which were revealed recently at the fifteenth meeting of the Deutsche Gesellschaft für Soziologie. Repeatedly, German sociologists exposed the political dangers latent in Weber's thinking, whereas American sociologists manifested greater interest in the substantive core of his work. It should be added that some colleagues objected to this very distinction—an attitude which, if carried to its logical conclusion, would cast doubt on the possibility of discussing different interpretations and, what is more, on the possibility of formulating scientific concepts in sociology.[2]

In such circumstances it is unprofitable to uphold this or that interpretation as being the only possible one. The many interpretations of Weber's work rather put one in mind of the saying of Jakob Burckhardt, to the effect that after a thousand years an interpreter would be able to discover in a sentence of Thucydides a meaning that had never been seen in that light before. Yet the multiplicity of interpretations is also limited by the number of meaningful lines of inquiry, even if this limitation can only be indicated in broad terms. Intellectual discourse and communication remain possible

---

[1] Commemorative address on the occasion of Max Weber's centenary, at the Free University of Berlin, 7 July 1964.

[2] Marianne Weber, *Max Weber, Ein Lebensbild*, Tübingen, J. C. B. Mohr (Paul Siebeck), 1926, pp. 174–5.

169

as long as we are prepared to make allowance for the limited perspective of our own approach to problems (what Max Weber called *Wertbeziehung*), and in principle to accept other approaches as long as they do not prevent the continuation of the intellectual dialogue. In the present case, I shall try to show that the open-ended quality of Weber's approach is one (I stress *one*) characteristic of his work, and that this offers prospects for comparative sociological studies which have an affinity with his scientific outlook. Let me say at once that I am more anxious to continue working along Weber's lines, because I find useful points of departure in his writings, than I am to add yet another interpretation to the many that exist already.

The attempt to provide an overview is aided by one concept contained in the work itself, that of 'rationalization.' In his introduction to *Gesammelte Aufsätze zur Religionssoziologie* Weber characterized the relevance of this concept in the following words: 'Anyone who is heir to the traditions of modern European civilization will approach problems of universal history with a set of questions, which to him appear both inevitable and legitimate. These questions will turn on the combination of circumstances which has brought about the cultural phenomena that are uniquely Western and that have at the same time—as we at least should like to imagine—a universal cultural significance.'[3]

Following this statement Weber enumerates these occidental cultural phenomena in the fields of science, art, the university, the civil service, and professionalism in general, jurisprudence and especially capitalism, which together point to related forms of rationalism based on technical calculation.

Therefore, the basic theme of Weber's scientific work seems clear, and I wish to emphasize its topicality. In his introduction to *Kapital* Marx pointed out that by its advanced industrial development England set the pattern for the economic development of other countries. On the other hand, Weber stressed and analysed the uniqueness of Western European history and social structure, and thus the fact that this historical process could not be repeated. True, he did not fully explore the problems which this perspective raised for the analysis of other social structures and their development. But it is well to remember the difficulty which modern social scientists encounter in seeking to free themselves from purely Western categories in their analysis of the so-called developing countries, in order to get back in their own way to the starting-point of Weber's analysis.

But this thematic characterization of Weber's work is nevertheless

---

[3] Cf. 'Universalgeschichtliche Probleme wird der Sohn der modernen europäischen Kulturwelt unvermeidlicher- und berechtigterweise unter der Fragestellung behandeln: welche Verkettung von Umständen hat dazu geführt, dass gerade auf dem Boden des Okzidents, und nur hier, Kulturerscheinungen auftraten, welche doch—wie wenigstens wir uns gern vorstellen—in einer Entwicklungsrichtung von universeller Bedeutung und Gültigkeit lagen?' (Weber *Gesammelte Aufsätze zur Religionssoziologie*, Vol. 1, p. 1. Tübingen, J. C. B. Mohr (Paul Siebeck).)

unsatisfactory. The concept of 'rationalization' makes it appear as though it were a question of straightforward development, say, from magic to scientific thought or from a primarily political to a primarily capitalistic orientation of economic enterprise.[4]

Of course, one can quote passages in Weber's work in which he describes the 'disenchantment of the world' in this way, but isolated quotations only lead to caricature. A study of the whole work shows on the contrary that for Weber the development towards increased rationality possesses a multiplicity of meanings and is highly problematic in character. Here are two examples of this. In *Antikes Judentum* (Ancient Judaism) the main theme is the decline of magic in religious belief as a result of Old Testament prophecy. More recent literature has, it is true, questioned Weber's sharp differentiation between prophecy and priesthood. But for our purposes it is sufficient to point out that Weber pursued the analysis of the decline of magic as far even as the ecstatic trances of the prophets. But then he also emphasized as sharply as possible the arrest of this dynamic power through the ritualized fidelity to the law which developed after the Babylonian captivity under the leadership of the Rabbinate. Here increased rationality (= decline of magic) first creates the great values of a monotheistic religion but then eventuates in the irrationality of formal rites and in the loss of inner meaning with regard to commandments originally rich in symbolic significance. Weber's famous treatise on Protestantism makes Calvin's teaching on predestination the cardinal point of the analysis. There is a conscious paradox in an approach which emphasizes at the same time the increased rationality of theological doctrine and the absolute and systematically conceived incomprehensibility of the Divine will. Yet here the paradox of rationality is still confined to the world of the intellect, whereas Weber was interested in the analysis of human conduct as well. At the heart of this analysis there is the religious fear of the believer for the salvation of his soul, evoked by doctrine and preaching. This fear provided the motive for the methodical ordering of life in which Weber saw the essence of the spirit of capitalism. But even at this core of what Weber understood by rationality, we find the same openness in his general conception. The systematization of the Puritan's way of life not only applies to his business, but extends to all other spheres as well. Every activity endangers man's salvation if it detracts from the fulfillment of his duty towards God. This holds good for art, which in most of its forms appeals to human sensuality; it holds good for sleep when it exceeds the requisite minimum. More generally, it holds good for the whole of our affective life, which binds us in love and friendship

---

[4] This is the view that led Talcott Parsons quite recently to describe Weber's work as that of a theorist of evolution. This interpretation entirely overlooks Weber's own, sharp, criticism of the concept of evolution, as well as the striking contrast between Weber's emphasis on the uniqueness of Western history and the tendency of most theorists of evolution, from Spencer to Parsons, to generalize.

to our fellow men but, for that very reason, leads us away from our work that is ordained by God and fulfilled only through trust in Him. Inner-worldly asceticism may, therefore, exert a rationalizing effect on the shaping of economic life, but at the same time it exacts a high price, an almost pathological numbness of natural feeling. Weber analysed this consequence in detail, especially in his contrast between Calvinistic and Lutheran piety, although perhaps on this point his description is not free from 'ideal typical' generalization.

It is clear, at any rate, that 'rationalization' is for Weber anything but a tendency developing in a straight line, even in Western society. This misleading impression is conveyed to the reader only because Weber consciously seeks to show the uniqueness of this society. Stressing this particular purpose repeatedly, he proceeds to analyse other types of rationality, especially in Chinese and Indian culture, in order to delineate more clearly the singularity of occidental rationalism. When analysing this singularity, Weber never loses sight of the multiple implications of this phenomenon. The controversy over *Die Protestantische Ethik* may have helped also to create an exaggerated impression of the importance of Puritanism in Weber's conception of occidental rationalism. To correct that impression one need only remember that Weber finds the origin of this singular development in ancient Judaism. Accordingly, Weber's main concern is to analyse the particularity of Western European civilization and the problematic character of its rationalist tendencies.

One can see the lasting significance of this theme as well as its time-bound limitations more clearly today than half a century ago. In the first place modern history has taught us that in Russia, Japan, and even in Germany the systematic way of life that favours industrialization must be traced to other factors than Puritanism or even religion. Recognition of this fact only serves to emphasize the singularity of each development, a theme Weber stressed with regard to the whole of occidental development. In the second place we must free ourselves today from a line of inquiry centred on Europe, even if we stress the singularity of occidental development. This perspective surely determined part of Weber's works. Yet it is evident today that this development has had political and ideological repercussions outside Europe which have again and again confronted the most diverse civilizations with a situation in which the main problem is not the autonomous development of a country but rather the clash between impulses emanating from Europe (ranging from the colonialism of the past to the medical and technical aid of today) and the indigenous social structures. However paradoxical it may seem, this process tends to confirm the 'positive critique' that Weber levelled at the theory of historical materialism. For the consequences of European influence have moved the Age of Ideology to a new level, with ideological and political independence now being considered in many countries a prerequisite of their economic development, a reversal of the causal nexus which dominated the thinking of Marx and can hardly be brought in line with it. A sort of vulgar Marxism may be popular in these countries today, but Marxism as a scientific theory is disproved by the course of history, particularly in these countries. Thus Weber's problem in the study of Protestantism has become less topical, because the historical and intellectual situation he confronted has been superseded.

Yet this thematic confrontation with Marxian theory is after all only part of Weber's work as a whole. We must remember that this work reflects not only the influence of Marxian ideas, but also of utilitarianism, the historical school, legal positivism, Dilthey's and Nietzsche's philosophies of life, Social Darwinism and the philosophy of Hegel. Thus, Weber's sociological work must be understood as a synthesis and continuation of the intellectual world of the nineteenth century. This is not the place for a closer analysis of this synthesis. Suffice it to say that one can observe this synthesis in the variety of intellectual confrontations which are contained in Weber's work. For Weber underscored the independent efficacy of ideas as against historical materialism; the role of ideas even in the striving for material gain as against utilitarianism; the indispensability of conceptual distinctions as against the historical school and Dilthey's philosophy of life; the historical preconditions and the limits of formal jurisprudence as against legal positivism; the universal significance of the Christian ethic as against Nietzsche's re- and devaluation of Christianity; the ethical importance and the problematic quality of the struggle for existence as against Social Darwinism, and the social conditioning of every creation of the mind as against the idealism of Hegel. Still, in every one of these confrontations with positions other than his own Weber found fruitful points of departure for his own thinking. It will be evident that this many-sided approach is responsible for the wealth of thought and the lasting effect of Weber's work but also for the difficulties arising from its lack of thorough systematization. Yet it seems to me that a systematic core can be extracted from his many-faceted writings and I shall now endeavour to substantiate this impression.

For this purpose I revert to a theme already broached, which I see as a thread running through Weber's lifework. Even the casual reader must be struck by the abundance of factual materials, on the one hand, and the 'casuistry' of definitions, on the other, which Weber himself describes as pedantic. Again and again we meet phrases in which Weber emphasizes this duality. Two citations will illustrate this point. In his work on the sociology of religion he says at one point that he takes the liberty to be '. . . "unhistorical" in the sense that the ethics of the several religions are presented systematically and in greater unity than has ever existed in the actual course of development. The abundance of contradictions existing within the different religions, of starting-points and offshoots in their development, have to be placed on one side so that the features important for us are often shown to be more logically connected and less in flux than they really were. This simplification would be a historical "falsification" if made arbitrarily. That, however, is not the case, at least not intentionally. On the contrary, the emphasis has been put consistently upon those features of an entire religion which were decisive in shaping the *practical* way of life, as well as on those which distinguish one religion from another.'[5]

A little further on, in reference to the analysis of systems of domination, it is stated that the kind of differentiation and terminology chosen '. . . by no means claims to be the only possible one, or even that all empirical systems of authority must conform "entirely" to any one of these types. On the contrary, the overwhelming majority of such systems represent combinations of, or a state of transition between, several types. In word-formations like "patrimonial bureaucracy" we are always being forced to express the fact that the phenomenon in question belongs to the rational form of authority with one part of its characteristics and to the traditional (in this case: estate) form with the other part. . . . Thus, the terminology suggested here does not seek to impose a distorting schematization on the endless variety of history, but only to provide serviceable points of reference for specific purposes.'[6]

One can summarize Weber's discussions of the problematic relation between evidence and concept under three points.

1. Historical reality is characterized by endless variety and by a fluidity of transitions so great as to exclude the possibility of dividing lines naturally inherent in the evidence.
2. All concepts brought to bear on the evidence are consequently constructions which are to serve certain purposes of inquiry and can only claim to be valid in this scientific and pragmatic sense.

---

[5] Cf. ' "unhistorisch" in dem Sinne zu sein, dass die Ethik der einzelnen Religionen systematisch wesentlich einheitlicher dargestellt wird, als sie es im Fluss der Entwicklung jemals war. Es müssen hier eine Fülle von Gegensätzen, die innerhalb der einzelnen Religionen lebten, von Entwicklungsansätzen und Zweigentwicklungen beiseite gelassen und also die für uns wichtigen Züge oft in einer grösseren logischen Geschlossenheit und Entwicklungslosigkeit vorgeführt werden, als sie in der Realität sich vorfanden. Diese Vereinfachung würde historisch "Falsches" *dann* ergeben, wenn sie willkürlich vorgenommen würde. Das aber ist, wenigstens der Absicht nach, nicht der Fall. Es sind vielmehr stets diejenigen Züge im Gesamtbilde einer Religion unterstrichen, welche für die Gestaltung der *praktischen* Lebensführung in ihren *Unterschieden* gegen andere Religionen die entscheidenden waren.' (Weber, *Religionssoziologie*, Vol. 1, p. 267.)

[6] Cf. 'mitnichten den Anspruch erhebt, die einzig mögliche zu sein, noch vollends: dass alle empirischen Herrschaftsgebilde einem dieser Typen "rein" entsprechen müssten. Im geraden Gegenteil stellt die überwiegende Mehrzahl von ihnen Kombinationen oder einen Übergangszustand zwischen mehreren von ihnen dar. Wir werden immer wieder gezwungen sein, z. B. durch Wortbildungen wie: "Patrimonial-bürokratie" zum Ausdruck zu bringen; dass die betreffende Erscheinung mit einem Teil ihrer charakteristischen Merkmale der rationalen, mit einem anderen der traditionalistischen—in diesem Falle: ständischen—Herrschaftsform angehört. . . . Die hier vorgeschlagene Terminologie will also nicht die unendliche Mannigfaltigkeit des Historischen schematisch vergewaltigen, sondern sie möchte nur, für bestimmte Zwecke, brauchbare begriffliche Orientierungspunkte schaffen.' (Weber, *Religionssoziologie*, Vol. 1, p. 273.)

3. From the contrast between the diversity of history and the simple, unidimensional character of concepts, it follows that logical deductions from a concept should only be used as a point of reference in the analysis of any body of evidence.

Let it be said, therefore—though with all due caution on a point of this kind—that Weber's work consists largely in the working out of these points of reference. This is meant as a statement of fact, not as criticism— in so far as it is properly applicable. Those who do not possess Weber's knowledge of history (and who today can claim that he does?) can hardly appreciate the psychological burden imposed on a scholar who undertakes the conceptualization of so formidable a body of evidence—for in such an endeavour all new material can easily appear as a threat to previous conceptual formulations and the latter just as easily as a schematic viola- tion of the evidence. Is it wrong to see a sublimated reflection of Weber's personality in this orientation of his work, an attempt to create meaning through conceptual tools as an expression of his strong sense of dignity in the face of the psychological threats to which he found himself exposed? This question is only noted here, it cannot be pursued. At any rate, many parts of Weber's work consist in the formulation of conceptual tools whereas their application in empirical analysis frequently remains a task to be performed. Indeed, Weber recognized this and stressed the limited importance of his preparatory work, though in other parts of course he went well beyond this level. But where his discussion is ideal-typical he did not always keep within the bounds of what can be attained analytically by the use of such ideal types.[7] Yet these concepts are formulated at a level that is most appropriate for the analysis of world history, and at that level they possess a systematic core of their own which should not be neglected.

Let us look simply at Weber's most general formulation, his definition of sociology. Here he says that social action must be understood through an interpretation of what sense his action makes to the person involved, and he proceeds at once to differentiate between 'action' and 'social action.' This distinction has not received the attention it deserves in my judge- ment. For, according to Weber, conduct makes subjective sense to the actor, but action should be called 'social' only if the actor relates the intended sense or meaning to the behaviour of others and orients himself accordingly. One should note the many intellectual positions which are implied here. For the emphasis on meaning (*Sinn*) already precludes a biological or a psychological reductionism in the interpretation of human

---

[7] A notable example of this is the uncertainty in Weber's own use of the material gathered from his study on Protestantism. Another example seems to me to be his use of 'ideal typical' formulations in his political prognoses. See also my contribution to the discussion at the fifteenth meeting of the Deutsche Gesellschaft für Soziologie. A contribution of the methodological importance is the recent article by Arthur Schweitzer, 'Vom Idealtypus zum Prototyp,' *Zeitschrift für die gesamte Staatswissenschaft*, Vol. 120 (January 1964), pp. 13–55.

conduct, and the further distinction between action and social action also constitutes a block against sociological reductionism. In this apparently so rudimentary definition of sociology one finds already evidence of Weber's opposition to the materialism of Marx and of Social Darwinism, to the pansociology of Durkheim (though I find no indication that Weber knew Durkheim's work) and to the pan-psychology of Freud, of which Weber apparently took some notice. On the positive side, Weber was influenced by the English empirical tradition and combined it in his own fashion with certain elements of German idealism. In this way he related meaning to human behaviour and thus separated it from Hegel's concept of the 'absolute spirit,' allowing for the possibility that men can make sense of, or give meaning to, their conduct. This is an impressive foundation of sociological thought on which Weber based his analysis of ideas and interests in the context of social stratification and his analysis of administrative organization and belief in legitimacy in the context of his types of domination.[8] I turn now to these two themes.

Weber's treatise on the 'Protestant Ethic' has the abiding merit of having shown that certain ideas underlie a form of economic action. On the other hand, important parts of his work on the sociology of religion deal with the contrary relationship, proceeding from the view that 'conduct motivated by religion or magic is oriented basically to achieve effects in this life.'[9] Weber did not regard these two lines of inquiry as paradoxical; rather he made both the systematic starting-points of his analyses. Quite deliberately he characterized the materialistic and the idealistic perspectives as equally legitimate heuristic principles. All tendency to generalize

---

[8] Weber's fundamental position was indeed formulated very early, but coincided in the main with that of other sociologists of his generation, with the important exception of Emile Durkheim. These corresponding intellectual points of departure can be gathered from Roscoe Hinkle's survey, 'Antecedents of the Action Orientation in American Sociology before 1935,' *American Sociological Review*, Vol. 28 (October 1963), pp. 705-15 and the sources quoted there. Similar parallels in the European area, which however blur important differences between Weber and authors such as Durkheim and Pareto, are discussed in H. Stuart Hughes' *Consciousness and Society* (New York, A. A. Knopf, 1961), *passim*. Despite these parallels, Weber offered a perspective peculiar to himself by reason first of the universal span of his thinking and also because of his characteristic conceptual treatment of this subject-matter, a reflection no doubt of his legal training. Important points of departure for Weber's concept of behaviour were taken from the German theory of penal law (see Gustav Radbruch's publication, *Der Handlungsbegriff in seiner Bedeutung für das Strafrechtssystem*, Berlin, J. Guttentag, 1904). This approach has affinities with that of Jakob Burckhardt and both no doubt show the influence of Schopenhauer. (Cf. my paper 'Max Weber and Jakob Burckhardt, syntheses of nineteenth-century themes,' submitted at the fifty-ninth annual meeting of the American Sociological Association, Montreal, 1964.)

[9] Cf. 'religiös oder magisch motiviertes Handeln, in seinem urwüchsigen Bestande, *diesseitig* ausgerichtet ist.' (Weber, *Wirtschaft und Gesellschaft*, Tübingen, J. C. B. Mohr (Paul Siebeck), 1956, Vol. 1, p. 245.)

the one or the other perspective by logical deductions should be left to the 'amateurs who believe in the "unity" of the "social psyche" and its reducibility to a single formula.'[10] Weber once expressed this attitude in the following, positive terms: 'Interests (material and ideal), not ideas, directly govern men's conduct. Nevertheless, "views of the world" created by "ideas" have frequently acted like switchmen indicating the lines along which action has been propelled by the dynamic of interest.'[11] In other words: ideas like interests have each a dynamic of their own. But each of these spheres must complement the other, if it is not to lose its dynamism, for interests without ideas are empty, and ideas without interests impotent.[12]

One can observe this confrontation in Weber's definition of classes and estates (*Stände*). The term 'class' applies to any group of people in so far as it possesses the same or similar powers of control over consumer goods, sources of supply, property, means of livelihood, qualifications for jobs, etc. But these common bases of interest only make common actions possible, they do not compel them. Class action on this basis ('*vergesellschaftetes Klassenhandeln*' as Weber puts it) becomes more likely when there is a direct opponent, when the common class situation has quantitative significance, when organization is technically and geographically simple and when there exists a '*leadership* towards clear goals, which are regularly imposed or interpreted by non-class members (intelligentsia).'[13] Class, therefore, is the name given to every group formation brought about by a community of interests and by facilitating circumstances, so that shared ideas (that go beyond material interests) come into play—but only when clear goals are formulated by non-class leaders. The separation of interests from ideas could hardly be put more strongly.

Just the opposite applies to the concept 'estate' as defined by Weber. An estate is based on the assessment of social prestige and thus on a subjective element in contrast to the class situation which is determined by the power to dispose of material goods. Prestige depends upon family, education and way of life; it is maintained by excluding outsiders on the

---

[10] Cf. 'Dilettanten überlassen, die an die "Einheitlichkeit" der "Sozialpsyche" und ihre Reduzierbarkeit auf eine Formel glaul en.' (Weber, *Religionssoziologie*, Vol. 1, pp. 205–6.)

[11] Cf. 'Interessen (materielle und ideelle), nicht: Ideen, beherrschen unmittelbar das Handeln der Menschen. Aber: die "Weltbilder," welche durch "Ideen" geschaffen wurden, haben sehr oft als Weichensteller die Bahnen bestimmt, in denen die Dynamik der Interessen das Handeln fortbewegte.' (Ibid., p. 252.)

[12] A formulation of this view, corresponding to the spirit of Weber's statement, is to be found in Otto Hintze's 'Kalvinismus und Staatsräson in Brandenburg zu Beginn des 17ten Jahrhunderts,' *Historische Zeitschrift*, Vol. 144 (1931), p. 232.

[13] Cf. 'Führung auf einleuchtende Ziele, die regelmassig von Nichtklassenzugehörigen (Intelligenz) oktroyiert oder interpretiert werden.' (Weber, *Wirtschaft und Gesellschaft*, Vol. 2, p. 179.)

basis of rules governing the institutions of marriage, of social intercourse (commensality), and of the monopolistic appropriation (or rejection) of certain types of economic opportunity. Of course, an estate and a class can be combined in the most diverse ways. But the class's powers of control are not in themselves either the basis of social prestige or qualifications for membership in an estate, any more than the absence of material possessions as such is synonymous with social disqualifications. Therefore, the formation of an estate is attributed to an ideal held in common by members of the group; this idea in turn has vital social and economic consequences. Similarly, the group formation of a class is determined by a material position shared by members of the group and this shared position forms the basis for the influence of guiding ideas that are brought to the group from the outside. Weber's work shows that he was primarily concerned with the tensions and overlaps between class and estate, between interest and idea, for in this he saw the dynamic of historical development. But the analysis of such tensions and overlaps depended upon a prior, clear-cut separation of concepts, which for him was an indispensable tool of scientific work in general.[14]

Similar considerations apply to Weber's sociology of domination. My closing remarks are devoted to this theme, because here conceptual analysis is closely related to Weber's idea of social structure. Discussion of this point serves to enhance our understanding of his work, and, beyond that, to provide a contribution to modern sociology. In following this thought I shall not attempt to decide where questions of interpretation verge on a further development of Weber's ideas.

To begin with, it should be pointed out that Weber develops the distinction between society and the State in his own way. Classes and estates are basic aspects of society, respectively accentuating group-formation on the basis of material interests (*Vergesellschaftung*) and of feelings of affinity (*Vergemeinschaftung*). Weber derived these concepts from Toennies, but also reinterpreted them as processes in his own characteristic way. The point is that such contrasting concepts should not be reified. In this respect Weber had been influenced too much by utilitarian ideas, and hence thought too much along nominalist lines, ever to lose sight in his own formulations of the basic discrepancy between concept and reality. When Weber refers to *Vergemeinschaftung* instead of *Gemeinschaft* (community), he means that in the social relationships thus designated feelings and ideas of solidarity prevail while common material interests are correspondingly subordinated. (The reverse statement applies to his use of *Vergesellschaftung*.) Accordingly, estates and classes are two important examples of contrasting types of group-formation which overlap in diverse ways with those based on the household, on ethnic, religious or economic relationships. In all these cases we have to do with group-formations on the basis of which members of the group can 'force their will upon the

---

14 In my books on Weber's sociological work, I have used this starting-point as the basis for my presentation of the comparative sociology of religions.

behaviour of others.'[15] Weber analysed this type of power (which is based on group-formations in society) with special reference to economic and religious behaviour. However, a very different type of power is represented by 'domination by virtue of authority (the power of command and the obligation to obey).'[16] This then is the nominalistic form in which Weber continued the distinction between society and the State which had strongly influenced German thought during the nineteenth century. However, in so doing he altered the intellectual basis of this distinction by making room for 'ideal interests' in his concept of society (especially through his broad use of the concept 'estate'), and for 'material interests' in his concept of the State. Thereby, the traditional concept of society was divested of its crass materialism, and the traditional concept of the State of its equally crass idealism. I may add that the recent literature on these themes hardly mentions this evidence of Weber's intellectual independence not only in relation to Marxism but also to the idealization of the State.

Weber's analysis of domination distinguishes between administrative organization and the belief in legitimacy, a set of concepts which parallels the distinction between interests and ideas. Weber's concern is clearly indicated by this question: 'on what ultimate principles does the "validity" (*Geltung*) of a system of domination rest, i.e. the claim to obedience which the "officials" [recognize] towards the ruler and which the ruled [recognize] towards both [the officials and the ruler].'[17] For Weber these principles on which systems of domination ultimately rest, consist in beliefs, namely the belief in rational regulations, the sanctity of tradition, or the gift of grace (charisma), possessed by a person. Such beliefs sustain the legitimacy of legal, traditional or charismatic domination. As always, Weber emphasizes that any given system of domination can be analysed only with the aid of several such abstractions and so must be understood as a combination of different elements. Analogous considerations apply to the respective administrative organizations, such as bureaucracy, the patriarchal household staff, or the circle of the close, personal retainers or disciples of the charismatic ruler. All this is well known.

Less familiar but much more important is the peculiar dynamic of these concepts, which illustrates the systematic openness of Weber's approach on which I commented earlier. For each system of domination remains 'valid' only within limits, and when these are ignored or exceeded for too long, the type of domination either changes its form or loses its original, authoritative character altogether. Charisma is a 'supernatural quality of a personality,' which in its original meaning proved itself by miracles, thereby gaining recognition from the ruled and in turn making that

---

[15] Cf. 'eigenen Willen dem Verhalten anderer aufzuzwingen.' (Weber, *Wirtschaft und Gesellschaft*, Vol. 2, p. 542.)

[16] Cf. 'Herrschaft kraft Autorität (Befehlsgewalt und Gehorsamspflicht).' (Ibid., p. 549.)

[17] Cf. 'auf welchen letzten Prinzipien die 'Geltung' einer Herrschaft, d. h. der Anspruch auf Gehorsam der 'Beamten' gegenüber dem Herrn und der Beherrschten gegenüber beiden, gestützt werden kann.' (Ibid., p. 549.)

recognition their sacred duty.[18] True, charismatic authority unconditionally demands acceptance of its *claims* to legitimacy, but the belief in its legitimacy is by no means unconditional. For, if the test of this claim remain forever wanting, then the 'person favoured by the gift of grace is shown to be forsaken by his God or his magic or heroic powers.'[19] Seen from the point of view of the ruled, this means that their belief in the lawful claims of this authority may well spring from 'enthusiasm or necessity and hope' ('*Begeisterung oder Not und Hoffnung*') but that secretly they desire or hope for tests which will confirm its legitimacy. It is certainly characteristic of charismatic domination that the ruler interprets these desires or hopes as disbelief and demands unconditional acceptance of this interpretation. But the desire of the ruled for signs of confirmation remains.

The same applies to the other types. The legitimacy of traditional domination rests on the 'sanctity of established structures and powers of command' ('*Heiligkeit attüberkommenen ordnungen und Herrengewalten*'); accordingly, authority is exercised by the *person* of the ruler, not by means of statutes. However, the commands of a ruler are legal not only when they conform to tradition, but also when they proceed from the 'arbitrary will of the master, on whom tradition confers a certain latitude.'[20] Hence, traditional domination possesses a characteristic 'duality of rule that is tradition-bound as well as free from tradition.' This freedom from tradition refers to the arbitrary will of the personal ruler, who may have the right to ignore tradition since his will is absolute, but who can thereby imperil his own traditional authority.

Finally, I allude to the corresponding 'duality of rule' in the case of legal domination. In his *Rechtssoziologie* (sociology of law) Weber paid by far the most attention to this type, but for that very reason the systematic aspect may easily be lost in the mass of detail. Legal authority rests upon the idea 'that any law whatever . . . can be *enacted*, that all law constitutes a universe of abstract rules,' and that any superior who issues commands obeys the same impersonal normative order as do those who are ruled.[21] In another passage, but in a similar context, Weber points out that it is not possible to define a political association—and *mutatis mutandis* a legal system—by specifying its aim, because such associations or legal systems have pursued the most varied aims at one time or

---

[18] In this and the following definitions, I quote Weber's text, avoiding however, wherever possible, the pedantry of his formulation. Whether the rendering is faithful will appear by reference to the quoted passages. Cf. 'als ausseralltäglich geltende Qualität einer Persönlichkeit . . .'. (Ibid., Vol. 1, p. 140.)

[19] Cf. 'zeigt sich der charismatische Begnadete von seinem Gott oder seiner magischen oder Heldenkraft verlassen.' (Ibid.)

[20] Cf. 'Kraft der freien Willkür des Herrn, welcher die Tradition den betreffenden Spielraum zuweist.' (Ibid., p. 130.)

[21] Cf. 'dass beliebiges Recht . . . gesatrt werden könne, dass jedes Recht ein Kosmos abstrakter Regeln sei.' (*Ibid.*, p. 125.)

another without thereby losing their defining characteristics.[22] Be it noted, however, that this is a question of how best to formulate a concept. It does not mean at all that purposes are unimportant for an understanding of political associations or the legal type of domination. On the contrary, the most important aspect of Weber's *Rechtssoziologie* consists in the confrontation between formal and substantive rationality in the law, i.e. between formal versus substantive purposes to be achieved through legal means. Here Weber was particularly interested in the development of formal rationality, especially in the history of Western law, but at the same time he emphasizes the limits of this type of rationality arising from considerations of natural law as well as through the 'antiformal tendencies in the development of modern law.'[23] Here again we can speak of a 'duality of rule,' since the existence of the legal order depends on the persistence of overlaps and tensions between formal and substantive rationality in the law, and is in fact defined by that persistence. Similarly, charismatic domination is defined by the tension between the claim to unconditional recognition, on the one hand, and the desire for signs of grace, indeed for miracles, on the other. The same applies to traditional domination, which upholds the sanctity of the established order as well as the arbitrary will of the ruler, and retains its structure as long as this tension continues.

This way of conceptualizing a social structure is of the greatest importance in my opinion. For it enables us to connect the unfolding of social phenomena with the persistence of a certain over-all structure, and in this way we grasp the developments compatible with this structure at the same time that we obtain criteria for assessing the replacement of one structure by another. I should like to conclude by citing two examples.

If legal authority has its existence in the tensions between the formal and the substantial rationality of law and administration, then the exaggerated ascendance of one or the other tendency must endanger the existence of the legal order. Tension of course means that this danger is always present, but that the political task (in the sense of upholding legal authority) consists in keeping the balance between antagonistic tendencies. When the balance is upset, because, for instance, some principle of material justice destroys the formal rationality of the law, we have the principle of the totalitarian State, in which formal legality can be violated at any time through the prerogative of the Party as the ultimately valid principle of representing the people. Here I see the connexion between Weber's conception and the theory of the 'Dual State' which was formulated by Professor Ernst Fraenkel twenty-five years ago.

The second example relates to traditional domination. The ruler who acts arbitrarily can appeal to the tradition sustaining him, but when he regularly infringes upon the limits set by tradition, he runs the risk of jeopardizing the legitimacy of his own position. This applies to the charis-

---

[22] Ibid., p. 30.

[23] Cf. 'antiformalen Tendenzen in der modernen Rechtsentwicklung.' (Ibid., Vol. 2, p. 501.)

matic ruler as well, who may regard every desire of his subjects for a proof of his gifts as disloyalty or treason, who does not care for their physical and spiritual welfare, but who may unwittingly cast doubt upon the supernatural inspiration of his personal claim to rule. Recent history reminds us that a charismatic ruler may very well try to avoid this test by claiming unquestioned validity for every one of his utterances, while making the executive agencies responsible for the actions which can justify his claim to rule in the eyes of the faithful. Under modern conditions, the day of reckoning may thus be put off for a long time, since now the balance between the claim to authority and the test of its validity is impossible. On the contrary, executive agencies are put in the position of placing the tools of administration at the disposal of absolute commands. But now the ruler evades responsibility for these commands by shifting the blame for failure on to the executive agencies, while these agencies in turn evade responsibility by reference to the absolute commands which they have merely obeyed. Thus, both charismatic domination and bureaucratic administration become caricatures. There are seeds of danger in all exercise of authority. Today, we know that in this particular combination the dangers of charisma and the dangers of bureaucracy were escalated through interaction at a disastrous cost to all humanity.

It is appropriate to close this address in memory of Weber on a political theme which shows that some of his most abstract concepts can be of great assistance for an understanding of extremely topical and controversial problems. I have tried to show that Max Weber's work possesses a thematic and a systematic core, which provides important leads for further sociological research today—forty-four years after his premature death. I think we honour Weber's memory best by continuing his and our work in the spirit of his own ascetic scientific ideal.

SUMMARY AND EVALUATION
OF CHAPTER FIVE

A thorough evaluation of Weber's approach to sociology and his historical–comparative works is beyond the goal of this chapter. Even small parts of his work—for example, his discussion of "interpretive" understanding and the prescription for carrying this out or his Protestant ethic thesis—have generated much controversy.

We must remember that Weber's goal was to understand concrete actions through discovering *how they are significant to us*. He took this to be the most "satisfying" pursuit for the cultural scientist. Since actions can be significant to us in many different ways, there is therefore no single valid approach to studying them. The scientist must begin to analyze the confused experience of history with reference to values, but he must also understand historical events causally in order to understand which of the *possible* outcomes of a chain of events was the real one.[1]

---

[1] Raymond Aron, *German Sociology* (New York: Free Press, 1964), pp. 76–78.

The outcome is problematical until it occurs. In the process of under-standing the event we must integrate it with the larger configuration of events to which it belongs (according to the values with which we associate it). Weber thought that both history and sociology could contribute some-thing to the analysis—history, the concrete detail from which we begin and to which we impute some meaningfulness; and sociology, a knowledge of the concepts and other factors that constitute causal probabilities in the production of a cultural event. Weber thus linked interpretative under-standing and causal explanation together into a single approach.

We must not confuse the concepts and chains of causation that we visualize in our minds with the real events of the world as they unfold. The concepts that we form only partially illuminate what is happening, but the skillful use of concepts can help us reduce some of the com-plexity of the cultural world and give us insight into its dynamics, as the article by Bendix indicated. Historical reality evinces endless variety and fluidity; we need all the tools available to us—conceptual distinctions, laws of regularity, and others—in order to understand it from different points of view.

Weber's work presents several problems. First, not all sociologists can be expected to agree upon and work within his conception of the field of sociology. To require that sociology deal only with action as it is meaningful to the actors is too narrow. Second, though he transcended crass idealism, he still seems to imply erroneous argument. He thought that since sociology deals with "mindful" phenomena ("significating" actors), the relation of theory to fact in social science *must* differ from that in physical science because the theories' presuppositions derive from one among many possible viewpoints of the researcher.[2] Finally, although Weber endeavored to show that subjective phenomena must be studied in their objective manifestations, his theory of explaining actions by reference to motives still entails some difficulty. While he did caution against care-less imputations of motives and stated good reasons why claims for their existence must remain guesses,[3] he did not specify just *how* to explain actions in terms of motives nor how to deal with the various problems that might be encountered in the process.[4]

Weber's lasting contribution to social science lies in his recognition of social reality as highly diverse, meaningful, and complex in its causal links and interdependencies. The outcome of an event is not indeterminate; it depends on the effects of many factors—factors that may influence other events differently. His contribution also lies, and perhaps this is most important, in the diligence and scope of his historical–comparative re-

---

[2] W. G. Runciman, *A Critique of Max Weber's Philosophy of Social Science* (New York: Cambridge University Press, 1972), pp. 38–41.

[3] Max Weber, *The Theory of Social and Economic Organization*, A. M. Hen-derson and Talcott Parsons (Trans.) and Talcott Parsons (Ed.) (New York: Free Press, 1964), pp. 96–97.

[4] See Robert Brown, *Explanation in Social Science* (Chicago: Aldine, 1963) for a thorough treatment of these problems.

search, as we have seen in the article by Andreski. Weber was constantly interested in what was unique about contemporary Western civilization. Analysts sometimes believe that Weber opposed Marx's mode of analysis—that Weber stressed the role of ideas in economic activity in order to refute Marxian analysis. Such was not the case. Weber apparently had great respect for Marx's ideal model of historical development;[5] when Delbrück once attempted to speculate that Weber was not a materialist, Weber himself interrupted him, saying, "I really must object to this; I am much more materialistic than Delbrück thinks."[6] As Bendix noted, Weber saw his writing simply as the development of *another* point of view and the attempt to reveal the interplay between ideal *and* material conditions or interests. His classic statement on the matter is still instructive: "Not ideas, but material and ideal interests, directly govern men's conduct. Yet very frequently the 'world images' that have been created by 'ideas' have, like switchmen, determined the tracks along which action has been pushed by the dynamic of interest."[7]

SELECTED BIBLIOGRAPHY

Abel, Theodore. *The Foundation of Sociological Theory*. New York: Random House, 1970.

American Sociological Review, 30 (April 1965). See articles by Reinhard Bendix, Paul Lazarsfeld and Anthony Oberschall, Edward Shils, and Guenther Roth.

Aron, Raymond. *German Sociology*. New York: Free Press, 1964 (paperback).

Aron, Raymond. *Main Currents in Sociological Thought II*. New York: Basic Books, 1967.

Barnes, Harry Elmer, (Ed.). *Introduction to the History of Sociology*. Chicago: University of Chicago Press, 1948. Chap. XIII.

Bendix, Reinhard. *Max Weber: An Intellectual Portrait*. Garden City, N.Y.: Doubleday, Anchor Books, 1962.

Bendix, Reinhard, and Guenther Roth. *Scholarship and Partisanship: Essays on Max Weber*. Berkeley: University of California Press, 1971.

Birnbaum, N. "Conflicting Interpretations of the Rise of Capitalism: Marx and Weber." *The British Journal of Sociology*, 4 (June 1953), 125–140.

Blum, Alan F., and Peter McHugh. "The Social Ascription of Motives." *American Sociological Review*, 36 (February 1971), 98–109.

Brown, Roger. *Explanation in Social Science*. Chicago: Aldine, 1963.

Cahnman, Werner J. "Ideal Type Theory: Max Weber's Concept and Some of Its Derivations." *The Sociological Quarterly*, 6 (Summer 1965), 268–280.

---

5 Weber, *Social and Economic Organization*, p. 103.

6 Quoted in Runciman, *Max Weber's Philosophy of Social Science*, p. 5.

7 H. H. Gerth and C. Wright Mills (Eds.), *From Max Weber: Essays in Sociology* (New York: Oxford University Press, 1958), p. 280.

Cahnman, Werner J., and Alvin Boskoff, (Eds.). *Sociology and History: Theory and Research.* New York: Free Press, 1964.

Eisenstadt, S. N., (Ed.). *The Protestant Ethic and Modernization.* New York: Basic Books, 1968.

Fallers, L. A. "Max Weber's Concept of 'Traditional Authority.' " Unpublished paper presented at 1966 annual meeting of the American Political Science Association, New York. Copyright by the American Political Science Association, 1966.

Freund, Julien. *The Sociology of Max Weber.* New York: Vintage Books, 1969.

Gross, Llewellyn, (Ed.). *Symposium on Sociological Theory.* Evanston, Ill. Harper & Row, 1959. See especially Chaps. II, III, and IV.

Grünbaum, Adolf. "Causality and the Science of Human Behavior." In Herbert Feigl and May Brodbeck (Eds.), *Readings in the Philosophy of Science.* New York: Appleton, 1953. Pp. 766–778.

Hughes, H. Stuart. *Consciousness and Society.* New York: Vintage Books, 1961 (paperback).

Lipset, Seymour Martin, and Richard Hofstadter, (Eds.). *Sociology and History: Methods.* New York: Basic Books, 1968.

Mayer, J. P. *Max Weber and German Politics.* 2d ed. New York: Hillary House Publishers, 1956.

Miller, S. M. *Max Weber.* New York: Crowell, 1963 (paperback).

Mitzman, Arthur. *The Iron Cage: An Historical Interpretation of Max Weber.* New York: Knopf, 1970.

Nettler, Gwynn. *Explanations.* New York: McGraw-Hill, 1971.

Parsons, Talcott. *The Structure of Social Action.* New York: Free Press, 1949.

Rudner, Richard S. *Philosophy of Social Science.* Englewood Cliffs, N.J.: Prentice-Hall, 1966 (paperback). See especially Chap. 4.

Sahay, Arun, (Ed.). *Max Weber and Modern Sociology.* London: Routledge, 1971.

The Sociological Quarterly, 5 (Autumn 1964), entire issue.

Sociology and Social Research, 51 (April 1967) articles by Murray Wax, Theodore Abel, Carl Baar, and John Rhoads.

Tawney, R. H. *Religion and the Rise of Capitalism.* New York: New American Library, a Mentor Book, 1958.

Udy, Jr., Stanley H. " ' Bureaucracy' and 'Rationality' in Weber's Theory." *American Sociological Review*, 24 (December 1959), 791–796.

Zeitlin, Irving M. *Ideology and the Development of Sociological Theory.* Englewood Cliffs. N.J.: Prentice-Hall, 1968.

SIX

Georg Simmel

"It seems ironical that the prerequisite for insight into the workings of society, as Simmel achieved, [requires that] one must remain detached from its very operations."

—STUDENT COMMENT

General Introduction

Georg Simmel, the youngest of seven children, was born in Berlin in 1858, the same year in which Emile Durkheim was born.[1] Simmel was the son of Jewish parents who had been nominally converted to Protestantism and was still young when his father, an owner of a chocolate candy business, died.

Simmel's education was in Berlin, first at the *Gymnasium* and then at the University of Berlin where he studied history, psychology, philosophy, and Italian language and culture. Berlin had become a place of great intellectual mix by this time, an era of industrial expansion in

---

[1] Biographical material has been drawn from various sources: Lewis A. Coser, *Masters of Sociological Thought* (New York: Harcourt Brace Jovanovich, 1971); K. Peter Etzkorn (Ed. and Trans.), *Georg Simmel: The Conflict in Modern Culture and Other Essays* (New York: Teachers College Press, 1968); Donald N. Levine (Ed.), *Georg Simmel: On Individuality and Social Forms* (Chicago: University of Chicago Press, 1971); Nicholas J. Spykman, *The Social Theory of Georg Simmel* (New York: Atherton, Atheling Books, 1966); Kurt H. Wolff (Ed.), *Essays on Sociology, Philosophy and Aesthetics by Georg Simmel et al.* (New York: Harper Torchbooks, 1965); Kurt H. Wolff, "The Challenge of Durkheim and Simmel," *American Journal of Sociology*, 63 (May 1958), 590–596; Kurt H. Wolff (Trans. and Ed.), *The Sociology of Georg Simmel* (New York: Free Press, 1950); Kurt H. Wolff and Reinhard Bendix (Trans.), *Georg Simmel, Conflict and the Web of Group-Affiliations* (New York: Free Press, 1955).

Germany. With this came the rapid creation of new social forms and ideas, which Simmel both observed and took part in.[2] At Berlin, Simmel prepared a dissertation on "Psychological and Ethnological Studies of Music," which his committee rejected because it contained too many "misspellings, stylistic errors . . . [and, according to one member of his committee, because] . . . Simmel is entirely too confident in his conclusions."[3] In this study Simmel considered the sources and uses of vocal music and even included empirical research on yodeling, which he considered to be among the "most primitive forms of musical expression."[4] A second dissertation on Kant, written a year earlier, was accepted instead. Outside of his immediate professors, those intellectual figures that seem to have influenced Simmel the most were Kant, Goethe, Schopenhauer, Nietzsche, Hegel, and Heraclitus.

Simmel taught from 1885 to 1900 as a *Privatdozent* (a low-status, low-paying position) and from 1900 to 1914 as a "Professor Extraordinary" (a title that sounded more prestigious than it was) at the University of Berlin.[5] Four years before his death in 1918, he gained the more clearly prestigious title of full professor at the University of Strasbourg. But, alas, by then, because of the war, the university's traditional teaching and scholarly functions were hampered. Simmel received little or no salary much of his life—only student fees—and lived mainly on an inheritance left him earlier.

Simmel was a prodigious writer. More than two dozen books, (some collected posthumously) and 180 articles were published.[6] Some of Sim-

---

[2] Coser, *Masters of Sociological Thought*, pp. 203–205.

[3] Etzkorn, *Conflict in Modern Culture*, p. 127.

[4] *Ibid.*, p. 126. One of Simmel's hypotheses concerning the expression of emotions through rhythmic activities is that when we are excited, we can sense the beating of the heart and pulse more markedly.

[5] Wolff, *Sociology of Georg Simmel*, p. xviii.

[6] Simmel's major books are as follows (though the titles are translated here, the works themselves are for the most part only excerpted in English, as indicated below): *Social Differentiation* (1890), *Problems of the Philosophy of History* (1892), *Introduction to the Philosophy of Morals* (1892–1893), *The Philosophy of Money* (1900), *Sociology* (1908), *Philosophy of Culture* (1911), *Goethe* (1913), *Rembrandt* (1916), *Major Problems of Philosophy* (1910), *The War and Spiritual Decisions* (1917), *Basic Questions of Sociology* (1917), *Perspectives on Life: Four Chapters in Metaphysics* (1918), and *The Conflict in Modern Culture* (1918).

Simmel's *Sociology of Religion* is translated in full by Curt Rosenthal (New York: Philosophical Library, 1959). In addition to the articles translated and published in American journals, such as the *International Journal of Ethics, Annals of the American Academy of Political and Social Science, American Journal of Sociology* (under the editorship of Albion Small of the University of Chicago), and *International Monthly*, the most accessible sources of his works in English are the books mentioned in footnote 1 (some

mel's personal notes were confiscated from his son by the Nazi Gestapo just before his son emigrated to the United States.

Though the general milieu of Simmel's time was essentially the same as that of Weber's, his life was encompassed by quite a different set of circumstances. Two questions often arise: Given Simmel's brilliance and great erudition, why did he not become a full professor much earlier in life? and, Why has he not been given a more prominent place in American sociology up to now? While these problems must be dealt with separately, Simmel's unorthodox style of sociological analysis—to be discussed last— pertains to both.

In considering the question of Simmel's slow promotion and am- biguous status in academe, we must take several factors into account. Being Jewish, he was undoubtedly discriminated against in some instances. But perhaps of greater importance was the structure of universities and their relation to the larger society in the Germany of his day.[7] Even then, universities tended to hire and promote academicians who could be identified with a particular specialty and who showed promise of sticking to a full life of scholarship in that particular subject. Simmel's imaginative and integrative mind, which knew no boundaries, could not be easily fitted into such a departmentalized institution. Consequently, he taught in a wide range of subjects and wrote essays on the diverse social events that caught his attention rather than comprehensive treatises on society or history. Furthermore, academicians were by and large peacemakers with the Fatherland and content to devote their energies to the purities of their disciplines. Although Simmel tended to avoid the controversy of current affairs by using events only as illustrations of broader principles, he did take a critical stance against restrictions on intellectual freedom and remained the champion of man's individuality, which was being diminished by the increasing number of cultural conventions and prescriptions. When

---

of which include articles from the journals). The material in these books comes from various of Simmel's publications: Spykman's *The Social Theory of Georg Simmel* (from *Sociology*); Wolff's *The Sociology of George Simmel* (from some journal articles and from *Sociology* and *Basic Questions of Sociology*); Wolff and Bendix's *Conflict and the Web of Group-Affiliations* (from *Sociology*); Wolff's *Essays on Sociology* (largely from *Philosophy of Culture* and *Sociology*); Etzkorn's *The Conflict in Modern Culture* (from *The Conflict in Modern Culture, Philosophy of Culture,* and journal articles); Levine's *On Individuality and Social Forms* (largely from Simmel's *Sociology, The Philosophy of Money, Problems of the Philosophy of History,* and *Perspectives on Life*).

Lewis A. Coser has shown that whereas before 1900 an equal number of Simmel's articles were published in scholarly and nonscholarly journals, after 1900 most of them were published in nonscholarly journals (*Masters of Sociological Thought*, p. 213).

[7] Coser, *Masters of Sociological Thought*, pp. 205–211.

wrangling did occur in the universities, it took place because of conflict between "schools" of thought rather than because of the politics of the day.

This left a vacuum in the university. Social criticism was lacking, and challenges to the dominant ideas in the scholarly disciplines were difficult to mount from within, especially for younger scholars. So, the vacuum was filled in part by the "invisible" university—the Bohemian intellectuals who engaged in wide-ranging, radical discussions in salons, parlors, and other places where a circle of friends might get together. It appears that these gatherings of the counterculturalists appealed to Simmel as much as the sedate university. He may have enjoyed the edification he received in the Bohemian setting in spite of what it cost him. His marginality in academe was thus partly self-imposed.

It should be noted, however, that Simmel was highly acclaimed by many academicians of his time. By 1910 he had been recognized as the most important German sociologist, and in the same year he was selected as the lead-off speaker at the German Society for Sociology. So his slow progress can probably be ascribed to his having offended a few important faculty members by his reluctance to footnote anyone else in his writing, by his disregard of academic etiquette, and by his tendency sometimes to overimpress. It is said that Simmel sometimes chose a very mundane object or event about which to launch long, spirited monologs in the presence of distinguished scholars. And because of his ethnic background, some pressures might have been applied to university administrators to keep Simmel in junior positions for so long. Many full professors were quite comfortable, and few were willing to assist an upstart, especially one of Simmel's brilliance and critical abilities.

Simmel compensated in part for his lack of institutional status with his admirable lecturing, however. His diction and delivery were considered to be impeccable, and the talks themselves, finely honed creations. Ideas hit him with great intensity; he examined each one thoroughly, all the surprising facets, in a manner so engrossing that it kept his listeners spellbound. Simmel sought no disciples, but, then, his style was not such that it could have been easily imitated anyway. It was distinctly his own.

Specific factors can also be adduced to explain Simmel's minor reputation in American sociology. Up to this time, the little attention he has received has been in the form of rather perfunctory credit for a few ideas: sociability, social forms and content, the functions of social conflict, social types such as the coquette, the stranger, the poor, and the influence of the size of a group on its internal relationships. To be sure, only recently have more English translations of his works become available, but this cannot account for the full explanation. What has been lacking is an appreciation of Simmel's methodology. There has been little understanding of his concepts and ideas, which were the product of his encounter with the social world and the way he tried to interpret that world. Moreover, Simmel's approach to sociology was very different from the one that has become institutionalized in American circles today.

According to Simmel, the purpose of sociology is to study how people's goals shape social forms (and vice versa) and to compare given forms, apart from people's goals, in diverse settings so as to discover their common patterns. Such a method might demonstrate, for instance, that the strategies of Christ and Castro, although differing in specifics, have certain features in common. Wilhelm Windleband and Heinrich Rickert, two philosophers of Simmel's time, had maintained that sociology differs from history in its analytical approach: whereas history views events ideographically, as a series of unique occurrences, sociology views them generally, in search of universal principles. Simmel, however, felt that the distinction between the two disciplines lies in their respective method: history constructs reality in terms of how the individual deals with it selectively and synthesizes it, while sociology studies the properties of social conditions, which are different from the properties of individuals taken separately. Simmel made a useful distinction between the social (Simmel's concept of sociality) and the sociological. The social area involves what goes on between people; the sociological area involves what the sociologist perceives as important about the social and the tools he fashions to identify and analyze the matters of importance to him. In Simmel's view, a sociologist brings forth hypotheses about social events; his own work is replete with them. But these hypotheses were the product of Simmel's immediate perception of ways in which a particular situation was similar to or different from another. He presented them in their most tentative form; since he did not regard them as laws, he did not seek to interrelate them for the purpose of constructing a general explanatory theory of society or even a general theory of some major type of sociation such as conflict.

Simmel believed that the contents of situations develop from the cultural activities of social, religious, artistic, and scientific life. History and sociology study the contents after they are formed, whereas general sociology, the third level of analysis, studies "the whole of historical life insofar as it is formed societally."[8]

Simmel's method, as Donald N. Levine has well expressed it, was "to select some bounded, finite phenomenon from the world of flux; to examine the multiplicity of elements which compose it; and to ascertain the cause of their coherence by disclosing its form."[9] In other words, he felt that it is the observer's responsibility to communicate everything he is able to see of a social event (including the hidden dynamics or contradictions it embodies), establish what makes it comprehensible, and often

---

[8] Wolff, *Sociology of Georg Simmel*, p. xxxiii.

[9] Levine, *On Individuality and Social Forms*, p. xxxi.

show why it is different from what it first appeared to be. Because each of Simmel's analyses is thus complete in itself, his work as a whole appears to have no unity. In fact, however, the constancy of his method throughout constitutes a unifying thread.

Simmel used four basic principles in his analysis of social events: form, reciprocity, distance, and dualism.[10] He defined *form* as the structure that the mind of the observer imposes on the contents of the world. Thus, for example, the observer may perceive a dyad, a triad, a competitive or superordinate relationship, and so forth. By *reciprocity* Simmel meant the inherent tendency of some phenomena to so balance or limit each other that only together do they achieve a degree of completion. This concept is part of Simmel's idea of relativity, which he formulated as a result of reading Heraclitus. If something exists, it exists relative to something else: a cultural rule obtains part of its meaning from other rules; without a patient there would not be a physician; and the master is always limited to some extent by the slave since if the master were to kill the slave, he could no longer pursue the objectives of a master. Simmel conceived of *distance* as the extent of separation between one individual's private space and another's. He noted, for example, that conflict reduces the distance between people by bringing them into close contact; friendship is a relationship built upon the person in his totality; the relation with a prostitute is one that is based on calculation and physiological function—the sexual favor is depersonalized by its mediation through money. Finally, Simmel regarded *dualism* as a state in which counterbalancing or contrasting elements together determine the nature of an event. Hence, a relationship that is informal must at the same time involve some formality, and vice versa; what *appears* to be competitive behavior actually entails cooperation also; and so on.

Levine has indicated the main areas in which Simmel exercised creativity and the stages of his intellectual development.[11] According to Levine, it is important to see that Simmel's analyses of both cultural and social forms proceeded in the same manner in spite of the philosophical aspects of the former. Simmel started his cultural analysis at the level of the experiencing individual. His experience is shaped along a cognitive, aesthetic, or evaluative line. Action at this level is simply proto-culture; that is, they are primary cultural actions that are useful to the individual for satisfying his needs but do not have a life or momentum of their own because they are not established and shared by the rest of society. Gradually, these patterns, like a musical refrain, detach themselves from their immediate, practical context and then generally develop according

---

[10] Ibid., p. xxxii.

[11] Levine, *On Individuality and Social Forms*, p. xiv.

to a dynamic of their own. In so doing, they become separate spheres, or worlds, external to the individual; at this, the second, level, the world of music, for example, becomes cultivated *for its own sake.* Individuals can in turn draw on this objective culture for their own edification and growth.

At the highest level, each cultural world seeks to organize its contents in accordance with its own unifying principle, so that within it one perceives reality from a specific point of view—the practical, the aesthetic, the scientific, or the religious, for instance—each attempting to become all-inclusive. Simmel saw a tension or a warring between the subjective proto-culture, which is circumspectly developed by the individual and enlarged by the growing, synthesizing personality through time, and the objective culture, which has developed through time according to a logic or requirements of its own and threatens to engulf the individual, reduce his individuality,[12] and restrict the creative, shifting process in which his needs arise and change.[13]

Simmel believed that a similar tension exists between man and his social forms. In the geometry of social space, social activities can assume only a limited number of forms, such as competition, subordination, and distant or close relations.[14] Like cultural forms, social forms are capable of separating from life and becoming distinct worlds. However, unlike cultural worlds, social worlds organize actions in terms of particular viewpoints—for example, the relations among the players of an orchestra rather than the aesthetic relations among the musical sounds they make.

Simmel also perceived in the development of social forms the three levels discernible in the growth of cultural forms. He saw, first, that people, urged by pressing needs and impulses, engage in the practical interactions of everyday life. These emerging and passing acts—for example, waving good-bye, asking a person for directions, helping one in need, and so on—are a kind of *proto-sociality*; they, in other words, constitute primary sociality that is useful for the particular goals at hand but has no permanence. Simmel did most of his sociological analysis at this, the lowest, level. At the next level, relationships or social circles become more firmly established and thus become objective social forms. Because these forms are reenacted in predictable ways, they attain some autonomy from the life process. Finally, at the highest level, they become the building blocks of larger institutional structures such as families, clubs, and other social systems. They can also serve as models for social play—pure sociability— of which conversation for the sake of conversation is a conspicuous example. Another example of such social play is the enjoyment of the game

---

12 Ibid., p. xx.

13 Ibid., p. xxxvi.

14 Kant's influence is present here.

of coquetry for its own sake, apart from the serious goal of erotic gratification in a relationship.[15] Form (coquetry) and content (erotic need) are thus separated. Any area of serious social life may likewise be expressed as a "game."

Simmel's stand for individuality was an important part of all of his work. Indeed, he lived his analysis. He viewed the elaboration of the social world more favorably than that of the cultural world because larger and more diverse social circles allow more individuality; more different groups may intersect a person's life and thus enrich it. He thought that the cultural world was more rigid but that the individual could, nevertheless, draw on cultural forms for the enrichment of his own personality. An individual's life is his own creative journey during which he seeks some wholeness. Individuals, whether considered in the large building block of society (family, club, etc.) or in smaller forms, are the main focus of Simmel's interest, not large historically formed societies in which the individual is lost.

We must return now to Simmel's conception of society and his mode of sociological analysis. In the universities of his day in Germany, it was difficult to establish a place for sociology as a bona fide discipline. Historical idealism had staked out for itself the area of the unfolding social events of history with respect to actors as spiritual or mental agents. Positivism had taken as its province the world of external physical nature. Weber had (reluctantly) identified himself as a sociologist, but the recognition he received in that capacity probably resulted in large part from his work in macro-historical sociology—from *The Protestant Ethic and The Spirit of Capitalism*, for example. Simmel did not follow this macro-historical tradition except in part in his *Social Differentiation*. He undertook, rather, to delineate sociology analytically from history and from other disciplines that studied social relations as well, such as economics and jurisprudence. In so doing, he unfortunately intimated that formal sociology was to be restricted to the study of only the abstracted forms-of-sociation, a dictum that Simmel did not rigidly adhere to himself.[16]

Be that as it may, Simmel's approach to sociology as a formal discipline was his major contribution. He realized that social analysts must abstract from the complexity of people's actions for, with, and against one another, their associations and dissociations, their processes of binding and unbinding. While such social events always have a mental aspect to them in that they can be visualized by the actors and are influenced by their motivations and feelings, this does not make sociology and psychology

---

[15] See Wolff, *Sociology of Georg Simmel*, pp. 50–51.

[16] Simmel's ambivalence about this will be discussed in the Summary and Evaluation at the end of this chapter.

equivalent.[17] Social properties emerge from the interaction of individuals, which, at an unstructured level, Simmel regarded as proto-sociality. Every-day interactions, and the forms-of-sociation they embody, are always in the making. They have a validity of their own. Yet, they are not a fixed entity or organic whole whose development obeys macro-laws of nature, such as Comte and Spencer envisioned. Forms-of-sociation are both *more* than the individual because he is acted upon by (and acts upon) others and are *less* than he because his full individuality is never involved in sociation. They develop into a society and become restrictive to the individual only when they become strong or persistent enough to develop into larger institutional structures.

It is Theodore Abel's contention that Simmel did not intend the study of the forms-of-sociation in itself to be the main goal of sociology. The goal was, rather, to use the concepts of forms-of-sociation to formulate hypothetical laws explaining how these forms come about and change and what effects or functions they have in the situations in which they occur. Accordingly, Simmel abstracted the constant forms from the variable activities of life—religious, economic, governmental— and filled his essays with the numerous hypotheses that issued from his analytical mind.

Simmel's vignettes of social types, which illuminate some of these forms-of-sociation, are delightful to read, whether one selects "the stranger, the miser, prostitution or conflict." To give the reader some sense of Simmel's analysis, we quote at length from Abel's summary of Simmel's interpretation of conflict.[18]

> [Simmel found] that the greater the cohesion, or the more closely united a group is, the more intense the conflict within it is; that conflict is a means of reestablishing unity and cohesion of a group when it has been threatened by hostile feelings among its members; and that conflict is a means of preserving gradation and divisions in a social system, as in Hindu society, for example. Furthermore, Simmel established that the more complete the exclusion of personal elements in a conflict, the sharper, more bitter, and more relentless the struggle between them is, as manifest, for example, in legal contests; that objectification of goals intensifies the severity of the struggle between groups with opposing interests; that conflicts between parties that were originally united are highly passionate; that the more intense the struggle between two groups, the more the unity of each group concerned is strengthened; that a common opponent often creates a unity that did not formerly exist;

---

[17] See Levine, *On Individuality and Social Forms*, pp. xxiii, xxiv.

[18] Theodore Abel, *The Foundation of Sociological Theory* (New York: Random House, 1970), p. 83. For Simmel conflict was a very integral process of life itself. It has many uses. For example, through conflict a person can demarcate himself from others and thus assert his individuality.

and, finally, that a contest fought between group members by means of objective values or social services is advantageous to the group and therefore is usually fostered by it.

These observations both edify the curious enquirer and provide guidelines for the scientific researcher.

Introduction to Selections 6.1 and 6.2

Theodore Abel, one hundred years after the birth of Simmel, offers an overview of Simmel's contribution in Selection 6.1. Simmel delineated the field of sociology so as to escape the charge that it aspired to become the study of the whole human realm. He felt that, as a science, it should study only select phenomena from human process, namely, forms-of-sociation. Simmel's concepts, which combine generality with concreteness, guided efforts at empirical research.

Several propositions characterize Simmel's conception of sociology and his approach to it: (1) social existence is expressed in reciprocal action; (2) it constitutes a realm worthy of independent study; and (3) the effects of social variables in given situations remain a large area for exploration.

Abel next corrects certain stereotypes. One is that because Simmel considered sociology as the study of forms, he was only a formalist. But, as Abel explains, in viewing the discipline thus, Simmel was simply emphasizing that despite the diversity of social events, patterns can be identified and studied. The other stereotype is that Simmel showed no concern for technical scientific procedures. In answer, Abel points out that Simmel lived at a time when research methodology and institutes were in their infancy and that he did the best he could with what he had. Moreover, Abel believes there is evidence to indicate that Simmel would have made use of more sophisticated methods if they had been available.

Abel concludes by indicating some of the more recent trends in sociology of which Simmel would have approved.

Robert A. Nisbet, in his "Comment," largely agrees with Abel's appraisal of Simmel but notes that, as we mentioned in Chapter Two, Comte's sociology did not consist entirely of sweeping generalizations about the progress of Humanity as a whole; he also accomplished some micro-analysis of social ties, which provides some continuity between the earlier European sociology and the "Simmelian" analysis. In short, both Abel and Nisbet are impressed with Simmel's keen sense of observation, dissection, and interpretation of the flux of social life.

Rigid distinctions, among science, art, and philosophy are not to be found in Simmel's work. His approach was a unique combination of all three disciplines. In Selection 6.2, an unusual essay, Murray Davis demonstrates how Simmel used in his sociology the insight that he gained from his sense of art. He points out that Simmel's chaotic-appearing essays of social reality actually cohere around the themes of (1) art as a visual phenomenon; (2) art as a new, integrated world separate from life; and (3) art as universalization through particularization.

1. Because Simmel viewed society as visual rather than audile art, that is, music, he was primarily interested in social types and the arrangements of social space rather than the sequential development of society over time. He further preferred to view social reality as visual art (e.g., painting) instead of tactile art (e.g., sculpture). According to Simmel, only rarely is man the sculptor, creating new forms with his hands. All too often he is, tragically, merely the painter, contemplating already established forms that fill his social space and imprison him. In this outlook, Simmel resembles both Freud, who held that man's sociocultural conventions are inimical to his basic nature, and Weber, who believed that magic and charisma are being lost to the planned procedures deadening everyday life. In Simmel's visualization of a static social reality, those forms that man, the reactor, is capable of creating are only minor and limited, incidental to society at large. He is largely a contemplator in a world without time.

2. When art is objectified in a particular work, it stands on its own, separate from the dialectics and forces of real life. In similar fashion, Simmel thought, the diverse social forms, the individual, and the social types separate from one another and organize themselves into their own worlds. Thus, the individual studying social phenomena is faced with a dilemma: on the one hand, he must separate the object of his interest from the rest of society if he is to study it at all, and, on the other hand, he risks the danger that in studying it for its own sake he will contribute to its tendency to organize itself according to its own rationale. The individual can enjoy his autonomy from and enrichment in these worlds and, at the same time, lament his fragmentation as he is pulled apart by them. Life is, then, forever threatening to "come undone" (to reach "ruin") because the demands of the social worlds for their own symmetry impinge on the individual, who requires asymmetry and challenge to grow. If there is to remain any individuality, the figure (person) must contrast with the ground (the social environment).

The concept of distance is the tool that Simmel used in his analysis of the internal workings of social processes—the social relations between both superior and inferior as well as between those sharing and those not sharing particular experiences or knowledge. Distance can also be the measure of the observer's lack of affinity with the observed.

3. In Simmel's view one can comprehend art as universalization, the depiction of enduring human themes, through particularization, indi-

vidual painting, sculptures, and so on. He harmonized such metaphysics with his sociological method by pointing out the relation between the universal and the particular in social phenomena as well: since the individual gives up part of his individuality in order to participate in generalized social life, the universals of this "societalized" condition can be deciphered in even the small, trivial activities in which the individual engages.

6.1

The Contribution of Georg Simmel: A Reappraisal*

THEODORE ABEL

In honoring the memory of Georg Simmel on the hundredth anniversary of his birth we pay homage to one of the truly great men in the history of sociology. Simmel's accomplishment far surpasses that of the ordinarily creative scholar who leaves behind him some important land-mark or who erects a monument to himself with a *magnum opus* along some well-trodden path of intellectual enterprise. He belongs to the small company of men who have opened up an entirely new path of inquiry and whose pioneering work set the direction for others to follow.

What Simmel initiated has become the tradition from which the present body of sociological knowledge has grown. Whatever other features they may possess, all contributions that are sociologically relevant embody the approach and viewpoint which Simmel was the first to make explicit. For this reason Simmel can justifiably be regarded as the founder of modern sociology. In order to understand how this came about the state of sociology prior to Simmel's formulation of his trail-blazing ideas must be briefly considered.

Sociology in Simmel's Time

From its inception in the second half of the eighteenth century, the idea of a science of society followed a plan which is most fully and systematically stated in the works of Auguste Comte. The plan included the notion of an over-all science which was to take the place of the philosophy of history. This science was to interpret the essence, the meaning, and the direction of human development, not theologically and metaphysically, but in the manner of physical and biological science. To the

---

* A slight revision of a paper read at the Durkheim–Simmel Centenary Session of the annual meeting of the American Sociological Society, August, 1958.

pursuit of these goals of the philosophy of history by means of the scientific method, Comte gave the name "Sociology."

In Comte's program the task of sociology is the formulation of the laws according to which the Human Realm maintains itself, and the laws according to which the content of this Realm originates, grows, and changes. The key concepts in this scheme are Order and Progress, the datum is Universal History, the subject Humanity. The program tacitly assumes that the factual basis for dealing with the problems of human society in a comprehensive manner had been already established. According to Comte's view, sociologists can authoritatively contemplate the whole social realm and every study of any aspect of it must take its bearings from this holistic view. This is one part of Comte's program.

The second part proposes nothing less than the reorganization and reform of society by sociologists. For it seemed axiomatic that the discovery of the rational order upon which the statics and the dynamics of society rest would make possible the design of blue-prints for its perfect organization.

With hardly an exception, every writer in the nineteenth century who published his work under the aegis of sociology followed the Comtean program. Each one who wrote a general treatise tried to propound a new over-all explanatory principle that could account for all manifestations of social life. Racial, geographical, psychological, economic, and social factors were each singled out to serve as a basis for such explanation. The result was an accumulation of diverse and overlapping interpretations of the nature of social order that lacked continuity and was full of blind-alleys. At the same time, the writers who were proposing schemes for social reform also followed Comte and claimed the authority of science for their proposals in the name of his sociology.

Critique of the Comtean Program

In the latter part of the nineteenth century the difficulties inherent in the Comtean program became more and more apparent. In European universities sociology failed to gain academic recognition and was even actively opposed, as was the case in Germany. Some of the arguments advanced against it, particularly by Wilhelm Dilthey, were unanswerable. According to Dilthey, if sociology attempted to encompass all that actually happens in the "Human Realm," it could not be a science. It would merely provide a label for a string of unrelated, ambitious works, each advocating a different explanatory theory. As early as 1881 Dilthey clearly and forcefully argued in favor of advancing our knowledge of society, culture, and personality by way of cumulative, analytical, and experimental studies conducted by specialized disciplines.[1]

In the United States, where a social science movement flourished and sociology did gain academic recognition, other difficulties in the

---

[1] W. Dilthey, *Einleitung in die Geisteswissenschaften*, second edition (first edition, 1833), Berlin: Teubner, 1922, pp. 113–123.

Comtean program were revealed. There was, first, the dilemma in which the individual student of sociology found himself: the emphasis on sociology as a general science meant that there were only two alternatives open to him. He could invent his own explanatory principle for organizing the data of human history. Or, if he lacked the originality for this task, he could become an exponent of one of the masters.

Secondly, there was the more serious handicap that confronted those who desired to apply sociological knowledge to social planning. The laws and principles propounded in sociological writings were too vague and too sweeping to be applicable in practical circumstances. Especially lacking was a guiding viewpoint and a special approach which could be identified with sociology and give professional status to its practitioners.

Simmel's Resolution of the Dilemma

These difficulties pointed to the need for drastic revision, if not abandonment, of the Comtean program. It is at this crucial point that Simmel advanced the ideas which provided a new prospect for sociology and helped to inaugurate the era of specialized, cumulative research based on a specific sociological approach.

Simmel's interest in sociology grew from his earlier work on the problems of ethics. In the course of his studies he was faced with the problem of the cause for the growth of individuation in historical times. In the volume *Social Differentiation* (1890), he presents a theory in which the process of individuation is correlated with the breakup of primary groups. He attributes this phenomenon to the formation of larger groups or the differentiation of specialized groups out of more inclusive ones. As a result of this process there follows an increase in the incidence of multiple group membership which he views as the necessary sociological condition of individuation.

This work received high praise from Dilthey, who was one of Simmel's most influential teachers.[2] Dilthey encouraged Simmel to develop the general theoretical implications of the study for he saw in it the prototype of a new and needed specialized field of investigation. Beginning in 1890 and continuing in a series of articles, Simmel did just this. He developed a theory and demonstrated its application in several brilliant studies of human relations which are as fresh and significant today as they were fifty years ago.

In Germany the prejudice against sociology was so deeply ingrained that it was twenty years before Simmel's ideas began to be recognized academically. But the reaction in the United States was different. Here, because of a deep-felt need for a more workable specification of the subject matter of an established enterprise which, however, was faced with an impasse, Simmel's reception was almost immediate and favorable.

---

[2] *Ibid.*, p. 421.

Clear-minded scholars like Albion W. Small, who made *The American Journal of Sociology* available to Simmel (and other European sociologists) for the publication of his writings, were quick to recognize the value of his ideas as a means for resolving their impasse. In due time the change from the synthetic to the analytic approach greatly helped to establish continuity in research and to produce a steady development of theory. In this conceptual and methodological expansion and refinement of Simmel's ideas the works of Ross, Thomas, Park, Burgess, Wiese, Znaniecki, Becker, and Merton constitute major links.

Simmel's Theory

What were Simmel's ideas that played such a large role in bringing about this new development in sociology? They have become so thoroughly ingrained in our habits of thought that they appear self-evident, perhaps, and require little elaboration here. This is as it should be with every genuine accomplishment. But it is altogether in order to recall that it once required an especially brilliant mind to conceive and to explicate what today is part of our common intellectual heritage.

As I see it, the main propositions laid down by Simmel are:

1. That the *social* is a mode of existence which concretely expresses itself in the reciprocal relations of human beings, and that the unity of a society is a derivative of these relationships and does not precede them.

2. That the *social phase* of human existence can be viewed as distinct from the personal and cultural phases. The justification of sociology as a special science rests upon this fact.

3. That for sociological purposes a *society* is best conceived, not as composed of biophysical units, but as consisting of the modes of reciprocity, the patterns of interrelated activities in which human beings act for, with, and against each other. If they are conceived in this way societies can increase or diminish in a fashion that is independent of their numerical population, a point that as yet has not been fully explored.

4. Finally, that the *social*, in its manifold modes, generates a functional effectiveness which produces specifiable results in its influence upon human conduct. The social is determined, but it is also determining.

It follows from these considerations that:

First, the special sociological approach can be defined as the attempt to ascertain the functional influence of social factors in specific cultural-historical situations; and

Second, a sociological proposition is any statement of a correlation, a law, or, in general, any uniformity in which at least one of the independent variables is a social factor. Durkheim's law of suicide and Max Weber's hypothesis in his sociology of religion are familiar examples of such propositions.

The fruitfulness of his theoretical proposals was demonstrated by Simmel's own writings. His subtle, perceptive, and discerning mind produced a veritable horn of plenty of significant sociological studies. As a total output by a single person, the wealth of original contributions made by Simmel has yet to find its equal.

Reappraisals

The title of this paper calls for a reappraisal of Simmel's contribution. I will consider this task in two contexts. First, I will take up certain misapprehensions about Simmel's work that have been perpetuated by certain textbooks and which distort the proper view of his contribution. Second, and in conclusion, I will try to point out in what ways Simmel's thought is relevant for the evaluation of some current trends in sociology.

Formalism. One of the most serious misapprehensions of Simmel's work results from the summation of his views under the heading of formalism or formal sociology. This terminology has fostered the idea that Simmel advocates *formal* analysis of sociological data akin to geometry or grammar. Superficial support for this argument can be found, but only by stressing some of Simmel's pronouncements to the exclusion of others, and, particularly, by ignoring the nature of the procedure exemplified in his concrete studies.[3]

The current rejection of Simmel's awkward phrasing of the difference between sociology and the other social sciences, derived from the distinction between form and content, is correct. Simmel's numerous studies clearly show that he had no intention of assigning a procedure empty of concrete reference to sociology. In making the distinction between formal and non-formal social science, Simmel simply wished to convey the idea that, as human beings relate themselves to each other in pursuit of individual and common interests, they do so in ways that are patterned and that repeat themselves under different circumstances. He called these ways "forms-of-sociation."

It is important to note that these three words should not be separated because Simmel was not referring to forms as such, but to the form of a particular content, namely, sociation. Instead of forms-of-sociation he might just as well have spoken of "modes of reciprocity" or "types of transactions." Pattern, structure, type, even social process, are appropriate equivalents for Simmel's "form." The association of "formalism" with Simmel seems, in all simplicity, to be a result of his accidental use of the word "form" rather than a reflection of close inspection of the essential nature of his contribution.

Simmel's Scientific Stature. A second misapprehension is the conclusion that Simmel lacked the interest and disposition of the scientist, that he was essentially a philosopher, and that his ideas and findings, therefore, have little relevance for the technically-minded professional

---

[3] Omar K. Moore has called my attention to the fact that recent development in the theory of games makes it possible to treat forms-of-sociation as pure forms. Should this prove to be the case, such findings would merely show the applicability of formal analysis to sociological concepts, but would not establish it as a basic sociological procedure.

sociologist of today. This viewpoint neglects substance for outer appearance. It ignores a number of things. In the first place, it overlooks the fact that Simmel made his studies long before the technical proficiencies of modern research design were developed. Secondly, it discounts the fact that Simmel worked under great handicaps. Although he taught at the University of Berlin, he received no academic recognition or assistance until shortly before his death. He earned his living by lecturing and writing magazine articles, a fact which, as Lewis Coser has shown, largely accounts for his literary style.[4] For the material for his studies, Simmel was wholly dependent upon his own resources, his personal observations, and his discerning reading. Thirdly, this viewpoint ignores the fact that Simmel was aware of the preliminary character of his formulations. He called for the perfection of methods for the investigation of forms-of-sociation which would eventually provide more extensive, precise, and systematic sociological knowledge.[5]

The extent to which Simmel thought along modern lines about the need for codified data is illustrated by a little-known episode that occurred in 1910. In that year, Simmel, with Max Weber and a few other scholars, organized the German Sociological Society, not only to facilitate the exchange of ideas, but for the express purpose of organizing systematic research. At the time the group planned to make two studies, one, of the newspaper, and the other, of the German clubs—the so-called Vereine. The outline for the sociology of the newspaper calls for content analysis, for the study of journalism as a profession, its diverse social functions in different countries, its role in the power struggle, and the contribution of the press to the molding of modern man. In his report of the preparation for the research, Max Weber, who, with Simmel, was the moving spirit of this group, conceived of the task in a manner that was twenty-five years ahead of his time. For example, Weber asked: "Where is the material for such a research job to be found? The materials are the newspapers themselves and we will have to proceed at the beginning very unglamorously, with scissors and measuring stick, to find out how the content of the newspaper has changed quantitatively during the last generation. Only after such careful quantitative investigations can one hope to turn to qualitative ones." Or, again, commenting on the questionnaire to be used in the study of the Vereine, Weber stated that: "the data with which we will have to cope in the beginning will be very dry and trivial. But without such dry and trivial work, which requires the outlay of large sums of money and prodigious labor, nothing can be accomplished." He added: "you can see that the concrete research planned is not such that one can count on achieving brilliant results within a few years. The public will have to show a lot of patience. Furthermore, besides unselfish devotion to the scientific task, substantial financial resources are required. We have to

---

[4] Lewis A. Coser, "Georg Simmel's Style of Work: A Contribution to the Sociology of the Sociologist," *American Journal of Sociology*, 63 (May 1958), pp. 635–640.

[5] See especially *Soziologie, Leipzig*: Duncker & Humboldt, 1908, pp. 16–17.

recognize that, in order to carry out research on a large scale, the sociologist will have to depend on public support."[6]

Needless to say, the studies had to be abandoned, for the era of foundations had not yet dawned. It is clear, however, that both Simmel and Weber were fully aware of scientific research requirements from the very beginning of their sociological work.

Simmel and Current Trends in Sociology

What would have been Simmel's attitude toward current trends in sociology? His writings contain many clues which permit one to draw reasonable inferences about probable answers to this question without engaging in undue speculation. It is clear, for example, that Simmel would have given full support to the "structural functional" approach.

It would not be difficult to show that, in the last analysis, the investigation of forms-of-sociation, requested by Simmel, involves the determination of their functions with regard to social life. In retrospect, we can see that what was fresh and significant in Simmel's studies was not the specification of this or the other mode of reciprocity—for, obviously, conflict, subordination, the stranger, secrecy, and so on were well known phenomena—but the discovery of their unsuspected and unintentional functions. One example, to which Simmel systematically referred, is the differential effect of various forms-of-sociation on the process of group integration. Another important problem which he investigated was the role played by forms-of-sociation in resolving or integrating the dilemma of polarities in social life. Simmel viewed polarities as constituting the dynamic element in human life: man has to strive continuously to reconcile them. He must somehow bring together, for example, the individual and the group, the need for conformity and for individuation, the need for stability and for flexibility, into harmonious working arrangements. As a model of such functional analysis, Simmel's study of fashion makes clear that fashion (among other things) mitigates the conflict between the need to conform to conventions and the need for individual distinctiveness, by permitting the simultaneous satisfaction of both.[7]

Of other important developments in recent sociology, it is reasonably certain that Simmel would have welcomed the emphasis given to scientific methodology. There can be no doubt, however, that he would have voiced several warning signals which, in my opinion, we would do well to heed today.

---

[6] Max Weber, *Gesammelte Aufsaetze zur Soziologie und Sozialpolitik*, Tuebingen: Mohr, 1924, p. 441. Cf. also Marianne Weber, *Lebenserinnerungen*, Bremen: Storm, 1948, pp. 375–409, for an account of the relationship between Weber and Simmel; and the same author's *Max Weber, Ein Lebensbild*, Tuebingen: Mohr, 1926, pp. 425–431, for details of Weber's efforts on behalf of the German Sociological Society.

[7] Georg Simmel, "Fashion," *American Journal of Sociology*, 62 (May 1957), p. 551.

First of all, he would have cautioned us against regarding the codification of data—those reported in the *American Soldier*, for example—as distinctive contributions to sociology. Such studies, of course, furnish indispensable material for arriving at valid sociological propositions. The latter, however, are the result of a process which requires an act of creative imagination. For enduring sociological discoveries demand three progressive steps: the gathering of data, their codification, and interpretation of the data which combines the intellectual method of science with the intuitive insights of a highly sensitive and creative mind. Thus a recent interpretation which Simmel probably would have regarded as a distinct contribution to sociology is Merton's study of role-sets.[8] Evidently, this study could not have been made without the large amount of codified data on roles and reference group behavior gathered by many investigators. However, its findings are not logically deducible from the data. They are the result of an act of creative synthesis which transcends the data and illuminates them at the same time.

Simmel would further warn us not to blur the distinctive nature of the phenomena of the human realm. He would urge that the specifically human factors be given due consideration. To the current injunction (voiced by Merton and others) that we search for middle-range theories, Simmel thus would have added the request that we also use middle-range concepts, that is, concepts that stand between the definitions of particulars and what Einstein termed the "free concepts" employed in physico-mathematical equations.[9] Useful sociological concepts like status, Gemeinschaft, relative deprivation, and solidarity, combine generality with concreteness. The latter consists in that element of the concept which evokes personal experience and might be derived from self observation and which, therefore, constitutes the meaningful content of the concept. This content is irreducible. Nothing relevant can be said of human conduct in total abstraction from phenomenal and experiential reference.

There is another ramification of this viewpoint the nature of which is indicated by the following statement by Simmel: The study of forms-of-sociation must "include study of the peculiar characteristics . . . which [they] take under the influence of the particular environments in which they are realized. If, for example, we investigate the formation of aristocracies, we must not only examine the . . . separation of the . . . homogeneous masses, but . . . we must take into consideration . . . the modifications which different stages of production and variations in the dominant ideas of the times bring about."[10] Clearly, this admonition means that Simmel would have taken the side of such scholars as Max Weber, who insist that sociological theory cannot be built in total abstraction from the

---

[8] Robert K. Merton, "The Role Set: Problems in Sociological Theory," *British Journal of Sociology*, 8 (June 1957), pp. 106–120.

[9] Albert Einstein, "Physics and Reality," *Journal of the Franklin Institute*, 221 (March 1936), pp. 349–382.

[10] Georg Simmel, "The Problem of Sociology," *Annals of the American Academy of Political and Social Science*, 6 (November 1895), p. 417n.

historico-cultural actuality from which it derives its data. Simmel would not have gone as far as Weber. Weber regarded sociology as a generalizing discipline which is an adjunct to history. But Simmel would insist that every significant formulation in sociology is, or implies, a piece of history, either past or present.

In view of these considerations, it is clear that Simmel would have ruled out from sociology proper generalizations which ignore what Znaniecki called the "humanistic coefficient." He also would have favored models of social action of the kind Weber called "ideal types" rather than the dimensional models favored by such exponents of a Scientific sociology as Stuart C. Dodd.

But Georg Simmel, in his own way and faced by problems that we do not confront today, was a master contributor to the scientific study of social life. His thought is as alive and significant now as it was when it was uttered. Even more so, I should think, since we, with the additional experience gained in the last fifty years, can be much more appreciative of the importance of Simmel's contributions than were his contemporaries.

C O M M E N T / ROBERT A. NISBET

When one's agreement with a paper is as substantial as mine is with Theodore Abel's, there remains nothing, really, but the time-honored privilige of splitting a few hairs and, since even these are few, of adding a few observations that do not flow directly from the paper itself.

Thus, although Abel's essential argument about Comte is unexceptionable, it is still worth noting that there is an important section of the *Positive Polity* that goes beyond the argument. I am referring principally to the second volume of this often fantastic work where, in his analyses of kinship, religion, and other associational ties, Comte frequently, in spite of himself, comes close to fulfilling the promise of the sub-title of the work, "A Treatise on Sociology."

Here we have something, I believe, that approaches the heart of modern sociology: a serious and at times penetrating analysis of the social bond. Admittedly, even here the treatment suffers from the infusions of religiosity and humanitarian sentimentality which Comte, in his last years, was unable to resist injecting into everything that his mind touched. Whatever its inadequacies by the standards that such men as Simmel and Durkheim were later to give sociological study, however, at least this analysis of the social bond is distinguishable from that philosophy of history for which Comte is best known and to which Abel has confirmed himself.

I do not wish to go overboard on Comte. He was not, for all his importance, one of the towering minds of his age. But too close a concentration upon such matters as the law of three stages and the other elements of his *Positive Philosophy* may tend to hide the important fact that no small amount of later sociology, and I would not exclude the Germans, can fairly be seen as a secularization of Comte's religion of humanity.

I must also demur somewhat on Abel's reappraisal of Simmel as a formal sociologist. I do this in admiration of what is personally involved. After all, the common characterization of Simmel as a sociologist of forms owes a very great deal, in this country at least, to Abel's own profound study of the emergence of German sociology, published a quarter of a century ago.[1] But I am inclined to think that the earlier Abel has more validity on this matter than the present Abel seems willing to grant. For Simmel is very eloquent about the claims that "pure sociology" will be a crucial area of the larger field; and that the object of pure sociology is the abstraction of the element of sociation from the heterogeneity of contents and purposes which life reveals. Pure sociology thus proceeds, Simmel tells us, like grammar, which isolates the forms of languages from their contents. Elsewhere he compares sociology in this sense to geometry, also a study of forms in abstraction from content.

The evidence is convincing, I believe, that the earlier Abel is still sound. What the present paper does make clear and important, however, is the fact that when Simmel set himself to the study of actual forms, he lost a good deal of his purity. For this we may be grateful. Had Simmel held chastely to his methodological commandments when he turned to such subjects as secrecy, subordination, and the stranger, sociology would be the poorer. Form and content cannot, in practice, be separated, and although there is a pleasantly tantalizing note in Simmel's earlier call to the forms, his own superb studies of concrete forms of association make him less than, and a great deal more than, a formal sociologist. On this point, Abel is emphatically right.

He is also right in his succinct evaluation of Simmel's chief contributions to contemporary sociology. There is much warrant for saying that of all the pioneers Simmel is the most relevant at the present time. This is not to make any invidious comparisons among the Titans themselves, for such relevance is determined as much by the character of research interests at any given time as it is by the genius of the man. I mean merely that Simmel seems to hold all of the timely appeal today that Weber and Durkheim, for example, did two decades ago—and may well hold again, depending upon popular currents of thought and inquiry. To move from Simmel's pages to current work in the study of small groups, motivation, roles, status, and human interaction is not as difficult, I should say, as from the writings of either Durkheim or Weber.

It is the *microsociological* character of Simmel's work that may always give him an edge in timeliness over the other pioneers. He did not disdain the small and the intimate elements of human association, nor did he ever lose sight of the primacy of human beings, of concrete individuals, in his analyses of institutions. Patterns of obedience, loyalty, subordination, friendship, and influence change, to be sure, from age to age; they are

---

[1] Theodore Abel, *Systematic Sociology in Germany*, New York: Columbia University Press, 1929.

modified and given color by shifting institutional patterns of culture and power. Simmel was not unaware of these, as his keen insights into the Renaissance and other historical ages make plain. But he knew also that there is continuity of the fundamental elements of association; that, irrespective of the gross differences of ages and institutions, dyads and triads possess certain continuing or repetitive elements, and that these are often as influential upon decision-making and power structures as the changing phases of politics and culture.

For these and related reasons, then, there is a relevance to Simmel that is likely to make him a perennial source of inspiration to all who are concerned with the springs of human behavior. If we are less struck by concern with historical processes in Simmel than we are in Weber's work, for example, nevertheless it is incorrect to accuse Simmel of being unhistorical. It is impossible to read his brief—all too brief—passages on the social roots of the Renaissance, on the rise of party government in modern England, and on certain of the social structures of the Middle Ages without realizing Simmel's profound interest in history and the value of his insights for historians, as well as sociologists.

The same is true of politics. Everyone who has written about Simmel has commented on his aloofness to the overt issues and controversies of politics in his own age—at least until the outbreak of the first World War. And nowhere in Simmel's writings do we ever see as direct a concern with political processes, past or present, as we do in Weber's. Simmel's treatment of modern socialism, perceptive as it is, does not compare in sweep or depth of insight with the discussions of the same subject by Weber or by Michels.

Yet it would not do to dismiss him as ethereally non-political, for in a vast amount of Simmel's work there is constantly before us the yield of a mind sensitive to the psychosocial elements of political behavior—the micro-elements, as, again, they may be depicted. What, after all, is the point of his matchless treatment of subordination and superordination if it is not clarification of the political? The same point holds for his discussions of secrecy, of *tertius gaudens, divide et impera*, and other characteristic sections of his analysis. I believe that it is in some of the "inner histories" of politics—the diaries of Harold Ickes, for example, or Churchill's history of the second World War—that Simmel's political insights become most suggestive. Here we are so often in the intimate recesses of politics, and Simmel possessed abundantly, if only in an academic way, what Cardinal de Retz once called "the terrible gift of intimacy."

This preoccupation with the intimate and repetitive in life marks his kinship with the great essayists. Had Simmel lived in an age or a culture that prized the essay, he would, I am sure, have devoted himself to this difficult literary form, and used it to convey his wisdom. How clear is the likeness of outlook between Simmel and Francis Bacon, or the incomparable Montaigne. Compare their treatments of conventionality, of fear, of power, love, friendship, abasement, pride, and it is apparent that in Simmel there lie the essential elements of a great essayist. All elements save one: form! But this was more the fault of the age, and perhaps of the language, than of the man.

I cannot resist noting, finally, somewhat in the fashion of the moral essayist, how often there is an affinity between the small or intimate and the lasting in social thought. Those who strike for the great sweeping systems—as Comte, Spencer, Ward, and Buckle did in the nineteenth century—do so seemingly at their peril. Charles Horton Cooley was largely concerned with the small, with the microcosm, and his work is still fresh for us today when only antiquaries turn to men who in Cooley's day were thought immortal. This is even more the case for Simmel. It is also likely, I think, that less of Simmel's personal genius will be lost in the nameless body of advancing knowledge—the common fate of even great contributors in the history of science—than will be true of Durkheim and Weber. This is merely another way of saying that in Simmel's work there is a larger element of irreducible humanism and that, as with Darwin and Freud for example, it will always be possible to derive something of importance from him directly that cannot be absorbed by the impersonal propositions of science.

6.2

Georg Simmel and the Aesthetics of Social Reality*

MURRAY S. DAVIS

Arthur Salz (1959) once said he learned from his teacher Georg Simmel, the following about society: "[Simmel] conceives of sociology as the study of the forms of sociation. But whoever speaks of forms moves in the field of aesthetics. Society, in the last analysis, is a work of art."

Society is a work of art? The comparison is an intriguing one. In this article I will try to show that it constitutes Simmel's central vision, and that around this aesthetic model the overwhelming profusion of Simmel's sociological insights—that on first reading appear in such chaotic dissociation from one another—actually cohere. Of course, not all of Simmel's sociology can be reduced to his aesthetics, but I think it will greatly aid our comprehension of the unity of Simmel's work if we consider the ways in which much of it can.

There are three aspects of Simmel's aesthetics which underlie his sociology: (1) his particular conception of the *artistic modality*; (2) his particular conception of the *artistic product*; and (3) his particular conception of the *artistic method*. Let us proceed to discover the way in which Simmel conceives each of these components of his aesthetics, and to trace the way in which each of these aesthetic motifs runs through his treatment of social reality.

The Artistic Modality: Visual

Simmel's conception of society is based not on all the sensory modalities in different aesthetic genres, but only on art that is essentially visual (Duncan, 1959:111, 117; Walter, 1959:154). In fact, he (1968a:86–87) states explicitly that ". . . in art, there is absolutely no other point of

* The author wishes to thank Lewis Coser for his encouragement of this project, and Donald Levine for his valuable criticism.

reference besides purely optical processes."[1] This visual bias of his model has several repercussions on his thinking.

First, it means that Simmel does not see the fundamental elements of art and of society as developing through time, as he would have done had he drawn his model from the audile arts, whose tonalities and rhythms immediately draw the listener into the future or remind him of the past.[2] Instead, Simmel conceptualizes the fundamental elements of art and society as atemporal configurations in space, as his critics point out: ". . . if Bergson repeatedly asks that we admit the importance of time, Simmel is just as insistent in stressing the significance of *space*. If Bergson is concerned with passage and duration, with the movement and change of the object observed, Simmel is preoccupied with the object's *stability*" (Lipman, 1959:121; emphasis mine).

Being preoccupied with stable elements and forms leads Simmel to be ". . . more concerned with a *taxonomic analysis* of these forms than with a search for the causes that permit specific men to mobilize and to direct the energies of others. His formalism diverts him from causal questions . . ." (Walter, 1959:160–161; emphasis mine) and from developmental questions:

> [Simmel's] reliance upon a spatial (or pseudo-spatial) frame of interpretation tends to emphasize the *static* and extended aspect of the self [and to] neglect those more dynamic aspects, less readily visualized, which are also essential to a just conception of individuality: only cursorily or obliquely does Simmel confront such problems as power, integrity, productivity, and growth (Lipman, 1959:137; emphasis mine).

Second, while the contrast between the visual arts and the audile arts can show us a reason for Simmel's ahistorical perspective on society, the contrast between the visual arts and the tactile ones can help us clarify his ambivalent view of human nature. In Simmel's time, the objects of the tactile arts, such as a sculpture or a building,[3] implied, phenomeno-

---

[1] It is interesting how little music concerned Simmel after his doctoral dissertation (1882) on the subject. Though he later went on to write books or articles on a poet (Goethe), a painter (Rembrandt), a sculptor (Rodin), and an architect (Michaelangelo), he never wrote anything on a musician.

[2] Simmel did have an early flirtation with historicism (of the evolutionist, social Darwinist, variety), which can be seen in his works on social differentiation, the philosophy of history and the philosophy of morals. But he takes great care in his major work on sociology (1908) to distinguish the sociological approach from the historical. Occasionally, Simmel does discuss a feature of social life in its historical context, such as the urban experience, or individuality, or the organization of groups, but even here he usually does so merely for the purpose of comparison and not for the purpose of a detailed delineation of its development.

[3] Walter (1959) asserts that Simmel's artistic model is architecture, but this is wrong. Not only would this contradict Walter's (1959:162) own view of Simmel's essential passivity, but most of Walter's (1959:152) supporting illustrations are actually drawn from geometry.

logically, the hand of their creator. The tactile arts were seen as revealing man as a forger of the forms of the world, where as the visual arts (like painting) were seen as portraying man as a contemplator of a world already formed. (Considering the recent "active" paintings of Jackson Pollack and "passive" sculptures of Henry Moore, this kind of control between the visual and the tactile arts no longer has the same force.)[4]

Throughout Simmel's thinking runs an ambiguous—sometimes tragically ambiguous—conception of the human predicament: at times Simmel sees man as the creator of the forms of culture and of society—forms man creates in order to satisfy his needs and serve his purpose; at other times Simmel sees man as having to endure those forms which he had previously made—forms which now neither serve nor satisfy, but which now master him. In the previous generation, Marx and Nietzsche could limit this latter view—man as passive sufferer—to the present and, hence, could hope for a better future. But Simmel, like his contemporary Freud, finds the conflict between man and his social and cultural creations to be eternal, and to be a struggle which man is continually losing. Except for the brief moment of creation, man must suffer his own creations, endure his past organizations of his cultural and social worlds. If he is to master them at all, he can do so only internally, only through contemplation.[5] To view, to point, to name, to symbolize, to describe, and thus, by this damming off, to hold back and to direct momentarily a channel of the ongoing stream of life, is the very best man can hope to achieve. But, even so, almost immediately the very tools and concepts by which he separated part of life from its source unite with what they have cut off: from this conjugation there springs a new hybrid creature which, following its own logic, its own pattern of development, grows out of man's control and hence augments still further that objective environment (that environment of cultural objects) which determines and delimits him.[6] In point of

---

[4] Toward the end of his life, Simmel himself began to feel an "active" mode of painting was possible. In "The Conflict in Modern Culture" (1968e:15–17), he discusses the relation between the then avant-garde movement of "active" Expressionism and the prevailing school of "passive" Impressionism.

[5] Two recent commentators on Simmel bring out this point. Walter (1959: 162) states: "Simmel internalizes and psychologizes freedom, moving it from the realm of external relations to the inner life." And Weingartner (1962:183) adds: "Simmel feels deeply the need to dominate the current of experience and to transcend it. But for him, mastery does not primarily mean manipulation. Unlike John Dewey, whose goal is to use and change the world, to bend it to the will of men, Simmel's hope and need is to grasp it intellectually, to comprehend it, to contemplate it." On this point, Simmel's thinking seems to be dominated by a stoicism which is, in part, an aspect of his Kantian inheritance.

[6] This exposition of Simmel's view of the relation between man and his creations is a précis of his crucial and brilliant, but unfortunately difficult and neglected, article "On the Concept and the Tragedy of Culture" (1968c). Only three years later, however, in one of his last works, "The Conflict in

illustration, how Simmel would have sighed to see the progeny of his few pages on dyads and triads: those hundreds of recent articles on small-group research which fill the sociology journals and which provide the corpus of an already recognized field of specialization within sociology, complete with its own ground rules and requirements.

Notice how similar this position is to Weber's notion of the "routinization of charisma" (Bendix, 1962; Shils, 1965). Weber shows how charismatic leaders (embodiments of the life force) are continually bursting through the old forms of social organization and creating new ones, though these new ones slowly become routinized through traditionalization or bureaucratization until the next charismatic leader comes along. On this point both Weber and Simmel are attempting to reconcile their dual heritage of Nietzsche (life) and the neo-Kantians (form). The difference between Weber and Simmel is one of emphasis. The former stresses social processes that are predominantly external to man; the latter stresses cultural processes that are predominantly internal to him. Both focus on historical periods when social energy was declining as it becomes entrapped and dissipated in elaborate cultural forms and social organizations, but Simmel (at least until the last period of his life) pays even less attention than Weber to historical periods of "negative entropy" when available social energy was increasing.[7]

Modern Culture" (1968e) (written in 1914, but not published until 1918), he seems to have partially retracted this pessimistic view of man's fate. Here he asserts that the life force of the subjective spirit may yet overcome the dying forms of the objective world, and he gives examples of how it appears to be doing so already in the fields of art, philosophy, ethics, and religion—though even here he (1968e:25) concludes, again on a pessimistic note, that the conflict between life and form is eternal.

The model of human development put forth in Simmel's "On the Concept and the Tragedy of Culture" (1968c) anticipates by more than fifty years the model of human development put forth in Peter Berger and Thomas Luckmann's *The Social Construction of Reality* (1966). The only major difference between their two models is that Simmel views man as developing through the externalization and reinternalization of cultural artifacts, whereas Berger and Luckmann view man as developing through the externalization and reinternalization of social institutions.

[7] Though this is not the place to discuss the natural science models that form the basis of Weber's and Simmel's social thought, it should be noted that much of early twentieth-century German social theory is actually derived from one of the nineteenth century's greatest contributions to physical theory: the Second Law of Thermodynamics. This so-called "law of entropy" states, in one phrasing, that energy systems tend towards equilibrium, i.e., towards an equal diffusion of energy—in other words, everything runs down. The physical law of entropy served for pessimists the same function the biological law of evolution served for optimists: both provided a "scientific" foundation in nature for their contrary views on social life.

Weber, of course, did write one major work on a historical period of "negative entropy" when available social energy was increasing: *The Protest-*

It is not clear what caused Simmel to see man as more reactive than active. Perhaps it was the helpless position of German intellectuals during his lifetime. Perhaps it was the fact that both society and culture in neo-rococo, *fin-de-siècle* Germany were composed of an enormous number of outworn institutions and lifeless values. Certainly it was also affected by Simmel's inability to swim easily through the gelatin of German academic life (Coser, 1958). In any case, the fact remains that Simmel, like Burckhardt before him, saw man as no longer a Cesare Borgia, consciously forging the state and the institutions of society as the artist creates a work of art. At best, now, man's creations are limited to small new forms in the interstices and margins of a social world already given: his imagination can guide only his sociable relations during coffee breaks in the alcoves of great institutions, grace notes to a social symphony whose main themes already have been scored.

The final implication of the fact that for Simmel art is essentially a visual phenomenon concerns geometry, the mathematics on which visual aesthetics, and hence much of Simmel's sociology, is based.[8] (Geometry became the foundation of painting, sculpture, and architecture—Simmel's three main aesthetic interests—during the Classical period and its Renais-

---

ant *Ethic and the Spirit of Capitalism* (1958) (first published in 1904). But he intended his study of this dynamic historical period to provide a contrast with what he took to be the decline of German society at the start of the twentieth century. His studies of other civilizations focused, for the most part, on the routinization of the social energy that originally inspired their distinctive character.

The optimism of Simmel's last works, "The Conflict in Modern Culture" (1968e) and his *Perspectives on Life* (untranslated) (which were written during the social euphoria around the beginning of World War I), must also be excepted from the generally pessimistic trend in his thinking. It seems reasonable to suppose, for anyone as dialectical as Simmel, that the moribund philosophy of his middle years would provide fertile soil for the development of a vitalist philosophy in his old age.

[8] Unfortunately, the English translations of Simmel's sociology often blur its geometric basis. Attempts to make him "relevant" to the present by translating his key terms into modern sociological jargon instead of into their literal equivalents purchase this relevance at the cost of obscuring the unity of his thought. Perhaps the worst example of this distortion of his meaning is Reinhard Bendix's translation of Chapter 6 of Simmel's *Sociologie* as "The Web of Group-Affiliations" (Simmel, 1955:125–195) instead of the literal "The Intersection of Social Circles."

Simmel's geometric sociology is seen most clearly in Chapter 9 of his *Sociologie*, "Space and the Spatial Ordering of Society." This chapter is still untranslated, except for its famous "Note on the Stranger" (1950a: 402–408), which begins: "If wandering is detachment from every fixed point in space, it is the conceptual opposite of attachment to such a point. The sociological form of the 'Stranger' represents the synthesis, so to speak, of both these properties. This phenomenon is another indication that spatial relationships not only determine, but also symbolize, human relationships" (author's translation).

sance revival.) Simmel (1968b; 1950a:87–177) sometimes considers aesthetic and sociological topics in terms of their *quantitative* rather than *geometric* properties, but usually he analyzes both aesthetic and sociological phenomena from the point of view of Euclid, not Pythagoras.

Geometry, as a visual mathematics, has two essential features: it abstracts geometric forms from the empirical world, and it systematizes these forms it abstracts. Simmel thinks sociology—like geometry—is also able to abstract its own subject matter (social forms) from one object in the empirical world and to apply (generalize) the results of this abstraction to other empirical objects:

> Sociology, the discipline that deals with the purely social aspects of man . . . , is related to the other social sciences in the same way geometry is related to the physical sciences. Geometry studies the forms through which any material becomes an empirical phenomenon—though these forms, like social forms, themselves exist only in abstraction. Both geometry and sociology leave to other (physical and social) sciences the investigation of the contents which the forms make real (i.e., which the forms turn into empirical phenomena). . . . Just as geometry discovers forms of spatial relationship which hold for all objects, so sociology discovers forms of social relationship which hold for all men (even though their contents, materials, and interests differ) (1959a:320; Simmel quoted by Walter, 1959: 152; author's translation).

However, Simmel believes sociology—unlike geometry—is not yet able to organize its own forms systematically, especially because it is more difficult to isolate social forms as completely as geometric forms and more difficult to apply the few social forms already isolated to as wide a range of empirical objects as geometric forms (1959a:321–324). Nevertheless, Simmel tries to develop his sociology as a science of the social world in direct parallel to geometry as a science of the physical world.

Simmel's use of the visual science of geometry as a model for his sociology reinforced several of the important tendencies of his thinking which were mentioned above. For one thing, his sociology was deflected away from historical analysis inasmuch as geometric forms have no temporal dimension. For another, his sociology became concerned less with changing the world than with contemplating it inasmuch as geometry was concerned more with merely gazing at the forms it abstracted from empirical phenomena than with the processes by which empirical phenomena came to be organized by these particular forms and not others. Thus, insofar as Simmel viewed the social world geometrically—or, more generally visually and aesthetically—he saw it from the static perspective of the passive observer rather than from the dynamic perspective of the active creator.[9]

---

[9] Simmel did, of course, consider works of art from the point of view of the individual who actively created them in his writings on Michaelangelo, Rembrandt, Goethe, and Rodin, but I think it is significant that he did not write on any specific individual or group who actively created a new social form.

The Artistic Product:
A New Integrated World
Separated from Life

The second characteristic of art upon which Simmel bases his sociology is the assumption that the productions of art are "wholly separated from life" (1950b:43). More specifically,

> . . . the essence of a work of art is, after all, that it cuts out a piece of the endlessly continuous sequence of perceived experience, detaching it from all connections with one side or the other . . . . the real object interacts with everything that surges or hovers around it, but the content of a work of art cuts off these threads, fusing only its own elements into a self-sufficient unity. Hence, the work of art leads its life beyond reality (1959b: 245; 1959c:267).

The common thesis that art is a reality independent of life places Simmel with the late nineteenth- and early twentieth-century French and English "art for art's sake" schools. The struggle for the autonomy of art is the best known instance of the general movement toward the autonomy of all cultural forms which was flourishing at the turn of the century. One of Simmel's most important contributions to social thought is his discovery of the growing autonomy of all social forms as well (1950a:380–381; 1950b:40–43). In effect, Simmel here is generalizing Karl Marx's assertion of the growing autonomy of economic processes, to all social and cultural processes. "The 'fetishism' which Marx assigned to economic commodities represents only a special case of this general fate of the contents of culture" (1968c:42).

Much of Simmel's analysis of specific social phenomena consists of his attempt to show that this theme of "separation from life" runs through such diverse social forms (among many others) as "faithfulness" (1950a: 379–387), "sociability" (1950b:43–57), and the "adventure."

> A part of existence, interwoven with the uninterruptedness of that existence, yet nevertheless felt as a whole, as an integrated unit—this is the form common to both the work of art and the adventure . . . . the work of art exists entirely beyond life as a reality; the adventure, entirely beyond life as an uninterrupted course which intelligibly connects every element with its neighbors (1959b:245).

(Simmel, 1959b: 247–248, has even claimed that life itself may be detached from some more cosmic process, and, hence, can itself be seen as an adventure.)

From this theorem that art and certain social processes become separated from the life which created them, Simmel (1950b:44–45) draws the corollary that each of these separated processes has a place outside itself, in life, from which to draw materials that it can reshape with its own forms in its own medium.

> What may be called the art drive, extracts out of the totality of phenomena their mere form, in order to shape it into specific structures that correspond with this drive. In a similar fashion, out of the realities of social

life, the 'sociability drive' extracts the pure process of sociation as a cherished value . . . . As a sociological category, I thus designate sociability as the play form of sociation. Its relation to content-determined, concrete sociation is similar to that of the work of art to reality.

Just as life produces the forms of art which in turn draw their content from life again, so sociation produces the social form of sociability which likewise then draws its content from social life. This process of "selection from life" as a characteristic of both artistic and social modes is well illustrated by the "art of coquetry":

> . . . eroticism has elaborated a form of play: coquetry. . . . If the erotic question between the sexes turns about consent or denial . . . coquetry [plays] hinted consent and hinted denial against each other to draw the man on without letting matters come to a decision. . . . And this freedom from all the weight of firm content and residual reality gives coquetry that character of vacillation, of distance, of the ideal, which allows one to speak with some right of the 'art'—not of the '[artifice]'—of coquetry (1949:258).

This new sphere not only separates itself from life and selects its materials from life, it also organizes and forms these materials into a new unity. Again the model is art: ". . . art . . . cuts out a piece of the endless continuous sequences of perceived experience . . . giving it a self-sufficient form as though defined and held together by an inner core" (1959b:245). This tendency toward organization may be seen on the level of the individual:

> Culture . . . is a process whereby the individual interiorizes the objects he finds everywhere about him. . . . They become his objects in that they are the objects of a unified personality; they are integrated into the course of his life. . . . Cultivation means treating one's own life as an object which must be continually shaped (Simmel quoted by Weingartner, 1962:72, 78, 76).

And on the level of society: "The essence of societal formation . . . [is] that out of closed units—such as human personalities more or less are—a new unit emerges" (1959d:341).

Lewis Coser (1965:14) has suggested that Simmel is a functionalist thinker in that he "considers the individual's social actions not in themselves, but in relation to those of other individuals and to particular structures and processes." I would make the further suggestion that, for Simmel, functionalism is not only a methodological principle, but also an ontological feature of his subject matter. Whatever Simmel deals with seems to be trying to organize the materials in its environment into a unity around itself according to its own principles. This is true of the core of Simmel's Kantian world, the mind: "The essential accomplishment of the mind may be said to be its transformation of the multiplicity of the elements of the world into a series of unities. In the mind, things separated in space and time converge in the unity of a picture, a concept, a sentence" (1959c:267). But in Simmel's world, as opposed to Kant's, the mind is not the only thing which organizes. We have already seen organizations by the work of art, by the adventure, by the individual, and by the society. Simmel's world possesses many such centers of organization, and, hence, looks more like Leibniz's *Weltanschauung* of self-actualizing monads or, even, the primitives' animistic world-view than Kant's.[10]

This world composed of multiple conflicting centers of organization affects both the sociologist who observes it and the individual who has to live in it. Since each area of life is trying to organize the same materials around its own principles, the sociological observer, freezing the movement at any point of time, can choose from among several centers the one around which he may say the material is being organized, for, like an optical illusion, the whole picture changes with every slight adjustment of focus. As for the individual living in this world, he finds himself continually fluctuating between the existential ecstasy of being able to draw each of these centers into his own life and the existential agony of being pulled apart by them into theirs.

> From the moment that man began to say 'I' to himself, . . . from the same moment in which the contents of the soul were formed together into a center point, . . . everything connected with the center point [had to form] a unit, self-contained and self-sufficient. But the contents with which the 'I' must organize itself into its own unified world do not belong to it alone. [Insofar as these contents are integrated into various outside worlds] they do not wish to dissolve into . . . the 'I.' [In fact,] through these contents the exterior worlds grasp the 'I' and seek to draw *it* into *them*. They aim to break up the centralization of cultural contents around the 'I' and reconstitute [these cultural contents] according to *their* demands (1968c:40).

Simmel (1968d:71–72) describes the essential feature of the organization of the newly created aesthetic and social worlds with the terms "symmetry," "balance," and "equilibrium" to contrast them with the spontaneous, impulsive, disorganization of their source in life: "The origin of all aesthetic themes is found in symmetry. . . . It is possible to discover through an analysis of the role of symmetry in social life how apparently purely aesthetic interests are called forth by materialistic purposes, and how . . . aesthetic motives affect forms which seem to obey only functional purposes." (At those rare times when Simmel, 1959e, discusses life as balanced, he always does so in order to show the instability of its equilibrium; for instance, when he deals with architecture, which he defines as the balance between the striving of the spirit and the necessities of nature, he does so in the context of "the ruin.")

Simmel (1959e:264–265; 1949) then uses these concepts of "order" as the criterion of the extent to which these aesthetic and social organizations have separated from life:

----

[10] Simmel seems to have been aware of his own movement from Immanuel Kant to Gottfried Leibniz. After his doctoral dissertation on music was rejected, what was accepted in its place was his earlier essay on Kant's "monadology."

Wherever we perceive aesthetically, we demand that the contradictory forces of existence be somehow in equilibrium, that the struggle between [spirit] and [nature] come to a standstill. . . . If [sociation] is interaction at all, it appears in its purest and most stylized form among equals, just as symmetry and balance are the most notable forms of artistic stylizing.

A society organized according to socialist principles would be the most symmetrical, most harmonious, and hence most aesthetic of all conceivable societies:

> Without any doubt, certain ideas of socialism are based on aesthetic values. That society as a whole should become a work of art in which every single element attains its meaning by virtue of its contribution to the whole; that a unified plan should rationally determine all of production, instead of the present rhapsodic haphazardness by which the efforts of individuals benefit or harm society; that the wasteful competition and the fight of individuals against individuals should be replaced by the absolute harmony of work— all these ideas of socialism no doubt meet aesthetic interest. Whatever else one may have against it, these ideas at any rate refute the popular opinion that socialism both begins and ends exclusively in the needs of the stomach (1968d:74).

But this most symmetrical, most harmonious, most aesthetic of all conceivable societies would also be, Simmel implies, the most separated from the pulsating forces of life.

Though Simmel sometimes compares, in static distinction, these newly formed aesthetic and social worlds with the ground out of which they evolved, more often he is concerned with describing the dynamic process by which aesthetic and social worlds separate from, and contrast with, their ground. Matthew Lipman (1959:124) speaks of this "figure-ground motif" as being one of Simmel's most common analytic techniques:

> Certainly the figure-ground opposition is an important conceptual instrument for Simmel, for he often speaks of individuality as a pattern whose pronouncedness must be seen against the background of what it is not—of what contrasts with, or even contradicts it. (This chiaroscuro technique makes quite plausible his interest in Rembrandt—especially since Rembrandt used that technique for the purpose of intense individuation.)

Simmel rarely deals with anything in itself; instead, he nearly always relates it spatially to whatever is around it. For example, he contrasts the building with the surrounding countryside, the parts of the face with the whole, and the stranger with the group. He makes these comparisons in order to bring out the point that different objects are necessary to each other because they reciprocally define each other. Furthermore, he often connects the individual object not to any objects in its spatial environment, but, more specifically, to those things around it from which it arose or was differentiated. This he does both in his aesthetics (the handle against the bowl) and in his sociology (the individual against the group). Occasionally, this contrast of figure and ground actually shows the individual actively emerging from his ordinary background (as Michaelangelo's statues seem to struggle out from their stone). Lipman continues:

> The individual stands over against the common or the general; the individualized experience contrasts with the ordinary, commonplace experience. We prize the individual in this sense, not because of its intrinsic value, but because it occurs in a context of triviality, monotony, mediocrity. . . . The greater the routinization of the world, the more the genuine individual stands boldly in relief against it.

But more often Simmel considers the ground (a group, for example) to be constantly hovering, constantly oppressing the emerged individual, constantly threatening to swallow him up again.

Along with how artistic products and social processes relate externally to their ground, Simmel also deals with how their elements relate internally to one another. Simmel (1968d:77–80) treats these internal relations of aesthetic and social phenomena under the concept of "distance." With the exception of Simmel's discussion of the relation between intimacy and discretion in terms of distance (1950a:321–322), Donald Levine (1959:23) has pointed out most of the important social phenomena which Simmel examines in the light of this concept throughout his writings:

> Simmel wrote a pioneering and penetrating account of the influence of physical distance on human relations. Furthermore, nearly all of the social processes and social types treated by Simmel may readily be understood in terms of *social distance*. . . . Conflict is considered a kind of social interaction because the individuals concerned are, despite their antagonism, relatively close. . . . Domination and subordination, the aristocrat, and the bourgeois, have to do with relations defined in terms of 'above' and 'below.' Secrecy, arbitration, the poor man, and the stranger are some of the topics related to the inside-outside dimension (emphasis mine).

Finally, Simmel (1968d:77; 1959f: 304–305; Weingartner, 1962:127, 164) analyzes, in terms of distance, not only the generation and inner relation of objects, but also their separation from the observer. It is the observer's varying "distance" from these objects which distinguishes the various modes by which he experiences them. Not only do aesthetic and sociological modes of experience involve a different distance between the observer and his objects, but so do practical, scientific, historical, religious, and metaphysical modes.

This concern with "distance" is an especially distinctive feature of modern times, Simmel (1968d:78–80) wrote in 1896. The degree to which the observer is trying to increase his distance from his objects may be seen in recent developments in painting and social relations, as well as in literature and science.[11] The cause of this increasing desire for distance in modern culture and society? Simmel blames "the steadily deeper penetration of a money economy":

---

[11] Only in his last works, particularly in "The Conflict in Modern Culture" (1968e), did Simmel feel the time was about due for an end of "distance" from things and a return to experiencing them in their "immediacy."

Money is placed between man and man, between man and product, as a mediator. . . . Money, by the enlargement of its role, has placed us at a wider and more basic distance from the object. . . . Our contact with [things] becomes interrupted, and we sense them only through intermediaries, which can never fully express their genuine, unique and immediate being. Thus the most diverse features of modern art and culture seem to have in common . . . a tendency to increase the distance between man and his objects, which finds its most distinct form in the area of aesthetics.[12]

The Artistic Method: Universalization through Particularization

Simmel (1968d:69) defines aesthetic comprehension, and hence the sociological comprehension (and, ultimately, all the modes of comprehending experience) modeled on it, as revealing the immediate relation between the individual and the universal. Unlike inductive logic which ascends from the individual to the universal slowly through intermediate steps, aesthetic comprehension bridges this gap immediately, by a sudden leap: "The essence of aesthetic contemplation and interpretation for us consists in the following: What is unique emphasizes what is typical, what is accidental appears as normal, and the superficial and fleeting stands for what is essential and basic." So too our sociological comprehension of social relations gives us the intuitive insight that, in order for the human individual to relate at all to his surrounding society, he must somehow carry within him the social universal (1959d).[13]

Another of Simmel's major contributions to social theory is his shift in the locus and magnitude of the units which embody these social universals. Simmel (1949:271: 1950b:56–57) claims that these social universals should be sought for not in the large, outstanding, and famous instances of individuals where Hegel and Nietzsche looked for them, but rather in the apparently low, mean, and trivial particulars of social

---

[12] It is remarkable how similar Simmel sounds in this passage to the early Marx—especially since Simmel in 1896 was not likely to have known Marx's *Economic and Philosophic Manuscripts* which, though written in 1844, were not published until 1932.

[13] The human individual, of course, is more than the mere particularization of a social universal, for, as Simmel (1959d:347–348) states, "The a priori of empirical social life consists of the fact that life is not entirely social. Part of our personalities are reserved from entering into [social] interaction. . . . Society, therefore, is a structure which consists of beings who stand inside and outside of it at the same time. . . . Between a society and its component individuals a relation may exist as if between two parties." (Unlike the American tradition of Charles H. Cooley and George H. Mead, but like the European tradition of Sigmund Freud, this quotation shows that, for Simmel, the individual and the society, while interconnected, are not completely "two sides of the same thing.") Nevertheless, Simmel (1950b:11) asserts that it is the specific task of sociological comprehension to study the individual only insofar as he partakes in more general social processes.

life.[14] Just as each of the smallest details in classical art reproduces the essential form of the work as a whole, so mere sociable conversation, seemingly about trivia, can reveal the essential processes of society, and even life itself:

> In all art, in all the symbolism of religious life, even in the complex formu-
> lations of science, we depend on a certain faith or feeling that phenomena
> which seem merely fragmented or superficial are in fact connected to the
> deepest and most comprehensive aspects of reality and therefore of life
> itself. . . . Art perhaps reveals the secret of life: the fact that we cannot
> be relieved of the real pressures of life merely by looking away from them,
> but only by reshaping and reexperiencing them in the unreal world of play.
> . . . The more serious a person, the more he finds relief and freedom in
> sociability. In sociability, he enjoys, as in a dramatic production, a concen-
> tration and transformation of effort that simultaneously dilutes and sub-
> limates all the tasks and seriousness of life so that its heavy burdens
> are felt only faintly, their weight reduced to mere stimulation (author's
> translation).

It seems appropriate to end this inquiry into the unity of Simmel's thought by considering how well Simmel's own procedure in treating his various subject matters agrees with those ontological features of his world which we have noted. Though it is commonly agreed that Simmel's greatness lies in his imaginative thoughts, I would add that the logical consistency by which he combines those insights should not be overlooked in any assessment of his stature, for Simmel's methodology harmonizes completely with his metaphysics. Simmel does not merely postulate the fact that any particular subject matter embodies universal principles, he actually discusses each object of his interest "in an ever expanding context, until the context comes to include the whole of existence" (Weingartner, 1962:152).

Consider Simmel's (1968d:69) definition of "aesthetic pantheism": "Every point contains within itself the potential of being redeemed to absolute aesthetic importance. To the adequately trained eye, the totality of beauty, the complete meaning of the world as a whole, radiates from every single point." Might we not say then that what Simmel has produced —in all his writings on the human condition taken together—is a true Aesthetics of Social Reality?

Conclusions

We have seen how Simmel's views on society are derived from his aesthetics, specifically from his conception of the artistic modality, the artistic product, and the artistic method. Simmel's tendency to look at social phenomena visually led him to conceive of man as merely the con-

---

[14] At about the same time, Freud, too, was claiming that he could use his patients' trivial everyday actions and words and dreams as clues and symptoms which revealed the peculiar warp that constituted their essential personal nature.

templator of the ahistorical social forms he once created but now can
no longer control. But while man is predominantly passive, his social
products are not. These social products, having become autonomous from
the organic processes which engendered them, are now active agents in
their own right, organizing the materials of social life around themselves
in an orderly—sometimes even symmetrical— manner. It is the sacred task
of the sociologist—standing between relatively weak mankind on the one
side and mankind's relatively strong social creations on the other—to
reconcile the two. Through the method of suddenly grasping for the
social universals in the most trivial particulars of human existence, the
sociologist hopes to comprehend coherently for men their otherwise overwhelming social reality.

Simmel attempted to establish a sociology that had its foundation in
aesthetics. He thus created a discipline whose orientation is quite different from that of Marx, who grounded his sociology in economics and
political science—from that of Durkheim, who grounded his sociology in
biology and statistics—and from that of Weber, who grounded his sociology
in history and anthropology.[15] These other sorts of sociologies have had
their day. Perhaps the time has come to give Simmel's its due.

REFERENCES

Bendix, Reinhard. 1962. *Max Weber: An Intellectual Portrait*, New York:
Anchor Books.
Berger, Peter, and Thomas Luckmann. 1966. *The Social Construction of
Reality*. New York: Scribners.
Coser, Lewis. 1958. "The Stranger in the Academy." In Lewis Coser (ed.),
Georg Simmel. Englewood Cliffs, N.J.: Prentice-Hall.
————. 1965. *Georg Simmel*. Englewood Cliffs: Prentice-Hall.
Duncan, H. D. 1959. "Simmel's Image of Society." In Kurt Wolff (ed.),
George Simmel 1858–1918. Columbus: Ohio State University Press.
Levine, D. 1959. "The Structure of Simmel's Social Thought." In Kurt Wolff
(ed.), *Georg Simmel 1858–1918*. Columbus: Ohio State University Press.
Lipman, M. 1959. "Some Aspects of Simmel's Conception of the Individual."
In Kurt Wolff (ed.), *Georg Simmel 1858–1918*. Columbus: Ohio State
University Press.
Salz, A. 1959. "A Note From a Student of Simmel's." In Kurt Wolff (ed.),
Georg Simmel 1858–1918. Columbus: Ohio State University Press.
Shils, E. 1965. "Charisma, Order and Status." *American Sociological Review*
30 (April):199–213.
Simmel, Georg. 1949 (orig. 1910). (E. Hughes, trans.). "The Sociology of
Sociability." *American Journal of Sociology* 55 (November):254–261.

---

[15] Although Durkheim took great pains to separate social phenomena from
biological phenomena, his sociology borrowed many concepts from biology,
such as "organic solidarity," "function," and "pathology," which continue to
influence sociological thinking.

————. 1950a (orig. 1908). "Sociologie." In Kurt Wolff (trans.), *The Sociology of George Simmel.* New York: Free Press.

————. 1950b (orig. 1917). "Fundamental Problems in Sociology (Individual and Society)." In Kurt Wolff (trans.), *The Sociology of Georg Simmel.* New York: Free Press.

————. 1955 (orig. 1908). "Sociologie." In Reinhart Bendix and Kurt Wolff (trans.), *Conflict and the Web of Group-Affiliations.* New York: Free Press.

————. 1959a (orig. 1908). "The Problem of Sociology." In Kurt Wolff (ed.), *Georg Simmel 1858–1918.* Columbus: Ohio State University Press.

————. 1959b (orig. 1911). "The Adventure." In Kurt Wolff (ed.), *Georg Simmel 1858–1918.* Columbus: Ohio State University Press.

————. 1959c (orig. 1911). "The Handle." In Kurt Wolff (ed.), *George Simmel 1858–1918.* Columbus: Ohio State University Press.

————. 1959d (orig. 1908). "How is Society Possible?" In Kurt Wolff (ed.), *Georg Simmel 1858–1918.* Columbus: Ohio State University Press.

————. 1959e (orig. 1911). "The Ruin." In Kurt Wolff (ed.), *Georg Simmel 1858–1918.* Columbus: Ohio State University Press.

————. 1959f (orig. 1896). "On the Nature of Philosophy." In Kurt Wolff (ed.), *Georg Simmel 1858–1918.* Columbus: Ohio State University Press.

————. 1968a (orig. 1906). "On the Third Dimension in Art." In K. Peter Etzkorn (ed. and trans.), *Georg Simmel: The Conflict in Modern Culture and Other Essays.* New York: Teachers College Press.

————. 1968b (orig. 1896). "On Aesthetic Quantities." In K. Peter Etzkorn (ed. and trans.), *Georg Simmel: The Conflict in Modern Culture and Other Essays.* New York: Teachers College Press.

————. 1968c (orig. 1911). "On the Concept and the Tragedy of Culture." In K. Peter Etzkorn (ed. and trans.), *Georg Simmel: The Conflict in Modern Culture and Other Essays.* New York: Teachers College Press.

————. 1968d (orig. 1896). "Sociological Aesthetics." In K. Peter Etzkorn (ed. and trans.), *Georg Simmel: The Conflict in Modern Culture and Other Essays.* New York: Teachers College Press.

————. 1968e (orig. 1918). "The Conflict in Modern Culture." In K. Peter Etzkorn (ed. and trans.), *Georg Simmel: The Conflict in Modern Culture and Other Essays.* New York: Teachers College Press.

Walter, E. V. 1959. "Simmel's Sociology of Power: The Architecture of Politics." In Kurt Wolff (ed.), *Georg Simmel 1858–1918.* Columbus: Ohio State University Press.

Weber, Max. 1958 (orig. 1904). *The Protestant Ethic and the Spirit of Capitalism.* New York: Doubleday.

Weingartner, Rudolph H. 1962. *Experience and Culture: The Philosophy of Georg Simmel.* Middletown, Conn.: Wesleyan University Press.

**SUMMARY AND EVALUATION
OF CHAPTER SIX**

Simmel represented a unique blend of the scientist and humanist. In his attempts to delineate sociology from other disciplines he recognized the feature that distinguishes its subject matter: social properties emerge from the complex interactions *between* individuals. Simmel's interest in these social relations, the micro-determinants of human conduct, contrasts with Durkheim's concern with collectivities, the macro-determinants. According to Simmel, sociology is the scientific study of these emergent characteristics of life. He conceived of and practiced an abstracting–generalizing method for the study of these phenomena. As long as the *questions* for research remained important and the insightful skills of the observer–scientist as an individual were allowed to exercise themselves, he was not at all averse to the development of sophisticated tools of research. Simmel was adept at conceptualizing the character of social processes and comparing these in different settings so as to arrive at their regularities. Insofar as his approach avoided the presumption of a dichotomy between the individual and social life, it foreshadowed the thinking of George Herbert Mead. His dialectic thought allowed him to hold in focus forces at both the individual and the extra-individual levels and to concentrate on the fusion process that takes place when initially opposite themes or forces become complementary to and definitive of a new, though ever-changing, reality.

Simmel was a humanist in several respects. He had an abiding concern for the survival of individuality in the face of what he took to be the enlargement of autonomous cultural worlds. Individuals are imperfect expressions of their ideal selves; but they continue to strive. Simmel's humanism aligned with the view sometimes called phenomenology[1] in that he found everyday events of life interesting and considered them from the actor's point of view—his "world as lived." In this, Simmel assumed that all such data have a certain validity—that, in other words, what the individual is trying to do is real to him. The direct apprehension by the observer of these intentions of the actor is an art that Simmel cultivated well.

Previous conservative philosophers such as Comte had directed attention away from the individual. And Spencer viewed society as a totality evolving in accordance with laws of nature. Even conflict theory largely took society as the real entity from whose parts, or from whose economic understructure, change emanated. Simmel, Don Martindale contends, represented the "sociologist of democracy."[2] He did not see the individual as self-sufficient or capable of his own enrichment; nor did he lean toward an

---

[1] Edward A. Tiryakian, "Existential Phenomenology and the Sociological Tradition," *American Sociological Review*, 30 (October 1965), 679–680. We accept James L. Heap and Phillip A. Roth's contention that Simmel, as well as other sociologists, was not a true (Husserlian) phenomenologist because he did not primarily seek what stands behind (or before) the given mundane world of objects that are believed by the actors to exist or analyze how these objects are made to exist ("On Phenomenological Sociology," *American Sociological Review*, 38 [June 1973], 354–367).

[2] Don Martindale, *The Nature and Types of Sociological Theory* (Boston: Houghton Mifflin, 1960), p. 246.

aristocratic society, in which the individual is forced into strict cultural molds, or toward the crowd, where the individual is simply swept along. Rather, Simmel stood for the discerning individual who could freely build his social life with others and yet not be locked in by its edifice. He believed that where diverse groups have the freedom to form and assemble, the individual's opportunity to enrich his life is enlarged. "Group pluralism" is therefore part of both Simmel's sociology and political philosophy.

How much of an impact has Simmel had on American sociology? A somewhat small one, we should guess. To be sure, his inspiration has lasted in the form of some of the concepts he fashioned: social types, the functions of conflict, and the significance of numbers in small groups, for example. Especially at the University of Chicago, his legacy was evident in the fresh and vital empiricism of the 1920s and 1930s, as Abel stated in Selection 6.1. But these remained rather discrete studies. Simmel fashioned no integrated conceptual scheme. Sociology in the United States went on to separate itself from questions concerning the philosophy of culture (regarding the control of man's spirit by his cultural creations). Furthermore, as Donald N. Levine[3] notes, one of the major attempts to synthesize sociology —Talcott Parsons' *The Structure of Social Action*—left Simmel out.[4] In fact, Parsons made quite a different set of assumptions about the problems and realities of social life, which he saw largely in terms of the Hobbesian problem of order: social life in the long run requires consensus on higher-order values because there is nothing else that can integrate activities into a unified plan or create a sense of duty; the fulfillment of social expectations is the goal of interaction and therefore shape and guide that interaction; the actor assumes as his frame of reference a situation that is already largely defined both socially and culturally. To Simmel things were quite different: social realities are dualisms, precarious fusions of opposites; sociation is always in the making in interaction; social transactions keep the protoforms in existence; distance and intimacy are some of the numerous elements of social relations in flux; the life process is continually straining to free itself from rigid elaborated social and cultural forms.

This alternative reality to which Simmel drew our attention, together with his artistic method of observation and analysis, will, when properly appreciated, give him an eminent place in American sociology.

SELECTED BIBLIOGRAPHY

American Journal of Sociology, 63 (May 1958), entire issue: "Durkheim-Simmel Commemorative Issue."

Blau, Peter. *Exchange and Power in Social Life.* New York: Wiley, Sons, 1964.

---

[3] Donald N. Levine (Ed.), *Georg Simmel: On Individuality and Social Forms* (Chicago: University of Chicago Press, 1971), p. lvi.

[4] Talcott Parsons, *The Structure of Social Action.* (New York: McGraw-Hill, 1937).

Caplow, Theodore. *Two against One: Coalitions in Triads.* Englewood Cliffs, N.J.: Prentice-Hall, 1968.

Coser, Lewis A., (Ed.). *Georg Simmel.* Englewood Cliffs, N.J.: Prentice-Hall, Spectrum Books, 1965.

Etzkorn, K. Peter, (Ed. and Trans.). *Georg Simmel: The Conflict in Modern Culture and Other Essays.* New York: Teachers College Press, 1968.

Levine, Donald N., (Ed.). *Georg Simmel: On Individuality and Social Forms.* Chicago: University of Chicago Press, 1971.

Lyman, Stanford, and Marvin B. Scott. *A Sociology of the Absurd.* New York: Appleton, 1970.

Spykman, Nicholas J. *The Social Theory of Georg Simmel.* New York: Atherton, Atheling Books, 1965.

Weingartner, Rudolph. *Experience and Culture: The Philosophy of Georg Simmel.* Middletown, Conn.: Wesleyan University Press, 1960.

Wolff, Kurt H., (Ed.). *Essays on Sociology, Philosophy, and Aesthetics by Georg Simmel et al.* New York: Harper & Row, Harper Torchbooks, 1965.

SEVEN

Emile Durkheim

"I see our society as both mechanical and organic. To
an extent middle-class Anglo values are pressuring everyone
to become alike, but our increase in industrialization has
brought about the division of labor, bringing about, in some
respects, a special kind of anomie because of the specialization of work, yet making everyone mutually dependent."

—STUDENT COMMENT

General Introduction

Emile Durkheim (1858–1917) was born of Jewish parents in Epinal,
France.[1] He remained quite independent in his own thought, especially
from the Enlightenment philosophies mentioned in Chapters One and Two.
As an agnostic, he was able to maintain a "cool," detached analysis of
religion, and, being Jewish, he remained deeply interested in the moral
level of society, but without being committed to a particular dogma.
Between 1885 and 1886, Durkheim traveled and studied in Germany. In
1892, he completed his French dissertation on *The Division of Labor in
Society* at the University of Paris. His other dissertation, in Latin, was on
Montesquieu. Durkheim's broad knowledge and his keen logic made him
a fine scholar. Personally, he was a very austere and serious man, lacking
in humor.

In 1896, the first position in sociology in France was created for
Durkheim at Bordeaux, where he had been teaching for about nine years.
In 1902 he became a professor at the University of Paris, receiving the
title of "professor of the science of education and sociology" there in

---

[1] For a concise biography of Durkheim see Robert Bierstedt, *Emile Durkheim*
(New York: Dell, 1966), pp. 19–37.

1913. He was a superb lecturer, who evidenced verbally the same precision of thought that he displayed in his writings. In 1915, during World War I, one of his sons died in the service of his country. Durkheim took this very hard and died himself less than two years later. Durkheim, like Weber, is one of the scholars of the nineteenth and early twentieth centuries most frequently quoted by American sociologists today.

An assessment of his times would require considerable discussion.[2] The chaos of the revolution and the postrevolutionary period in France had subsided, but the problems of unity were still as acute as they were when Comte lived. A reevaluation of eighteenth-century liberal thought was emerging, though a humanism, which failed to excite Durkheim, still dominated the scene. Sociology was becoming independent of psychology, and Durkheim's work bolstered the separation.[3]

Durkheim's sociology opposed itself to certain other views, especially individualism, psychologism, certain types of socialism, and all attempts at supernatural explanations of social phenomena in general. He not only assumed the priority of society over the individual, as Comte had done, but also wished to show that general social ideals and categories of experience emerge from the conditions of social life through human interaction and that attempted explanations of these social facts at the level of the individual prove inadequate. Early in Durkheim's writing, in *The Division of Labor in Society*, we see his theme: the structure of social relations shapes the behavior of the members of society.

Durkheim was a positivist in that he assumed the determination by group forces, or "currents," of the individual's consciousness and behavior and, more importantly, in that he insisted upon the incontrovertible reality of social facts. He considered such facts observable "things" independent of the subjective will of particular persons. They are

---

[2] See Robert A. Nisbet, *Emile Durkheim* (Englewood Cliffs, N.J.: Prentice-Hall, Spectrum Book, 1965), especially pp. 1–28.

[3] Some of Durkheim's works, with their original publication dates, are *The Division of Labor in Society* (1893), George Simpson (Trans.) (New York: Free Press, 1964); *The Rules of Sociological Method* (1895), Sarah A. Solovay and John H. Mueller (Trans.) and George E. G. Catlin (Ed.) (New York: Free Press, 1964); *Suicide* (1897), John A. Spaulding and George Simpson (Trans.) and George Simpson (Ed.) (New York: Free Press, 1966); *The Elementary Forms of Religious Life* (1912), Joseph Ward Swain (Trans.) (New York: Free Press, 1947). Others are *Sociology and Philosophy*, D. F. Pocock (Trans.) (New York: Free Press, 1953); *Education and Sociology*, Sherwood D. Fox (Trans.) (New York: Free Press, 1956); *Professional Ethics and Civic Morals*, Cornelia Brookfield (Trans.) (New York: Free Press, 1958); *Socialism and Saint-Simon*, Charlotte Sattler (Trans.) and Alvin W. Gouldner (Ed.) (Yellow Springs, Ohio: Antioch Press, 1958); *Moral Education*, Everett K. Wilson and Herman Schnurer (Trans.) and Everett K. Wilson (Ed.) (New York: Free Press, 1961).

the group's ways of thinking, acting, and feeling. Durkheim conceptualized these social facts as being (analytically) external to the individual, constraining upon him, and general (i.e., shared by many different actors).[4] They arise out of people's collective interaction, which is not understandable on the level of individual psychology. In other words, society, in its "internal" workings, produces a *new order* of facts distinct from those pertaining to the individual; it has, accordingly, what Durkheim perceived as a *collective* "conscience," which is manifested in such observable phenomena as legal codes, statistics (pertaining to rates of different types of group behavior), and religious dogma. He felt that we can learn something about a society's collective conscience by compiling data on these facts. Durkheim's quest, then, was to establish a sociology that would empirically establish naturalistic, rather than psychological or metaphysical, explanations of social facts.[5] He believed sociology could thus demonstrate that some social facts explain others—for example, that the degree of social cohesion affects the rate of suicide in a society. This insight, together with the disciplined scientific method Durkheim developed, is his most important contribution to sociology.

From where, if not the psychological make-up of individuals, does the collective conscience emerge? What is its basis? Durkheim suggested that the source could be found in the "efficient causes," in the "morphology," or distinctive features, of a society: the number of people, their proximity to one another, their distribution in space, their paths of communication, and the frequency and intensity of their interaction. These characteristics determine the societal realities and imperatives that people share. New ideals, for example, arise during periods when, as in the Renaissance, people engage in vigorous mental interaction, when they seem to fuse into a single life of purpose and reach beyond themselves. Society thus represented for Durkheim a moral reality that emerges from nature but, at the same time, participates in an order unlike any other, psychological or biological. Without the operation of this reality, through the constraints of moral rules, for instance, there could be no orderly

---

[4] See *The Rules of Sociological Method*, pp. 1–13. Because of the emphasis by some critics on the "externality" of social facts in Durkheim's works we refer to his conception of society as a reality *sui generis*, that is, above and apart from individuals. In this idea Durkheim seems to have been most influenced by Emile Boutroux at the *Ecole Normale*. We will return to the controversy on externality in the Summary and Evaluation, following the articles.

[5] Durkheim's famous dictum regarding the proper analysis in sociology is the following: "The determining cause of a social fact should be sought among the social facts preceding it and not among the states of individual consciousness. . . . The function of a social fact ought always to be sought in its relation to some social end" (ibid., pp. 110–111). One should find the efficient cause first and then, quite importantly, the *social* rather than individual end it serves.

social life, and individual needs would run rampant. Laissez-fairists and Utilitarians were naive in thinking a society could operate as a system of contracts devised for the enlargement of individual wants without the force of collective moral rules, which give these contracts their meaning and obligatory character; and socialists were naive in forgetting that moral progress must accompany economic progress, which produces the material resources for the satisfaction of more wants, especially a moral progress that would foster an individual whose self-regulation and discernment would reflect group ideals.

How was Durkheim affected by his times? How did he view the times? He has been described as a conservative (see Selection 1.1, by Nisbet), somewhat on the order of Comte, and even as a reactionary. Actually, the independence of Durkheim's thought makes it difficult to classify him.

Lewis Coser contends that Durkheim's conservatism shaped his approach to society and the level of his analysis. By conservatism Coser means the "inclination to maintain the existing order of things or to reinforce an order that seems threatened."[6] Change is not a complete anathema to the conservative, but he believes that it should be made only in a specific way in a localized area, usually slowly, and with all due respect for the larger context in which the pathological part to be corrected is functioning, So, too, Durkheim was reluctant to disturb the normal articulation of function, structure, and meaning in a society—the balance of its contributing elements.[7]

Unlike radicals or liberals, who tend to weigh the realities of society against some nonexistent, more perfect, ideal, conservatives tend to assess the abnormal in relation to the frequently existing condition of the normal. This inclination of conservatives is, however, confounded in the rare cases where what is general, and thus normal, in a society is actually pathological, as, for example, an elaborated division of labor that does not serve the society or general interest well. It is not clear what this general interest is, nor through what groups it operates; yet Durkheim assumed that one does exist.

At the same time, Durkheim believed, with liberals, in the importance of justice, the free expression of democracy, and tolerance (as a Jew, he especially appreciated this quality); but he arrived at these views by a different route. His image of man was different from theirs.[8] To Durkheim the liberal view was too one-sided and too simplistic. Cate-

---

[6] Lewis A. Coser, "Durkheim's Conservatism and Its Implication for Sociological Theory," in Lewis A. Coser, *Continuities in the Study of Social Conflict* (New York: Free Press, 1967), pp. 156–157.

[7] Nisbet, *Emile Durkheim*, p. 28.

[8] See Joseph Neyer, "Individualism and Socialism in Durkheim," in Kurt H. Wolff (Ed.), *Essays on Sociology and Philosophy* (New York: Harper & Row, Harper Torchbooks, 1960), p. 32.

gories like authority and autonomy, which liberals—and even many conservatives—saw as largely exclusive and often contradictory, Durkheim saw as compatible. Without authority no autonomy was possible, and without some autonomy abusive authority could not be challenged. He displayed the insight he derived from the tension between these principles in such works as *Suicide*. Durkheim believed in rational science and viewed it as a descriptive and explanatory system, both theoretical and practical; but, like Comte, he also viewed it as a system capable of giving an account of the individual's place in society that would have the same function in moral education as the old "mythologies" had.[9] He envisaged a science of ethics, which would help select the goals of a society on the basis of "objective" criteria of social health and social pathology. Education would help implant in the individual an appreciation of the greater being of society.

It was clear to Durkheim that individualism, truly and properly conceived, could not emerge from the dominant Spencerian conception of society as the product of discrete agreements among persons, contracted for the purpose of carrying on necessary activities. Individualism develops only as the person becomes absorbed in society—becomes part of the larger body that his activities help sustain. The explanation of morality in terms of the consciences, faculties, and (self-discovered) rights of somewhat self-sufficient persons is likewise defective, according to Durkheim. He defended individualism only because, and to the extent that, the group's higher conscience is embodied in the individual.

The Encyclopedists were too much against the Church of their time, Durkheim thought, to see that religion (a collection of shared beliefs and practices that have a special authority) was an extremely important phenomenon for society; he seems to have arrived at this insight very suddenly in 1895 while teaching a course in religion.[10] By discovering the latent and subtle functions of religion, science would show the importance of retaining it in some form or other. Indeed, morality depends on the individual's finding something *beyond himself* to regard as the basis of values and to respect as authority. In Durkheim's estimation, the group fulfills these needs; it regulates the individual's otherwise unlimited wants by defining through its norms what is properly due him and, at the same time, provides his strength and inspiration to be free.

Solidarity, especially the extent to which a moral unity characterized a society, was of lasting concern to Durkheim. It cannot be achieved by gratuitously creating within society a special priesthood, as Comte had once suggested, whose purpose would be to avoid crises; it must come, instead, through the development of general norms and values in the context of real, everyday life. Durkheim saw the possibility that a large

---

9 Neyer, "Individualism and Socialism in Durkheim," p. 41.

10 Bierstedt, *Emile Durkheim*, pp. 28–29.

proliferation in the division of labor could bring about much diversification among interest groups within society. It is futile to attempt to check this growth, especially if it contributes to the overall good; moreover, only in concert with such developments can higher individualism *gradually* emerge. But even organic solidarity (the coordination of specialized parts for the overall good of a society), one of the several types of solidarity described in Selection 7.1, is not sufficient in itself to integrate a society. Durkheim called upon occupational groups in the more highly differentiated societies to assume some of the integrative functions, such as the nurturance of allegiance and duty to the larger social whole, heretofore provided by the common conscience in the smaller, more homogeneous society. As social relations become more interdependent, the individual becomes more autonomous since now, although he is still an organic part of society, he is not constrained by the absolutism of a shared mechanical mentality. What is lost in normative integration, which itself produces a certain like-mindedness, is gained in functional integration, which effects the coordination of more specialized activities and can also result in greater autonomy for the individual. Durkheim's concepts of mechanical and organic solidarity—to be discussed further below—reflect these changes in sentiment and in the quality of social relationships.

There are definite interrelationships among the division of labor in society, suicide, and religion—Durkheim's three main areas of analysis. Both *Suicide* and *The Division of Labor in Society* (referred to below as *DOL*) furthered Durkheim's singular goal of demonstrating empirically his doctrine that one can study society by investigating positive (observable) facts. These two works are also explorations of insights that are products of his blend of conservatism and liberalism. He undertook his analysis in *DOL* with an optimism shared by Montesquieu and Rousseau. Like them, Durkheim believed that natural laws govern the progressive development of society and that a society is stronger if its individuals can *freely* give their labor in some activity for the good of the whole. In the liberal tradition, he thought that without this willing cooperation of individuals within a society, the social order is unsteady, and without the provision of varied opportunities in the division of labor, the individual cannot grow and perfect himself. This idea has much to do with Durkheim's distinction between *mechanical* solidarity—a type of social unity or integration that derives from a simple (duplicative) division of labor and encourages a harsh like-mindedness of thought and belief—and *organic* solidarity—a type of unity that derives from the interdependence of specialized labor. In the condition of mechanical solidarity, the individual is, in a way, forcibly made to cooperate because there are few specialties that might enable him to grow in accordance with his social propensities, and he cannot think for himself because there is little room in the closed group "mind" for divergent thoughts.

But Durkheim's optimism could not sustain him. He came to realize that the functional integration of specialized roles in the organic society did not suffice. The division of labor was just that: a scheme of specialization; it lacked the common beliefs, sentiments, and usages that are required to make of a society a real community. He later turned his attention to the study of religious behavior in part because he realized that the division of labor itself was unable to provide social unity. Moreover, *DOL* was a demonstration for Durkheim that as the social density (interaction frequency) increases per social unit, the structure of society (mechanical or organic) also changes, as does its form of morality and law. Without this change in structure the increased interaction could not be accommodated.

In *Suicide* Durkheim subjected the concept of social regulation to a careful empirical analysis. Whereas in *DOL* he desired to demonstrate that mechanical and organic societies represent different collective consciences, as well as attempted to show empirically that each correlates with a different pattern of law. (And what could be more representative of a purely social, yet superindividual, factual thing than law?) In *Suicide* Durkheim brought to bear more "objective" data, specifically, suicide statistics, in order to test hypotheses about expected differences in suicide rates between groups in which the individual is differently regulated. He showed this regulation actually at work in *Suicide*, having shown its more general embodiment in laws in *DOL*. Durkheim's conservative inclination was to acknowledge that a person flounders when he is not regulated by society, as the phenomenon of suicide demonstrates; but his liberal inclination was to praise the individualism of a person who has reached the point of fulfilling the group within himself and can think on his own and resist any excessive or harmful group coercion. He believed that in the organic society, the individual has some autonomy and can consequently think for himself because the collective conscience, manifested in homogeneous thought, cannot operate in a rigid, immediate manner. Empirically, Durkheim found that more independent thought occurs among Protestants than among Catholics. However, suicide is higher among Protestants, not so much because of lack of restriction on their thought, but because they are not encouraged to nurture themselves in the group when failure or other vicissitudes of life occur. In short, they lack opportunities for participation in general communal activities on account of their individualism.

Both *Suicide* and *DOL* are arguments against the individualistic conception of society, such as that of the Utilitarians or contract theorists.[11] In *Suicide* Durkheim showed that while self-destruction seems to be a highly individualistic act, its varying rates are not explicable at the level of individual motives or biological facts; he did, however, consider such factors in explaining lower suicide rates for women than for men. In *DOL*

---

[11] The remainder of this introduction owes much to Nisbet, *Emile Durkheim*, pp. 49–102.

Durkheim demonstrated that the division of labor could neither have developed out of individual wants nor have expanded out of the desire for greater happiness. Rather, the increasing division of labor was a response to the social need for unity as society increased in density.

The two works also reflect both Durkheim's sociology of politics and his diagnosis of the troubled times in nineteenth-century France. He did not favor excessive control over the individual by the state, on the one hand, or by kin, religious, or other organic primary groups, on the other. Instead, in *DOL* and in another work, *Professional Ethics and Civic Morals*, he prescribed strengthening the new intermediary occupational associations and giving them legal recognition so as to *balance* the possible tyrannies from either the "top" or the "bottom" of society. He also suggested that the state could be used positively by intermediate groups to check the excessive control of primary groups over the individual and that intermediary groups could check the power of the state, should that be necessary. Durkheim believed that modern society had broken up too many important groups—kin, religious, and neighborhood groups, for example, which had meaningfully incorporated the individual—without replacing them with new forms of regulation. This analysis came out most forcefully in his conception of egoistic suicide, whose high rates, he felt, were precipitated by the loss of tradition, authority, cohesion, and stability. These conditions were threatening to cause a reversion of society to the animal level because without morally binding rules (and their force in action), human life becomes just that—an animal existence.

Furthermore, *Suicide* and *DOL* evidence Durkheim's evolutionism. Robert A. Nisbet has eloquently expressed the point that while Durkheim's empirical analysis remained in the forefront of his work, there was an underlying evolutionary view, fortunately lacking in the optimism of others who believed that modern society represented an advanced stage in progress.[12] As for his work on suicide, we have already mentioned that Durkheim's interest in the phenomenon derived partly from his alarm over the way modern society, spurred by Enlightenment and social contract philosophies, was drifting toward a dangerous individualism. He found that suicide was rare in "lower societies" and believed that boredom, anxiety, and despair actually increase as societies become civilized. A certain evolutionary assumption forms the background for *DOL* also. Toward the middle of the book, Durkheim unexpectedly came to see that the organic society cannot be an entirely new type, for it does not have the common sentiments, beliefs, and usages needed to hold it together. The organic society emerges from the mechanical and tends to nurture the individualistic conscience, but it still contains part of the strong collective conscience of the earlier type. Here it should be noted that the interplay

---

[12] Ibid., pp. 95–98.

of these two consciences represents a force for social change, as do the alterations in morphology, mentioned above.[13] In his study of religion, Durkheim hoped that by examining the operation of the sacred in "simpler" societies (e.g., the Australian Aborigines), he would see its functions and social base in complex societies more clearly.

Finally, in his works on religion Durkheim developed his moral view of society most fully. He believed that goals must derive from society in order to have authority. They are sanctioned by rules, which constitute the heart of society and are its distinctive feature, but nothing in man himself will compel him to adhere to them. He must first internalize the goals of the group into his need disposition. Once this has occurred, his actions will have a dutiful character because they will be oriented to these goals. Society will persist only as long as men act dutifully. No force other than that coming from society itself has the authority to cause them to act in behalf of something beyond themselves. Religion adds forcefulness to this authority because it brings men together in the name of symbols of fellowship. Engaging in religious rituals recharges the goals of the group.

Introduction to Selections 7.1, 7.2, and 7.3

The articles selected for this chapter elaborate on major parts of Durkheim's thought. In the first article, J. A. Barnes discusses Durkheim's conception of two forms of the division of labor (mechanical and organic). In the next, Barclay D. Johnson clarifies Durkheim's theoretical ideas contained in *Suicide*. Finally, Gregory P. Stone and Harvey A. Farberman note a development in the later works of Durkheim. They contend that perhaps beginning as early as 1898, in spite of his apparent impressions of society as *the* great "being" from which all our categories of experience and even our image of Divinity spring, he was starting to view society as a creation of symbolic interaction and to examine the very processes by which society's rules are internalized by the actor.

Barnes critically follows the threads of argument that Durkheim sets forth in *DOL*. Robert Bierstedt has remarked on the difficulty of understanding this book since it was written early in Durkheim's career, when his ideas remained in their "formative" stage.[14] The philosophical background of the book has already been hinted at above: Durkheim believed that the division of labor is the central feature of society and that an appropriate morality and collective conscience must accompany changes in this division in order to give it cohesion.

According to Barnes, when Durkheim used the term morality, he seemed to have in mind the solidarity of a society—an aspect not itself an

---

[13] Ibid., p. 94.
[14] Bierstedt, *Emile Durkheim*, p. 48.

externally observable or social fact. He distinguished several types of solidarity: (1) *positive* (as opposed to the anomic or forced "abnormal" type), which Durkheim assumed all societies require; (2) *mechanical*, which produces cohesion through similarity of parts; and (3) *organic*, which produces cohesion through differences among parts. Though the meaning of solidarity is not clear, it appears to refer to those social arrangements that enable an individual to identify (directly in the mechanical type, indirectly in the organic) with a collectivity larger than himself. Durkheim took what he called *dynamic density*—the number of people able to act and react to one another—as a measure of solidarity.

To solidarity is linked the notion of conscience—again not a directly observable fact—of which Durkheim distinguished two types: (1) a *common* or *collective* (common to the whole group; hence, a manifestation of society in the individual), which predominates in the mechanical society; and (2) *individual* (personal and distinct, rendering each person an individual), which predominates in the organic society. Durkheim considered law, an external and social fact in his estimation, as an indicator of conscience.

Barnes thinks that the division of labor and its operations are unfortunately not well defined. Durkheim advanced the statement that ". . . if it [the division of labor] progresses in a continuous manner in the course of social development, it is because societies become regularly denser and generally more voluminous [in dynamic density];[15] yet we cannot be sure that things could be otherwise, for the division of labor and dynamic density in a society seem to be one and the same thing. Is "division of labor" just another name for "dynamic density"? Or is dynamic density more amorphous, and does is precede the specialization of division of labor?

Durkheim postulated that predominantly repressive laws and a low degree of dynamic density characterize the mechanical solidarity type of society, while predominantly restitutive laws and a high degree of moral density characterize the organic solidarity type of society. Barnes notes that because Durkheim's terms are unclear and proper historical evidence is lacking, it is difficult to test this hypothesis. The weight of the evidence that does exist does not seem to support it, however, especially with respect to type of law and solidarity. Another proposition—that the division of labor springs from accommodative specialization in response to population growth—also seems dubious when the possibilities of alternative responses to population growth are considered.[16]

---

[15] *DOL*, p. 262.

[16] Instead of producing greater specialization, increased population growth might lead to greater dispersion or to fission of the population. It has also been speculated that the process of specialization precedes (makes possible) population increments.

In spite of these weaknesses, Barnes finds important contributions in the book. Durkheim accomplished one of his goals in that he found (or thought he found) a connection between the type of division of labor in a society and its moral life, as evidenced in forms of law. He also anticipated that a higher moral or dynamic (interaction) density can only arise in accompaniment with a more highly differentiated division of labor. Thus the division of labor intervenes between and accommodates the connection between the solidarity of a society and the frequency of inter-action of individuals.

Durkheim dropped the distinction between mechanical and organic solidarity in his subsequent work. It showed up again only faintly in *Suicide*.[17]

Johnson's article, "Durkheim's One Cause of Suicide," begins with the conceptual distinctions Durkheim made among causes of suicide. He identified two social conditions affecting suicide rates: *integration*, the extremes of which are *altruism* and *egoism*, and *regulation*, the extremes of which are *fatalism* and *anomie*. While every degree of integration and regulation corresponds to an approximate rate of suicide, Durkheim noted that the rates are highest at the extremes of both conditions and lowest at their midpoints, or *moderate* levels. Since any given society combines integration and regulation, its expected suicide rate is determined by measuring the levels of *both* conditions.

However, in Johnson's estimation, "a closer examination of *Suicide* justifies another, quite different, formulation." He believes that altruistic suicide must be eliminated from the scheme because this type is largely characteristic of tightly integrated societies. But the examples given by Durkheim are so diverse (societies such as Japan, India, and China, as well as small preliterate ones) that the meaning of integration is ambiguous. More importantly, Durkheim had no statistics on the actual suicide rates in these societies. It is likely that Durkheim would have found that, except in the army, high integration protects against suicide. Johnson feels, too, that fatalistic suicide must be eliminated because of lack of data and because Durkheim fell back on nonsocial explanations for the two cases in which he did examine data (he found higher rates for childless married women than for married women with children, and

---

[17] Perhaps one of the reasons for dropping it was that it appeared to lead to a contradiction. Durkheim had a personal preference for the organic society. In *Suicide* he expressed the idea that higher (denser) interaction is associated with low suicide rates. Yet in *DOL* high interaction is a char-acteristic of organic societies that were also thought to bring with them more boredom, anxiety, and so on, and consequently higher suicide rates. The contradiction was only apparent, however, because Durkheim found that the organic society in which suicide was high actually had an "unhealthy" (although high) division of labor, rather than a truly organic one.

for unmarried men than for married men of the same age). Moreover, Johnson finds that there are conceptual problems in differentiating egoism from anomie. He concludes, in fact, that they are one and the same. Of Durkheim's four original subcategories of integration and regulation, then, Johnson retains only one: egoism-anomie.

Johnson ends by discussing the difficulty of interpreting egoism in Durkheim's work. Is it, as Talcott Parsons believes, a freedom of inquiry sanctioned by church authority and maintained by the strong common conscience embodied in the general norms of self-reliance and independence from group support? Or is it, as Johnson holds, the existence of a weak and poorly integrated social organization, like that of the Protestants? In opposition to Parsons, he maintains that by egoism Durkheim meant, rather, the *loss* of common conscience and the *loss* of regulation over the individual. Therefore, Durkheim was actually dealing with only *one* factor— we might call it "cohesion"—as the cause of suicide. According to Johnson, when Durkheim's theory of suicide is thus modified, it stands as one of the ". . . few approximations to a scientific law that [sociology] has found."

In our final selection, Stone and Farberman trace in Durkheim's career his gradual movement toward the analysis of the processes by which "society gets into people and acts through them." Every theory presumes some image of man—man's endowment, his relation to society, or his modes of operation as a social animal. Durkheim's theory is no exception. Although individual men were not his focus, Durkheim was led to confront the question of man and society by the very way his theory of society developed.

Stone and Farberman explain that Durkheim first assigned man the role of "moving particle" in society; in *DOL* man is the contained, who simply has the type of individuality that his society, the container within which he moves as a particle, engenders. In *Suicide*, Durkheim shifted to the implicit view of man as a "conductor of societal energy." He saw suicide as one of the consequences of low group cohesion suffered by the individual. But society's mold is not everywhere the same; hence, suicide rates vary. Finally, in his study of religion, Durkheim entertained yet another view: the reality that is the foundation of religious experience does not conform objectively to the *idea* believers have of it; he therefore assumed that they, the contained, have some role in creating their container since religion is a representation of society. This ties in with Durkheim's theory of the social origins of knowledge. He is a precursor of Karl Mannheim, who held that much knowledge consists of social *constructions* of reality, which, if they are to be maintained, must be believed in, interpreted similarly, and acted on in such a way that they can come true.

In summary, Stone and Farberman show that once Durkheim had begun to view the collective conscience as being more internal to man, it lost some of the rigidity and mechanical character he had imputed to it earlier. Having changed his thinking in this respect, Durkheim was more prepared to see man in the capacity in which George Herbert Mead later saw him—as a creative and perceptive agent in society. Mead (to be discussed in Chapter Eight) believed that the individual shares his existence with the other through the use of gestures; the meanings of these gestures arise through the assessment of the other's conduct as the individual engages in role playing and in the internal conversation of the mind. Actions, feelings, and thoughts, then, are bound up in these gestures and communicated to others. The individual can anticipate the future of an act by referring to concepts about action sequence acquired in the past. In this way the definitions and coercions ascribed to "society" exist.

Simpson has said that to give Durkheim credit, as Parsons does, along with Freud, "for one of the most fundamental of all psychological discoveries—the internalization of culture in the structure of personality— is certainly stretching the point."[18] Stone and Farberman agree that Durkheim never got that far; however, they do think he had arrived at the essentials that might have contributed to understanding such internalization of culture.

---

[18] George Simpson, *Emile Durkheim* (New York: Crowell, 1963), p. 3.

7.1

Durkheim's Division
of Labour
in Society

J. A. BARNES

Introduction

The first edition of Emile Durkheim's *The Division of Labour in Society: A Study of the Organization of the Higher Societies* was published in 1893 while the author was professor of social science at the University of Bordeaux. It constituted the major of the two theses which he presented at the University of Paris for his doctorate. Durkheim had previously published several reviews and articles, but this was his first book. He gained his doctorate and his book made a significant impact, for it so annoyed the orthodox economists that for some time he could not obtain a teaching post in Paris (Mauss 1958:2). The book went to five French editions, the only work by Durkheim to do so, and was first published in an English translation in 1933. It has been described by its translator as Durkheim's greatest work (Simpson 1933:4). Yet despite these indications of importance, some critics have seen little value in the book. Thus, in his *History of Ethnological Theory*, where he devotes fifteen pages to Durkheim, Lowie has absolutely nothing to say about the *Division of Labour*. Its translation into English was greeted in the pages of the *American Journal of Sociology* with the comment:

> Published when the author was thirty-five years old, the work accepts as accurate the crude misconceptions of the 1880's concerning the life of primitive man as set forth in the books of those who were no more competent to describe them than a botanist would be to write a treatise in his field without ever having seen a plant. . . .
>
> Not to be severe with a writer who, forty-one years ago, accepted what is now known to be untenable, it would at least seem that extended discussion of an argument based on abandoned premises might be considered an unnecessary expenditure of energy (Faris 1934:376).

The English translation is poor. The development of social conditions, as well as the findings of scientific research, during the seventy years that have elapsed since the work was first published have cumulatively demonstrated the falsity of many of its substantive propositions. If then we are to understand in what context the *Division of Labour* is still of

241

interest, we have to look elsewhere than at introductory courses on occupational specialisation, or social evolution, or the changing patterns of legal organisation, or any other of the various themes discussed in the book. We need, however, go only to the very first sentence in the book to find the answer: 'This book is pre-eminently an attempt to treat the facts of the moral life according to the method of the positive sciences' (*DOL*[1] 32).

Here we have a clear statement of Durkheim's programme, a programme worked out in subsequent publications and which remained not far from the centre of his intellectual goal throughout his life. In this book we can easily see the beginnings from which his later studies on suicide, education, law and religion developed. In order to understand what Durkheim meant by 'collective representations' or by 'anomie' we have to study not only his *Elementary Forms of the Religious Life* and his *Suicide*, but also those sections of the *Division of Labour* where these concepts are first discussed at length (for religion, see *DOL* 288–9; for suicide, see *DOL* 246). *The Rules of Sociological Method*, published a year later, was, Durkheim said, implied in the *Division of Labour* (*Rules* lx).

Durkheim proclaims that he intends to study moral facts by the methods of science. We have come to realise, perhaps more explicitly than did Durkheim, that one of the distinguishing marks of science is that it is cumulative, and that each generation of investigators incorporates the discoveries of its predecessors into its established corpus of organised understanding. In the humanities, things are different; Sartre and Auden in no sense supersede Shakespeare and Homer. In philosophy, Plato and Aristotle are never out of print. But in science, Euclid and Hippocrates are either incorporated or discarded and have become only of historical value; the cartographer does not go back to Anaximander before drawing a map. Likewise, if sociology is scientific, as Durkheim stated it should be, we do not need to go back to Durkheim, and certainly not to his first major work, to discover how to tackle a new analysis of social phenomena. For, if what he had to say is true, it should long ago have become part of the corpus of sociological propositions and theorems utilised by subsequent sociologists or even in Durkheim's own later work. It is an indication of Durkheim's lack of clarity as a writer that it is, alas, still necessary to return to the *Division of Labour* for guidance on how to interpret his later writings and for clarification on the validity of the many diverse criticisms that have been levelled against Durkheim as a sociologist. But more importantly, it is also an indication that, for one reason or another, Durkheim's efforts to make sociology scientific have not been wholly successful and that we can still read him for help in interpreting the results of current

---

[1] References to Durkheim's own writings are indicated as shown:

DOL   *The Division of Labor in Society.* Simpson, G. (trans.). New York: The Free Press, 1947.

Rules   *The Rules of Sociological Method.* Solovay, S. A., & J. H. Mueller (trans.). Chicago: Chicago U.P., 1938.

1953   *Sociology and Philosophy.* Pocock, D. F. (trans.). London: Cohen & West.

enquiries. The organised corpus of positive science still remains an unfulfilled programme.

According to Mauss, Durkheim intended, while still at the *École Normale*, to write an account of the relationship of individualism and socialism but later recast the plan of his thesis to deal with the relation between the individual and society. The book was outlined in 1884 while he was teaching in a *lycée* near Paris, and was first written in 1886 after he had returned from his year in Germany. It was presented as a doctoral thesis seven years later (Mauss 1958:1). This thesis was not merely an academic exercise, for it arose at least in part out of Durkheim's concern for the revival of French society following the defeat of France in the Franco-Prussian war and his book stresses the necessity of political action, even if the details are left unspecified. He says:

> we should judge our researches to have no worth at all if they were to have only a speculative interest . . . there is a state of moral health which science alone is able to determine competently . . . science, in furnishing us the law of variations through which moral health has already passed, permits us to anticipate those coming into being, which the new order of things demands. If we know in what sense the law of property evolves as societies become larger and denser, and if some new growth in size and density make new modifications necessary, we shall be able to foresee them, and foreseeing them, will them beforehand. Finally, comparing the normal type with itself—a strictly scientific operation—we shall be able to find if it is not entirely in agreement with itself, if it contains contradictions, which is to say, imperfections, and seek to eliminate them or to correct them. (*DOL* 33–4)

Durkheim called for action in the world of learning, in part as a necessary preliminary to political action in the nation. He was directly concerned with the establishment of sociology as an academic discipline recognised in France, and although, at least in the first edition of his book, his national political comments are mainly negative, his arguments have immediate implications for the academic politics of the time on this issue. In his later writings he sets out in greater detail his pleas for the separation of sociology from philosophy and its development as, in some sense, a special kind of psychology (*DOL* 359–62; cf. Benoît-Smullyan 1948:501, n. 7). Likewise, in the second edition of *Division of Labour*, issued in 1902, he added specific political proposals, entitled 'Some notes on occupational groups,' aimed at restoring the country to a better state of social health. These were followed by practical suggestions for· social changes in a variety of fields, advocated in many publications.

Perhaps because this was Durkheim's first major work, the intellectual climate in which he had been trained, and against which he was now rebelling, had a decisive influence on the form of his argument. Unfortunately Durkheim never succeeded in freeing his presentation of sociological argument from the intellectual heritage he sought to repudiate, and much of the difficulty now experienced in understanding what Durkheim means or, to an even greater extent, in understanding why he wrote in the way he did, stems from our ignorance of the men and positions that

Durkheim was attacking. Simpson, Durkheim's translator, may go too far in trying to reduce Spencer to Durkheim's Dühring when he says, in justification of his editorial policy of not giving references to Spencer's original works:

> Where Durkheim quotes Spencer in order to criticize him adversely, as in the majority of cases, there would seem to be no reason for being interested in Spencer's ideas after Durkheim has finished with them. (*DOL* x)

Yet it is Durkheim's attack on Herbert Spencer—who had been translated into French by Espinas and Ribot—and on the utilitarian tradition going back to Adam Smith, that led to Durkheim's being identified as an anti-individualist and therefore a social realist (Parsons 1960:119; (Peyre 1960:24; Alpert 1939:150). In the later chapters of the *Division of Labour* Durkheim advocates a political individualism in which social harmony, or specifically organic solidarity, is achieved only by each individual being free to exercise his talents and fulfil his natural ambitions. But this political stance was overshadowed by his attack on utilitarianism and by his use of many of the same metaphors as the social realists. For the modern reader, his intellectual position is further complicated by what seems to be his frequent use of biological and organic analogies that seem at first glance to put him in the camp of the man he is attacking: Spencer. His commentators argue that Durkheim fought against the use of analogies drawn from biology (Peyre 1960:24), but by present standards he did not fight hard enough (*e.g. DOL* 217–8). Similarly, the attention given by Durkheim to Comte has to be seen in the light of Comte's persisting influence in French thinking as providing the stereotype of sociology—over-ambitious, imprecise and heretical.

Durkheim began his professional career when evolutionary doctrines in anthropology were at their height, and the notion of a broad transition from savage to civilised is taken for granted in his work without specific discussion of the assumptions that have to be made. Some of his commentators note that Durkheim was an opponent of unilinear evolution (Parsons 1937:372); yet Durkheim expects his readers to know what is meant by social evolution and brings forward evidence that conforms to late nineteenth century canons in support of the particular kind of evolutionary process he was seeking to establish. Formally, he treats evolution as a process, but in fact he argues most of the time in merely dichotomous terms, primitive versus civilised, and does little towards demonstrating that there are societies at intermediate points on the scale. The nearest he gets to doing this is in comparison of the legal codes of five societies, the ancient Hebrews, the Romans of the fifth century, the Franks under Salic law, the Burgundians and the Visigoths. Yet, even here, Durkheim is interested merely in demonstrating that there are quantitative differences between one code and another, and he neither correlates these with other features of the societies nor works out how these five societies might be regarded relative to one another. He merely asserts in a footnote that 'if the genealogical tables of social types could be completely drawn up, it would resemble a tufted tree, with a single trunk, to be sure' (*DOL* 141,

n. 21; *cf.* Alpert 1939:196–8). It has been said that the subtitle of the *Division of Labour* should be *Against Dilletantism*, but Durkheim's efforts to establish sociology as a professional specialism have given an appearance of amateurism to much of his own work. His arguments remain, however, despite the inadequate evidence he was able at the time to muster in their support.

Some commentators have drawn attention to the similarities between Durkheim's typology, when seen as dichotomous, and the views of Tönnies on *Gemeinschaft* and *Gesellschaft*. Earlier, Maine had made a distinction between societies based on status and those based on contract, and Spencer's division of societies into industrial and military was along similar lines. Redfield's folk-urban continuum may be viewed as a modern essay in the same tradition (Bohannan 1960:88; Freeman & Winch 1957: 461), and even Robert Park's sacred and secular societies, Albion Small's cultures and civilisation, and Riesman's tradition-oriented and other-directed personalities have been fitted into the same pattern. The fact that this simple analytical procedure still yields interesting results shows how far we still are from a satisfactory calculus of societies.

Concepts

In the course of his work Durkheim introduces a number of concepts which he links by several propositions. Concepts and propositions are intermingled in his presentation, and it is often not clear whether a concept is deliberately introduced as an analytical tool or as the name of some phenomenon already existing in the real or metaphysical world. For our purposes it may be convenient to try to unravel this mixture. Let us take first his battery of concepts.

Durkheim deals with a plurality of discrete societies, each containing a number of human beings, individuals who belong to the society. Each individual has some qualities that are merely human, common to all humanity, and he has other distinctive qualities that derive from heredity, presumably his own physical ancestry seen as distinct from the ancestry of anyone else. The individual has aptitudes and ambitions and holds ideas and beliefs; he has feelings, the most relevant feeling in the context of the *Division of Labour* being that of feeling coerced. Within a single society, individuals are grouped either into segments, sub-units of society largely similar to one another, or into organs, sub-units that are characteristically different from one another.

By examining societies the observer discovers facts about them. In the *Rules* Durkheim says that social facts are to be treated as things and this slogan has been widely misunderstood. Benoît-Smullyan (1948:501) has noted that Durkheim employs the name 'thing' for four different concepts and that hence his methodological premise may be read in four ways. The interpretation that Durkheim claims as his own in the *Rules* (xliii), is that sociology deals only with external observable facts, but this is not always borne out in his writings. In the *Division of Labour* he distinguishes several kinds of facts. Internal facts, the events and phenomena that occur in the minds of individuals, necessarily escape us. We can study these internal facts only through the external facts that are an expression of, and which in some sense symbolise, the internal facts. The notion of exteriority, of being external, Durkheim applies in two ways. Some facts are external to the observer; they belong to the intractable reality the observer records and which he seeks to understand; he cannot alter the external facts to fit his theories, but his theories must be fitted to them. But Durkheim also designates some facts as external because they are experienced or perceived by the actor as external to him.

One sub-class of external facts contains social facts. These are characterised not only by their exteriority, but also by the constraint that they exert and by their generality. The main social facts that Durkheim discusses are laws and customs, for these are clearly external and observable. In the *Division of Labour* he is not much concerned with that other kind of social fact, social statistics, which was later to form the basis of his enquiry into suicide. It is easy to agree that a law constrains those to whom it applies, but again we find that Durkheim uses the notion of constraint in a variety of ways. Sometimes constraint means the need to conform to social standards, but at other times constraint is used for pressure stemming from persons with prestige or authority, or else for mere mechanical necessity (Lacombe 1926:40–8). In the view of Benoît-Smullyan, who distinguishes seven different meanings of constraint in Durkheim's writings, he fails to distinguish between collective constraint, as in the enforcement of a law; cultural determination, in the acceptance of the ambient scale of values by adolescents growing up in a culture; physical determination, where geographical and other material facts limit possibilities; and psychological compulsion, as when individuals in a crowd act in unison in a distinctive way (Benoît-Smullyan 1948:529). By shifting from one kind of constraint to another, Durkheim is able to set out his propositions in forms difficult either to verify or to disprove.

Laws and customs are then general in that they apply widely throughout a society, and they exert constraint. They and other external facts enable us to infer the presence of internal facts, the most relevant internal fact being that of social solidarity. In view of the insistence that social facts must be explained by other social facts, and that these are the facts with which the sociologist has to operate, it is important to stress that, by Durkheim's definition, social solidarity is not itself a social fact. He says:

> But social solidarity is a completely moral phenomenon which, taken by itself, does not lend itself to exact observation nor indeed to measurement. To proceed to this classification and this comparison, we must substitute for this internal fact which escapes us an external index which symbolizes it and study the former in the light of the latter (*DOL* 64).

Despite this, Durkheim's book is arranged around the distinction between two kinds of solidarity. We are therefore in the unsatisfactory position of having to distinguish between two sub-types of a phenomenon which is not itself defined or observable. We have to take solidarity for granted. Durkheim divides solidarity into two types, positive and negative, and then further divides positive solidarity into two types, mechanical and organic. All three kinds of solidarity are present in every real society, but in varying proportions, and it is possible to distinguish them analytically.

Mechanical solidarity binds the individual directly to the society without any intermediary (*DOL* 129) and is predominant in those societies belonging to the collective type, in which the beliefs and sentiments of each member are the same, not merely because of their common humanity but because of their common membership in a specific society. Organic solidarity arises when the members or sub-units of a society differ from one another but depend on one another and are controlled or constrained or regulated by one another or by some single specialised sub-unit. Durkheim justifies his use of terms by saying:

> The term [mechanical solidarity] does not signify that it is produced by mechanical and artificial means. We call it that only by analogy to the cohesion which unites the elements of an inanimate body as opposed to that which makes an unity out of the elements of a living body. . . . The individual conscience, considered in this light, is a simple dependent upon the collective type and follows all of its movements, as the possessed object follows those of its owner (*DOL* 130).

On the other hand, organic solidarity is produced by the division of labour in society, so that each member has his own specific activity which makes some contribution to the lives of other members. No member can live alone, for each depends on the activities of others for his own well-being. He says:

> In effect, on the one hand, each one depends as much more strictly on society as labour is more divided; and, on the other, the activity of each is as much more personal as it is more specialized. . . . This solidarity resembles that which we observe among the higher animals. Each organ, in effect, has its special physiognomy, its autonomy. And, moreover, the unity of the organism is as great as the individuation of the parts is more marked. Because of this analogy, we propose to call the solidarity which is due to the division of labour, organic (*DOL* 131).

Organic and mechanical solidarity together constitute the two forms of positive solidarity, in contradistinction to negative solidarity. Durkheim makes little use of the concept of negative solidarity. He says that it does not produce any integration by itself (*DOL* 129), and that it corresponds to a certain class of legal rules; but in fact he uses the term as a synonym for the rules themselves, those rules that define rights to real property. As far as I can tell, he makes no distinction between real property and chattels and hence speaks of the 'solidarity of things,' another synonym for negative solidarity or 'real solidarity' (*DOL* 116). He says that these rules 'do not cause the people whom they put in contact with one another to concur; they do not demand any co-operation; but they simply restore or maintain, in the new conditions which are produced, this negative solidarity whose circumstances have troubled its functioning' (*DOL* 118).

He mentions yet another kind of solidarity, industrial or contractual solidarity (*DOL* xviii, 200) attributed to Spencer. Durkheim refers to it principally to show that it is spurious. It would be the solidarity of a society in which individuals, each with his own goals and values, were linked only by a vast system of particular contracts (*DOL* 203) spontaneously entered into. Durkheim refutes this principally by reference to the limitations placed by every known society on the kinds of contracts that are valid and by the existence of elaborate legal machinery for regulating and enforcing contracts (Parsons 1960:119–20). 'For everything in the contract is not contractual' (*DOL* 211), and it is in the non-contractual elements that we can find the true sources of organic solidarity (*cf.* Parsons 1937:319, where he says Durkheim was mistaken). Indeed, in his eagerness to overthrow the Hobbesian view of society, and to reject the randomness of individual goals, Durkheim almost overlooks the similarity between such solidarity as there may be in spontaneous contractual relations and his own organic solidarity. Indeed, in a later passage, he reinstates contractual solidarity as one of the important varieties of organic solidarity (*DOL* 381).

Durkheim makes a distinction between laws and customs. By law, he means a law as written in a code of laws. There are two sub-categories of law, repressive and restitutive, classified according to the kinds of sanctions attached to them. Some sanctions, says Durkheim, 'consist essentially in suffering, or at least a loss, inflicted on the agent. They make demands on his fortune, or on his honour, or on his life, or on his liberty, and deprive him of something he enjoys. We call them repressive. They constitute penal law.' 'As for the other type it does not necessarily imply suffering for the agent, but consists only of *the return of things as they were*, in the re-establishment of troubled relations to their normal state' (*DOL* 69). Restitutive laws are further divided into two types, those dealing with real rights, *i.e.* rights over things, as mentioned above, and those dealing with interpersonal rights, and it is these that Durkheim makes use of as the external sign of the inward organic solidarity. The concept of custom is not divided up in the same way, and Durkheim has little to say in this book about custom other than to treat it as a feeble version of the law. He says:

'The acts which custom alone must repress are not different in nature from those the law punishes' (*DOL* 301). 'Normally,' he says, 'custom is not opposed to law, but is, on the contrary, its basis.' 'If, then, there are types of social solidarity, which custom alone manifests, they are assuredly secondary; law produces those which are essential and they are the only ones we need to know' (*DOL* 65–6).

The individuals who together make up a society are thought of as each having a conscience or consciousness, what we might call a value system, and this conscience can be analysed into its parts.

'There are in each of us . . . two consciences: one which is common to our group in its entirety, which, consequently, is not ourself, but society living and acting within us; the other, on the contrary, represents that in us which is personal and distinct, that which makes us an individual. . . . However, these two consciences are not in regions geographically distinct from us, but penetrate from all sides' (*DOL* 129–30). The social component of the conscience, the common or collective conscience (*cf. DOL* 79), is itself divided into two parts. There is an affective element consisting of sentiments and 'phenomena of sensibility,' and there is a representative element consisting of ideas and doctrines (*DOL* 170). As with solidarity and laws, the proportions in which these different varieties of conscience are found in different individuals in any society, and in different societies, vary. It is with the manner in which these proportions vary, relative to one another, that Durkheim is principally concerned.

Solidarity, law and conscience are three of Durkheim's variables, and only one of these is readily accessible to scientific observation. There is, therefore, the likelihood of the whole system of analysis becoming tautologous and self-fulfilling, were it not for the fourth variable, the division of labour, an aspect of social morphology. It is this variable that gives the book its title, and which perhaps provided the newest element in Durkheim's thesis. The concept of division of labour seems nowhere to be defined explicitly and, as we shall see, there is no clear distinction between what we would call specialisation and fragmentation of activities. Durkheim merely says:

> . . . co-operation . . . does not come about without the division of labour. To co-operate, in short, is to participate in a common task. If it is divided into tasks qualitatively similar, but mutually indispensable, there is a simple division of labour of the first degree. If they are of a different character, there is compound division of labour, specialization properly called. (*DOL* 124).

The division of labour, however, is only what we would call an intervening variable for, in Durkheim's terms, it is 'a derived and secondary phenomenon' which 'passes on the surface of social life.' He therefore warns us against mistaking a superficial division of labour, acquired by imitation or diffusion, for the genuine article (*DOL* 282, n. 30). The division of labour is likewise not to be confused with mutualism, whereby two mutually hostile societies 'exchange products in a more or less regular manner' (*DOL* 281–2), nor with differentiation 'pure and simple,' as when certain persons specialise in crime, for this is the 'very negation of solidarity' (*DOL* 353). Thus, to this extent, Durkheim admits as division of labour only those kinds of occupational specialisation which satisfy the relationship between division of labour and social solidarity that he is seeking to demonstrate.

As befits a scientist, Durkheim recognizes the value of measurement and uses several quantitative concepts. Yet, in many cases no attempt is made to provide rules for determining these quantities operationally, and we are given only statements about 'larger' and 'smaller' and the like. Durkheim refers to the volume of social life (*DOL* 198), the volume of a legal code (*DOL* 205), the size and intensity of various phenomena. Indeed, he gives considerable attention to the way in which a given component, in the law or in the conscience, can vary in size both absolutely and relatively to the other components. Most of his commentators have overlooked this aspect of Durkheim's methodology, but it is interesting to note that the analytical tool of concomitant variation, which Durkheim develops considerably in *Suicide*, is present in embryonic form in the *Division of Labour.*

'Vivacity' (*DOL* 237) is another apparently quantitative concept, but the notion of quantity and measurement is most developed in Durkheim's use of 'density.' He deals with 'material density' which we would call population density, and 'moral or dynamic density of society,' which is the relation between 'individuals sufficiently in contact to be able to act and react upon one another' and 'the active commerce resulting from it' (*DOL* 257). The 'condensation of society' and 'social density' (*DOL* 260) seem to be synonyms for population density.

There are two other analytical concepts by which Durkheim tries to link his four variables: 'function' and 'type.' He says: 'To ask what the function of the division of labour is, is to seek for the need which it supplies' (*DOL* 49). Endless confusion has followed Durkheim's popularisation of this term, and I cannot unravel this confusion here. It must be sufficient to note that in Merton's terminology Durkheim is concerned with 'latent function' rather than with manifest or mathematical function (Merton 1949:22, 62). In the *Division of Labour* the term 'function' is restricted to beneficial function. Thus in one of his numerous biological analogies Durkheim says, with reference to crime:

> . . . cancer and tuberculosis increase the diversity of organic tissues without bringing forth a new specialization of biologic functions. In all these cases, there is no partition of a common function, but, in the midst of the organism, whether individual or social, another is formed which seeks to live at the expense of the first. In reality, there is not even a function, for a way of acting merits this name only if it joins with others in maintaining general life (*DOL* 353–4).

Frequently in his book Durkheim refers to the 'collective type' as opposed to the 'individual type' (*DOL* 106–33). The English-speaking reader at least asks 'type of what?' and the answer is not immediately clear. Sometimes it seems that the collective and individual types are types of conscience in which one or the other corresponding component predominates; at other times it seems that these are types of society in which consciences of these kinds are to be found. In either case, Durkheim uses his types as what we would call polar or ideal types.

Durkheim also uses a batch of evaluative concepts, usually in adjectival form. He describes phenomena as 'abnormal' (*DOL* 190), 'decadent' (*DOL* 196), 'pathological' (*DOL* 196, 271) or 'morbid' (*DOL* 219). These words seem to be interchangeable, and are contrasted with another set: 'normal' (*DOL* 375), what 'ought to be' (*DOL* 190), 'healthy,' 'spontaneous' (*DOL* 377) and the like. This use of terms springs from Durkheim's conviction that scientific enquiry provides the only reliable basis for political action, but it involves him in considerable difficulties in his efforts to find a scientific basis for the good.

Finally, he introduces a useful typology of sanctions. This is fairly straightforward and I need not discuss it, for it has become part of the general stock-in-trade of social enquiry (*DOL* 69; *cf.* Radcliffe-Brown 1952: 205–19).

Propositions

Using this conceptual scheme, Durkheim makes several substantive propositions. Many of these are made *en passant*, but two central theses emerge from the book. Firstly, it is asserted that societies may, in broad terms, be placed on a morphological and at least partly historical continuum. At one end of the continuum are primitive societies; these are characterised by internal differentiation into similar segments with negligible division of labour, legal codes that are mainly repressive, a collective conscience that predominates in each individual member's mind over the individual component, low moral density, small population and mechanical solidarity. At the other end are the higher societies characterised by internal differentiation into many distinct organs, a great division of labour, a legal code that is predominantly concerned with restitutive regulation of inter-personal rights, a collective conscience that constitutes only a modest portion of the mind of each individual, high moral density, large population and organic solidarity. As we have seen, solidarity and conscience are internal facts, so that essentially the first proposition amounts to no more than saying (though Durkheim might protest at this) that the extent of the division of labour in a society is correlated positively with moral density and with the predominance of restitutive laws concerned with inter-personal rights in its legal code, and correlated negatively with the predominance of repressive laws.

The second proposition is that a society's movement away from the primitive and towards the higher end of the continuum is due to a causal chain running as follows. A society begins to increase in population and to have a higher population density. Consequently, the struggle for existence becomes more acute and, in order to survive, members of the society develop a division of labour. Durkheim says:

> Thanks to [the division of labour] opponents are not obliged to fight to a finish, but can exist one beside the other. Also, in proportion to its development, it furnishes the means of maintenance and survival to a greater number of individuals who, in more homogeneous societies, would be condemned to extinction (*DOL* 270).

The increasing division of labour then leads to a higher moral density, a decline in the collective component in the conscience, a shift in the structure of the law, and the growth of organic solidarity at the expense of mechanical solidarity.

This proposition has been described as the only serious attempt anywhere in Durkheim's writings to provide an explanation of social change (Benoît-Smullyan 1948:518), but there is little evidence to support it (*cf.* Schnore 1958:627). Durkheim devotes almost as much space to attacking the arguments of his opponents as he does to putting forward evidence for his own assertions. He does not discuss the many possible alternative responses to increased competition (*cf.* Alpert 1939:94). He relies quite heavily on the argument by elimination, in which he puts forward an array of alternatives and advances arguments to eliminate all but one, which is then declared to be proved correct. However, I think that one reason why the evidence advanced by Durkheim appears to us to be so inadequate is that, although the whole book is proclaimed to be an analysis according to the manner of science, in fact Durkheim continually tries to show that in some sense his conclusions are inherent in his definitions, and do not require the support of fresh empirical data. It is significant that in this his first book there is comparatively little appeal to the facts of history and ethnography, whereas in his later writings he is much more closely concerned with the analysis of specific facts. As Lévi-Strauss remarks: 'Durkheim struggled between his methodological attitude, which made him consider social facts as "things," and his philosophical formation which uses those "things" as a ground on which the fundamental Kantian ideals can be firmly seated. Hence, he oscillates between a dull empiricism and an aprioristic frenzy' (Lévi-Strauss 1945:528). In the *Division of Labour* we are still in the realm of the philosophy of history and have not yet entered the fresh fields of sociological enquiry. In fact, it would be quite difficult to prove this second proposition by reference to the facts, since even the division of labour is hard to quantify and there is little conclusive evidence for the level of moral density at any time anywhere. In any case, Durkheim hedges his assertion by introducing several secondary factors, though he does not discuss what logical difference there is between a primary cause and a secondary factor (Alpert 1939:96). Heredity has influenced the division of labour (*DOL* 305), particularly among the more primitive societies. The physical environment may cause a segment of society to specialise its activities and become an organ with a recognised function (*DOL* 263). As the scale of social interaction becomes wider, the real entities symbolised by the collective representations become more numerous, and hence the common conscience becomes more abstract (*DOL* 287), and its characteristic dogma is the cult of the individual (*DOL* 107, 172). Under conditions of social change the wisdom of the aged is less revered and the bonds of tradition are loosened, as, likewise, they are in cities where the aged are comparatively less numerous than they are in the country. Hence individuals feel freer to follow their own inclinations and there is greater diversity in occupations (*DOL* 294–6). It is then a multiple chain of causation that Durkheim is putting forward, and it is difficult to either verify or disprove it.

Part of the first main thesis, that the division of labour is positively correlated with the predominance of restitutive laws concerned with interpersonal rights and negatively with the predominance of repressive laws, is easier to tackle, and indeed to disprove, and its disproof in turn throws doubt on the second proposition. Durkheim supports his arguments with some comparative evidence on legal codes which I have already mentioned, but the evidence is confined to one part only of the correlation. He shows that various legal codes do differ from one another, but only takes for granted the corresponding differences in the division of labour.

Durkheim speaks only in general terms of the level of the division of labour in specified societies, and some of his critics too have not been very successful in giving precision to this term. Thus, for example, one attempt to disprove the 'primitive communism theory,' *i.e.* that the division of labour is non-existent in the primitive world, using material of the kind available to Durkheim, managed to assert that among the Aranda of central Australia there were seven distinct domestic functions performed by women and three by men, and that in the whole of Aranda activities there were ten different occupations for men and three for women. The unreliability of this method of analysis is shown by the fact that this same investigator found only one recognised domestic activity for women among the Warramunga and none for men (Watson 1929). Yet, in fact, these two tribes are quite close to one another and in the division of labour they are almost identical.

But the main weakness of the first thesis is that the ethnographic evidence shows that, in general, primitive societies are not characterised by repressive laws. Durkheim took his evidence on legal codes from classical antiquity and early Europe, and some historical progression of the kind he had in mind may have taken place there, though even in this area Merton holds he was mistaken (Merton 1934:326). But this progression cannot be extended to the primitive world, where legal codes do not exist in writing, if at all. In stateless societies almost all jural rules are, in these terms, restitutive rather than repressive. Indeed, it is interesting that in an enquiry based on evidence from forty-eight societies, and aimed to test whether or not Tönnies, Durkheim, Park, Small, Maine, Redfield and Riesman are all talking in different terms about the same dimension of societal complexity, the authors have, perhaps unconsciously, quite overlooked what Durkheim had to say about the development of law. They examine eight variables in terms of greater or less societal complexity, as suggested by these theorists, and equate punishment by government action with greater complexity, and punishment by the person wronged with less complexity (Freeman & Winch 1957:461, 463). Yet, the ethnographic record shows that it is governmental action that is typically repressive, and redress by self-help that is restitutive. As Nisbet (1965:30) notes, it is perhaps significant that in his later writings Durkheim does not refer at all to social solidarity generated by repressive laws.

Durkheim is on firmer ground when he correlates the division of labour with moral density, though this is hard to state quantitatively. In the *Division of Labour* Durkheim weakens his own case somewhat by treating moral and material density as interchangeable, and in the *Rules* he corrects this fault. Herskovits cites Durkheim's proposition:

> The division of labour varies in direct ratio with the volume and density of societies, and, if it progresses in a continuous manner in the course of social development, it is because societies become regularly denser and generally more voluminous (*DOL* 262).

Herskovits comments: 'It is not possible to document this statement, especially in its dynamic aspects. Yet if the quantitative precision it implies is not insisted upon the position carries a considerable validity' (1952:142).

Thus the difficulty of testing Durkheim's main assertions in this book lies partly in the absence of data with historical depth from an adequately wide range of societies, and partly from the fact that his propositions involve terms which, on his own definitions, are not accessible to observation. Mechanical and organic solidarity and collective and individual types of conscience may be handy names for recognised constellations of observable facts concerned with legal systems, occupational specialisation, population density and population size. But they cannot be more than mere names unless independent criteria are introduced by which their existence can be proved or disproved. This Durkheim singularly failed to do. The term 'solidarity' did come to have a clear meaning later, in the writings of Léon Bourgeois, but his book, *La Solidarité*, was published after the *Division of Labour* (Alpert 1939:178; 1941; Richter 1960:1).

Despite this lack of operational definition, the notion of social solidarity remains central to Durkheim's argument. Forms of the division of labour are assessed as normal or pathological according to the kind of social solidarity they engender. We have noted earlier that Durkheim rejected the notion of professional crime as an example of the division of labour. Nevertheless he does admit three kinds of the division of labour that he classes as exceptional or pathological (*DOL* 353–4). First there is the division of labour characterised by chronic conflict between capital and labour. This anomic form arises because there is inadequate contact between the various organs of society, and this in turn is due in part to the lack of juridical determination of the rights of capital and labour (*DOL* 367), and in part to the fact that, as organised society develops, the producer cannot appraise the market for his product at a glance. Hence production becomes unregulated and there are periodic crises (*DOL* 370). This is pathological, for under normal conditions, the worker is 'not a machine who repeats his movements without knowing their meaning, but . . . he feels he is serving something' '. . . this essential character of the division of labour . . . is above all a source of solidarity' (*DOL* 372–3).

Yet, if under-regulation and insufficient contact lead to an anomic division of labor, too much regulation may lead to another pathological form, the forced division of labour. There is no spontaneity if people are linked to their functions only by constraint, and we have only an imperfect and troubled solidarity. Durkheim here has in mind caste societies, and he goes on to distinguish between inequality of income and status, which is not necessarily bad, and inequality in what he calls the external conditions of conflict (*DOL* 379), which is bad. Overregulation, or occupational specialisation by prescription rather than by achievement, prevents that desirable state of affairs in which social inequalities exactly express natural inequalities and labour is divided spontaneously. This is achieved by contracts spontaneously entered into and adhered to (*DOL* 377).

Finally, in some societies, the functional activity of each worker is insufficient to produce the required degree of solidarity. Durkheim does not give any modern examples of this pathological condition, but notes approvingly that as societies advance there is less leisure. 'In societies which are exclusively agricultural and pastoral, labour is almost entirely suspended during the season of bad weather.' But as we advance, work becomes a 'permanent occupation' and 'if sufficiently strengthened, a need.' The division of labour makes individuals solidary 'not only because it limits the activity of each, but also because it increases it' (*DOL* 394–5).

Developments

Before making some assessment of the *Division of Labour*, it may be convenient to note some of the developments that have sprung from it. In a sense, the greatest of these is the work of Durkheim himself for, as already mentioned, the seeds of much of his subsequent writings, the *Rules*, *Suicide* and *Elementary Forms* are to be found in the *Division of Labour*. In the *Rules* he stresses the autonomy of social facts to a greater extent than in the *Division of Labour*, so that the physical environment and factors of heredity become less admissible as links in the chain of social causation. The collective conscience is conceived in the *Division of Labour* as containing an affective component, but it is the cognitive or representative element that is mainly dealt with. In later work, particularly in the *Elementary Forms*, these representative elements begin to acquire an autonomy of their own, their coercive force on the individual is stressed, and hence the affective element comes also to be stressed at the expense of sentiments arising in the individual component of the conscience. In the *Division of Labour* the collective conscience is linked closely with the fact that the members of a society are, and perceive themselves to be, similar to one another; Durkheim is concerned with culturally homogeneous, and not plural, societies. But in *Suicide* the collective conscience is seen as merely the system of moral beliefs and sentiments common to members of a society (Parsons 1937:337; *cf. DOL* 129) whether or not they have the same occupations and social statuses. Durkheim's next step is to concentrate on these ideas and beliefs rather than on the legal codes and occupational groupings, so that sociology comes to be the study of systems of ideas rather than systems of action (Parsons 1937:446). This trend is now in full flood in French anthropology under the leadership of Lévi-Strauss, on whom the mantle of Mauss has descended and who may be regarded as Durkheim's heir.

We can distinguish, at least analytically, between the collective conscience existing as an entity on its own, independent of any individual manifestation, and any individual's imperfect comprehension of it. But Durkheim is never clear on this distinction and his fumbling towards it exposes him to the charge of advocating a group mind. Some modern writers assert that the distinction can be understood by analogy with the laws of grammar, which unconsciously constrain the speech of even the

ignorant unschooled peasant. Durkheim accepted the existence of the unconscious mind in an article he published in 1898 (Durkheim 1953:21–3;
cf. Neyer 1960:61–2). Yet Lévi-Strauss comments:

> The solution of Durkheim's factitious antinomy lies in the awareness that
> these objectivated systems of ideas are unconscious or that unconscious
> psychical structures underlie them and make them possible. Hence their
> character as "things" and at the same time the dialectic—I mean un-
> mechanical—character of this explanation. (Lévi-Strauss 1945:528).

While Molière allows Monsieur Jourdain to discover merely that he has
been talking prose all his life without knowing it, Lévi-Strauss makes him
obey the rules of grammar as well.

A no less fruitful consequence of Durkheim's book has been the
development of the notion of organic solidarity through Mauss' study of
exchange as an integrating mechanism, as seen in his book *The gift*. Durkheim in the *Division of Labour* still regards social solidarity as derived in
part from such non-social factors as 'The affinities that the community of
blood brings about' (*DOL* 175), but in later work his followers have expanded the social causes of solidarity. The exchange of goods and services
through the division of labour is seen to be only one source of the multiplex
and diverse social ties that bind together the members of a differentiated
society.

I have already referred to the work of Radcliffe-Brown on the classification of sanctions, where, as in his writings on law and in his use of
the concept of function, he follows Durkheim closely. Yet it is curious
to note how little influence Durkheim seems to have had on anthropology
in America, at least until quite recently. Lowie, despite devoting a chapter
to Durkheim in his *History of Ethnological Theory*, managed to write his
three major books on social organisation (*Primitive Society*, *Social Organization* and *The Origin of the State*) without a single reference to Durkheim.
Even more surprising is that in the weighty *Anthropology Today*, with 966
pages and fifty bibliographies, there are only four references to Durkheim,
two of these being by Lévi-Strauss. This is the more remarkable in that it
was an anthropologist, Radcliffe-Brown, who was partly responsible for
introducing Durkheim's work to sociologists in America, as Nisbet (1964:4)
stresses. Durkheim's writings on religion were closer to American anthropological interests prior to 1950 than anything he had to say about
social organisation, and the former may have become so much a part of
anthropological thinking that direct citation was unnecessary. Yet the
apparent irrelevance of the *Division of Labour* for studies of social organisation is strange. Since Durkheim, there have been only two serious
attempts to study the division of labour on a world-wide scale. The first
was in 1915 by Hobhouse, Wheeler and Ginsberg, and the second in 1959
by Udy in a book whose title exactly mirrors Durkheim's—*Organization of
Work: A Comparative Analysis of Production among Non-industrial Peoples*.
In neither book is there any reference to Durkheim. It seems that his book
is already part of prehistory.

Assessment

There are two ways of looking at the *Division of Labour*. Either we can see it as a contribution towards the defeat of the social nominalists, and of Spencer in particular, and towards the establishment of sociology as a recognised professional academic discipline in France; or else we can view it as a contribution to present-day thinking about social cohesion, legal development, occupational specialisation and so on. The latter, if fully developed, would take us too far for our present purpose and would, as I have already suggested, yield rather meagre results. To explore the former would require a much greater knowledge of Durkheim's philosophical and sociological adversaries than I have. All I can do is to offer a few comments on points of Durkheim's method that, even seventy years after he wrote, still seem relevant.

In the first place, Durkheim seems to have been very poorly served by his terminology. He wrote, so Alpert claims, in as mechanical an idiom as possible (Alpert 1939:85) for polemical reasons and hence it is not surprising that some people took him literally. He was misunderstood by Malinowski, who said that Durkheim claimed that there was 'slavish, fascinated, passive obedience' to social codes (Malinowski 1926:4; Alpert 1939:208). He did not support syndicalism (Parsons 1937:339), nor did he advocate the fascist corporate state (Richter 1960:196), although both these accusations were brought against him. He has been accused of breaking his own canons of explanation by saying that the cause of the growth of organic solidarity is to be found in a non-social fact, the growth of population, and on this score his latest defender (Schnore 1958:624) gives the impressive list of Alpert, Benoît-Smullyan, Parsons and Sorokin as all having misunderstood Durkheim. All of these are points of substance and he can scarcely be excused on the grounds that he could not be expected to write clearly about everything he had to say. More serious in his confusion about the average, the normal, the healthy and the ideal. In *Rules*, Durkheim says that the normal type is identical with the average type and that every deviation from this standard is a pathological phenomenon (*Rules*:64; Benoît-Smullyan 1948:504), but he never followed consistently even this clear, if surprising, statement. Halbwachs points out that the rising suicide rate, which Durkheim regarded as so undesirable, should, by Durkheim's own criteria, be judged to be quite normal (Benoît-Smullyan 1948:529, n. 21). In the earlier *Division of Labour* there is greater confusion, for Durkheim writes that sickness is not 'part of the normal type of old age. On the contrary, the illnesses of old age are abnormal facts just as those of the adult' (*DOL* 433, n. 22). He seeks to identify the 'normal moral fact for a given social type' by the repressive diffuse sanction attaching to it (*DOL* 435), but while this may work for rules of conduct it cannot apply to phenomena like crime rates. Peristiany (1953:viii-xx) devotes most of his introduction to the translation of Durkheim's *Sociology and Philosophy* to commenting on these points, but Durkheim's usages still remain confused for me. It is perhaps significant that the longest discussion of these concepts in the *Division of Labour* occurs in that portion of the preface to the first edition which was omitted from the second and subsequent editions. There would seem to me to be a fundamental conflict between Durkheim's attempt to look at values relativistically, in the context of the society in which they are held, and his insistence at the same time that certain social conditions are intrinsically pathological. This conflict is obscured by lack of clarity about the status of the norm, which is equated at one moment with the average and at another with the healthy, with what ought to be. Unfortunately this particular confusion still persists, at least terminologically.

Alpert claims that Durkheim recognized the integrative value of conflict in social life (Alpert 1941:173; *cf.* Richter 1960:194) but there is little in the *Division of Labour* to support this view. Indeed, the contemptuous dismissal of what Durkheim calls mutualism, limited co-operation between enemies, and his restriction of the concept of function to beneficial function, suggest that he looked upon internal conflict as essentially unhealthy and destructive of solidarity. Solidarity and integration are seen as good in themselves, and the more the better. The concept of altruism is used a little in the *Division of Labour* (*DOL* 196, 197, 228) but it is not linked to suicide, while those suicides which by the criteria of *Suicide* would be classed as altruistic are here referred to as not 'true suicide' (*DOL* 246–7). Hence there is no need to discuss the dangers of excessive integration. Instead, as we have seen, Durkheim argues that the division of labour produces solidarity only if it is spontaneous, not forced (*DOL* 376–7). There must be external equality so that 'harmony between individual natures and social functions cannot fail to be realised, at least in the average case. For, if nothing impedes or unduly favours those disputing over tasks, it is inevitable that only those who are most apt at each kind of activity will indulge in it.' 'It will be said that it is not always sufficient to make men content, that there are some men whose desires go beyond their faculties. This is true, but these are exceptional and, one may say, morbid cases' (*DOL* 376). The freedom to find the right niche in society can be secured only by conscious action on the part of the state, and only by this action can a society based on organic solidarity survive, since it cannot rely on its weak collective conscience. Hence 'liberty itself is the product of regulation. Far from being antagonistic to social action, it results from social action' (*DOL* 386).

It is true that in the politically most controversial section of the *Division of Labour* Durkheim protests that this idyllic state of affairs is far from being realised in contemporary France. He might have been surprised to find that it was to be in Soviet Russia between the wars that his notions of the connexion between organic solidarity and the division of labour found most explicit expression, in the stress on the social value of the humblest tasks performed by factory workers (Friedmann 1955:49). This view is found in the poem 'The funeral' by Stephen Spender (1955:53), published in the early 1930s.

Death is another milestone on their way.
With laughter on their lips and with winds blowing round them

They record simply
How this one exceeded all others in making driving belts.[2]

However, it should be remembered that similar sentiments are to be found in a seventeenth century poem by George Herbert (1941:185).

> A servant with this clause
> Makes drudgerie divine:
> Who sweeps a room, as for thy laws,
> Makes that and th' action fine.

Divine determinism and dialectical materialism both provide the solidarity Durkheim reserved for applied positive science.

But Durkheim's recipe for harmony in twentieth century industrial society tallies neither with the changes in industrial organisation since his day, brought about by increased mechanisation, nor with the findings of industrial psychology. Georges Friedmann ends his discussion of 'Durkheim's thesis and the contemporary forms of the division of labour' by saying:

> During the half-century which has followed the publication of this report, the forms taken by specialisation in industrial society have only enlarged the gap between the ideal consequences of the division of labour as Durkheim expounded them and the real effects that we observe in our societies. (Friedmann 1955:58).

In much the same spirit, Richter writes that Durkheim never investigated political institutions with anything like the care he gave to his work on suicide and religion. He says:

> The limitations of Durkheim's political thought are nowhere more clear than when put in the perspective of twentieth century totalitarianism. (Richter 1960:199, 204).

The virtues of the *Division of Labour* must be found elsewhere. Negatively, it provided arguments against utilitarianism. Positively, it was the first substantial statement of the view that values, beliefs and aspirations were not randomly distributed throughout the population, nor diffused independently from one society to another, nor directly derived from a common humanity. Rather, they were to a significant degree shared by members of a society by reason of their membership. The form and content of these common values were likewise connected with the forms of organisation of the society, so that a change in organisation was followed, sooner or later, by a change in values, and vice versa. We take all this so much for granted that we tend to forget where it came from.

REFERENCES

Alpert, Harry J. 1939. *Emile Durkheim and His Sociology*. (Studies in history, economics and public law 445). New York: Columbia U.P.

---

[2] Quoted with acknowledgments to the author and the publishers, Messrs. Faber & Faber.

―――― 1941. Emile Durkheim and the Theory of Social Integration. *J. Soc. Philos.* 6, 172–84.

Benoît-Smullyan, Emile 1948. The Sociologism of Emile Durkheim and His School. In *An Introduction to the History of Sociology* (ed.) Barnes, Harry Elmer. Chicago: Chicago U.P.

Bohannan, Paul 1960. Conscience Collective and Culture. In Wolff, K. H. (ed.) 1960.

Faris, Ellsworth 1934. Emile Durkheim on the Division of Labor in Society. Review in *Am. J. Sociol.* 40, 376–7.

Freeman, Linton C. & Winch, Robert Francis 1957. Societal Complexity: An Empirical Test of a Typology of Societies. *Am. J. Sociol.* 62, 461–6.

Friedmann, Georges 1955. La thèse de Durkheim et le Formes Contemporaines de la Division du Travail. *Cah. Intern. Sociol.* 19, 45–58.

Herbert, George 1941. *The Works of George Herbert.* Oxford: Clarendon Press.

Herskovits, M. J. 1952. *Economic Anthropology: A Study in Comparative Economics.* New York: Knopf.

Hobhouse, L. T., Wheeler, G. C. & Ginsberg, M. 1915. *The Material Culture and Social Institutions of the Simple Peoples: An Essay in Correlation.* London: Chapman & Hall.

Lacombe, Roger E. 1926. *La Méthode Sociologique de Durkheim: Étude Critique.* Paris: Alcan.

Lévi-Strauss, Claude 1945. French Sociology. In *Twentieth Century Sociology* (eds.) Gurvitch, G., & W. E. Moore, New York: Philosophical Library.

Lowie, R. H. 1937. *The History of Ethnological Theory.* London: Harrap.

Malinowski, B. 1926. *Crime and Custom in Savage Society.* London: Kegan Paul, Trench, Trubner.

Mauss, Marcel 1958. Introduction to the First Edition. In *Socialism and Saint-Simon*, Durkheim, Emile. Yellow Spring, Ohio: Antioch Press.

Merton, R. K. 1934. Durkheim's Division of Labor in Society. *Am. J. Sociol.* 40, 316–28.

―――― 1949. *Social Theory and Social Structure: Towards the Codification of Theory and Research.* New York: The Free Press.

Neyer, Joseph 1960. Individualism and Socialism in Durkheim. In Wolff, K. H. (ed.), 1960.

Nisbet, R. A. 1965. *Emile Durkheim . . . with Selected Essays.* Englewood Cliffs, N.J.: Prentice-Hall.

Parsons, Talcott 1937. *The Structure of Social Action.* New York: The Free Press (2nd ed., 1949.)

―――― 1960. Durkheim's Contribution to the Theory of Integration of Social Systems. In Wolff, K. H. (ed.) 1960.

Peristiany, J. G. 1953. Introduction. In *Sociology and Philosophy*, Durkheim, Emile. London: Cohen & West.

Peyre, Henri 1960. Durkheim: The Man, His Time, and His Intellectual Background. In Wolff, K. H. (ed.) 1960.

Radcliffe-Brown, A. R. 1952. *Structure and Function in Primitive Society: Essays and Addresses.* London: Cohen & West.

Richter, Melvin 1960. Durkheim's Politics and Political Theory. In Wolff, K. H. (ed.) 1960.

Schnore, Leo F. 1958. Social Morphology and Human Ecology. *Am. J. Sociol.* 63, 620–34.

Simpson, George 1933. Emile Durkheim's Social Realism. *Sociol. Soc. Res.* 18, 3–11.

Spender, Stephen 1955. *Collected poems 1928–1953.* London: Faber & Faber.

Udy, Stanley Hart, Jr. 1959. *Organization of Work: A Comparative Analysis of Production among Non-industrial Peoples.* New Haven: H.R.A.F. Press.

Watson, Walter T. 1929. A New Census and an Old Theory: Division of Labor in the Preliterate World. *Am. J. Sociol.* 34, 632–52.

Wolff, Kurt H. 1960 (ed.). *Emile Durkheim, 1858–1917; A Collection of Essays with Translations and a Bibliography.* Columbus, Ohio: Ohio State U.P.

7.2

Durkheim's One Cause of Suicide*

BARCLAY D. JOHNSON

Although Durkheim's *Suicide* is among the most widely read classics in our field, sociologists rarely seek to clarify the theory it contains. The present paper is devoted to this task. I shall formulate Durkheim's theory in a manner harmonious both with his own words and with the demands of logical consistency. In the process, I shall call attention to certain inconsistencies in his argument, and try to resolve them. Since this is primarily an attempt to understand Durkheim, I shall not attempt to "improve" the theory by introducing changes of my own invention.

The aforementioned purpose is a restricted one, and should be clearly distinguished from several related endeavors. Some of the things I will *not* attempt to do are the following: (1) Evaluate Durkheim's empirical claims about suicide rates of particular groups.[1] This is a study in theory, not an examination of the incidence of suicide. (2) Review studies of suicide rates carried out since Durkheim's day.[2] (3) Interpret and collate the work of various authors who have elaborated such Durkheimean concepts as "integration" and "anomie."[3] (4) Present a new theory of suicide, or new data pertaining to suicide.[4]

---

* I am grateful to Neil J. Smelser, Kenneth E. Bock, Max Heirich, and R. Stephen Warner for their help in the preparation of this paper.

[1] For comments on this question, see Jack P. Gibbs, "Suicide," in Robert K. Merton and Robert A. Nisbet (eds.), *Contemporary Social Problems*, New York: Harcourt, Brace and World, 1961, pp. 222–261, *passim*.

[2] *Ibid.* On the question of the validity of suicide statistics, see Warren Breed, "Occupational Mobility and Suicide Among White Males," *American Sociological Review*, 28 (1963), esp. pp. 181–182. A recent review of data on suicide is in Louis I. Dublin, *Suicide*, New York: Ronald Press, 1963.

[3] On concepts of "integration," see Werner S. Landecker, "Types of Integration and Their Measurement," in Paul F. Lazarsfeld and Morris Rosenberg (eds.), *The Language of Social Research*, Glencoe, Ill.: Free Press, 1955, pp. 19–27. On concepts of "anomie," articles and books have been appearing at an astonishing rate, to a great extent stimulated by Robert K. Merton, "Social Structure and Anomie," in *Social Theory and Social Structure*, New York: Free Press, 1957, Ch. 4.

[4] Theories of suicide rates are offered in at least two recent books: Andrew F. Henry and James F. Short, Jr., *Suicide and Homicide*, Glencoe, Ill.: Free

Of course we want to move beyond Durkheim. But this craving should not deflect all our attention from his classic study, for *Suicide* remains worthy of close examination in its own right.[5]

An Initial Formulation of the Theory

Durkheim's starting point is the observation, not original with him, that self-destruction occurs with varying frequency in different populations, and he intends his theory to explain this variation among social environments in the incidence of suicide, not the suicides of particular individuals.[6] Durkheim contends that suicide rates depend on two variable social conditions. He calls these independent variables social *integration* and social *regulation*. Together, the two determine the incidence of suicide in any group: to any given level of integration and regulation, an approximate rate of suicide corresponds.

A society, group, or social condition is said to be *integrated* to the degree that its members possess a "common conscience"[7] of shared beliefs and sentiments, interact with one another, and have a sense of devotion to common goals. *Altruism* is Durkheim's name for a high level of integration. His two main examples of altruism are primitive peoples and the army. Altruistic societies such as these have many suicides be-

---

Press, 1954, and Jack P. Gibbs and Walter T. Martin, *Status Integration and Suicide*, Eugene: University of Oregon Press, 1964. Both books appear to have grown, in part, out of careful study of Durkheim's *Suicide*. Gibbs and Martin (pp. 5–10) mention briefly a number of the points about Durkheim's book that I have made in the present essay.

[5] All references to an English edition are to Emile Durkheim, *Suicide, A Study in Sociology* (trans. by John A. Spaulding and George Simpson; ed. by George Simpson), Glencoe, Ill.: Free Press, 1951.

[6] The question of Durkheim's *unit of analysis* occasionally troubles readers of *Suicide*. One sometimes wonders whether it is societies and groups, or social conditions (for example, widowhood or poverty), or perhaps even individuals. The feeling that implicitly Durkheim's unit of analysis is the individual arises especially in his discussion of the "Individual Forms of the Different Types of Suicide" (Book II, Ch. 6). Often in this chapter, and on occasion elsewhere, Durkheim seems to be estimating the probability that some particular individual will kill himself. The reason may be a paradoxical one: the very intensity of Durkheim's desire to prove that society is a reality *sui generis* leads him, most clearly in *The Rules of Sociological Method*, to point out that one's own experience shows that something *external* to the individual *constrains* him to act in certain ways. Durkheim, in a sense, focusses on the individual precisely to demonstrate that a social reality exists "outside" of him. But to conclude that this individual is in fact the unit of analysis would be to misapprehend the very aim of Durkheim's intellectual career, which was to show that society is real.

[7] The expression "common conscience" is taken from Durkheim's *Division of Labor in Society*. The *concept*, unchanged from the earlier book, is present in *Suicide* though the phrase is not.

cause they stress individual renunciation, even though suicide may not be specifically prescribed.[8]

At the low end of the integration scale is the condition Durkheim calls *egoism*. Egoism exists when the common conscience is weak (that is, few common beliefs and sentiments are present), interaction is limited, and dedication is to self-interests rather than to those of the collectivity. Egoism is characteristic of Protestants, Frenchmen, and unmarried people, among others. Groups such as these, although at the opposite end of the scale from altruism, also display a high rate of suicide. In a condition of weak integration, life derives no meaning and purpose from the group, and it is readily surrendered.[9]

Thus, both high and low levels of integration cause high suicide rates. But between altruism and egoism lies a third social condition of *moderate* integration, in which suicides are few.[10] Durkheim never names this condition, but examples of it appear in passages of *Suicide* that draw a contrast between either an egoistic or an altruistic group and another group with a lower suicide rate. Thus, Protestant society is egoistic and causes many suicides, while the Catholic and Jewish religions are moderately integrated and have few suicides.[11] The army is altruistic and has many suicides, while civilian society, at least in such nations as Italy, Austria, and England, is intermediate in integration and has few suicides.[12]

Regulation and suicide have exactly the same relationship: either a low or a high level of regulation causes many suicides, while a moderate level causes few. Durkheim assigns the term *anomie* to a state of low regulation. When society has only weak control over the individual, his passions are apt to burst forth, he may become disoriented, and he will perhaps kill himself. Anomie occurs among businessmen, especially during booms and depressions, and among widows and divorced people.[13]

But a *high* degree of regulation can also engender suicide: ". . . there is a type of suicide the opposite of anomic suicide, just as egoistic and altruistic suicides are opposites." When a state of *fatalism* prevails, social regulation is intense: ". . . futures [are] pitilessly blocked and passions violently choked by oppressive discipline." This social cause of suicide occurs among childless married women, very young husbands, and slaves.[14]

---

[8] *Suicide*, Book II, Ch. 4, esp. pp. 220–223.

[9] *Ibid.*, Chs. 2 and 3, esp. pp 209–210.

[10] *Ibid.*, pp. 236, 364.

[11] *Ibid.*, pp. 157–160.

[12] *Ibid.*, p. 236.

[13] *Ibid.*, Book II, Ch. 5, esp. pp. 246–254, 258. Although contemporary sociologists make a great to-do about "anomie," Durkheim asserted that egoism is a far more common cause of high suicide rates in modern societies than is anomie. *Ibid.*, pp. 356, 358.

[14] *Ibid.*, p. 276, ftn. 25. Durkheim's discussion of fatalism is *not* confined to his famous footnote on the subject, even though the expression "fatalistic suicide" appears only in that footnote, and the word "fatalism" does not appear in *Suicide* at all. The other, more extended passages he devotes to the subject are on pp. 177–179, 188–189, 274–276.

Durkheim never explicitly asserts that *moderate* regulation engenders few suicides. But this view is unmistakably implied. Whenever he locates a group at either pole of the regulation scale, he offers in contrast another group, lying between the poles, which has fewer suicides. Thus, the weak regulation experienced by businessmen exposes them to the danger of anomic suicide, whereas the greater regulation to which poor people are subject protects them against suicide.[15] Correspondingly, the over-regulated husband of tender years is prone to fatalistic suicide, while the less-regulated, older husband is less likely to kill himself.[16]

In short, Durkheim identifies three significant levels of integration, and three of regulation, and to each level he assigns a suicide rate, whether it be high or low.

The discussion should not, however, stop here. It is important to note Durkheim's implication that every society is to some degree integrated *and* regulated as well. The very definitions of these dimensions imply that any society or group stands at some point on each of them. Thus, the *nine* combined states of integration and regulation are the total number of significant social conditions. If we know, for example, that some particular group is egoistic, this fact does not by itself permit us to predict its suicide rate. We must also learn whether its level of regulation is anomic, moderate, or fatalistic. These relations among integration, regulation, and suicide are represented in Figure 1.

Cells 2, 4, 6, and 8 in Figure 1 represent Durkheim's claim that any one of the four causes of suicide, occurring by itself, causes a high rate of suicide. The figure also calls attention to his implicit view that in fact a low rate of suicide corresponds to only one social condition. Since he assumes that an extreme value of *either* independent variable is sufficient to cause a high rate, a low rate will occur only if a group is both moderately integrated and moderately regulated (Cell 5).

Finally, Figure I suggests that two of the causes of high suicide rates can coexist, a possibility that Durkheim explicitly acknowledges by discussing what he calls the "mixed types" of suicide. Egoism, anomie, and altruism ". . . are very often combined with one another, giving rise to composite varieties; characteristics of several types will be united in a single suicide."[17] He mentions three possible mixed types, "ego-anomic," "anomic-altruistic," and "ego-altruistic."[18] There seems to be no inconsistency in saying that a group can be both unintegrated and unregulated, or both highly integrated and unregulated (Cells 1 and 3 in Figure 1). But if every group stands at *one* point on the integration dimension, no group can be at once egoistic and altruistic.[19] Further, to this error of commission, Durkheim adds an error of omission, for he makes no mention of

---

[15] *Ibid.*, pp. 254–258.

[16] *Ibid.*, pp. 275–276.

[17] *Ibid.*, pp. 287–290.

[18] *Ibid.*, p. 293.

[19] The society Durkheim describes in his discussion of this strange mixture appears, on reflection, to be a case of pure egoism. *Ibid.*, p. 289.

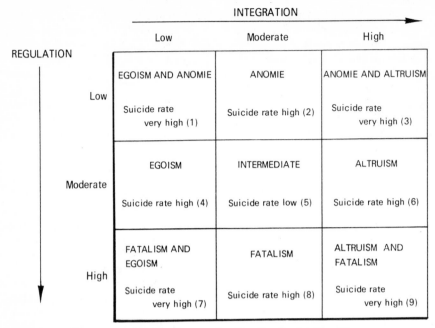

Figure 1.   Suicide Rate under Varying Social Conditions

fatalism. Yet, if both regulation and integration exist to some degree in every group, and if fatalism is a high degree of regulation, then fatalism might occur in conjunction with either egoism or altruism (Cells 7 and 9 in Figure 1.

Therefore, to impart internal consistency to Durkheim's analysis, we must subtract the odd blend of egoism and altruism, and add the two combined forms of fatalism, producing the four possible combined social causes of suicide in the four corner cells of Figure 1.

For the sake of simplicity I have written as if only three values exist for each of the two independent variables. In many passages, however, Durkheim treats both integration and regulation as *continuous* variables. The suicide rates themselves, of course, are spread over a wide range, rather than being concentrated in three clusters.

Figure 2 represents the theory interpreted in this way and summarizes my initial formulation. The midpoints of integration and regulation are, respectively, the vertical and horizontal lines that cross at the center of the figure. Groups located at this point of intersection have the lowest suicide rates. Moving in any direction from the midpoint, one encounters, as if following a topographical map, ever higher rates of suicide. Each succeeding circle corresponds to a higher rate until, at the four corners, one finds groups with peak rates of suicide. (Figure 2 is intended, not as a source of testable hypotheses, but as a visualization of the initial formulation of Durkheim's theory I have worked out here. Further specification,

INCREASING DEGREES OF INTEGRATION

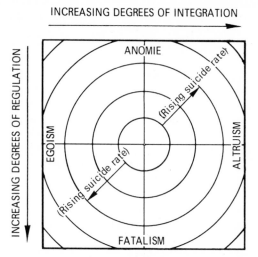

Figure 2. Suicide Rate under Varying Social Conditions

as in assigning a specific suicide rate to each concentric circle and deciding upon definite empirical indicators of integration and regulation,
might imply that in fact the line corresponding to each suicide rate is not
a circle but an ellipse, or some irregular form, or even that some lines
differ in shape from others.)

Reformation, Part I: Eliminating
Altruism and Fatalism

Using Durkheim's theory as formulated in Figure 2 as a point of
departure, I shall now contend that a closer examination of *Suicide* justifies
another, quite different formulation. The first step is to eliminate altruism
and fatalism from Durkheim's range of data. I do not mean to imply that
these conditions do not exist, or even that they do not generate suicide,
but rather that under Durkheim's own premises he cannot legitimately
study altruistic and fatalistic groups.

Almost all Durkheim's examples of altruism are what he calls "primitive." Altruism is "a moral characteristic of primitive man." Between
altruism and egoism ". . . there is . . . all the difference between primitive
peoples and the most civilized nations."[20] What he means by "primitive
peoples" is not entirely clear. Sometimes they are small nonliterate tribes,
as when he contrasts such societies with ancient city-states.[21] On other
occasions he includes among altruistic societies major civilizations such
as India, China, and Japan.[22]

---

[20] *Ibid.*, pp. 223, 227.

[21] *Ibid.*, p. 332.

[22] *Ibid.*, pp. 222–224.

This ambiguity about the word "primitive" helps explain Durkheim's inadequate measures of integration (and, therefore, of altruism) in non-Western societies. He seems to accept as proven his conclusion from the *Division of Labor* that any small society must be tightly integrated. Even if small size were acceptable as proof of altruism, however, it hardly follows that China, India, and Japan are altruistic.

Durkheim's indices of the effect, suicide rates, are almost as unconvincing as his measures of the cause, integration. As evidence that suicides do occur he cites customs requiring, or at least recommending, suicide; that is, in the absence of statistics he infers that suicides occur in primitive societies from the norms that recommend them.[23] Obviously, an inference of a high suicide *rate* from norms alone is of dubious validity, as Durkheim himself recognizes in his analysis of egoism. The difference between Protestant and Catholic rates of suicide cannot be attributed to the different teachings of the two religions, since each condemns suicide equally.[24] The stronger common conscience of the Catholic religion, not its condemnation of suicide, accounts for its lower suicide rate.[25]

Durkheim's sources of information about non-Western societies are even more dubious, being confined to the impressions of ancient authors, early anthropologists, historians, and travelers. Furthermore, Durkheim's authorities describe no society as highly integrated or as experiencing many suicides. Instead, they say that individuals are governed by a sense of duty (which Durkheim accepts as evidence of high integration), and that occasionally people who feel this sense of duty kill themselves.

Clearly, Durkheim's own standards rule out, as proper objects of study, all societies but those modern nations for which moral statistics are available. That is, they rule out all but one of his examples of altruism.[26] This remaining example is the army. If military society is in fact highly integrated, its high rate of suicide constitutes the single empirically demonstrated exception to the proposition that egoism (low integration) promotes suicide while a higher degree of integration protects against it.

The reasons for ruling out fatalism as a proper object of study are equally strong. Durkheim devotes only a few pages to the subject, in part because it "has so little contemporary importance."[27] Just as anomie and egoism are modern phenomena, fatalism and altruism are most often found in pre-modern and non-Western societies. His examples of this sort of fatalism are slaves, and others who suffer from "excessive physical and moral despotism." The available evidence, at least regarding the incidence of suicide, is no better than the evidence for most of his examples of altruism.

---

[23] *Ibid.*, p. 363. See Harry Alpert, *Emile Durkheim and His Sociology*, New York: Russell and Russell, 1961, p. 203.

[24] Durkheim, *op. cit.*, pp. 169–170.

[25] *Ibid.*, pp. 156–157.

[26] Durkheim does mention prison society as another modern example of altruism, but the reference is brief, rather uncertain, and without suicide statistics. *Ibid.*, p. 346, esp. ftn. 45.

[27] *Ibid.*, p. 276, ftn. 25.

Durkheim offers two contemporary examples of fatalism; the first is childless married women. This case requires a brief consideration of the complex relations between sex and suicide. Among men, suicide is less common among the married than among the single. The suicide rate of married men is lower, furthermore, whether they have children or not.[28] The suicide rate of married women is also lower than the rate of single women, and suicide is very rare among married women who have children. But among *childless* married women suicide is more common than among single women. Durkheim concludes that the presence of children, and not marriage itself, protects women from suicide. Among women, marriage in itself actually aggravates the tendency to suicide.[29]

How does Durkheim account for these curious data? Whether he has children or not, a married man is protected by ". . . the regulative influence exerted upon him by marriage . . . the moderation it imposes on his inclinations and . . . his consequent moral well-being." Single men, then, suffer from an anomic social environment, while married men are nearer the midpoint on the regulation scale.

Childless married women, on the other hand, are prone to fatalistic suicide because of the "inflexible rule" that marriage imposes. Marriage can be

> . . . a very heavy, profitless yoke for them. Speaking generally, we now have the cause of that antagonism of the sexes which prevents marriage favoring them equally: their interests are contrary; one needs constraint and the other liberty.[30]

These words may be true. But they contradict Durkheim's initial theoretical premise because they do not attribute the suicide rate of childless married women to purely social causes. Marriage is a "profitless yoke" for women, and they need liberty, not solely because of the nature of marriage itself. Women respond differently than men to the same social environment, as a result of organic and psychological differences. In short, childless married women are not a persuasive example of fatalism.[31]

Similarly, the second modern example of fatalism is not explained by strictly social causes. Generally speaking, marriage immunizes men against suicide, but, among very young husbands, the suicide rate is higher than among single men of the same age. As in the case of childless married

---

[28] *Ibid.*, p. 176, Table XXI, pp. 186, 189.

[29] *Ibid.*, pp. 188–189.

[30] *Ibid.*, p. 274.

[31] If one pieces together Durkheim's widely scattered remarks on the subject of various female suicide rates, the following inconsistent (and rather curious) doctrines of womanhood are to be found: (1) Women participate in social life, but find it a hardship and need liberty. (The case of childless married women.) (2) Women participate in social life, but *in a different way* from men. (*Ibid.*, p. 341.) (3) Women have weak moral and intellectual needs, are unaffected by society, and in fact *do not participate* in society. (*Ibid.*, pp. 166, 272, 299, 385.) So muddled and fluctuating a doctrine must have been made up as circumstances required, quite after the fact.

INCREASING DEGREES OF INTEGRATION

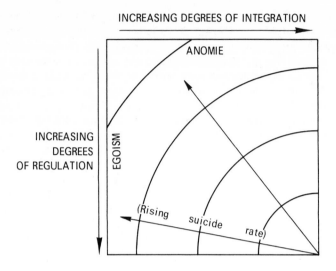

Figure 3.   Suicide Rate under Varying Social Conditions
(The Theory with the Reformulation Half-Completed)

women, a single social condition, marriage, affects men differently depending on their age. Very young husbands show a high suicide rate "because their passions are too vehement at that period and too self-confident to be subjected to so severe a rule."[32] The strength of the passions, and not the nature of marriage, accounts for this alleged example of fatalism.

Altruism and fatalism should be excluded from Durkheim's theory, then, because, with the single exception of the army, all the cases he cites either lack evidence or are not explained in purely social terms.

A Flaw in the Theory

With the elimination of fatalism and altruism my reformulation of Durkheim is half completed. The theory as it now stands is represented in Figure 3. But there is a serious flaw in the theory. I shall argue that to overcome this flaw, egoism and anomie should be equated, for integration and regulation are in truth one dimension, rather than two.

The flaw is a consequence of Durkheim's assumption that the suicide rate depends on *two* social variables, integration and regulaton, though in *Suicide* he seldom locates a group on *both* dimensions at once. Typically he locates a group on the integration scale (by saying it is egoistic, perhaps), *or* on the regulation scale (by calling it, for example, anomic). Definite predictions of the suicide rate do not follow from Durkheim's usual procedure.

---

[32] *Ibid.*, p. 275.

For example, his description of Protestantism permits us to say that it "tends toward" egoism; that is, it lies to the left of the mid-point on the integration scale in Figure 4. The Catholic Church, on the other hand, lies at the right-hand end of the integration scale, where suicides due to low integration occur at the lowest rate. On this basis, Durkheim predicts a higher suicide rate among Protestants. The trouble is that in so doing he does not take into account the possible effects of regulation on suicide. Each group must be given some approximate position on *both* dimensions if a determinate prediction is to be generated. Otherwise, all we can say is that the Catholic rate is somewhere on line (1) in Figure 4, and the Protestant rate, somewhere on line (2). If Catholicism is very unregulated (anomic), so that its exact position is at C, and Protestantism is less anomic and therefore at P_1, then the Protestant suicide rate should be the lower of the two. Even if Protestant society were extremely unintegrated (egoistic), with its rate at some point along line (3), it still might not have a high suicide rate: if Protestantism were at P_2 and Catholicism, at C, the two rates would be identical. In short, even to predict a group's relative position requires that one locate each group on *both* dimensions at once.

Reformulation, Part II: Egoism and Anomie are Identical

Suicide contains a number of reasons for concluding that "egoism" and "anomie" are merely two different names for the same thing. First of all, if egoism and anomie can be equated, so that integration and regulation

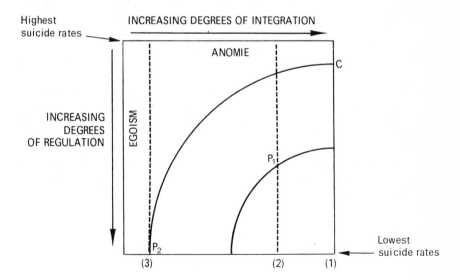

Figure 4. Hypothetical Social Conditions and Suicide Rates of Catholicism and Protestantism

are really only one dimension, then one needs only to know which of any two groups is more egoistic and anomic, to predict which of the two will have the higher suicide rate. Thus, equating egoism and anomie resolves the flaw I have found in Durkheim's theory and makes his predictions determinate. Even if other considerations did suggest a distinction between egoism and anomie, the predictive power gained would be a strong reason for equating them.

The Two Usually Occur Together.   A second reason is that Durkheim occasionally observes that the two conditions usually occur together. Egoism and anomie, he says at one point, "are usually merely two different aspects of one social state."[33] Although he does not say that the correlation between egoism and anomie is perfect, one is inclined to infer from any very close association between two rather "soft" variables that the two are in fact one.

This is not to say, of course, that egoism and anomie are not two different *aspects* of one state. All that must be established to eradicate Durkheim's flaw is that the two conditions coincide *empirically*, so that if one grows or declines the other must also. Nevertheless, I shall argue that not only do the two coincide empirically, but there is not even a conceptual distinction between them.

Durkheim's Definitions.   The two arguments just offered are indirect and merely suggestive: my strongest argument is that Durkheim's very definitions of the terms make egoism and anomie identical.

Anomie is the more easily understood of the two. Quite consistently Durkheim defines it as a weakness of social regulation. The "individual," that is, the analytical individual, the unsocialized man, has no means of self-regulation.[34] If a social component of the personality exists, however, it limits and disciplines the unsocialized part, so that anomie cannot exist.[35] When this social component is weak, the self-interested passions expand and ambitions become limitless. Modern businessmen, for example, suffer from this condition: ". . . industry . . . has become the supreme end . . . [and] the appetites thus excited have become freed of any limiting authority."[36] Similarly, in most societies marriage "regulates the life of passion" yet in modern societies in which divorce is easily attained, anomie prevails generally, even, to a degree, among those who are married.[37]

Durkheim's definition of egoism is more complex. From the many things he says about egoism, I have extracted these essential aspects of the concept:

---

33 *Ibid.*, p. 288.

34 *Ibid.*, pp. 247–248.

35 *Ibid.*, p. 250.

36 *Ibid.*, p. 255.

37 *Ibid.*, pp. 270, 271.

1. Lack of interaction among the members of society;
2. No common conscience. Since passions and goals are to be found in the social component of the personality, the absence of a common conscience means that such purposes and goals will be lacking too.

These two ingredients of egoism reinforce each other: If people do not interact, they will not acquire the goals that social life might provide,[38] and men without purpose are not drawn together in social activity.[39] Together, lack of interaction and the absence of a common conscience imply a third condition, which must be added to the definition:

3. Lack of social regulation.
   Thus, anomie is one aspect of egoism. This is especially evident when Durkheim contrasts egoistic groups with other, more integrated ones, as in the following passages:

> When society is strongly integrated, it holds individuals under its control, considers them at its service . . .[40]
> Egoistic suicide results from the fact that society is not integrated at all points to keep all its members under its control.[41]
> Judaism, in fact, like all early religions, consists essentially of a body of practices which minutely regulate all the details of existence and leave only a small place to individual judgment.[42]
> Obviously, the less numerous confessions, facing the hostility of the surrounding populations, in order to maintain themselves are obliged to exercise severe control over themselves and subject themselves to an especially rigorous discipline.[43]

These passages, taken from several different parts of *Suicide*, strongly suggest that anomie, the absence of social regulation, is by definition one characteristic of egoism.[44] Moreover, if all of the properties of egoism vary together, so that if any one increases or decreases, the others must also, then anomie and egoism must *coincide empirically*. If one is present, the other will be also.[45]

---

[38] *Ibid.*, p. 214.

[39] *Ibid.*, p. 225.

[40] *Ibid.*, p. 209.

[41] *Ibid.*, p. 373.

[42] Émile Durkheim, *Le Suicide, Étude de Sociologie* (nouvelle édition), Paris: Presses Universitaires de France, 1960, p. 160, my trans.

[43] Durkheim, *Suicide* (translated edition), p. 156.

[44] Henry and Short have also observed that lack of social regulation is one property of egoism. *Op. cit.*, p. 74.

[45] At least two commentators on Durkheim have assigned to anomie more than one of the properties of egoism. See Sebastian De Grazia, *The Political Community*, Chicago: University of Chicago Press, 1963, p. xii, and Don Martindale, *The Nature and Types of Sociological Theory*, Boston: Houghton Mifflin, 1960, p. 88.

But it remains to be shown that the two conditions are *conceptually identical*. Such a conclusion can be defended on the grounds that when Durkheim creates what purports to be a separate concept, anomie, from one aspect of egoism, he contradicts one of his own principles. His definitions of mechanical and organic solidarity in the *Division of Labor*,[46] and of egoism in *Suicide*, seem to derive from the working principle that several dimensions coinciding empirically should be regarded as one, conceptually. Each end of such a multifaceted dimension is then assigned a single name, and treated as a single concept. According to Durkheim's own practice, then, a legitimate definition of anomie must encompass not only the absence of social regulation but the other two aspects of egoism as well. Anomie and egoism are thus identical conceptually as well as empirically.

An Explicit Distinction. Perhaps recognizing that egoism and anomie are very similar, if not identical, Durkheim makes at least one attempt to distinguish them explicitly. My fourth argument for equating the two conditions is that he fails in this attempt.

Much of Durkheim's book is an attempt to distinguish the social conditions that cause suicide rates; this procedure yields a set of "aetiological types" of suicide. The "individual forms" corresponding to these types, that is, the psychological manifestations of each social cause of suicide, are the morphological types. They are, quite explicitly, "derived from" the aetiological types.[47] But if the morphological types depend logically on the aetiological types, there can be only as many of the former as there are of the latter. In short, if egoism and anomie are identical social conditions, they cannot have distinguishable psychological manifestations.

Durkheim asserts that he can identify such distinct manifestations. He forgets, however, that the morphological types are not logically independent, and uses them to "complete the setting forth of" (*achève de montrer*) the differences between egoism and anomie. Thus, egoistic suicide occurs when "reflective intelligence . . . is excessively affected," whereas anomic suicide takes place when "emotion becomes over-excited and unruly."

> In one case, thought, by dint of turning in upon itself, no longer has a purpose; in the other, passion, no longer recognizing any limit, lacks a goal. The first loses itself in an infinity of dreams, the second, in an infinity of desires.[48]

There is, certainly, a difference between reflective intelligence and emotion. But it does not, in Durkheim's scheme, correspond to a difference

---

[46] See Barclay D. Johnson, *Emile Durkheim and the Theory of Social Integration*, unpublished M.A. thesis, University of California, Berkeley, 1964, Ch. 2.

[47] Durkheim, *Suicide* (translated edition), p. 277. Here Durkheim, following his usual practice, does not mention fatalism, his fourth social cause of suicide.

[48] Durkheim, *Le Suicide*, p. 324, my trans. See also Durkheim, *Suicide* (translated edition), pp. 356, 357.

between social conditions, and if excessive reflection and emotion have the same social cause, they cannot vary independently. Once again, then, egoism and anomie are, as social conditions, one and the same.[49]

An Implicit Distinction? Although Durkheim's efforts to distinguish *explicitly* between egoism and anomie come to naught, one might still find an *implicit* distinction between the two in his book. Parsons claims to have done so, and a number of more recent authors have followed him.[50] But Parsons' claim is an ill-founded one. His position is that Durkheim implicitly links anomie with the *strength* of the common conscience and egoism, with its *content*. Anomie is present where common sentiments and social regulation are weak, whereas egoism occurs where a common sentiment places a high value on the individual. I have no quarrel with Parsons' view of anomie, but I must challenge his interpretation of egoism.

Parsons derives this interpretation largely from Durkheim's discussion of Protestantism. Durkheim says that Protestants are ruled by a "spirit of free enquiry." Parsons contends that this spirit is a shared sentiment maintained by the religious authority of the Protestant church.[51] But on the contrary, Durkheim asserts that it is a *breakdown* of collective sentiments which has led Protestants to pursue truth independently of any social authority. Protestant society is weak and poorly integrated. This absence

---

[49] Elsewhere (*ibid.*, pp. 241, 258) Durkheim attempts another distinction between egoism and anomie, which cannot be considered here for reasons of space. See Johnson, *op. cit.*, pp. 119–121.

[50] Parsons wants to show that Durkheim is moving toward a "voluntaristic" theory of action, which stresses the content of shared sentiments as a basis of individual choice among possible lines of conduct. Apparently this aim leads Parsons to ignore some of the confusion in Durkheim's own mind about what egoism really is, and to choose the far less plausible of two interpretations of egoism.

More generally, in his effort to show that Durkheim is moving from "positivism" to voluntarism, Parsons sometimes reads more into Durkheim than is actually there. By exaggerating the "biologizing" tendency of the *Division of Labor*, and misinterpreting the meaning of egoism in *Suicide*, Parsons finds Durkheim undergoing a great shift: In the first book, man is pushed around by physical forces (the pressure of population); in *Suicide*, the contents of common sentiments, or the subjective meaning the actor assigns to his experience, is an important cause of action. Parsons' documents his interpretation of Durkheim so sparsely that the distortion is visible only through a very close reading of his book, and of Durkheim's books as well. See Talcott Parsons, *The Structure of Social Action* (2nd ed.), Glencoe, Ill.: Free Press, 1958, Ch. 8, and pp. 460–469.

Perhaps Gouldner and Lipset followed Parsons to reach a similar misinterpretation. See Alvin Gouldner, "Introduction" to Emile Durkheim, *Socialism*, New York: Collier, 1962, pp. 16, 25, and Seymour M. Lipset, "Religion and Politics in the American Past and Present," Survey Research Center publication SRC A31, University of California, Berkeley, 1964, pp. 113–114.

[51] Parsons, *op. cit.*, pp. 332–333.

of integration, and of the shared sentiments accompanying it, forces individuals to find purposes and meanings for their lives independently.

> . . . if Protestantism concedes a greater freedom to individual thought than Catholicism, it is because it has fewer common beliefs and practices. Now, a religious society cannot exist without a collective *credo* and the more extensive the *credo* the more unified and strong is the society. . . . Inversely, the greater concessions a confessional group makes to individual judgment, the less it dominates lives, the less its cohesion and vitality. We thus reach the conclusion that the superiority of Protestantism with respect to suicide results from its being a less strongly integrated church than the Catholic church.[52]

I find no basis in this passage for Parsons' view that egoism exists when a shared sentiment dictates free inquiry.

Parsons also refers briefly to egoism in the family,[53] but again the notion of a shared respect for the individual simply cannot be found in Durkheim's discussion. Instead, "in a family of small numbers, common sentiments . . . cannot be very intense" because only a small group participates in the "active interchange of views and impressions."[54] It is the weakness, not the content, of the common conscience which is important.

Durkheim does discuss the condition Parsons calls egoism, but not until Book III of *Suicide*, long after the end of his analysis of egoism. In Book III, he speaks of the respect for human personality as an intense collective sentiment which derives from the collectivity.[55] Clearly, egoism and this respect for personality are not the same thing at all. Egoism implies a low level of interaction, yet sustenance of a shared sentiment requires a high level. Egoism implies the absence of common conscience, yet shared respect for personality means that a common conscience must exist. Egoism signifies lack of social regulation, yet a shared sentiment implies regulation.

> This cult of man is something, accordingly, very different from the egoistic individualism above referred to, which leads to suicide. Far from detaching individuals from society and from every aim beyond themselves, it unites them in one thought, makes them servants of one work. For man, as thus suggested to collective affection and respect, is not the sensual, experiential individual that each one of us represents, but man in general, ideal humanity as conceived by each people at each moment of its history.[56]

Occasionally, Durkheim contradicts his usual view of egoism and the cult of personality, and his confusions help to account for Parsons' misunderstanding. At several points he speaks as if the cult of personality

---

52 Durkheim, *Suicide* (translated edition)., p. 159.

53 Parsons, *op. cit.*, p. 334.

54 Durkheim, *ibid.*, p. 202.

55 *Ibid.*, p. 335.

56 *Ibid.*, pp. 336–337.

prevailed in his time, as if it is upon it that "all *our* morality rests."[57] But this notion contradicts other, more powerful lines in his thought. If a strong common respect for the individual existed in Durkheim's time, then his whole analysis of modern egoism (and, since it is indistinguishable from egoism, of anomie as well) must be considered invalid. The common conscience in a given society cannot be simultaneously strong and weak.

Nonetheless, if the cult of personality and egoism coexist empirically, they must somehow be reconciled theoretically. Durkheim toys with the position that the two are somehow compatible, so that egoism is "associated with" respect for individuality in civilized nations.[58]

> . . . in societies and environments where the dignity of the person is the supreme end of conduct, where man is a God to mankind, the individual is readily inclined to consider the man in himself as a God and to regard himself as the object of his own cult. When morality consists primarily in giving one a very high idea of one's self, certain combinations of circumstances readily suffice to make man unable to perceive anything above himself. Individualism is of course not necessarily egoism, but it comes close to it; the one cannot be stimulated without the other being enlarged. Thus, egoistic suicide arises.[59]

Since Parsons equates the cult of personality with egoism, he may have relied heavily on this passage. But it is a hopeless muddle, an attempt to reconcile two irreconcilable views of the modern world, and thus hardly a suitable proof text for the Parsonian view. If "man is a God to mankind," the "man" who is worshipped is not the self-interested individual as he actually is, but a shared conception, "man in general, ideal humanity."[60] The situation in which "morality consists primarily in giving one a very high idea of one's self" cannot be egoism, since egoism means that moral sentiments are very weak, nor can it be the cult of personality, since this involves respect for ideal man, not real man.

Durkheim's confusion must be acknowledged. But the evidence strongly suggests that his primary view is that egoism implies not a strong common sentiment of respect for the individual, but rather the weakness of the common conscience. Since this weakness, and the resulting absence of social regulation, is also defined as anomie, I conclude once again that egoism and anomie are identical.

Conclusion

This paper has dealt almost exclusively with *theoretical* problems in *Suicide:* What are Durkheim's concepts? What are the logical relations among these concepts? What hypotheses do these relations generate? Are there inconsistencies in his reasoning? How can they be resolved?

---

[57] *Ibid.*, p. 334, italics added. See also passage quoted above from p. 335.

[58] *Ibid.*, p. 227.

[59] *Ibid.*, pp. 363–364.

[60] *Ibid.*, p. 337.

As an approach to these problems, I have constructed a simpler formulation of Durkheim's theory, first by eliminating altruism and fatalism from the range of relevant phenomena, then by showing that egoism and anomie are identical. My final reformulation of the theory can be stated as follows: The *more* integrated (regulated) a society, group, or social condition is, the *lower* its suicide rate. Another way to say exactly the same thing is this: The *higher* the level of egoism (anomie) prevailing in a society, group, or social condition, the *higher* the suicide rate.

Finally, a word about the relation of the theory in its final form to Durkheim's data: Once altruism and fatalism are eliminated, the single case in *Suicide* that clearly contradicts the theory is the army. It is the one instance of a highly integrated group with a high suicide rate. But the many empirical cases of egoism and anomie that Durkheim offers appear to support the theory. Therefore, although much work remains to be done, I am inclined to concur with Merton's judgment that Durkheim's theory of suicide is among the few approximations to a scientific law that our discipline has found.[61]

---

[61] Merton, *op. cit.*, pp. 96–99.

7·3

On the Edge of Rapprochement: Was Durkheim Moving toward the Perspective of Symbolic Interaction?

GREGORY P. STONE AND HARVEY A. FARBERMAN

After the publication in 1912 of *The Elementary Forms of the Religious Life*, Emile Durkheim turned almost at once to the epistemological problems raised by that work in a series of lectures on "Pragmatism and Sociology," delivered at the Sorbonne in 1913 and 1914.[1] Durkheim's concern with pragmatism (especially the work of Charles Peirce, William James, and John Dewey) shortly before his death in 1917 is almost patent evidence of the direction his theoretical development was taking at the culmination of his sociological inquiries.[2] However, he was unable to make the full transition which, indeed, would have required a revolutionary transformation of his ontological position.

This article will focus on the development of Durkheim's thought in the direction of symbolic interaction. In addition, some attention will be paid to objective and metaphorical barriers blocking the transition. In accomplishing these things, the notion of metaphor will be central to our argument.[3] Moreover, we shall not be concerned here with any substan-

---

[1] The first five and the thirteenth and fourteenth lectures, reconstructed from student notes, have been translated by Charles Blend in Kurt H. Wolff (ed.), *Essays on Sociology and Philosophy by Emile Durkheim et al.* (New York: Harper & Row, 1964), pp. 386–436.

[2] The *account* of Durkheim's theoretical development in Talcott Parsons, *Structure of Social Action* (New York: Free Press, 1949), pp. 301–470 remains the best exegetic treatment available. Obviously we question Parsons' interpretation of the development as moving inexorably toward an impasse with idealism. In all fairness, it should be noted that *Pragmatisme et Sociologie* did not appear until 1955, eighteen years after Parsons had completed his study.

[3] On metaphor, see *inter alia* Kenneth Burke, *Permanence and Change* (Indianapolis, Ind.: Bobbs-Merrill, 1965), pp. 94–96.

tive exegesis of Durkheim's works. We presume substantive knowledge on the part of the reader.

Every sociological theory or perspective implies some image of man, communication, society, and their interrelations. Our contention is that the development of Durkheim's sociological thought was marked by significant metaphorical changes, particularly in respect to the image of man. Two additional metaphors proved less yielding and provided powerful obstacles to thoroughgoing theoretical reformulation: first, the image of communication as interaction or action in parallel;[4] second, the image of society as. a container of communication and individual contents.

Metaphorical Development of Durkheim's Theory

To deal with the metaphors of man, society, and communication which are presupposed by any sociological theory is to carry critical analysis into a highly debatable area. For metaphors are frequently implicit in theory, and, in the final analysis, implications are always made by the critic. Confronted by the explication of his presuppositions, the theorist may well deny them, or, acknowledging them, may alter his theoretical statement in a fundamental way so that they no longer obtain. In Durkheim's case, metaphors became more explicit as his thought developed, until, in *The Elementary Forms of the Religious Life*, critical confrontation with the presuppositions underlying his thought produced a crucial philosophical impasse. Our treatment of the metaphorical development in Durkheim's theory, then, is a kind of *tour de force* and necessarily oversimplified. Questions will undoubtedly be raised by the reader, but, hopefully, this will lead to a necessary re-examination of Durkheim's contributions by symbolic interactionists.

A further caveat must be entered before our treatment begins. To assert that some image of *man* is presumed by a sociological theory is not to assert that individual *men* are the theorist's central objects of inquiry. Durkheim was always centrally concerned with the nature of society or the nature of the social bond. Yet, the implicit view of man and its progressive alteration had a critical impact on his conceptualization and study of society. The more Durkheim began to understand that the fabric of society—collective representations—was a creation of man, the more he altered his image of man and, consequently, his image of society.

The development of Durkheim's thought can be interpreted as an elaboration on the mechanistic metaphor, changing from a view of man as a moving particle, to a conductor of societal energy, to a transformer

---

[4] On this view, "symbolic *interaction*" is a misnomer, and we would prefer to return to Mead's original designation of the perspective as "social behaviorism." However, since the former phrase has so much currency in sociological circles, we will use it, explicitly recognizing its inadequacies. On the distinctions among "self action," "interaction," and "transaction," see John Dewey and Arthur F. Bentley, *Knowing and the Known* (Boston: Beacon Press, 1960), pp. 103–43.

of society itself. Until the very end of this development, society is seen as a container and energizer of these individual particles. It is a reality *sui generis* and made up of materials distinctively its own, collective representations of social facts exterior to and constraining of its individual contents So is any container distinguished from the things it contains.

The Division of Labor. Key terms in this work—density, volume, and dynamic or moral density—suggest the metaphorical raiment which cloaks and disguises genuinely social phenomena in a vocabulary more appropriate to physical energy systems. If a bounded area (the container) is overpopulated in such a way that the enclosed moving particles cannot avoid colliding with one another, something must give—some new process must be set in motion. What occurs is a progressive differentiation of the particles and their movements in an increasing division of labor. At one time (under conditions of mechanical solidarity) particles are alike, their movements relatively undifferentiated, and they have access to all "corners" of the container's space. They collide relatively infrequently with one another, given their small numbers and the relatively large volume of the container. With increasing numbers and density, the container, in a metaphorical sense, must expand and develop internal compartments to minimize collisions and facilitate the "existence" of the whole.[5]

To be sure, mere material density is not enough. The concentrated population must engage in communication as well as collison. Density, therefore, has a moral or social dimension, and Durkheim recognizes that "there are particular, exceptional cases . . . where material and moral density are *perhaps* not entirely in accord."[6] Nevertheless, the moral

---

[5] This image of society persists through the *Elementary Forms*, e.g., "Society supposes a self-conscious organization which is nothing other than a classification. . . . To avoid all collisions, it is necessary that each particular group have a determined portion of space assigned to it: in other terms, it is necessary that space in general be divided, differentiated, arranged, and that these divisions and arrangements be known to everybody." Emile Durkheim, *The Elementary Forms of the Religious Life*, translated by Joseph Ward Swain (New York: Collier Books, 1961), p. 492 (hereafter cited as *Elementary Forms*). Yet, on the very next page, Durkheim writes: "Consequently things can no longer be contained in the social moulds according to which they were primitively classified; they must be organized according to *principles which are their own*, so logical organization differentiates itself from the social organization and become autonomous." *Ibid.*, p. 493. Italics ours. Here our main point is anticipated. It becomes increasingly difficult for Durkheim to maintain his image of society as a container. As most readers will know, Hughes has also seen the problems posed by Durkheim's metaphor, or "mechanistic vocabulary." However, Hughes, like Parsons, sees these difficulties leading Durkheim into an idealism. This, of course, is farthest from our mind, and, we think, Durkheim's. See H. Stuart Hughes, *Consciousness and Society* (New York: Vintage Books, 1958), pp. 278–87.

[6] Emile Durkheim, *The Division of Labor in Society*, translated by George Simpson (New York: The Free Press, 1947), p. 260, note 11. Italics ours.

dimension of density is decidedly underplayed when Durkheim states his central proposition in the main text of the *Division of Labor:*

> The division of labor varies in direct ratio with the volume and density of societies, and, if it progresses in a continuous manner in the course of development, it is because societies become regularly denser and generally more voluminous.[7]

The image of man as a particle persists, as individuality, *per se*, becomes merged with the changing character of the container induced by the progressive differentiation of the contents. Thus, "individuality is something which the society possesses."[8] Later, discussing the weakening of the collective *conscience* (the "walls" of the container) brought on by the emergence of organic solidarity, Durkheim observed:

> This is not to say that the [collective *conscience*] is threatened with total disappearance. . . . There is even a place where it is strengthened and made more precise: that is the way in which it regards the individual. As all the other beliefs and all the other practices take on a character less and less religious, the individual becomes the object of a sort of religion. We erect a cult in behalf of personal dignity which, as every strong cult, already has its superstitions.[9]

Even as man approaches a condition where he can feel more actor than acted upon, he reaches that condition precisely by being acted upon by external and constraining forces.

If in the *Division of Labor* Durkheim maintained a consistent image of man, his conception of society must be said to have vacillated. In explaining the transition to organic solidarity, the moral dimension of society was de-emphasized. Yet, at the end of this major work, Durkheim turned to the "abortive" forms of the division of labor. This led him once again to a consideration of variations in containers—the moral dimension. Compartmentalization may proceed in a disjointed way, as in the anomic division of labor. Compartments may be sealed too tightly as in caste societies. Finally, the container may become overcompartmentalized so that *particular* motion is so severely constricted that it may be brought to a standstill.

The Rules. Reconsidering his magnificent effort in the *Division of Labor*, Durkheim emerged filled with unbounded enthusiasm and perhaps somewhat starry-eyed. He had discovered what social facts *were* and felt he had a firm grasp on their method of study. Sociology as a science could at last be clearly distinguished from philosophical speculation.

His conception of social facts as exterior to and constraining of individual conduct led him back to a reconsideration of societal variation—the moral dimension. Moral density, as "dynamic density," had replaced material density in Durkheim's conceptualization of the necessary condi-

---

[7] *Ibid.*, p. 262.

[8] *Ibid.*, p. 130.

[9] *Ibid.*, p. 172.

tions for the proliferation of the division of labor.[10] He specifically acknowledged his error: "We made the mistake, in our *Division du travail*, of presenting material density too much as the exact expression of dynamic density."[11] Durkheim, thus, was led to a recasting of the metaphor of society as a generalized container—a return of the moral dimension. There were many societies; many varieties of containers. Individual acts, however, remained irrelevant—constrained by the character of the container: "When . . . the sociologist undertakes the investigation of some order of societal facts, he must consider them . . . independent of their individual manifestations."[12] What better test, then, of sociological method than to investigate the "ultimate" individual act—the suicide?

Suicide. In *Suicide*, Durkheim's view shifts from a conception of man as the thing contained, the moving particle, to man as a conductor. Society is no longer seen as purely a container, but as an energizer of individual conduct. Different societies "energize" man in different ways.[13]

Subsequently, communication is viewed by Durkheim as exchange: ". . . conversation and all intellectual communication between men is an exchange of concepts."[14] On this view also, man may be seen as a kind of conductor of the energy generated by society. Pushing the metaphor almost to the absurd—absolutely rhetorically—we might conceive egoistic suicide as a consequence of "overloading" the conductor; altruistic suicide as implying a short circuit—the faulty conductor must be replaced in the interest of maintaining an efficient generator. Anomic suicide is the mark of a defect in the generator. With no more current, the conductor atrophies, rusts, or otherwise falls into disuse.

But not all individuals in societies or social segments characterized by faulty circuits or power-losses commit suicide. Durkheim, then, reviews the extreme position he assumed in *The Rules*. In the Preface to the second edition, written in 1901, four years after the publication of *Le suicide*, he observed:

> Because beliefs and social practices thus come to us from without, it does not follow that we receive them passively or without modification. In reflecting on collective institutions and assimilating them for ourselves, we individualize them and impart to them more or less personal characteristics.

---

[10] Emile Durkheim, *The Rules of Sociological Method*, translated by Sarah A. Solovay and John H. Mueller and edited by George E. G. Catlin (Chicago: Univ. of Chicago Press, 1938), pp. 113–15.

[11] *Ibid.*, p. 115, note 22.

[12] *Ibid.*, p. 45.

[13] Parsons' interpretation is quite compatible on this point: "Instead of the *conscience collective* being contrasted with organic solidarity, there now are two types of influence of the *conscience collective*, and set over against both of them the state where its disciplining influence is weak, at the polar extreme altogether absent. In so far as this weakening of discipline is present, the state of *anomie* exists." Parsons, *op. cit.*, p. 336.

[14] *Elementary Forms*, p. 482 .

Similarly, in reflecting on the physical world, each of us colors it after his own fashion, and different individuals adapt themselves differently to the same physical environment. It is for this reason that each one of us creates, in a measure, his own morality, religion, and mode of life. There is no conformity to social convention that does not comprise an entire range of individual shades. It is nonetheless true that this field of variations is a limited one. It *verges on non-existence.* . . .[15]

Although he tried, Durkheim could not wish the individual away. The stage, at last, was set for him explicitly and directly to confront his formerly implicit views of man, society, and communication.

The Elementary Forms. In the concluding section of *The Elementary Forms of the Religious Life*, when Durkheim attempts to secure the foundation of religious experience in society, the culmination and subsequent erosion of the mechanistic metaphor occur. Man is seen as a transformer of reality,[16] for Durkheim notes clearly that, with respect to religious experience, "it does not follow that the reality which is its foundation conforms *objectively* to the idea which believers have of it."[17] From this point on, the metaphor of society as a container cannot be maintained, for Durkheim begins to see the contained as the creator of the container. The force of collective definition, when universalized and objectified *through symbolization*, comes to the fore. The collective representation, itself, even though it is impersonal and exterior and may take a religious form, is a precipitate of collective action and *formulation.*[18] Indeed, the religious cosmos is no more than a magnified, transformed, and dramatized image of ordinary life. As Durkheim suggests, "Men alone

---

[15] Durkheim, *The Rules of Sociological Method*, pp. lvi–lvii, note 7. Italics ours.

[16] In his preface to the second edition of *The Rules*, Durkheim specifically recognizes the transforming character of human association: "Whenever certain elements combine and thereby produce, by the fact of their combination, new phenomena, it is plain that these new phenomena reside not in the original elements, but in the totality formed by their union. . . . What we say of life could be repeated for all possible compounds. The hardness of bronze is not in the copper, the tin, or the lead, which are its ingredients and which are soft and malleable bodies; it is in their mixture. The fluidity of water and its nutritional and other properties are not to be found in the two gases of which it is composed but in the complex substance which they form by their association. Let us apply this principle to sociology." *The Rules of Sociological Method*, pp. xlvii–xlviii. However, the transformation remains physical—biological and chemical. In *The Elementary Forms*, Durkheim's view of the transforming function of communication undergoes a profound change.

[17] *Elementary Forms*, p. 465. Italics ours.

[18] As Durkheim says, "This is because society cannot make its influence felt unless it is in action, and it is not in action unless the individuals who compose it are assembled together and act in common." *Ibid.*, p. 465. Note the persistent conception of "communication" as parallel action and not transaction.

have the faculty of conceiving the ideal, of *adding something* to the real."[19] Why does man idealize the real? Because, in the throes of religious passion, "man does not recognize himself; he feels transformed and consequently he transforms the environment which surrounds him."[20]

We find that Durkheim's metaphor of man has shifted from that of a particle-in-motion to a conductor, to a particle physiochemically transformed and transforming, to a creative human transformer of the world around him. Man has, in his collective existence, become the source of reality. The consequences for this sociological epistemology seem bold and clear to us, and Durkheim asks the pertinent question, "what has been able to make social life so important a source for the logical life?"[21] The answer focuses on the development of concepts in society. Concepts are depicted as impersonal, fixed, and immutable—of themselves, static. If a concept changes, "it is not because it is its nature to do so, but because *we* have discovered some imperfection in it; it is because it had to be rectified."[22] By implication, the collective representation is becoming the internalized concept rather than the exterior and constraining social fact. It becomes part of the content of society rather than the material from which the "walls" of society are constructed. This signals a fundamental change in Durkheim's conception of society, but the reformulation is given no definitive statement. The concept is seen as a tool of collective existence—if it is imperfect or not useful, *we* change it.[23] It is only by thinking with concepts, moreover, that the realm of impersonal and stable ideas is reached—the realm of truth. Once man becomes conscious of this realm of ideas,

> and, in so far as he believes that he has discovered their causes, he undertakes to put these causes into action for himself, in order that he may draw from them by his own force the effects which they produce; that is to say, he attributes to himself the right of making concepts.[24]

So man does more than formulate concepts; he passes collective judgment on their acceptability:

> It is not enough that they be true to be believed. If they are not in harmony with the other beliefs and opinions, or, in a word, with the mass of the other collective representations, they will be denied: minds will be closed to them; consequently it will be as though they did not exist.[25]

Although Durkheim saw truth as characterized by "stability" and "impersonality," he could not but acknowledge that it was a collective for-

---

[19] *Ibid.*, p. 469. Italics ours.

[20] *Ibid.*

[21] *Ibid.*, p. 480.

[22] *Ibid.*, p. 481. Italics ours.

[23] At this point, Durkheim falls squarely in the camp of *social* pragmatism, as opposed to the *subjective* pragmatism of James and, occasionally, Dewey. This is a major distinction to which we shall return.

[24] *Ibid.*, p. 485.

[25] *Ibid.*, p. 486.

mulation, hence, temporally and societally specific. "To be sure," he writes, "we cannot insist too much upon the different characteristics which logic presents at different periods in history; it develops like the societies themselves."[26] In his statement on the method he used for investigating religion, he writes, "social facts vary with the social system of which they form a part; they cannot be understood when detached from it."[27] Clearly Durkheim has apprehended the temporal and locational relativity of truth. Thus, we are not surprised when he muses:

> In a word, the old gods are growing old or already dead, and others are not yet born. . . . There are no gospels which are immortal, but neither is there any reason for believing that humanity is incapable of inventing new ones.[28]

Obviously Durkheim has placed the realm of the gospel (or truth) squarely within the domain of human intervention. The metaphor of society as a container is no longer compatible with the main thrust of Durkheim's intellectual thought.

The Problem of Truth

In what may be his most radical statement, Durkheim analyzes the rhetorical power of both science and religion down to the base of collective faith. In effect, the truth value of a concept is guaranteed less by its objective reference than by the faith that it mobilizes:

> Today it is generally sufficient that [concepts] bear the stamp of science to receive a sort of privileged credit, because we have faith in science. But this faith does not differ essentially from religious faith. . . . science continues to be dependent upon opinion at the very moment when it seems to be making its laws; for, as we have already shown, it is from opinion that it holds the force necessary to act upon opinion.[29]

There can be no doubt then that Durkheim apprehended truth as a function of a larger consensus. In his opinion the ultimate insurance against irrational elements in truth was the emergence of a new form of intersocietal, cosmopolitan life. Much in the way Mannheim's relational conception of truth rested on the surmounting of barriers by divergent groups in communication, so Durkheim saw the depreciating importance of the social segment and the concomitant upsurge of the transnational life as a

---

[26] *Ibid.*, p. 487.

[27] *Ibid.*, p. 113.

[28] *Ibid.*, pp. 475–76. It is difficult to refrain from the observation that, today, more than a half century after Durkheim made these remarks, some segments of Christianity seem to be catching up with the past. We refer to the "Is God dead?" controversy.

[29] *Ibid.*, pp. 486–87. The reader ought really to compare this conception of science with the conception stated in *The Rules*. For Durkheim, science, just as religion, develops as a cult based on faith. We cannot help but observe at this time that the "new left" is precisely a cult without faith, and, if we may, we hope wistfully that science will be *a* faith without cults.

filter for the elimination of "bias."[30] The greater its dispersion in collective opinion, the more autonomous the development of truth; or the wider the societal base of truth, the less is the emergence of truth inhibited by society. But, alas, the flow of humanity is the flaw of tragedy: "Really and truly human thought is not a primitive fact; it is the product of history; it is the ideal limit towards which we are constantly approaching, but which in all probability we shall never succeed in reaching."[31] As Mead might well have said, we premise our acts on a future of which we are certainly uncertain.

Given the general direction of his statements at the conclusion of the *Elementary Forms*, it is not surprising that Durkheim turned immediately to a consideration of the pragmatic reaction against the classical conceptions of truth, mind, and reality. He had already consulted and cited James's *Varieties of Religious Experience* and *Principles of Psychology* in the concluding sections of the *Elementary Forms*.

Truth and Pragmatism

In his lectures on pragmatism and sociology, Durkheim had arrived at the seminal insight that "today's truth is tomorrow's error"[32]—a proposition which confounded most of the assumptions of nineteenth-century European philosophy and which forced him to look elsewhere for an epistemology consonant with his theoretical advances in sociology. He turned to pragmatism. Not only was Durkheim already familiar with the work of James, but James had a spokesman and critic who had the ear of European intellectuals, namely the Englishman, F. C. S. Schiller. Moreover, both Durkheim and James were influenced, if in different ways, by Charles Bernard Renouvier—Durkheim as a student and James through careful reading of Renouvier's works. Each must have been impressed with Renouvier's rejection of the Kantian dichotomy between noumena and phenomena—James settling on the notion of truth as experiential, Durkheim on the notion of "presentations" as facts.

In his review of pragmatism, Durkheim observed that Peirce, James, Schiller, and Dewey were in agreement: no exterior, impersonal, and complete truth, irrespective of its source (intellection or sensory perception) could be a living and compelling truth without taking the realm of

---

[30] It seems almost unnecessary to point out Mannheim's profound distinction between relativistic and relationistic conceptions of truth. See Karl Mannheim, *Ideology and Utopia*, translated by Louis Wirth and Edward Shils (New York: Harcourt, Brace, and World, 1963), pp. 78–80. Mannheim's epistemology is premised on a dialectic, and this is precisely the process that Durkheim misses. For Durkheim cosmopolitanism is accomplished when collective representations "spill over the walls" of the container and engulf the world at large. Suddenly, the fabric of the "walls of the container" becomes its content. This is an additional flaw in the transition of Durkheim's metaphor that ought, one day, be examined by the critical theorist.

[31] *Ibid.*, p. 493.

[32] Emile Durkheim, "Pragmatism and Sociology," in Wolff (ed.), *op. cit.*, p. 409.

goals, means, and choices (the realm of human purpose) into account. In fact, to conceive truth as "given," i.e., "out there," divorces it from human life and action.

Any conception which makes truth independent of the intervention of man, as the argument goes, implies a theory of mind (and reality) which eliminates man as an agent of influence on truth. For, if the best that mind can do is merely to describe the out-there-given truth, then man becomes a passive recorder of an established and impinging universe. This image is, of course, unacceptable to pragmatism which postulates the inextricable connection of thinking and living or of mind and existence. Hence, in the early statements of James, truth must be conceived as having a "personal character," and this conception persists throughout the work of James.

To root truth in existence, is to place it in the realm of means, ends, and choices. From this perspective, truth is seen as a matter of *efficacious* choice with respect to an end-in-view which itself is dictated by human interest. Truth, then, devolves around the matter of assessing the efficacy of means, and its detection requires an examination of consequences. More important to our argument is the fact that, for James, the detection of truth *also* requires an examination of the personal psychology of any individual who asserts the truth value of his statements. Truth becomes a very personal and, by implication, pluralistic affair. There is the further implication that, to the degree individual interest (or consciousness) lends relevance (for the individual) to certain aspects of reality by bringing them into a means-end schema, mind must be conceived as an additive principle. In searching for solutions, mind converts unformulated sensuous experience into formulated reality, but, for James, reality is *personally* formulated.[33] It was against such a position, no doubt, that Bertrand Russell

---

[33] Durkheim clearly understood the fundamental distinction between experience and formulated reality: "Sensual representations are in a perpetual flux; they come after each other like the waves of a river, and even during the time that they last, they do not remain the same thing. . . . We are never sure of again finding a perception such as we experienced it the first time; for if the thing perceived has not changed, it is we who are no longer the same. On the contrary, the concept is, as it were, outside of time and change; it is in the depths below all this agitation; it might be said that it is in a different portion of the mind, which is serener and calmer. . . . It is a manner of thinking that, at every moment of time, is fixed and crystallized." See *Elementary Forms*, p. 481. It is at this point that Durkheim cites James. However, as we shall see, Durkheim could never conceptualize the concept as personal. The distinction, of course, persists in pragmatism and has received its most extensive formulation in Dewey's *Experience and Nature*. For a fundamental reformulation that brings the distinction squarely into the perspective of symbolic interaction, see Harry Stack Sullivan, "The Illusion of Personal Individuality," in Helen Swick Perry, Mary Ladd Gawel, and Martha Gibbon (eds.), *The Collected Works of Harry Stack Sullivan*, II (New York: W. W. Norton, 1964), pp. 198–226, especially p. 214.

was reacting when he proclaimed that, at least James's work "is only [another] form of the subjective madness which is characteristic of most modern philosophy."[34]

Russell's criticism, however, echoed a far earlier one; for, after considering the major alternatives offered by the pragmatists in opposition to the classical position, Durkheim said rather decisively, "Pragmatism . . . claims to explain truth psychologically and subjectively." He went on to argue in the same passage:

> . . . the nature of the individual is too limited to explain by itself alone all things human. Therefore, if we envisage individual elements alone, we are led to underestimate the amplitude of the effects that we have to account for. . . . But men have always recognized in truth something that in certain respects imposes itself on us, something that is independent of the facts of sensitivity and individual impulse.[35]

What Durkheim was reacting to in the pragmatic resolution was the persistent strain of subjective nominalism embodied in a psychological, as opposed to a sociological, conception of mind. With a purely individualistic theory of mentality, one could hardly arrive at a phenomenon "that is independent of the facts of sensitivity and individual impulse." And this is precisely the position that Durkheim had already developed in his extensive analyses of collective representations. A purely psychologistic perspective could never account for a collectively established universal. Hence, while Durkheim appears extremely sympathetic to the pragmatic rejection of the classical views and, indeed, seems to resonate, if ambivalently, not only with the notion of a living truth but also with an instrumentalistic formulation of mind as well as an emergent conception of reality, he could not resonate with an atomistic or elementaristic psychology. He was literally forced to reject the subjective pragmatism of James.

Durkheim required a *social* theory of mind which could be built on a conception of society as a "synthesis of human consciousness."[36] Such a theory would apprehend concepts as collectively established representations somewhat free from, but not insensitive to, the fact of individual percipience. Truth, in this way, while neither a detached given nor a simple consequence of individual adjustment, could be conceived as an emergent collective reconstruction.

Possibilities of Convergence with Symbolic Interaction

The social theory of mind which Durkheim was on the edge of discerning, but for which no support was forthcoming in the subjective pragmatism available to him at the time, appears full blown in the work of

---

[34] Bertrand Russell, *A History of Western Philosophy* (New York: Simon and Schuster, 1954), p. 818.

[35] Durkheim, "Pragmatism and Sociology," in Wolff (ed.), *op. cit.*, pp. 429–30.

[36] *Elementary Forms*, p. 479.

George Herbert Mead. In Mead's work, we find a *social* pragmatism based on a conceptualization of mind which accounts, by way of a theory of significant symbols, for the linkage between any particular communicative act and universal meaning. The heart of Mead's work rests on the proposition that mind develops out of and sustains itself within an objective phase of experience. This objective phase of experience is, of course, what is captured in Mead's concept of the significant symbol or universal and Durkheim's concept of a collective representation.[37] In each case the symbol (or representation) is an objectification and universalization of particular experiences. Neither Mead nor Durkheim confused the universality of the symbol with its generality. For each, the objective meaning of the symbol is universal in the sense that it has currency within some social circle. As Durkheim put it:

> This universality of the concept should not be confused with its generality: they are very different things. What we mean by universality is the property which the concept has of being communicable to a number of minds, and in principle, to all minds; but this communicability is wholly independent of the degree of its extension. A concept which is applied to only one object, and whose extension is consequently at the minimum, can be the same for everybody. . . .[38]

This idea is pervasive in Mead, and it seems unnecessary to provide cited examples of the distinction.

Although Durkheim speaks of the *property* of concepts as being communicable, the main force of his argument leads him away from this conception. In the first place, while any particular symbol objectifies experience, it may be replaced by any other symbol in that more than one symbol may evoke the objectified experience:

> . . . as far as religious thought is concerned, the part is equal to the whole; it has the same powers, the same efficacy. The debris of a relic has the same virtue as a relic in good condition. The smallest drop of blood contains the same active principle as the whole thing.[39]

More important, the symbol, *per se*, is irrelevant. "Surely," Durkheim writes, "the soldier who falls while defending his flag does not believe that he sacrifices himself for a bit of cloth."[40] And Mead also insists on the irrelevancy of the concrete symbol or object:

---

[37] Roscoe C. Hinkle, Jr., has incisively established the relationship between the significant symbol of Mead and the collective representation of Durkheim. See his, "Durkheim in American Sociology," in Wolff (ed.), *op. cit.*, pp. 278–79.

[38] *Elementary Forms*, p. 482, note 9. Here Durkheim remains attached to the metaphor of the symbol, or collective representation, as a *thing*. On this point, he vacillates, and the vacillation is never resolved.

[39] *Ibid.*, p. 261. Although he was speaking of religion, as we have shown earlier (pp. 156–57), we may generalize the implication to all knowledge.

[40] *Ibid.*, p. 260.

. . . one has a nail to drive, he reaches for the hammer and finds it gone, and he does not stop to look for it, but reaches for something else he can use, a brick or a stone, anything having the necessary weight to give momentum to the blow. Anything that he can get hold of that will serve the purpose will be a hammer. That sort of response which involves the grasping of a heavy object is a universal.[41]

In short, the meaning or relevance of symbols for both Mead and Durkheim was not in the character of the symbols themselves but in the responses that they mobilized.

On this point, Durkheim becomes explicit:

The concept is universal, or at least capable of becoming so. A concept is not my concept: I hold it in common with other men, or, in any case can communicate it to them. It is impossible to make a sensation pass from my consciousness into that of another; it holds closely to my organism and personality and cannot be detached from them. All that I can do is to invite others to place themselves before the same object as myself and leave themselves to its action.[42]

Here, we see that Durkheim is, indeed, on the edge of apprehending Mead's profound conceptualization of a universe of discourse:

This universe of discourse is constituted by a group of individuals carrying on and participating in a common social process of experience and behavior, within which all these gestures or symbols have the same or common meanings for all members of that group, whether they make them to other individuals, or whether they overtly respond to them as made or addressed to them by other individuals. A universe of discourse is simply a system of common or social meanings.[43]

And for Mead, the meaning of the "hammer" is in its use, or the meaning of the symbol in the response that is made to it.

In such a way, Durkheim comes to the very edge of conceiving society as a universe of discourse, but he can not move over that edge. He holds up the symbol and awaits the action of others, and their action is construed as common or parallel. Above all, he does not inquire into his own action—how he might respond to the symbol he holds up as he waits on the action of others. Durkheim has no notion of concert, transaction, or role-taking.

Obstacles to Convergence

Although James asserted, in effect, that we have as many selves as we have group affiliations, this statement seems not to have influenced his psychologistic conception of mind. Consciousness, for James, was

---

[41] George Herbert Mead, *Mind, Self and Society* (Chicago: University of Chicago Press, 1934), p. 83.

[42] *Elementary Forms*, pp. 481–82.

[43] Mead, *op. cit.*, pp. 89–90.

instrumental for bringing the *individual* into a more serene adjustment to the problematics of his existence. Thought was an instrument of individual existence. James did not speak of maintaining concerted, ongoing trans- actions. In other words, the means-end schema was not anchored in the transactive context. To repeat, this subjective pragmatism was unacceptable to Durkheim. It is our contention that he could easily have accepted Mead's *social* pragmatism, had it been made explicit to him at the time. Social pragmatism conceives consciousness as instrumental for the maintenance of concerted conduct. Mind is social, shared, and objective. It acts to bring individuals into a more serene adjustment to the problematics of *their* existence. But mind, for Mead, is never epiphenomenal. It is a *conversa- tion* rooted in action. Thus, the pragmatic truth is the *conception* that keeps the conversation going or permits the conversation to overcome temporary interruptions. Even pragmatic truth for the person emerges from the dialogue—the dialogue between experience and formulation, or, as Mead would have it, the dialogue between the "I" and the "me."

In the final stages of his sociological inquiry, Durkheim would almost assuredly have accepted the position of social pragmatism, even down to the rooting of personal truth, *or faith*, in the internalized conversation between the "I" and the "me." How else could he have secured the foun- dation of scientific knowledge in the bedrock of faith?[44] Such a conception of truth transcends the subjective perspective. This transcendence, how- ever, can never be detached from the individual response, for the repre- sentative symbol or the objective phase of experience is established ultimately in the concerted response in which the individual, of course, plays a part. As Durkheim barely hinted in his discussion of the genesis of concepts: "The general only exists in the particular; it is the particular simplified and impoverished."[45] This is a formulation of the universal which Mead elaborates in his discussion of meaning:

> Meaning is that which can be indicated to others while it is by the same process indicated to the indicating individual. In so far as the individual indicates it to himself in the role of the other, he is occupying his per- spective, and as he is indicating it to the other from his own perspective, and as that which is so indicated is identical, it must be that which can be in different perspectives. It must therefore be a universal, at least in the identity which belongs to the different perspectives which are organized into the single perspective. . . .[46]

---

[44] See p. 115, above. Durkheim speaks of "collective faith," but the conver- sation between the "I" and the "me" is precisely one's participation in a collective dialogue. Any resolution of the dialogue places one in a universe of discourse—a social circle.

[45] *Elementary Forms*, p. 480. Again, this marks a transformation of Durk- heim's metaphorical view of the individual, since he speaks of the concept "impoverishing" individual experience. Literally, Durkheim has "discovered" the individual and doesn't know what to do with him!

[46] Mead, *op. cit.*, p. 89.

Hence, the universal is not in the stimulus but in the collective response. As soon as we consider the response, however, we are in a position to see the essential difference between Mead and Durkheim.

As a social psychologist concerned primarily with the emergence of mind and self, Mead began from a *process* orientation; as a worried sociologist concerned with explaining solidarity or the moral value of social life, Durkheim worked from an "entity" orientation. For Durkheim a collective representation was a social "fact"—a *thing*—which in its symbolic form existed outside of man and constrained him into using it, like money or language. While it is true that it emerges out of collective life, any given individual is constrained by it. Mead, however, looks at symbols rather than the language that they comprise. Such symbols are implemented in an ongoing conversation and may be altered—indeed, they are always in the process of becoming—as responses are played back upon them by individuals. This implies that the individual is entirely capable of transforming the collective dialogue by making crucial unanticipated responses to symbols that have become conventionally established. Such unanticipated responses arise out of the individual's self-indicative or interpretive capacities.

Although Durkheim also allows for modification of the collective representation, such changes are seen as nonprocessual or mechanistic. Durkheim notes that in assimilating (not producing!) concepts, one must

> assimilate them to himself, for he must have them to hold intercourse with others; but the assimilation is always imperfect. Each of us sees them after his own fashion. There are some which escape us completely and remain outside of our circle of vision; there are others of which we perceive certain aspects only. There are even a great many which we pervert in holding, for as they are collective by nature, they cannot become individualized without being retouched, modified, and consequently falsified. Hence comes the great trouble we have in understanding each other. . . .[47]

What Durkheim is referring to are sources of ambiguity. Notice that these sources have a spatial and locational tone which removes them from the social process. Mead takes the opposite tack. Ambiguity, for him, is part and parcel of the social process. Individuals because of their *interpretative* capacities may misformulate the conceptual meaning of any given symbol. More important is Mead's core distinction between the "I" and the "me." This distinction takes into account the fact that an individual can never be certain of his own next action. If the "I" is interpreted as a principle of pure, hence meaningless, experience, an individual can not know what he is doing until he has done it. In other words, one must have an experience before one can formulate it by referring it back to a conceptual framework—a universe of discourse or the collective *conscience*. If every activity sequence contains an element of uncertainty, or unpredictability, then each act, whether in mental, verbal, or physical

---

[47] *Elementary Forms*, p. 484.

form, becomes a source of change. The ongoing conversation is always in motion.

Now Durkheim could not comprehend such an ontology. For him, as we have shown, "communication" was either collision, chemical synthesis, or action-in-parallel. Durkheim never grasped the essence of communication as conversation or transaction. Moreover, society was implicitly viewed as a constraining container of its individual human particles. The walls were made of collective representations, symbols, or social facts. Men might be variously attached to them, energized by them, or cement them more firmly together as they exchanged them. When Durkheim finally came to see that the particles made the symbols or that the symbols themselves were the "things contained" and threatened to spill out over the walls that had been built by the symbols, he was confounded and groped for a new epistemology and, implicitly, a new ontology. The classical European solutions had already been transcended, and the new American pragmatism had not been fully enough developed to provide him convincing solutions—solutions in which he could have faith. He was certainly on the edge of symbolic interactionism, but he died in 1917, perhaps disenchanted by the death of his only son in World War I. At any rate, all the essentials were there, and he could not grasp them. In our view no social theorist had ever come further over the course of his lifetime.

SUMMARY AND EVALUATION OF CHAPTER SEVEN

Durkheim was a rigorous scholar, divorced from loyalty to any party or province of France. He gave a new cast to sociological theory, offering a model that was both testable and relevant to the key issues of social structuralism.[1] Furthermore, his social theory was informed with the unique view that man cannot fulfill his humanity apart from society and that within some kind of organic society he may acquire autonomy as well. To the end Durkheim was concerned about the moral quality of society—how it could continue to generate that commitment to rules nowhere else found in nature. He promoted the cause of religion on a generic level—in that he believed its importance lay in its reaffirmation of the life man shares in the greater being of society; even when the belief in specific divinities had passed, man must remain religious by transferring his sense of reverence directly to the group.

Durkheim's analysis of religion was perceptive. Why are weight-watchers, alcoholics, and others, more effective in overcoming their debility when they join a group? Is it not that in the group they have a power

---

[1] Structuralism, as understood here, is the theory that the difference in the predominant behavior patterns of two groups results from the difference in the operating norms and contingencies for behavior under these norms and not from the difference in individuals *qua* individuals. For a sophisticated discussion of this theory and some of the problems in testing it empirically see Matilda White Riley, *Sociological Research* (New York: Harcourt Brace Jovanovich, 1963), pp. 700–739.

and a communion greater than themselves? Moreover, if men *construct* social orders and if they must believe in them in order to make them work, is not religious behavior—that is, group reaffirmation of values—necessary if these orders are not to come undone?

Running through Durkheim's researches is a common thread: social phenomena cannot be understood at the level of individual goals or acts. Because of this emphasis, he is sometimes referred to as an "agelicist"— one who "maintains the reality *sui generis* or the causal priority of the social group *qua* group . . . [and holds that] the social group precedes and constitutes the individual."[2] This impression should not serve as the singular label for Durkheim. By itself it does not tell us of the greater subtleties of his view nor how he put it to work in his research. He meant of course, that there were patterns of social relations already established in our society before we were born. They may even appear external to us if we fail to abide by them and receive some punishment as a result. By taking a strong stand against individual factors in all explanations of social patterns, Durkheim may have been premature, but he wished to note that collective patterns are not *fully* understood with reference to the actions of *particular* individuals in *particular* situations. On the animal level, *each* organism is equipped with its own regulatory system, which develops *separately* for each even though it is duplicated by all the members of the species. This is not so on the human level, however.

Furthermore, although we do not know whether Durkheim understood analytic abstraction as we use the term today,[3] Robert A. Nisbet has argued eloquently against the stereotype that Durkheim reified society—in other words, believed that society acts independently of the people who constitute it. Having discovered a whole social fabric distinct from contracts, Durkheim had to discuss it in distinctive terms in order to make an impression on the many thinkers of his day who were enamored of individualism; it is solely for this reason that he used such phrases as *sui generis*. Durkheim himself insisted that society exists only *in action*. In *The Elementary Forms of Social Life* he conceived of the interplay between the individual and society, and, after emphasizing that all our human traits come from society and only from society, he says,

> But, on the other hand, society exists and lives only in and through individuals. If the idea of society were extinguished in individual minds and the beliefs, traditions and aspirations of the group were no longer felt and shared by the individuals, society would die. We can say of it what we just said of the divinity: it is real only insofar as it has a place in human

---

[2] Emile Benoit-Smullyan, "The Sociologism of Emile Durkheim and His School," in Harry Elmer Barnes, *An Introduction to the History of Sociology* (Chicago: University of Chicago Press, 1948), p. 499.

[3] An abstraction by itself cannot act since it has no concrete existence; it is an inextricable aspect of some object or event. Thus, for example, we understand that the weight (of the book) crushed the cracker under it or that the rules (of a society of people) caused the man to get angry when someone stole his property.

consciousnesses, and this place is whatever one we may give it. . . . [S]ociety cannot do without individuals any more than these can do without society.[4]

Durkheim seemed to be treating society *as if* it had an existence of its own separate from individuals. This is a perfectly acceptable methodological procedure, which A. R. Radcliffe-Brown and Bronislaw Malinowski, two great social anthropologists heavily influenced by Durkheim, made much use of later. If we can *conceive* of society in this way, then a whole new set of events may be visible; for example, we may see society as a system of exchanges whose constraints are not fully the product of individuals. Even George Caspar Homans's attack on Durkheim is not severe. He only insists that sociologists admit that in their so-called sociological explanations they tacitly use or assume certain kinds of psychological explanations or that psychological propositions are needed to explain the more general sociological propositions.[5] Most sociologists are willing to own up to this. But society is real, for the purposes of analysis, if it has real consequences, and who would want to argue that suicide is not a real consequence! The role given to psychological factors is indeed small—in *Suicide*, for example, they only "excite" the individual to kill himself— but Durkheim was trying to establish the real facts of *society*, not of the psyche.

There have been criticisms of Durkheim's *Suicide*. Most of them have already been discussed by Johnson in Selection 7.2; egoism and altruism were not truly paired opposites; Durkheim shifted ground to rationalize why Jews had a lower rate of suicide than Protestants in spite of the fact that Jews had high education; and Durkheim brought in psychological variables to explain some of the different suicide rates in different categories of people. Another criticism is that we cannot be sure the *same* individuals who might have been under anomic stress committed suicide since Durkheim only correlated types of groups and *rates* of suicide within the group.[6] The book is, however, a landmark. George Simpson contends that "*Suicide* can be looked upon as the first modern piece of distinguished, empirical, monographic research in sociology."[7] Today, suicidologists, scholars devoted to the study of self-destruction, have formed an association and continue to carry out empirical research as the result of Durkheim's inspiration.

Another area of study that Durkheim hinted at derives from his mor-

---

[4] P. 347 (of the 1915 edition published by George Allen & Unwin of London) as quoted in Robert A. Nisbet, *Emile Durkheim* (Englewood Cliffs, N.J.: Prentice-Hall, Spectrum Books, 1965), p. 53.

[5] See George Caspar Homans, "Contemporary Theory in Sociology," in R. E. L. Faris (Ed.), *Handbook of Modern Sociology* (Skokie, Ill.: Rand McNally, 1964), pp. 961–973.

[6] See Hanan C. Selvin, "Durkheim's *Suicide*: Further Thoughts on a Methodological Classic," in Nisbet, *Emile Durkheim*, pp. 125–129.

[7] George Simpson, *Emile Durkheim* (New York: Crowell, 1963), p. 4.

phological conception of society. It is translated today as social ecology, the subject of which is the symbiotic and commensalistic activities of social units and the locations resulting from these processes in physical space.[8] Communities can be visualized as machines that interact with the environment of physical resources and acquire a structure, or a characteristic arrangement of units in space, as a result of this utilization of resources and the distribution of utilities. Certainly this arrangement for sustaining the life of the community creates some parameters that determine social life and interaction.

Marvin E. Olsen has attempted to clarify the concept of anomie by suggesting that Durkheim gave it two different meanings.[9] In *Division of Labor in Society* he described it as "inadequate procedural rules to regulate the complementary relationship among the specialized and interdependent parts of a complex social system," while in *Suicide* he defined it as "inadequate moral norms to guide and control the actions of people and groups in the interests of the total social system."[10] Olsen proposes to call the former phenomenon "discordance," and the latter, anomie. He then notes that there are sources of both normative (anomic) and functional (discordant) malintegration in a society *other* than those noted by Durkheim—inconsistent values or lack of centralized coordination, for instance.

In conclusion, we must again stress that Durkheim was interested in several problems simultaneously: the causes of the structure of a society; the cause of different patterns of actions and the social ends they serve; and the way society produces the expression of our art and religion and the very categories of our thought. Durkheim must be appreciated in terms of where his career started and where it ended. We repeat the closing lines of the article by Stone and Farberman above: "[N]o theorist had ever come further over the course of his lifetime."

SELECTED BIBLIOGRAPHY

Alpert, Harry. *Emile Durkheim and His Sociology*. New York: Columbia University Press, 1939.

American Journal of Sociology, 63 (May 1958), entire issue: "Durkheim–Simmel Commemorative Issue."

American Sociological Review, 24 (August 1959): articles by Robert Bellah, Harry Alpert, and Bruce Dahrenwend.

Barnes, Harry Elmer, (Ed.). *An Introduction to the History of Sociology*. Chicago: University of Chicago Press, 1948. Chap. XXVII, (this is Chap. IX in the abridged paperback edition).

---

[8] See Otis Dudley Duncan and Leo F. Schnore, "Cultural, Behavioral, and Ecological Perspectives in the Study of Social Organization," *American Journal of Sociology*, 65 (September 1959), 132–146.

[9] Marvin E. Olsen, "Durkheim's Two Concepts of Anomie," *The Sociological Quarterly*, 6 (Winter 1965), 37–44.

[10] Ibid., p. 40 and p. 41, respectively.

Bierstedt, Robert. *Emile Durkheim.* New York: Dell Publishing Company, 1966 (paperback).
Clark, Terry Nichols. *Prophets and Patrons: The French University and the Emergence of the Social Sciences.* Cambridge: Harvard University Press, 1973.
Giddens, Anthony, (Ed.). *Emile Durkheim: Selected Writings.* New York: Cambridge University Press, 1972.
Lukes, Steven. *Emile Durkheim: His Life and Work.* London: Allen Lane, 1973.
Madge, John. *The Origins of Scientific Sociology.* New York: Free Press, 1962. Chap. II.
Nisbet, Robert A. *Emile Durkheim.* Englewood Cliffs, N.J.: Prentice-Hall, Spectrum Book, 1965.
Olsen, Marvin E. "Durkheim's Two Concepts of Anomie," *The Sociological Quarterly,* 6 (Winter, 1965), 37–44.
Parsons, Talcott. *The Structure of Social Action.* New York: Free Press, 1949.
Simpson, George. *Emile Durkheim.* New York: Crowell, 1963.
Wallwork, Ernest E. *Durkheim: Morality and Milieu.* Cambridge, Mass.: Harvard University Press, 1972.
Wolff, Kurt H., (Ed.). *Essays on Sociology and Philosophy by Emile Durkheim et al.* New York: Harper & Row, Harper Torchbooks, 1964.
Zeitlin, Irving M., *Ideology and the Development of Sociological Theory,* Englewood Cliffs, N.J.: Prentice-Hall, 1968.

EIGHT

George Herbert Mead

"Having visited a number of foreign countries, I believe that Mead's conception of social communication and the gesture are very important in our world for understanding. For example, individuals from Latin countries get very close to the other person when speaking. We Americans are put off by such 'pushiness.' "

—STUDENT COMMENT

General Introduction

George Herbert Mead (1863–1931) was born in Hadley, Massachusetts, the son of a clergyman, Hiram Mead.[1] In 1870 Hiram moved his family to Oberlin, Ohio, where he taught at Oberlin Theological Seminary until his death in 1881. George Mead enrolled at Oberlin College and read prodigiously. Colleges then were usually closely tied to religious bodies, which scrutinized new discoveries or ideas in any field of learning. Though an unassuming person, Mead apparently rebelled against this close supervision, but never lost his moral concern for society. He completed a masters degree at Harvard and several years of study in Germany, where he was influenced by both Wilhelm Wundt and G. Stanley Hall in physiological psychology. In 1891 Mead married Helen Castle, with whom he had one child. Mead's first teaching position, offered him by John Dewey, was at the University of Michigan, where Mead became a good friend of Charles Horton Cooley. Three years later, in 1894, Mead followed Dewey to the newly founded University of Chicago and remained there for the rest of his life. He died in 1931 before he could take up the duties of a new position that he had accepted at Columbia University.

---

[1] The following biography is drawn from David Wallace, "Reflections on the Education of George Herbert Mead," *American Journal of Sociology*, 72 (January 1967), 396–408.

The Chicago setting, in which Mead did his writing, was a bustling one. He circulated among many different groups, which must have added inspiration to his concept of taking roles from different points of view, and the presence of a large, anonymous urban scene must have stirred his interest in the symbolism of interaction. The city was a place where the community life of rural environs had broken down. In these new conditions it was important to study the processes that connect individuals and enable them to survive.

Mead represented a new subdivision in sociology, sometimes referred to as symbolic-interactionist social psychology. This school of thought arose among scholars in both sociology and psychology who investigated the symbolic–cognitive and social aspects of behavior simultaneously.

Closely acquainted with philosophy himself, Mead lived at a time when some moral philosophers were radically reorienting their thinking along the lines of pragmatism and evolution. Out of this new orientation Mead forged a social psychology that was both very different from any formulated previously and highly profound in its insights and hypotheses. His social psychology caught the spirit of the scientific age and the spirit of individual ruggedness expressed in both the Protestantism of the day and frontier America.

Yet it is difficult to understand Mead, perhaps because he was so imaginatively philosophical in the development of his concepts and because his posthumously published books consisted, in large part, of notes that he certainly would have revised, edited, and organized had he published them himself.[2] We shall here attempt to impart an initial understanding of his ideas; Selections 8.1, 8.2, and 8.3 will then further clarify and elaborate on them.[3]

---

[2] Mead's major works are found in the following: *Philosophy of the Present* (1932), Arthur E. Murphy (Ed.) (LaSalle, Ill.: Open Court); *Mind, Self, and Society* (1934), Charles W. Morris (Ed.) (Chicago: University of Chicago Press); *Movements of Thought in the 19th Century* (1936), Merritt H. Moore (Ed.) (Chicago: University of Chicago Press); *Philosophy of the Act* (1938), Charles W. Morris (Ed.) (Chicago: University of Chicago Press); *George Herbert Mead on Social Psychology* (1956), Anselm Strauss (Ed.) (Chicago: University of Chicago Press); *Selected Writings* (1964), Andrew J. Reck (Ed.) (Indianapolis: Bobbs-Merrill); *George Herbert Mead* (1968), John W. Petras (Ed.) (New York: Teachers College Press). For a complete bibliography see Natanson, footnote 3.

[3] See the introduction in Strauss, footnote 2, and the following: Bernard N. Meltzer, *The Social Psychology of George Herbert Mead* (Kalamazoo, Mich.: Center for Sociological Research, Western Michigan University, 1959); Paul E. Pfuetze, *The Social Self* (New York: Bookman Associates, 1954); Maurice Natanson, *The Social Dynamics of George Herbert Mead* (Washington, D.C.: Public Affairs Press, 1956); Gregory P. Stone and Harvey A. Farberman (Eds.), *Social Psychology through Symbolic Interaction* (Waltham, Mass.: Ginn–Blaisdell, 1970).

The guiding idea for Mead was evolutionism. It was not that he employed biological explanations for human conduct—he shunned them, in fact; rather, evolution suggested that not only do animal forms continually diverge and develop in an *open process* of adaptation, but so does human action. Human action is also intelligent because in a pragmatic way human organisms adjust their behavior on the basis of the real effects it does have or the effects they imagine it might have. Human organisms are distinguished from other organisms in that they become aware of themselves as both the initiator of actions and the object of others' actions. This allows human beings to make a complex *mutual* adjustment of their actions to one another. Nonhuman organisms may "gesture" to one another; that is, they may act toward others of their species in such a way that their action provokes a response or an "answer" from them; but there is presumably no assessment of the meaning of such responses on the part of the principles. There is none because self-awareness and self-reflexiveness are lacking.

When the self becomes an object to itself, it can think, plan, feel, and act toward itself and can indicate to itself what and who it is. This reflexiveness occurs in a setting with others who may be present either physically or imaginatively, in the mind of the actor, as they appeared in previous encounters, for example.

In Mead's view, the actor evaluates himself not from the single standpoint of the self, but from the collective standpoint of what he believes others think of him. He identifies with others and is motivated by their approval.[4] Others, relationships, settings, the self—all can become objects having meaning to the actor. The social context is always present because meaning is necessarily *shared.* Meaning is imputed to objects after some negotiation on the part of the actors and often after each has inferred the meaning from the type of response observed in the other.

Combined action of actors makes a community, and symbols, although ever changing in meaning, provide the medium of community. Mind is the process of "minding." It is the process of symbolling as the self indicates to the self the meaning of objects in a context where others and their responses are taken into account by the actor. Self and other, mind and society, are part of the same process of creating, sharing, and indicating meaning. If the self could not be both subject and object (from the point of view of the other), none of this would be possible.

For Mead, mind and self evolve through interaction with others. The child acquires a self as he acquires symbols. His self develops as he becomes aware of others and their actions and reactions concerning him. He becomes an object to himself by taking the roles of others. His identity

---

4 Tamotsu Shibutani, *Society and Personality: An Interactionist Approach to Social Psychology* (Englewood Cliffs, N.J.: Prentice-Hall, 1961), pp. 239–240.

is found in the rudimentary self—"I am not ball, not bed, not mommy"—and is anchored in the responses of others. The child also takes charge of his own socialization. When he assumes the roles of others, he can stimulate himself by engaging in the *internal dialogue* and the *imaginative rehearsal*. These techniques help him anticipate what his actions and meanings would be if he were others. In the internal dialogue, the child speaks the roles of others. Because he can hear his own remarks he stimulates himself in the same way that adults stimulate each other. The dialogue is between himself and the others, and the child carries out the rehearsal imaginatively without engaging in overt action with them.

The child may do this in the *play*, where he gives some external validation to the rehearsed dialogue. In the play, the child as a sole actor puts himself in the place of another: she is the mommy, the doll, the baby; he is the service station operator pumping gas, the motorist. It is play because it involves only taking the place of one other at a time and is not regarded as authentic—"for real"—interaction. But play is the work of little children.

In the *game* the actor must take the role of the other among many actors whose behavior is simultaneously relevant to him. The baseball game is a favorite example, although any plurality of people in action might be used as an illustration. Here, concerted action rather than simply action-in-parallel takes place. It is the result of the actor's taking all the other positions imaginatively (and observing them in action), then inferring the rules of the game, that is, the collective meanings that guide it in its course. The actor actually has a conception of the game from the attitude, or tendency to act, of each member. This conception is the *generalized other*.

The individual *binds*, or manipulates, time. This idea appears in Mead's philosophy of the act and his philosophy of the present, both of which play a part in his social behaviorism. The symbol is crucial to the process of binding time. Symbolling permits the human organism to react to the conception of any object without reacting to the object itself and to envisage the end of the organism's own act without performing the act itself. We can talk about trees, for example, without taking the time to go out and get one; and we can economize action by assessing possible outcomes without taking the time for each of the overt performances. Symbolization makes of the world something it isn't. A triangular, flat board on the ground becomes "second base," which derives its significance from the different actions involving the base. Symbolization shortens the time between actions and consequences and allows the past as well as the future to be present in human action. We have two concepts here: the act and the perspective (pasts and futures sliding together in a present).

The act is the process by which the organism adjusts to its environment. Among humans the act begins with an impulse stage and ends with a consummation stage.[5] It can be short or long, simple or complex. The importance of the act lies in the perceptions we have of what is occurring and what should be attended to. The outcome is somewhat indeterminate because each person selectively perceives and interprets stimuli, thus directing the act along rather unique lines. The act is guided by the "me" aspect of the self, which is the self's past organization, but it emerges with the "I," a novel and somewhat surprising conclusion. The "me" controls; the "I" creates.

The present is the perspective from which anyone acts. But not everyone's present is the same. The present may consist of the features that the individual selects from the past and the future to which he is now acting as objects. Knowing one's present involves knowing the meanings of these relevant features.

Society is a universe of meaning and an aggregation of actions. It is generated in the generalized other, which gives stability and integration to the diverse selves, but is ever changing. Society is also people engaging in interaction that results from their communication of meanings. Society is possible because meanings develop, signifying (1) what the person to whom a gesture is directed should do, (2) what the gesturer plans to do, and (3) what the joint action that arises through the articulation of the acts of both will be.[6] Individuals fit their actions together on the basis of their identities—he is a "boy," a "farmer"; I am a "failure," a "date"; and so on—and the way they define situations—as a "holdup," a "class," or the like. The result is never definitive. Because you can pick up on yesterday's uncompleted interaction, the "me" demonstrates a stability. That the outcome is likely to be different today from what it would have been yesterday, had you completed it then, indicates the surprise of the "I."

Introduction to Selections 8.1, 8.2, and 8.3

Selection 8.1, Herbert Blumer's "Society as Symbolic Interaction," is provocative and polemical. Blumer emphasizes Mead's belief that individuals are truly acting organisms because they develop selves and engage in self-indicating behavior. They are not just stimulated; they select and construct objects. No existing or previous psychology fully catches the spirit of this view. The complexity with which the individual

---

[5] See Shibutani (*Society and Personality*, pp. 65–70) for a description of all of the stages of the act.

[6] Herbert Blumer, *Symbolic Interactionism* (Englewood Cliffs, N.J.: Prentice-Hall, 1969), p. 9.

constructs his line of action is matched only by the complexity with which he fits his actions together with others. The individual seeks to ascertain the intention and direction of the acts of others by taking the role of others.

Blumer prefers Mead's symbolic interactionist view of society to other sociologies that see the individual as compelled by external "forces," impelled by "antecedent" factors, or pliantly coerced by the "organization" of the group or society. Blumer believes that one cannot bypass the individual and the process of self-indication in which he engages. Social organization may shape a situation or provide some preexisting definition of it by virtue of the shared symbols people coming to the situation already possess. But the situation is not always prestructured, so there is usually room for reinterpretation. At bottom, only individuals, separately or together, act. And unless we understand the interpretation process in terms of the acting unit, we will pursue a groundless sociology and miss the realities in which individuals create and manage new institutions.

It is difficult to say exactly what the "self" is. Some suggest that it is only an analytic fiction that the researcher creates for the purpose of better understanding behavior. Ely Chinoy defines the self as the awareness of the feelings about one's own personal and social identity.[7] Blumer, in Selection 8.2, suggests that Mead saw the self not as a structure, which ignores its acting nature, but as a process. This view especially characterizes the "I self," which is impulsive and spontaneous and is capable of the novel response to a situation, rather than the "me self," which is conceived in retrospect and represents a selected set of consequences from the acting "I self." The individual objectifies the self by using others as mirrors. In his observations of others he assesses the meanings of their gestures by inferring what the meanings would be for him if he were they. The role-taking process is thus a reflexive one. Whether or not the individual's assessments of meaning are correct can be determined only by his actually playing the others' roles or some different role related to theirs in their presence. If the gestures that he makes toward them while playing their roles evokes the responses he expects, then his assessment is apparently correct. One can practice in advance for such encounters through what, as we have already mentioned, Mead called the rehearsal. Here an individual engages in an entirely internal dialogue by being both himself and the other.

According to William H. Desmond (in Selection 8.3), the similarities in the thoughts of certain psychoanalytic thinkers and those of Mead are quite striking, especially in view of the apparent absence of communication between them. Desmonde devotes most of his attention to Mead, whom he regards as the one who moved social psychology

---

[7] Ely Chinoy, *Society* (New York: Random House, 1967), pp. 78–79.

toward naturalism by providing it with a methodology for the observation of its subject matter and an evolutionary-processual view that freed it from fixed dualistic concepts. Mead was not, however, fully in accord with behaviorism since he wished to include in his social psychology data on the early, unobservable phase of an action, during which covert *ideas* organize and prepare the actor for the movement that follows. One of the early, observable phases in an ongoing act is the gesture, which indicates the direction and the goal of the progressing movement. In a later phase, the actor sees the consequences of his action; having this knowledge, he can control his action in the future by aligning the early stages with the consequences he desires to produce. Mead assumed that the central nervous system provides the mechanism for doing this, but a human being is not *compelled* to complete an action he has begun in any one particular way. He can select, in the midst of the progressing movement, from a number of alternative ways of carrying it out. Moreover, since language makes possible the sharing of significant symbols, individual A can potentially respond to his own gestures in the same way as would individual B. This makes the gesture significant to both. Thus, before completing an action, A can anticipate what B's reaction will be and can change the outcome of his action in accordance with it. This process is called reflexiveness and is at the heart of all introspection (the inner rehearsal of the actor's actions and the other's reactions) and sociality. Mind, then, involves the individual's ability "to take the role of the other toward [his own] developing action." On a small scale, the actor creates new relationships because of the interaction between the "me" ("the internalized role of the other towards the beginnings of a response" by the actor) and the "I" (the actor's eventual response, from a range of alternatives, to the imported reaction). On a larger scale, the actor creates new social forms because of his ability to internalize the organized roles and attitudes of a whole group (the generalized other) and respond to it.

For both Mead and Freud, reason, reality, and mind are the products of interaction between the organism and the environment, and both men developed parallel concepts to analyze this process. Mead"s "inner forum" parallels Freud's fantasy, or dreamwork. According to Mead, the organism's tension with its environment is indicated by the presence of the "me" and "the generalized other" and the temporary resolution in the "I," whereas for Freud it is manifested by the resolution of the id impulses in the Oedipus complex. Furthermore, Freud's notion of the weakening of the ego in situations where the individual is enthusiastically swept up by a crowd is similar to Mead's fusion of the "I" and "me" in the religious or patriotic experience. .Desmonde concludes by showing further parallels between Mead and Harry Stack Sullivan, Paul Schilder, J. L. Moreno, and Norbert Wiener.

We might elaborate briefly on Desmonde's remark that "his [Mead's]

attitude toward psychoanalysis seems to have been somewhat negative."
This attitude apparently stymied communication between Mead and psychoanalysts. Several reasons for this might be suggested, although they
apply more to some analysts than others.[8] First, sociologists and social
psychologists have objected to the use of psychoanalytical concepts whose
operations have not been well enough defined to permit scientists to compare observations from subject to subject;[9] among these concepts are
"death wish" and "castration complex," for example. If the analyst claims
that the operation of such forces can be detected only in his own private
way, then they are of little utility to science, for the analyst cannot be
proved wrong about their degree of existence. Second, it has often been
objected that psychoanalysts impute well-developed, complex feelings in
very young individuals. Critics believe that an infant cannot be jealous
of the sexual position of the father vis-à-vis the mother if he knows
nothing of the experiences that allow him to form such a feeling and
make such fine discriminations among individuals. Finally, psychoanalysts
have often asserted not only that childhood experiences are crucial to
adult character formation (and are even modified as the organism passes
through different biological stages), but also that given child-rearing
practices, for example, weaning, have a determinative effect on specific
adult character patterns. Such beliefs are quite questionable, although
they do have heuristic merit; that is, they may suggest some directions
for careful research to take.

---

[8] See Philipp G. Frank (Ed.), *The Validation of Scientific Theories* (New
York: Crowell-Collier and Macmillan, 1961), Chap. III, "Freud's Psycho-
analytic Theory." See also Harold Orlansky, "Infant Care and Personality,"
Psychological Bulletin, 46 (January 1949), 1–48; William Sewell, "Infant
Training and the Personality of the Child," *American Journal of Sociology*,
58 (September 1952), 150–159.

[9] We do not claim that Mead's social psychology is entirely free from this
defect—if it should be called that—either.

8.1

Society as Symbolic Interaction
HERBERT BLUMER

A view of human society as symbolic interaction has been followed more than it has been formulated. Partial, usually fragmentary, statements of it are to be found in the writings of a number of eminent scholars, some inside the field of sociology and some outside. Among the former we may note such scholars as Charles Horton Cooley, W. I. Thomas, Robert E. Park, E. W. Burgess, Florian Znaniecki, Ellsworth Faris, and James Mickel Williams. Among those outside the discipline we may note William James, John Dewey, and George Herbert Mead. None of these scholars, in my judgment, has presented a systematic statement of the nature of human group life from the standpoint of symbolic interaction. Mead stands out among all of them in laying bare the fundamental premises of the approach, yet he did little to develop its methodological implications for sociological study. Students who seek to depict the position of symbolic interaction may easily give different pictures of it. What I have to present should be regarded as my personal version. My aim is to present the basic premises of the point of view and to develop their methodological consequences for the study of human group life.

The term "symbolic interaction" refers, of course, to the peculiar and distinctive character of interaction as it takes place between human beings. The peculiarity consists in the fact that human beings interpret or "define" each other's actions instead of merely reacting to each other's actions. Their "response" is not made directly to the actions of one another but instead is based on the meaning which they attach to such actions. Thus, human interaction is mediated by the use of symbols, by interpretation, or by ascertaining the meaning of one another's actions. This mediation is equivalent to inserting a process of interpretation between stimulus and response in the case of human behavior.

The simple recognition that human beings interpret each other's actions as the means of acting toward one another has permeated the thought and writings of many scholars of human conduct and of human group life. Yet few of them have endeavored to analyze what such interpretation implies about the nature of the human being or about the nature of human association. They are usually content with a mere recognition that "interpretation" should be caught by the student, or with a simple realization that symbols, such as cultural norms or values, must be introduced into their analyses. Only G. H. Mead, in my judgment, has sought to think through what the act of interpretation implies for an understanding of the human being, human action, and human association. The essentials of his analysis are so penetrating and profound and so important for an understanding of human group life that I wish to spell them out, even though briefly.

The key feature in Mead's analysis is that the human being has a self. This idea should not be cast aside as esoteric or glossed over as something that is obvious and hence not worthy of attention. In declaring that the human being has a self, Mead had in mind chiefly that the human being can be the object of his own actions. He can act toward himself as he might act toward others. Each of us is familiar with actions of this sort in which the human being gets angry with himself, rebuffs himself, takes pride in himself, argues with himself, tries to bolster his own courage, tells himself that he should "do this" or not "do that," sets goals for himself, makes compromises with himself, and plans what he is going to do. That the human being acts toward himself in these and countless other ways is a matter of easy empirical observation. To recognize that the human being can act toward himself is no mystical conjuration.

Mead regards this ability of the human being to act toward himself as the central mechanism with which the human being faces and deals with his world. This mechanism enables the human being to make indication to himself of things in his surroundings and thus to guide his actions by what he notes. Anything of which a human being is conscious is something which he is indicating to himself—the ticking of a clock, a knock at the door, the appearance of a friend, the remark made by a companion, a recognition that he has a task to perform, or the realization that he has a cold. Conversely, anything of which he is not conscious is, *ipso facto*, something which he is not indicating to himself. The conscious life of the human being, from the time that he awakens until he falls asleep, is a continual flow of self-indications—notations of the things with which he deals and takes into account. We are given, then, a picture of the human being as an organism which confronts its world with a mechanism for making indications to itself. This is the mechanism that is involved in interpreting the actions of others. To interpret the actions of another is to point out to oneself that the action has this or that meaning or character.

Now, according to Mead, the significance of making indications to oneself is of paramount importance. The importance lies along two lines. First, to indicate something is to extricate it from its setting, to hold it apart, to give it a meaning or, in Mead's language, to make it into an object. An object—that is to say, anything that an individual indicates to himself—is different from a stimulus; instead of having an intrinsic character which acts on the individual and which can be identified apart from the individual, its character or meaning is conferred on it by the individual. The object is a product of the individual's disposition to act instead of being an antecedent stimulus which evokes the act. Instead of the individual being surrounded by an environment of pre-existing objects which play upon him and call forth his behavior, the proper picture is that he constructs his objects on the basis of his on-going activity. In any of his countless acts—whether minor, like dressing himself, or major, like organizing himself for a professional career—the individual is designating different objects to himself, giving them meaning, judging their suitability to his action, and making decisions on the basis of the judgment. This is what is meant by interpretation or acting on the basis of symbols.

The second important implication of the fact that the human being makes indications to himself is that his action is constructed or built up instead of being a mere release. Whatever the action in which he is engaged, the human individual proceeds by pointing out to himself the divergent things which have to be taken into account in the course of his action. He has to note what he wants to do and how he is to do it; he has to point out to himself the various conditions which may be instrumental to his action and those which may obstruct his action; he has to take account of the demands, the expectations, the prohibitions, and the threats as they may arise in the situation in which he is acting. His action is built up step by step through a process of such self-indication. The human individual pieces together and guides his action by taking account of different things and interpreting their significance for his prospective action. There is no instance of conscious action of which this is not true.

The process of constructing action through making indications to oneself cannot be swallowed up in any of the conventional psychological categories. This process is distinct from and different from what is spoken of as the "ego"—just as it is different from any other conception which conceives of the self in terms of composition or organization. Self-indication is a moving communicative process in which the individual notes things, assesses them, gives them a meaning, and decides to act on the basis of the meaning. The human being stands over against the world, or against "alters," with such a process and not with a mere ego. Further, the process of self-indication cannot be subsumed under the forces, whether from the outside or inside, which are presumed to play upon the individual to produce his behavior. Environmental pressures, external stimuli, organic drives, wishes, attitudes, feelings, ideas, and their like do not cover or explain the process of self-indication. The process of self-indication stands over against them in that the individual points out to himself and interprets the appearance or expression of such things, noting a given social demand that is made on him, recognizing a command, observing that he is hungry, realizing that he wishes to buy something, aware that he has a given feeling, conscious that he dislikes eating with someone he despises, or aware that he is thinking of doing some given thing. By virtue of indicating such things to himself, he places himself over against them and is able to act back against them, accepting them, rejecting them, or transforming them in accordance with how he defines or interprets them. His behavior, accordingly, is not a result of such things as environmental pressures, stimuli, motives, attitudes, and ideas but arises instead from how he interprets and handles these things in the action which he is constructing. The process of self-indication by means of which human action is formed cannot be accounted for by factors which precede the act.

The process of self-indication exists in its own right and must be accepted and studied as such. It is through this process that the human being constructs his conscious action.

Now Mead recognizes that the formation of action by the individual through a process of self-indication always takes place in a social context. Since this matter is so vital to an understanding of symbolic interaction it needs to be explained carefully. Fundamentally, group action takes the form of a fitting together of individual lines of action. Each individual aligns his action to the action of others by ascertaining what they are doing or what they intend to do—that is, by getting the meaning of their acts. For Mead, this is done by the individual "taking the role"of others —either the role of a specific person or the role of a group (Mead's "generalized other"). In taking such roles the individual seeks to ascertain the intention or direction of the acts of others. He forms and aligns his own action on the basis of such interpretation of the acts of others. This is the fundamental way in which group action takes place in human society.

The foregoing are the essential features, as I see them, in Mead's analysis of the bases of symbolic interaction. They presuppose the following: that human society is made up of individuals who have selves (that is, make indications to themselves); that individual action is a construction and not a release, being built up by the individual through noting and interpreting features of the situations in which he acts; that group or collective action consists of the aligning of individual actions, brought about by the individuals' interpreting or taking into account each other's actions. Since my purpose is to present and not to defend the position of symbolic interaction I shall not endeavor in this essay to advance support for the three premises which I have just indicated. I wish merely to say that the three premises can be easily verified empirically. I know of no instance of human group action to which the three premises do not apply. The reader is challenged to find or think of a single instance which they do not fit.

I wish now to point out that sociological views of human society are, in general, markedly at variance with the premises which I have indicated as underlying symbolic interaction. Indeed, the predominant number of such views, especially those in vogue at the present time, do not see or treat human society as symbolic interaction. Wedded, as they tend to be, to some form of sociological determinism, they adopt images of human society, of individuals in it, and of group action which do not square with the premises of symbolic interaction. I wish to say a few words about the major lines of variance.

Sociological thought rarely recognizes or treats human societies as composed of individuals who have selves. Instead, they assume human beings to be merely organisms with some kind of organization, responding to forces which play upon them. Generally, although not exclusively, these forces are lodged in the make-up of the society, as in the case of "social system," "social structure," "culture," "status position," "social role," "custom," "institution," "collective representation," "social situation," "social norm," and "values." The assumption is that the behavior of people as members *of a society* is an expression of the play on them of these kinds of factors or forces. This, of course, is the logical position which is necessarily taken when the scholar explains their behavior or phases of their behavior in terms of one or other of such social factors. The individuals who compose a human society are treated as the media through which such factors operate, and the social action of such individuals is regarded as an expression of such factors. This approach or point of view denies, or at least ignores, that human beings have selves—that they act by making indications to themselves. Incidentally, the "self" is not brought into the picture by introducing such items as organic drives, motives, attitudes, feelings, internalized social factors, or psychological components. Such psychological factors have the same status as the social factors mentioned: they are regarded as factors which play on the individual to produce his action. They do not constitute the process of self-indication. The process of self-indication stands over against them, just as it stands over against the social factors which play on the human being. Practically all sociological conceptions of human society fail to recognize that the individuals who compose it have selves in the sense spoken of.

Correspondingly, such sociological conceptions do not regard the social actions of individuals in human society as being constructed by them through a process of interpretation. Instead, action is treated as a product of factors which play on and through individuals. The social behavior of people is not seen as built up by them through an interpretation of objects, situations, or the actions of others. If a place is given to "interpretation," the interpretation is regarded as merely an expression of other factors (such as motives) which precede the act, and accordingly disappears as a factor in its own right. Hence, the social action of people is treated as an outward flow or expression of forces playing on them rather than as acts which are built up by people through their interpretation of the situations in which they are placed.

These remarks suggest another significant line of difference between general sociological views and the position of symbolic interaction. These two sets of views differ in where they lodge social action. Under the perspective of symbolic interaction, social action is lodged in acting individuals who fit their respective lines of action to one another through a process of interpretation; group action is the collective action of such individuals. As opposed to this view, sociological conceptions generally lodge social action in the action of society or in some unit of society. Examples of this are legion. Let me cite a few. Some conceptions, in treating societies or human groups as "social systems," regard group action as an expression of a system, either in a state of balance or seeking to achieve balance. Or group action is conceived as an expression of the "functions" of a society or of a group. Or group action is regarded as the outward expression of elements lodged in society or the group, such as cultural demands, societal purposes, social values, or institutional stresses. These typical conceptions ignore or blot out a view of group life or of group action as consisting of the collective or concerted actions of individuals seeking to meet their life situations. If recognized at all, the efforts of people to develop collective acts to meet their situations are subsumed under the play of underlying or transcending forces which are lodged in society or its parts. The individuals composing the society or the group become "carriers," or media for the expression of such forces; and the interpretative behavior by means of which people form their actions is merely a coerced link in the play of such forces.

The indication of the foregoing lines of variance should help to put the position of symbolic interaction in better perspective. In the remaining discussion I wish to sketch somewhat more fully how human society appears in terms of symbolic interaction and to point out some methodological implications.

Human society is to be seen as consisting of acting people, and the life of the society is to be seen as consisting of their actions. The acting units may be separate individuals, collectivities whose members are acting together on a common quest, or organizations acting on behalf of a constituency. Respective examples are individual purchasers in a market, a play group or missionary band, and a business corporation or a national professional association. There is no empirically observable activity in a human society that does not spring from some acting unit. This banal statement needs to be stressed in light of the common practice of sociologists of reducing human society to social units that do not act—for example, social classes in modern society. Obviously, there are ways of viewing human society other than in terms of the acting units that compose it. I merely wish to point out that in respect to concrete or empirical activity human society must necessarily be seen in terms of the acting units that form it. I would add that any scheme of human society claiming to be a realistic analysis has to respect and be congruent with the empirical recognition that a human society consists of acting units.

Corresponding respect must be shown to the conditions under which such units act. One primary condition is that action takes place in and with regard to a situation. Whatever be the acting unit—an individual, a family, a school, a church, a business firm, a labor union, a legislature, and so on—any particular action is formed in the light of the situation in which it takes place. This leads to the recognition of a second major condition, namely, that the action is formed or constructed by interpreting the situation. The acting unit necessarily has to identify the things which it has to take into account—tasks, opportunities, obstacles, means, demands, discomforts, dangers, and the like; it has to assess them in some fashion and it has to make decisions on the basis of the assessment. Such interpretative behavior may take place in the individual guiding his own action, in a collectivity of individuals acting in concert, or in "agents" acting on behalf of a group or organization. Group life consists of acting units developing acts to meet the situations in which they are placed.

Usually, most of the situations encountered by people in a given society are defined or "structured" by them in the same way. Through previous interaction they develop and acquire common understandings or definitions of how to act in this or that situation. These common definitions enable people to act alike. The common repetitive behavior of people in such situations should not mislead the student into believing that no process of interpretation is in play; on the contrary, even though fixed, the actions of the participating people are constructed by them through a process of interpretation. Since ready-made and commonly accepted definitions are at hand, little strain is placed on people in guiding and organizing their acts. However, many other situations may not be defined in a single way by the participating people. In this event, their lines of action do not fit together readily and collective action is blocked. Interpretations have to be developed and effective accommodation of the participants to one another has to be worked out. In the case of such "undefined" situations, it is necessary to trace and study the emerging process of definition which is brought into play.

Insofar as sociologists or students of human society are concerned with the behavior of acting units, the position of symbolic interaction requires the student to catch the process of interpretation through which they construct their actions. This process is not to be caught merely by turning to conditions which are antecedent to the process. Such antecedent conditions are helpful in understanding the process insofar as they enter into it, but as mentioned previously they do not constitute the process. Nor can one catch the process merely by inferring its nature from the overt action which is its product. To catch the process, the student must take the role of the acting unit whose behavior he is studying. Since the interpretation is being made by the acting unit in terms of objects designated and appraised, meanings acquired, and decisions made, the process has to be seen from the standpoint of the acting unit. It is the recognition of this fact that makes the research work of such scholars as R. E. Park and W. I. Thomas so notable. To try to catch the interpretative process by remaining aloof as a so-called "objective" observer and refusing to take the role of the acting unit is to risk the worst kind of subjectivism—the objective observer is likely to fill in the process of interpretation with his own surmises in place of catching the process as it occurs in the experience of the acting unit which uses it.

By and large, of course, sociologists do not study human society in terms of its acting units. Instead, they are disposed to view human society in terms of structure or organization and to treat social action as an expression of such structure or organization. Thus, reliance is placed on such structural categories as social system, culture, norms, values, social stratification, status positions, social roles and institutional organization. These are used both to analyze human society and to account for social action within it. Other major interests of sociological scholars center around this focal theme of organization. One line of interest is to view organization in terms of the functions it is supposed to perform. Another line of interest is to study societal organization as a system seeking equilibrium; here the scholar endeavors to detect mechanisms which are indigenous to the system. Another line of interest is to identify forces which play upon organization to bring about changes in it; here the scholar endeavors, especially through comparative study, to isolate a relation between causative factors and structural results. These various lines of sociological perspective and interest, which are so strongly entrenched today, leap over the acting units of a society and bypass the interpretative process by which such acting units build up their actions.

These respective concerns with organization on one hand and with acting units on the other hand set the essential difference between conventional views of human society and the view of it implied in symbolic interaction. The latter view recognizes the presence of organization in human society and respects its importance. However, it sees and treats organization differently. The difference is along two major lines. First, from the standpoint of symbolic interaction the organization of a human society is· the framework inside of which social action takes place and is not the determinant of that action. Second, such organization and changes in it are the product of the activity of acting units and not of "forces" which leave such acting units out of account. Each of these two major lines of difference should be explained briefly in order to obtain a better understanding of how human society appears in terms of symbolic interaction.

From the standpoint of symbolic interaction, social organization is a framework inside of which acting units develop their actions. Structural features, such as "culture," "social systems," "social stratification," or "social roles," set conditions for their action but do not determine their action. People—that is, acting units—do not act toward culture, social structure or the like; they act toward situations. Social organization enters into action only to the extent to which it shapes situations in which people act, and to the extent to which it supplies fixed sets of symbols which people use in interpreting their situations. These two forms of influence of social organization are important. In the case of settled and stabilized societies, such as isolated primitive tribes and peasant communities, the influence is certain to be profound. In the case of human societies, particularly modern societies, in which streams of new situations arise and old situations become unstable, the influence of organization decreases. One should bear in mind that the most important element confronting an acting unit in situations is the actions of other acting units. In modern society, with its increasing criss-crossing of lines of action, it is common for situations to arise in which the actions of participants are not previously regularized and standardized. To this extent, existing social organization does not shape the situations. Correspondingly, the symbols or tools of interpretation used by acting units in such situations may vary and shift considerably. For these reasons, social action may go beyond, or depart from, existing organization in any of its structural dimensions. The organization of a human society is not to be identified with the process of interpretation used by its acting units; even though it affects that process, it does not embrace or cover the process.

Perhaps the most outstanding consequence of viewing human society as organization is to overlook the part played by acting units in social change. The conventional procedure of sociologists is (1) to identify human society (or some part of it) in terms of an established or organized form, (2) to identify some factor or condition of change playing upon the human society or the given part of it, and (3) to identify the new form assumed by the society following upon the play of the factor of change. Such observations permit the student to couch propositions to the effect that a given factor of change playing upon a given organized form results in a given new organized form. Examples ranging from crude to refined statements are legion, such as that an economic depression increases solidarity in the families of workingmen or that industrialization replaces extended families by nuclear families. My concern here is not with the validity of such propositions but with the methodological position which they presuppose. Essentially, such propositions either ignore the role of the interpretative behavior of acting units in the given instance of change, or else regard the interpretative behavior as coerced by the factor of change. I wish to point out that any line of social change, since it involves change in human action, is necessarily mediated by interpretation on the part of the people caught up in the change—the change appears in the form of new situations in which people have to construct new forms of action. Also, in line with what has been said previously, interpretations of new situations are not predetermined by conditions antecedent to the situations but depend on what is taken into account and assessed in the actual situations in which behavior is formed. Variations in interpretation may readily occur as different acting units cut out different objects in the situation, or give different weight to the objects which they note, or piece objects together in different patterns. In formulating propositions of social change, it would be wise to recognize that any given line of such change is mediated by acting units interpreting the situations with which they are confronted.

Students of human society will have to face the question of whether their preoccupation with categories of structure and organization can be squared with the interpretative process by means of which human beings, individually and collectively, act in human society. It is the discrepancy between the two which plagues such students in their efforts to attain scientific propositions of the sort achieved in the physical and biological sciences. It is this discrepancy, further, which is chiefly responsible for their difficulty in fitting hypothetical propositions to new arrays of empirical data. Efforts are made, of course, to overcome these shortcomings by devising new structural categories, by formulating new structural hypotheses, by developing more refined techniques of research, and even by formulating new methodological schemes of a structural character. These efforts continue to ignore or to explain away the interpretative process by which people act, individually and collectively, in society. The question remains whether human society or social action can be successfully analyzed by schemes which refuse to recognize human beings as they are, namely, as persons constructing individual and collective action through an interpretation of the situations which confront them.

8.2

Sociological Implications of the Thought of George Herbert Mead

HERBERT BLUMER

My purpose is to depict the nature of human society when seen from the point of view of George Herbert Mead. While Mead gave human society a position of paramount importance in his scheme of thought he did little to outline its character. His central concern was with cardinal problems of philosophy. The development of his ideas of human society was largely limited to handling these problems. His treatment took the form of showing that human group life was the essential condition for the emergence of consciousness, the mind, a world of objects, human beings as organisms possessing selves, and human conduct in the form of constructed acts. He reversed the traditional assumptions underlying philosophical, psychological, and sociological thought to the effect that human beings possess minds and consciousness as original "givens," that they live in worlds of pre-existing and self-constituted objects, that their behavior consists of responses to such objects, and that group life consists of the association of such reacting human organisms. In making his brilliant contributions along this line he did not map out a theoretical scheme of human society. However, such a scheme is implicit in his work. It has to be constructed by tracing the implications of the central matters which he analyzed. This is what I propose to do. The central matters I shall consider are (1) the self, (2) the act, (3) social interaction, (4) objects, and (5) joint action.

The Self

Mead's picture of the human being as an actor differs radically from the conception of man that dominates current psychological and social science. He saw the human being as an organism having a self. The possession of a self converts the human being into a special kind of actor, transforms his relation to the world, and gives his action a unique character. In asserting that the human being has a self, Mead simply meant that the human being is an object to himself. The human being may perceive himself, have conceptions of himself, communicate with himself, and act toward himself. As these types of behavior imply, the human being may become the object of his own action. This gives him the means of interacting with himself—addressing himself, responding to the address, and addressing himself anew. Such self-interaction takes the form of making indications to himself and meeting these indications by making further indications. The human being can designate things to himself—his wants, his pains, his goals, objects around him, the presence of others, their actions, their expected actions, or whatnot. Through further interaction with himself, he may judge, analyze, and evaluate the things he has designated to himself. And by continuing to interact with himself he may plan and organize his action with regard to what he has designated and evaluated. In short, the possession of a self provides the human being with a mechanism of self-interaction with which to meet the world—a mechanism that is used in forming and guiding his conduct.

I wish to stress that Mead saw the self as a process and not as a structure. Here Mead clearly parts company with the great bulk of students who seek to bring a self into the human being by identifying it with some kind of organization or structure. All of us are familiar with this practice because it is all around us in the literature. Thus, we see scholars who identify the self with the "ego," or who regard the self as an organized body of needs or motives, or who think of it as an organization of attitudes, or who treat it as a structure of internalized norms and values. Such schemes which seek to lodge the self in a structure make no sense since they miss the reflexive process which alone can yield and constitute a self. For any posited structure to be a self, it would have to act upon and respond to itself—otherwise, it is merely an organization awaiting activation and release without exercising any effect on itself or on its operation. This marks the crucial weakness or inadequacy of the many schemes such as referred to above, which misguidingly associate the self with some kind of psychological or personality structure. For example, the ego, as such, is not a self; it would be a self only by becoming reflexive, that is to say, acting toward or on itself. And the same thing is true of any other posited psychological structure. Yet, such reflexive action changes both the status and the character of the structure and elevates the process of self-interaction to the position of major importance.

We can see this in the case of the reflexive process that Mead has isolated in the human being. As mentioned, this reflexive process takes the form of the person making indications to himself, that is to say, noting things and determining their significance for his line of action. To indicate something is to stand over against it and to put oneself in the position of acting toward it instead of automatically responding to it. In the face of something which one indicates, one can withhold action toward it, inspect it, judge it, ascertain its meaning, determine its possibilities, and direct one's action with regard to it. With the mechanism of self-interaction the human being ceases to be a responding organism whose behavior is a product of what plays upon him from the outside, the inside, or both. Instead, he acts toward his world, interpreting what confronts him and organizing his action on the basis of the interpretation. To illustrate: a pain one identifies and interprets is very different from a mere organic feeling and lays the basis for doing something about it instead of merely responding organically to it; to note and interpret the activity of another person is very different from having a response released by that activity; to be aware that one is hungry is very different from merely being hungry; to perceive one's "ego" puts one in the position of doing something with regard to it instead of merely giving expression to the ego. As these illustrations show, the process of self-interaction puts the human being over against his world instead of merely in it, requires him to meet and handle his world through a defining process instead of merely responding to it, and forces him to construct his action instead of merely releasing it. This is the kind of acting organism that Mead sees man to be as a result of having a self.[1]

The Act

Human action acquires a radically different character as a result of being formed through a process of self-interaction. Action is built up in coping with the world instead of merely being released from a pre-existing psychological structure by factors playing on that structure. By making indications to himself and by interpreting what he indicates, the human being has to forge or piece together a line of action. In order to act the individual has to identify what he wants, establish an objective or goal, map out a prospective line of behavior, note and interpret the actions of others, size up his situation, check himself at this or that point, figure out what to do at other points, and frequently spur himself on in the face of dragging dispositions or discouraging settings. The fact that the human act is self-directed or built up means in no sense that the actor necessarily exercises excellence in its construction. Indeed, he may do a very poor job in constructing his act. He may fail to note things of which he should be aware, he may misinterpret things that he notes, he may exercise poor judgment, he may be faulty in mapping out prospective lines of conduct, and he may be half-hearted in contending with recalcitrant dispositions. Such deficiencies in the construction of his acts do not belie the fact that his acts are still constructed by him out of what he takes into account. What he takes into account are the things that he indicates to himself. They cover such matters as his wants, his feelings, his goals, the actions of others, the expectations and demands of others, the rules of his group, his situation, his conceptions of himself, his recollections, and his images of prospective lines of conduct. He is not in the mere recipient position of responding to such matters; he stands over against them and has to

---

[1] The self, or indeed human being, is not brought into the picture merely by introducing psychological elements, such as motives and interests, along side of societal elements. Such additions merely compound the error of the omission. This is the flaw in George Homan's presidential address on "Bringing Man Back In" (*American Sociological Review*, XXIX, No. 6, 809–18).

handle them. He has to organize or cut out his lines of conduct on the basis of how he does handle them.

This way of viewing human action is directly opposite to that which dominates psychological and social sciences. In these sciences human action is seen as a product of factors that play upon or through the human actor. Depending on the preference of the scholar, such determining factors may be physiological stimulations, organic drives, needs, feelings, unconscious motives, conscious motives, sentiments, ideas, attitudes, norms, values, role requirements, status demands, cultural prescriptions, institutional pressures, or social-system requirements. Regardless of which factors are chosen, either singly or in combination, action is regarded as their product and hence is explained in their terms. The formula is simple: Given factors play on the human being to produce given types of behavior. The formula is frequently amplified so as to read: Under specified conditions, given factors playing on a given organization of the human being will produce a given type of behavior. The formula, in either its simple or amplified form, represents the way in which human action is seen in theory and research. Under the formula the human being becomes a mere medium or forum for the operation of the factors that produce the behavior. Mead's scheme is fundamentally different from this formula. In place of being a mere medium for operation of determining factors that play upon him, the human being is seen as an active organism in his own right, facing, dealing with, and acting toward the objects he indicates. Action is seen as conduct which is constructed by the actor instead of response elicited from some kind of preformed organization in him. We can say that the traditional formula of human action fails to recognize that the human being is a self. Mead's scheme, in contrast, is based on this recognition.

Social Interaction

I can give here only a very brief sketch of Mead's highly illuminating analysis of social interaction. He identified two forms or levels—non-symbolic interaction and symbolic interaction. In non-symbolic interaction human beings respond directly to one another's gestures or actions; in symbolic interaction they interpret each other's gestures and act on the basis of the meaning yielded by the interpretation. An unwitting response to the tone of another's voice illustrates non-symbolic interaction. Interpreting the shaking of a fist as signifying that a person is preparing to attack illustrates symbolic interaction. Mead's concern was predominantly with symbolic interaction. Symbolic interaction involves *interpretation,* or ascertaining the meaning of the actions or remarks of the other person, and *definition,* or conveying indications to another person as to how he is to act. Human association consists of a process of such interpretation and definition. Through this process the participants fit their own acts to the ongoing acts of one another and guide others in doing so.

Several important matters need to be noted in the case of symbolic interaction. First, it is a formative process in its own right. The prevailing practice of psychology and sociology is to treat social interaction as a neutral medium, as a mere forum for the operation of outside factors. Thus psychologists are led to account for the behavior of people in inter- action by resorting to elements of the psychological equipment of the participants—such elements as motives, feelings, attitudes, or personality organization. Sociologists do the same sort of thing by resorting to societal factors, such as cultural prescriptions, values, social roles, or structural pressures. Both miss the central point that human interaction is a positive shaping process in its own right. The participants in it have to build up their respective lines of conduct by constant interpretation of each other's ongoing lines of action. As participants take account of each other's on- going acts, they have to arrest, reorganize, or adjust their own intentions, wishes, feelings, and attitudes; similarly, they have to judge the fitness of norms, values, and group prescriptions for the situation being formed by the acts of others. Factors of psychological equipment and social organi- zation are not substitutes for the interpretative process; they are admis- sible only in terms of how they are handled in the interpretative process. Symbolic interaction has to be seen and studied in its own right.

Symbolic interaction is noteworthy in a second way. Because of it human group life takes on the character of an ongoing process—a con- tinuing matter of fitting developing lines of conduct to one another. The fitting together of the lines of conduct is done through the dual process of definition and interpretation. This dual process operates both to sustain established patterns of joint conduct and to open them to transformation. Established patterns of group life exist and persist only through the con- tinued use of the same schemes of interpretation; and such schemes of interpretation are maintained only through their continued confirmation by the defining acts of others. It is highly important to recognize that the established patterns of group life just do not carry on by themselves but are dependent for their continuity on recurrent affirmative definition. Let the interpretations that sustain them be undermined or disrupted by changed definitions from others and the patterns can quickly collapse. This dependency of interpretations on the defining acts of others also ex- plains why symbolic interaction conduces so markedly to the transforma- tion of the forms of joint activity that make up group life. In the flow of group life there are innumerable points at which the participants are re- defining each other's acts. Such redefinition is very common in adversary relations, it is frequent in group discussion, and it is essentially intrinsic to dealing with problems. (And I may remark here that no human group is free of problems.) Redefinition imparts a formative character to human interaction, giving rise at this or that point to new objects, new concep- tions, new relations, and new types of behavior. In short, the reliance on symbolic interaction makes human group life a developing process instead of a mere issue or product of psychological or social structure.

There is a third aspect of symbolic interaction which is important to note. In making the process of interpretation and definition of one another's acts central in human interaction, symbolic interaction is able to cover the full range of the generic forms of human association. It embraces equally well such relationships as cooperation, conflict, domination, exploitation, consensus, disagreement, closely knit identification, and indifferent concern for one another. The participants in each of such relations have the same common task of constructing their acts by interpreting and defining the acts of each other. The significance of this simple observation becomes evident in contrasting symbolic interaction with the various schemes of human interaction that are to be found in the literature. Almost always such schemes construct a general model of human interaction or society on the basis of a particular type of human relationship. An outstanding contemporary instance is Talcott Parsons' scheme which presumes and asserts that the primordial and generic form of human interaction is the "complementarity of expectations." Other schemes depict the basic and generic model of human interaction as being "conflict," others assert it to be "identity through common sentiments," and still others that it is agreement in the form of "consensus." Such schemes are parochial. Their great danger lies in imposing on the breadth of human interaction an image derived from the study of only one form of interaction. Thus, in different hands, human society is said to be fundamentally a sharing of common values; or, conversely, a struggle for power; or, still differently, the exercise of consensus; and so on. The simple point implicit in Mead's analysis of symbolic interaction is that human beings, in interpreting and defining one another's acts, can and do meet each other in the full range of human relations. Proposed schemes of human society should respect this simple point.

Objects

The concept of object is another fundamental pillar in Mead's scheme of analysis. Human beings live in a world or environment of objects, and their activities are formed around objects. This bland statement becomes very significant when it is realized that for Mead objects are human constructs and not self-existing entities with intrinsic natures. Their nature is dependent on the orientation and action of people toward them. Let me spell this out. For Mead, an object is anything that can be designated or referred to. It may be physical as a chair or imaginary as a ghost, natural as a cloud in the sky or man-made as an automobile, material as the Empire State Building or abstract as the concept of liberty, animate as an elephant or inanimate as a vein of coal, inclusive of a class of people as politicians or restricted to a specific person as President de Gaulle, definite as a multiplication table or vague as a philosophical doctrine. In short, objects consist of whatever people indicate or refer to.

There are several important points in this analysis of objects. First, the nature of an object is constituted by the meaning it has for the person or persons for whom it is an object. Second, this meaning is not intrinsic to the object but arises from how the person is initially prepared to act toward it. Readiness to use a chair as something in which to sit gives it the meaning of a chair; to one with no experience with the use of chairs the object would appear with a different meaning, such as a strange weapon. It follows that objects vary in their meaning. A tree is not the same object to a lumberman, a botanist, or a poet; a star is a different object to a modern astronomer than it was to a sheepherder of antiquity; communism is a different object to a Soviet patriot than it is to a Wall Street broker. Third, objects—all objects—are social products in that they are formed and transformed by the defining process that takes place in social interaction. The meaning of the objects—chairs, trees, stars, prostitutes, saints, communism, public education, or whatnot—is formed from the ways in which others refer to such objects or act toward them. Fourth, people are prepared or set to act toward objects on the basis of the meaning of the objects for them. In a genuine sense the organization of a human being consists of his objects, that is, his tendencies to act on the basis of their meanings. Fifth, just because an object is something that is designated, one can organize one's action toward it instead of responding immediately to it; one can inspect the object, think about it, work out a plan of action toward it, or decide whether or not to act toward it. In standing over against the object in both a logical and psychological sense, one is freed from coercive response to it. In this profound sense an object is different from a stimulus as ordinarily conceived.

This analysis of objects puts human group life into a new and interesting perspective. Human beings are seen as living in a world of meaningful objects—not in an environment of stimuli or self-constituted entities. This world is socially produced in that the meanings are fabricated through the process of social interaction. Thus, different groups come to develop different worlds—and these worlds change as the objects that compose them change in meaning. Since people are set to act in terms of the meanings of their objects, the world of objects of a group represents in a genuine sense its action organization. To identify and understand the life of a group it is necessary to identify its world of objects; this identification has to be in terms of the meanings objects have for the members of the group. Finally, people are not locked to their objects; they may check action toward objects and indeed work out new lines of conduct toward them. This condition introduces into human group life an indigenous source of transformation.

Joint Action

I use the term "joint action" in place of Mead's term "social act." It refers to the larger collective form of action that is constituted by the fitting together of the lines of behavior of the separate participants. Illustrations of joint action are a trading transaction, a family dinner, a marriage ceremony, a shopping expedition, a game, a convivial party, a debate, a court trial, or a war. We note in each instance an identifiable and distinctive form of joint action, comprised by an articulation of the acts of the participants. Joint actions range from a simple collaboration of two individuals to a complex alignment of the acts of huge organizations or institutions. Everywhere we look in a human society we see people engaging in forms of joint action. Indeed, the totality of such instances—in all of their multitudinous variety, their variable connections, and their complex networks—constitutes the life of a society. It is easy to understand from these remarks why Mead saw joint action, or the social act, as the distinguishing characteristic of society. For him, the social act was the fundamental unit of society. Its analysis, accordingly, lays bare the generic nature of society.

To begin with, a joint action cannot be resolved into a common or same type of behavior on the part of the participants. Each participant necessarily occupies a different position, acts from that position, and engages in a separate and distinctive act. It is the fitting together of these acts and not their commonality that constitutes joint action. How do these separate acts come to fit together in the case of human society? Their alignment does not occur through sheer mechanical juggling, as in the shaking of walnuts in a jar or through unwitting adaptation, as in an ecological arrangement in a plant community. Instead, the participants fit their acts together, first, by identifying the social act in which they are about to engage and, second, by interpreting and defining each other's acts in forming the joint act. By identifying the social act or joint action the participant is able to orient himself; he has a key to interpreting the acts of others and a guide for directing his action with regard to them. Thus, to act appropriately, the participant has to identify a marriage ceremony as a marriage ceremony, a holdup as a holdup, a debate as a debate, a war as a war, and so forth. But, even though this identification be made, the participants in the joint action that is being formed still find it necessary to interpret and define one another's ongoing acts. They have to ascertain what the others are doing and plan to do and make indications to one another of what to do.

This brief analysis of joint action enables us to note several matters of distinct importance. It calls attention, first, to the fact that the essence of society lies in an ongoing process of action—not in a posited structure of relations. Without action, any structure of relations between people is meaningless. To be understood, a society must be seen and grasped in terms of the action that comprises it. Next, such action has to be seen and treated, not by tracing the separate lines of action of the participants —whether the participants be single individuals, collectivities, or organizations—but in terms of the joint action into which the separate lines of action fit and merge. Few students of human society have fully grasped this point or its implications. Third, just because it is built up over time by the fitting together of acts, each joint action must be seen as having a career or a history. In having a career, its course and fate are contingent on what happens during its formation. Fourth, this career is generally orderly, fixed and repetitive by virtue of a common identification or definition of the joint action that is made by its participants. The common definition supplies each participant with decisive guidance in directing his own act so as to fit into the acts of the others. Such common definitions serve, above everything else, to account for the regularity, stability, and repetitiveness of joint action in vast areas of group life; they are the source of the established and regulated social behavior that is envisioned in the concept of culture. Fifth, however, the career of joint actions also must be seen as open to many possibilities of uncertainty. Let me specify the more important of these possibilities. One, joint actions have to be initiated—and they may not be. Two, once started a joint action may be interrupted, abandoned, or transformed. Three, the participants may not make a common definition of the joint action into which they are thrown and hence may orient their acts on different premises. Four, a common definition of a joint action may still allow wide differences in the direction of the separate lines of action and hence in the course taken by the joint action; a war is a good example. Five, new situations may arise calling for hitherto unexisting types of joint action, leading to confused exploratory efforts to work out a fitting together of acts. And, six, even in the context of a commonly defined joint action, participants may be led to rely on other considerations in interpreting and defining each other's lines of action. Time does not allow me to spell out and illustrate the importance of these possibilities. To mention them should be sufficient, however, to show that uncertainty, contingency, and transformation are part and parcel of the process of joint action. To assume that the diversified joint actions which comprise a human society are set to follow fixed and established channels is a sheer gratuitous assumption.

From the foregoing discussion of the self, the act, social interaction, objects, and joint action we can sketch a picture of human society. The picture is composed in terms of action. A society is seen as people meeting the varieties of situations that are thrust on them by their conditions of life. These situations are met by working out joint actions in which participants have to align their acts to one another. Each participant does so by interpreting the acts of others and, in turn, by making indications to others as to how they should act. By virtue of this process of interpretation and definition joint actions are built up; they have careers. Usually, the course of a joint action is outlined in advance by the fact that the participants make a common identification of it; this makes for regularity, stability, and repetitiveness in the joint action. However, there are many joint actions that encounter obstructions, that have no pre-established pathways, and that have to be constructed along new lines. Mead saw human society in this way—as a diversified social process in which people were engaged in forming joint actions to deal with situations confronting them.

This picture of society stands in significant contrast to the dominant views of society in the social and psychological sciences—even to those that pretend to view society as action. To point out the major differences in the contrast is the best way of specifying the sociological implications of Mead's scheme of thought.

The chief difference is that the dominant views in sociology and psychology fail, alike, to see human beings as organisms having selves. Instead, they regard human beings as merely responding organisms and, accordingly, treat action as mere response to factors playing on human beings. This is exemplified in the efforts to account for human behavior by such factors as motives, ego demands, attitudes, role requirements, values, status expectations, and structural stresses. In such approaches the human being becomes a mere medium through which such initiating factors operate to produce given actions. From Mead's point of view such a conception grossly misrepresents the nature of human beings and human action. Mead's scheme interposes a process of self-interaction between initiating factors and the action that may follow in their wake. By virtue of self-interaction the human being becomes an acting organism coping with situations in place of being an organism merely responding to the play of factors. And his action becomes something he constructs and directs to meet the situations in place of an unrolling of reactions evoked from him. In introducing the self, Mead's position focuses on how human beings handle and fashion their world, not on disparate responses to imputed factors.

If human beings are, indeed, organisms with selves, and if their action is, indeed, an outcome of a process of self-interaction, schemes that purport to study and explain social action should respect and accommodate these features. To do so, current schemes in sociology and psychology would have to undergo radical revision. They would have to shift from a preoccupation with initiating factor and terminal result to a preoccupation with a process of formation. They would have to view action as something constructed by the actor instead of something evoked from him. They would have to depict the milieu of action in terms of how the milieu appears to the actor in place of how it appears to the outside student. They would have to incorporate the interpretive process which at present they scarcely deign to touch. They would have to recognize that any given act has a career in which it is constructed but in which it may be interrupted, held in abeyance, abandoned, or recast.

On the methodological or research side the study of action would have to be made from the position of the actor. Since action is forged by the actor out of what he perceives, interprets, and judges, one would have to see the operating situation as the actor sees it, perceive objects as the actor perceives them, ascertain their meaning in terms of the meaning they have for the actor, and follow the actor's line of conduct as the actor organizes it—in short, one would have to take the role of the actor and see his world from his standpoint. This methodological approach stands in contrast to the so-called objective approach so dominant today, namely, that of viewing the actor and his action from the perspective of an outside, detached observer. The "objective" approach holds the danger of the observer substituting his view of the field of action for the view held by the actor. It is unnecessary to add that the actor acts toward his world on the basis of how he sees it and not on the basis of how that world appears to the outside observer.

In continuing the discussion of this matter, I wish to consider especially what we might term the structural conception of human society. This conception views society as established organization, familiar to us in the use of such terms as social structure, social system, status position, social role, social stratification, institutional structure, cultural pattern, social codes, social norms, and social values. The conception presumes that a human society is structured with regard to (1) the social positions occupied by the people in it and with regard to (2) the patterns of behavior in which they engage. It is presumed further that this inter-linked structure of social positions and behavior patterns is the over-all determinant of social action; this is evidenced, of course, in the practice of explaining conduct by such structural concepts as role requirements, status demands, strata differences, cultural prescriptions, values, and norms. Social action falls into two general categories: conformity, marked by adherence to the structure, and deviance, marked by departure from it. Because of the central and determinative position into which it is elevated, structure becomes necessarily the encompassing object of sociological study and analysis—epitomized by the well-nigh universal assertion that a human group or society is a "social system." It is perhaps unnecessary to observe that the conception of human society as structure or organization is ingrained in the very marrow of contemporary sociology.

Mead's scheme definitely challenges this conception. It sees human society not as an established structure but as people meeting their conditions of life; it sees social action not as an emanation of societal structure but as a formation made by human actors; it sees this formation of action not as societal factors coming to expression through the medium of human organisms but as constructions made by actors out of what they take into account; it sees group life not as a release or expression of established structure but as a process of building up joint actions; it sees social actions as having variable careers and not as confined to the alternatives of conformity to or deviation from the dictates of established structure; it sees the so-called interaction between parts of a society not as a direct exercising of influence by one part on another but as mediated throughout by interpretations made by people; accordingly, it sees society not as a system, whether in the form of a static, moving or whatever kind of equilibrium, but as a vast number of occurring joint actions, many closely linked, many not linked at all, many prefigured and repetitious, others being carved out in new directions, and all being pursued to serve the purposes of the participants and not the requirements of a system. I have said enough, I think, to point out the drastic differences between the Meadian conception of society and the widespread sociological conceptions of it as structure.

The differences do not mean, incidentally, that Mead's view rejects the existence of structure in human society. Such a position would be ridiculous. There are such matters as social roles, status positions, rank orders, bureaucratic organizations, relations between institutions, differential authority arrangements, social codes, norms, values, and the like. And they are very important. But their importance does not lie in an alleged determination of action nor in an alleged existence as parts of a self-operating societal system. Instead, they are important only as they enter into the process of interpretation and definition out of which joint actions are formed. The manner and extent to which they enter may vary greatly from situation to situation, depending on what people take into account and how they assess what they take account of. Let me give one brief illustration. It is ridiculous, for instance, to assert, as a number of eminent sociologists have done, that social interaction is an interaction between social roles. Social interaction is obviously an interaction between *people* and not between roles; the needs of the participants are to interpret and handle what confronts them—such as a topic of conversation or a problem—and not to give expression to their roles. It is only in highly ritualistic relations that the direction and content of conduct can be explained by roles. Usually, the direction and content are fashioned out of what people in interaction have to deal with. That roles affect in varying degree phases of the direction and content of action is true but is a matter of determination in given cases. This is a far cry from asserting action to be a product of roles. The observation I have made in this brief discussion of social roles applies with equal validity to all other structural matters.

Another significant implication of Mead's scheme of thought refers to the question of what holds a human society together. As we know, this question is converted by sociologists into a problem of unity, stability, and orderliness. And, as we know further, the typical answer given by sociologists is that unity, stability, and orderliness come from a sharing in common of certain basic matters, such as codes, sentiments, and, above all, values. Thus, the disposition is to regard common values as the glue that holds a society together, as the controlling regulator that brings and keeps the activities in a society in orderly relationship, and as the force that preserves stability in a society. Conversely, it is held that conflict between values or the disintegration of values creates disunity, disorder, and instability. This conception of human society becomes subject to great modification if we think of society as consisting of the fitting together of acts to form joint action. Such alignment may take place for any number of reasons, depending on the situations calling for joint action, and need not involve, or spring from, the sharing of common values. The participants may fit their acts to one another in orderly joint actions on the basis of compromise, out of duress, because they may use one another in achieving their respective ends, because it is the sensible thing to do, or out of sheer necessity. This is particularly likely to be true in our modern complex societies with their great diversity in composition, in lines of interest, and in their respective worlds of concern. In very large measure, society becomes the formation of workable relations. To seek to encompass, analyze, and understand the life of a society on the assumption that the existence of a society necessarily depends on the sharing of values can lead to strained treatment, gross misrepresentation, and faulty lines of interpretation. I believe that the Meadian perspective, in posing the question of how people are led to align their acts in different situations in place of presuming that this necessarily requires and stems from a sharing of common values, is a more salutary and realistic approach.

There are many other significant sociological implications in Mead's scheme of thought which, under the limit of space, I can do no more than mention. Socialization shifts its character from being an effective internalization of norms and values to a cultivated capacity to take the roles of others effectively. Social control becomes fundamentally and necessarily a matter of self-control. Social change becomes a continuous indigenous process in human group life instead of an episodic result of extraneous factors playing on established structure. Human group life is seen as always incomplete and undergoing development instead of jumping from one completed state to another. Social disorganization is seen not as a breakdown of existing structure but as an inability to mobilize action effectively in the face of a given situation. Social action, since it has a career, is recognized as having a historical dimension which has to be taken into account in order to be adequately understood.

In closing I wish to say that my presentation has necessarily skipped much in Mead's scheme that is of great significance. Further, I have not sought to demonstrate the validity of his analyses. However, I have tried to suggest the freshness, the fecundity, and the revolutionary implications of his point of view.

8.3

G. H. Mead and Freud:
American Social Psychology
and Psychoanalysis

WILLIAM H. DESMONDE

George Herbert Mead (1863–1931) is now esteemed as one of the most creative thinkers in the pragmatist movement of the twentieth century. In the view of Charles W. Morris, an outstanding disciple, "the analytical depth and scientific precision he gave to the naturalistic theory of personality" entitles Mead to a permanent place among the founders of social psychology. Though to date, Mead's work has exerted greater influence on psychologists and sociologists than on philosophers, he has been acclaimed a creative mind of the first rank by such writers as John Dewey and Alfred North Whitehead.[1]

What is particularly remarkable about Mead's work in the present setting is that so far as any one now knows he independently developed a social psychology which, in many respects, closely resembles the clinically-derived theories of psychoanalysis. Mead's extraordinary influence on American social psychology and the recent efforts to integrate his views with those of Freud deserve closer attention than they have yet achieved. The significance of Mead and these undertakings for the future of psychoanalysis in America may be immense.

The Influence of Darwin

Mead was a contemporary and close friend of the sociologist Charles Horton Cooley[2] and the philosopher, John Dewey. Like Freud and Dewey, Mead derived his basic orientation from the impact of Darwin's theory

---

[1] For an evaluation of Mead's work and excerpts from his key writings, see now: *The Social Psychology of George Herbert Mead*, ed. Anselm Strauss (Chicago: University of Chicago Press, 1956), esp. pp. iv-xvi (in introduction); also, Grace C. Lee, *George Herbert Mead: Philosopher of the Social Individual* (New York: King's Crown Press, 1945).

[2] Cooley's development is described and appraised in Edward C. Jandy, *Charles Horton Cooley* (New York: Dryden Press, 1942).

upon nineteenth-century thought. Darwin's indications that man is an organism functioning in accordance with natural laws gave a fresh impetus to the scientific investigation of the determinants of human behavior. It was confidently anticipated by many people all over the world that the application of scientific method of human phenomena would bring about the solution of numerous age-old problems in social relations. Freud was born three years before and Mead, four years after the publication (1859) of Darwin's *Origin of Species.* Writing of his youthful ambitions, Sigmund Freud said:

> . . . the theories of Darwin, which were then of topical interest, strongly attracted me, for they held out hopes of an extraordinary advance in our understanding of the world. . . .[3]

As for the influence of Darwin upon George Herbert Mead, Charles W. Morris wrote:

> It has been the philosophical task of pragmatism to reinterpret the concepts of mind and intelligence in the biological, psychological, and sociological terms which post-Darwinian currents of thought have made prominent, and to reconsider the problems and task of philosophy from this new standpoint . . . the outlines of an empirical naturalism based on biological, psychological, and sociological data and attitudes are clearly discerned, a naturalism which sees thinking men in nature, and which aims to avoid the inherited dualism of mind and matter, experience and nature, philosophy and science, teleology and mechanism, theory and practice. It is a philosophy which, in terms used by Mead, opposes 'the otherworldliness of the reason . . . of ancient philosophy, the otherworldliness of soul . . . of Christian doctrine, and the otherworldliness of the mind . . . of the Renaissance dualisms.'[4]

Not only did Darwin's theory enable man to regard himself scientifically, but it emphasized the concept of process in the consideration of personality. It is difficult for us to appreciate today the extent to which the concept of process was neglected in thought prior to the time of Darwin. Nature was regarded as consisting of fixed, unalterable substances which existed independently of one another. These substances or essences possessed static forms which did not undergo transformations in time, but were eternal. If the recently deceased pioneer social psychologist, Kurt Lewin, is to be believed, the Aristotelian world-view which Western civilization had inherited divided the world into classifications which were unchangeable and immutable:

> In modern quantitative physics dichotomous classifications have been entirely replaced by continuous gradations. Substantial concepts have been replaced by functional concepts.

---

[3] Sigmund Freud, *An Autobiographical Study* (London: Hogarth Press, 1946), p. 9.

[4] In his introduction to George Herbert Mead's *Mind, Self, and Society* (Chicago: The University of Chicago Press, 1934), p. x.

Here also it is not difficult to point out the analogous stage of development in contemporary psychology. The separation of intelligence, memory, and impulse bears throughout the characteristic stamp of Aristotelian classification; and in some fields, for example, in the analysis of feelings (pleasantness and unpleasantness) or of temperaments, or of drives, such dichotomous classifications as Aristotle's are even today of great significance. Only gradually do these classifications lose their importance and yield to a conception which seeks to derive the same laws for all these fields, and to classify the whole field on the basis of other, essentially functional, differences.[5]

Darwin demolished this conception of fixed species; his work led to the acceptance of the notion of process. Nature was now viewed as a continuum, and all natural objects, including organisms, were part of an eternally changing, ceaselessly dynamic matrix. Psychic phenomena, too, were part of this process. It was no longer possible to regard men as possessing fixed, unalterable attributes or "traits." Instead, the mind was to be viewed as arising developmentally. Both Mead and Freud started from the assumption that psychic phenomena are evolutionary emergents subject to causal laws. Horney observed:

> I regard as the most fundamental and most significant of Freud's findings his doctrine that psychic processes are strictly determined.[6]

If man is to be conceived as a natural, determined phenomenon, the problem arises of fitting the organism into the universal causal nexus. Mead fought against any type of artificial dualism between organism and environment. An "organism" must be conceived as a temporary equilibrium within a field of force, an equilibratory state which comes into existence, maintains itself in a position of relative stability for a period of time, then literally disintegrates back into the nexus from which it emerged. Organism and environment, Mead wrote, are mutually determinate; each is in a continual state of reciprocal reconstruction. A similar concept of equilibration appeared in Freud's metapsychology:

> As a result of theoretical considerations, supported by biology, we assumed the existence of a death-instinct, the task of which is to lead organic matter back into the inorganic state; on the other hand, we supposed that Eros aims at complicating life by bringing about a more and more far-reaching coalescence of the particles into which living matter has been dispersed, thus, of course, aiming at the maintenance of life . . . both would be endeavoring to re-establish a state of things that was disturbed by the emergence of life.[7]

---

[5] Kurt Lewin, *A Dynamic Theory of Personality* (New York: McGraw-Hill, 1935), p. 4.

[6] Karen Horney, *New Ways in Psychoanalysis* (New York: W. W. Norton, 1939), p. 18.

[7] Sigmund Freud, *The Ego and the Id* (London: Hogarth Press, 1947), p. 55.

Thus, both Freud and Mead basically regarded human nature as a resultant of a physical state of ever-changing equilibration. Abandoning the conception of personality as a fixed, unchanging set of pre-ordained faculties, both sought to show the emergence of complex psychic phenomena from an environmental matrix.

Mead's "Social Behaviorism"

By destroying the mind-body dualism, Darwin's theory gave impetus to those philosophies which regarded mind and body as parts of a natural process. It was now contended that all psychic phenomena could be observed and understood in the same manner as other natural processes, with the aid of measuring instruments and laboratory controls. The influential American school of behaviorism constituted one such effort to make psychology a natural science. George Herbert Mead's "social behaviorism" was an attempt to correct many of the crudities of early behavioristic psychology.

Mead's criticisms began with an objection to the dismissal of introspection by many of the objective psychologists. By rejecting introspection as a methodological tool, the behaviorists tended to regard it as a non-existent phenomenon. *Mead, however, believed that the scope of behaviorism could be extended to include the neglected introspective phenomena.*

Furthermore, Mead stated that the behaviorists' description of the organism was based on an abstraction of the individual from the social process in which actions occur. The consequences of this artificial abstracting was a conception of individuals acting and reacting to each other, on the causal model of billiard balls. It was Mead's contention that the behaviorists were merely considering the external aspect of the total behavior of the organism. Actually, stimulus and response are meaningful only when viewed as part of a complete communicative situation.

Mead also rejected the notion that organisms passively respond to stimuli. He contended that the organism dynamically selects its stimuli; it does not react to perceptions. The organism to a great extent determines its environment.

> . . . attention enables us to organize the field in which we are going to act. Here we have the organism as acting and determining the environment. It is not simply a set of passive senses played upon by the stimuli that come from without.[8]

Mead thus opposed the British associationist school, in regarding the organism as a dynamic, forceful agent molding the world around it, rather than existing as a mute receptacle for stimuli which are later associated.

Mead began the construction of his "social behaviorism" by considering the function of gestures in social acts. An "idea," he stated, is the

---

[8] *Mind, Self, and Society*, p. 24.

early, unobservable stage in an ongoing act directed toward an environmental goal. Before an organism makes any overt movements, an inner mobilization of energy takes place, which no other organisms (except with special instruments) can observe. The mistake of the early behaviorists was to study merely one part of the complete act—the last, overt stages—thereby ignoring the initial stages, which occur behind the organism's epidermis. Ideas, therefore, are attitudes: the internal organization and preparation for the developing act. Hence, if we regard ideas as "inner" or "private" phases in ongoing acts, it becomes possible to construct a naturalistic theory of introspection.

Some of the early stages in an ongoing act are objectively observable. The initial aspect of the overt phase of an action indicates to other organisms the direction and goal of the progressing movement. These initial actions, said Mead, borrowing from Wundt, are gestures.

> The term 'gesture' may be identified with these beginnings of social acts which are stimuli for the response of other forms.[9]

For example, when a person draws back his arm and clenches his fist, this indicates to the other organisms that the former is going through the initial phase of a striking movement. Similarly, the roar of a lion is a gesture which displays readiness to attack. The gesture of "A" is a sign to "B" of "A's" complete act. It is through such observed preparatory movements that an organism's intentions become known to other individuals.

However, gestures are usually part of a complex social situation. The social situation in its simplest form consists, for Mead, in the "conversation of gestures," in which a gesture on the part of one individual evokes a preparatory movement on the part of the second person, and this gesture on the part of the second calls out a response in the former, and so on. For example, dog "A" makes a preparatory action toward springing at the throat of dog "B"; this gesture causes "B" to spring back; and this springing-back action of "B" is in turn a stimulus to "A."

But as yet, according to Mead, no communication need have taken place between the dogs—the gestures are *non-significant*, in that neither organism is aware of the effect of its gestures upon the other. In order for communication to take place, each organism must obtain cognition of the reaction of the other individual to his own behavior. This involves a temporal organization of the act, whereby the consequences of actions are already present while the behavior develops.

> The later stages of the act are present in the early stages—not simply in the sense that they are all ready to go off, but in the sense that they serve to control the process itself. They determine how we are going to approach the object, and the steps in our early manipulation of it.[10]

---

[9] *Ibid.*, p. 43.

[10] *Ibid.*, p. 11.

That is to say, when we stretch out our hand to pick up a book, the neural process that will activate the later clenching reaction has been already initiated before the clenching occurs; these processes exert an influence upon the phases of action which are already in progress. Mead cites the phenomenon of the hurdle runner. Several seconds before he jumps the hurdle, and while he is rapidly running toward it, the runner is timing himself so that he will be in the proper position to leap over the hurdle when he finally reaches it.

On the basis of such phenomena, Mead assumed that the central nervous system provides a mechanism whereby our behavior is organized with reference to the future. In so doing, he explained the determination of the present by the future, without resorting to obsolete versions of teleological concepts.

Furthermore, the capacity of the later phases of an act to control the earlier stages makes the organism an intelligent being, rather than a mere automaton acting on the basis of conditioned reflexes, as was the crude belief of the early behaviorists.

Now before any given act is completed, there are a number of alternative ways of carrying out the movement. Since the later stages of the developing action determine the earlier phases, it is possible for the organism to select one of these alternative ways of completing the motion. In this manner, rational conduct is possible, as over against behavior which is determined in advance by instincts, as in the lower forms of life.

> It is the entrance of the alternative possibilities of future response into the determination of present conduct . . . which decisively contrasts intelligent conduct or behavior with reflex, instinctive, and habitual conduct. . . .[11]
> Rational conduct always involves a reflexive reference to self, that is, an indication to the individual of the significance which his actions and gestures have for other individuals.[12]

The temporal organization of the act provides a necessary condition for the existence of communication. Effective sociality requires that organism "A" be capable of responding to its own response in the same way as does organism "B," the other participant in the social situation. But Mead rejects Tarde's conception of a "faculty" of imitation, and isolates the mechanism whereby symbols achieve significance.

The first condition for the existence of significant symbols is that organism "A" have present within it the same possibilities for response as has organism "B." The second condition is that organism "A" be capable of responding to its own responses, through the use of some sense-modality, in the same way as would "B."

Language meets these conditions, for we can hear what we are saying, and thus evoke in ourselves the same ideas (preparations to act) as are

---

11 *Ibid.*, p. 98.
12 *Ibid.*, p. 122.

evoked in the other organism. Thus, by means of the verbal response, we can simultaneously respond as would the other, while at the same time evoking the other's response by our action. Hence, in advance of our completion of a social action, we can already anticipate the response of the other. And, since our behavior is temporally organized, this anticipation works back on the ongoing act, and may cause the selection of a different alternative course of action than we originally intended.

In general, then, whenever organism "A" makes a gesture of any sort, to which "A" can at the same time respond in the same way as would "B," then "A" is making a significant gesture. And only when organisms can employ significant gestures does sociality exist.[13]

Through its capacity to use significant symbols, a given organism can take two or more roles simultaneously. The other's point of view is called out along with the given organism's perspective. For Mead, "mind" is the ability of an organism to take the role of the other toward its developing action. Mind emerges in the social act when the person is able to obtain cognition of the perspective of the other individual, and hence is able to modify his original response in the light of his knowledge of how the other may react to that response.

> Mind arises in the social process only when that process as a whole enters into or is present in the experience of any one of the given individuals involved in that process. . . . It is by means of reflexiveness—the turning-back of the experience of the individual upon himself—that the whole social process is thus brought into the experience of the individuals involved in it; it is by such means, which enable the individual to take the attitude of the other toward himself, that the individual is able consciously to adjust himself to that process, and to modify the resultant of that process in any given social act in terms of his adjustment to it. Reflexiveness, then, is the essential condition, within the social process, for the development of mind.[14]

Once reflexivity comes to exist, the entire social act is imported within the individual. Society is internalized, and serves to alter the original developing acts of the person. A complete social act can thus be internally carried out within the organism, without any overt movements necessarily taking place. This inner rehearsal of projected actions constitutes introspection.

That is to say, communication exists because organisms are capable of responding to their own response in the same manner as the other.

---

[13] It is interesting to compare Mead's "significant symbol" with Max Weber's definition of sociality: "Action is social in so far as, by virtue of the subjective meaning attached to it by the acting individual, it takes account of the behavior of others and is thereby oriented in its course." Talcott Parsons, *Max Weber: The Theory of Social and Economic Organization* (New York: Oxford University Press, 1947), p. 88.

[14] *Mind, Self, and Society*, p. 134.

The individual thus can, at the same time, take the role of the other, as well as act out its own role. Through this mechanism the unification of roles or perspectives occurs, and common viewpoints become possible.

By being able to take the role of the other, the organism becomes capable of looking at itself and observing itself as do other organisms. And taking the role of the other toward the beginnings of an act can occur even if the other organism is not in the field of perception. Thus, the social act is internalized.

The "I" and the "Me"

As a result of the internalization of the social act, the "inner forum" comes into being. The organism rehearses internally various types of possible social relations. Mead denotes the internalized role of the other toward the beginnings of a response the "me." That is to say, the "me" is the other person's reaction, implanted within the organism, toward the initial stages of the given organism's developing actions. It is in this manner that it is possible for other people to influence permanently our lives. A person who is important to us is internalized in the form of a "me" which modifies the course of our ongoing behavior. The altered, or adjusted, response of the organism to the imported reaction of the other is termed by Mead the "I."

> The 'I' is the response of the organism to the attitudes of the others; the 'me' is the organized set of attitudes of others which one himself assumes.[15]

Personality is the resultant of the interaction between the "I" and the "me"; the organism is perpetually beginning acts, then taking the attitude of the other toward this act, and finally readjusting the ongoing behavior in accordance with the anticipated reactions of the other.

> Now this is the highest expression of sociality, because the organism not only passes from one attitude to another, by means of a phase which is a part of all these attitudes, but also comes back on itself in the process and responds to this phase. It must get out of itself in the passage and react to this factor in the passage.[16]

Through man's capacity to readjust his developing acts to his anticipations of the future, he achieves freedom. The knowledge of what is necessary enables us to make an appropriate adjustment to that reality when it eventuates. We are not bound by the past, but can utilize the past to prepare for the future.

---

[15] *Ibid.*, p. 175.

[16] George Herbert Mead, *The Philosophy of the Present* (Chicago: Open Court Publishing Co., 1932), p. 86.

As Patrick Mullahy has pointed out,[17] the fact that society is imported within us is not incompatible with the uniqueness of each individual. According to Mead, innovation always can arise through the readjustment of the original ongoing act to the "me." The "I" is the source of all novelty and individuality, for by this readjustment new social forms come into being. We do not passively adapt ourselves to the reactions of others, but we actively create new relationships to other individuals. Because of the "I," we live in a constant state of growth, in which fresh perspectives are continually being created.

> By its own struggles with its insistent difficulties, the human mind is constantly emerging from one chrysalis after another into constantly new worlds which it could not possibly previse.[18]

The world of interpersonal relations is in a continual state of flux, for each individual is occupied in reconstructing the social group, by means of the "inner forum"—the interaction between the "I" and the "me."

> [It is the possession of] . . . mind or powers of thinking which enables human individuals to turn back critically, as it were, upon the organized social structure of the society to which they belong, and to reorganize or reconstruct or modify that social structure.[19]

One of Mead's most fruitful concepts is the "generalized other," which is the importation of the social organization within the individual. In group situations, such as games, the individual must adjust his actions, not merely to one other person (the "me"), but to the entire community. In a baseball game, for example, a person must act in accordance with the organized roles of every other member of the group.

> . . . in a game where a number of individuals are involved, then the child taking one role must be ready to take the role of everyone else. If he gets in a ball nine he must have the responses of each position involved in his own position. He must know what everyone else is going to do in order to carry out his own play. He has to take all of these roles.[20]

It is through the internalization of the organized attitudes of the entire group that the individual develops a complete self, according to Mead. The manifold functions of a society, its cooperative processes and institutions, are possible only insofar as the individual can carry within himself the numerous roles of the other people involved in group situations, and can extend these group attitudes to larger social organizations.

---

[17] " A Philosophy of Personality," *Psychiatry*, XIII (1950), p. 436.

[18] George Herbert Mead, "Scientific Method and the Moral Sciences," *International Journal of Ethics*, XXXIII (1923), 33: p. 246.

[19] *Mind, Self, and Society*, p. 308.

[20] *Ibid.*, p. 151.

It is in the form of the generalized other that the social process influences the behavior of the individuals involved in it and carrying it on, i.e., that the community exercises control over the conduct of its individual members; for it is in this form that the social process or community enters as a determinative factor into the individual's thinking.[21]

In the mature individual, the "inner forum" becomes more than an inner conversation with one other person; it becomes an imaginative discourse with a large group of other individuals who are organized into a cooperative enterprise.[22] And, just as in the case of the "me," the adjustment of the organism to the role of the generalized other causes the creation of new social forms.

There are certain occasions, Mead wrote, when all of the members of the group achieve a very close relationship, because of some common venture in which all are engaged. In such situations, each person has a feeling of being identified with the other members of the group. Inspired by this sense of closeness or identity, a sense of exaltation develops. This feeling is at the core of all religious experiences, according to Mead.

In a situation where persons are all trying to save someone from drowning, there is a sense of common effort in which one is stimulated by the others to do the same thing they are doing. . . . In the case of team work, there is an identification of the individual with the group; but in that case one is doing something different from the others, even though what the others do determines what he is to do. If things move smoothly enough, there may be something of the same exaltation as in the other situation. There is still the sense of directed control.[23]

This phenomenon is found mainly in religion, patriotism, and team work; it consists of a fusion of the "I" and the "me." That is to say, the internalized response of the other toward the given organism's ongoing act is such as to permit a harmonious merging of the two components. In these situations, there is agreement between the "I" and the "me" in the inner forum, and there results, according to Mead, "a peculiarly precious experience," which involves "the successful completion of the social process."[24]

The self under these circumstances is the action of the 'I' in harmony with the taking of the role of the others in the 'me.'[25]

[21] *Ibid.*, p. 155.

[22] Mead's "generalized other" is remarkably similar to Emile Durkheim's conception of the "collective representation." See for example, Durkheim's *The Elementary Forms of the Religious Life* (New York: Macmillan, 1915), p. 271.

[23] *Mind, Self, and Society*, p. 273.

[24] *Ibid.*, p. 275.

[25] *Ibid.*, p. 277.

In the fusion of the "I" and the "me," it may be said that Mead terminates his task of expressing psychic phenomena in terms of "social behaviorism." For here the dualism of environment and organism against which he fought is finally destroyed, and the mutual interdetermination of these two aspects of nature is clarified.

Mead and Freud

We have seen that both Mead and Freud were stimulated by Darwin's theory to regard man as a natural phenomenon which could be scientifically investigated. Both sought to find the determinants for human conduct, and both regarded mind as a social emergent. The results of their inquiries are surprisingly similar.

For example, the Freudian "ego" is formed to a great extent out of identifications taking the place of cathexes on the part of the Id which have been abandoned. Rationality is hence a bio-social development resulting from the precipitations of affect-percept-musculature coordinations arising from adjustment to the environment. Mead's treatment of the development of the reality-principle is rather similar:

> The awakening social intelligence of the child is evidenced not as much through his ready responses to the gestures of others, for these have been in evidence much earlier. It is the inner assurance of his own readiness to adjust himself to the attitudes of others that looks out of his eyes and appears in his own bodily attitudes.
>
> If we assume that the object arises in consciousness through the merging of the imagery of experience of the response with that of the sensuous experience of the stimulation, it is evident that the child must merge the imagery of his past responses into the sensuous stimulation of what comes to him through distance senses.[26]

For Mead as for Freud, the sense of reason or reality arises through partial identifications with others—the progressive implantation of "me's" within the organism. For both thinkers, intelligence (the ability to coordinate affects, percepts, and muscular innervations so as to realize goals) is built up from the causal nexus by means of the experiences acquired in this process. For neither investigator is mind an isolated monad somehow implanted within the individual—a pre-determined entity which interacts with other similarly constituted minds. Rather, mind is a social emergent. Freud wrote:

> We must conclude that the psychology of the group is the oldest human psychology; what we have isolated as individual psychology, by neglecting all traces of the group, has only since come into prominence out of the

---

[26] George Herbert Mead, "The Mechanism of Social Consciousness," *Journal of Philosophy*, (1912), p. 403.

old group psychology, by a gradual process which may still, perhaps, be described as incomplete.[27]

While Mead stated:

Inner consciousness is socially organized by the importation of the social organization of the outer world.[28]

For both Mead and Freud, the individual's capacity to respond to his own developing act as would the other person is the basic mechanism for the development of mind. By being in this fashion able to take the perspective of the other toward the ongoing behavior, the organism internalizes the social situation. An "inner forum" develops which acts to check, modify, or block the ongoing action.

Mead's "inner forum" thus parallels the Freudian conception of the fantasy or dream-work. In both instances, imaginative social behavior is carried out, under the control of a censoring agency representing the role of other persons in the environment.[29] Mead also developed the notion that the roles of non-human, physical objects are likewise internalized,[30] and serve as a check upon the individual's ongoing behavior.

Mead's conception of the "me"—the internalized role of the other, standing over against the developing act—is obviously very similar to the Freudian superego, in that it serves as an agency which restricts human conduct. Insofar as the father-image is a representation of the social organization of the group, the superego is identical with the "generalized other," as is apparent from a comparison of the following statements by Freud and Mead.

Freud declares:

It is easy to show that the ego-ideal answers in every way to what is expected of the higher nature of man. In so far as it is a substitute for the longing for the father, it contains the germ from which all religions have evolved. The self-judgment which declares that the ego falls short of its ideal produces the sense of worthlessness with which the religious believer attests his longing. . . . The tension between the demands of conscience and the attainments of the ego is experienced as a sense of guilt.[31]

Mead writes:

We approve of ourselves and condemn ourselves. We pat ourselves on the back and in blind fury attack ourselves. We assume the generalized

---

[27] Sigmund Freud, *Group Psychology and the Analysis of the Ego* (London: Hogarth Press, 1945), p. 92.

[28] See *Journal of Philosophy*, IX (1912), p. 406.

[29] *Ed. note:* For Freud, uncensored fantasy often issues in behavior which is non-realistic and anti-social in varying degrees.

[30] George Herbert Mead, *The Philosophy of the Act* (Chicago: The University of Chicago Press, 1945).

[31] *Group Psychology*, p. 49.

attitude of the group, in the censor that stands at the door of our imagery and inner conversation.[32]

As has been noted, both Freud and Mead conceived of the organism as a continuously equilibrating physical system. In the process of mutual interdetermination of environment and organism, instincts or drives make their appearance. For Mead, a basic notion is that of the "act"—the external or internal behavior of an individual in achieving an end. Complex mental phenomena, such as ideas, are viewed as preparations to act; they differ from overt behavior only in that they are not, being behind the opaque epidermis, easily observable as the initial phases in developing actions.

The homeostatic tendencies of the human organism were prominent in Freud's system from the start, as a number of recent writers have observed.[33] In his writings after 1920, the date of *Beyond the Pleasure Principle*, the two phases in the interdetermination of organism-environment become the life and death instincts. Eros seeks to maintain the integrity of the organism as a forceful, dynamic agent within a field of force, while Thanatos strives to disintegrate the individual. The id is the source of all energy; when the life instinct is dominant, it comprises the creative force in personality. The continuous descent toward death is delayed by the introduction of fresh tensions stemming from Eros.

Thus, both Mead and Freud conceived of motivation as arising from the equilibration of an organism within an environment. The "initial phases in a developing act" of which Mead spoke are hence to be compared with Freud's "id impulses."

But neither the id impulses nor the "ongoing act" remain unchanged by reality. For Freud, they are modified by either the ego or superego; analogously, in Mead, they are regulated by either the "me" or the "generalized other." What Mead denotes as the "I"—the readjustment of the developing behavior to the internalized role of the other—is quite similar to the Freudian "sublimated id impulse": the blocked impulse seeks another outlet, or appears in disguised form.

Mead's inner forum thus closely resembles the psychoanalytic conception of anxiety. The internalization of the social situation within the organism results in an inner conversation between the individual and a person external to him. The internalized dialogue between the "I" and the

---

[32] George Herbert Mead, "The Genesis of the Self and Social Control," *International Journal of Ethics*, XXXV (1924–5), p. 272.

[33] *Ed. note*: A number of recent discussions explore this issue: Ernst Kris' introduction to Sigmund Freud, *The Origins of Psychoanalysis: Letter to Wilhelm Fliess, Notes and Drafts: 1887–1902*, ed. Maria Bonaparte, Anna Freud and Ernst Kris (New York: Basic Books, 1954), esp. pp. 14–17; Kenneth Mark Colby, *Energy and Structure in Psychoanalysis* (New York: Ronald Press, 1955); Nigel Walker, "Freud and Homeostasis," *British Journal for the Philosophy of Science*. Vol. XXIV (1956); *idem*, "A New Copernicus?" *Freud and the 20th Century*, ed. Benjamin Nelson (New York: Meridian Books, 1957).

"me" results from the tension between the ongoing impulse and the re-action of the other person to the consummation of that impulse.

However, according to Mead, the gap between the "I" and the "me" breaks down in the religious and patriotic experience, in which there is a fusion between the ongoing act and the internalized role of the other. This phenomenon may be compared with the resolution of the Oedipus complex, which causes a removal of the barriers existing between the person and his father. For both Freud and Mead, religion has a social matrix, and relates to the reconciliation between the individual's ongoing acts and the internalized role of the other.

It is very instructive to compare Mead's theory of the fusion of the "I" and the "me" in group enthusiasm with Freud's conception of the function of the ego and superego in mass psychology.

According to Freud, in group phenomena, such as the formation of a mob, there is a weakening of the ego, and the reasoning powers of the individuals are swept away in a surge of abandonment to autism. The leader of the group usurps the followers' superego; and, as a parent-sub-stitute, brings them beneath his quasi-hypnotic influence. Mead's descrip-tion of the fusion of the "I" and the "me" in group enthusiasm parallels Freud's group psychology to an astonishing degree; present are the same feeling of self-abandonment, emotion of unity with the group, and sense of release. The following account of mass psychology, written by Mead, might well have been penned by Freud himself:

> A mob is an organization which has eliminated certain values which have obtained in the interrelation of individuals with each other, has simplified itself, and in doing that has made it possible to allow the indi-vidual, especially the repressed individual, to get an expression which otherwise would not be allowed. . . . The repression which existed has disappeared and he is at one with the community and the community is at one with him.[34]

Thus, insofar as the father-image represents the social organization of the community, Mead's concept of the fusion of the "I" and the "me" is identical with the resolution of the Oedipus complex, in that the bar-riers existing between a given person and authority are removed, along with the resolving of the interpersonal conflict.

Lines of Influence and Recent Developments

It is most improbable—no evidence has ever been adduced to indicate —that Freud was influenced by Mead. Did any influence run the other way? Was Mead at any of the significant points along the road affected by the available fund of Freud's ideas or any of his publications? On this question there is no ready answer.

---

[34] *Mind, Self, and Society*, p. 218.

John Dewey, for some years a colleague of Mead at Chicago and closely associated with Mead's thought throughout the latter's life, answered the question in the negative. Responding to the present writer's inquiry on this head, Dewey wrote:

> 504 South Street
> Key West, Florida
> March 13, 1948

Dear Mr. Desmonde:

I'm sorry not to be able to assist you on the topic of your question. I left Chicago in 1905; up to that time I do not know of any special influence exerted by Freud on Mead—no more I mean than upon any cultivated person of psychological interests. I should be surprised to learn that Freud shaped any of Mead's basic points of view but of course it's possible he had more influence after I left Chicago than I was aware of.

I have no information as to the 1909 lectures. I am reasonably sure that Mead would have had himself a biological explanation of most of the things Freud attributed to the "unconscious."

> Yours truly,
> John Dewey

The present writer is strongly disposed to accept this view. Scholars are currently striking balances of the divergences and of the convergences of the two men. Thus far, they have tended to stress the former as against the latter. A full review of this question must be left to the future.[35]

Here we must be content to survey traces of the influence of or approximations to Mead's thought in the work of four men and movements in the last two decades. These four are among the most notable attempts to achieve a comprehensive social psychiatry in which the concepts of Mead and Freud are integrated. They are:

---

[35] *Ed. note:* Anselm Strauss concludes: "Toward the development of a theory of childhood development Mead has little to offer—he is here no competitor to Sigmund Freud or Harry Stack Sullivan—but, again his concern with such matters as language and the "generalized other" provide a framework for a certain kind of developmental account. . . . His *I* and *Me*, for instance, although superficially similar to Freud's *Id* and *Superego*, represent quite a different formulation of the relations of man to society and man to biological nature; and there is in Mead no trace of speculation about basic human drives toward self-consistency or self-realization." *The Social Psychology of George Herbert Mead*, XV-XVI. In their comprehensive recent survey of *Theories of Personality* (New York: John Wiley, 1957), Calvin S. Hall and Gardner Lindzey place Freud at the very center of current developments; Mead, on the other hand, is accorded only one half-page. Nothing is said about convergences between the two. For further discussion of this question, see note 43 below.

A. Harry Stack Sullivan and Interpersonal Psychiatry
B. Paul Schilder
C. Moreno and Psychodrama
D. Psychological schemes growing out of the development of Cybernetics and Information Theory.

We shall discuss them in turn.

Harry Stack Sullivan   Sullivan started from the same assumption as Mead did—that mind is a social emergent. The self-dynamism arises out of the communicative situation (the empathic relation) between the child and its parents.

According to Sullivan, the self-dynamism is built up from experiences of disapproval and reward; the self becomes more and more like a microscope, focusing on those performances of the child which bring either approbation or punishment. The rest of the personality remains outside of the reflexive acts of the self-dynamism. This theory is obviously very similar to Mead's notion of the "me" standing over against the ongoing act as a modifying agent, eliminating all of the behavior of which the other person disapproves.[36] In both Mead and Sullivan the self is the result of reflected appraisals.

Sullivan's statement that anxiety appears whenever the built-in self-dynamism disapproves of the person's behavior is also very similar to Mead's "inner forum," in which a conflict goes on between the ongoing act and the internalized role of the other.

Thus, throughout Sullivan's theory of personality, as in Mead's "social behaviorism," the internalized role of the other comes to control and modify the ongoing acts of the individual in his interpersonal relations.

Paul Schilder   As we have seen, Mead's main effort was to show that mind is a social emergent, and that the role of a given individual is a function of the internalized role of other people. Furthermore, he sought to explain these phenomena behavioristically, i.e., in terms of the theory of the organism as a natural process.

Conclusions very like these will be found in the work of Paul Schilder. In his celebrated study, *The Image and Appearances of Body* (1937), Schilder showed that the body-image is derived from taking the role of other individuals. Like Mead, Schilder sought to elucidate the socio-neurophysiological basis for role-taking. He, too, insisted that organisms do not merely passively perceive stimuli, but instead build up their roles, or body-images, as the result of adjustments to the environment which require the active use both of musculature and the perception organs.

---

[36] It is well known that Sullivan was greatly influenced by the philosophy of George Herbert Mead. However, I have not been able to obtain any data bearing on the specific nature of this influence. The striking parallelism between the two points of view is obvious.

Schilder quite deliberately sought to merge Freud and Gestalt theory. Reviewing his own development, he came to see the convergence of his ideas with those of American social psychology and philosophy, notably the work and thought of James and Dewey.

Schilder writes:

A psychology of this kind necessarily places emphasis on the action and does not consider the organism in its psychic and somatic aspects as a theoretical entity with merely perceptive qualities (perceptions, imaginations, and thoughts). Perception and action, impression and expression, thus form a unit, and insight and action become closely correlated to each other. Human action, badly misjudged in the philosophy of Bergson, and artificially separated by Kant into practical reasoning and pure reasoning, is thus restored to its full dignity. It is easy to see that the pragmatism of James and the instrumentalism of John Dewey express the same principle in a philosophic way. I have come, in this respect also, in my previous formulations (e.g., in my *Ideen zur Naturphilosophie*) nearer to the trend of American philosophy than I realized at that time.[37]

According to Schilder's findings, the body-image develops gradually, as a result of the child learning to differentiate its own body from the surrounding environment. Mead puts a related point as follows:

In the organization of the baby's physical experience, the appearance of his body as a unitary thing, as an object, will be relatively late, and must follow upon the structure of the objects of his environment. This is as true of the object that appears in social conduct, the self. . . . The earliest achievement of social consciousness will be the merging of the imagery of the baby's first responses and their results with the stimulation of the gestures of others. . . . The child's early social percepts are of others. After these arise incomplete and partial selves—or 'me's'—which are quite analogous to the child's percepts of his hands and feet, which precede his perception of himself as a whole.[38]

J. L. Moreno The similarities between the views of Mead and those of Moreno have frequently been noted. Seeking to integrate Freudian thought and sociological research, Moreno hit upon theoretical constructs and therapeutic techniques which parallel Mead as clearly as they seek to extend Freud.

One of the major contributions of Mead's "social behaviorism" was to show that introspection and fantasy-construction are derived from the social environment. That is to say, the "inner forum" consists of an internalized rehearsal of social actions. There is an inner dialogue between the "I" and the "me," with the internalized role of the other person acting as a modifying agent upon the ongoing act.

---

[37] Paul Schilder, *The Image and the Appearance of the Human Body* (London: Kegan Paul, 1935), p. 8.

[38] See *Journal of Philosophy*, IX (1912), p. 403.

The similarities between Mead's theory and Moreno's therapy are evident. In the Psychodrama, a personality is expressed, according to Moreno, by the way he acts out an assigned role in the therapeutic theatre, and by the roles which this individual prefers to play. The varying ability and desire of a patient to act out different parts may be designated, in Mead's system, as the way in which the initial phases of developing acts are determined by the anticipated reactions of others.

The Psychodrama can be interpreted as an objectification of what Mead calls the "inner forum." Moreno assigns various "auxiliary egos" to the patient, who acts out his fantasies in their presence. That is to say, these "auxiliary egos" are actually the "me's" or internalized roles of others, which stand over against the patient's ongoing acts.[39]

Cybernetics and Information Theory　Mead's conception of the regulation of the ongoing act by the internalized role of the other has recently received added support by Norbert Wiener's principles of cybernetics. Like Mead, Wiener realized that reflexivity (the feed-back) is an essential condition for the existence of mind, and that this occurs by means of a temporal organization of the act, whereby the future stages of the behavior are known in advance, and regulate the developing phases of the ongoing motions. Wiener states:

> The central nervous system no longer appears as a self-contained organ, receiving inputs from the senses and discharging into the muscles. On the contrary, some of its most characteristic activities are explicable only as circular processes, emerging from the nervous system into the muscles, and re-entering the nervous system through the sense organs, whether they be proprioceptors or organs of the special senses. This seemed to us to mark a new step in the study of that part of neurophysiology which concerns not solely the elementary processes of nerves and synapses but the performance of the nervous system as an integrated whole.[40]

At this very moment, there is, extraordinary activity in the elaboration of "information theory," the name given to the schema evolved by Wiener and his co-workers. The awareness of Mead's significance in this development recedes as the process of codification makes increasing use of refined conceptual models and mathematical tools. A similar treatment is being accorded to the Freudian system as information theory moves into the new terrain of psychoanalysis. The distinctive features remain no less significant despite the indifference to these special problems by mathematical model-builders now fusing information theory with "small group dynamics."

---

[39] Moreno was aware of the work of Mead, and correctly criticized him for over-emphasizing the factor of language in communication. See *Psychodrama*, Vol. I (New York: Beacon House, 1946), p. 157.

[40] Norbert Wiener, *Cybernetics* (New York: John Wiley, 1948), p. 15.

Conclusion

Despite the similarity between Mead's "social behaviorism" and the theories of Freud, Sullivan, Schilder, and Moreno no psychoanalytic writer is known to have had an influence upon "social behaviorism." Mead was aware of the similarity between the "me" and the dream censor, but, in general, his attitude toward psychoanalysis seems to have been somewhat negative. He especially opposed Freud's emphasis upon sexual factors in personality. In turn, with the exception of Sullivan, Mead has hardly exerted any influence upon the psychoanalytic writers.

In recent days Mead's influence has perhaps been greatest in developments in theoretical sociology. His conception of the role of individual, as standing over against the organized attitudes of the other members of the group (represented internally by the generalized other) has become prominent in the field of the sociology of professions, occupations, and status-structures, as well as in social psychiatry.[41] The generalized other as a determinant of the individual's thinking is a major contribution to the sociology of knowledge. Mead's conceptual apparatus provides an instrument for studying the phenomena of sincerity and deception in social relations.[42] Yet Mead's most important contribution doubtless remains his analysis of the mechanisms of communication which underlie human relatedness at its core and personality in its emergence.[43]

Much fresh research needs to be done in the extant materials, including unpublished letters, before it will be possible to resolve or measure the influence of Freud on Mead.

In an article exploring the impact of Freud on American sociology in America, E. W. Burgess seems to adopt the position taken by the author of the present work. It may be noted, however, that Professor Burgess emphasizes the influence of psychoanalytic notions upon Freud's disciples. Burgess writes:

Mead's analysis of the act appears to show little or no Freudian influence but an integration of psychoanalytic concepts into the analysis of the stages in the act carried through by Mead's disciples has undoubtedly enriched the value of this instrument for research. E. W. Burgess, "The Influence of Sigmund Freud upon Sociology in the United States." American Journal of Sociology, XLV. 3 (November 1939), p. 372.

---

[41] Ed note: See now Harrison Gough "A Sociological Theory of Psychopathy," (1948), reprinted in Mental Health and Mental Disorder, ed. Arnold M. Rose (New York, W. W. Norton, 1955) 271–83; Bingham Dai, "A Socio-Psychiatric Approach to Personality Disorganization," (1951), ibid., pp. 314–24, esp. 321–22; also, the recent papers of John P. Spiegel in Psychiatry.

[42] I have discussed this topic in Self-Actualization: Loving and Strategic. Unpublished doctoral dissertation, Columbia University, 1951.

[43] Ed. note: For an appraisal of this aspect of Mead's thought, comparing him with the noted Jewish philosopher, Martin Buber; see Paul E. Pfuetze, The Social Self (New York: Bookman Associates, 1954).

Another bit of evidence—one from Mead's own pen—seems to suggest, if only by indirection, that Freud may have exerted a significant measure of influence on the elaboration of Mead's views. Evaluating the life work of Cooley, with whom he was so frequently linked, Mead writes:

> He (Cooley) did not feel it to be his primary task to state the whole of human behavior in scientific terms which would be equally applicable to primitive impulses and to the so-called higher expressions. *It followed that the beginnings of behavioristic and Freudian psychology did not attract him or suggest new avenues of approach.* (Mead, "Cooley's Contributions to American Social Thought." *American Journal of Sociology*, XXXV. 5 (March 1930), pp. 693–706, at p. 705.)

Mead *did* seek to "state the *whole* of human behavior in scientific terms." He *was* influenced by the beginnings of behavioristic psychology. Does this passage not seem to imply, therefore, that Freudian psychology "attracted" Mead or "suggested new avenues of approach" to him? (B. N.)

SUMMARY AND EVALUATION OF CHAPTER EIGHT

Mead viewed the self and society in process and showed that they were merely opposite sides of the same coin. His major concepts were the self, others, role taking and role playing, the generalized other, gestures, imaginative rehearsal, the play, the game, and the act. He wove these into a social psychology that allows us to see actors creating, sharing, and negotiating meaning by taking the role of the other, a process made possible by their distinctively human ability to regard their own actions and selves as objects.

The act is a complex phenomenen, which actors are capable of guiding because they have an end-in-view at the very beginning. The drama of human society consists in the ways they coordinate their different lines of action with ever-changing meanings. Individual actors always interpret and formulate experience. If this is true, why isn't *everything* constantly changing? Mead's answer lies in the "me." A person, the "I," cannot know what he has done in full until he has done it. But having done it, he does not randomly interpret it in any one or all of the infinite ways possible. He interprets it only in terms of the "me," which is in part the societal usages and definitions shared by others. Nevertheless, Mead largely presented man as a being of great creativity.

We must note several criticisms of Mead's sociology, however. One shortcoming is his failure to concern himself with the power structures that are capable of holding individuals to the dominant view of reality. Mead must be faulted for not considering the role that power plays in determining whose meanings receive priority. For this reason his optimistic democracy is inadequate; it implies a "give-and-take" process among persons, each regarding the other's point of view as equal to his own, and neglects to see power as a fact of life also.

In addition, Mead may have made the separation between humans and nonhumans too dogmatic. Charles Horton Cooley postulated an innate tendency toward sociality within the human organism. Mead would not. Furthermore, it is not clear that all nonhuman animals lack the ability to self-indicate.

Finally, Mead's explanation of the source of meaning also presents problems. He believed that meaning lies in the response of the other and nowhere else. Technically, this cannot be correct; meaning lies in the *coincidence* (or approximate coincidence) of the response of individual A (the other) with the response anticipated in A by individual B.

One of the most important implications of Mead's work has been forcefully expressed by Herbert Blumer.[1] Blumer's argument is that we would carry out social science research differently today if we had a thorough appreciation of Mead's sociology. According to Blumer, our images of society influence our methodology—the instruments and designs that we use in conducting social research. He believes that research methods should be in harmony with the empirical character of the social world—its wholeness, changeability, and obdurateness—rather than that of the physical world, as they are now. Blumer's point is that much of present-day sociological method and analysis is mistaken because it is not founded on the "root image" of man and society as Mead conceived it. "[T]he four customary means [of investigating the social world]—adhering to scientific protocol, engaging in replication, testing hypotheses, and using operational procedure—do not provide the empirical validation that genuine empirical social science requires. They give no assurance that premises, problems, data, relations, concepts, and interpretations are empirically valid. Very simply put, the only way to get this assurance is to go directly to the empirical social world."[2]

Blumer believes there are no easy answers or shortcuts. We must study the empirical world *directly* and maintain an abiding respect for it. Our concepts must be provisional and sensitive to the flux that is to be found there. Methods based on the assumption of interrelated "factors" or "entities," conceived in the minds of researchers as determinants of man's behavior, must be discarded. Only the *interaction* of real people provides the stuff of man's world—the same stuff that is responsible for its change.

A somewhat different view is offered by Norman K. Denzin.[3] For him the methodological considerations of symbolic interactionism require that (1) an investigation must be deemed incomplete until the researcher takes the role of the other (the subject) and thereby brings the symbols together with the interaction he is studying; (2) the symbols and self-conceptions of those being studied must be linked to the social circles in which they

---

[1] Herbert Blumer, *Symbolic Interactionism* (Englewood Cliffs, N.J.: Prentice-Hall, 1969), pp. 1–60.

[2] Ibid., p. 32.

[3] Norman K. Denzin, "The Methodologies of Symbolic Interaction: A Critical Review of Research Techniques," in Gregory P. Stone and Harvey A. Farberman (Eds.), *Social Psychology through Symbolic Interaction* (Waltham, Mass.: Ginn–Blaisdell, 1970), pp. 447–465.

arise; and (3) research methods must be capable of capturing the processual elements of human interaction. Denzin goes on to describe how each of the major research techniques now in use in sociology can be of use to the symbolic interactionist—even the survey, which many symbolic interactionists have been adverse to using up to this point.

But Denzin does not discuss what types of *analyses* of the data generated by these different methods would be in keeping with the symbolic interactionist perspective. The problem is that some of these methods are not designed to study *interaction* at all (at least not first hand, as Blumer recommends, since the surveyor may be only *asking about* people's interaction and not observing it). With many of these methods the researcher acquires data that represent the *products* of interaction (e.g., buying decisions or attitudes) or both the products and the general circumstances of interaction (e.g., the relationship of education to mobility on an aggregate level). Blumer insists that interaction itself be the focus of sociological investigation and proposes a method of both exploration and inspection (analysis) for symbolic interaction research.

Blumer, as a symbolic interactionist, would like us to observe social life "as it is"—on its own terms. How can this be done? Anything we see depends on a way of seeing. Joan Huber's[4] recent attack on symbolic-interactionist "theory" is pertinent at this point. Her argument is complex, but she faults symbolic interactionism on essentially two points. First, she points out that, for Mead, each organism is its own everyday scientist. Solutions, or truths, are seen as emerging in the behavior of the problem-solving person. Pragmatism is taken to be the logic by which truth emerges and is certified. Truth is therefore regarded as a process emerging *in nature*—from the actions and events themselves, each stage carrying the solutions for the problems of the previous stage. But the accumulation of everyday experience and solutions is not the same as science, Huber argues. Intersubjectivity (organisms agreeing on what works) is not the same as interobjectivity (procedures for judging the validity of knowledge). Modern science is logical–theoretical as well as empirical. Logic stipulates in advance how truth is to be obtained. And logic is needed to *organize* experience into word-pictures (theories), whose truth depends on the amount and type of evidence favoring hypotheses (instances of the theory). Experiences in themselves have no logic; facts do not speak for themselves.

Modern-day symbolic interactionists do not believe in the evolution of an ever-higher truth in nature, but they do speak of keeping the researcher's mind open so that theory can *emerge* in the field situation in conjunction with the feedback from the subjects being studied (in whose lives the researcher participates, if possible, by using the self–other orientation). Herein lies the second weakness of the symbolic interactionist's emergent view of theory, according to Huber: what is seen (and depicted in the theory) is a product of the agreements reached by the

---

[4] Joan Huber, "Symbolic Interaction as a Pragmatic Perspective," *American Sociological Review*, 38 (April 1973), 274–284.

participants or the influence of those who are most powerful. The problem throughout is the reluctance of the symbolic interactionist to interpose between man and his pursuit of knowledge some word-pictures and procedures in terms of which attempts can be more readily judged as valid or invalid.

Other writers and analysts have built on Mead. Irving Goffman,[5] who takes the more pessimistic attitude that the world of social encounters is always threatening to come undone, has nevertheless given an insightful account of the presentation of the self in everyday life by utilizing the language of drama—upstage, downstage, backstage, props, identity kits, and so on. According to Cuzzort, Goffman often sees interaction sustained by rather flimsy devices, and there is often a "phoniness" about people as they direct others' attention away from their stigmas. Reality is only what people are willing to treat it as and cannot be sustained by those who are uncooperative or unprepared.[6] Harold Garfinkel[7] has explored the hypothesis that there is a large, symbolic, taken-for-granted world, which, if violated or suspended, bars individuals from interaction and often leads to embarrassment, anger, or confusion.

Reality is negotiable because it can be seen and constructed from so many different points of view. A person is deviant not because he has committed a particular act, but because people's reactions define the act as deviant, thereby possibly setting the person on his wayward course. As they sustain their definition, they provide him with opportunities for the deviant "career."

Mead explored a new domain for sociology, with much profit for the discipline. The implications of his thought are numerous: to understand a person's action we must discover how *he* (the actor) constructs his world (his social and physical objects); inaccurate role taking is a source of problems in diverse human relationships—affecting workers in industry and spouses in the family alike; and individuals are constantly changing their identities and thus their performances. This last Meadian principle was discovered by a group of fraternity men who secretly befriended a shy girl on an American campus and treated her as popular and important for a year; they found that she had actually become popular and important and stayed so after their "experiment"! Even behavior-modification psychologists (who are growing in number) cannot dispense with symbolic-interaction approaches, in spite of their denials. When they give a patient a "token" for "good" behavior, the patient (according to the principles of strict "behaviorism") should *eat* the object. But he doesn't. Instead, it is altogether likely that such a reward helps modify the patient's behavior because the meaning attached to the token makes him feel better.

---

[5] Irving Goffman, *The Presentation of Self in Everyday Life* (Garden City, N.Y.: Doubleday, 1959).

[6] See R. P. Cuzzort, *Humanity and Modern Sociological Thought* (New York: Holt, Rinehart and Winston, 1969), pp. 173–192.

[7] Harold Garfinkel, *Studies in Ethnomethodology* (Englewood Cliffs, N.J.: Prentice-Hall, 1967).

For many admirers of Mead's work, its most important virtue is his view of man as a creative individual, constantly making the world anew. This idea turns the tables on one hundred years of previous thought in sociology: Whereas Comte and others looked for natural laws that define perimeters of human behavior, Mead pointed out that people *create* these perimeters themselves.[8]

SELECTED BIBLIOGRAPHY

Blasi, Anthony J. "Symbolic Interactionism as Theory." *Sociology and Social Research*, 56 (July 1972), 453–465.

Blumer, Herbert. *Symbolic Interactionism.* Englewood Cliffs. N.J.: Prentice-Hall, 1969.

Farberman, Harvey A. "Mannheim, Cooley, and Mead: Toward a Social Theory of Mentality." *The Sociological Quarterly*, 2 (Winter 1970), 3–13.

Manis, Jerome G., and Bernard N. Meltzer, (Eds.). *Symbolic Interaction.* Boston: Allyn and Bacon, 1967.

Meltzer, Bernard N. *The Social Psychology of George Herbert Mead.* Kalamazoo, Mich.: Center for Sociological Research, Western Michigan University, 1959.

Miller, David L. *George Herbert Mead: Self, Language and the World.* Austin: University of Texas Press, 1973.

Natanson, Maurice. *The Social Dynamics of George Herbert Mead.* Washington, D.C.: Public Affairs Press, 1956.

Pfuetze, Paul E. *The Social Self.* New York: Bookman Associates, 1954.

Rose, Arnold, (Ed.). *Human Behavior and Social Processes.* Boston: Houghton Mifflin, 1962.

Sheff, Thomas J. "Toward a Sociological Model of Consensus." *American Sociological Review*, 32 (February 1967), 32–46.

Shibutani, Tamotsu. *Society and Personality: An Interactionist Approach to Social Psychology.* Englewood Cliffs, N.J.: Prentice-Hall, 1961.

The Sociological Quarterly, 7 (Summer 1966), entire issue: "The Self and Related Concepts."

Stone, Gregory P., and Harvey A. Farberman (Eds.). *Social Psychology through Symbolic Interaction.* Waltham, Mass.: Ginn–Blaisdell, 1970.

Stoodley, Bartlett H., (Ed.). *Society and Self.* New York: Free Press, 1963.

Strauss, Anselm, (Ed.). *George Herbert Mead on Social Psychology.* Chicago: University of Chicago Press, 1956.

---

[8] I am indebted to my colleague, Barbara Kalkas, for this insight.

NINE

Karl Mannheim

"Are there ultimate truths apart from what society believes
to be true?"

—STUDENT COMMENT

"[I]t was never clear to me—and seemingly never clear to
Mannheim—how . . . 'democratic planning' was to occur
or how a 'collectively agreed value policy' was to emerge."

—STUDENT COMMENT

General Introduction

Karl Mannheim (1893–1947) was born of Jewish parents in Budapest, where he attended school and also began his university studies. Part
of Hungary's small middle class,[1] he was, like some persons of his social
position rather marginal as a Jewish intellectual. Mannheim was a member
of the Society for Social Sciences, a positivistically oriented group in which
the works of sociologists in other countries were discussed. At the same
time, he belonged to another group, led by Georg Lukács, which took
the more judgmental stance that man's condition is one of increasing
spiritual impoverishment and loss of human dignity.

Mannheim married a fellow student, Juliska Lang, a psychologist.
In 1919, after completing his doctoral dissertation on structural analysis,
he received a position in philosophy at the University of Budapest. Because of his (loose) connections with the Soviet regime, he lost this
appointment within a few months and fled to Germany. Here, in 1925,
he secured a teaching position (as an unsalaried lecturer) at the University of Heidelberg, where he had studied earlier, and then, in 1929,

---

[1] See Lewis A. Coser, *Masters of Sociological Thought* (New York: Harcourt,
1971), pp. 441–449.

became professor of sociology and economics at Frankfort University. Although Mannheim was sympathetic to the labor movement in Germany, he remained aloof from political activity and wrote most of his works on the sociology of knowledge, including his now famous *Ideology and Utopia.*

In 1933, Mannheim escaped the Hitler regime by emigrating to England, where he taught at the London School of Economics and, in 1946, became professor of education at the University of London. In England, he turned toward education for the reconstruction and stabilization of society, thus sharply altering the course of his career, and wrote *Diagnosis of Our Time* and *Man and Society in an Age of Reconstruction*, among other works.[2] Mannheim accepted the directorship of UNESCO in 1947, but died before he could assume his duties.

Mannheim's philosophy and sociology are difficult to understand. He started out with questions largely belonging to epistemology: in what relationship does the knower stand to the known, and how is it that he can claim to know anything at all? From there Mannheim moved, almost imperceptibly, to the problem of obtaining sociocultural knowledge: can the knower be objective, and does he have special problems in knowing the characteristics of society, the object of his study? Mannheim's task was even larger; he wanted to know how historically situated man achieves the freedom to see beyond his society, to escape some of the limitations of being a mere product of his society. The other side of this question— how society itself can be transformed and kept free—also engaged Mannheim. His sociology of knowledge, his major work and his contributions to which Mannheim viewed as tentative, reflected these changing interests. It evolved from a way of *interpreting* modes of thought, in Mannheim's early period, to, later, the basis for a proposed *solution* for the crises confronting modern man (see Selection 9.2 by Remmling for a discussion of these changes). Can the sociology of knowledge, which shows the susceptibility of what is known to the viewpoint of the knower, also provide the toleration for different groups' viewpoints and the vision to reach beyond them?

Mannheim believes that objects are not *ontic*, that is, they do not

---

[2] Mannheim's major works, written during his years of residence in both Germany and England, are the following (dates of composition given after titles): *Essays on the Sociology of Knowledge* (1921–1930), Paul Kecskemeti (Ed.) (London: Routledge & Kegan Paul, 1952); *Ideology and Utopia* (1929–1931), Louis Wirth and Edward Shils (Trans.) (New York: Harcourt, 1936); *Essays on Sociology and Social Psychology* (1922–1938) (London: Routledge & Kegan Paul, 1953); *Essays on the Sociology of Culture* (early 1930s) (New York: Oxford University Press, 1956); *Man and Society in an Age of Reconstruction* (New York: Harcourt, 1940); *Diagnosis of Our Times* (London: Routledge & Kegan Paul, 1943); *Freedom, Power and Democratic Planning* (New York: Oxford University Press, 1950, published posthumously).

have real beings.[3] Since they cannot speak for themselves, what an individual knows of them depends on his way of looking at them. This frame of reference, or perspective, interposes itself between the knower (subject) and the known (object). Mannheim started with a critical epistemology: without a perspective an individual cannot find anything; yet with one, he finds only what the perspective allows him to find.[4] The object changes as the frame of reference changes—only a dogmatist could hold otherwise. A work of art, for example, from one point of view is simply an acrylic; from another, surrealism; and from another, avant garde. What something is on the existential level, Mannheim believed, remains the same; what changes is one's *way* of knowing it, which is a matter of "logic" whose validity is not to be confused with empirical truth, that is, *what* we know about something. The mind, which originates the way of looking at something, has a creative role. But it is, we shall see, also historically and socially situated.

In Mannheim's view, there can be no absolute truth because change takes place in the very presuppositions, or norms, on which truth, rightness, and all that is taken as existing are based. To know what these presuppositions are is the goal of "structural analysis," a method that attempts to arrive at a total view of things. It is based on neology, the study of the categories of knowledge—the terms in which things can be known. One can make a structural analysis of all types of intellectual creations. Such an analysis of art objects, for example, would entail considering the discrete elements of their existence, then very carefully constructing a transcendental motif that incorporates their essence and gives unity to their changes through history. This fusion of the situated particular with the overriding general is called *interpretation*, a process in which the pretheoretical becomes theoretical. Man refuses to relinquish this propensity for theoretical understanding because it gives him the meaning of objects in a broader sense than his mere experience of objects can; moreover, it marks man as distinct. He wishes to know what spheres

---

[3] In addition to Mannheim's main writings mentioned above, our discussion draws on Kurt H. Wolff's useful summary in his introduction to Kurt Wolff (Ed.), *From Karl Mannheim* (New York: Oxford University Press, 1971), pp. xi–cxxxiii.

[4] This was one of the main bases for the extension of Mannheim's thought, and he seems to have been slightly affected by the logical positivists. In effect, Mannheim implied that what exists depends on one's finding operations; it is unclear whether or not he would have concluded, in addition, that what cannot be specified in observational operations cannot be presumed to exist. Or, he was suggesting that truth is obtained according to a criterion, and without the specification of some criterion, truth "in itself" cannot be said to exist. This latter position—the idea that knowledge is intimately linked up with action—seems to have been one of the foundations on which he later based his activism and pragmatism.

of meaning objects objectify, what principles govern the emergence of novel cultural manifestations. This extrinsic (abstract) interpretation is a "higher" form of understanding than that gained through a knowledge of any field of culture (art, social philosophies, etc.) in itself (the intrinsic interpretation). What an action or an action product documents (its interpretation) does not depend on the intention of the actor. (An influence of Freud on Mannheim.)

Mannheim himself made a structural analysis of *Weltanschauungen*, that is, men's philosophies of society, or outlooks on the world. Since history and society change a great deal (compared with nature), so do *Weltanschauungen*. It is difficult to interpret these for a number of reasons: several *Weltanschauungen* may be prevalent at the same time in (especially modern) society; the same element, for example, pacifism, may have a different meaning, or function, in two different *Weltanschauungen*; and the exact connection between the *Weltanschauung* of a category of people and their experiential, social, economic, and political base in society is not easy to ascertain, nor the way the *Weltanschauung* influences knowledge. One of Mannheim's major studies was the structural analysis of the conservative *Weltanschauung*, which had become an integrated object, overarching style of thought. Because of challenges from philosophers hostile to their views, conservatives reviewed and legitimated the present social order on the basis of the so-called truth that the parts of societies are organically connected, according to a "necessary," or natural, plan deeply rooted in the past.

The historical method of structural analysis was still most prominent in Mannheim's analysis at this point in his career.[5] That is, he believed that one can understand conservatism by interpreting it as the product of conservatives who are historically situated actors, belonging to a particular era or epoch. It is limited and relative. History, as Hegel emphasized, is a constant process of change. Later, largely as a result of confrontation with Marxian ideas, Mannheim introduced the sociological analysis of *Weltanschauungen* in order to enrich his historical method. Through sociological analysis, one can show the compatibility or harmony among a group's stratum position (generation, religion, economic status, etc.), its attitudes and aspirations, and its outlook on the world. The reality from which a *Weltanschauung* springs is a *social*, and changing reality, but not just economic. The analyst must then regard his construction of the world view of the group under consideration as an ideal type and must carefully assess its fit and utility with reference to its actual influence on the group's way of thinking.

Mannheim's sociology of knowledge was largely prompted by the Marxist concept that the dominance of particular ideas in a society

---

[5] About 1924. See Wolff, *From Karl Mannheim*, p. xxviii.

depends on the control of major power resources by the "ideators," whose dominance, in turn, depends on their relationship to the material and social means of production. However, Mannheim shunned what he considered to be the vulgarization of this concept, namely, the notion that the ideas of an individual or group turn out to be nothing but the reflection in consciousness of the objective economic actions entailed in making a living. He could not believe that "from the socially established way in which man bakes bread or cobbles shoes, his conscious activity, however complex, could be explained."[6] In Mannheim's view, to judge cognition, ideas, and knowledge only in terms of their effectiveness in promoting the economic interest of the "ideators" is crudely ideological. He would not accept such an approach because it considers one assertion to be as good as any other and concludes that objectivity is therefore impossible. Moreover, the tendency to regard the thought of all groups as merely the instrument for promoting their material interests would foreclose the operation of rationality where it is still possible. That is, it would prevent the comparison of different points of view in the hope of finding the one that might be more correct. Instead of accomplishing this, however, vulgar Marxism succeeds only in mystifying. All knowledge is deemed arbitrary from this point of view since it is considered only as a mask for group interests.

Marxism presented Mannheim with a more general and important problem, the necessity of answering the question facing German historical idealism at this time: if an individual's ideas can only be understood with reference to his age, why cannot they simply be reduced to the material circumstances of which Marx spoke? Mannheim's response was that ideas are *both* material and spiritual. He believed, therefore, that one must reconcile the individual with the realities of society in a way that properly recognizes the uniqueness of the human spirit. One must, in other words, recognize the impossibility of *totally* confining the spirit within the context of social structure.

Mannheim lived during the modern age, a period characterized chiefly by the growing awareness of the relativity of all things. People have come to accept the idea that as their society or groups change, their points of view about the world also change. Mannheim explained this new thinking as the result of the transformation in the structure of society since the Enlightenment. The market economy of modern society replaced the tyrannies of political or religious authority, which had previously enforced a consensus of thought, with considerable indirect control over the individual; it consequently placed upon the individual the responsibility of being aware of social changes. A plurality in society and points of view

---

[6] Jacques Barzun, *Darwin, Marx, Wagner* (Garden City, N.Y.: Doubleday, Anchor Books, 1958), p. 133.

became possible not only because the social structure was now indeed highly differentiated, but also because man was now free to perceive this mix for himself. Such rapid change made the old social forms obsolete, so that any claims to absolute truth were easily suspect. Old myths about the necessity of the given forms of society and ways of thinking broke down and could no longer guarantee the interests of the powerful. According to Mannheim, this made possible the formation of a true, noncoerced consensus in society. He believed that the opportunity to view positions as relative is a prerequisite to *correcting* them rather than an invitation to debunk them. The spirit of freedom and truth could now hold broader sway in society.

What Mannheim feared, however, was the decline of utopian thought and the corresponding ascendance of a fully rationally mastered society, which would make a thing of man himself (a possibility Weber, too, had feared). He believed that in such a society thinking, the means by which man elevates himself above his existence and achieves the ecstasy of utopia, would stop because everything would be seen in the same way— in terms of cause and effect. Only if man can choose the point of view by which he interprets the world around him can his thinking be free.

Broadly conceived, thought is existentially influenced when it is not immanent (when it does not issue from the object of thought itself) and when it can be shown to be influenced by extratheoretical factors (tendencies other than those of the mind alone). Thought and its products are affected by the thinker's (or group's) frame of reference, which is, in turn, affected by the thinker's (or group's) position in society. This seems especially true of sociohistorical knowledge and less true, Mannheim believed, of highly "rational" knowledge such as mathematics, in which the frame of reference or presuppositions of truth are virtually uniform.[7]

We are necessarily more intimate with sociohistorical knowledge because it is anchored in a set of values. The objects of the human sciences are also incorporated into the process of cognition and come to be what they are in part because of cognition. This does not mean, however, that a degree of objectivity in the study of cultural–intellectual phenomena is unattainable, nor that we are stuck in a morass of relativism in which no reliable knowledge is possible. Relativism does accept one important insight—that historical thinking is bound up with the concrete position in the life of the actor; it presents difficulties because it fails to accept another *equally important* insight which Mannheim termed relationism—that the evaluation of such knowledge should not be based on *static* prototypes of truth in which the subjective standpoint of the knower is absent. This caveat does not apply to such statements as

---

[7] "[T]he more compelling and rational a thought is, the less is it caused empirically" (Wolff, *From Karl Mannheim*, p. xxiv).

$2 \times 2 = 4$ because their truth is presumably the same regardless of one's perspective. But it does apply to a claim for the truth of social knowledge. In Mannheim's words, "there are spheres of thought [especially the cultural–intellectual] in which it is impossible to conceive of absolute truth existing independently of the values and position of the subject and unrelated to the social context."[8] He was proposing that the very foundations of knowledge change with changes in society and history. Unlike the old epistemologists, who needed to believe in an absolute sphere of truth, Mannheim was able to suspend judgment while searching for the view(s) that entails the "optimum" truth.

As we stated earlier, Mannheim's interests changed radically after his emigration to England in 1933. He was in a new milieu, and the war years brought a new sense of urgency. He marveled at the absence of rancor among groups espousing different points of view. He perceived that this was the result of a larger consensus among them, something that seemed to have been lacking in Germany. In England Mannheim lacked the prestige (and insulation) of the professorship he had occupied in Germany. Being a man of interest, he spoke to many audiences and in this way assimilated the new climate. At the same time, his zest for constructive action fed on the new philosophies of democracy and pragmatism, which gave him a new sense of optimism. He now considered the possibility of observing the development of knowledge as it is linked up with action. Again, this time by making commitments to action, Mannheim tried to avoid the malaise of relativism. Man and society would have to be reconstructed; planning for freedom and democracy would have to go ahead. Three books of this period (1933–1957) mark his general interest in societal engineering and indicate some shifts in what he perceived to be the problems and requirements: *Man and Society in an Age of Reconstruction, Diagnosis of Our Time,* and *Freedom, Power, and Democratic Planning.* He now viewed sociology as "the most secularized approach to the problems of human life."[9]

The problem for the modern world was that neither laissez-faire nor unplanned regulation was adequate. Mannheim, especially in what Gunter Remmling refers to as stages 2 and 3 of his development (Selection 9.2, believed that more training for substantive rationality (the interpretation of the overall direction and goals of a society) was necessary. He came to see democracy, of which he was initially skeptical, as crucial to planning, for it encourages the individual to be more competent and fosters leadership among the masses. The new realities of the industrial mass state had to be recognized: the tendency to repress and renounce impulsive satisfactions, the quick grasp for leadership, the manipulation of

---

[8] Mannheim, *Ideology and Utopia,* p. 79.

[9] Wolff, *From Karl Mannheim,* p. cxxix.

mass communication, new problems in the relationship between man and the machine, and leisure. Mannheim proposed giving power in small amounts and only to those who *merit* it and have the confidence of the people. Planning is both desirable and necessary (although the question, Who plans the planners? haunted him); and the liberal value of free development of the personality is its goal.

In *Diagnosis of Our Time*, Mannheim examined the conditions that produce totalitarianism (in societies that *were* planned), especially the emotional factors, so that man might know how to avoid these developments in the future. He was especially interested, however, in the crisis of values in modern society and how both education and religion (Christianity) might be enlisted to inculcate those values necessary for planning for freedom. Mannheim now supplemented his earlier structural approach with a social psychology. In his final work, *Freedom, Power, and Democratic Planning*, Mannheim was concerned about the undesirable effects of power centralization after the war. He warned that democratic vigilance would be necessary.

Introduction to Selections 9.1 and 9.2

Mannheim's escape from relativism was evidenced by his attempt to clarify the notion of ideology and its role in thought. He saw an antithesis between ideology, which is, in one sense, the fictions that are used and propagated to stabilize a social order, and utopia, the "orientation which transcends reality and which at the same time breaks the bonds of the existing order."[10] Both ideologies and utopian thought may transcend reality: The difference is that ideologies are "ideas which never succeed *de facto* in the realization of their projected contents"[11] because they cannot pass over into action in such a way as to alter the social order with which they clash. Individuals who subscribe to ideologies fall prey to a "false consciousness"; they fail to understand that such ideas are chimerical or that in order to realize them they must *change* their very life situations. These visions are necessarily unattainable because their projections are out of touch with social realities, but the implicit strictures on thought prevent the everyday person from gaining this insight. Mannheim saw utopian thought, on the other hand, as part of the answer to the estrangement between individuals and their culture since he felt that through it they would seek changes in their life situations. He discussed four main types of utopian mentality in historical order: the orgiastic chiliasm of the Anabaptists, the liberal humanitarian idea, the conservative idea, and the socialist–communist utopia.

---

[10] Mannheim, *Ideology and Utopia*, p. 192.

[11] Ibid., p. 194.

As we noted above, Mannheim suggested that the theoretical basis of knowledge must be revised in terms of relationism, the idea that the very criteria and categories of truth change with the perspective of the knower. Relativism, the older static ideal, would not incorporate this change and thus was forced into the nihilistic position of rejecting all claims to truth. In relationism, objectivity can take on a new meaning. Essentially, one must attain objectivity with respect to knowledge *indirectly*, by understanding the perspective of the individual or group making claims to truth and by knowing what effect this perspective has on such claims. How one specifically accomplishes this touches on Mannheim's treatment of ideology, which we discuss below.

The problem of the validity of knowledge now arose. If knowledge depends upon one's perspective, is truth outside of or beyond the particular perspective at all possible? Mannheim first attempted to answer affirmatively by asserting that ideas are "right" if they succeed in facilitating adjustment to a given situation at a particular historical stage. He himself later saw this view as unsatisfactory, for, as Robert K. Merton points out,[12] it begs the question, How does one determine what a correct adjustment is? Mannheim attempted to salvage the idea of validity in other ways, for example, by making it depend on the scope of an individual's assertions: a claim for only partial knowledge has the possibility of being valid, while a claim for complete knowledge does not.

Mannheim's most serious attempt to avoid relativism, however, was his effort to neutralize the distorting effects of ideology on knowledge by bringing *out into the open*, the relationship of ideology to the life situations of its advocates. He believed that by means of specific counteractions one could rise above distorted thought and gain greater objectivity. He distinguished several conceptions of ideology, which are described by John K. Rhoads in Selection 9.1. The *particular conception of ideology* involves claims by an individual based on errors in logic or fact and motivated by personal interests. These distortions are correctable at the level of individuals on the basis of standards they share. In the *general conception of ideology*, an *entire* system of thought, generally propounded by a group rather than an individual, is considered suspect because it has been influenced by the group's concrete situation. The individual merely mirrors the outlook of the group, whose assumptions he is incapable of questioning. Again, one must oppose such views by revealing their connection with group interests. The idea that only the thinking of one's opponents is determined in this way is called the *special form of the total conception of ideology*.

12 Robert K. Merton, "Karl Mannheim and the Sociology of Knowledge," in Robert K. Merton, *Social Theory and Social Structure* (New York: Free Press, 1968), p. 557.

The final concept leads directly into Mannheim's sociology of knowledge. In contradistinction to the special form of the total conception, the *general form of the total conception of ideology* supposes that the thinking of *all* groups is determined. When *both* parties to a conflict are prepared to recognize the situated effects on their outlooks, the effects of ideology can be neutralized. At this point the exchange becomes nonevaluative because the defense of one party's view and the attack on the adversary's yield to analysis. The search for a larger objectivity can then proceed. But who is to pursue the higher synthesis? Mannheim's answer was the intelligentsia since they are presumably recruited from constantly *varying* social strata and life situations. Presumably, they are therefore less passionately tied to any particular point of view and their vision can therefore reach further.

The essay by Rhoads is concerned solely with Mannheim's sociology of knowledge, the area of development for which he is most frequently credited in sociology. Rhoads begins with a discussion of the production of cultural knowledge in German historiography, which had to face the problem that sociocultural history changes and the cultural scientist's views are affected by his place in the social order. Mannheim took the position that to demonstrate validity for statements of sociocultural fact, one must see the way in which they are related to the thinkers' life situations.

For the purpose of clarifying Mannheim's formulations of the sociology of knowledge, which are not easily grasped, Rhoads distinguishes his several major conceptions—*Weltanschauung*, relativism, agnosticism, relationism. After describing Mannheim's development of the general conception of the total conception of ideology, just outlined above, Rhoads presents several methods of relational thinking, the last of which goes beyond perspectivism to a type of synthesis.

There are weaknesses and errors in Mannheim's sociology of knowledge, as Rhoads indicates. However, one cannot ignore the importance of the task assayed by Mannheim for the world today, especially in view of the need to reconcile the competing claims of hostile groups.

In Selection 9.2, Gunter Remmling attempts to map the major shifts that occurred throughout Mannheim's entire career. It is therefore a fitting article for this part of our volume. At the same time, Remmling brings into focus some of the events to which Mannheim was responding when he made his shifts in position.

In the first stage, the one largely analyzed by Rhoads in the foregoing article, Mannheim defined his approach to the sociology of knowledge, drawing on the views and ideas of many other scholars. His is called a radical sociology of knowledge of the "functional" variety since all aspects of culture, including knowledge, are viewed as determined by society (the absolute stratum) through intervening processes in which the mind of the perceiving individual defines the objects of his world. However, these objects of the mind are the products of the particular *Weltanschauung* of the individual, who is bound by the historical conditions in which he lives. (i.e., from a given standpoint of the individual within these conditions). Mannheim believed that the sociology of knowledge could serve mankind by enabling the individual not only to unmask the other's thought, through refuting the ideology in which it is cloaked, but also his own as well, thus allowing for more consideration of the other's point of view. The intellectual, who lacks gross political and economic attachments, is capable of greater objectivity and is thus suited to the task of mediation.

In the second stage, Mannheim became more the pragmatic societal engineer. He sought to avert totalitarian episodes by reconstructing society in such a way as to prevent those crises, stemming from internal contradictions, on which totalitarian movements so often feed. A looser relation between thought and social structure was now admitted.

During his third phase, a direct response to the outbreak of war, Mannheim gave more serious consideration to the nonrational, or emotional, aspects of man's behavior and assessed the ability of ethical systems such as Christianity to enlist man's energies toward a planned social order. Remmling describes this last phase as one in which Mannheim more carefully took social power into consideration.

9.1

Karl Mannheim's Sociology of Knowledge
JOHN K. RHOADS

In order to understand Karl Mannheim's formulations of the sociology of knowledge, it is necessary to face the question of what he meant by knowledge. What he meant was generally shared by German-speaking historians, philosophers, and other scholars in the nineteenth and early twentieth centuries. On the one hand there was the majestic knowledge of mathematics and natural science, whose objects of study exist in space; on the other there was the knowledge gained by the cultural disciplines, whose objects of study are the actions, thinking, and products of men. Although men exist in space and fall within the universe of objects studied by science, behind their actions and material creations are thoughts, intentions, and volitions presumed to be unanalyzable from a purely scientific standpoint. Thoughts proceed in a nonphysical universe not determined by the laws of natural science. If the methods of mathematics and natural science cannot be applied to the sphere of human action and thinking, the epistemological problem arises of the validity of cultural knowledge.[1] Does an assertion about men's actions in a given period of history have the same kind of truth-value as the proposition that $2 \times 2 = 4$? Mannheim's attempt to find an answer to the vexing question of validity led him to formulate the various concepts and orientations identifiable as his version of the sociology of knowledge.

Let us examine in greater detail the character of cultural knowledge. It was widely assumed by scholars within the Idealistic philosophical tradition that the actions and thinking of men are in the final analysis unique. Hence, it is impossible to generalize about them and analyze them in terms of analytical scientific frameworks like the laws of the classical economics.[2] However, it *is* possible to interpret the richness and variety of their meaning, which is to be intuitively grasped by the cultural scientist divested of his own predispositions in order to understand them from the historical actor's own viewpoint. The assumption was generally held that action and thinking occur in specific historical contexts, which shape them

---

[1] Talcott Parsons, *The Structure of Social Action* (New York: Free Press, 1949), pp. 473–474.

[2] Ibid., p. 476. The scholars of the Idealistic tradition refused to accept the classical economics of Adam Smith and others.

and which must be taken into account in comprehending them. Theorizing in the cultural sciences accordingly took the form of detecting meaningful unities among cultural events. Since each action is modified by its context, all the parts form a meaningful unity provided by that context. There was a further assumption that human history is constituted by a succession of holistic contexts, each of which forms a meaningful unity different from the others in the historical sequence. It became the task of the cultural scientist and historian to grasp somehow these wholes. Synthesis rather than analysis was the order of the day.

These unique historical configurations are expressible as ideas, for their unities are meaningful unities. For example, Werner Sombart, writing within the tradition we are discussing, characterized the capitalist system as acquisitive, competitive, and rational. It was an easy jump from such meaningful contexts to the concept of an overarching "spirit of an age" or "global outlook," which provides an entire civilization with its unity. The task then becomes to fit every part of an epoch into this global outlook or *Weltanschauung*. The kind of knowledge Mannheim most frequently had in mind when he spoke of historically determined knowledge was the *Weltanschauung* of any given historical era. It was such knowledge to which the method of the sociology of knowledge was to be applied.

In an early essay Mannheim advanced the position that the spirit of an epoch, its *Weltanschauung*, is over and above, apart from, the cultural objectifications that express it. *All* cultural objectifications, such as art, religions, legal codes, literary works, and ethical maxims, are vehicles for its meaning.[3] The global outlook of a civilization is over and above men's cultural creations that carry it, yet it is discoverable by a comparative analysis of cultural products. In this essay Mannheim held out the possibility of a single global outlook but adduced no examples. The purely hypothetical possibility of only one source of unity for any civilization is corroborated by his later writings in which he stated there are always a number of *Weltanschauungen* competing for dominance.[4] For example, in the first half of the nineteenth century liberalism and conservatism were two polar outlooks struggling for acceptance.[5] The notion of a unity of outlook in civilization was somewhat compromised by the ceaseless struggle of contending views.

Although nowhere does Mannheim present a comprehensive account of what kinds of meaning and knowledge are contained within any *Weltanschauung*, there are clues in his formulations and examples. Global outlooks make purely factual observations as in conservative historicism's observation that irrational factors are important in any society's development.[6] They also express value-judgments, exemplified by bourgeois liberal-

[3] Karl Mannheim, *Essays on the Sociology of Knowledge*, ed. Paul Kecskemeti (London: Routledge and Kegan Paul, 1952), pp. 38–42.

[4] Mannheim, *Essays on the Sociology of Knowledge*, pp. 180–181.

[5] Karl Mannheim, *Ideology and Utopia*, trans. Louis Wirth and Edward Shils (New York: Harcourt, 1936), pp. 307–308.

[6] Ibid., p. 120.

ism's commitment to the use of reason in developing political ends and the means to attain them.[7] Therefore, parliamentary discussions and debates as institutionalized forms of reason are positive values. In addition, they hold out goals for the society to collectively strive for. An example is the revolutionary goal of the millennial kingdom on earth of the Anabaptists, who subscribed to a "Utopian" world view.[8] Concepts like freedom, categorical frameworks, and standards of conduct are also to be found. These are examples of the kinds of meaning that constitute the knowledge of world views, which must be interpreted and understood by the cultural scientist.[9]

An obvious question suggested by this discussion is how true can such heterogeneous kinds of knowledge be? The question goes to the core of Mannheim's sociology of knowledge, for he was not content merely to delineate the constituents of global outlooks and their reflections in cultural products. He was tormented by the more difficult question of which global outlooks approximate truth most closely. Indeed, he described the situation in the modern world of competing outlooks and points of view as "the contemporary predicament of thought," in which a fundamental agreement is lacking.[10] The problem in the light of such a predicament becomes one of overcoming the distressing relativity of views within modern man's situation.

Now truth to Mannheim is not to be found in the relationship of an assertion to what it refers—a definition propounded by logicians. Rather, by truth, particularly cultural-historical truth, he meant an attribute of existence, more specifically an attribute of the historical process itself. The distinction between truth as discourse and truth as existence is an important one, for Mannheim's commitment to the latter directs attention to history itself. What does one discover when he contemplates history? The most obvious recognition is that history continually changes, consisting of contending and evolving *Weltanschauungen*. If truth is located in history but history continually changes, it follows that cultural-historical truth changes. The changing character of historical truth contrasts dramatically with the kind of truth embodied in the timeless proposition that $2 \times 2 = 4$ and in the timeless generalizations of the classical mechanics. The changing character of cultural knowledge and the timeless, absolute knowledge of mathematics and natural science give rise to Mannheim's distinction between "static and dynamic thought."[11]

---

[7] Ibid., pp. 122–123.

[8] Ibid., pp. 211–219.

[9] In essays subsequent to "*On the Interpretation of Weltanschauung*," Mannheim modified somewhat the ontological status of a global outlook by characterizing it as an ideal-type. The outlook of an epoch is a methodological device constructed by the sociologist of knowledge, and no intellectual creation embodies all of its dimensions. See Mannheim, *Ideology and Utopia*, pp. 210–211, 307–308.

[10] Ibid., pp. 5–13.

[11] Karl Mannheim, *Essays on the Sociology of Knowledge*, pp. 84–97.

Furthermore, there is extreme variability in the way historical knowledge is gathered both at different times and by different historians. The very categories utilized to describe historical processes vary as in the example given by Mannheim of the concept of evolution.[12] In Western countries outside Germany the concept of evolution resulted in a view of history as an atomized causal sequence of evolutionary stages, whereas in Germany evolution was conceived as a series of dialectical transformations. Students of history also disagree on the facticity of what they report and employ different selective principles to decide what facts are relevant. Such disagreements lead to pessimistic judgments about the objectivity of history. Furthermore, underlying the varying historical categories and selective principles is the standpoint of the student of culture, whose own social location affects his choices. Thus, a German scholar would likely interpret historical change differently than an English scholar and a positivist differently than a historicist, a Marxist, and a Hegelian.[13] By way of contrast, one gets no inkling of the nationality, class, or occupational location of a natural scientist from his statements about his subject; his standpoint does not affect his assertions. The changes that occur in the knowledge of natural science consist strictly in the discovery of hitherto unknown truths and the correction of errors. Such linear progress does not seem to be in evidence in the cultural fields.

The impact of the cultural scientist's social location on his interpretations of the global outlooks of other historical epochs in the final analysis boils down to the problem of his own values interfering with his historical understanding. Is it possible for a member of one epoch permeated by a given outlook to completely understand the outlook of a different epoch? The cultural scientist and historian are participants in the very historical process they strive to discover—a problem that does not hinder the efforts of the natural scientist. Mannheim's attempt to find a solution to this problem guided his formulations of the sociology of knowledge.

From the foregoing discussion can be detected two distinct but related problems that make the validity of cultural-historical knowledge problematic. The first of these is the change of knowledge itself through historical periods. Moreover, it is imprudent to hold that these changes are in the nature of an accumulation of truths and a gradual elimination of errors. The second problem is the difficulties faced by the cultural scientist in understanding those world views alien to his own perspective, for his own values hinder an adequate grasp. According to Mannheim, the social location of the student of culture reflects itself in his understanding of culture.

A final distinction between natural and historical knowledge relating to the latter's validity deserves comment. Social-historical events must be understood in terms of their meanings, which is to say that the cultural scientist must apply *verstehen*. An example given by Mannheim is a family,

---

[12] Ibid., p. 100.

[13] Ibid., p. 102.

which must be understood by the conceptions its members have of their situations. Family norms are as much a part of their situations as the landscape and furniture, and they must be grasped in terms of what they mean.[14] Cultural phenomena, unlike physical events, cannot be reduced to a cluster of correlations among purely external, observable facts. It is quite obvious that the method of interpretation (*verstehen*) must also be employed in the historical understanding of global outlooks and world perspectives. The difference between the observation of externals and the understanding of internal processes of thought is clearly a factor separating the natural and the cultural sciences.

In the light of the foregoing differences between scientific and cultural-historical knowledge Mannheim outlines three possible epistemological positions pertaining to their validity.[15] The first holds that any thinking that manifests the impact of the thinker's life situation cannot be true. This position Mannheim refers to as relativism. It obviously rules out all cultural-historical knowledge as possessing validity on the assumption that the social position of the asserter penetrates those of his thoughts that refer to historical and cultural events. Such knowledge is merely relative—relative, that is, to the standpoint of the thinker. The only valid knowledge would be that of mathematics and natural science, in which it is impossible to infer anything about the mathematician when he states that $2 \times 2 = 4$. According to Mannheim, this epistemological viewpoint was worked out by philosophers after natural science had originated.

The second position holds that the validity of any thinking that can be demonstrated to reflect the life situation of the thinker is indeterminate. It is impossible, for example, to ascertain whether the political statements made by a liberal or a conservative have any grain of truth. This epistemology would obviously make it impossible to determine either the truth or falsity of cultural-historical knowledge. One could characterize this position as agnostic.

Mannheim rejects both of these distasteful positions for a more satisfying one that holds that the extent to which a given unit of cultural-historical knowledge is valid can be ascertained *only* by recognizing the way in which it is related to the thinker's life situation. The tables are turned on relativism, which disbars knowledge subject to this distortion from possessing validity. This position Mannheim refers to as relationism. According to him epistemologies are created by philosophers only after certain kinds of knowledge are discovered. Relativism reflects the general philosophical stance of positivism, which served to legitimate natural scientific knowledge *ex post facto*.[16] Now the time is at hand for thinkers to create a new epistemology that will legitimate and clarify cultural-historical knowledge. The possibility of relationism is Mannheim's attempted fulfillment of this need, and, as we shall see, relationism incorporates the sociology of knowledge.

---

[14] Karl Mannheim, *Ideology and Utopia*, pp. 43–46.

[15] Karl Mannheim, *Ideology and Utopia*, pp. 283–286, 78–80.

[16] Karl Mannheim. *Ideology and Utopia*, pp. 288–290.

The theoretical ground has been prepared for the appearance of a relational epistemology, certain advances in the thinking of cultural scientists and philosophers having occurred that suggest its outlines. In the first place, states Mannheim, there has occurred the "self-relativization of thought."[17] This is the recognition that thinking is not an autonomous sphere but reflects, expresses, and is the concomitant of factors other than thought. This is to say that it is not possible to offer a complete explanation of the appearance of an idea in terms of another idea. In the second place, those factors to which thought is relativized, of which it is an expression, are recognized to be social, especially economic. Preceding the cognizance of the impact of socio-economic factors, for which positivism was mainly responsible, was the attempt to account for thinking as the emanation of a religious sphere.[18] In this case thinking emanates from a suprahistorical source, namely God. In the third place, the "unmasking turn of mind" materialized. The unmasking mind attempts not to refute the ideas of an opponent by demonstrating with evidence or logic their falsity, but rather disintegrates them by revealing the function they serve in his life situation.[19] The focus shifts from the truth or falsity of what an opponent states to how his statements serve his interests.

The mind that attempts to unmask a person or group by these techniques leads Mannheim to his various conceptions of ideology,[20] which in turn eventuate into the sociology of knowledge and its bearing on relationism. By the particular conception of ideology Mannheim means the statements made by an individual that are viewed with skepticism by an opponent. The statements can range all the way from deliberate and conscious lies to half consciously held distortions, which the individual himself may only dimly recognize. The opponent who is making an ideological attack on the veracity of these statements endeavors to comprehend them by going beyond their surface meaning. He interprets them with reference to the individual's life situation, including his class position and other group identifications. Not only does the particular conception involve an understanding of the underlying meanings, but the opponent also attempts to discredit the statements by showing how their distortions serve some economic or psychological interest of the one who makes them. Ideological thinking goes beyond understanding and attacks thinking. An example of a particular ideological attack would be the demonstration that an individual who argues for a tariff holds a central position in an industry threatened by foreign competition.

The total conception of ideology goes beyond the particular conception. In the total conception it is a total *Weltanschauung* that is under attack, and the target is most likely some group or collectivity rather than a single individual. It is also not only a question of isolated statements that are viewed with skepticism, but a total way of thinking. The world

---

[17] Karl Mannheim, *Essays on the Sociology of Knowledge*, pp. 137–139.

[18] Ibid., pp. 139–140.

[19] Ibid., pp. 140–141.

[20] Karl Mannheim, *Ideology and Utopia*, Ch. II, *passim*.

outlook is constructed not by a single individual, but by a group whose circumstances predispose its members to think along certain lines, although not every member shares completely in the outlook. Again, it is not only a question of the substance of the outlook that is at focus but also its categorical framework and formal style. In ideological clashes on the total level, the opposing groups talk past each other, for even their criteria of truth diverge. Therefore, it is difficult for a Marxist and a bourgeois liberal to fully understand each other's viewpoints. Despite the more inclusive and extended context of the attacks, the total shares with the particular conception the attempt to relate the thoughts and ideas to the life situations of the group espousing them and thereby discredit them.

Another pair of concepts of ideology according to Mannheim is the special and the general. This pair refers not, as in the case of the particular and the total, to the scope of the thinking, but rather to the number of groups under attack. The special conception of ideology assumes that only the outlooks of one's adversaries are socially determined, whereas the general conception assumes the social determination of all thinking, including that of one's own group. The Marxists held to the special conception, for the viewpoint of the proletariat is not subject to socially determined error. Marx took a giant step in bringing about the unmasking turn of mind. Later on the ideological weapon he forged became adopted by all contending groups. Putting these two pairs of ideological conceptions together, Mannheim arrives at the general conception of the total conception of ideology, which develops into the sociology of knowledge.

The appearance of the various conceptions of ideology provides the fundamentals of the approach to the sociology of knowledge. When the objective of a scholar is solely to understand the meaning of an outlook in terms of the existential background of the group that embraces this outlook, the general conception of the total ideology becomes "transformed into a method of research in social and intellectual history generally."[21] The objective is no longer to destroy the credibility of a political opponent, but rather to reconstruct a sociologically oriented history of ideas by demonstrating how they are related to social factors. One can say that ideas are existentially determined by extra-theoretical factors, and all systems of thought must be explained in terms of them. When this method is utilized to research the history of ideas, it becomes the non-evaluative sociology of knowledge.

Examples of the penetration of ideas by social factors are the diverse definitions different groups offer of freedom. An old-style German conservative in the early nineteenth century meant by it the right of each estate to exercise its privileges, the landowners to expect services from the peasants and the latter to expect security from the landowners. A romantic-conservative Protestant meant by it the inner freedom of each individual to live according to his own conscience. A liberal meant by it the availability of the same privileges to everyone, that all have the same

---

[21] Karl Mannheim, *Ideology and Utopia*, p. 78.

rights at their disposal. This is an egalitarian definition.[22] These examples illustrate that the economic and religious statuses of groups are correlated with their views about an idea.

It also needs to be recognized that not only is the content of thinking penetrated by existential factors but also the formal categories of thought. As a case in point, the aforementioned German conservative applied morphological categories to history, in which everything is related to everything else and at the same time is preserved in all its uniqueness. This approach stabilizes tradition. On the other hand, the groups on the left analyze history in smaller, more general units in order to distinguish causal and functional patterns. This type of analysis facilitates the recombining of units in novel ways in order to bring about change.[23] Thus, formal styles of thinking are also situationally determined, and modes of analysis are tailored to political objectives.

The non-evaluative approach as a method of research does not cope with validity. It does not inquire into the truth of a group's outlook, but interprets and explains it in terms of situational factors. It relates all systems of ideas to the total structure of historical reality. Nevertheless, it is impossible, states Mannheim, to avoid indefinitely the question of validity. When the cultural scientist not only explains outlooks but also assesses their validity by utilizing the sociology of knowledge, the non-evaluative approach slides over into the evaluative conception of the sociology of knowledge. Moreover, the matter of truth and falsehood is lifted from the arena of practical politics and elevated to the level of science. Relationism is the way in which the evaluative approach copes with the validity of knowledge.

The validity of cultural-historical knowledge is the most pervasive theme running through Mannheim's discussions and relationism is bound up with this theme. What does he mean by relationism? Although his explication of the notion is not so precise or clear as we would like, he does suggest several somewhat related strategies of how the sociologist can think relationally.

One way to ascertain whether the norms legitimated by a particular global view are invalid is to determine whether an individual with good intentions is able to comply with them. If this is impossible one can rightly conclude that those norms are invalid.[24] The reason for the impossibility of conformity is that the moral code calls for actions that maladjust individuals to the situations they face, their situations being determined by the historical stage at that moment. Mannheim gives the example of the rule prohibiting the taking of interest on loans. The taboo against usury was formulated in a precapitalist society based on intimate neighborly relations, and the prohibition was not only enforceable but functional in that setting. However, the taboo became increasingly unrealistic with the

---

[22] Karl Mannheim, *Ideology and Utopia*, p. 273.

[23] Ibid., pp. 274–275.

[24] Karl Mannheim, *Ideology and Utopia*, pp. 94–96.

growth of commerce, yet the church continued to incorporate the idea in its world view. The anticapitalistic perspective was an ideological one, which obscured the nature of the emerging economic order in order to stabilize old values.

Another example of a distorted perspective is evident in a landed proprietor who runs his estate as a capitalistic enterprise but who still describes his relationships to his workers in the terms of a patriarchal order. According to the latter the proprietor undertakes certain obligations to his workers irrespective of the cost. This description reflects an older perspective, true at one time, but now a distortion.[25] Both examples require the examination of ideas with reference to historical, situational factors, bringing into play the sociology of knowledge.

A second method of relational thinking, closer to the core of relationism as Mannheim conceives it, is the translation of different perspectives of a given phenomenon into one another in order to elicit a common denominator. A multiplicity of perspectives of an object is always possible, each one reflecting the social position of the perceiver. The multiplicity of perspectives does not deny the object's objective character, which becomes more completely revealed as different perspectives of it are put together and mutually translated. It is a question of partial views of the truth leading to a more comprehensive view. Mannheim refers to this type of relational thinking as perspectivism.[26]

As perspectives are compared and their common elements extracted, the resulting perspective becomes increasingly formalized and abstract. The purely formal properties of the phenomenon are emphasized. The truth of this observation, states Mannheim, is corroborated by a general trend toward abstractness in thinking, which results from the amalgamation of increasingly heterogeneous groups.

His most significant formulation of relationism is similar to perspectivism but goes somewhat beyond it. This is Mannheim's well-known notion of the synthesis of perspectives into a scientific politics. Since every perspective of phenomena is only partial, there is the possibility of an integration of many mutually complementary points of view into a comprehensive whole.[27] The possibility of a synthesis, which will result in a truer perspective than any by itself, stems from the fact that all possible perspectives emerge out of the same historical context. Since, as we have learned earlier, each historical context is an integrated meaningful unity, the various parts are intimately related. Mannheim contends that a given historical reality is too complex for any *one* view to grasp in its entirety. Synthesis involves the putting together of a number of partial perspectives rather than distilling a common denominator.

The operations to achieve a synthesis are not spelled out in any clear

---

[25] Karl Mannheim, *Ideology and Utopia*, p. 96.

[26] Ibid., pp. 296–302.

[27] Karl Mannheim, *Ideology and Utopia*, p. 149. The possibility of a synthesis was foreshadowed in some of Mannheim's earlier essays, although not in detail. See Mannheim, *Essays on the Sociology of Knowledge*, p. 90.

way by Mannheim. He does make several things clear, however. The synthesis is not an additive process, for the sociologist does not merely add together all existing perspectives the way a mathematician adds to get the sum of parts. The divergence of categorical apparatuses of perspectives introduces qualitative distinctions. It is also clear that the synthesis, like the other methods of relational thinking, must apply the sociology of knowledge; each perspective of a given historical phenomenon must be related to the existential conditions of the group whose perspective is being understood. Then the validity of each perspective will be shown to be *particularized* to certain contexts. Another aspect of the synthesizing process is the need for the synthesizers to engage in dialogue with the representatives of all perspectives being studied.[28] This is necessary to understand the perspectives from the points of view of those holding them. Finally, it is certain that there will be no final synthesis; the synthesizing process continues because history changes and the perspectives on history continue to change. Relational thinking is truly dynamic and not subject to the errors of the older epistemological view that truth is absolute and static.

As the synthesizing proceeds toward more comprehensive views, a truly scientific politics comes into being. Now with a more total, presumably more valid perspective, the ground is prepared for a science of politics that yields guidelines for the formation of political policy. The kinds of policies that such a science suggests include the formation of treaties with foreign powers, taxation policies, and the handling of strikes.[29] Mannheim distinguishes these decisions from purely administrative routines like the application of a law to a particular case by a judge. These administrative routines have been rationalized, whereas the sphere of authentic political decision-making has not yet become subject to rational criteria. The scientific politics based on relational thinking is also differentiated from such current subjects in universities as history, sociology, political theory, social psychology, and statistics, which may be useful to political leaders but which do not add up to a science of politics. Thus, a more valid cultural-historical knowledge dependent on a new epistemology leads to practical political consequences. What begins as a method of research eventuates into a method of social reconstruction.

An important question remains: what group should be responsible for performing the relational synthesis? Mannheim's answer comes through loud and clear—the intelligentsia.[30] There are two justifications for assigning the function of the relational synthesis to this group. In the first place, by virtue of their work they are not so firmly anchored in a particular sector of the economic system as, say, entrepreneurs and proletarians,

---

[28] Karl Mannheim, *op. cit.*, pp. 183–184. Mannheim develops this dialogue into a technique of pedagogy in transmitting the scientific politics.

[29] Karl Mannheim. *Ideology and Utopia*, p. 113.

[30] He is vague, however, about what groups in contemporary society belong to the intelligentsia, alluding to the *rentier* strata, some government officials, and members of the liberal professions.

and hence are relatively classless. They are "socially unattached," which is not to imply that they lack economic interests, but their outlooks are not so thoroughly unconsciously determined as those of other groups. Essential to relational thinking is the awareness of the determinants of one's own outlook so that he can control knowledge through the subjection of one-sided viewpoints. In the second place, their educations enable them to understand clashing ideological positions as they arise in history— indispensable for the synthesizing task. Modern education is a microcosm of the conflicts raging in society at large, so the intelligentsia are not likely to become captives of any single *Weltanschauung*. Thus, Mannheim belongs to a long line of intellectuals beginning with Plato who wanted to see political decisions entrusted to the thinkers and scholars.

These formulations constitute Mannheim's most important contributions to the sociology of knowledge. Since his essays were written, other sociologists have contributed to its theoretical development and have conducted empirical studies within its framework. There is little doubt of the lasting value of his work. Yet there are many difficulties evident in his approach, some of which are more troublesome than others. Let us analyze a few of them.

First, an assumption underlying his approach to the validity of knowledge is that the latter's truth-value is somehow affected by demonstrable influences on whoever advances it. If it can be shown that certain factors influence the thinking process of the formulator of an idea, somehow the latter's validity is rendered doubtful. This according to Mannheim is true of all cultural-historical knowledge. In order to escape from a morass of relativism, he tried to turn this observation to good advantage by suggesting that if these influences are brought to light, then the first step will have been taken to ascertain the idea's validity. Now the validity of an idea *depends* upon a revelation of its determinants.

Nowhere does Mannheim examine this assumption. Yet it is quite obvious that any proposition can be judged from standpoints different from the standpoint of why the assertor stated it. These standards of judgment can be ethical, esthetic, legalistic, religious, logical, and scientific. As a matter of fact probably *any* statement can be judged from more than one point of view. For example, the statement that the class struggle bursts asunder the fabric of capitalism can be judged as ethically good or bad, as theologically repugnant, or even as beautiful, if one sees beauty in predictable outcomes. It can also be scientifically judged by scrutinizing observable trends in existing and previous capitalistic societies. These standards of judgment are separable from the observation that those who assert the proposition are workingmen whose situation in the factory is deplorable. If one is interested in the scientific truth of a statement, then different criteria are brought to bear, such as, for example, the weight of the evidence, than those that decide how such a statement came to be expressed. Therefore, Mannheim is in error for stating that social determinants are relevant to the ascertainment of its validity.

A second, closely related impediment to a satisfactory formulation is

Mannheim's assumption that mathematical and natural scientific knowledge are exempt from the impact of determinants. No one can detect, for instance, the class position of him who states $2 \times 2 = 4$. Hence, its validity is unimpaired from that source. However, a little reflection easily reveals that a whole host of determinants affect the thinking of a physicist, such as his training in this subject, his knowledge of a language, the state of his nervous system, etc. Indeed, some of these determinants are distinctively social as, for example, the funding he receives from government to perform his research. Hence, this distinction between natural scientific and cultural-historical knowledge is a false distinction, which is not to deny, obviously, the possibility of other differences.

Third, Mannheim fails to offer a clear definition of knowledge. The suggestion that cultural-historical knowledge appears as *Weltanschauungen* conceals basically heterogeneous ideas. Two examples center on the well-known distinction between value-judgments and factual assertions. Factual statements are provable or disprovable in the light of empirical evidence, and it makes no sense to speak of the scientific status of value-judgments. That aspect of conservatism that envisages history as an unfolding of social wholes must be judged according to different standards than that aspect that upholds class privilege as a good thing. The former can be scientifically tested, whereas the latter cannot. Therefore, the quest for the scientific truth of cultural-historical knowledge can succeed only when directed toward scientifically determinable cultural-historical knowledge. The heterogeneity of what Mannheim includes as knowledge is further evidenced by goals, concepts, categorical frameworks, and norms.

Fourth, the notion that intellectuals are unattached and "freely floating" when contrasted with others has never been substantiated. Mannheim presents little proof for this conclusion. Lewis Coser rightly points out that he has created a *deus ex machina* in the unattached intellegentsia, who are presumed to have greater immunity than others from the penetration of their thinking by their social locations.[31] Certainly the universities in the modern world are a focus of economic interests and pressures, which one could plausibly entertain as exerting influences on the thinking of their personnel.

Finally, Mannheim is vague about the modes of relationship between existential determinants and the ideas they affect. His writings reveal a number of possibilities including the casual determination of ideas by social factors, a harmony between them, a correspondence, and a conjunction.[32] The imprecision of the word "determination" not only leaves his formulations ambiguous but also renders empirical research difficult.

It is generally agreed among contemporary sociologists, who are re-

---

[31] Lewis A. Coser, *Masters of Sociological Thought* (New York: Harcourt, 1971), p. 436.

[32] Robert K. Merton, *Social Theory and Social Structure*, revised and enlarged edition (New York: Free Press, 1957), pp. 498–499. Merton has traced in Mannheim's writings his variable characterizations of the modes of relations.

luctant to take up epistemological and other philosophical questions,[33] that the least satisfactory aspects of Mannheim's sociology of knowledge pertain to the validity of knowledge. There is also substantial agreement on the lasting value of the purely sociological dimensions of the relationship between thinking and factors in the thinker's context. For those intrigued especially by the scientific aspects of the sociology of knowledge, Mannheim's fertile essays are milestones in the latter's development.

BIBLIOGRAPHY

Berger, Peter L., and Thomas Luckmann. *The Social Construction of Reality.* Garden City, N.Y.: Doubleday, 1967.

Coser, Lewis A. *Masters of Sociological Thought.* New York: Harcourt, 1971.

Mannheim, Karl. *Essays on the Sociology of Knowledge*, ed. Paul Kecskemeti. London: Routledge and Kegan Paul, 1952.

Mannheim, Karl. *Ideology and Utopia*, trans. Louis Wirth and Edward Shils. New York: Harcourt, 1936.

Merton, Robert K. *Social Theory and Social Structure*, revised and enlarged edition. New York: Free Press, 1957.

Parsons, Talcott. *The Structure of Social Action.* New York: Free Press, 1949.

---

[33] For example, see Merton, *op. cit.*, pp. 502–508 and Peter L. Berger and Thomas Luckmann, *The Social Construction of Reality* (Garden City, N.Y.: Doubleday, 1967), pp. 12–14.

9.2

Karl Mannheim: Revision of an Intellectual Portrait

GUNTER W. REMMLING

Karl Mannheim's name is firmly linked with the sociology of knowledge which is chiefly known for its preoccupation with the problematic connections between sociocultural factors and thought in its various manifestations. Mannheim's resolute research led him into an intellectual frontier which Louis Wirth has well designated as an area of "dangerous thought."[1] A disquieting inquiry into sacred institutions and beliefs constituted part of Mannheim's investigation. Therefore, he invited numerous attacks and criticisms. But, we have to turn to Mannheim's few defenders for the much needed elucidation of his complex sociology. Notably, Louis Wirth and Paul Kecskemeti have provided significant interpretations of his work.[2] My analysis of Mannheim's ideas adopts a comprehensive frame of reference.[3] This research intention calls for the formulation of specific assumptions.

The Hypothesis

Mannheim's picture as here developed is a dynamic one which has undergone significant changes. Since he lived in continuous contact with

---

[1] Louis Wirth, "Preface" to Karl Mannheim, *Ideology and Utopia: An Introduction to the Sociology of Knowledge* (translated by Louis Wirth and Edward Shils, 2nd edition, New York: Harcourt, Brace and Company, 1940), pp. xvi-xvii.

[2] Cf. *ibid.*, pp. xiii-xxxi. Cf. also his "Modern German Conceptions of Sociology," *American Journal of Sociology*, XXXII (November 1926), pp. 461–470, and "Karl Mannheim," *American Sociological Review*, XII (June 1947), 356–357. Cf., furthermore, his "Ideological Aspects of Social Disorganization," *American Sociological Review*, V (August 1940), 472–482. Paul Kecskemeti, "Introduction," in Karl Mannheim, *Essays on the Sociology of Knowledge* (translated by Paul Keckskemeti, London: Routledge and K. Paul, 1952), pp. 1–32.

[3] Cf. also Gunter W. Remmling, "Karl Mannheim, 1893–1947," *Archiv für Rechts- und Sozialphilosophie*, XLIII/2 (May 1957), 271–285.

the realities of a world experiencing rapid transformations, these changes in his thinking follow an inherent logic.

The hypothesis here presented is that Mannheim's thinking has undergone four changes, which we shall refer to as phases of his intellectual development. They are briefly described below:

First Phase: Mannheim accepts an absolute historism as the basis of his thinking and his interpretation of sociocultural reality. He develops his radical sociology of knowledge which claims, in contrast to Scheler's moderate view, that all thoughts in the human studies are determined in form and content by nontheoretical factors. He expands the concept of ideology from Marx's total and special one into one that is total but general. Thus, all knowledge becomes existentially determined. In answer to the charge of relativism, he develops a number of defensive arguments, among them the assertion that the "socially unattached intelligentsia" has access to truth since this group is supposedly not attached to any specific existential position.[4]

Second Phase: Mannheim's epistemological, ontological, and methodological theorizing that lead to the formulation of his radical sociology of knowledge, and the total suspicion of ideology give way to a new interest in the crisis of our age. Mannheim develops a theory of social planning as his answer to the problems of modern industrial societies. He demands now that man himself be reconstructed to ensure a lasting reconstruction of society. The key problem becomes the development of the formerly dominant "functional rationality" into a "substantial rationality."[5]

Third Phase: Mannheim realizes that his earlier emphasis on rationality was one-sided and out of tune with the essential nature of man. Therefore, he integrates emotional and volitional factors into his so far purely

---

[4] Cf. Karl Mannheim, "Historismus," *Archiv für Sozialwissenshaft und Socialpolitik*, 52, 1924, pp. 1ff., and "Das Problem einer Soziologie des Wissens, "*Archiv für Socialwissenschaft und Sozialpolitik*, 53, 3, 1925, pp. 601 ff. For his ontological and conceptual theorizing against Marx see K. Mannheim, *Ideology and Utopia*, pp. 62–84. His central argument concerning the expansion of the concept of ideology is: "We add here another distinction to our earlier one of 'particular and total,' namely that of 'special and general.' While the first distinction concerns the question as to whether single isolated ideas or the entire mind is to be seen as ideological, and whether the social situation conditions merely the psychological manifestation of concepts or whether it even penetrates to the noological meanings, in the distinction of special *versus* general, the decisive question is, whether the thought of all groups (including our own) or only that of our adversaries is recognized as socially determined." (pp. 68–69).

[5] See the major work of this second phase: Karl Mannheim, *Man and Society in an Age of Reconstruction. Studies in Modern Social Structure* (New York: Harcourt, Brace and Company, 1940), pp. 51–57. The book was written originally in German, and the English edition has been substantially enlarged and revised. Cf. Karl Mannheim, *Mensch und Gesellschaft im Zeitalter des Umbaus* (Leiden: A. W. Sijthoff, 1935).

rationalistic scheme of social planning. His main concern is now the meaning of values and religion. Mannheim hopes that these two non-rational elements will enlist the active support of men for the construction of a fundamentally and militantly democratic society. The major problem now is how to create an adequately strong value system and how to rejuvenate Christianity for the purposes of social reconstruction.[6]

Fourth Phase: Mannheim turns his attention finally to the problem of political power. Although he retains his concept of social planning as ultimately developed in his third phase, he again shifts his interest to a new field of inquiry and starts to develop his critical sociology of power as a unique presupposition to a political sociology. This stage of his intellectual development remained rather rudimentary as a consequence of his untimely death.[7]

We can summarize as follows the major concepts and problems around which Mannheim's studies have centered during the different stages[8] of his intellectual development:

First phase: sociology of knowledge
Second phase: social planning
Third phase: values and religion
Fourth phase: the control of power

I shall now trace this development more closely.

It is frequently said that Mannheim's sociology of knowledge reflects nothing but the situational standpoint of the German university professor

---

[6] The principal book on this phase is: Karl Mannheim, *Diagnosis of our Time* (London: Routledge and K. Paul, 1943).

[7] Cf. Karl Mannheim, *Freedom, Power, and Democratic Planning* (New York: Oxford University Press, 1950).

[8] The different phases are not of equal importance. The main transition occurs between phase one and phase two. Here Mannheim's thinking undergoes significant alterations. Compared to his estrangement from the radical sociology of knowledge, his subsequent changes no longer indicate basic transformations of his style of thinking but rather subtle shifts of interest and major concern.

The importance of the transition from phase one to phase two becomes especially apparent in the new conception of ideology as it appears in the main publication of the second phase. While the original total term as developed in *Ideology and Utopia* was a razor-sharp conceptual tool that limited man's search for truth with iron consistency, the new concept is not dogmatic but rather elastic. In the second phase ideology is used as a descriptive term that no longer has any inevitable determining consequences. The Mannheim of the second phase indicates that ideologies can be eliminated: "These are the sociological conditions in which ideologies are unmasked. . . This is the moment of scepticism . . . productive for science, as it destroys the petrified habits of thought of the past." (K. Mannheim, *Man and Society in an Age of Reconstruction*, p. 129). For further instances of Mannheim's looser application of the concept see *ibid.*, pp. 9, 29.

during the earlier part of the twentieth century. We shall see, however, that Mannheim changes from the German professor to the social and political strategist whose career ends with the call to a leading position in UNESCO.

The First Phase: Genesis of the Radical Sociology of Knowledge

Karl Mannheim was born in Budapest in 1893. From 1929 to 1933 he taught sociology at the University of Frankfurt/Main. In 1933 he emigrated to England where he lectured at the London School of Economics and Political Science. After World War II broke out, he edited the *International Library of Sociology and Social Reconstruction* which he had previously founded. In 1945, he accepted the chair in pedagogy at the University of London. A few weeks before his death he was offered the directorship of the European branch of UNESCO. He died in London on January 9, 1947, at the age of 53.

Karl Mannheim's sociology of knowledge is one area within the larger field known as the sociology of culture, which can be defined as a theory of the relationships between culture and society. These relationships can be studied by using the methods of analytic sociology. In this instance, the ways of acquiring and disseminating knowledge emerge as the object of cognition. This analytically oriented sociology of culture is closely related to the sociology of knowledge although it does not lead directly into this latter problem area. Only a sociology of culture conceived of as a research method oriented towards the humanistic studies connects up with the sociology of knowledge. Such a discipline shows culture to be dependent upon society in a specific way. The moderate branch of this sociology of culture is represented primarily by Max Scheler who claims that the "real factors" or social conditions do not determine the actual form or content of knowledge. Social reality, he states, has the moderate function of making it possible to achieve certain types of knowledge only at certain periods of history.[9]

The radical branch, in contrast, emphasizes that all aspects of culture are determined by society. It, in turn, contains two subdivisions. One approach establishes a causal determination of culture; the other proclaims a functional state of dependency. While Karl Marx is customarily associated with the idea of causal determination, Mannheim's radical sociology of knowledge belongs to the functional variety of absolute cultural sociology.

Like any other sociology of knowledge, Mannheim's theory rests on certain premises that are based upon the epistemological discoveries of

---

[9] Cf. Max Scheler, "Vorrede" and "Einleitung" in M. Scheler (ed.), *Versuche zu einer Soziologie des Wissens*, Schriften des Forschungs-instituts für Sozialwissenschaften in Köln (München und Leipzig: Duncker & Humblot, 1924), and M. Scheler, *Die Wissensformen und die Gesellschaft* (Leipzig: Der Neue-Geist-Verlag) 1926.

Kant and the exponents of critical philosophy. As its object of cognition a sociology of knowledge establishes the dependence of knowledge on social reality. Yet this premise would be meaningless were it derived from a crude realism that confronts the subject of perception with an autonomous object which has merely to be registered in photographic fashion. In the case of naive realism, perceiving man could never exert any influence upon the object of cognition. Such influence is conceivable only if we assume that the object of cognition is constituted by a creative act of the perceiving individual.[10]

Thus, the particular question raised by the sociology of knowledge presupposes the object-constituting function of cognition, as such function was affirmed by the Copernican turn of Kant.

Thanks to the widening of criticistic epistemology by Wilhelm Dilthey, by other representatives of *Lebensphilosophie* and by exponents of historism, Kant's insights—thus far limited to nature—could now at last be applied to the sphere of intellect (*Geistige Welt*). The preobjective material becomes the essence of an objective world only in the process of understanding (*Verstehen*). Kant's statement concerning the lawful order of the objects of the physical sciences is valid also in the world of ideas. Order, and in the case of the human studies, the meaningful order of the world does not originate in the objects but rather in the structure of the perceiving mind.

It was in this sense that Dilthey discussed the "Establishment of the Historical World in the Human Sciences."[11]

The object of the human sciences is also incorporated into the process of cognition and is considered to be dependent on, or at least codetermined by specific object-constituting formative factors which are located on the side of the perceiving subject. In analogy to Kant, these formative factors may be called "categories of understanding" (*Kategorien des Verstehens*).

The consistent philosophical historism which marks Mannheim's early conceptual frame is partially rooted in Dilthey's foundation of the human sciences. It was Dilthey's proclamation that every *Weltanschauung* is historically determined and therefore both limited and relative, that became the decisive germ which was later to develop into Mannheim's total historism which, in turn, interprets "each and every part of the mental-psychic world as being in a state of flux, of becoming."[12] While Mannheim now

---

[10] Cf. Immanuel Kant, *Critique of Pure Reason* (translated by Norman Kemp Smith, London: Macmillan & Co., Ltd., 1956), p. 22. Kant argues: "If intuition must conform to the constitution of the objects, I do not see how we could know anything of the latter *a priori*, but if the object (as object of the senses) must conform to the constitution of our faculty of intuition, I have no difficulty in conceiving such a possibility."

[11] Wilhelm Dilthey, *Der Aufbau der geschichtlichen Welt in den Geisteswissenschaften*, Gesammelte Schriften, (Leipzig-Berlin: B. G. Teubner, 1927), VII.

[12] Karl Mannheim, "Historismus," p. 3.

applies the category of totality to aid his search for the unifying principle of this change, he also sees historical development as a meaningful process of becoming which is guided by a "principle of order." In this recourse to Hegel's idea of an inspirited and entelechial unfolding of history we find the other root of Mannheim's historism. The central question of Mannheim's sociology of knowledge, which tries to unravel the relationships between knowledge and society, reflects his attempts to solve the problem of the historical nature and unity of mind and life.

Thus, Mannheim develops his early system against a larger intellectual background. Hegel's philosophy of history propels his search for the deeper meaning, for the unity behind the constant change of history. Marx, whose theory of ideologies represents the first attempt at research in the spirit of a sociology of knowledge, forces Mannheim to clarify and delimit his own position. Georg Lukács is significant because of his endeavors to revive the Hegelian elements in the Marxist system, and because of his attempts to understand history as the genesis of class consciousness, i.e., the ideal type of thinking that is adequate to reality. Rickert and Windelband connect Mannheim with neocriticism. Max Weber teaches him to view functionally the relationships between superstructure and substructure and opens the approach to an elastic cultural sociology. His controversy with Max Scheler over the latter's moderate sociology of knowledge lends valuable impulse to Mannheim's thinking. Husserl provides him with the tool of the phenomenological method. Without all this equipment Mannheim would have been unable to overcome the limitations of Scheler's ontology. From this position Mannheim finally reaches an understanding of Heidegger's novel explication of the question concerning being (*Seinsfrage*).

Mannheim distinguishes between two different interpretations of mental products in establishing the sociology of knowledge as the central science. He declares the sociology of knowledge to be an extrinsic interpretation of thought products.[13] The immanent interpretation is based upon an understanding of the intellectual content; it is thereby limited to the theoretical content of knowledge. The extrinsic interpretation is based upon the understanding of manifestations; it sees culture content as the manifestation of an absolute stratum (*Absolutschicht*).

This differentiation between two types of interpretation enables Mannheim to designate a logical place for the sociology of knowledge within the scientific system. Along with a few other disciplines such as psychoanalysis, the sociology of knowledge stands opposite the traditional human sciences which seek the immanent meaning of mental products via *Geistverstehen*. Thus, cultural sociology interprets culture, and the sociology of knowledge interprets knowledge through the understanding of manifestations as an examination of the *ens realissimum*: social reality. In other

---

[13] Cf. Karl Mannheim, "Ideologische und soziologische Interpretation der geistigen Gebilde," Jahrbuch für Soziologie, II (ed. by G. Salomon, Karlsruhe: G. Braun, 1926), pp. 424 ff.

words, the sociology of knowledge as an extrinsic interpretation functionally relates intellectual statements and judgments to social reality as the absolute stratum.

Mannheim claims in support of the sociology of knowledge that its fundamental thesis was not established arbitrarily. Rather, the sociology of knowledge must be understood as the conceptual expression of contemporary historical experience which has social reality at its vital center and which conceives of all manifestations of life as dependent upon the socioeconomic orders and their transformations.[14]

The idea of an "existential determination of knowledge" forms the central theme of Mannheim's sociology of knowledge. By equating reality to social reality he establishes the actual relevance (*Geltungsrelevanz*) of societal life for all intellectual utterances. According to Mannheim, the method of sociology of knowledge becomes effective only where content and form of judgment are dependent on a specific constellation of social life. Thus, the concept of "socio-existential determination of knowledge" expresses the theory that the absolute stratum, i.e., societal life centered around socio-economic orders not only has importance for the realization of judgments *hic et nunc*; that it not only possesses factual relevance (Faktizitätsrelevanz); but also that it influences the content, form, and structure of intellectual utterances.[15]

This peculiar influence of the absolute stratum upon the products of thinking is not direct; rather, it is mediated by the carrier of knowledge, by the space- and time-bound and always historical subject of cognition. This perceiving subject is always fitted into the historical-social process of life in a specific way; he always has a particular "stand-point" in the all-embracing totality of life. Therefore, an object of cognition never totally discloses itself to man. Rather, every agent of cognition sees only a partial aspect and that only from his own cognitive standpoint (*Denkstandort*).

Presumably this perspective extends into the product of thinking. Now, the term *Aspektsruktur* is introduced to point out how a perceiving individual uses an object, which of its elements he grasps, and how he constructs a context in the process of thinking. Apart from thought products of the type $s = \frac{g}{2}t^2$ or $2 \times 2 = 4$, the results in the human sciences which rest on *weltanschaulichen*, metaempirical presuppositions can only be formulated as "*Aspekstrukturen.*" The existentially determined standpoint of thinking thus extends via *Aspekt-struktur* into the content of a judgment, leaving its imprint on the entire utterance since it exerts a decisive influence even upon the categorical apparatus.[16]

The first period of Mannheim's work ends with his article *Wissens-*

---

[14] Cf. Karl Mannheim, "Das Problem einer Soziologie des Wissens," pp. 632 f.

[15] *Ibid.*, p. 635.

[16] Karl Mannheim, *Ideology and Utopia*, pp. 26, 243 f. and 263 f.

soziologie (sociology of knowledge), published in 1931.[17] In it Mannheim still attempts to clarify epistemological and ontological issues concerning a sociology of knowledge that follows the main stream of *Kultursoziologie* and tends towards a problem awareness resting on the larger question of a sociology of the mind.

Mannheim's theorizing in this first period must be understood against the background of the Weimar Republic. Political and social life of this period resembled a kaleidoscopic display, with the observer witnessing constant changes of the most varied philosophical, political, social, and cultural tenets.

Because of these and other experiences and influences, including Marxist economic determinism and the various methods of unmasking ideologies that were advanced by Nietzsche, Freud, and Marx, Mannheim in time came to a basic doubt regarding man's intellectual behavior. The impact on him of *Lebensphilosophie* and historism increased and accentuated his doubts and distrust until he eventually arrived at the question of the basic meaning of mind and culture.

The Second Phase:
Social Planning

In 1933, Mannheim left Germany for England, and his thinking began to change. Any attempt to explain these changes must take into account four factors over and above the obvious influence of his new English environment.

1. The effects of psychoanalysis, *Lebensphilosophie*, existentialism, and extreme historism had touched off an intellectual unrest on the continent resulting from a fundamental societal crisis. This upheaval was the ultimate climax of a great disillusionment that started with Nietzsche and spread after the *auto-da-fé* of World War I. But when Mannheim reached England, he left behind him this lightning, as the England of the early thirties had hardly been touched by this crisis.

2. After 1930, Mannheim lost interest in historical materialism. The old formula maintaining the existential determination of the mind diminishes in importance.

3. This development was strengthened when after 1933, Mannheim turned towards western sociology and moved away from the Hegel-Marx-Dilthey sequence. Like Pareto and Ortega y Gasset, Mannheim approached the problem of the élite.[18] He abandoned his earlier construction of a

---

[17] Cf. Karl Mannheim, "Wissenssoziologie" in Alfred Vierkandt (ed.), *Handwoerterbuch der Soziologie*, (Stuttgart: F. Enke, 1931).

[18] For a statistical approach to this problem see Vilfredo Pareto, *The Mind and Society* (New York: Harcourt, Brace, 1935), par. 2027 ff. Cf. also José Ortega y Gasset, *The Revolt of the Masses* (New York: New American Library, Mentor Edition, 1950), pp. 91 ff. For a comparison between Marx and Pareto see Raymond Aron, "Social Structure and Ruling Class," *British Journal of Sociology*, I, nos. 1 and 2 (1950).

"socially unattached intelligentsia." Instead a positivist sociology must determine how an élite will emerge from the masses. The methodological monism, resulting from the absolute historism of Mannheim's first period, was not extinct. Mannheim assimilated social psychology, instrumentalism, and pragmatism. He began to think more and more in terms of ecological approaches and established contact with similar schools in American pragmatism.

4. His observation of political life in England led to a slow but steady recovery of faith in democracy, the functional value and vitality of which he had begun seriously to question at the end of his first period.

In the central work of this second phase[19] Mannheim raises new questions that differ from the ones that concerned him during his first phase in Germany.

In the introduction to *Man and Society*, Mannheim declares that contemporary western society suffers from the antagonism between two coexisting contradictory principles, *laissez-faire* and unplanned regulation.

In the later stages of capitalistic democracy the *laissez-faire* principle had failed to establish the equilibrium expected, *qua definitionem*, and had resulted in the reign of economic superstructures with consequent dangerous economic and social crises. Mannheim, therefore, thought it necessary to transform man's thinking and behavior before he would be able to fashion social relations in the spirit of a new principle. A realistic and fully developed system of social planning, Mannheim believed, would help to overcome the frictions created by the incompatible principles of *laissez-faire* and unplanned regulation, and would spare the western democracies the *salto mortale* into totalitarian solutions of civilization's crisis. However, reasoned Mannheim, even under democracies society would unavoidably need to be reconstructed. At this point Mannheim formulated his second thesis: Without a reconstruction of man, there can be no reconstruction of society.

Mannheim develops the ideas expressed in *Man and Society* on the basis of a correlation among psychic, social, and cultural symptoms of crisis. The mental and psychic confusion of the individual is interrelated with the unrest and fermentation of society. The nonmaterial aspects of culture reflect this social malady. Only the integration of individual and social forces, based on rational goal-striving and sober insight into the actual efficacies of both forces, can create a genuine culture as an adequate and creative form of expression.

The Third Phase:
Values and Christianity

A change of interest and approach in *Diagnosis of Our Time*, Mannheim's next work, marks his entrance upon a third phase.[20] This collection

---

[19] K. Mannheim, *Man and Society*.

[20] K. Mannheim, *Diagnosis of our Time*.

of lectures and essays, written mostly in 1941 and 1942, was intended to complete the ideas put forth during his second period. This was his response to the crisis of continental society. The outbreak of war against Nazism now stimulated Mannheim in an attempt to support and amplify his original intention—to alleviate the crisis by means of a rational planning of society—through the postulate of moral and religious rearmament.

Diagnosis of Our Time serves two functions. The book is a popular version of ideas developed in *Man and Society*; it also moves the struggle for a new value system and a revaluation of Christianity into the spotlight. First and foremost, Mannheim wishes to assist those groups that are striving towards an understanding of the present crisis. He renounces the systematic, "academic" form of presentation in order to utilize the findings of scientific sociology for this important task.

The ultimate importance of this book transcends the recognition of its functional pragmatism. When Mannheim wrote *Man and Society*, he demanded a conscious development of substantial rationality and the education of all members of society towards the elevated standard of this intellectual attitude. The realization of an idea like "planning for freedom" presupposed this process. But now in *Diagnosis of Our Time*, Mannheim stresses the volitional and emotional aspects of this operation. In keeping with his terminlogy we can infer that his demand for substantial morality now supersedes that for substantial rationality.[21] Consequently, Mannheim analyzes the question of whether or not Christianity might help to create values meaningful to a planned social order. He enters fully into a discussion of a value system adequate and generally significant enough to meet the critical needs of the day. Such a well-integrated and functional value system is essential to generate enthusiasm and activity that would be instrumental in realizing the objective of planning for freedom.

The Fourth Phase:
The Problem of Power

Mannheim's last work, *Freedom, Power, and Democratic Planning*,[22] was published posthumously in 1950. The book discusses many questions raised earlier and, ultimately, opens a fourth phase in Mannheim's career which, however, was never fully developed due to his untimely death.

This fourth and last phase adds the problem of power to those of social planning, values, and Christianity. Mannheim focuses his attention upon the controversy between power and freedom which a planned democracy must try to solve. To use the words of his students, Mannheim is no longer a detached critical observer, but has grown into a political

---

[21] Mannheim distinguishes between substantial and functional rationality and maintains that the latter characterizes the limited thought processes of the common soldier when compared to the larger view accessible to the leader of large scale operations. Industrialization has furthered functional rationality. See K. Mannheim, *Man and Society*, p. 54.

[22] Karl Mannheim, *Freedom, Power, and Democratic Planning*.

and social strategist who tries to understand so that others may be able to act.[23] This book once again shows how rapidly and determinedly Mannheim could respond to the actual sociohistorical constellation. The problems now posed are mainly a theoretical echo to the over-all political situation emerging after World War II. Mannheim views the phenomenon of power and the "power complex" as the greatest danger of the post-war period. The neurotic power complex emerging along with the unfolding of industrial capitalism is fostered by the critical development of recent sociopolitical circumstances, and often reaches the dimensions of a collective compulsion. The negative aspects of a striving for power come more and more to the fore. The most essential postulate that Mannheim proclaimed shortly before his death, therefore, reads: Democratic vigilance is necessary to control power in whatever disguise it may appear.

The controlling function should be delegated to democratic "control stations." Mannheim is convinced that this development would then unavoidably lead to the postulate for an integration of these control stations into a uniform world-authority that must co-ordinate the secondary power centers. These endeavors, however, must be carefully watched to ensure that there will be no abuse of power at the highest level—the global control stations.

As the phenomenon of power develops into a crucial issue with a community or a nation, it also casts a menacing shadow across the globe that the Second World War has split into two primary centers of power.

In his last book Mannheim also returns to the major theme of his post-emigration period. But by now the question of planning benefits from Mannheim's greater insight and experience. His approach embraces greater appreciation of structural defects in modern society, an understanding of various "social techniques" aimed at correcting these defects, the recognition of forces emanating from the world of values and beliefs, and a keen awareness of potential dangers lurking in the phenomenon of power.

Still Mannheim is enough of a realist to recognize that a powerful government authority is necessary. Without such a strong centralized authority the planning project could never be realized. However, he links this positive aspect of power with the existence of democratic government which the public holds responsible. In the final analysis, Mannheim's program stands and falls with his belief in the success of the process of "fundamental democratization" that must produce a mature public able to force governments to resign whenever necessary.

Summary and Conclusion:
The Intellectual Portrait Revised

Karl Mannheim develops a keen sense for the important constellations in sociopolitical reality early in his career and subsequently arrives at the

---

[23] Cf. *ibid.*, p. xii (Introduction by Ernest K. Bramsted and Hans Gerth).

main thesis of his sociology of knowledge concerning the "gliding of standpoints," largely as a result of his experiences with the Weimar Republic with its kaleidoscopic rate of change. He perceives socio-historical reality as a constant flux and hypostatizes the theoretical expression of this approach, i.e., historism, so that it becomes fundamental to his intellectual existence. From Dilthey's *Lebensphilosophie* he assimilates the concept of *Verstehen* (understanding) as the second integral of his initial approach. His peculiar intellectual consistency leads him into the dangerous proximity of a norm-destroying, self-corroding relativism. After various attempts to overcome the problem of relativism, he arrives at the dubious construction of a so-called "socially unattached intelligentsia" that is allegedly able to rise above the unavoidable chaos of diverse standpoints.

Undoubtedly, the historicist thesis concerning the gliding of standpoints contains an optimistic element introduced by compensating mechanisms such as those contained in the concept *"consensus ex post"* and the idea that the socially unattached intelligentsia engages in adjusting and synthesizing activities. The different standpoints following upon one another represent, in final analysis, a process that leads *in infinitum* towards truth.

This optimistic element in Mannheim's first period rests on a metaphysical and speculative basis, embodies an attempt to outshine despair emerging in the wake of a radical sociology of knowledge. However, the optimism of his post-emigration period is more down-to-earth and of a more practical nature. Mannheim wants to get things done. This later optimism has its roots in the robust philosophy of pragmatism and in a readiness to invade reality with an active and creative spirit. Much of its energy stems from the experience of the Anglo-Saxon environment in which Mannheim regained his belief in the possibility of overcoming social crises. Mannheim exemplifies the intellectual emigrant who grows with his widening horizons. He benefits from his access to new knowledge and by accepting this challenge he becomes a man who, henceforth, must offer new ideas.

Mannheim benefits also in terms of method. After his emigration he gains access to fruitful philosophical and social-scientific trends which free him from his early methodological monism. In other ways too this experience with a different political and social reality redeems him from the compulsive idea that every thought is inevitably ideological. Benefiting from various new approaches and freed from one-sidedness and extravagance, his earlier labors now find fruitful application to the social problems at mid-century.

His harassing philosophy of doubt gives way to ideas that are more in tune with constructive action. With American pragmatism as his ally, Mannheim fuses thought and action and, ultimately, develops his challenging theory of social planning.

During the fight against Fascism—an enemy welded together by a totalitarian *Weltanschauung*—Mannheim begins to understand the gigantic power inherent in those psychic and mental forces that originate beyond the realm of mere day-to-day living. He recognizes the need to enhance his rational theory of planning through the introduction of volitional and emotional elements. The nihilism of modern existence which is primarily *zweckrational*[24] has to be overcome; the enthusiastic commitment of man to an idea has to be awakened. Mannheim calls for the revival of so-called "primary experiences" that are common to all men and that can take the place of the psychic instigation practiced by totalitarian systems. Mannheim elaborates his theory of paradigmatic experience[25] and appeals to the representatives of Christianity to mobilize the forces of genuine and realistic religiosity, so that men may be integrated in deep, supra-existential spheres of experience.

After World War II, Mannheim once more responds to the current political constellation. His last thoughts are directed to helping those forces that try to lessen those dangerous tensions resulting from a bifurcation of power, from the global split into two belligerent camps. Mannheim pursues the entangled problem of power into many areas of human life. He attempts to X-ray governmental apparatus, the economy, army, party mechanism, press, and the often invisible groupings of modern society. He establishes the first conceptual framework for his own political sociology which culminates in the idea of planning for freedom, in the suggestion of a third way, in the acknowledgment of Aristotle's golden middle path.

SUMMARY AND EVALUATION OF CHAPTER NINE

Mannheim succeeded in establishing (1) that there can be no certainty about knowledge because knowledge hinges on perspectives that change; (2) that one can more fully understand intellectual and all cultural phenomena by perceiving them as expressions of the spirit of an age (and the grasp of this higher meaning allows man to transcend the causally located and understood events of history); (3) that a sociological analysis of thought must show by analyzing the metapremises (tacit assumptions and categories anchored in social structure and life circumstances, which underlie thought itself) of a group what kinds of world views such premises are in harmony with and the extent to which such views are anchored in the group's life situation; (4) that a planned society is possible and desirable; and (5) that fictions underlie every social order (and we live in a time when these are increasingly exposed, and utopian transformations of the social order, in which action reflects a more desirable reality, are attempted).

The criticisms of Mannheim's sociology of knowledge have already been well put by Rhoads at the end of his article: The *validity* of an idea does not depend upon a revelation of its determinants. Highly rational

---

[24] The term is used in accordance with Max Weber's distinction between *wertrational* and *zweckrational*, whereby the latter *modus operandi* has to be understood as social action in terms of rational orientation to a system of discrete individual ends.

[25] Cf. Karl Mannheim, *Diagnosis of our Time*, p. 137.

(e.g., mathematical) thinking is also affected by situational–historical determinants. Mannheim's definition of knowledge (or processes involved in knowledge, cognition, ways of thinking, grounds for knowing, perspectives, world views, and content of knowledge as distinguished from forms of knowledge, etc.) is too heterogeneous to have much precision. The type of relationship between knowledge and the social location of the producers is unclear; at different times Mannheim suggests that knowledge is influenced by the social location, is causally determined by it, or is simply in accord with it.[1] Finally, the belief that the intelligentsia are more detached and can, therefore, accomplish a synthesis, borders on wishful thinking on Mannheim's part.

Sociology studies cultural objects. Knowledge of culture is gotten via the mind of an investigator who is socially situated in society. At the same time the investigator is an actor who, as others, can grasp what the cultural objects he is studying are by applying the cognitive process of *verstehen* to them. A man kisses a woman. By *verstehen* that act becomes an object of significance to both the participants and the observer. Because cultural objects stem from social life, and because our very knowledge of them is also part of our culture, Mannheim introduced the sociology of knowledge. And because the investigator is socially situated and must see these objects through a perspective that influences *verstehen*, Mannheim explored the problems of epistemology—our knowledge of knowledge.

Part of Mannheim's problem was his assertion that social phenomena differ from the physical because we incorporate social phenomena in the process of cognition or because we not only think about, but act on (and in action create), them. For these reasons the way we know social science knowledge must presumably differ from the way we know physical science knowledge. The matter goes back to Weber's reference to a meaningfully adequate, as opposed to a causally adequate, account of a sociohistoric event. It is of course true that in asking what a priest is doing when he shakes an object, sprinkles powder, utters words, and so on, we are looking for the meanings that make something called "mass" significant to the participants. We would not ask a swinging pendulum what its action means to it. We may also ask what the priest's intentions are and if they are adequate for him to accomplish what he is doing. In these considerations we seek a meaningful account of the genesis of the action.[2] However, does the attempt to determine the truth of the state-

---

[1] See Robert K. Merton, "Karl Mannheim and the Sociology of Knowledge," in Robert K. Merton, *Social Theory and Social Structure* (New York: Free Press, 1968), pp. 552–556. In addition, Lewis A. Coser concludes that since Mannheim changed from the view that perspectivist thought is necessarily ideological to the weaker idea that it *might* merely represent a *partial* view and that the social location of the thinker *is not irrelevant* to the determination of the truth of the assertion, the initially bold claims of the sociology of knowledge are finally reduced to a mere whimper (*Masters of Sociological Thought* [New York: Harcourt, 1971], p. 436.

[2] Mannheim, *Ideology and Utopia* (New York: Harcourt, 1936). p. 294.

ment, "The larger the religious organization, the more formal the mass," require a meaningful account of its genesis? And if not, is the answer a type of social science knowledge that is different from meaningful knowledge, even though the truth of the proposition may be reflected in the actions of the actors? Mannheim would have called a proposition of the type advanced above a *formalization* of knowledge; concerning such, he simply contended that "there is still a minimum of evidence of the investigator's general direction of interest which would not be entirely eliminated."[3] In other words, Mannheim's claim seemed to be that the investigator's intimacy with his own situation and the social world at large still leaves its mark: it has in all likelihood led to the development of his *interest* in organizational size and formality in the first place or affects the way he formulates the proposition. This does not, however, separate social from physical knowledge since a physicist or a biochemist would have his problems shaped by his (socially formed) interests, too.[4]

In credit to Mannheim, and in conclusion here, we may say that his attempt to link Marx's materialist conception of society with the idealist view of the intentionally acting actor was commendable. The preliminary attempt to view thought with reference to social structure was fruitful and will continue to be deserving of a great deal of research in the future. Finally, his attempts to come to terms with the problems of modern mass society and the future of democracy remains a compelling area of investigation and interpretation for us all.

SELECTED BIBLIOGRAPHY

Adler, Franz. "The Range of Sociology of Knowledge." In Howard Becker and Alvin Boskoff (Eds.), *Modern Sociological Theory*. New York: Holt, Rinehart and Winston, 1957. Pp. 396–423.

Berger, Peter L., and Thomas Luckmann. *The Social Construction of Reality*. Garden City, N.Y.: Doubleday, 1967.

Boskoff, Alvin. *Theory in American Sociology*. New York: Crowell, 1969. Chap. VIII.

Connolly, William E. *Political Science and Ideology*. New York: Atherton, 1967.

Curtis, James E., and John W. Petras (Eds.). *Sociology of Knowledge*. New York: Praeger, 1970.

Holzner, Burkart. *Reality Construction in Society*. Cambridge, Mass.: Schenkman Publishing Company, 1968.

Maquet, J. J. *The Sociology of Knowledge*. Boston: Beacon, 1951.

---

[3] Ibid., p. 303.

[4] Mannheim's point is, of course, that knowledge of social reality is socio-existentially determined and that sociology, as the study of the social bases underlying the shaping of cognition, would be a useful aid in determining the validity of such knowledge. The fact that these bases change makes such knowledge especially problematical.

Merton, Robert K. *Social Theory and Social Structure.* New York: Free Press, 1968. Chap. XV.

Remmling, Gunter W. *Road to Suspicion.* New York: Appleton, 1967.

Remmling, Gunter W. "Philosophical Parameters of Karl Mannheim's Sociology of Knowledge." *The Sociological Quarterly,* 12 (Autumn 1971), 531–547.

Stark, Werner. *The Sociology of Knowledge.* New York: Free Press, 1958.

Wagner, Helmut R. "Mannheim's Historicism." *Social Research,* 19 (September 1952), 300–321.

Walter, Benjamin. "The Sociology of Knowledge and the Problem of Objectivity." In Llewellyn Gross (Ed.), *Sociological Theory.* New York: Harper & Row, 1967. Pp. 335–357.

Willer, Judith. *The Social Determination of Knowledge.* Englewood Cliffs, N.J.: Prentice-Hall, 1971.

Wolff, Kurt H. "The Sociology of Knowledge and Sociological Theory." In Llewellyn Gross (Ed.), *Symposium on Sociological Theory.* Evanston, Ill.: Harper & Row, 1959. Pp. 567–602.

Wolff, Kurt H., (Ed.). *From Karl Mannheim.* New York: Oxford University Press, 1971.

TEN

Social Theory Revisited

Sociology is an outgrowth of the age-old tendency of man to ask questions about his social existence, its products and causes. In objective and procedure, sociology drew on the methodology that originated with physical science in the fifteenth and sixteenth centuries. Disciplined sociology was born in the midst of crisis and change in European societies in the eighteenth and nineteenth centuries. Although sociology resembles, and may in the future resemble even more, physical science in logical structure, the sociologist's inevitable participation in the very phenomena he seeks to understand, explain, or control sets sociology off from physical science in spirit and in ultimate use. Edward Shils refers to this in calling sociology an act of self-interpretation.[1] There is also something about social phenomena—their multifacetedness, changeability, and complexity perhaps—that distinguishes them from physical phenomena in degree if not kind. Sociology gropes for an outlook and method suitable to such a subject matter, even if this means the adoption of many diverse outlooks and methodologies.[2]

Sociologists, at least some of them, have also sought to be interpreters—diagnosticians—of their age and of the future of man and society. This penchant was noticeable in the writings of the theorists covered in this book, especially in the works of Comte, Marx, Weber, and Mannheim. Those who have undertaken this task have stimulated much debate and disagreement concerning how to judge the features of power and equity in society.[3] Every sociologist has his own view of society and conjectures

---

[1] Edward Shils, "The Calling of Sociology," in Talcott Parsons et al. (Eds.), *Theories of Society* (New York: Free Press, 1961), p. 1420.

[2] See Leon H. Warshay, "The Current State of Sociological Theory: Diversity, Polarity, Empiricism, and Small Theories," *Sociological Quarterly*, 12 (Winter 1971), 23–45.

[3] Many examples could be cited. For a defense of modern society see Shils, "Calling of Sociology," and Seymour Lipset's defense of *The First New Nation* in his debate with Irving Horowitz, in "The Birth and Meaning of America," *Sociological Quarterly*, 7 (Winter 1966), 3–20. The critical attack is exemplified in C. Wright Mills, *The Power Elite* (New York: Oxford University Press, 1956), and Thomas Ford Hoult, "Who Shall Prepare Himself for Battle?" *The American Sociologist*, 3 (February 1968), 3–7.

about why it works well this way or that. These diagnoses—part of the baggage he carries to his work—influence the theories he constructs.[4]

Sociology in the United States, seeking to legitimate itself in a climate of pragmatism, social change, and social problems, became very empirical between 1920 and 1945. Sociologists grew in numbers as colleges grew and job opportunities in business, industry, and government enlarged. Areas of specialization in the field proliferated, and research procedures became more intensified. Several reactions to these developments occurred. One was the attempt by Talcott Parsons (and others)[5] to synthesize a framework for a general theory of action that would draw the various social sciences together and provide a conceptual guide for locating the different problems studied by sociologists themselves.

Another reaction was radical sociology,[6] the main roots of which were in the depression and postdepression period in the United States. The depression encouraged sociologists to look beyond the narrow focus in which social problems had been viewed and now saw them as products of the larger structure and inadequacies of society. Radical sociology rejected the so-called value-neutrality stance that Weber had urged the sociologist to assume in relation to politics and political affairs. The new movement grew as regulative and coordinative institutions in mass society became more centralized. It asserted that modern society was oppressive and without conscience and that many sociologists were, advertently or inadvertently, accomplices of the insensitivity by virtue of the way they fashioned their research questions and served "intelligence" data to those in power. Supporters of radical sociology called for the sociologist to use his knowledge in the task of constructing a more "humane" society.

The theories of the classical period took shape in a milieu of growing rationality and technical efficiency. The strength and type of government, the character of industrialization, and the size and place of the middle classes in France, England, and Germany were crucial conditions that influenced the topics and assumptions of Comte, Spencer, Marx, Weber, and Durkheim. In England, as we have seen, industrialization got off to a vigorous start, the middle classes grew, and the government facilitated the satisfaction of their needs and remained, for a while at least, unobtrusive. In Germany the imitative industrialization was carried out under the auspices of a strong government, but one that remained aloof from the middle classes. Thus, Weber dealt at length with types of authority, legitimation, and the merit of the middle-class Protestant ethic, while Spencer wrote on evolutionism, taking less interest in Weber's problems since, in England, the middle classes were dealt with less paternalistically. Marx, writing

---

[4] See Ralf Dahrendorf, *Essays in the Theory of Society* (Stanford, Calif.: Stanford University Press, 1968), esp. Chap. I; and Alvin W. Gouldner, *The Coming Crisis of Western Sociology* (New York: Avon Books, 1970), esp. Chap. II.

[5] See Talcott Parsons and Edward Shils (Eds.), *Toward a General Theory of Action* (New York: Harper & Row, 1962).

[6] See references to Mills and Hoult in footnote 3, above.

from a more marginal position than Weber, saw the capitalistic system destroying human relations and consequently sought to hasten its passage, while retaining some of its production virtues under the authority of the proletariat. Nationhood was less problematical in Germany and England than in France, where the clamor for power by a multitude of factions and the sharp break from the medieval past exacerbated the problems of industrialization. Both Comte and Durkheim, therefore, took the problem of social order as central.

We have tried in each chapter of this book to relate the theorist's life to his work and discuss the merit that the theoretical ideas themselves may have had on their own. Some stereotypes about these theorists hopefully have been qualified. A few might be reviewed here. Comte was not just a "science worshipper." He may have been zealous and overly confident about the virtues and promises of science, but he dared to dream of a world in which man would realize himself through science, free himself from crippling ignorance, and yet appreciate the moral and traditional aspects of social life. In his sociological analysis, Comte came to terms with the existing realities of society, noting especially the positive and negative tendencies of the industrial revolution and its impact on the division of labor.

Spencer expected the better adaptation of man to his circumstances to result in greater happiness and viewed society as a whole in progressive evolution. But he was not just a "grand evolutionist," leaving progress to the lawful workings of nature. He gathered a great deal of data on institutions in societies the world over and classified them carefully in an investigation that gave sociology a serious cast, as befits a science. And there is still a great deal of interest in the directional change of societies and the intermediate stages of social development, subjects that Spencer pioneered.

Marx's analysis of social change, which called attention to the dynamic inherent in capitalist production, has never been rivaled. According to the stereotype, however, he saw the stages of capitalistic exploitation as inevitable. Such was not the case. He gave us the spirit rather than the letter of a method of analysis by which we can assess the various impacts that changes in economic relations have on social organization.

Weber is remembered chiefly for having pioneered "interpretive" sociology—the *verstehende* method. Actually, something much deeper resulted from his work. He was interested in apprehending the value-significance of social actions that makes them distinctive on the human level. At the same time, however, he was careful not to ignore the external verification of such apprehensions. Weber always made cautious use of mental constructions, which gave a hypothetical understanding of the order or interrelation of events, and consistently regarded them as tentative. Through his ideas we have learned that at the level of socio-historical events themselves we should be prepared to meet great complexity, change, and the varied functional and causal linkages that the world of cultural man exhibits.

Many accuse Simmel of having been too unsystematic and "philosophic." In fact, his approach was unified by his concerns about the direction of modern culture and by his interest in the eternal processes of reciprocity, duality, distance, and the like. Refusing to make peace with fixed and restrictive forms, he sought through his analysis to disclose the micro-processes in which man continually re-creates the social relations within his control.

Durkheim is supposed to have used agelicism as the framework for all of his analyses. The fact is, however, that his view shifted as the focus of his research shifted, and vice versa. He had a profound appreciation of the way rules, nonempirical reality, bring about real social consequences and of man's struggles to make real objects of rules by exerting effort, sacrificing, and punishing in their name. Durkheim also became interested in the process by which real actors construct the collective conscience.

Many of the theorists considered here knew of one another's work. Like sociologists today, they sometimes dismissed or disparaged their colleagues' ideas as they competed for prestige.[7] Although Spencer and Comte, for example, were familiar with each other's writings and even met on one occasion, neither had a great deal of regard for the work of the other. Spencer pointedly claimed to be studying not the evolution of intellect to the positive stage, but "real" *things* and the phenomena that constitute nature. Marx knew of Comte's writings also but said there was nothing "positive" about positivism; apparently referring to the emphasis Comte placed on the evolution of the intellect and to the role he assigned to intellect in the keeping of social order and the furtherance of progress. It is not clear if Weber was acquainted with Durkheim's work, but he did know of Marx's, which he esteemed highly. In particular, Weber praised Marx's conception of socioeconomic change as one of the greatest attempts at ideal type construction. Weber sought, however, to modify Marx's idea that causation derives exclusively from the economic sphere of society by showing the interplay between ideal and material interests.

Durkheim was familiar with the works of Comte, Spencer, Marx, and Weber. He gained some insights from Comte but deplored what he saw as Comte's attempt to produce solidarity in society by harking back to common beliefs. We have already indicated that Durkheim criticized Spencerian sociology for being naively individualistic. Durkheim also argued against the socialist programs, in part because he thought they overstimulated the desire for satisfaction of all consumption "needs"; moral needs were more important to him, especially the strength that derives from the individual's attachment to the group. Finally, Durkheim distrusted some of Weber's work because he feared that the German scholar was too closely involved with religious valuation.

Sociological theory, it has been said,[8] is often divided into two separate categories: one is the history of sociological thought which concerns comprehensive systems of philosophy, methodology, and sociological theory constructed by individual theorists; and the other is

---

[7] See Robert K. Merton, *On Theoretical Sociology* (New York: Free Press, 1967), pp. 53–56.

[8] Neil J. Smelser, *Sociological Theory: A Contemporary View* (New York: General Learning Press, 1971), pp. 1, 2.

systematic theory, which includes the more recent systems of theory that are the products of the accumulated effort of a large number of theorist–researchers and that apply criteria for theoretical adequacy generally accepted in modern science.[9] We have attempted to do both in this book, to present the system of each theorist and to evaluate the type of theory each produced, apart from its setting.

Theory in the broad sense, as we indicated in the Introduction to this book, aims at the construction of abstract statements that go beyond mere observations and indicate some kind of general connection between events, thus making possible the explanation of new events. Explanation is, then, the nub of the matter. In a way, we may construe the theories covered in this book as kinds of explanations that the early theorists developed and used and their successors have added to and refined. The full *logic* of these explanations is in many cases still quite obscure, but we shall nevertheless try to indicate the outlines and modes of comprehension of the several major types developed, even embryonically, by theorists in this book. In addition, we will mention several types developed more recently.

According to the *evolutionary* explanation, society is a system of interconnected parts that changes slowly, but continuously and smoothly, over a long period of time. The main theory explains social change as the result of *adaptation*, which occurs in response to major internal or external pressures or problems. The result is a given line of selection if the system survives at all. This explanation is quite vague since the types of problems are highly varied, the types of responses are diverse, and the judgment about whether the system is surviving (or how well) must be suspended until some time has elapsed. The effect of adaptation on the structure of the system might be either a more differentiated specialization of functions of parts or a less differentiated specialization. Up to this point in world history, evolutionists have usually found evidence of the former effect in societies. The evolutionary view, especially of William Graham Sumner, concerning the level of individual organisms or actors (the micro-level) has been that individuals unthinkingly adopt the ways of the group as habits. According to Sumner, some of these habits, such as thrift and industriousness, have survival value. Habits are taken as characteristic of the individual or group, just as in biological evolution physical traits are taken as characteristic of the species. Ideologically, evolutionists have usually favored a so-called natural process of slow, unfettered development of relations among substructures within the larger whole of society, whose requirements constitute demands on the functioning parts.

Another explanation, the macro-, or general, evolution theory, involves the idea that a system develops in stages, each stage limiting what the general nature of the system can be at a future stage.[10] This theory

---

[9] For an example of such criteria see the review by Joseph Berger and Morris Zelditch, Jr., of Talcott Parsons, *Sociological Theory and Modern Society*, in *American Sociological Review*, 33 (June 1968), 446–450.

[10] Macro-conflict theorists such as Marx may be included here. They assume a largely internal dynamic by which the system generates its own (radical) change.

actually has some of the features of a structural explanation, to be discussed below.

According to the *structural* explanation, such as that championed by Durkheim in *Suicide*, a society or a group has an interrelated set of parts. Any one of these parts exists and develops because it is compatible with the other parts with which it must relate in a kind of configuration. That is, to use George Caspar Homans's[11] example, it is possible to interpret the existence of matrilineality as the result of its compatibility with the constraints of a type of residence pattern at marriage, a certain system of authority over children, and other *already* established features of the group. It would follow, then, that a change in one part of a group would be followed by a change in others, although structural explanations are usually *synchronic*—concerned with the consequences of the present structure in operation here and now—rather than *diachronic*—relating to structural change over a period of time. An example of the latter is Marx's explanation of change in production relations as a consequence of the development and change of productive forces over time. Structural theory, in general, rests on the idea that because the parts of a group can fit together only in certain ways, they limit the possibilities of change; thus, the growth of a new part is determined by the configuration of the old. For example, suicide is the consequence of the structural characteristic of low group cohesion. One of the merits of this type of explanation is that a practice such as matrilineality does not have to be explained as intentionally designed and implemented by a society on account of its fit with other practices; its fit simply renders its growth more probable than that of another practice.

The view that behavior is the consequence of the structure or organization of a setting, system of relationships, or group has been touted as *the* model of a distinctively sociological (as opposed to a psychological) explanation since it concerns properties of groups (e.g., division of labor or mobility rate) rather than of individuals. To prove their theory, however, structuralists must show that behavior results *primarily* from the structure within which it occurs, not from the individuals qua individual because they, having been selected into a group, for example, may be predisposed to behave in a certain manner. Proof rests on the demonstration that a structured group, setting, or situation has influenced the behavior of individuals by shaping the conditions, parameters, and rewards of their *interaction.* Behavior is, in the last analysis, affected by interaction. In order to make such effects more understandable, however, one must supplement the structural explanation with various social–psychological explanations, which can show *how* the structure of a group is translated into predominant kinds (or rates) of behavior. Weber combined the two types of explanations by investigating the meanings or motives of hypothetical actors who would, for example, be producing capitalistic growth as a result of the structuring of their lives under ascetic Protestantism.

---

[11] George Casper Homans, "Contemporary Theory in Sociology," in Robert E. L. Faris (Ed.), *Handbook of Modern Sociology* (Skokie, Ill.: Rand McNally, 1964), pp. 961–963.

In order to show the effects of a structural feature on behavior, and thus that the structural explanation is useful for certain purposes, one has to find or construct two or more groups or settings in which the structures are the same (and the individuals are similar), except in one respect: only one group should have the feature that allegedly produces a difference in behavior. This is not always easy to do, and such a demonstration can run aground on the ecological fallacy, the erroneous assumption that the individuals who exhibit the predominant type of behavior in a group under investigation are necessarily the same individuals who are most affected by the structural conditions of that group; in fact, the individuals in each case may be different. Thus, for example, Durkheim's finding of a lower suicide rate in Catholic *areas* (or in "ecological niches" where Catholics predominate) than in Protestant areas does not prove a connection between religious structure and suicide rate unless it is Catholic *individuals* who less frequently commit suicide (and this is not necessarily the case at the aggregate level since not all individuals commit suicide and not all individuals in the areas studied by Durkheim were Catholic).[12]

A third type of explanation has been called *functional*, which is not to be confused with functional *analysis*, a method for disclosing simply what effect on other parts the change in structure or functioning of a particular part produces. Functional analysis, as Richard P. Appelbaum has indicated,[13] is easily aligned with evolutionary analysis since both utilize the concept of differentiation in an important way: evolutionary analysis is interested in how differentiation in a society comes about, while functional analysis is concerned with how new alignments among differentiated parts occur and what their consequences are.

Functional explanation is based on the idea that a part (activity, group, or rule) exists in a system because its function is to satisfy (even if only to a small degree) some need(s) or requisite(s) of the system. Durkheim developed some of the outlines of this type of explanation, but sociologists have become more conscious of its merits and shortcomings only quite recently. Homans,[14] among others, has noted some of the problems. It is difficult, for example, to specify what the universal needs of a society are, let alone the degree to which individuals and groups must fulfill them in order to insure the society's minimum survival. Moreover, few tests could effectively demonstrate the invalidity of a hypothesized social need. For societies in general the list of needs would be almost uselessly abstract, and for particular societies, almost unmanageably long (e.g., resistance to measles, "firewater," pollution, etc.).

---

[12] Quite a substantial literature exists on the methodology and pitfalls of structural explanation. Two examples are Donald I. Warren, "Structural Effects," unpublished ms., University of Michigan; and Matilda White Riley, *Sociological Research* (New York: Harcourt, 1963), pp. 700–739.

[13] Richard P. Appelbaum, *Theories of Social Change* (Chicago: Markham, 1970), p. 54.

[14] Homans, "Contemporary Theory in Sociology."

There is also the danger that on the basis of an examination of a part, one might draw an erroneous conclusion about what need it fulfills and, hence, what its function is. To rest an explanation of the origin of the part on such faulty reasoning would be equally faulty. For example, one might suppose on examining a man's face that he needed something to hang his spectacles on, and therefore the nose developed! But the nose was there long before a man "needed" a support for his spectacles. Likewise, the origins of such customs as the wailing ceremony and a pattern of inheritance cannot be explained in terms of their functions (the regrouping of society and the transfer of property in an orderly manner) if these customs existed before the needs they fulfill were present. The wailing ceremony and inheritance pattern might have *acquired* these functions, but their functions would merely explain or provide one reason for the *persistence* of these structures rather than qualify as explanations of their origins. Undoubtedly, through explicit human purpose some structures *are* brought into existence because of the functions they will serve. But reference to such purposes does not comprise the full explanation of the origins of even these structures.

Arthur L. Stinchcombe[15] has attempted to elucidate how a functionalistic process operates and to circumvent in part some of the problems of functionalism and its relation to human purposes. According to him, if a structure functions successfully to solve some problem or lessen some tension and thereby promote the survival of a system in a natural or desirable state then these beneficial effects will reinforce the structure and insure that *it* rather than some other structure will continue. Stinchcombe asserts that reinforcement may depend solely on the outcome of an equifinal process, in which systems that do not have such a structure (or something of its type) to handle a problem will finally die out or break down and those that do have them will continue. To return to one of the examples we gave above, a society that has accumulated property might very well be threatened with chaos if workable and effective rules of inheritance (structures with these functions) were not devised.

Functionalism has been criticized for its implied tendency toward conservatism; it intimates that in nature, if not by man's design, the tension is urgent, operational (e.g., regulatory) structures are "needed" to conserve or rescue the system, and those structures that work are difficult to abandon.[16]

Today, a sociologist chooses from among the three types of explanations considered thus far—the evolutionary, the structural, or the functional—on the basis of his assessment of the situation and the social

---

[15] Arthur L. Stinchcombe, *Constructing Social Theories* (New York: Harcourt, 1968), pp. 80–93.

[16] Critics have further complaints: adherents of this type of explanation assess functions (positive or negative) only with reference to the normative structure of society; they ignore the facts that norms are ideal, are not always reflected in actuality, and might be changing, and, moreover, that complex societies may subscribe to several different sets of norms.

problem that it exemplifies. Where patterns of interaction are relatively stable and/or the situation is well defined by rules and procedures—as in formal organizations—a structural explanation may carry the greatest weight because other processes, such as major, long-term technological change or changes in modes of learning among the actors, can be either discounted or considered only parenthetically. Structural change itself, on the other hand, might best be interpreted through an evolutionary explanation. Functionalism analyzes effects (or functions) in a special way: from the standpoint of the equilibrium of a system. Therefore, *when the system is surviving*, one can explain the continuation of a part in terms of its function if the function really has anything to do with fulfilling the requirements for the operation of the system. However, if flux among actors happens to be the focus of inquiry, other types of explanations are called for. To these we now turn.

One that is little developed but widely used in sociology is the *motive* explanation.[17] Some sociologists, however, do not fully acknowledge motives because they are not usually sufficient to explain conduct and because theorists often detect them in the course of faulty introspections. Weber paid much attention to motive explanations, as we have indicated in Chapter Five. Motive explanations clarify actions that involve a choice since neither tradition (or habit) nor a uniformly structured situation fully constrains them. Assuming that a person behaves according to a certain standard, we can explain a particular action (in part) as a response to a motive in harmony with such a standard (or biophysical condition) if he chose this action over another that was open to him. Or we can speculate that an individual would be likely to perform a certain action (rather than another open to him) if he had the opportunity to act on a particular motive. Knowledge of motives gives us a more intimate understanding of action on the human level since they distinguish most actions of humans from behaviors of nonhumans. Some sociologists are also interested in investigating more fully the conditions under which a person is likely to take one action or another (not just when he has accepted a clear standard), why one standard rather than another affects behavior, and how the operation of sanctions supplements the motive explanation of actions.

A second explanation focusing on individuals and their creative actions is the *symbolic-interactionist* type, championed, as we have learned, primarily by Mead. Such explanations may also refer to motives, but they rely more heavily on the notion that the social world, at least as expressed in the realities of individuals, is in a continuous process of formation—it is an emergent—and that its understructure consists of a constantly forming, breaking, and re-forming of meanings. The orientation is, strictly speaking, not "cause"-directed in the sense that identifiable

---

[17] See Erik Allardt, "Structural, Institutional, and Cultural Explanations," *Acta Sociologica*, 15, No. 1 (1972), 55–57; Robert Brown, *Explanation in Social Science* (Chicago: Aldine, 1963), esp. Chaps. VI–VIII; and Gwynn Nettler, *Explanations* (New York: McGraw-Hill, 1970), esp. Chap. III.

independent variables operate prior to behavior and effect it. The symbolic-interactionist view assumes much more of a simultaneity and cognitive and adaptive indeterminacy. This perspective is distinct from others because it is concerned with how action unfolds as a result of the dialogue of the "I" and "me" telescoped in the language-represented realities taken from the alternating standpoint of the self and other. Individuals adapt to one another and "read" the meanings of their adaptations; these readings then become the context for the next series of pragmatic actions. Throughout this process the self becomes both subject and object in a medium of symbols. This view is likely to gain ground, for it closely aligns itself with the increasingly popular notion that there is a realm of truth in experience that rational science has heretofore ignored and that the investigator, by immersing himself as fully as possible in the experiences of his subjects (despite the "liabilities" of "disturbing" them by his intrusion) can act as a conduit for this truth. We have already criticized symbolic interactionism in Chapter Eight, chiefly because it often ignores those social realities that are not constituted directly by the ideas of the participants. For example, understanding a class structure depends on knowing not only the meanings that people in it attach to a given rank, but also *how many* people are in the rank; this latter data may be completely unknown to the participants but may have important consequences for those who aspire to advance their social standing and for the scientist who is trying to predict rates of mobility. The symbolic-interactionist perspective also pays little attention to the societal coercions that make certain ways of defining the situation available to one actor and not to others.[18]

---

[18] There is emerging, partly from the Meadian view, a fundamental "existentialist" critique of "absolutistic" or "deductive" theory, which has remained the dominant approach to theory in sociology. The critique draws on the sociology of knowledge and holds that what theory "is" depends on one's view of man. The way of viewing is tied to the way of living. Deductive, rationalistic theory is made possible by a view of man that assumes some kind of relationship he is making to his environment, e.g., controlling. Its methodology, according to the critique, is borrowed from the natural sciences and entails the imposition of predetermined categories of meaning (of what man is like and doing) in a world in which largely external forces operate. This kind of theory is a "display of mind" that short-cuts the relationship between men and their actions and aids in creating (or sustaining) a reality in which abstractions guide practices by putting on them the limits of action or meaning assumed by the deductive theorist's image of the world. The existential view is that theory must incorporate man with reference to the meanings and real situations in everyday life and thereby illuminate a view of the world in which man is not the victim of his imprisonment within society, but the creator of alternatives. The existential critique harks back to the desire to restore "wholeness" to man's life and to seek the meaning of his existence and survival as a human being in mass society. See Alan F. Blum, "Theorizing," in Jack D. Douglas (Ed.), *Understanding Everyday Life* (Chicago: Aldine Publishing Company, 1970), pp. 301–319; and Peter K. Manning, "Existential Sociology," *The Sociological Quarterly*, 14 (Spring 1973), 200–225.

We shall now consider a third and final explanation that refers primarily to individuals, namely, the *behavioral,* or *"psychological,"* type. While it has no immediate relation to the theorists treated in this book, it does perhaps pertain to Sumner's references to pleasure and pain as the means by which folkways come about. It was most seriously introduced into sociology recently by Homans.[19] His leading proposition is that "men are likely to take actions that they perceive are, in the circumstances, likely to achieve rewarding results." The psychological view rests mainly on the so-called "law of effects" principle, which states that the effects of past actions are important in shaping similar actions in the present and future and, for specific actions, we must investigate the conditions under which the effects operated. Among other reasons Homans has for advancing such a view is his claim that, in spite of what sociologists say, they have no *distinctive* sociological explanations; they actually use some psychological explanations, along with whatever others they employ, which are in fact more truly general and powerful than those of Parsons (a sociologist). Furthermore, Homans adheres to the deductive set-of-laws type of explanation, which follows the logic of the physical sciences quite closely.

Many criticisms have been leveled against Homans's view: he has not actually fulfilled the deductive explanatory task, or, in other words, he has not logically derived the social patterns from the psychological propositions in a rigorous manner and has, thus, not explained them, even according to his own view;[20] he ignores the existence of "compositional effects"[21] (the process by which individuals monitor, correct, and complicate their own behavior); and his notion of reward and reinforcement is too vague or confined mainly to clinical types of settings.[22]

It appears that a large part of the controversy Homans has stirred stems from his disagreement with Parsonian sociology: Homans contends that since Parsonian sociology is modeled on a functionalist view that leaves individuals out and attributes needs or requisites to systems whose existence, Homans claims, is noncontingent (cannot be determined), Parsonian sociology is, therefore, not explanatory, let alone general or

---

[19] See Homans, "Contemporary Theory in Sociology" and also some of his other works: *Social Behavior, Its Elementary Forms* (New York: Harcourt, 1961); *The Nature of Social Science* (New York: Harcourt, 1967); and "Fundamental Social Processes," in Neil J. Smelser (Ed.), *Sociology (New York:* Wiley, 1967), pp. 27–78.

[20] Ron Maris, "The Logical Adequacy of Homans' Social Theory, *American Sociological Review,* 35 (December 1970), 1069–1081.

[21] Walter Buckley, *Sociology and Modern Systems Theory* (Englewood Cliffs, N.J.: Prentice-Hall, 1967), p. 111.

[22] See James A. Davis's review of *Social Behavior, Its Elementary Forms,* in the *American Journal of Sociology,* 67 (January, 1962), 458; and Kurt W. Back's review of *Behavioral Sociology* (New York: Columbia University Press, 1967), edited by Robert L. Burgess and Don Bushell, Jr., in the *American Sociological Review,* 30 (December 1965), 1098–1100.

distinctive. Much of his disagreement with other sociologists might be resolved if they specified rules of combination that showed how principles applying to individuals result in the formation of structures more characteristic of groups,[23] and if they recognized that Homans seems to take certain features of social life for granted that they generally do not, and vice versa. In other words, their "givens" are different. Homans attempts to show how individuals acquired given structures (e.g., the family farm pattern in the U.S.) through processes of reward and reinforcement rather than why one structure instead of another existed in the first place; other sociologists, however, usually take the behavior-learning processes for granted, treating them as constant.[24] Homans also asks only a specific "why" question: why, in terms of (the effects of) the reward for conduct of individuals, do given social patterns come about? It may well be that virtually all the purportedly sociological explanations now used by sociologists are interpretable in terms of Homans's psychological propositions; it remains to be seen if they are actually *reducible* to that level.

Another type of explanation that has been suggested is the *organizational*.[25] We treat this more as a framework for analysis or an orientation rather than a theory since it is quite broad and since not until one knows what is problematical about organizations can one select or construct an explanation to account for the problematical features. Organizational analysis provides a conceptual framework of elements such as norms, statuses, institutions, and so forth. We might wish to know how or why different styles of supervision over employees are successful under different conditions, why the organization changes, or how to explain linkages to other organizations. Organizations range from the formal to the informal, from the large to the small, and differ as widely as communities, businesses, and social or governmental service agencies. The typology of communities or societies such as Spencer's or Durkheim's and Weber's description of bureaucracy all can be viewed within organizational analysis.

Two other types of explanation resemble some of those that we have already discussed.

The so-called institutional analysis described by Daniel J. Koenig and Alan E. Bayer is akin to a broad organizational analysis since it sees institutions as crescive or enacted ways of satisfying personal and social needs.[26] It is therefore also akin to both evolutionary and functional

---

[23] See Murray Webster, Jr., "Psychological Reductionism, Methodological Individualism, and Large Scale Problems," *American Sociological Review*, 38 (April 1973), 269, 272.

[24] The compatibility and separate tasks of psychological and structural (sociological) explanations are nicely stated in Allan D. Coult, "The Structuring of Structure," *American Anthropologist*, 68 (April 1966), 438–443.

[25] See Warshay, "Current State of Sociological Theory," pp. 27, 28.

[26] Daniel J. Koenig and Alan E. Bayer, "The Institutional Frame of Reference in Family Study," in F. Ivan Nye and Felix M. Berardo (Eds.), *Emerging Conceptual Frameworks in Family Analysis* (New York: Crowell-Collier-Macmillan, 1966), p. 78.

explanations. Social exchange theory is also used to explain some features of organizations. This theory is built on the idea that individuals or groups become interdependent with others by providing them with things, activities, or feelings that they cannot provide for themselves, and vice versa; this process is mediated by shared institutional agreements and continues on the basis of a reward system in which profit equals reward minus cost (including the perception that it would be less rewarding or impossible to exchange elsewhere).

We shall close by attempting to describe certain broad trends that characterize the development of sociological theory over the period covered here from Comte to Mannheim. This must be done very cautiously since the trends are by no means unilinear; that is, an earlier characteristic of sociological theory is not necessarily completely replaced by a later development, but, rather, the two might exist today side by side, or the trend might have resulted in a complex of differentiated developments at a later stage.

First, there was major interest in the global analysis of society and social solidarity, which was eclipsed in part as concepts in sociology multiplied—concepts such as formal and informal relations, competition, succession, reference group, and so on. Weber, Durkheim, and Simmel were especially instrumental in exploring new facets of social life and fashioning concepts for the analytic tasks they set themselves.

Second, sociology began, with Comte, with a diagnostic concern for social order and stability. Interest then shifted, in Marx, Weber, Durkheim, Simmel and others, to an analysis of the actual workings of society, social groups, and interrelations. In the process, theorists suspended judgments of the "social problem" character of society in order to translate moral concerns into research questions that might yield a wider range, and the less visible connections of, events.

Related to the second trend are two subsidiary and parallel trends. There has been a shift, though not uniformly, from a concern for application, in which scientific investigation is measured by the usefulness of its data to society, to a concern for explanatory theory, in which scientific investigation is measured by its development of an abstract, organized body of knowledge. This has involved another development—the growth of a greater consciousness of the form that scientific theory should take and the criteria by which scientific theory should be judged. Durkheim's sociology is most relevant here, especially his approach to suicide.

Third, the assumption with which Comte, Spencer, and Marx began— that there were laws of nature driving history and determining the character of social order—came into serious question. Knowledge of such laws was of little use when interest turned to the study of some of the particular workings of society. Sociology became more cognizant of the complexity of relationships and "causes," and the mechanistic certitude supposed in the earlier, predominantly mono-causal explanations withered away.

Fourth, interest in the "exterior" worlds of individuals in their society was supplemented by divergent interests in the "interior" world of the actor alone or the actor in interaction. This is not to say that the latter replaced the former; rather, several different approaches became available, owing, to some extent, to a shift in Durkheim's sociology, but more importantly to the development of Weber's, Simmel's, and Mead's sociologies.

Fifth, a broad "speculative" style of inquiry gave way to a methodology of operationalism, sampling, testing, multivariate analysis, and research design questions. Although the research conducted by some of the theorists in this book was rigorous, such as Durkheim's and Weber's, the movement toward rigor that we allude to here resulted from more recent developments in statistical techniques, quasi-experimental methodologies, and the critical analysis and specification of the meaning of concepts.

Finally, a shift in institutional base occurred. Sociology became primarily situated in colleges and universities. The organization of societies of sociologists and the specialization and proliferation of interests developed as the number of sociologists grew. This resulted in the opening of new avenues of communication among sociologists.

SELECTED BIBLIOGRAPHY

General

Abel, Theodore. *The Foundation of Sociological Theory*. New York: Random House, 1970.

Aron, Raymond. *Main Currents in Sociological Thought II*. New York: Basic Books, 1967.

Aron, Raymond. *Main Currents in Sociological Thought I*. Garden City, N.Y.: Doubleday, Anchor Books, 1968.

Barnes, Harry Elmer, (Ed.). *An Introduction to the History of Sociology*. Chicago: University of Chicago Press, 1948. (Also, an abridged, paperback version is available from the same publisher. 1966.)

Becker, Howard, and Harry Elmer Barnes. *Social Thought from Lore to Science*. 3 vols. 3d ed., New York: Dover, 1961.

Becker, Howard, and Alvin Boskoff (Eds.). *Modern Sociological Theory: In Continuity and Change*. New York: Holt, Rinehart and Winston, 1957.

Borgatta, Eugene F., and Henry J. Meyer (Eds.). *Sociological Theory: Present-Day Sociology from the Past*. New York: Knopf, 1961.

Boskoff, Alvin. *Theory in American Sociology*. New York: Crowell, 1969.

Cohen, Percy S. *Modern Social Theory*. New York: Basic Books, 1968.

Coser, Lewis A. *Masters of Sociological Thought*. New York: Harcourt, 1971.

Coser, Lewis A. (Gen. Ed.). *Makers of Modern Social Science Series*. Englewood Cliffs, N.J.: Prentice-Hall.
  1. Coser, Lewis A. (Ed.). *Georg Simmel*. 1965.
  2. Meisel, James H. (Ed.). *Pareto & Mosca*. 1965.
  3. Nisbet, Robert A. (Ed.). *Emile Durkheim*. 1965.
  4. Wrong, Dennis (Ed.). *Max Weber*. 1970.

Coser, Lewis A., and Bernard Rosenberg (Eds.). *Sociological Theory: A Book of Readings*. 2d ed. New York: Crowell-Collier-Macmillan, 1964.

Cuzzort, R. P. *Humanity and Modern Sociological Thought*. New York: Holt, Rinehart and Winston, 1969.

Deutsch, Morton, and Robert M. Krauss. *Theories in Social Psychology.* New York: Basic Books, 1965.
Furfey, Paul Hanley. *The Scope and Method of Sociology.* New York: Harper & Row, 1953.
Gross, Llewellyn (Ed.). *Symposium on Sociological Theory.* New York: Row, Peterson, & Company, 1959.
Gross, Llewellyn (Ed.). *Sociological Theory: Inquiries and Paradigms.* New York: Harper & Row, 1967.
House, Floyd N. *The Range of Social Theory.* New York: Holt, Rinehart and Winston, 1929.
Hughes, H. Stuart. *Consciousness and Society.* New York: Vintage Books, 1961 (paperback).
Janowitz, Morris (Gen. Ed.). *Heritage of Sociology Series.* Chicago: University of Chicago Press.
1. Abrams, Philip. *The Origins of British Sociology: 1834–1914.* 1968.
2. Duncan, Otis Dudley (Ed.). *William F. Ogburn on Culture and Social Change.* 1964.
3. Eisenstadt, S. N. (Ed.). *Max Weber on Charisma and Institution Building.* 1968.
4. Faris, Robert E. L. *Chicago Sociology 1920–1932.* 1967.
5. Janowitz, Morris (Ed.). *W. I. Thomas on Social Organization and Social Personality.* 1966.
6. Reiss, Jr., Albert J. (Ed.). *Louis Wirth on Cities and Social Life.* 1964.
7. Schneider, Louis (Ed.). *The Scottish Moralists on Human Nature and Society.* 1967.
8. Strauss, Anselm (Ed.). *George Herbert Mead on Social Psychology.* 1964.
9. Turner, Ralph H. (Ed.). *Robert E. Park on Social Control and Collective Behavior.* 1967.
Lee, Alfred McClung (Gen. Ed.). *Major Contributors to Social Science Series.* New York: Crowell.
1. Davie, Maurice R. *William Graham Sumner.* n.d.
2. Gerver, Israel. *Lester Frank Ward.* 1963.
3. Lopreato, Joseph. *Vilfredo Pareto.* 1965.
4. Miller, S. M. *Max Weber.* 1963.
5. Rosenberg, Bernard. *Thorstein Veblen.* 1963.
6. Simpson, George. *Emile Durkheim.* 1963.
7. Simpson, George. *Auguste Comte.* 1969.
Loomis, Charles P. and Zona K. Loomis. *Modern Social Theories: Selected American Writers.* Princeton, N.J.: Van Nostrand Company, 1961.
Lichtenberger, James P. *Development of Social Thought.* New York: Appleton, 1925.
Madge, John. *The Origins of Scientific Sociology.* New York: Free Press, 1962.
Martindale, Don. *The Nature and Types of Sociological Theory.* Boston: Houghton Mifflin, 1960.

Merton, Robert K. *Social Theory and Social Structure.* Rev. and enl. ed. New York: The Free Press, 1957.

Merton, Robert K. *On Theoretical Sociology: Five Essays, Old and New.* New York: Free Press, 1967 (paperback).

Mihanovich, Clement Simon (Ed.). *Social Theorists.* Milwaukee, Wis.: Bruce, 1953.

Mills, C. Wright. *Images of Man: The Classic Traditions in Sociological Thinking.* New York: Braziller, 1960.

Mitchell, G. Duncan. *A Hundred Years of Sociology.* Chicago: Aldine, 1968.

Nisbet, Robert A. *The Sociological Tradition.* New York: Basic Books, 1966.

Odum, Howard Washington. *American Sociology: The Story of Sociology in the United States through 1950.* New York: McKay, 1951.

Parsons, Talcott. *The Structure of Social Action.* New York: Free Press, 1949.

Parsons, Talcott. *Sociological Theory and Modern Society.* New York: Free Press, 1967.

Parsons, Talcott, Edward Shils, Kasper D. Naegele, and Jessie R. Pitts (Eds.). *Theories of Society.* New York: Free Press, 1961.

Rose, Arnold M. *Theory and Method in the Social Sciences.* Minneapolis: University of Minnesota Press, 1954.

Ruitenbeek, Hendrik M., (Ed.). *Varieties of Classic Social Theory.* New York: Dutton, 1963 (paperback).

Sorokin, Pitrim A. *Sociological Theories of Today.* New York: Harper & Row, 1966.

Stark, Werner. *The Fundamental Forms of Social Thought.* New York: Fordham University Press, 1963.

Timasheff, Nicholas S. *Sociological Theory: Its Nature and Growth.* 3d ed. New York: Random House, 1967.

Vine, Margaret Wilson. *An Introduction to Sociological Theory.* New York: McKay, 1959.

Wallace, Walter L. *Sociological Theory: An Introduction.* Chicago: Aldine, 1969.

Anthropology

Bidney, David. *Theoretical Anthropology.* New York: Columbia University Press, 1953.

Harris, Marvin. *The Rise of Anthropological Theory.* New York: Crowell, 1968.

Lowie, Robert H. *The History of Ethnological Theory.* New York: Holt, Rinehart and Winston, 1937.

Specific Coverage

Aron, Raymond. *German Sociology.* New York: Crowell-Collier-Macmillan, 1964 (paperback).

Berger, Joseph, Barnard P. Cohen, J. Laurie Snell, and Morris Zelditch, Jr. *Types of Formalization in Small Group Research.* Boston: Houghton Mifflin, 1962.

Berger, Joseph, Morris Zelditch, Jr., and Bo Anderson (Eds.). *Sociological Theories in Progress.* Boston: Houghton Mifflin, 1966.

Blau, Peter. *Exchange and Power in Social Life.* New York: Wiley, 1964.

Boskoff, Alvin, and Werner J. Cahnman. *Sociology and History: Theory and Research.* New York: Free Press, 1964.

Brown, Robert. *Explanation in Social Science.* Chicago: Aldine, 1963.

Buckley, Walter. *Sociology and Modern Systems Theory.* Englewood Cliffs, N.J.: Prentice-Hall, 1967.

Catton, Jr., William R. *From Animistic to Naturalistic Sociology.* New York: McGraw-Hill, 1966.

Count, Earl W., and Gordon T. Bowles (Eds.). *Fact and Theory in Social Science.* Syracuse, N.Y.: Syracuse University Press, 1964.

Demarath III, N.J., and Richard A. Peterson. *System, Change, and Conflict.* New York: Free Press, 1967.

DiRenzo, Gordon J. (Ed.). *Concept, Theory, and Explanation in the Behavioral Sciences.* New York: Random House, 1966.

Gillin, John, et al. (Eds.). *For a Science of Social Man.* New York: Crowell-Collier-Macmillan, 1954.

Gouldner, Alvin W. *The Coming Crisis of Western Sociology.* New York: Basic Books, 1971.

Hofstadter, Richard. *Social Darwinism in American Thought.* Rev. Ed. Boston: Beacon, 1955 (paperback).

McKinney, John C. *Constructive Typology and Social Theory.* New York: Appleton, 1966.

Mills, C. Wright. *The Sociological Imagination.* New York: Grove, 1961 (paperback).

Natanson, Maurice (Ed.). *Philosophy of the Social Sciences: A Reader.* New York: Random House, 1963.

Nettler, Gwynn. *Explanations.* New York: McGraw-Hill, 1970.

Rex, John. *Key Problems of Sociological Theory.* London: Routledge & Kegan Paul, 1961.

Sjoberg, Gideon, and Roger Nett. *A Methodology for Social Research.* New York: Harper & Row, 1969.

Stern, Bernhard J. *Historical Sociology.* New York: Citadel, 1959.

Stinchcombe, Arthur L. *Constructing Social Theories.* New York: Harcourt, 1968.

White, Leonard Dupee (Ed.). *The State of Social Sciences.* Chicago: University of Chicago Press, 1956.

Willer, David. *Scientific Sociology: Theory and Method.* Englewood Cliffs, N.J.: Prentice-Hall, 1967.

Zeitlin, Irving M. *Ideology and the Development of Sociological Theory.* Englewood Cliffs, N.J.: Prentice-Hall, 1968.

Zetterberg, Hans L. *On Theory and Verification in Sociology.* 3d. ed., enl. Totowa, N.J.: The Bedminster Press, 1965.

Social Thought

Beach, Walter Greenwood. *The Growth of Social Thought.* New York: Scribner, 1939.

Becker, Howard, and Harry Elmer Barnes. *Social Thought from Lore to Science.* Vol. I. New York: Dover, 1961.

Bogardus, Emory E. *The Development of Social Thought.* 4th ed. New York: McKay, 1960.

Chambliss, Rollin. *Social Thought from Hammurabi to Comte.* New York: Holt, Rinehart and Winston, 1954.

Gittler, Joseph B. *Social Thought among the Early Greeks.* Athens: University of Georgia Press, 1941.

Gouldner, Alvin W. *Enter Plato: Classical Greece and the Origins of Social Theory.* New York: Basic Books, 1965.

Hertzler, Joyce O. *The Social Thought of the Ancient Civilizations.* New York: McGraw-Hill, 1936.

Martindale, Don. *Social Life and Cultural Change.* Princeton, N.J.: Van Nostrand, 1962.

Sociology of Knowledge and Sociology of Science

Barber, Bernard. *Science and the Social Order.* New York: Crowell-Collier-Macmillan, 1962 (paperback).

Berger, Peter L., and Thomas Luckmann. *The Social Construction of Reality: A Treatise in the Sociology of Knowledge.* Garden City, N.Y.: Doubleday, Anchor Books, 1967 (paperback).

Holzner, Burkart. *Reality Construction in Society.* Cambridge, Mass.: Schenkman Publishing Company, 1968.

Kuhn, Thomas S. *The Structure of Scientific Revolutions.* Chicago: University of Chicago Press, 1962.

Marsak, Leonard M. (Ed.). *The Rise of Science in Relation to Society.* New York: Crowell-Collier-Macmillan, 1964 (paperback).

Remmling, Gunter W. *Road to Suspicion: A Study of Modern Mentality and the Sociology of Knowledge.* New York: Appleton, 1967 (paperback).

Stark, Werner. *The Sociology of Knowledge.* New York: Free Press, 1958.

Willer, Judith. *The Social Determination of Knowledge.* Englewood Cliffs, N.J.: Prentice-Hall, 1971.

Name Index

Subject Index